Editors
Seamus Deane
Breandán Mac Suibhne

Consultant to the Editors
Ciarán Deane

Assistant to the Editors
Joan Arbery

Copy
Hilary Bell

Design
Red Dog Design Consultants
www.reddog.ie

Fonts
Headlines — Gill Sans 24/28
Body Copy Essays/Reviews — Sabon 9/12

Paper Stock
McNaughton's Challenger Offset

Field Day Review is published annually by
Field Day Publications in association with
the Keough-Naughton Institute for Irish
Studies at the University of Notre Dame.

ISSN 1649-6507
ISBN 978-0-946755-38-7

Field Day Review
Keough-Naughton Institute for Irish Studies
86 St. Stephen's Green
Dublin 2
Ireland

fieldday@nd.edu

FIELD DAY REVIEW
2008

ESSAYS

The Greenwich or Prime Meridian in south-east London. Photo: Fred Mayer/Getty Images.

Istanbul 28°57' E

Beijing 116°25' E

Athens 23°44' E
Seoul 127°00' E
Tokyo 139°45' E
Tehran 51°26' E

Jerusalem 35°13' E
Cairo 31°15' E

Riyadh 46°46' E

Hong Kong 114° E
Hanoi 105°54' E

Rangoon 96° E
Bangkok 100° E

Saigon 106°
Addis Ababa 38°
Bombay 72°
Colombo 79°
Lagos 3°

Nairobi 36°
Kuala Lumpur 101°
Singapore 103°

The Literary Greenwich Meridian

Thoughts on the Temporal Forms of Literary Belief

Pascale Casanova
For Pierre Bergounioux

A *sine qua non* of the existence of a world literary space is a measure of time shared by all international players. That is why I suggest the idea of a literary Greenwich meridian. The fact that the ordinary world was unified in part by the British invention and that there then followed the worldwide acceptance of the Greenwich meridian — the imaginary arbitrary line enabling the whole world to measure and thereby to share time — is, it seems to me, objective proof that:

1 an imaginary line can have objective measurable effects on the real order of the world;
2 the prerequisite to the political and economic unification

of the world rests to a great extent on an organization of time that enables all of the countries that recognize the Greenwich meridian to measure their position with respect to this line and thus to determine their own time.

In other words, this unification rests on universal recognition of a common clock that allows everyone, not to have the same clock-time, but to situate themselves with respect to the prime meridian. It also enables us to calculate the longitudes, designated in minutes and seconds, that is, to determine very precisely the location of every point on the face of the earth.[1]

The world of literature can be seen in the same way (at least to a certain extent and differentially according to the zones, territories or spaces). It can even be considered that it is precisely this specific measure of a particular time that enabled the world of literature to constitute itself, to unify itself gradually around this highly distinctive 'clock'. As the literary planet expanded, as new claims to literature's right of existence appeared, as new national literary spaces emerged over the nineteenth and twentieth centuries, protagonists gradually came to agree on a shared measure of (literary) time. Little by little, they agreed on the localization of a present (which I therefore suggest we call by homology the literary Greenwich meridian), which made it possible not only to situate oneself (and to be situated) with respect to other literatures, but also to implement strategies for drawing closer to this line, for rejecting it, laying claim to it, distancing oneself from it, discussing it, proposing other definitions, and so on.

Western philosophical tradition, as we know, makes a classic distinction between two aspects of time: collective or social time (also known as historical time), on the one hand, and inner time or psychological or existential time, on the other hand. Henri Bergson thus opposes scientific time to what he calls 'duration'.[2] However, when we pause to reflect, in terms of 'literary space', as I try to do, using Pierre Bourdieu's notion of 'field of artistic production',[3] we begin to think that it is not enough to describe and define these two kinds of time, that many other kinds of time exist side by side (both in our heads and in the world), and that these relatively separate worlds, these artistic or scientific worlds that operate relatively independently of political and social constraints generate their own tempo, their own temporality. Which means that these worlds have another way of counting time, another chronology, have important events other than those of the political or the historical world.

In other studies I showed that the progressive and relative process of unifying the international literary space has been first of all the history of the unification of (literary) time, through gradual and transnational agreement of all protagonists in this collective enterprise, on the specific way of measuring it. This unification gradually came about over the four centuries during which the Republic of Letters took shape, but it was probably in the first half of the nineteenth century that the unification was actually completed and that we can begin to glimpse its objective effects.

Such international unification of time is possible only if each party agrees to recognize one or several places as reference points that make it possible to measure time and to evaluate practices using universally recognized standards. In the world of literature, this unification is first effected in certain major literary capitals, which, at a given moment in the history of the structure and distribution of resources, embody specific power or even represent literary prestige ('prestige' being one of the major forms of power in the literary space). As a consequence, the places endowed with the most prestige 'territorialize' (to use an expression coined by Gilles Deleuze[4]) the literary present. Simply, unlike the ordinary social world, no one in the literary world clearly explains its structure; there is tacit

1   I would like to thank Bruce Robbins and Gayatri Spivak for having reminded me that some countries have modified their relative position in the world system of time zones. Hugo Chavez, for instance, recently created a new time zone set 30 minutes ahead of the old one (cf. bbc. news.co.uk, 9 December 2007, 'Venezuela creates own time zone'); India is 30 minutes ahead of Pakistan (UTC [Universal Time Coordinated] + 5h30), and Nepal marks its own difference by adding another 15 minutes (UTC + 5h45); Iran is another time dissident (UTC + 3h30). Opposition to the time system is clearly a way of challenging the dominant world order while recognizing its power: temporal dissidents merely want to mark an internal distinction while remaining within the world time system.

2   Henri Bergson, *Essai sur les Données Immédiates de la Conscience* (Paris, 1888); *Time and Free Will: An Essay on the Immediate Data of Consciousness* (London, 1910; New York, 2001).

3   Pierre Bourdieu, *The Field of Cultural Production: Essays on Art and Literature*, ed. and introd. by Randall Johnson (Oxford, 1993); see also *The Rules of Art: Genesis and Structure of the Literary Field*, trans. Susan Emanuel (Stanford, 1995).

4   See among others, Gilles Deleuze and Felix Guattari, *A Thousand Plateaus: Capitalism and Schizophrenia*, trans. Brian Massumi (Minneapolis, 1988).

Kathy Prendergast, *City Drawings Series* (Paris), 1997–, pencil on paper. Courtesy Kerlin Gallery, Dublin.

agreement on the one or two places where modernity is decreed, since it is more or less obvious to all protagonists of this world; but it is never explicitly stated for fear of disenchanting the reputedly quasi-magical mechanisms of literary consecration.

The literary meridian is not located in a single place. In fact, there are struggles between several centres vying for the monopoly to inscribe and impose the present. And that is why the criteria used at the literary Greenwich meridian are neither frozen nor set; they are always multiple, contradictory, plural. There are several competing measures of the present, several criteria of literary legitimacy, which exist side by side and vie with each other. And it is the presence and the concentration in these competing definitions of the most powerful

agencies of consecration and the investment of many members of literary circles in the discussions about the present of literary legitimacy that create or designate the literary capitals as places where literary time is continually engendered and reproduced.

It can be said that the two places, the two capitals that have been vying for this monopoly for nearly two hundred years are London and Paris, to which must of course be added, no doubt for at least the past fifty years, New York and Frankfurt. If these places are recognized, at different spots on the literary planet and for different reasons, as Greenwich meridians, it is because they provide writers from the zones most remote from the present, those desirous of entering the fray, those pretending to the title of writer, with 'certificates of modernity'. It is in Paris, London or New York, in effect, that we encounter what we euphemistically call the most *influential* literary critics, thus disguising the fact that the recognition they provide produces objective and measurable effects; it is there that the most consecrating translators and the most recognized publishers work, there that the most prestigious literary prizes are awarded, and so on. The major capitals embody the present because the decree of modernity they issue is *effective* (since everyone is convinced that the label 'modern' they award is grounded in 'literary reason') and because this decree is assumed to be authorized. These literary centres 'make' the modernity of the works that are, at any given moment, declared to be 'contemporary', in other words synchronous with the criteria of the present in use at the meridian.

E. P. Thompson, in his famous article on time-measurement and the changes it provoked in the organization of labour in England at the end of the eighteenth century, showed that it took the diffusion and imposition of clock-time on one and all, in other words the unification of social time, to overhaul the whole organization of labour.[5] In the sphere of literature, to refer to a shared, that is to a unified, time is to posit, beyond the diversity and idiosyncrasy of national times, aesthetic reference points common to all international protagonists; it is to engage in a discussion (even tacit) about the art of narrative using the same presuppositions; it is to be able to refer to the same great revolutions in the literary world, to the same major works of which it is said, precisely, that they *mark a date*. It is the great innovations in the literary world that, when they have been recognized, celebrated, remarked on, analysed as marking a date in 'literary history', change the measure of time, themselves become instruments for measuring the present, reset the clock to literary time: they become 'time-marks' (as in landmarks or bookmarks).

The Faulknerian Present

Let us take the case of the Faulknerian revolution, which was and remains in many respects, and in an extraordinarily important way, one of the measures of the present to which numerous writers in the world used to and continue to refer. Those who claimed William Faulkner as the true founder of their aesthetic position were, and still often are, in positions homologous to that of the American writer. They come from a rural world that is often economically disadvantaged and far away from the literary centres. Until the arrival of these new novelists, such regions typically produced novels that had not got beyond the stage of Naturalism and its beliefs: in other words, their writing dated to the preceding major revolution in the world novel, and writers referred to this writing, unaware that other standards had come to prevail in the world literary space. António Lobo Antunes in Portugal and Juan Benet in Spain, in the 1950s and 1960s; Mario Vargas Llosa and Gabriel García Márquez in Latin America at the end of the 1960s, all similarly recounted their discovery of Faulkner's work as a sort of revelation: it taught them that access to literary time was possible; for them, Faulkner represented, in very different contexts and at very different times, something they all acknowledged explicitly: not only a decisive influence but, above all, what might be called a 'temporal accelerator'. By this, I mean that he was a creator who enabled them, in spite of their geographical, and especially aesthetic, remoteness, to synchronize themselves with the present time of the art of the novel upon arriving in the world of literature.

In a 1981 article published in Lima, 'Faulkner in Laberinto', Vargas Llosa explained his fascination with Faulkner's novels in terms of a homology of their economic as well as cultural and literary positions. Speaking of Peruvian Amazonia, he wrote:

5   E. P. Thompson, 'Time, Work-Discipline and Industrial Capitalism', *Past and Present*, 38, 1 (1967), 56–97.

Kathy Prendergast, *City Drawings Series* (London), 1997–, pencil on paper. Courtesy Kerlin Gallery, Dublin.

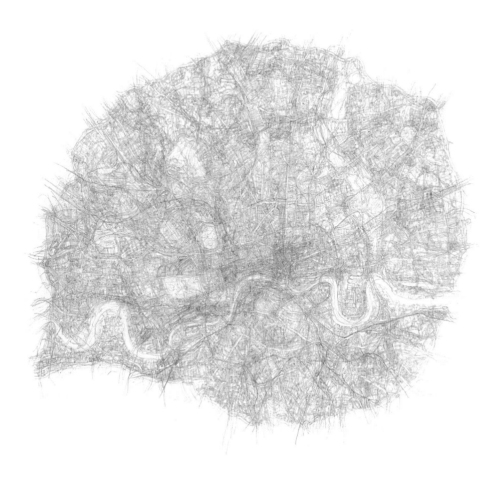

6   Mario Vargas Llosa, 'Faulkner in Laberinto', *Making Waves*, ed. and trans. John King (New York, 1996), 148–51. Emphasis added.

7   Claude Simon, who was one of the Nouveau Roman group, received the Nobel Prize for literature in 1985. He spent his childhood and teenage years in Perpignan, a town in southern France's Pyrénées-Orientales.

It is impossible not to think of Faulkner. This is the heart of Amazonia, far away, of course, from the Mississippi. The language, the race, the traditions, the religion and the customs are different. But the citizens of Yoknapatawpha County and those of the settlement in the department of Madre de Dios ... have a lot in common: violence, heat, greed, ... in short, life as an adventure in which the grotesque, the sublime and the tragic are enmeshed as inextricably as branches of trees in a wood. ... Faulkner's world was really not his alone. It was ours. ... in the turbulence and complexity of the world 'invented' by Faulkner, we readers in Latin America discovered, transfigured, our own reality and we learned that, as in Bayard Sartoris or Jenny du Pre, that *backwardness and marginality* also contain beauty and virtues that so-called civilization kills. He wrote in English, but he was one of our own.[6]

The diffusion pattern of Faulkner's innovation can be applied to France, that is to say, to French writers or those writing in French who come from the periphery of the national and/or colonial, in other words linguistic, literary space. With Faulkner begins one of the great genealogies of the French-language novel: Claude Simon, in particular, who lived in the south of France and who also identified strongly, in his beginnings, as a provincial writer remote from the centre, with Faulkner's South.[7] In the same line, we would have to analyse the case of the French- and Creole-speaking writers from

Martinique — above all Edouard Glissant (who devoted a long analysis to the American novelist in *Faulkner, Mississippi*[8]) but also his younger compatriots, Patrick Chamoiseau[9] and Raphaël Confiant; the case of the novelist Kateb Yacine,[10] certainly one of the greatest Algerian writers to have worked in French until now and who described his discovery of Faulkner on several occasions;[11] the case of the Algerian writer Rachid Boudjedra, who lays claim to the double ancestry of Faulkner and Claude Simon, which is a way of claiming the American's paternity twice over;[12] the case of Pierre Bergounioux (born in 1949 and native of the Corrèze, an isolated region of France's Massif Central); and of Pierre Michon (born in 1945, native of the Creuse, a region reputed to be the ideal-type of rural France). Bergounioux and Michon are today recognized as the two greatest French prose-writers of their generation. They have in common their attempt to restore, in a very classical prose, their rural and popular past,[13] to describe their region as paradoxically 'remote' more in terms of time than of space; and both have told how they were in a way 'liberated' from their relegation to the 'land of the past' by Faulkner's irruption into their lives as readers and writers.

Faulkner is what Michon calls 'the father of the text':

How can I confess that it is to Faulkner that I feel the closest? ... Well then, I affirm it ... my principal company on earth was that of Faulkner. ... and it was in his shadow and guided by his hand, as it were, that I began to write. I read him at a late age. I was over thirty. I hadn't written a line. I happened to read *Absalom! Absalom!*, which had been reissued in paperback: there, from the first pages, I found a father or a brother, something like the father of the text ... Indeed, what Faulkner gave me was permission to hack my way into language as with an axe, enunciative determination ... It is a violent freedom. He is the one who gives permission to

dare ... Because he was a barbarian. A barbarian from this barbarous country, a hick among this raggle-taggle bunch of Southern hicks; but spewing forth from this hinterland a prose that was more than Bostonian, much more than Yankee ... His inconceivable exploit was that he was something urbane, like Proust, for a pathetic salon of lynchers in stetsons, in Oxford, in the state of Mississippi — without ever ceasing to say he hailed from Oxford, Mississippi.[14]

And Bergounioux adds, in *Jusqu'à Faulkner*: 'When we have finally attained the present, by dint of forced marches, we will recognize the works that bear the outline of [Faulkner's] face because they free us from the shackles of the past.'[15] In other words, there are works that 'mark their time' because they change the formerly accepted time, they reset the clock; and others that situate themselves and are situated with respect to this new time and which lay claim to their access to the literary present by proclaiming their kinship with the latest 'time-mark book' (*œuvre-date*).

Literary unification, through the establishment of a shared time-measurement, is therefore by no means synonymous with progressive submission on the part of all protagonists, and writers in particular, to a uniformization of literary practices and aesthetics. Unification does not mean uniformization; does not signify reduction to formal, generic, thematic oneness or uniform and formless relegation to sameness. It is often believed that internationalization is synonymous with globalization, or in other words, generalization of a certain kind of narration, or editorial products stripped of their explicitly national features and targeted at the international bestseller market. Actually, the kind of internationalization I mean, and which is characteristic only of the most autonomous and best-endowed regions of the Republic of Letters, that is to say, the extension beyond the boundaries of national spaces, of a literary space having its

8 Translated by Barbara Lewis and Thomas Spear (Chicago, 1999).

9 See Patrick Chamoiseau, *Texaco*, trans. Rose-Myriam Rejouis and Valerii Vinokurov (New York and London, 1997); *Solibo Magnificent*, trans. Rose-Myriam Rejouis and Valerii Vinokurov (New York, 1998).

10 See Kateb Yacine, *Nedjma* (Paris, 1956); English translation by Richard Howard (New York, 1961; repr. Charlottesville, 1991).

11 Cf. Kateb Yacine, *Le Poète comme un boxeur: Entretiens 1958–1989* (Paris, 1994).

12 Rachid Boudjedra, *La Répudiation* (Paris, 1969).

13 See among others Pierre Michon, *Vies Minuscules* (Paris, 1984); *Masters and Servants* (San Francisco, 1997); *The Origin of the World*, trans. Wyatt Alexander Mason (San Francisco, 2002); Pierre Bergounioux, *Catherine* (Paris, 1984); *La Mort de Brune* (Paris, 1996).

14 Pierre Michon, 'Le Père du Texte', in *Trois Auteurs* (Lagrasse, 1997), 80–85. Unless otherwise indicated, the passages quoted from French works have been translated by Nora Scott.

15 Pierre Bergounioux, *Jusqu'à Faulkner* (Paris, 2002), 55.

Kathy Prendergast, *City Drawings Series* (Lima), 1997–, pencil on paper. Courtesy Kerlin Gallery, Dublin.

16 Viktor Shklovsky, 'Art as Device' and 'The Relationship between Devices of Plot Construction and General Devices of Style', in *Theory of Prose*, trans. Benjamin Sher (Champaign, 1990), 1–51.

17 I have borrowed the expression used by Quentin Skinner to explain the novelty of his historical approach. He thus talks about 'real history' to evoke the commonsense meaning of history as the succession of events, as opposed to the history of ideas of which he is a proponent. Cf. *Liberty before Liberalism* (Cambridge, 1998), esp. ch. 3, 'Freedom and the Historian', 101–20.

own operating laws, its own non-economic economy and entirely devoted to the art of literature, is the contrary of the reduction of all narrative to the commercial novel in its global version; it is a unification by struggle, through discussion about what is at issue, about form, about devices (to cite Viktor Shklovsky[16]). Thus the global reappropriation of the major narrative transformations realized by Faulkner in the case of the novel does not result in the generalization of his conceptions of narrative to the whole world of literature. The novel as it is written since Faulkner — in very different zones and periods of 'real history'[17] — is much more an instrument of specific struggle against the dominant productions in each of the national spaces in which it appeared. As we know, the international commercial novel is far from tolerating such liberties (for instance, forsaking the linear narrative, which itself is a global commercial standard).

Nevertheless, if we are to explain the difference between commercial globalization and literary internationalization, something needs to be said about the bipolar structure of the international literary space. One of the two poles, the relatively autonomous one, is the site of this internationalization and this circulation of texts that write the specific history of the literature. The other is the more heteronomous zone where the texts that are subject to the law and standards of the market are written and circulate and where the publishing practices most dependent on commercial standards develop. This is where use of the most popular novelistic procedures is generalized and rationalized; the effect is to simplify the translations by a process of denationalization in order to set in place a global system of publication; this is where certain forms of the most commercial brand of World Literature appeared. This editorial/ publishing and commercial pole has always existed; there have always been people to manufacture and sell popular literature; and of course they have never prevented the most independent protagonists of the literary world from existing. The novelty resides, it seems to me, in the unprecedented expansion of the market and, above all, in the confusion maintained between globalized texts and the most autonomous transnational texts.

Time-marks

Literary time is not just one dimension of literature among others. We know that time, like space, is what Kant calls a pure, or an *a priori* form of intuition; it is necessarily a part of any form of thought, and allows and organizes our access to thought or to knowledge. In other words, time is more than a simple category of thought: it is the very form of thought.

In the particular case of literary space, time is constitutive of both specific modes of thought and internal representations; it

organizes the whole space. But at the same time as it is a foundation, an *a priori* form of sensibility, as Kant says, or perhaps precisely because it is inseparable from the most basic operations of the structure, literary time and its effects are seldom described or even perceived as such. From the standpoint of collective experience, it belongs to what a long philosophical and anthropological tradition — revived by, among others, Harold Garfinkel[18] and Clifford Geertz[19] — has called 'common sense', that is, that which is so common (in both senses of the word) that it seems obvious that no one thinks to describe its workings. Time, as 'common sense', is so common that it is both recognized (in practice) and unrecognized (as an objective reality). Writers constantly refer to this measure of time; it is an instrument of evaluation, of anticipation; it provides the means to situate other people and things and to situate oneself. In a word, it is one of the implicit forms of knowledge that are indispensable to writers for finding their way, developing critical tools and locating reference points. And yet few recognize its existence. Its reality remains quasi-tacit: revealing its existence and its mechanisms might demystify the workings of a world that rests in great part on belief in enchantment.

As we shall see, this clock haunts equally those who feel 'late' in the competition and those who would impose themselves as the 'avant-garde', that is, as the bridgehead of modernity. In this case, the present can be measured against other artistic practices and disciplines. Thus, one of the French avant-garde groups, the Sound Poetry, founded in the 1950s by Brion Gysin, Bernard Heidsieck, François Dufrêne and Henri Chopin among others, arose from a strange 'observation': the 'lateness' of poetry. First of all with respect to pictoral innovations: 'Writing is fifty years behind painting', Brion Gysin declared at the time of his first 'permutations'; and then with respect to the upheavals occuring in the world of music in the same years. Bernard Heidsieck reports having had the idea of sound poems as an

18 Harold Garfinkel, *Studies in Ethnomethodology* (Oxford, 1984, [1967]), esp. ch. 3.
19 Clifford Geertz, *Local Knowledge: Further Essays in Interpretive Anthropology* (New York, 1983), esp. ch. 4, 'Common Sense as a Cultural System', 73–93.

20 Bernard Heidsieck, *Nous étions bien peu en … Poésie sonore 1950–1980* (Paris, Onestar Press, 2001), pages not numbered.

21 About this expression see also Pierre Bourdieu, *The Rules of Art*, 154–59.

22 Ernst Cassirer, *The Philosophy of Symbolic Forms*, 3 vols. (New Haven and London, 1953–1957 [1923–29]), esp. vol. 1, ch. 2.

active critic of intellectualist poetry, inspired by the musical revolution occurring in Paris around Pierre Boulez, compared with which the poets' 'lateness' seemed patent to him:

> … we were scarcely more than a hundred, packed into the Petit Marigny literally to soak up the musical revolution that could be heard there: an altogether other kind of music, unsuspected, was being played there: Viennese music, to be sure: Schönberg, Berg, Weber, but especially the music of those kids of the time who went by the name of Stockhausen, Nono, Bério, Boulez, by that of their master Messiaen, and above all — incredible bombshells — by the names of Varèse and Cage. If such a radical revolution was underway in music, it seemed to me a crying necessity that the same should be occuring in poetry. Each of the concerts confirmed me in this thinking, shouted to me that poetry deserved better than these languorous states in which it was vegetating …[20]

Furthermore, when it is partially described, this literary clock is rarely cast in temporal terms but rather in aesthetic terms. The reference of literary time-measurement is not the date as determined by ordinary linear chronology, imposed by the Roman calendar; it is the emergence and then the collective consecration of a text or a work that overturns what had hitherto been recognized as the current standard. It is the recognition, at the end of a long collective process, that a work, because of the innovations it brings to the art of narrative or poetry, marks a date (*fait date*[21]). An event in the literary (or artistic) sphere is a work, or a declaration, or a manifesto that marks a date, that is to say, creates a reference point, a break. To mark a date is to establish a reference point on the timeline that history will transform into a date, but which is not in itself temporal. To mark a date is to transform the existence of a work, whose irruption marks an unprecedented moment into time. A work that marks a date becomes the

yardstick by which subsequent works will be measured. The literary time-mark becomes the model to which are compared (including for rejection or refutation, which is another kind of recognition) those writers who, aware of this new measure, this innovation, claim it as a yardstick by which to measure their own practice. The literary time-mark opens an entirely new aesthetic period that would not have been possible without the appearance of this work, which is not to say that the works compared with it are simple imitations or reproductions. It means simply that some of those who recognize and celebrate this mutation begin to write (or pass critical judgements or publish) with respect precisely to this measure. Because of this, the work that marks a date can be said to be at once inseparably 'chronothetic', a *time-maker*, because it produces time; and 'legal' in the sense that it prescribes one of the aesthetic legalities of the literary world. I borrow this notion from Ernst Cassirer : for the German philosopher, the 'internal legality' of a symbolic form is the specific law that operates in it and in it alone.[22] But in the world of literature there is more than one law. There are several measures of time competing for the monopoly of legality. That is why there are also several literary time-marks — to which writers or literary protagonists are subjected.

Certain literary time-marks exercise their jurisdiction only in national literary spaces. In other words, these are works that do not refer to international literary time, but only to a particular national time. We do in effect find, in the Republic of Letters, multiple non-synchronous national literary times existing side by side in the world literary space and which continue and reproduce specific self-enclosed aesthetics independently of the international timeline and mode of rivalry. This explains the existence and perpetuation of 'national classics' that remain unknown at the international level.

And then there are works that, having been consecrated by authorities that are themselves international, become internationally 'legal' from the standpoint of the specific law and therefore exercise their dominion over a transnational territory. Here it must be noted that the Greenwich meridian has the force of temporal law only for those who recognize it, that is, for those writers who accept both its legality and the international clock, those aware of and interested in the latest innovations and the latest consecrations.

The Struggle for Modernity

The specific literary present bears the name 'modernity'. To be 'present', to be recognized as existing for the literary world is to be declared 'modern' at the moment under consideration. Declaration of modernity is one of the hardest consecrations to obtain for authors from the outlying zones of the literary space. It is the object of the most bitter and violent competition. In this way, time itself becomes one of the principal stakes of the struggles waged in the literary space. From the writers' standpoint, existence, that is to say, visibility, depends on the recognition they enjoy or do not enjoy as someone producing a work in accordance with the criteria of the present of which they claim to be contemporaries. To be contemporary, one must be modern; that is, one must be regarded as such, have the reputation of being modern, be designated as modern by those credited with the power to say and make others believe as much — like Sartre, in particular, who established Faulkner as one of the century's greatest writers by a single article published in 1937 in *Les Temps Modernes*.[23] Modernity is an unstable construction by definition, a stake in a rivalry *par excellence*, because the modern is always new, subject to loss of status in the very name of its definition. The only way to be truly modern, for a writer, is to challenge the present, or the latest aesthetic revolution as dated, by proposing a more-present present and thus becoming the latest certified modern.

Pretenders to this title will have to develop a series of highly sophisticated strategies. One of these is simply to declare oneself 'modern'. Which, at least in part, explains the persistence and the insistence of the term modernity in all literary movements and decrees claiming to innovate, from the premises of Baudelairian modernity to the very name of the journal founded by Sartre (*Les Temps Modernes*) via Rimbaud's battle cry 'One must be absolutely modern', or again, as in Spanish 'modernismo' founded by Rubén Darío at the end of the nineteenth century, or the Brazilian modernism of the 1920s, without forgetting Italian Futurism and even Velimir Khlebnikov's Futurianism, and so on. The labels 'Nouveau Roman', 'Nouvelle Vague' or even 'post-modernism' are clearly the same kind of strategies.

We see that Alain Robbe-Grillet, for instance, in the collection of articles that served as his manifesto, *For a New Novel*,[24] is trying to promote the modernity specific to the properly literary revolution he supports against the Sartrean novel that dominated the French literary space in the 1950s. In one of the texts, dated 1957, he writes: 'Whence the embarrassment we feel in the "committed" novels which claim to be revolutionary because they treat the condition of the workers and the problems of socialism. Their literary form, which generally dates from before 1848, makes them the most backward of bourgeois novels.'[25] To put it another way, to promote the Nouveau Roman, Robbe-Grillet moves Sartre's novels down a notch, refers them back to the past, but a literary past, that is to say, to devices that are more than a hundred years behind the times with respect to the specific present. Likewise, he entitles one of his articles 'Sur Quelques Notions Périmées' ('On Several Obsolete Notions').[26] These notions for him, in 1957, were: character, story, commitment, form and content. 'Périmé'[27] is a very interesting term because it belongs to the vocabularies of both economics and time. It means at once: 'something that has lost its value', in the sense of a currency that is no longer in use, and 'something whose sell-by-date has

23 'A propos de *Le Bruit et la Fureur: La Temporalité chez Faulkner*', in the *Nouvelle Revue Française* (July 1939); reprinted in *Situations* I (Paris, 1947), 65–75.

24 Alain Robbe-Grillet, *Pour un Nouveau Roman* (Paris, 1963); *For a New Novel: Essays on Fiction*, trans. Richard Howard (New York, 1965).

25 Robbe-Grillet, *For a New Novel*, 44.

26 Robbe-Grillet, 'On Several Obsolete Notions', in *For a New Novel*, 25–47.

27 'Outdated' might be a better translation.

Kathy Prendergast, *City Drawings Series* (Berlin), 1997–, pencil on paper. Courtesy Kerlin Gallery, Dublin.

28 Robbe-Grillet, *For a New Novel*, 28.
29 R. Mortier, *L'Originalité: Une Nouvelle Catégorie Esthétique au Siècle des Lumières* (Genève, 1982).

expired'. In other words, the notions that Robbe-Grillet calls obsolete are alleged to be both worthless on the non-economic market of literature and without temporal validity because they belong to the past. This text should be carefully reread to see how Robbe-Grillet makes use of all possible time metaphors in order to show that Sartre's system is defunct. Throughout the text, the New Novel is called: a *modern* story, a *modern* novel, as opposed to the 'dead system' characteristic of the Realist novel. The novel of characters, Robbe-Grillet asserts outright, belongs entirely to the past.[28] By branding these novelistic categories 'outdated', he uses a strategy frequently found in the Republic of letters: he proclaims the archaic character of the author he hopes to depose, the better himself to shine as the new holder of the title 'modern'.

Two Short Digressions

1 — The literary space has not, of course, been temporalized uniquely with reference to the 'modern'. In fact, this mode of aesthetic renewal and change is characteristic of the second half of the nineteenth and the twentieth centuries. This way of counting and of measuring time is in reality linked to the changes that appeared in the world of literature at the end of the eighteenth century, at least in France, as Roland Mortier showed in his book on the emergence of the category of 'originality'.[29] Beginning sometime around 1850, the pace of the renewals, the upheavals, the claims, the appearance of literary manifestos accelerated (e.g. for Romanticism, Symbolism, the Parnassus group) taking, at the start of the twentieth century, the shape of a 'permanent revolution', that is, of constitutive instability. The phenomenon known as 'historical

avant-gardes' is the most patent outcome of this logic. In this system of relentless competition, the quest for originality (that is, the rising value of novelty, which, at least from Baudelaire on, is known as modernity) has become the fundamental condition of artistic-literary legitimacy. Paris (in competition with London) became, between 1800 and 1960 more or less, as I tried to show, the capital city of literature, that is the site of the most powerful and the broadest consecrations. That is why the 'modern' régime of historicity, to borrow a concept from the historian François Hartog,[30] has expanded to cover the near totality of the literary world. Or to put it another way, in the last two centuries, the struggle for literary recognition has taken the shape of competition for modernity in so far as it is the very principle of literary legitimacy.

2 — This ongoing race for modernity is clearly the main force driving change and innovation in the world of literature. We can recognize, in this hypothesis, certain aspects of the thesis developed by the Russian Formalists, who were not preoccupied with literary time but with the question of change in literature, with 'literary evolution', to quote the title of a famous article by Yury Tynianov.[31] They posited that each significant new work shows a gap with respect to literature that Tynianov termed 'automatized'. According to the Formalists, this gap was constituted by the debanalization or the defamiliarization of the literary language, genre or procedures. Works that produce a new difference tend to replace — Boris Eikhenbaum says 'substitute' themselves for[32] — those that produced the earlier debanalization, which, having been diffused, became 'automatized'. I subscribe to Shklovsky's famous precept: 'A new form makes its appearance not in order to express a new content, but rather, to replace an old form that has already outlived its artistic usefulness.'[33] I would also follow the Formalists when it comes to the modality of change in literature, which they see as a break, a permanent revolution, and not, as

traditional literary history would have it, as the result of a peaceful and 'natural' passage of generations. Finally, I agree with their attempt, much more historicist in Tynianov than in Shklovsky, to reinsert the works they study into what they call a series or a system, a series of works to which each text makes implicit reference. In other words, and to put it differently, their major innovation was to relate literary change not to political or social history but solely to literature itself.

It remains, nevertheless, that their vision of change by successive gaps, by a continual sliding from debanalization to banalization, does not account for a number of important literary phenomena. The historicity and the practical effectiveness of the mechanisms of recognition have no place in their system, and, above all, they can in no way account for the existence and permanence of the classics. Yet we know that the literary world does not banalize all texts or refer them all back to the past. On the contrary, the debanalizing power of some texts endures long after the ordinary ageing that affects most works. And that is why, it seems to me, the Formalist view of literary change, however innovative it may be, does not truly account for the specificity and the complexity of the temporal struggles within what Tynianov calls each 'literary system'.

The Literary Past

The specific past is another modality of literary time. In the world literary space we find two kinds of texts that belong to the past. On the one hand are works that, having marked a date or having simply been declared to be 'in the present', that is to say, contemporaneous with what is regarded as the present at the time studied, are, owing to specific ageing mechanisms, banished to the past, where they gradually become outdated, 'automatized' or banalized. In this event, their legality, their aesthetic law, is no longer in force or, in other terms, their value no longer has authority. Reputed to have

30 Cf. François Hartog, *Régimes d'Historicité: Présentisme et Expériences du Temps* (Paris, 2003).

31 Yury Tynianov, 'On Literary Evolution', in Ladislav Matejka and Krystyna Pomorska, eds., *Readings in Russian Poetics: Formalist and Structuralist Views* (Cambridge, Mass., 1971), 68–78.

32 Boris Eikhenbaum, 'The Theory of the "Formal Method"', in Matejka and Pomorska, eds., *Readings in Russian Poetics*, 3–37.

33 Shklovsky, *Theory of Prose*, 20.

34 Georges Poulet, *Studies in Human Time* (Oxford, 1979).

35 Antonio Candido, *On Literature and Society*, ed. and trans. Howard S. Becker (Princeton, 1995), 126–29.

36 Paul Nizon, *L'Envers du Manteau*, translated from German by J. C. Rambach (Arles, 1997), 333.

37 Pierre Bergounioux, *Où est le Passé? Entretien avec Michel Gribinski* (Paris, 2007).

'become obsolete', they have faded into the past and have become a 'dead letter', another literary way of expressing devalorization.

Considered to be 'outdated' as well are works produced in areas of the literary universe that are far from the Greenwich meridian. When we take leave of the prime meridian and look at the literary space as a whole, we can see, in effect, literary regions that paradoxically can be defined as belonging to the past. This bipartition has to do with the distance of these spaces from the meridian, in other words with the practices and models that prevail in these regions and which remain more or less distant from those used and valorized in the region of the meridian. This implies that a temporal inequality constitutes or, to put it better, structures the totality of the space.

Typically, it is the writers themselves who have felt 'late' in this world, or who have experienced the effects of this specific past, who have best described the forms of literary immobilism of their native world. In other words, they are the ones for whom the literary present is not obvious, is not part of the air they breathe; it is they who are the most clear-sighted about the temporal inequality of the literary world and who, having understood this, proceed to afford a few glimpses, most often in the derealized mode of literature. And we find in many authors highly detailed representations of their native belonging to the territorialized past. In literature, this past is formulated according to two principal modalities: either in the temporal form of the anachronism or in the spatial form of the province, or, as Georges Poulet put it in his *Studies in Human Time*: 'On the anachronism of duration is superposed its counterpart, an anachronism of space.'[34]

A — Anachronisms

Antonio Candido, the great Brazilian literary critic, spoke clearly of the aesthetic anachronism of certain zones of the Latin American literary space. What is striking about Latin America, he writes, 'is the way esthetically anachronistic works were considered valid ... So, when naturalism was already only a survival of an outdated genre in Europe, among us it could still be an ingredient of legitimate literary formulas, such as the social novel of the 1930s and 1940s.'[35]

Paul Nizon, the Swiss-German writer who spent many years in Paris, penned some fine words on what he considered to be the Swiss anachronism. About his country, for example, he wrote that it was 'an anachronistic spiritual clearing ... A resin secreted into the heavy air, produced in a place sheltered from the wind.'[36] The word 'resin' is a perfect metaphor for a situation 'stuck' in an earlier state. True, it is characteristic of the past (and not only the literary past) that it is frozen, that nothing happens there that has not already happened, that nothing changes there. Consequently, literary anachronism is not only the past, in the sense of a former state: it is more particularly a stasis, a state of frozen conservation. The spaces that are far from the present, the 'anachronistic spiritual clearings', are immobilized in an earlier state, 'sheltered from the wind', that is to say, sheltered from the incessant movement, the perpetual renewal characteristic, as I have tried to show, of the aesthetic present.

No need to think of the places furthest from the centres: we can find regions of the country from the past, chunks of the past, in the literary spaces reputed to be closest to the present, for example in France. To live in the past is therefore one of the major themes of Bergounioux's writing. He has recently published a book entitled, precisely: *Where is the Past?*[37] In it he reflects on the territorialization of time, or rather on the localization of the past. Concerning his autobiographical enterprise, Bergounioux writes: 'What led me to conduct [these] apparently disparate investigations, which are nevertheless guided by a single principle, is the suddenness with which we have moved, my little compatriots and I, from the past, that is, the country we took for the present, the real, to present-day reality, whose tone is set by those central, enlightened, active places';[38] 'this past recommended itself by an opacity, an obstinacy that not only had triumphed over the efforts of its inhabitants to bring some enlightenment but which stuck so firmly to their feet that it disqualified them even when they attempted to flee it, to rid themselves of it';[39] 'the dreams offered to us partook of the anachronism that was an inseparable part of our particularity';[40] 'we had the chronic impression of living in the past and this impression ... was not unfounded. There is no absolute time. Duration always relates to a given place, to the stage of historical development it has achieved, and we were several years, decades, centuries — depending — behind those places where life was being invented, ... the big cities, Paris. Earlier ages had crystallized in things and lingered there as though beyond themselves'.[41]

Octavio Paz, too, evoked the question of anachronism connected with the objective and subjective existence of a measure of literary time. He did this in several texts: first of all in his famous 'Labyrinth of Solitude' (published in 1950), in which we find, among many others, this passage of extraordinary violence against his compatriots:

As people of the fringes, inhabitants of the suburbs of history, we Latin Americans are uninvited guests who have sneaked in through the West's back door, intruders who have arrived at the feast of modernity as the lights are about to be put out. We arrive late everywhere, we were born when it was already late in history, we have no past or, if we have one, we spit on its remains.[42]

This echoes almost word for word what Bergounioux has to say about his compatriots: 'We are late-comers to history.'[43]

Above all, Paz evokes the question of time and the sense of being behind the times in his Nobel Prize acceptance speech in 1990, entitled precisely: 'In Search of the Present'. In it he describes his personal and poetic trajectory as the headlong quest for a literary present from which he learned early on, as a Mexican, that he was structurally removed, and he explains his discovery, as a young boy, of a time other than the personal time of his childhood:

I felt literally dislodged from the present. ... I felt that the world was splitting and that I did not inhabit the present. My present was disintegrating: real time was somewhere else ... My time ... was a fictitious time. In spite of what my senses told me, the time from over there, belonging to the others, was the real one, the time of the real present. ... the modern was outside and had to be imported.[44]

Then, speaking of writing poetry, he adds:

[A]t that time I wrote without wondering why I was doing it. I was searching for the gateway to the present: I wanted to belong to my time and to my century. A little later this obsession became a fixed idea: I wanted to be a modern poet. My search for modernity had begun.[45]

Practically all of the components of perception of those who feel themselves to be 'belated' when they enter the international space are present, it seems to me: the present located in space (with a *gateway* by which one enters — a little later Paz talks about New York time or Paris time or London time)[46]; the necessity of importing a modernity that is lacking so as to have some chance of existing as a writer; the temporal domination of the centres that impose their tempo and their chronology; and the rapid realization that one must not only enter, but import, understand, seize this time, that is, this aesthetic measure, in order to have some chance of being recognized as a legitimate poet. Paz's practical understanding of this mechanism was so effective that his career was crowned by the Nobel Prize, which consecrated his recognition as a 'modern' poet.

38 Bergounioux, *Où est le Passé?*, 35: 'Ce qui m'a poussé à mener des enquêtes apparemment hétéroclites mais dont le principe est unique, c'est la soudaineté avec laquelle nous avons passé, mes petits compatriotes et moi, du passé, c'est-à-dire du pays que nous avions pris pour le présent, le réel, à la réalité actuelle, qui est celle dont les lieux centraux, éclairés, actifs donnent le ton.'

39 Bergounioux, *Où est le Passé?*, 39: 'ce passé se recommandait par une opacité, une opiniâtreté qui, non seulement, avaient triomphé des efforts de ses habitants pour le clarifier mais leur collaient si bien à la peau qu'il les disqualifiait encore lorsqu'ils prétendaient le fuir, s'en débarrasser.'

40 Pierre Bergounioux, *Kpélié* (Charenton, 1997), 43–45: 'Les rêves qu'on nous proposait participaient de l'anachronisme, indissociable de notre particularité.'

41 Pierre Bergounioux, *l'Héritage* (Charenton, 2002), 16: 'On avait l'impression chronique d'habiter le passé et cette impression [...] n'était pas infondée. Il n'existe pas de temps absolu. La durée est toujours relative à un endroit donné, au stade de développement historique auquel il est parvenu, et nous retardions de plusieurs années, décennies, siècles — c'est selon — sur les lieux où la vie s'inventait, ... les grandes villes, Paris. Des âges antérieurs avaient cristallisé dans les choses et s'attardaient comme au-delà d'eux-mêmes.'

42 Octavio Paz, 'Post-Scriptum', *The Labyrinth of Solitude, the Other Mexico and Other Essays*, trans. Yara Milos, Rachel Phillips Belash, Lysander Kemp (New York, 1982), 185.

43 Bergounioux, *Où est le Passé?*, 93.

44 Octavio Paz, *In Search of the Present: 1990 Nobel Lecture*, trans, Anthony Stanton (San Diego, 1990), 14–16.

45 Paz, *In Search of the Present*, 16–17.

46 Paz, *In Search of the Present*, 16.

47 T. S. Eliot, 'What is a Classic?', *Selected Prose*, ed. and introd. Frank Kermode (New York, 1975), 117.

48 Eliot, 'What is a Classic?', 115–31.

49 Eliot, 'What is a Classic?', 130.

50 A town in the department of Indre, in central France.

51 Pierre Michon, 'Le Temps est un Grand Maigre', in *Trois Auteurs*, 24–25. To 'provincialize', in other words to declare that a certain region or production is 'provincial', is one of the most effective strategies for discrediting (in literature or elsewhere) a cumbersome rival. In the historical domain, the success of Dipesh Chakrabarty's book *Provincializing Europe* (Princeton, 2000) shows the strategy is still in use and effective; and, therefore, that the stakes and weapons involved in the intellectual struggle are often linked to the specific time.

52 Vargas Llosa, 'Faulkner in Laberinto', 149.

B — Provincialism

The other, more unexpected, form in which the literary past is cast is that of the 'province'. It is an essentially relative term: the province exists only with reference to the capital: everything that is not 'from the capital' is provincial. This bipartition, which is more than spatial, is not restricted to France: the strong opposition between province and capital was exported to England, where 'to be provincial' has more or less the same connotations as the French expression; and it is found in Spain as well. In short, this bipartition has become a category of thought and a criterion of opposition that also belongs to the category of 'common sense'.

It is clearly in this sense that we should understand the distinction proposed by T. S. Eliot in his famous 1944 address as president of London's Virgil Society: 'What is a Classic?', a reference to the title of another famous address, that of the Frenchman Sainte-Beuve, to which I will return. As we know, in this text Eliot opposes 'mature literatures' that can stand on their own tradition and which have, according to his expression, 'a history behind [them]',[47] to 'provincial literatures'.[48] The literary province, according to Eliot, is a space-time that does not produce classics because it is lacking in tradition, and in its own history. Describing what he calls precisely literary provincialism, he says magnificently, '[it] is not a provincialism of space, but of time'.[49] Literary provincialism, in Eliot's terms, is what could be called a structural anachronism.

Michon, too, describes the sensation of the province he feels each time he passes through the little town of La Châtre:[50]

It is a provincial town the likes of which no longer exist. ... The slow pace is still there, nonetheless, the slow, unbearable life. They are there, behind the clusters of wisteria, the poets who failed to become poets, the lions that became dogs, the lovelorne who burned in vain until they were old maids, ... as the chill of the province gripped them, froze them, gently crushed them — and left them time, all the time they needed, to think it over.[51]

Vargas Llosa, in turn, evoking the homology between Peru and Yoknapatawpha County, writes:

Faulkner's America is underdeveloped and primitive, filled with rough and uncultured, prejudiced and gallant people, capable of extraordinary meanness and nobility, but incapable of breaking free of their visceral provincialism which makes them, from the moment they are born until their death, men of the periphery, wild and old fashioned, pre-industrial ...[52]

Usage of the Classics

Once a literary work has been certified and recognized as modern, writers and agents endowed with the power of consecration have still more ways to keep a work from oblivion. This is Stage Two of recognition, as it were. After accession to modernity as a provisional present, a work can accede to the continuous present. But the only works to attain this ultimate stage of consecration are those that achieve the status of 'classics'.

This is often a long-drawn-out process, at the end of which a work (or an author — in this case the two are one) is recognized by the most legitimate agents of consecration to be an absolute value, an undisputed monument. A classic is supposed to mark an unforgettable date in the specific history of the space; and at the same time it is regarded as a specific authority, an uncontestable work. Which means that, unlike all other works that must undergo continual competition, challenge and contestation concerning their value, the classic is exempt from fluctuations of taste and judgement, from struggles for evaluation, from all rivalries. The classic is, by definition, removed from the arbitrary

Kathy Prendergast, *City Drawings Series* (Moscow), 1997–, pencil on paper. Courtesy Kerlin Gallery, Dublin.

and uncertain index of literary values. In a way, in the Republic of Letters the classic stands as one of those works that is ineligible for competition, a very rare and highly sought after category. Because of this, the classic is not and cannot be relegated to the past. In other words, it has not been nor can it be surpassed, is not nor can it be stripped of its status. It belongs to an eternal literary present. This is clearly nothing other than the definition of immortality itself. This explains why many analysts, in very different worlds of thought and at very different times, have spoken of the classics in the same paradoxical terms as the 'eternal contemporary'. Its belonging to the present having been declared (and unanimously accepted) once and for all, this belonging makes it, whatever may happen, a 'contemporary'. In an article written in 1850, entitled 'What is a Classic?' and later revisited by Eliot, Sainte-Beuve writes: 'A true classic is an author who has enriched the human mind ... who has spoken to all in a personal style which also proves to be that of everyone, in a new style devoid of neologisms, a style both new and old, easily contemporaneous with all periods.'[53]

Much later, in 1960, and in a completely different intellectual world, Hans-Georg Gadamer too tackled the problem of defining the classic, in particular in *Truth and Method*.[54] In it, he seeks to show that, contrary to the claims of the social sciences (and history in particular), literature has no history, or that history cannot account for

53 Charles-Augustin Sainte Beuve, 'Qu'est-ce qu'un Classique?' [1850], in *Causeries du Lundi*, 3 vols. (Paris, 1874–76), vol. 3, 42: 'Un vrai classique c'est un auteur qui a enrichi l'esprit humain, ... qui a parlé à tous dans un style à lui et qui se trouve aussi celui de tout le monde, dans un style nouveau sans néologisme, nouveau et antique, *aisément contemporain de tous les âges*.'; emphasis added.
54 Hans-Georg Gadamer, *Truth and Method*, trans. J. Weinsheimer and D. G. Marshall, 2nd rev. edn. (New York, 1989), esp. second part, ch. 2-B-ii: 'The Example of the Classical', 285–89.

55 Alain Robbe-Grillet,
    *Préface à une Vie
    d'Écrivain* (Paris, 2005),
    123.
56 Jorge Luis Borges,
    'History of Eternity',
    Selected Non-Fictions, ed.
    Eliot Weinberger, trans.
    Esther Allen, Suzanne
    Jill Levine and Eliot
    Weinberger (London,
    2000).

the essential nature of literature. According to Gadamer, the very existence of the classics, their resistence to history, is proof of the supposed incapacity of history to account for literature and for its 'essential nature'. This is the major point on which historical criticism is caught out, he believes. Thus at the close of an argument totally different from Sainte-Beuve's, Gadamer writes, of the classic, that it is '[a work] contemporaneous with every present' and further on, logically: it is a work that is 'immediately accessible', which directly recalls Sainte-Beuve's 'easily' (*aisément*).

A work 'contemporaneous with all periods': this almost oxymoronic expression seems to me precisely what is at stake in the use and the manufacture of the 'classics'. The primary characteristic, the miracle of the classic, is its condition of eternal contemporary. However one defines present, the classic is forever *co-temporaneous*, existing in the same time as those works that are regarded as being 'of the present'. It is therefore not merely immortal: it also belongs to an eternal present, that is to say, it is recognized as existing in the same time as the moderns, but in a mode that exempts it from the indecisive character of modernity.

It could be shown that the kinship between the claim to modernity and the aspiration to the status of classic is such that one of the most effective strategies and one widely used by writers aiming for modernity is to claim a great classic as one of their contemporaries. In effect, as 'becoming a classic' is a lengthy process (since, generally speaking, the older one is the more chances one has of becoming a classic, and the older a classic, the more indisputable it is), one solution is to declare oneself the contemporary of a classic. If the classic is, whatever may come, contemporaneous with all periods, in other words, undisputed and indisputable, then to declare oneself the contemporary of an eternal contemporary is an excellent strategy for creating the possibility of being considered both a contemporary and a classic. Robbe-Grillet is unbeatable at this game: instead of Balzac, he chose Flaubert ('my friend

Flaubert,' he writes in a recent text to indicate his equality and his contemporaneousness with today's most admired author in France and the most renowned of the classical nineteenth-century novelists[55]); then he claims kinship with a series of more-or-less recently canonized writers who make up what could be called the canon or the classics of modernity: Proust, Kafka, Joyce, Faulkner, Beckett. And in so doing, he claims to be himself the contemporary of all these writers. Which gives him a good chance of being 'classicized'. Moreover, he will go down in history, as we know, with the label by which he is well known: 'pope of the Nouveau Roman', which is, one must concede, an excellent start to his announced canonization …

We see, through the different cases I have exposed, that the literary 'present' is the only temporal modality tolerated in the literary space. The only recognition, the only validity, in other words, the only possible form of legitimacy, is to belong, in one way or another, to the present. But what, then, can this perpetual contemporaneousness mean? I think that, among many other things, it means, in accordance with the representations most deeply rooted in our literary unconscious, that there is no such thing as time. That is why the temporal structure of the literary space is highly paradoxical, to say the least: one of its major functions might be to perpetuate the denial of literary history. Nevertheless, I by no means think we should conclude that any history of literature is impossible. On the contrary, I believe that a true collective reflection about literary time could lead us to rethink, I mean to take seriously, a new form of literary history that would also be, to quote Jorge Luis Borges, 'a history of eternity'.[56]

Translated by Nora Scott.

© *Pascale Casanova.*

This is a version of a lecture given at Yale University, in the French department, in December 2007.

Ibsen in Exile

Peer Gynt, or the Difficulty of Becoming a Poet in Norway

Toril Moi

1 'Blant samtlige mine bøger anser jeg *Peer Gynt* for den, der mindst egner sig til at forståes udenfor de skandinaviske lande' … 'den norske natur og det norske folkeliv' … 'fortrolig med vor literatur og med vor folkelige tænkemåde' … '[kende] personer og karakterer deroppe. … Er ikke alt dette nødvendigt for at finde nogen smag i dette digt?' Letter to Ludwig Passarges, the first German translator of the play, 19 May 1880, in the Norwegian Centenary Edition of Ibsen's collected works: *Hundreårsutgave: Henrik Ibsens samlede verke*, eds. Francis Bull, Halvdan Koht and Didrik Arup Seip, 21 vols. (Oslo, 1928–57), vol. 17, 399 [hereafter, *HU*]. Unless otherwise noted, all translations from Norwegian and Danish are mine.

Erik Werenskjold (1855–1938), detail of a portrait of Henrik Ibsen (1828–1906), Nasjonalgalleriet, Oslo, Norway. Photo: Getty Images.

'Among all my books, I consider *Peer Gynt* to be the least suited to be understood outside the Scandinavian countries,' Henrik Ibsen wrote in 1880 to Ludwig Passarges, a potential German translator. To appreciate his play, Ibsen thought, it was necessary to know 'Norwegian nature and the life of the Norwegian people', be familiar with 'our literature and our popular way of thinking', and also actually 'know persons and characters up there'. 'Isn't all this necessary to find this poem [*digt*] to one's taste?' he asked rhetorically.[1]

Norwegians have generally agreed. For generations, *Peer Gynt* has enjoyed a unique status in the Norwegian consciousness. It is consistently treated as the most essentially Norwegian of

Mark Rylance as Peer Gynt, with members of the cast as inmates in the insane asylum, in the Guthrie production of *Peer Gynt*, translated and adapted by Robert Bly from the original by Henrik Ibsen. Directed by Tim Carroll, set and costume design by Laura Hopkins, lighting design by Stan Pressner. 12 January – 2 March 2008 on the Wurtele Thrust Stage at the Guthrie Theater in Minneapolis. Photo © Michal Daniel, 2007

works. In spite of its obvious anti-Norwegian irony, the play has been promoted as a nationalistic paean to Norway and Norwegian culture. When I went to school, *Peer Gynt* was the only Ibsen play we absolutely had to study in Norwegian lessons. In 2007, a vogue for selecting literary canons swept Norway. When listeners to a popular radio programme chose the ten best books in Norwegian history, *Peer Gynt* was the only Ibsen play to make the list, at number six.[2] At the same time, the annual literary festival at Lillehammer launched its own canon of twenty-five works, selected by experts. Again, *Peer Gynt* was the only Ibsen play to make the list, extolled by the jury as the 'Canon within the canon' and as 'The core of Norwegian literature'.[3]

Peer Gynt also has its own festival; since 1967, its centenary year, it has been celebrated annually in the little mountain village of Vinstra.[4] Every August over 12,000 people come to see the play performed outdoors, in the mountain landscapes where the historical Peer is said to have hunted reindeer.[5] The spectacle takes place at the edge of the hauntingly desolate Gålå lake, where the sets are arranged so as to maximize the effect of the slow August sunsets. Edvard Grieg's music is a fundamental part of the show: a full symphony orchestra is engaged and the part of Solveig is usually performed by a well-known soprano. While professional actors are hired for the main roles, locals from Vinstra appear in small parts and as extras in the many crowd scenes. Tickets sell out the first day they go on sale, months before the festival takes place.

Growing up in Norway, I never really questioned the extreme canonization of *Peer Gynt*. Only after living abroad for many years did I begin to wonder why the Norwegians insist on the supreme value of this particular play. After all, many of Ibsen's later plays have been far more influential. Plays such as *A Doll's House* (1879), *Ghosts* (1880), *The Wild Duck* (1884) and *Hedda Gabler* (1890) helped to transform modern theatre. Internationally, Ibsen's contemporary plays opened the way for *Peer Gynt*, not the other way around. *Peer Gynt* did not even begin to be widely translated

2 See <http://www.dagbladet.no/kultur/2007/06/01/502278.html>.

3 'En kanon i kanon. Kjernen i den norske litteraturen.' See <http://www.aftenposten.no/kul_und/litteratur/article1811924.ece>. The twenty-five works are presented in chronological order.

4 For information about the festival, see <http://www.peergynt.no/?lang=en>.

5 A character called Per (or Peer) Gynt appears in folktales from the region. Whether there actually ever was a historical figure called Peer Gynt is by no means clear. After exploring the details, Francis Bull remains agnostic on the question (see Bull, 'Innledning', *HU*, vol. 6, 22–25).

6   *Peer Gynt* was translated
    into German several times
    in the 1880s, but this is
    the only exception to the
    rule. See Bull, 'Innledning',
    HU, vol. 6, 11.

7   '... et stort musikalsk
    tonemaleri, der antyder
    Peer Gynts omflakken i
    den vide verden', letter to
    Edvard Grieg, *HU*, vol.
    17, 124–25. See also Toril
    Moi, *Henrik Ibsen and
    the Birth of Modernism:
    Art, Theater, Philosophy*
    (Oxford, 2006), 127–29.

8   For information on early
    Scandinavian productions,
    see Bull, 'Innledning', *HU*,
    vol. 6, 11.

9   For a complete list of
    the repertoire of the
    Théâtre de l'Œuvre, see
    the exhibition catalogue
    *Le Théâtre de l'Œuvre
    1893–1900: Naissance du
    Théâtre Moderne* (Milano
    and Paris, 2005), 151–53.

10 Information on the 1896
    Paris production of *Peer
    Gynt* is taken from the
    International Repertoire
    Database for Ibsen plays
    (<http://www.ibsen.net/
    index.gan?id=96929>).
    For a wide-ranging
    account of Ibsen's status
    on European avant-garde
    stages in the 1890s,
    see Kirsten Shepherd-
    Barr, *Ibsen and Early
    Modernist Theatre,
    1890–1900* (Westport,
    1997).

11 According to the
    International Repertoire
    Database, by 21
    December 2007 *A
    Doll's House* had
    accumulated 965
    registered productions
    since it first opened in
    December 1879; *Hedda
    Gabler* had reached
    738; *Ghosts* 711; and
    Peer Gynt 674 (<http://
    www.ibsen.net/index.
    gan?id=2953&subid=0>).

12 The play itself is
    deliberately hazy on
    historical detail, but

until the 1890s.[6]

For years *Peer Gynt* was not produced at all. This is not surprising, since Ibsen originally conceived it as a closet drama, a play written to be read rather than performed. Belonging to his monumental middle phase, *Peer Gynt* (1867) joins Ibsen's two other revolutionary closet dramas, *Brand* (1866) and *Emperor and Galilean* (1873). Relatively quickly, however, Ibsen decided that *Peer Gynt* might be performed after all. His change of mind came about in the 'gap period' after he had finished *Emperor and Galilean* and before he had managed to write *Pillars of Society* (1877), the first of his magnificent series of contemporary plays. In January 1874, Ibsen wrote to Grieg, asking him to compose the music for the play, and outlined a remarkably pictorial plan for the stage version. At that point, Ibsen appears to have thought of *Peer Gynt* as a series of *tableaux vivants*. He also suggested that almost the whole of Act 4 (the one act set fully outside Norway, in North Africa) could be replaced by a 'great musical tone painting that suggests Peer Gynt's wanderings in the wide world'.[7]

February 1876 saw the opening of the Kristiania Theatre's production of *Peer Gynt* with Grieg's music. Ten years later, a theatre in Copenhagen also took a chance on the play. In the early 1890s, it was produced in Sweden, but the first production outside Scandinavia did not come until 12 November 1896, when *Peer Gynt* opened at Aurélien Lugné-Poë's Théâtre de l'Œuvre in Paris.[8] By opening here, *Peer Gynt* became part of the Symbolist avant-garde in France, joining plays like Maurice Maeterlinck's *Pelléas et Mélisande* (produced in 1893 as the inaugural show at the new theatre) and Alfred Jarry's *Ubu Roi*, which opened the following month, in December 1896.[9] In fact, in Lugné-Poë's pioneering production of *Peer Gynt*, Jarry himself turned up as a senior troll, and Anitra, the clever and seductive Arab woman, was played by Jane Avril, the cancan dancer celebrated in Toulouse-Lautrec's paintings.[10] Since then, *Peer Gynt* has become one

of Ibsen's most widely performed plays internationally. To date, only *A Doll's House*, *Hedda Gabler* and *Ghosts* have accumulated more productions.[11]

Against Ibsen's expectations, then, *Peer Gynt* has turned out to appeal as much to foreigners as to Norwegians. When Peer peels the onion and likens it to himself, the play's existential dimensions are laid bare. All over the world, directors have excelled in making audiences see that *Peer Gynt* is a drama about human existence and the meaning of life. Like all of Ibsen's plays, moreover, it is sufficiently open-ended to allow everyone to draw their own conclusions about its 'message': *Peer Gynt* appears to have something for everyone.

Like *Hamlet*, *Peer Gynt* is inexhaustible, and like *Hamlet*, it is daunting to any critic who ventures to write about it, and to any director who takes on the monumental task of making it come alive on stage. Christians and atheists, idealists and materialists, modernists and post-modernists have all appropriated it for their own purposes. Critics as well as directors have emphasized a huge variety of themes: it has been understood as a symbolic exploration of 'man's fate'; as an existentialist critique of bad faith and a celebration of human freedom; as either a critique or a celebration of identity understood as performance rather than essence; as a stark representation of a meaningless universe, anticipating Kafka and Beckett; and — particularly in the early days — as an ultimately Christian and idealist celebration of the redemptive powers of the 'eternal feminine'.

In this essay, however, I will leave aside the great universal themes that give the play such wide appeal. Instead, I will show that *Peer Gynt* can also be read as an exploration of what it meant for a poet and writer to be born in Norway in the first half of the nineteenth century.[12] That Ibsen only turned to this topic once he had left Norway is no accident: *Peer Gynt* is (among many other things) Ibsen's meditations on the necessity of exile for a Norwegian writer like himself.

It tells us that, had he remained in Norway, Ibsen would never have become Ibsen. By looking at what *Peer Gynt* has to say about Ibsen's relationship to Norway, I hope to make a contribution to a new tendency in Ibsen studies, namely the attempt to rethink what Tore Rem, in a recent essay on the reception of Ibsen in Ireland, calls 'the tension between the insider Ibsen and the outsider Ibsen, the writer within and without the nation, the nationalist versus the internationalist or cosmopolitan'.[13] To understand Ibsen's relationship to Europe, and the rest of the world, to decide whether Ibsen should be considered an internationalist or a cosmopolitan, it is also necessary to understand his relationship to Norway.

Ibsen finally felt free to comment on his situation as a Norwegian writer in *Peer Gynt*. It was to a great extent because of his departure from Norway in 1864 and the unexpected and unprecedented success of *Brand* in 1866.

Ibsen Leaves Norway

On 1 April 1864 Henrik Ibsen sailed from Christiania to Copenhagen.[14] The 36-year-old dramatist was heading south, to Rome, the city that to him, as to every other Nordic writer and artist of the period, stood as the very symbol of the European tradition in art and culture. By contrast, Ibsen's first biographer, Henrik Jæger, described mid-nineteenth-century Christiania as a provincial outpost, at least when considered from an artist's point of view: 'Surely many things can be said in praise of the Norwegian capital; but nobody in their right mind would call it a town where art and literature thrive.'[15]

Why did Ibsen leave in 1864? An obvious answer to this question would be that his decision was a pragmatic one — he left because he could not make a decent living in Norway. After the birth of his son Sigurd in 1859, Ibsen's economic situation had gone from bad to worse. In 1861 alone he was sued for debt ten times.

He barely escaped the usual punishment for debtors, namely hard labour at the Akershus fortress.[16] He was at that time director of the Kristiania Norwegian Theatre which had been struggling with serious financial difficulties for many years. On 1 June 1862 it had to close, and Ibsen lost his job.[17] In 1862 and 1863, Ibsen repeatedly moved his family to ever cheaper lodgings in ever more unappealing locations, and was regularly sued for debt. He was also developing a serious alcohol problem, and was occasionally seen drunk in the streets. Constantly scrounging for money, he more than once considered giving up writing entirely. The alternative career he had in mind was painting, which was not reassuring to his wife, Suzannah. According to his daughter-in-law, Bergliot (née Bjørnson), this led to conflicts in the marriage: 'It is no secret that he wanted to be a painter, but few people know that it cost Mrs. Ibsen many efforts to get him to give it up. Indeed, she herself says that "I actually had to struggle with him".'[18]

In the summer of 1862, Ibsen received a small state stipend to gather folktales in the Norwegian mountains.[19] His wanderings took him to the mountains around Vinstra, where for the first time he heard tales about a character called Peer Gynt. But mountain wanderings would not feed a family. In February 1863, Stortinget, the Norwegian parliament, voted to provide an annual salary for life for Ibsen's friend and rival, the poet and dramatist Bjørnstjerne Bjørnson. A few weeks later, Ibsen's application for the same honour was turned down. 'Bjørnson, clearly, was absolutely necessary to the nation, whereas Henrik Ibsen was not,' Ivo de Figueiredo comments.[20] However, the committee that turned down Ibsen's application let it be known that it might give him a travel grant instead. Ibsen immediately applied, claiming that he needed 600 Norwegian speciedaler for a year-long European *dannelsesreise*. The Norwegian word is a literal translation of the German *Bildungsreise*, a journey of cultural

scholars agree that the action is supposed to unfold in the first half of the nineteenth century (see, for example, Bull, 'Innledning', *HU*, vol. 6, 24).

13 Tore Rem, 'Nationalism or Internationalism? The Early Irish Reception of Ibsen', *Ibsen Studies*, 7, 2 (2007), 199. The work of scholars such as Pascale Casanova, Kjetil Jakobsen, Elisabeth Oxfeldt and Tore Rem instantly comes to mind. See Pascale Casanova, 'La Production de l'Universel Littéraire: Le "Grand Tour" d'Ibsen en Europe', in Eveline Pinto, ed., *Penser l'Art et la Culture avec les Sciences Sociales* (Paris, 2002), 63–80; Kjetil Jakobsen, *Kritikk av den reine autonomi: Ibsen, verden og de norske intellektuelle* (Oslo, 2004); Elisabeth Oxfeldt, *Nordic Orientalism: Paris and the Cosmopolitan Imagination 1800–1900* (Copenhagen, 2005); and Tore Rem, *Henry Gibson/Henrik Ibsen: Den provinsielle verdensdikteren* (Oslo, 2006).

14 Ivo de Figueiredo, *Henrik Ibsen: Mennesket* (Oslo, 2006), 270. (This is the first volume of Figueiredo's acclaimed new Ibsen biography; hereafter, *Mennesket*.)

15 Henrik Jæger, *Henrik Ibsen: A Critical Biography*, trans. William Morton Payne (Chicago, 1901), 159.

16 This paragraph is based on the detailed account of Ibsen's finances at the time in Per Kristian Heggelund Dahl, *Streiflys: Fem Ibsen-studier* (Oslo, 2001), 11–52.

17 Figueiredo, *Mennesket*, 236. What was left of

Kristiania Norwegian Theater (the theatre wrote the capital's name with a K long before it was legally required, to indicate its political nationalism) was taken over by Christiania Theater, which now became the only permanent theatre in the capital.

18 Bergliot Ibsen, *De tre: Erindringer om Henrik Ibsen, Suzannah Ibsen, Sigurd Ibsen* (Oslo, 1949), 40–41.

19 Figueiredo, *Mennesket*, 238.

20 'Henrik Ibsen var ikke uomgjengelig nødvendig for nasjonen. Men det var altså Bjørnson.' Figueiredo, *Mennesket*, 253.

21 Information based on Figueiredo, *Mennesket*, 253.

22 For more information on this play, see Moi, *Henrik Ibsen and the Birth of Modernism*, 178–87.

23 '[D]en fordrukne digter Henrik Ibsen', Francis Bull, *Tradisjoner og minner* (Oslo, 1946), 195.

24 Knut Hamsun, *Hunger*, trans. Sverre Lyngstad (London, 1998), 3.

25 '... tre Revolutioner, seks Korstog, et Par fremmede Invasioner og et Jordskælv'. Shaw was responding to the Copenhagen newspaper *Politiken*'s request for some lines to celebrate Ibsen's birthday. Responses from a range of British writers were published (in Danish) on 18 and 20 March 1898. Quoted in Rem, *Henry Gibson/Henrik Ibsen*, 283.

26 See Daniel Haakonsen, *Henrik Ibsen: Mennesket og kunstneren* (Oslo, 2003 [1981]), 86.

education. In the summer of 1863, Stortinget awarded Ibsen 400 speciedaler, less than he had applied for, but enough for him to begin making plans to leave.[21]

In October 1863, Suzannah and Sigurd left for Copenhagen, to stay with Suzannah's stepmother, the well-known writer Magdalene Thoresen (1819–1903). Still, the Italian journey was not yet a certainty. Ibsen was beset with debts, and the grant was too small to allow him to pay them off. Luckily that autumn he learned that his latest play, *The Pretenders*, a historical drama set in thirteenth-century Norway, had been accepted by the Christiania Theater, the only permanent theatre in town. Ibsen decided to stay in Norway that winter to help direct it.

That *The Pretenders* was to be produced was welcome news indeed. Artistically, the early 1860s had been a decidedly mixed period for Ibsen. In 1862, he finished *Love's Comedy*, a brilliant, radical critique of social norms for love and marriage. Far ahead of its time, *Love's Comedy* was excoriated by the critics and refused by the Christiania Theater.[22] In January 1864, *The Pretenders* opened to strong reviews. The play was performed eight times that spring which, by Christiania standards, was a fine success. Nevertheless, Ibsen's various efforts to get this play, or indeed any of his plays, produced at the Royal Theatre in Copenhagen failed.

However, by March 1864 Ibsen had settled his most pressing debts, and his friend Bjørnson whipped up a 'subscription' to fund Ibsen's trip. According to the literary historian Francis Bull, an elderly gentleman interviewed by him in the early 1900s remarked that, in 1864, the Christiania bourgeoisie was asked to contribute money so that the 'drunken poet Henrik Ibsen' could go abroad.[23] As soon as the ice on the Christiania fjord thawed, Ibsen sailed south. As he looked back on Christiania from the steamship that was taking him out to sea, Ibsen was well known in Norway, but nowhere else. He could not have known that he was not to return to live in the town the

novelist Knut Hamsun described as 'that strange city which no one leaves before it has set its mark upon him' for twenty-seven years.[24] Between 1864 and 1891, Ibsen visited Norway only twice — in 1874 and 1885. When he moved back to Kristiania (the spelling of the capital's name was made more 'Norwegian' in 1876) in 1891, he had become the most famous living dramatist in the world, the author of an unparalleled series of plays, beginning with *Brand* and ending (so far) with *Hedda Gabler*. His work inspired and sustained the new theatrical avant-gardes then emerging in the great cities of Europe. In 1898, George Bernard Shaw declared that Ibsen's impact on British cultural life had been approximately the same as the effect of 'three revolutions, six crusades, a couple of foreign invasions, and an earthquake'.[25]

Italy and the Success of Brand

Ibsen arrived in Rome on 19 June 1864, and initially he spent a good deal of time exploring the city, often in the company of the Hegelian art historian Lorenz Dietrichson. In search of information about Rome, its art, its traditions and its important sights, he borrowed a Danish translation of Madame de Staël's 1807 novel *Corinne, or Italy*.[26] Soon he was full of ideas. The first, and the one that would take the longest to complete, was to write a play about Julian the Apostate. It would take almost ten years before that idea was realized as the huge double play *Emperor and Galilean*. Instead, Ibsen began an early version of *Brand*, but work was slow and difficult, and by the summer of 1865 he was running out of money again. In an effort to economize, and escape the city heat, the Ibsen family spent the summer of 1865 in the village of Ariccia outside Rome.

One day in June, Ibsen had an errand in the city and took the opportunity to visit St. Peter's. Then, he writes to Bjørnson, he had a revelation: 'I immediately realized a strong

Isabell Monk O'Connor as Asa
and Mark Rylance as Peer Gynt.
Photo © Michal Daniel, 2007

and clear form for what I have to say.'[27] He
went home, put his old draft (now known as
the 'Epic *Brand*') aside, and started intense
work on a new version, a closet drama
in five acts, with a contemporary setting.
Three months later, *Brand* was finished.
On 15 March 1866 the play was published
in Copenhagen, and became an instant
sensation. While the leading Copenhagen
critics, as well as Bjørnson, were rather
hostile to this strange and unusual work,
ordinary readers were absorbed, and
challenged. Everywhere in Scandinavia,
people were passionately discussing *Brand*.
The book was reprinted in May, and there
were three more printings in that year alone.

For the first time in his life, Ibsen was
making serious money from his writing.
Suddenly, everything was going his
way. In May, Stortinget (the Norwegian
parliament) agreed to give him a 'poet's
salary' (*digtergasje*) for life, similar to
that granted to Bjørnson.[28] That month
Ibsen also received a travel grant from the

Society for the Advancement of the Sciences
in Trondheim, and in July, although no
application had been made, the government
awarded him an additional travel grant.

Ibsen's unexpected financial and artistic
success had immediate consequences. It
was as if he wanted to signal to the world
that he was transformed. First of all, he
shaved off his full beard, adopting instead
the imposing whiskers he was to keep for
the rest of his life. He bought new, highly
bourgeois clothes: overnight the dishevelled
poet turned into a gentleman in a velvet
jacket and elegant gloves. His friends
barely recognized him. Most strikingly, he
radically changed his handwriting. Before
1866, Ibsen wrote in a forward slanting
scrawl; after the success of *Brand*, he
suddenly produced the pedantic, backward-
leaning script of an accountant.

The success of *Brand* and the
improvement in Ibsen's finances also had
emotional and professional consequences.
Ibsen had written nine plays before he

27 '... der gik det med
engang op for mig en
stærk og klar Form for
hvad jeg havde at sige',
letter to Bjørnstjerne
Bjørson dated 12
September 1865, *HU*,
vol. 16, 110.
28 See Figueiredo,
Mennesket, 315.

Mark Rylance as Peer Gynt.
Photo © Michal Daniel, 2007

29 'Men en Rejse, som den jeg nu er ude paa, vender op og ned paa meget i et Menneske, og for mig har dette været til det bedre.' Letter to Magdalene Thoresen, dated Rome, 3 December 1865, *HU*, vol. 16, 117–18.

30 'Hvad der har været det afgjørende og betydningsfulde for mig er, at jeg kom i tilstrækkelig Frastand fra vort eget til at se Hulheden bagved alle de selvgjorte Løgne i vort saakaldte offentlige Liv og Jammerligheden i alt det personlige Frasemageri. ... [T]hi hernede er jeg ikke ræd for nogen Ting; hjemme var jeg ræd naar jeg stod inde i den klamme Flok og havde Følelsen af deres stygge Smil bagved mig.' Letter to Magdalene Thoresen, dated Rome, 3 December 1865 (*HU*, vol. 16, 118–19).

left Norway, but had never felt confident that he had a future as a writer. *Writer*, however, is not quite the right word. The word Ibsen mostly uses, in his plays and in his correspondence, is *Digter*, which, like the German *Dichter*, is usually translated as 'poet'. The word does not just mean someone who writes poetry, however, but, more generally, someone who makes things up, someone who uses the imagination to invent stories, images, ideas, and then gives them shape, whether in the form of poetry, plays, stories, or novels.

Finally, Ibsen felt assured that he was a poet, regardless of what the critics might say. The success of *Brand* gave him confidence, energy and imaginative power. That his breakthrough came with the first thing he wrote after leaving Norway must have made him think about the difference between writing in Norway and writing in Italy.

In December 1865, soon after finishing *Brand*, Ibsen sent a revealing letter to Magdalene Thoresen, in which he encouraged her to come to Italy. To go so far away, Ibsen writes, has turned him 'upside down', and the effects have definitely been 'for the better'.[29] Now that he lives

in Italy, he has seen the inauthenticity of Norwegian public life, and — above all — he has stopped fearing the judgement of his countrymen:

> What has been decisive and significant for me, is that I arrived at a sufficient distance from our own preoccupations to see that all the self-made lies in our so-called public life were hollow, and the personal phrasemongers pitiful. ... [F]or down here I am not afraid of anything; at home I was afraid when I stood in the oppressive [*klamme*] crowd, and felt their ugly smiles behind my back.[30]

Ibsen celebrated Christmas 1866 in Rome rather more opulently than usual. In early January 1867, he reported that he was already hard at work on a new play. In May, he and his family left for the island of Ischia in the Gulf of Naples, where he worked away on a new closet drama until mid-August, when he was scared by a small earthquake and immediately sought refuge in a *pensione* in Sorrento. There he stayed until he sent the last act of *Peer Gynt* off to his publisher, on 18 October 1867.

Three days before sending off the final pages of his play, Ibsen wrote to Thoresen to urge her to apply for a grant to travel to Italy:

> Many times I just don't understand how you can stand it up there! Life up there, as it now appears to me, has something indescribably boring about it; it bores the spirit out of one's being, bores the ability out of one's will; the curse of such small circumstances is that they make people's souls small.[31]

Ibsen's comments on the destructive effects of boredom call to mind Hedda Gabler, who complains that her only talent is to bore herself to death. Given the date of this letter, we should perhaps think of Peer as Hedda's cousin, as someone who, like her, suffers grievously under the pettiness of his circumstances, without having Hedda's pride and grandeur of soul.

'Peer, You're Lying': Peer as Poet

Ibsen is the least autobiographical of writers. The only significant exception to this rule is *Peer Gynt*. Indeed, Ibsen himself acknowledged that he had drawn on his own experiences as a young man for the early parts of the play: 'This poem contains much occasioned by my own youth; for 'Aase' — with necessary exaggerations — my own mother furnished the model.'[32] There are parallels between the fathers, too: Peer's father, Jon Gynt, squandered his considerable fortune, leaving his wife and son in poverty; Ibsen's own father, Knud Ibsen, was once a rich merchant in Skien, but had to declare bankruptcy when Henrik was just seven years old.

In the first three acts, Peer is represented as a talented but despised storyteller. The first lines of the play, so popular in Norway that many Norwegians know them by heart, announce the theme:

> AASE. Peer, du lyver!

> PEER GYNT (*uden at standse*). Nej, jeg gjør ej!
> AASE. Naa, saa band paa, det er sandt!
> PEER GYNT. Hvorfor bande?
> AASE. Tvi; du tør ej!
>   Alt i hob er Tøv og tant!
> PEER GYNT (*staar*). Det er sandt — hvert evigt Ord![33]

> AASE: Peer, you're lying!
> PEER GYNT (*without stopping*): I am not!
> AASE. Well, then, swear it's true!
> PEER GYNT. Why swear?
> AASE. Ah; you daren't! It's all rubbish!
> PEER GYNT (*stops*). It's true, every word![34]

These characters live in a world that has no category for fiction: if a story is not true, they assume it must be a lie. Peer shares the concepts of his world: he is not in a position to claim poetry or fiction for himself. If his mother and his so-called friends say that his stories are lies, he will deny it by claiming that they are the gospel truth. Since he is in fact recycling old folktales by turning them into tales about himself, this is a self-defeating strategy. In such a world, a young poet has no chance to become conscious of his own talents.

So, right at the outset of the play we are plunged into a society that has no cognizance of — let alone respect for — the products of the imagination. In this world, fiction — or rather *digtning*, poetry — cannot be understood as anything but lies. To have a lively imagination is simply a sin. In Act 5, when Peer returns as an old man to the village of his youth, the bailiff calls the young Peer Gynt a 'vederstyggelig Digter', a phrase that literally means 'an abominable poet' or 'an abominable maker-up of stories'.[35] In this context, the adjective is to be taken as an inherent part of the noun. It is difficult to render this phrase, with its succinct disparagement of fiction, poetry, and the imagination, in English. Michael Meyer has 'a damned liar';

31 'Jeg begriber mangegange ikke hvorledes Du holder ud deroppe! Livet deroppe, saaledes som det nu staar for mig har noget ubeskrivelig kjedende ved sig; det kjeder Aanden ud af ens Væsen, kjeder Dygtigheden ud af ens Vilje; det er det forbandende ved de smaa Forholde, at de gjør Sjælene smaa.' Letter to Magdalene Thoresen, dated Sorrento, 15 October 1867 (*HU*, vol. 16, 188). (Ibsen may have just Norway in mind, or both Denmark and Norway, since his stepmother was living in Copenhagen. Yet Ibsen himself never lived in Denmark; what he knew from experience was life in Norway.)

32 'Dette digt indeholder meget, som har sin foranledning i mit eget ungdomsliv; til 'Aase' har, med fornødne overdrivelser, min egen moder afgivet modellen.' Letter to Peter Hansen, dated Dresden, 28 October 1870 (HU, vol. 16, 318).

33 *HU*, vol. 6, 59. All Norwegian quotations from the play are from Henrik Ibsen, *Peer Gynt: Et dramatisk Digt, HU*, vol. 6.

34 Henrik Ibsen, *Peer Gynt*, trans. Michael Meyer (London, 1963), 29; punctuation slightly edited.

35 *HU*, vol. 6, 208.

Mark Rylance as Peer Gynt and
Bill McCallum as the Head of
the Asylum.
Photo © Michal Daniel, 2007

36 Ibsen, *Peer Gynt*, trans.
Meyer, 153; Henrik
Ibsen, *Peer Gynt: Play
in Five Acts*, trans.
Christopher Fry (Oxford,
1970), 141; Henrik Ibsen,
*Peer Gynt: A Dramatic
Poem*, trans. Peter Watts
(London, 1970), 188;
Henrik Ibsen, *Peer Gynt:
A Dramatic Poem*, trans.
John Northam (Oslo,
1995), 143. Hereafter,
Northam's translations
will be cited as *Northam*.

Christopher Fry 'an appalling story-teller';
Peter Watts 'a most shocking romancer', and
John Northam 'a terrible yarn-spinner'.[36]
But one scene in *Peer Gynt* shows the power
of fiction, when Peer eases his mother's way
to death by holding her in his arms and
imagining that they are reaching the gates of
Paradise together. Because he loves her, and
because she believes in him, and in his love,
and because he is absolutely not telling this
story to show off, his story truly comforts
his dying mother.

Peer's relations with the other young
people in the village echo Ibsen's admission
that 'at home I was afraid when I ... felt their
ugly smiles behind my back'. Like Henrik,
Peer fears his fellows' judgement, and drinks
to get the courage to face them. Finding no
sympathy and no understanding, he acts out,

as the psychoanalysts put it, by engaging in
rash, violent and shocking actions, to show
them that he is worth something after all.
Ultimately, the consequences of his own
rashness in running away with Ingrid, the
bride at Hægstad, forces him into exile.

Peer, in short, comes across as something
like Ibsen's negative alter ego: a talented
poet who never wrote a line. That the play
intends us to see Peer as someone who
should have become a poet is made clear in
Act 5. After his encounter with the bailiff
and his other acquaintances from his youth
comes the scene in which Peer peels the
onion and discovers that he has no core.
Then he catches a glimpse of Solveig's cabin,
and hears her singing. Filled with horror
and remorse, he runs through the night,
stumbling across a barren, burnt-out plain.

Mark Rylance as Peer Gynt, with Jim Lichtscheidl and Tyson Forbes as Trolls.
Photo © Michal Daniel, 2007

In his panic and fear he hears the voices of some balls of thread rolling on the ground:

Vi er Tanker;
du skulde tænkt os! — [37]

We are thoughts;
You should have thought us! — [38]

A little later he hears voices in the air:

Vi er Sange;
Du skulde sunget os! — [39]

We are songs;
You should have sung us! — [40]

Peer Gynt, then, can be read as a nightmare about how Norway necessarily will destroy a young man with genuine literary talent. On a different level, however, it can be read as evidence that a *truly* great poet (Henrik as opposed to Peer) will manage to turn the circumstances that undermined Peer's poetry into rich sources of inspiration — provided he no longer has to live in Norway. Refusing to settle for easy solutions, *Peer Gynt* conveys a subtle understanding of the interplay between Peer's character and his surroundings. While it is true that Peer lacks existential courage and seriousness, it is also true that his friends, even his own mother, never take him seriously. They all constantly challenge him to put on an act, to perform for them. (The best examples are the scenes at the wedding at Hægstad in Act 1.) In so far as Ibsen at this time thinks of performance as theatrical, as an inauthentic mask for the self, Peer — and his jeering but eager listeners — are degraded by his performances. Peer spends his life claiming to be himself, only to discover that he has simply moved from one role to the next, from capitalist slave-trader to desert prophet, and emperor of the madhouse in Cairo. In such a life, poetry in the Romantic and idealist sense of a realization of human freedom that takes the form of an uplifting vision of truth,

37 *HU*, vol. 6, 213.
38 *Northam*, 147, punctuation amended.
39 *HU*, vol. 6, 214.
40 *Northam*, 148.

Mark Rylance as Peer Gynt.
Photo © Michal Daniel, 2007

41 *HU*, vol. 6, 227.
42 *Northam*, 159.

beauty and goodness can have no place. Ibsen, then, interweaves the theme of the impossibility of becoming a poet in Norway with the play's fundamental contrast between being oneself (*at være sig selv*) and being selfish (*at være sig selv nok*). To be selfish is the motto of the trolls in the Hall of the Dovre Boss (*Dovregubben*; Northam's translation), who are obvious caricatures of Norwegians and Norway. After escaping from the trolls, Peer carries their motto with him; for the rest of his life, he takes his selfishness as evidence of his authenticity.

In Act 5, Peer meets the ageing Dovre Boss again. It turns out he is on his way to join the theatre in Christiania:

> Jeg vil gaa til Komedien.
> De søger i Bladet nationale Subjekter
> — 41

> I'll try acting instead.
> They're asking for national types in the
>   paper — 42

Given that the character of the Dovre Boss is the very archetype of a character from the old folktales treasured by the national Romantics who dominated Norwegian cultural life in the 1850s, these brief lines tell us that by 1867 Ibsen thinks that national Romanticism is no longer capable of generating anything but hollowed-out theatricality. The final exit of the Dovre Boss is Ibsen's satirical farewell to his own long involvement with nationalism.

There is a delicious irony in the thought that the real thing — the head troll, the actual Dovre Boss himself — now has to go on stage to perform what he is, namely a 'national type'. In Act 5, it is the scene in which the old Peer Gynt learns that his younger self was considered an 'abominable poet' and most especially so in the story he tells in response to the name, that elaborates most profoundly, and most ironically, on the idea that Peer (and Ibsen) live in an age when people can no longer tell the difference between theatre and reality.

*The Devil Who did not Know How to Play
to His Audience*

Peer has returned to his home village as an
old man, arriving at the Hægstad farm just
as the last property of the legendary Peer
Gynt is being sold at a public auction (the
goods were originally acquired by the farmer
at Hægstad after Aase's death). The occasion
has attracted a large crowd and caused much
drinking and merriment.

The auction imagery was particularly
pregnant with meaning for Ibsen, for in
the summer of 1866 Bjørnson finally told
him that in June 1864 all the furniture,
clothes and belongings (including personal
letters) belonging to him and Suzannah
had been sold at an auction in Christiania
to cover a small part of his debts. Ibsen
was particularly furious at learning that
his private papers had been handed over
to complete strangers.[43] No wonder, then,
that the auction scene in *Peer Gynt* is one
of Peer's most desperate moments. In a
sequence hovering on the edge between
dream and reality, Peer appears to offer
up for auction all the hopes, dreams and
delusions he ever clung to in his life. He
behaves in such a wild fashion that the
bailiff comes to calm him down. Peer asks
him about the legendary Peer Gynt, whose
property is being sold:

> PEER GYNT. ... Men sig mig, hvem var
>   Peer Gynt?
> ...
> LENSMANDEN. Aa, der siges at han var
>   en vederstyggelig Digter!
> PEER GYNT. En Digter —?
> LENSMANDEN. Ja, — alt, som var
>   stærkt og stort,
> det digtet han ihob at *han* havde gjort. [44]
>
> PEER GYNT. ... But tell me, who was
>   Peer Gynt?
> ...
> BAILIFF. Oh, a terrible yarn-spinner— so
>   his repute is.
> PEER GYNT. A spinner — ?

> LENSMANDEN. Yes, — everything
>   under the sun
> he'd cobble together as marvel's *he*'d
>   done. [45]

The name of poet or writer (*Digter*) makes
Peer stop and reflect. At this moment, after
symbolically stripping himself of his past, he
for the first time begins to develop something
like serious self-reflection. An old man
remarks that Peer Gynt has probably long
since been hanged in some foreign country.
Peer is about to leave, when suddenly,
without explanation, he stops and offers to
tell the audience a tall tale (*en Skrøne*). There
are few stage directions in *Peer Gynt*, but here
Ibsen feels the need to insert one: Peer 'moves
closer, a strange expression comes over
him'.[46] Then follows a story about the devil's
performance on stage in San Francisco. While
the details of the story itself may be somewhat
obscure to most Norwegians, the punchline
has become proverbial; *see facing page*. It is
in the scene immediately following this story,
with its famous conclusion, that we find Peer
sitting alone, peeling the onion in search of
the kernel that does not exist.

Why does Peer tell this story just after he
has learned that Peer Gynt is a poet? Why
does an 'uneasy silence' fall over the crowd
after he has told it? In short, how does Peer
'size up' (the Norwegian word is *beregne*,
to calculate, to measure) his audience here?
And, above all, what is he really talking
about? I can think of five elements that come
together to indicate some answers.

First, Peer tells this story fully conscious
that he is putting on a performance. The
'strange expression' that comes over him
indicates that he is putting on a mask,
the mask of an actor. In this respect, this
performance is wholly deliberate, and wholly
calculating, in a way his storytelling as a
young man was not. There is here a split or
a distance between Peer as actor and Peer
as himself, a split that is the very basis for
self-knowledge, but which also tells us that
there may be something theatrical about self-
knowledge itself, in so far as it encourages us

43 See Ibsen's letter to
    Bjørnson, dated Rome,
    October 1866; *HU*, vol.
    16, 169–70. See also
    Figueiredo, *Mennesket*,
    319.
44 *HU*, vol. 6, 208.
45 *Northam*, 142–43.
46 Peer 'kommer nærmere;
    der glider ligesom en
    fremmed Mine over
    ham' (*HU*, vol. 6, 209).
    Northam, 143.
47 *HU*, vol. 6, 209–10.
48 *Northam*, 143–44.

Mark Rylance as Peer Gynt
peeling the onion. Photo ©
Michal Daniel, 2007

I San Franzisco jeg grov efter Guld.	In San Francisco I dug after gold.
Hele Byen var af Gjøglere fuld.	The city crammed, all the freaks it could hold.
En kunde gnide paa Fiol med Tæerne;	One scraped the fiddle — with his toes, if you please;
en anden kunde danse spansk Halling paa Knæerne	another danced sarabands, down on his knees;
en tredje, hørte jeg, gjorde Vers	a third one recited in verse, so it's said,
mens hans Hjerneskal blev boret igjennem paatvers	while having a drill pass clean through his head.
Till Gjøgler-Stævnet kom ogsaa Fanden;	The devil, too, joined this freakish band; —
vilde prøve sin Lykke, som saa mangen anden.	he wanted, like others, to try his hand.
Hans Fag var *det*: paa en skuffende Vis	His line was this: — in a lifelike stunt,
at kunne grynte som en virkelig Gris.	just like a genuine pig, he'd grunt.
Hans Personlighed trak, skjønt han ej var kjendt.	Though he wasn't a name, his persona drew.
Huset var fuldt og Forventningen spændt.	The house was full, expectations grew.
Frem traadte han i Kappe med svajende Fliger;	He came on in a cape of swirling habit;
man muss sich drappieren, som Tyskeren siger.	man muss sich drapieren, as the Germans have it.
Men ind under Kappen, — hvad ingen vidste, —	But under the cloak — and quite unsuspected —
havde han forstaaet en Gris at liste.	he's managed to sneak in a pig undetected.
Og nu begyndte da Præstationen.	And now commenced the presentation.
Fanden, han kneb; og Grisen gav Tonen.	The devil's pinch; the pig's remonstration.
Det hele blev holdt som en Fantasi	The whole thing produced as a fantasy
over Grise-Tillværelsen, bunden og fri; —	over porcine existence, imprisoned and free;
till Slutning et Hvin, som ved Slagterens Stikk; —	to end with, a shriek as the slaughterman slew; —
hvorpaa Kunstneren bukked ærbødigt, og gik. —	there the artist, respectfully bowing, withdrew. —
Emnet blev af Fagmænd drøftet og dømt;	Experts debated and judged several ways;
Stemningen blev baade lastet og berømt; —	the performance was greeted with censure and praise; —
nogle fandt Røstens Udtrykk for tyndt;	one thought the vocal expression lacked feel;
andre fandt Dødsskriget altfor studeret; —	another, the death-shriek too mannered, oppressive; —
men alle var enige om: qva Grynt	but all were agreed on one thing – that qua squeal,
var Præstationen yderst outreret. —	there the performance was wholly excessive. —
Se, *det* fik Fanden fordi han var dum	So that's what he got for being so dense,
og ikke beregned sit Publikum.	and not sizing up his audience.
(*han hilser og gaar. Der falder en usikker Stillhed over Mængden.*)[47]	(*He takes his leave. An uneasy silence falls over the crowd.*)[48]

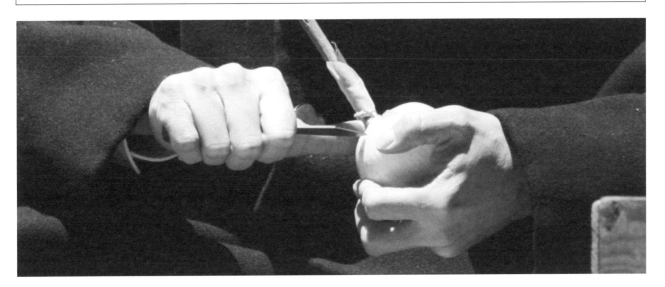

to look at ourselves, at our own performances, as if we were looking at another.

Second, he is now addressing the same audience as before, when he was young; several members were present at the Hægstad wedding in Act 1. This audience represents Norway and the Norwegians, and their impact on Peer.

Third, the story is an extended theatre metaphor. It is about a mountebank who acts for money, who draws great crowds, and who steps out on stage to perform his routine.

Fourth, the story takes pleasure in satirizing Norwegian critics and their aesthetic norms. The 'experts' conclude that the real pig's squeal was 'wholly excessive'. The critics, Ibsen seems to say, refuse even to consider that there might be truth in the performance, or, in other words, the critics seek to aestheticize away anything authentic in a performance. The last thing they want on stage is genuine existential angst. Critics will theatricalize everything, and particularly theatre. (This begins to explain why Ibsen needed to turn to the closet drama at this stage of his career.)

Fifth, the devil's performance can be read as a self-conscious reference to the play *Peer Gynt*. The devil performs a 'fantasy / over porcine existence, imprisoned and free', ending with the last howl at the slaughterhouse. This is not a bad image of *Peer Gynt*, which surely can be described as a fantasy over human existence, imprisoned and free, ending with the fear of death. In Norwegian the parallel is even more obvious, since Ibsen places the word *grynt* (grunt, squeal), so similar to *Gynt*, in a highly stressed position:

> men alle var enige om: qva Grynt
> var Præstationen yderst outreret. —

> but all were agreed on one thing — that
>   qua squeal,
> there the performance was wholly
>   excessive. —

The entire story adds up to an elegant allegory of art, theatre and authenticity, of audiences and critics, and of the relationship between existence and aesthetics. The devil is said to be stupid (*dum*; 'dense' in Northam's translation). Audiences and critics, however, are equally stupid, for they completely fail to see through the devil's trickery. The audience and the critics expect theatre; the devil gives them reality disguised as theatre. Or rather, the devil *almost* gives them reality: the pig's final squeal is said to be '*as if* knifed by the butcher'. Nothing indicates that the devil actually kills his squealing pig there and then (there would have been blood). The experts, however, are not interested in the reality of the pig's squeal. By calling it excessive or outré, they indicate, rather, that it violates their criteria for successful aesthetic utterances. In other words, an artist who takes risks, who does something unusual, will be criticized to death. There will be no understanding, just the injunction to stay within the narrow bounds of established taste. To give a Norwegian audience the real thing — real art — is to cast pearls before swine.

There is much 'self-anatomy' here, as Ibsen once acknowledged.[49] Assessing his own Gyntian existence, Peer realizes that he has never known how to distinguish between life and fantasy, theatre and authenticity. As a result, his whole life has been one inauthentic performance (there is the onion metaphor again). He has been no better than the devil's audience, he realizes. By telling this bitingly aggressive tale to his old 'friends', he accuses them too: they turned him into a superficial performer; he did not even know that he had willingly complied.

The story about the devil who failed properly to calculate his effects on his audience is also a critique of theatre as an art form. On this point, Ibsen remains quite Romantic. In his *Antitheatrical Prejudice*, Jonas Barish points out that Romanticism in general distrusted the theatre.[50] The Romantics wanted the 'poetry of the heart', absolute, radical authenticity, the

49 See letter to Peter Hansen, dated Dresden, 28 October 1870 (*HU*, vol. 16, 318).

50 See Jonas Barish, *The Antitheatrical Prejudice* (Berkeley, 1981).

51 Barish, *Antitheatrical Prejudice*, 327.

52 Quoted in Barish, *Antitheatrical Prejudice*, 326.

53 See particularly ch. 6, on *Emperor and Galilean*, in Moi, *Henrik Ibsen and the Birth of Modernism*.

54 '[Peer Gynt] ble skreven i Syditalien, på Ischia og i Sorrento. Saa langt borte fra den tilkommende læsekreds blir man hensynsløs.' Letter to Peter Hansen, dated Dresden, 28 October 1870 (HU, vol. 16, 318).

55 Bjørnstjerne Bjørnson, Review of Peer Gynt, Norsk Folkeblad (Christiania), 23 November 1867. Consulted online at ibsen.net <http://www. ibsen.net/index. gan?id=228&subid=0>.

56 'give en afsluttet, bestemt, klar og sikker Fremstilling av Idealet.' Clemens Petersen, Review of Peer Gynt, Fædrelandet (Copenhagen), 30 November 1867, consulted online at ibsen.net <http://www. ibsen.net/index. gan?id=229&subid=0>. For an account of idealist aesthetics, and its effects on Ibsen, see Moi, Henrik Ibsen and the Birth of Modernism, particularly ch. 3.

57 '[T]hi Idealet ... det mangler.' '... der er ingen Poesi'.

58 'Hverken 'Brand' eller 'Peer Gynt' er egenlig Poesi.'

59 'Begrebet Poesi skal i vort Land, i Norge, komme og bøje sig efter Bogen.' Letter to Bjørnstjerne Bjørnson, 9 December 1867 (HU, vol. 16, 198– 99).

60 For an account of Knut Hamsun's famous attack on Ibsen, in a lecture delivered in Kristiania in October 1891, with Ibsen present, see Ivo de Figueiredo, Henrik Ibsen: Masken (Oslo, 2007), 417–20.

outpourings of a human soul in its most private moments.[51] For them, the very act of 'playing' a scene, rather than reading it inwardly, was enough to make it theatrical, and thus inauthentic. 'Eloquence is heard, poetry is overheard,' wrote John Stuart Mill.[52] The Romantics, then, often turned to closet drama as an alternative to the degrading theatricality of the actual stage. In his early years outside Norway, Ibsen used the closet drama as a kind of theatre laboratory, as a place for critique and experimentation with language and form. This effort reached a peak in Emperor and Galilean, after which Ibsen felt able to move out of the Romantic and idealist tradition, and invent new forms of theatre.[53]

Peer's story does not please the audience at all: they become uneasy. It is tempting to conclude that, like the devil, Peer has failed to 'size up' his audience. But this would be wrong. Rather than failure, we are seeing open revolt: Peer no longer wants to give his audience what they are looking for. Turning his back on the crowd, he despises them. Such defiance and such courage are easier to find when one is in fact far away from one's audience. In a letter from 1870, Ibsen explains that: '[Peer Gynt] was written in the South of Italy, at Ischia and in Sorrento. At such a distance from one's future reading audience, one gets ruthless'.[54] Far from his homeland, then, and no longer afraid, Ibsen turned Peer Gynt into a masterly critique of the conditions of art and artistic production in Norway.

'My Book is Poetry'

Peer Gynt positively glows with Ibsen's new-found courage and energy — he never again produced a more alive play. Some of his first readers felt the jolt. Bjørnson immediately realized that Peer Gynt was a great satire of Norway and Norwegians, and praised its comic spirit. Ibsen's exposure of Norwegian egoism, vanity and cowardice made him laugh out loud, Bjørnson reported, in an otherwise somewhat mixed review.[55] But the judgement Ibsen was eagerly waiting for was that of the leading Danish critic, Clemens Petersen.

Petersen's verdict was not favourable. A major proponent of the then dominant idealist aesthetics, Petersen wrote that for a work to be poetry (Poesi), or art, it 'has to offer a complete, determinate, clear and assured representation of the Ideal'.[56] In his view, Peer Gynt was far too one-sided, too angry, too satirical, to satisfy this demand: 'The Ideal is missing,' he concluded, 'this is not poetry'.[57] And he added, for good measure, that 'neither Brand nor Peer Gynt are really poetry'.[58]

Ibsen was furious. 'My book is poetry; and if it isn't it will become so,' he wrote to Bjørnson. 'The concept of poetry shall in our country, in Norway, come to shape itself after this book.'[59] Not merely the reply of a self-confident writer, this was a declaration of war. Ibsen no longer feels that the petty aesthetic norms of his home country are capable of measuring his worth. As if to drive the point home, he gave Emperor and Galilean, his next big closet drama, the pointedly cosmopolitan subtitle A World-Historical Play. Ibsen did not return to Norway until he had become so famous that no one in his homeland (except the young rebel Hamsun) would even think of criticizing the Master.[60] As for Peer Gynt, Ibsen turned out to be right. His 'poem' has long since become the most canonical text in the language.

Some of the ideas in this essay were first presented in a lecture written for the Peer Gynt festival at Vinstra in August 2007. The Norwegian text of that lecture was published as 'Peer Gynt i eksil: Meditasjoner om norskhet', in Rasmus Stauri, ed., Per Gynt Stemnet 1. – 12. August 2007 (Vinstra, 2007), 11–18.

London Pub.d Sept.r 21 1793 by S W.m Fores N.3 Piccadilly

Oh: DEAR WHAT CAN THE MATTER BE

Radicalism, Visual Culture, and Spectacle in the 1790s

John Barrell

I

Early in 1794, during the alarm created by the war with the new French Republic and the popular movement in Britain for universal manhood suffrage, Daniel Isaac Eaton's periodical *Politics for the People; or, A Salmagundy for Swine* published a series of verses that claimed to describe some of the caricatures displayed in the window of a printseller in Coddletown, the imaginary rotten borough from which one of the periodical's correspondents, Gregory Grunter, sends occasional reports.[1]

The printshop belongs to a man called 'JACOBIN', whose name strikes terror in the loyal burghers of the borough, and especially in its alarmist mayor, Gaffer Greybeard. The caricatures Jacobin is selling include images of three enemies

1 *Politics for the People; or, a Salmagundy for Swine*, 2 vols. (London, 1794–95), vol. 2, 52–54.

Fig. 1. Isaac Cruikshank, *Oh Dear What Can the Matter Be*, S.W. Fores, 21 September 1793. Courtesy of the Lewis Walpole Library, Yale University.

of parliamentary reform and keen supporters of the war against the French Republic. Isaac Cruikshank's satire *Oh Dear What can the Matter Be* (fig. 1) is an attack on the duke of Richmond, Master of the Ordnance, whom the opposition press blamed for failing to supply the British army with sufficient artillery during the siege of Dunkirk. William Dent's *Call of the House* imagines Prime Minister William Pitt as a kind of corrupt Christ, scattering the loaves and fishes of patronage, or bribery, on his venal supporters. A third satire is described as representing 'the Arch Apostate'. Richmond and Pitt, both formerly vigorous supporters of parliamentary reform, have a fair claim to this title, but the verses themselves leave no doubt about who is intended:

> Arm'd cap-a-pee, with *spectacles* and
> *lance*,
> To kill the millions of OPPRESSED
> *France*,
> With ghastly smiles behind his gorgon
> shield,
> ST. OMER's JESUIT, trembling, takes the
> field,
> His coat of mail, his carcase, and his
> spear,
> And all his pranks, the wretched SWINE
> must bear.

This is Edmund Burke, once the enemy of government corruption and the friend of democratic revolution, now the defender and beneficiary of state bribery and the man who had orchestrated, so British radicals believed, the alliance of kings against France. In the print devoted to him — and it is not clear that Eaton has any one specific print in mind — Burke appears as an amalgam of two characters he had assumed in various recent caricatures: Don Quixote, or rather Don Dismallo, Knight of the Woeful

Fig. 3. James Gillray, *Presages of the Millenium*, H. Humphrey, 4 June 1795. Courtesy of the Lewis Walpole Library, Yale University.

Presages of the MILLENIUM;... with _ The Destruction of the Faithful, as Revealed to R.Brothers the Prophet & attested by MB Halhead Esq
And _ œer the Last Days began I look'd & behold, a White Horse & his Name who sat upon it was Death & Hell followed after him & Power was given unto him to kill with the
Sword, & with Famine & with Death; And I saw under him the Souls of the Multitude , those who were destroy'd for maintaining the word of Truth & for the Testimony. _

2   To trace Burke's appearance in caricature in these two guises, see Nicholas Robinson, *Edmund Burke: A Life in Caricature* (New Haven and London, 1996), index, under the entries: Burke 'as Don Dismallo', 'as Don Quixote', 'as Jesuit'.

3   David Alexander, *Richard Newton and English Caricature in the 1790s* (Manchester, 1998), 34.

Countenance, unaware that the age of chivalry was long gone; and the Jesuit priest, supposed Catholic, supposed friend of the Catholic Church in France, and abettor of the Prince of Wales's clandestine and illegal marriage to the Catholic Mrs. Fitzherbert.[2]

From 1793 until the end of the century there were very few anti-government caricatures of the kind Eaton imagines being published, almost none indeed that appear to emerge from a point further left on the political spectrum than that occupied by the Foxite Whigs. To some degree we have concealed from ourselves the overwhelmingly loyalist character of political graphic satire in the 1790s by our habit of finding ambiguities in caricatures that do not seem to have been noticed at the time, as well as by the assumption that, because James Gillray, the leading caricaturist of the decade, was so hostile to Pitt, he must have been hostile too to the policies of

Pitt's ministry. After the foundation of the Association for the Preservation of Liberty and Property against Republicans and Levellers in late 1792, and the appearance, early in 1793, of affiliated associations throughout England, keen to hunt out sedition wherever they could find it, the very notion of a Jacobin printshop in London, let alone in a rotten borough where Eaton imagines it, is almost *beyond* imagining.

Before the great political polarization of 1792, William Holland, whom *The Times* indeed described as a 'Jacobin' publisher,[3] ran a printshop in fashionable Oxford Street, where he published the satires produced by his brilliant teenage protégé Richard Newton. Holland was indicted in December 1792 for selling Thomas Paine's *Address to the Addressers*, but apparently with the aim of stopping him selling radical caricatures. With the same aim, the Birmingham publisher William Belcher was also

FarmerLOOBY manuring the Land.

IS LOOBY only fit
To dung the verdant plain?
Yes, LOOBY has got wit
To fack the golden grain.

A TOAST.

MAY every Tyrant fall from power and flate,
To be made Ploughmen quickly be their fate;
But that fome care of thefe fine Lads be taken,
May KATE be made to boil their broth and bacon.

Fig. 4. Anon., *Farmer Looby Manuring the Land*, no publication details (1794). Trustees of the British Museum.

prosecuted for publishing Paine's *Address*.[4] The pornographer John Aitkin, who with the brothers John and James Roach had taken over the publication of *Harris's List of Covent-Garden Ladies*, the long-established guide to the more expensive prostitutes working in London, was prosecuted and fined in 1795 for publishing the list, with the effect, if not the intention, of putting a stop to the radical caricatures he had published, very occasionally, in the preceding years.[5] As a small final act of defiance he produced in July *Billy's Hobby Horse* (fig. 2), just after the open-air general meeting of the London Corresponding Society at St. George's Fields depicted in the right distance, with Pitt driving George III as John Bull as a broken down packhorse loaded with the weight of taxes imposed to pay for the war. This was a moderately offensive literalization of Gillray's famous *Presages of the Millenium* (fig. 3) of the previous month, in which Pitt rode the king in the figurative shape of the white horse of Hanover.[6] But apart from the prints published by Holland and Aitken, there is almost nothing by way of radical culture published during the heyday of the

LCS. In 1794, probably, there appeared an anonymous, undated woodcut, *Farmer Looby Manuring the Land* (fig. 4), which Dorothy George describes as 'a crude and cheap print probably sold for a penny'. It depicts George III, breeches down, about to shit; the legend includes a wish that all tyrants should soon be made ploughmen. Probably in 1795 the strange caricature of the faceless, featureless king, *Plan of Mud Island, off the Kingdom of Corsica* (fig. 5), was published to celebrate the pointless accession to the British Empire of George's newest realm, too barren to exploit, too costly to defend. The print sold no more than twenty copies before the plate was 'privately purchased', presumably by an outraged loyalist, and the image suppressed.[7]

There was a brief flowering of anti-government caricature in the last two months of 1795, a protest led by the relatively liberal Piccadilly printseller S. W. Fores against the infamous Two Bills introduced in November, and in particular against the increase in the penalties for seditious libel set out in the Treasonable Practices Bill. But thereafter, except for a brief return to political caricature by Newton before his death in 1798, there is once again almost nothing. In short, what Eaton's caricatures in verse purport to describe, a series of anti-government and anti-loyalist caricatures exhibited in a Jacobin printshop window, to the consternation of men in power and authority, is a fantasy. They describe caricatures that have ceased to be produced, they write what cannot be engraved, conjuring up satires in verse as if to supply their absence from the shops.

When at the end of the eighteenth century satirical prints are described as if seen in printshop windows, the point is always that there they are available to be seen by a promiscuous public, but one chiefly made up of those who cannot afford to buy them (fig. 6); and this is usually regarded as a serious social and political problem, 'a great and public nuisance', as the periodical the *Ranger* put it in 1794.[8] During the brief

4 Vic Gatrell, *City of Laughter: Sex and Satire in Eighteenth-Century London* (London, 2006), 493–94.

5 *Courier*, 10 June 1795; *True Briton*, 10 November 1795. The circumstances of the suppression of *Harris's List* are described by Hallie Rubenhold, *The Covent Garden Ladies* (Stroud, 2006), 309–13, according to whom (309) Aitkin died before the prosecution of James Roach in February 1795. In fact, he was not sentenced until November of that year.

6 British Museum, no.8655 in Dorothy George, *Catalogue of Political and Personal Satires Preserved in the Department of Prints and Drawings in the British Museum*, vol. 7 (London, 1942).

7 George, *Catalogue*, vol. 7, 115–16.

8 *Ranger*, 15 (5 April 1794), 170.

Fig. 5. Anon., *Plan of Mud Island, off the Kingdom of Corsica*, no publication details (1794). Trustees of the British Museum.

Fig. 6. Anon., *Caricature Shop*, P. Roberts, September 1801. Courtesy of the Lewis Walpole Library, Yale University.

flowering of anti-government caricature at the end of 1795, it became the turn of the Treasury-funded newspaper, the *True Briton*, to worry that in printshop windows 'the most seditious *Publications*' were now being 'exhibited to the gaping multitude'.[9] 'As to these here print shops,' says a character in a novel of the early 1790s, 'I see no manner of use they are of, except to make people spend their time in gaping at what does not belong to them.'[10] Versions of this anxiety are frequently found in the late eighteenth century. Sometimes the prints that seem to cause most anxiety are those that threaten to corrupt by their sexual content, sometimes by their politics. The radical essayist and schoolmaster Vicesimus Knox even goes so far as to suggest that among the causes of the anti-Catholic Gordon Riots in 1780 was the exhibition of caricatures of leading politicians in shop windows, where they must 'diminish and destroy that reverence, which is always due to legal authority, and established rank'.[11] This is exactly Eaton's idea in *Politics for the People*: a wish that the popular radical movement could, through caricature, through the printshop window, reach this plebeian public on the street, and teach it to despise, not to admire, its masters. The wish is presumably entertained for the very reason that strikes anxiety in so many writers: the fact that caricatures can communicate to the illiterate, as seditious pamphlets cannot, and the fact that visual imagery was supposed to communicate with an immediacy beyond that of language, and thus was more liable to inspire an immediate response.

In fact, however, the popular societies working for a radical reform of parliament in the 1790s produced very little significant visual political culture. This is surprising for all sorts of reasons, which means this essay will have nothing very tidy or decisive to say about why it may have turned out that way. The movement for universal manhood suffrage was fostered in the 1780s by the Society for Constitutional Information, whose very name suggests that it was aware

that achieving its aim would require the invention of a new, popular, political culture. The plebeian societies that developed in London, Sheffield, Edinburgh and elsewhere in the 1790s understood this to be their task too, hence the decision of the LCS that for every meeting of its affiliated divisions held to discuss specific proposals and policies, they were to hold another at which political texts were read aloud and discussed, with everyone present obliged to contribute. Hence, too, the remarkable number and variety of radical publications produced by plebeian publishers in London, especially in 1794 and 1795: pamphlets, periodicals, poetry, songs, satires of every kind, and so on. Some of the output of these publishers was recycled from more polite sources, but by 1795 a significant proportion of popular radical publications appears to have been written by plebeian authors.

The variety of these publications shows that the popular radical movement, especially in London and Sheffield, was also thoroughly committed to exploring the means of propaganda at its disposal. The Committee of Secrecy of the House of Commons, reporting on the evidence that had been collected following the arrests and the seizures of papers in May and June 1794, which led to the treason trials of later that year, became fascinated by what it saw as the dangerous resourcefulness of radical propaganda. Some of that fascination is no doubt to be put down to the alarmism which, for many loyalists, hugely magnified the threat posed by the movement. The committee no doubt exaggerated the propensity to enthusiasm among those to whom this propaganda was addressed, and so exaggerated also its likely effect, but it was not wrong to insist upon the ingenuity with which the movement attempted to win adherents. The movement, the committee reported, used 'every possible artifice' to disseminate its principles. 'Some of these means', it told the Commons,

may at first sight be considered as too

9   *True Briton*, 23 December 1795. For more on this topic, see Gatrell, *City of Laughter*, 210–12.

10 Anon., *Terentia, A Novel. By the Author of The Platonic Guardian, &c.*, 2 vols. (London, 1791), vol. 1, 69.

11 Vicesimus Knox, 'On the Effect of Caricatures Exhibited at the Windows of Printsellers', in his *Winter Evenings; or, Lucubrations on Life and Letters*, 2 vols., 3rd edn. (London, 1795), vol. 1, 140.

12 *The Parliamentary History of England*, 36 vols. (London, 1806–20), vol. 32, col. 708.

13 The number of the supposedly seditious issue of Wilkes's periodical *The North Briton*.

14 Arthur H. Cash, *John Wilkes: The Scandalous Father of Civil Liberty* (New Haven and London, 2006), 119, 219.

15 Cash, *John Wilkes*, 160, 210, 212, 222.

16 Gatrell, *City of Laughter*, 485.

trivial to be mentioned on an occasion of this importance, but they appear to your Committee in a very different light, when they recollect that an essential part of such a plan as has been in agitation, was to seduce and corrupt the thoughtless and uninformed, and to make use of the channels of communication best adapted to this purpose. The appearance of insignificance and levity, which belongs at first sight to this part of the system, is, in truth, only an additional proof of the aim and industry with which it has been pursued. The measures employed for this purpose appear to have been deliberately prepared, and every contrivance used to mix them (in the shape most likely to captivate attention) with the ordinary occupations and amusements of those on whom they were intended to operate.

These measures include lectures 'calculated from their very extravagance to catch the attention of the audience' on 'every topic … that could inflame their minds'; 'violent' handbills, covering 'every point that could excite discontent', secretly but widely circulated; political satires in the form of mock playbills; songs, seditious toasts, and 'a studied selection of the tunes which have been most in use in France since the revolution'. By all these means the popular reform societies are accused of 'endeavouring to render deliberate incitements to every species of treason familiar to the minds of the people'.[12]

'Every artifice', 'every contrivance', 'every topic'; 'every point', 'every species of treason': the report is concerned to suggest that the propaganda effort of the popular reform societies is as comprehensive as could possibly be imagined. It is so carried away by its rhetoric that, even as it points out the danger inherent in the kind of irreverent levity that caused Knox such anxiety in political caricatures, it does not notice that the societies have nowhere been found making any marked use of visual propaganda. It reveals a remarkable contrast between the popular radical movement in the 1790s and other political movements and societies in the late eighteenth century that the former made no attempt to give themselves or their beliefs any visual identity, except for a few like John Thelwall who, with no employers or customers to propitiate, could at least wear their hair cropped as a visible badge of principle. The members of polite political clubs of course could afford to wear uniforms, custom-made buttons, coloured cockades, as the popular societies could not. But think how ubiquitous in the 1760s were images of the radical John Wilkes or the number 45[13] on everyday objects: on tobacco papers, ballads, prints, broadsides, buttons, buckles, snuffboxes, brooches, earthenware or porcelain mugs, teapots and punchbowls.[14] Think of the use made of the visual by the plebeian Wilkites of the 1760s who wore blue cockades and carried old boots on demonstrations to symbolize the ministry of Lord Bute, and petticoats to stand for the alleged petticoat government of the Dowager Princess of Wales, or who simply chalked the number 45 on every door so that even the innumerate soon learned the ciphers that added up to 'Wilkes and Liberty'.[15] There is no obvious equivalent attempt by the radical societies of the 1790s to convey meanings and spread ideas by visual means.

We cannot put this down entirely to government or loyalist repression. As Vic Gatrell has pointed out, it was far harder to bring a charge of seditious libel against those who sought to convey unwelcome political meanings by images than it was to prosecute the publishers of political pamphlets.[16] To prosecute seditious libels, the law officers had to state precisely what they took the meaning of the supposed libel to be, and to convince the jury that their reading of it was correct. Even when everyone understood perfectly well the meaning of an image, a picture, a symbol, there was an irreducible indeterminacy about the visual, which made paraphrase or ekphrasis always inadequate, and made the defence that the image had been misunderstood always available. The written

word was regarded as far less indeterminate and so far easier to prosecute, and yet the radical movement in its heyday was responsible for an astonishingly high volume of print publications — so many in 1795 that the attorney general was forced to admit that the publication of seditious libels was far too prevalent to be controlled by legal means.

II

There is arguably one obvious exception to the claim that the reform societies, for all the urgency of their propaganda effort, for all their apparent need to communicate with the less than fully literate, did not seek to disseminate the reform agenda by visual means: the token coinage issued by Thomas Spence, the Newcastle-born writer and propagandist who in the 1790s was living in London and was a member of the LCS.[17] From the mid-1780s or so to the end

of the century, there was an extraordinary explosion of copper token coinage throughout Britain. The main reason for this was the shortage of low-denomination specie: virtually none had been minted since the 1750s. Some manufacturers took advantage of this situation by manufacturing tokens, and selling them in bulk at about 70 per cent of their face value to whoever would circulate them.[18] Until 1797, when the government commissioned Matthew Boulton to make a new copper coinage, this was perfectly legal, and in the remote parts of the kingdom tokens probably continued in circulation for some years after that.

Some tokens bore the names of businesses, were probably given as wages to employees, and were 'payable' — redeemable for current coin; most were not payable but were still widely accepted. These were followed by tokens issued by shopkeepers, which became fashionable in the early 1790s. These were not usually payable and were intended rather

Fig. 7. Four tokens by Spence referring to his token coinage: from top to bottom, Lord George Gordon (D & H 696); boxers and a coining press (D & H 740); a turnstile (D & H 715; Spence's shop was in Little Turnstile near Lincoln's Inn); a highlander and a coining press (D & H 742). Notice the contrast between the uncirculated and circulated condition of nos. 740 and 742.

Fig. 8. The radicals acquitted in the treason trials: from top to bottom, Thomas Hardy (D & H 1025); John Horne Tooke and 'Pandora's breeches' (D & H 841); Tooke again (D & H 1046); John Thelwall and Minerva (D & H 866).

Fig. 9. Tokens referring to political trials and to the London Corresponding Society: from top to bottom, Daniel Isaac Eaton's game cock (D & H 203); Eaton, with game cock and swine (D & H 301); Thomas Erskine & Vicary Gibbs (D & H 1011); the fable of the bundle of sticks and the dove of peace (D & H 286).

17 The best general accounts and catalogues of the political tokens and catalogues of the 1790s are: R. Dalton and S. H. Hamer, *The Provincial Token-Coinage of the 18th Century* (London, 1967 [1910–17]); Laurence Brown, *A Catalogue of British Historical Medals 1760–1960, Vol. I, The Accession of George III to the Death of William IV* (London, 1980); R. C. Bell, *Political and Commemorative Pieces Simulating Tradesmen's Tokens 1770–1802*, 2nd edn. (Felixstowe, 1988); and Arthur W. Waters, *Notes Gleaned from Contemporary Literature, &c., Respecting the Issuers of the Eighteenth Century Tokens Struck for the County of Middlesex* (Leamington Spa, 1906) and *Notes on Eighteenth Century Tokens* (London, 1954).

18 Waters, *Notes on Eighteenth Century Tokens*, v.

19 According to C. Shephard, 'The enthusiasm was the most prevalent and regular in the latter part of the year 1794', see 'Essays on the Provincial Half-Pennies. Essay II. — The History of the Modern Provincial Half-Pennies', *Gentleman's Magazine*, 68 (February 1798), 120.

20 See [Thomas Spence], *The Coin Collector's Companion* (London, 1795); Charles Pye, *Provincial Copper Coins or Tokens* (London and Birmingham, 1795), [Samuel Birchall], *An Alphabetical List of Provincial Copper-Coins of Tokens* (Leeds, 1796); James Conder, *An Arrangement of Provincial Coins, Tokens,*

as advertisements or durable substitutes for trade cards, but the shortage of specie certainly led to some of these being circulated as well. By the middle of the 1790s, many thousand different copper tokens had been produced, and they were being avidly collected,[19] which stimulated yet further production, including tokens bearing loyalist or radical political propaganda, sometimes even loyalist propaganda on one side and radical on the other. The craze for token-collecting was fed by the publication of numerous descriptive catalogues produced between 1794 and 1798, including one by Spence,[20] and by numerous articles on the phenomenon of tokens and token-collecting in the *Gentleman's Magazine* and four or five other magazines.[21] Non-payable tokens began to be produced in great quantity, entirely to be sold to collectors. For a year or so, this was Spence's main line of business (fig. 7), his most reliable source of income, and he was describing himself as 'T. Spence, Dealer in Coins',[22] though by early 1797 his money difficulties forced him to sell his dies to another large scale manufacturer of tokens for collectors, Peter Skidmore.

Radical tokens were usually the size of a penny, halfpenny or farthing, and it is convenient to think of them as of two kinds, though the kinds overlap. There were, to begin with, a few penny- and halfpenny-sized coins known by collectors as 'medalets', small medals struck in large editions in imitation of those issued to celebrate military and naval victories, for example, except that these commemorated the victories of the reform movement in the courts. Of those acquitted in the great show trials for treason and sedition in 1793 and 1794, for instance, there are four different medalets for the polite radical John Horne Tooke, and three for Thomas Hardy, founder of the LCS, and two for Eaton. None of these is now thought to have been issued by Spence, but he did produce medalets of John Thelwall and of himself, commemorating their acquittals and release from custody following the collapse of the 1794 treason trials. There

is at least one medal showing the head of Thomas Erskine, lead counsel for the defence in those trials, and another purporting to show Erskine together with Vicary Gibbs, his junior in the trials. The reverses of these medals usually bear information relating to the treason trials, often the names of the jurors to whom the medals were probably presented (figs. 8 and 9).

These radical portrait-medals, for obvious reasons, were nothing like as desirable to collectors as the other variety of political token issued by Spence, halfpennies and farthings bearing designs, sometimes satirical like caricatures, or with political messages dressed up as folk wisdom or animal fables, with a brief, often punchy, legend explaining the political point. Marcus Wood has discussed these very effectively in his *Radical Satire and Print Culture*.[23]

Among serious collectors of tokens, Spence quickly acquired a bad name. This was partly, of course, on account of the political content of his tokens. To collect them, one antiquary declared, was to drink 'from the very ditch of this dirty traffic'.[24] Spence's tokens, thundered another, were 'contemptible in execution, and infamous in representation; ... beyond the revolutions of ages, and the decay of empires, they will carry the marks of his infamy to the final dissolution of the world'.[25] The engraver Charles Pye, who issued a collection of engravings of tokens for the use of collectors, found them 'so infamously base, that ... they are a disgrace to the age we live in, and such as I don't think proper to admit into my collection'. He had compiled his catalogue with the help of Sarah Banks, the sister of Sir Joseph Banks, and if he shared the Bankses' ultra-loyalist politics, he could hardly have tolerated Spence's.[26]

Writers on token-collecting were desperate to regulate the production of tokens so that they could imagine some end to their pursuit, and their chief objection to Spence was his practice of continually varying the combination of dies on the reverse and the obverse of his tokens. The medalet or token he produced of his own head, for example, is known with eighteen different dies on the reverse, and almost every token he made is known with a variety of reverses. Pye, James Conder and many others accused him of mixing 'the obverses and reverses ... on purpose to make variety', so as *'to impose upon the publick'*.[27] Other token manufacturers did this too, but if it was an offence, Spence was the worst offender, interchanging his numerous dies, as a correspondent of the *Gentleman's Magazine* put it, 'almost beyond the powers of calculation'.[28]

Wood argues that by this practice, in which 'almost any combination for the obverse and reverse of a token was both possible and effective ... Spence promulgated his ideas through an ever varying series of juxtapositions'.[29] This may be too much a literary critic's view of things. We can try to persuade ourselves that the endless combining of dies was at the very heart of Spence's politicizing project: that he was inviting those who found a token in their change to make out a relation between its two sides, and thus to learn to think for themselves about politics by making hitherto unperceived connections. It seems more likely that the bewildering variety of combinations issuing from Spence's shop taught those who came across these tokens to discount the idea that the two sides were meant to be related to each other at all.

The most interesting but also the most puzzling contemporary comment on Spence's tokens was made by a contributor to the *Gentleman's Magazine* in 1797, who described visiting Spence's shop on Little Turnstile, where he saw

> many many thousands of different tokens lying in heaps, and selling at what struck me to be very great prices. These, therefore, could not be considered as struck for limited sale. I confess, considering the number I saw struck, and what the subjects of them were, I thought myself justified in supposing that it was the intention to circulate them very widely.[30]

The correspondent is clearly confused by what Spence was about. Knowing him to be what loyalists liked to call 'a violent democrat', he wants to believe that Spence is at the centre of a vast propaganda network, preparing to spread sedition by circulating his tokens by the thousand throughout the kingdom. He knows, however, that Spence is really in business for some quite other purpose. The tokens in Spence's shop were selling at prices many times higher than their notional face value; his farthings at twelve or sixteen times their face value. They were obviously not for circulation either as coin or as propaganda, and this writer is the only one in the 1790s who pretends that they are, if only for a moment. He knows they were being made to feed the insatiable desire of collectors, and the primary effect, perhaps even the primary purpose, of their radical messages was to attract publicity and the attention of collectors.

Spence's tokens are usually discussed as if they circulated in shops, taverns and street markets, spreading the radical word to the uncommitted poor. Wood claims that Spence's tokens were circulating in Hastings, Birmingham, Newcastle, in Worcestershire, in Munster,[31] but apart from in Newcastle, where Spence's brother certainly sold them, this seems to be based on a misunderstanding. What happened was that, after he sold them to Skidmore, impressions from Spence's dies turn up on tokens manufactured in, or simply depicting, provincial locations. This belief, however, in the wide circulation of his tokens has meant that too much has been made of their propaganda value. It is perfectly clear that the commemorative medalets by Spence and others, of Hardy, Tooke, Thelwall and so on, and of Erskine and Gibbs, were designed for general circulation. They frequently turn up very well rubbed and worn, and have clearly been used like general trade tokens as a substitute for current coin. It is most unusual, on the other hand, to come across circulated examples of the much more inventive side of Spence's practice, the

and Medalets (Ipswich, 1798); [T. Prattent and M. Denton], *The Virtuoso's Companion and Coin Collector's Guide*, 8 vols. (London, 1795–97); and *The Virtuoso's Guide in Collecting Provincial Copper Coins* (London, 1795). On the first page of their unpaginated Introduction, Dalton and Hamer, *Provincial Token-Coinage of the 18th Century*, also mention Christopher Williams, *A Descriptive List of the Provincial Copper Coins* (London, 1795), but I have not seen this and cannot find it in any library catalogue.

21 See the following articles in the *Gentleman's Magazine*: R. Y[oung], 66 (September 1796), 752–55; Charles Pye, 66 (December 1796), 991–92; 'Civis' (= James Wright, FASS), 67 (January 1797), 31–34; Young, 67 (April 1797), 267–70; 'Civis', 67 (January 1797), 270–71; C. Sh[ephard], 'Essays on the Provincial Half-Pennies': 'Essay I', 68 (January 1798), 10–13; 'Essay II', 68 (February 1798), 119–22; 'Essay III', 68 (March 1798), 212–15; 'Essay IV', 68 (September 1798), 741–43; 'Essay V', 68 (October 1798), 829–32; 'Essay VI', 69 (March 1799), 206–09. There are articles on token-collecting in the *Monthly Magazine* in December 1796, 867; February 1797, 110; March 1797, 177; May 1797, 351; June 1797, 441; September 1797, 183, and no doubt many thereafter.

22 He describes himself thus on the title page of *The Coin Collector's Companion*.

23 Marcus Wood, *Radical Satire and Print Culture 1790–1822* (Oxford, 1994), 68–82.

24 *Gentleman's Magazine*, 66 (September 1796), 754.

25 *Gentleman's Magazine*, 68 (October 1798), 830.

26 Pye, 'Advertisement', *Provincial Copper Coins or Tokens*, unpaginated.

27 *Gentleman's Magazine*, 66 (December 1795), 991, and see Conder, *Arrangement of Provincial Coins, Tokens, and Medalets*, second page of the unpaginated 'Address to the Public'.

28 *Gentleman's Magazine*, 68 (February 1798), 122.

29 Wood, *Radical Satire and Print Culture*, 71.

30 *Gentleman's Magazine*, 67 (April 1797), 269.

31 Wood, *Radical Satire and Print* Culture, 69.

32 Francis Place Papers, British Library Add. MS 27808, fos. 182–85.

33 *Gentleman's Magazine*, 67 (April 1797), 32.

34 The section that follows derives from the Introduction and notes to John Barrell, ed., *Exhibition Extraordinary!! Radical Broadsides of the Mid 1790s* (Nottingham, 2001).

35 Barrell, *Exhibition*, x, 9–12.

36 Barrell, *Exhibition*, xiv.

halfpenny and farthing tokens with designs like caricatures or with political messages dressed up as animal fables. Some were no doubt thrown by Spence to children in the street, as Francis Place, the LCS member and first historian of the society tells us,[32] in the expectation that they would quickly be spent and circulated, but the bulk seem to have disappeared in mint condition into the cabinets of gentleman and lady collectors, who may have enjoyed a mild alarmist thrill on seeing their message — may even, like one of the correspondents to the *Gentleman's Magazine*, have claimed to find them infamous, disgraceful — but probably did not feel in much danger of being radicalized by them. Safely laid out in drawers, such 'sedition pieces', as the Scots collector James Wright put it, 'can produce no effect more important than that of licentious caricatures, which excite laughter, or incur contempt'.[33] If we measure them by their likely effectiveness rather than by their marvellous wit and invention, Spence's tokens, fascinating as they are, were not an important contribution to the creation of a visual radical propaganda.

III

Another variety of propaganda with strong visual impact and appeal is the mock playbill, a satirical genre that the Committee of Secrecy listed as among the most apparently trivial but in fact dangerously resourceful examples of the reform societies' attempts to corrupt the uncommitted and ignorant. The first of these, which may in fact have been an example of loyalist black propaganda, appeared in 1793, but the heyday of the radical mock playbill came after the committee's report, from the end of 1794 to the middle of the following year.[34]

The point of the playbills was to represent politics, as conducted by Pitt and his government, as a theatrical spectacle. Though the events they pretended to advertise were not always plays — they

could be processions, conjuring shows with Pitt as conjurer, art exhibitions and so on — they were advertised in a way that often represented Pitt's government as attempting to rule by overawing its subjects with the spectacle of power and privilege. And the point, of course, is that once you see politics as spectacle, it ceases to overawe: it is recognized as just another show, and not a very good one either; one that is fake, tawdry, and ridiculous. These playbills usually began life as satires contributed to the columns of Foxite or radical newspapers, but it was when they were reprinted by jobbing radical printers, in the same format as the advertising playbills stuck up in the street, that they became such an inventive form of propaganda and one with strong visual appeal. The most famous of them was a bill advertising the first of a series of imaginary magic shows supposed to be put on by Pitt in the House of Commons, except that Pitt has become Gulielmo Pittachio (fig. 10), and has adapted some of his tricks from the real-life celebrated Italian illusionist Giuseppe Pinetti.[35] Using every font in the printer's shop in the manner of a real playbill and decorated with stock woodblocks, this advertisement is ready to take its place among the real advertisements stuck up on the dead walls of London and wait to draw the kind of crowd that gathered in front of printshop windows.

The first Pittachio advertisement was written by the poet Robert Merry, and a number of others of those that originally appeared in newspapers seem to emanate from the circle around Richard Brinsley Sheridan at Westminster and Drury Lane.[36] Though the printers who turned these newspaper columns into broadside advertisements probably did so without the permission of the original authors and editors, the mock playbills do represent an interesting collaboration of a sort between polite authors and plebeian printers. The most inventive of these printers was the radical Methodist poet and bookseller Richard Lee, who looked beyond the

37 For Lee, see John Barrell, *Imagining the King's Death: Figurative Treason and Fantasies of Regicide 1793–1796* (Oxford, 2000), 604–22, and (especially) Jon Mee, 'The Strange Career of Richard "Citizen" Lee: Poetry, Popular Radicalism and Enthusiasm in the 1790s', in Timothy Morton and Nigel Smith, eds., *Radicalism in British Literary Culture, 1659–1830* (Cambridge, 2002), 151–66.

38 Barrell, *Exhibition*, 64–67.

Fig. 10. [Robert Merry], *Wonderful Exhibition!!!*, London 1794/5. Bodleian Library, University of Oxford, John Johnson Collection.

Fig. 11. *Grand Order of Procession*, London, Richard Lee [1795]. All Rights Reserved. The British Library Board.

GRAND ORDER OF PROCESSION

AT THE FIRST FORMAL ENTRY OF

LOUIS XVII.
Into His City of Paris.

April 1. (A. D. ——*not yet positively determined*)

Hatchet-men, Crowned with Laurel, His Serene Highness, the Duke of BRUNSWICK at their head.
ROYAL LEGION,
Cooks, Dancing Masters, and Fidlers.—Court Buffoons ten a Breast.
The beautiful Animal, called a FAVOURITE, Male and Female.
Demireps four and four; interspersed with PRINCES OF THE BLOOD, *Dignified Clergy*, and *Emigrant Nobleffe*.—Drunken MONKS, singing *Te Deum*.—VOLUNTARY NUNS, conducted by their Fathers, with the affistance of Ropes.—*A Parisian, comme il faut* ; Chapeau bras, laced coat, paper ruffles, ne'er a fhirt.
A Troop of MARRIED WOMEN, efcorted by ABBES;
their Hufbands at a refpectful diftance: "CIVIL SOCIETY" in a Wreath over their Heads.
An OPERA GIRL mounted on a MINISTER of STATE, a PRIEST at Top.
"SOCIAL ORDER"
brayed by Mr. CANNING, elegantly dreffed in a fuit of *Fuftain*, with a beautiful Plume of *Parrot* Feathers.
Emblems of Agriculture;
viz. a broken Plough drawn by one lean Cow, and an Afs.
Statue of *Commerce*, hiding her Face. Right Hon. Mr. WYNDHAM fupporting a label, "*Redeunt Saturnia Regna*." The Cardinal Virtues comprifed in a fingle figure, finely executed, though not after the antique; his knee bent, and head upon the Ground. Potraits reprefenting The ARTS (of *Bowing, Scraping, Cringing, Lying*.) A Gentleman Penfioner, with a *Cornu Copid*. Grand Painting, Supported by

TAX GATHERERS,
richly decorated; the fubject taken from life. viz. *Want* fhowering rags on *Induftry*. Beautiful Tranfparency, the BASTILE rifing from its ruins, furmounted by the words "*Lettres de Cachet*," in coloured lamps.
The SOLICITOR GENERAL, in a *poppy* fuit, with a garland of *Totums*, unveiling *Treafon*.
A fanciful figure, ftuffed with ftraw, in a vaft *patch work* covering compofed entirely of *party coloured* fhreds.
Grand Chorus of Spies,
Reciting, with enthufiasm, the moft wonderful difcoveries, and ingenious inventions of this or any other Century. Mr. REEVES, fupporting a label "*Auricular Confeffion*." The ATTORNEY GENERAL, Grand Inquifitor, *Explorator feliciffimus*, &c. &c. &c. Carrying a flag; on one fide "Half an hour's fufpenfion to all Friends of Freedom." On the reverfe, "Eternal fufpenfion to all provifions in its Favour."
The Duke of PORTLAND, dreffed out with Ribbons, proclaiming *Security*.
The Earl of MANSFIELD, fhouting *Indemnification* ; His Son, the young Auditor in his arms.
A TRIUMPHAL CAR.
Drawn by Spaniels completely harneffed ; Mr PITT, feated majeftically
in a Superb fuit of *changeable* Silk ; the young

MONARCH
on his Knee ; the EMPEROR and King of PRUSSIA one on each hand, carefsing the great War Minifter ; the *Sardinian* Potentate from behind ; all of them ftriving who fhall make the moft of him.
Waggons of Britifh Coin;
An infcription over each "Every one that afketh, receiveth; and he that feeketh findeth."
Regiments, compofed of Troops juft releafed from the Rod, or refcued from the Rope, forming the main body of the Britifh Army ;
preceeded by the Flower of ditto.—viz. A Company compofed entirely of Colonels in their teens ;
Mafter JENKINSON, fenoir in Command.

At the BRITISH TREE of LIBERTY, No. 47, Hay-Market ; may be had a variety of Patriotic Publications, including the following. Liberty Songs. Precious Morfels ; on the blefsed Times we live in. Letter from John Bull to the Pope. Harlequin Stadtholder. Tribute of civic Gratitude an Addrefs to Triumphant Patriotifm. Nebuchadnezzar's Decree for a Faft. Pittachio's Exhibition 2 Parts, Muftapha's Adoration of the Sultan Pittander 2 Parts Muftapha's Vifion's. Dundaffio's Eating Match. Exhibition of the Swinifh Multitude. a Letter to a King. Letter to a People. Duke of York's New March. The Genius of Liberty. Proclamation of Liberty, Equality, Fraternity. Rights of Swine. The Return of Liberty. The Tree of Liberty, &c. &c.

polite Whigs for the material of his mock advertisements.[37] Lee's most remarkable contribution to this style of textual/visual propaganda was two wonderful mock advertisements announcing imaginary spectacles of revolution and counter-revolution. He may perhaps have written as well as designed these himself, for they seem to appear in no previous publication. The first, *Grand Order of Procession* (fig. 11), provides a satirical prospect of the final triumph of the counter-revolution in France; it offers itself as an All Fools' Day joke, and it may well have appeared on, or in time for, 1 April 1795.[38] The satire imagines the final restoration of the Bourbon king in the person of little Louis Capet, the eleven-year-old former dauphin, now Louis XVII, who enters Paris in triumph, sitting on the bony knee of William Pitt, with everyone and everything most corrupt about the *ancien régime* returning in triumph with him. The contrast between the tiny king and the huge font used to proclaim him 'MONARCH' is typical of Lee's mischievous touch. The procession, with its emblematic figures, and portable texts, paintings, transparencies, and other images, suggests one of the great pageants that were staged in Paris after the Revolution, in a style cheerfully inappropriate to the resurgent *ancien régime*.

The second of this pair — *An Entire Change of Performances?* (fig. 12) — provides a carnivalesque view of the final triumph of the revolution in Britain, a riotous satire in which the 'Swinish Multitude', British sans-culottes, stage a revolution in London, seizing the government from Pitt and the theatre from Pittachio. In most of the other mock playbills, the vulgar are imagined as the audience at the theatre of politics, an active 'popular' or even 'public' opinion that will hiss Pitt from office, but in the expectation that they will then cheer Fox to the stage; will applaud, huzza, be enthralled by the spectacle of power passing from the Pittites to the Foxites, from one set of hereditary aristocrats and polite career politicians to

An entire Change of Performances?

THE Public having been for a long Series of Years entertained at a Prodigious Expence, with the unrivall'd Deceptions of PITTACHIO, and his Fellow Profeffors in the Black Arts; they are now inform'd that Fiction muft give way to Truth, and Reality fupply the Place of Delufion!———In cofequence of which,

The Swinifh Multitude

will difplay a Variety of Wonderful Performances, exhibiting ftriking Proofs of their Wifdom, Strength, and Activity, having (to Accommodate the Tafte of the Mobility of this Country), received a courfe of Leffons in the Firft Schools of Paris.———In the Firft place they will agreeably furprize the Spectators with the various Manoevres of

STORMING A TOWER,

which will be done without the Aid of Military Tactics, and unretarded by the regular Operations of a Siege, yet performed with a Dignity, and compofure fuch as never before was witnefsed in a HERD OF SWINE.

N.B. This performance will be Peculiarly interefting to ACQUITTED FELONS.

Secondly, they will with the utmoft Eafe, and Facility (to prove the exquifite refinement of their Tafte) metamorphofe a

PALACE INTO A PIG-STYE,

And then Transform a

TREASURY CHEST INTO A HOG TROUGH.

After which the Audience will be amufed with a Scene reprefenting the infide of a Minifter of State's WORKSHOP, wherein will be exhibited a Brilliant Variety of *Coxcombs*, and Coronets; Stars and Garters; Places and Penfions. The firft of thefe *Baubles* the PIGS will actually hand from the Shelf, and turn it to the

CAP OF LIBERTY

To the marvellous Satisfaction of all prefent———With the *Garters*, they will in a moft ludicrous manner perform the Office of JACK KETCH on certain wicked, and notorious Malefactors, who it is already decreed fhall be

REWARDED according to their WORKS.

Thirdly, This inimitable Troop of Performers will moft Effectually

DEMOLISH A BASTILLE

And plant on the ruined Bulwark of Defpotifm

THE TREE OF LIBERTY.

Fourthly, they will proceed to regulate and Purify

A Houfe of Ill-Fame, or, a Den of Thieves

(not a Hundred Miles from St. Stephen's———) containing ample Materials, which after mature deliberation and a fair *Trial* (though not a Nine Day'sOne), will befound *incorruptibe* and fit for decorating and ornamenting

The LAMP IRONS in PARLIMENT STREET.

The whole to conclude with a moft diverting Difplay of

PIGS IN PATTENS.

Vivant la People Soveraigne.

A Variety of other Performances are preparing, and will be announced to the Public in due Time.

At the BRITISH TREE of LIBERTY, No. 47, Hay-Market; may be had a variety of Patriotic Publications, including the following. Liberty Songs.-Precious Morfels ; on the blefsed Times we live in.--Letter from John Bull to the Pope.--Harlequin Stadtholder.--The Tribute of civic Gratitude an Addrefs to Triumphant Patriotifm.--Nebuchadnezzars Decree for a Faft, Pittacchios Exhibition 2 Parts. Muftapha's Adoration of the Sultan Pittander 2 Parts---MuftaphaVifion's. Dundaffio's Eating Match.--Exhibition of the Swinifh Multitude. Letter to a King. Letterto a People. Duke of York's New March. The Genius of Liberty. Proclamation of Liberty, Equality and Fraternity. Rights of Swine. The Return of Liberty. The Tree of Liberty, &c. &c.

39 Barrell, *Exhibition*, 68–69.
40 See William Hamilton Reid, *The Rise and Dissolution of the Infidel Societies in this Metropolis* (London, 1800), 6.

another; and will overlook the fact that the Foxites offer them at most only a very moderate political reform. By contrast, *An Entire Change of Performances?* is the only advertisement that represents the swinish multitude as actors as well as audience in the imagined revolution. They have learned the arts of revolution from the people of Paris and will storm the Tower of London as the Parisians stormed the Bastille, will turn the king's palace into their own quarters ('A PIG-STYE') and force their snouts into the Treasury ('HOG TROUGH') previously reserved for feeding the ravenous appetites of pensioners and placemen. The swine will seize the crown and turn it into a 'CAP OF LIBERTY'; that is, they will proclaim a republic and will hang the worst criminals of the previous regime. Finally, they turn their attention to the corrupt and criminal Houses of Parliament, try the members, and hang them, French-style, from lamp posts in the street outside. The dance concluding the entertainment is performed by female swine, 'PIGS IN PATTENS', whose feet will make an appropriately rough music to end this carnival of revolution. Once again, Lee has had about as much fun as you can have with a collection of fonts and a single frame, offering us immediate visual pleasure as well as the pleasure of imagining the future spectacle he describes. The font changes with bewildering, staccato intensity, as one revolutionary act leads to another. Unusually in these broadsides, the engraved vignettes seem not selected from stock but entirely appropriate to the text: the warlike oak and peaceful olive entwined round a lance bearing the cap of liberty, and, below, the insignia of king, Church, and judicial punishment in the form of an executioner's axe, all smashed or overthrown.[39]

This was probably not, however, an attempt at creating a visual culture that the reform societies would choose to be associated with: Lee was distinctly off-message. While the societies were attempting to insist that they were demanding little more than universal manhood suffrage

and peace with France, Lee was cheerfully looking forward to bloody revolution on the streets of London and the execution of George III and his ministers. Lee was both too hard line and too pious for the leaders of the LCS, and though he styled himself the printer to the society, he was apparently expelled in 1795 for refusing to sell Paine's *Age of Reason* and Constantin François de Volney's *Ruins*.[40] He escaped prosecution only because the government, following its defeat in the treason trials, chose to avoid confronting the radical movement in the courts of law for most of 1795. Eventually, however, late in the year, he was arrested for selling a handbill that recommended king-killing. He escaped and fled to Philadelphia, but with his arrest, and the imminent threat of new legislation directed against radical booksellers, the production and sale of these playbills came to an end.

The mock advertisements mobilize a language with which any reader of newspapers, anyone indeed walking the streets of London, would have been thoroughly familiar. Advertisements for plays, pantomimes and other shows, often in the form of small playbills but with less typographical pizzazz, were printed on the front page of most newspapers, frequently in the most prominent place: the left-hand column. Playbills were stuck up on every dead wall in London and in every major town in the country. By its sheer ubiquity, the language of theatre advertising could address both the polite and the vulgar much more effectively than the language, or rather the languages, of formal political debate, which differed widely according to the class identity of author and supposed audience. The layout and typography of playbills were equally familiar, immediately recognizable: they were the most conspicuous, attention-seeking, visually enjoyable advertisements around, and if radicals succeeded in pasting them up alongside other, genuine advertisements, it must have doubled the pleasure they already offered by their wit and design. They no doubt succeeded

THOMAS MUIR.

JOSEPH GERRALD

Fig. 13. T. Holloway after Thomas Banks, *Thomas Muir*, no publication details, cropped copy. Private collection.

Fig. 14. S. W. Reynolds after C. Smith, *Joseph Gerrald*, London, S. W. Reynolds, 25 November 1795. Private collection.

sometimes: in his lines on street advertising in the London of the 1790s William Wordsworth writes of 'advertisements of giant size' pasted to 'dead walls', one of which, he suggests, 'is peradventure one in masquerade'.[41] It is probable that this was one of these political mock advertisements. Wordsworth was living in Lincoln's Inn in early 1795, in the months when almost all of these bills were produced.

Still, as an attempt to provide the popular reform movement with a propaganda that had visual appeal and impact, the mock playbills did not perhaps amount to much. They were produced for a few months only, and though their imagined destination was as street advertising, there cannot have been many radicals brave enough to risk pasting them up in public. They suffered the fate, too, of Spence's tokens, in that they were clearly regarded as collectables. It sometimes looks as though London in 1795 was like Paris in 1968, with the distributors of radical propaganda outnumbered two to one by eager collectors, for whom the curiosity value of these plebeian publications

outweighed any damage they threatened to the established order. And as with tokens, the collectors influenced the production of what they were collecting, and some radical printers, notably George Riebau, the publisher of the prophecies of Richard Brothers, the nephew of Almighty God, turned every newspaper satire they could find into broadsides, which had no real connection with advertising and little visual appeal, but which provided collectors with something more to collect.

IV

A few of the medalets of Hardy, Tooke, Thelwall and others (fig. 8) were made by Spence, more by Peter Kempson of Birmingham, some by other manufacturers; others still were probably commissioned by the LCS, some struck as private speculations, but they all seem to have been intended for general circulation as well as for keepsakes and souvenirs. These were the tokens that spread the radical message in the street;

41 William Wordsworth, *The Prelude* (1805), Book 7, 213–14.

THOMAS HARDY.

JOHN THELWALL.

42 See Hardy, 'Memoir of Thomas Hardy' (1832), in David Vincent, ed., *Testaments of Radicalism: Memoirs of Working-Class Politicians 1790–1885* (London, 1977), 70.
43 Christina Bewley, *Muir of Huntershill* (Oxford, 1981), 107.
44 Horace, *Odes* III, 3, lines 1–4, but line 2 is omitted on the print; Lord Byron, *The Poetical Works of Lord Byron* (London, 1945), 5.

these were the images by which the radicals chose that the reform movement should be represented. They portray the leaders of the societies as men of virtue and gravitas; because they commemorate acquittals, they show them not as trying to overthrow the constitution but as trusting firmly that juries of freeborn Englishmen will vindicate their character and conduct. The small amount of visual propaganda that the societies themselves appear to have approved and even sometimes sponsored was almost all of this kind: serious, ennobling portraits of the heroes or martyrs of the radical cause.

When Hardy, a few weeks before his arrest, went down to Portsmouth to say a final goodbye to his close friend and colleague Maurice Margarot and the other reformers who had been sentenced in Edinburgh to be transported to New South Wales, he found Thomas Banks, the republican sculptor, Royal Academician and member of the Society for Constitutional Information, on board the transport ship the *Surprize*.[42] He was taking a cast of the head of the Scots reformer Thomas Muir to

make a relief portrait, nowadays known only by a contemporary engraving by Thomas Holloway (fig. 13), with appropriately heroic verses chosen from James Thomson's *Seasons* by the poet Anna Barbauld.[43] Another of the Scottish martyrs on board the *Surprize*, Joseph Gerrald, was engraved by S. W. Reynolds wearing his hair loose and unpowdered as he famously had done at his Edinburgh trial (fig. 14); the original painting was by C. Smith, 'painter to the Great Mogul', as he called himself, and publisher of the newspaper closest to the LCS, the *Telegraph*. The print bears a motto in Latin adapted from Horace, lines which Byron would later translate as: 'The man of firm and noble soul / No factious clamours can control; / No threat'ning tyrant's darkling brow / Can swerve him from his just intent'.[44]

When the leaders of the LCS, Hardy, Thelwall and John Richter, were in the Tower awaiting their trials for high treason, they were visited by Richter's brother Henry, a professional artist, who made portraits of them to be published in the radical

Fig. 17. Richard Newton, *Soulagement en Prison*, watercolour study for a lost aquatint. Courtesy of the Lewis Walpole Library, Yale University.

Fig. 18. William Hogarth, *A Midnight Modern Conversation*, pub. Hogarth, 1732–33. Private collection.

Fig. 19. Richard Newton, *Promenade in the State Side of Newgate*, William Holland, 5 October 1793, Art Gallery of Ontario, Toronto. Gift of the Trier-Fodor Foundation, 1989. © AGO.

45 See Claudette Hould, Stéphane Roy, Annie Jourdan and Rolf Reichardt, *La Révolution par la Gravure: Les Tableaux Historiques de la Révolution Française* (Vizille, 2002); for some useful remarks on the history of this manner of portraiture, see Marcia Pointon, *Hanging the Head: Portraiture and Social Formation in Eighteenth-Century England* (New Haven and London, 1993), 65–66.

46 Perhaps most famously Henri-Félix-Emmanuel Philippoteaux's painting *Le Dernier Banquet des Girondins*, first exhibited at the Paris Salon, 1850, now in the Musée de la Révolution Française at Vizille; see Philippe Bordes and Alain Chevalier, *Catalogue des Peintures, Sculptures et Dessins* (Vizille, 1996), 151–53, which illustrates other examples of the subject.

periodical the *Register of the Times*, and for separate sale and circulation (figs. 15 and 16). They show men dignified and steadfast of purpose, with Thelwall in particular, hair cropped and holding a scroll, looking like a hero of the Roman Republic transplanted into eighteenth-century London. The plain style of these images was typical of portrait-heads that illustrated many of the periodicals of the 1790s, but it may have been influenced too by the *feuilles volantes*, if any had been blown over to Britain, which the previous year had begun to be issued in Paris by François Bonneville and which would later be collected under the name *Portraits des Personnages Célèbres de la Révolution*, the unassuming forerunner of the more elaborate portraits published in the more famous *Tableaux Historiques de la Révolution Française*.[45]

The primary efforts by way of radical portraiture were Newton's pair of group-portraits of 1793, *Promenade in the State Side of Newgate* and *Soulagement en Prison*. These are not in the heroic vein appropriate to men facing transportation or a trial on a capital charge: as Ian McCalman has argued, these images depict 'British Jacobin civility, symbolically representing the fine manners and morals of radical *philosophes* under the most testing and uncivilized circumstances'. *Soulagement* (fig. 17) intriguingly anticipates a number of heart-wrenching nineteenth-century images of the Girondins, some gloomy, some spirited, some self-consciously heroic, sharing their last supper in prison on the eve of their execution.[46] These British reformers, however, spared the prospect of imminent martyrdom, are all good humour and good cheer. The image most obviously recalls William Hogarth's definitive picture of impolite sociability, the drunken debauch *A Midnight Modern Conversation* (fig. 18): Newton's point, however, is to show that the political prisoners caught up in Pitt's 'terror' exhibit the very opposite of the appallingly impolite behaviour of Hogarth's drunks. The *Promenade* (fig. 19) derives from its own first version, *A Peep into the State Side*, a jovial caricature of the kind an artist is allowed to make of his friends for circulation amongst themselves. When the scene got enlarged, repopulated and reworked, all that was left of the caricature were the cheerful smiles, now slightly muted, the expressions of men too schooled in philosophy and politeness to allow the injustice of their lot to dampen their spirits. It is hard to agree, however, with McCalman's description of these images as 'radical counterpropaganda'.

Fig. 20. Tokens and caricatures by Thomas Spence. Top to bottom, left to right: a laden ass, (D & H 716–23); a man on all fours (D & H 1099–1105); *The Contrast* and *The Civil Citizen*, both pub. Spence, 1796.

Who would buy them? How would they circulate? As a half-guinea subscription-print, the *Soulagement* was probably not on sale to the public at all; the *Promenade*, priced at seven shillings and sixpence, appears in Newton's famous watercolour of Holland's shop, hung high on the walls. It was presumably available for purchase, but its sale must have been entirely among the friends and relations of those it depicted, plus perhaps one or two Home Office spies. If these images were propaganda, their job was to boost morale, to lift the spirits of the faithful, not to win converts to the radical cause, and the same is presumably true of all the portraits, except those on the copper tokens.

With these portraits in mind, it is worth returning to the question of the dearth of radical caricature in the 1790s. Both Lee and Spence tried their hand at caricatures of a sort. Spence etched a few of his designs

for tokens and published them as small prints just a few inches square (fig. 20). To illustrate a song, Lee published one caricature, *A Cure for National Grievances* (fig. 21), obviously an amateur effort that he may well have etched himself. These little images arguably do most of the job of explaining why, when textual political satire was the stock-in-trade of the booksellers most closely associated with the popular radical movement, there was so little radical caricature. Plebeian radical publishers could afford neither the services of professional caricaturists, nor the expenses of printmaking, because, at retail prices of two shillings and upwards, the members of, and sympathizers with, the popular radical movement could not have afforded the finished product.[47] Lee's usual price for his textual satires was one penny, so for two shillings they could have bought twenty-four copies of *A Cure for National Grievances*

47 For more on the prices of caricature, see Gatrell, *City of Laughter*, 244–45.

48 Gatrell, *City of Laughter*, 493.

49 On the LCS, respectability and caricature, see Gatrell, *City of Laughter*, 579–80. Notice, however, that Francis Place, whom Gatrell uses as the prime representative of radical entrepreneurial respectability, wrote in 1835 that Gillray and Thomas Rowlandson were among the artists who had helped raise art to the flourishing condition he believed it was in by 1835: see the Francis Place Papers, British Library Add. MS. 27,828, vol. 40: iv, fos. 163–64.

50 Thomas Holcroft, *A Narrative of Facts, Relating to a Prosecution for High Treason* (London, 1795), 13; John Thomson Callender, *The Political Progress of Britain* (Philadelphia, 1795), 86; Daniel Stuart, *Peace and Reform, against War and Corruption*, 4th edn. (London, 1795), 119n.

51 John Gale Jones, *Sketch of a Political Tour through Rochester, Chatham, Maidstone, Gravesend, &c.* (London, 1796), 19.

or twenty-four mock playbills, or the same number of Lee's standard-issue, eight-page satirical pamphlets.

Perhaps, as Gatrell has suggested, more could have been attempted in the way of radical caricature 'had there been a greater will to take risks'.[48] But it may be a mistake to assume that radicals in general would have chosen to produce propaganda in the form of graphic satire if only they had had the will or the money to do so. Perhaps some would — Lee possibly, or Eaton, or the literary blackmailer Charles Pigott — but it is by no means certain, at least before 1796 when the LCS lost the bulk of its membership, that the majority of popular radicals in London, least of all the majority of activists, would have wanted such a thing. It is doubtful that radicals who controlled their own image as carefully as they did, in order to assert their ownership of the high ground of heroic public virtue and rational civility, would have wished to be associated with images that represented their opponents in the same humiliating visual vocabulary as loyalist caricatures used for the opponents of the government or for the French.[49] A good number of radical writers — Thomas Holcroft, James Thomson Callender, Daniel Stuart — write with disgust about loyalist caricatures of the Foxite Whigs,[50] and would no doubt have thought that to degrade one's opponents by such means was at the same time to degrade oneself. It was one thing to enjoy caricatures that represented Pitt or his drinking companion and cabinet colleague Henry Dundas, or even the king, as arrogant, drunk or foolish, as John Gale Jones among the LCS leaders admits to doing.[51] It would have been quite another for the popular radical movement to become associated with the production of such impolite images.

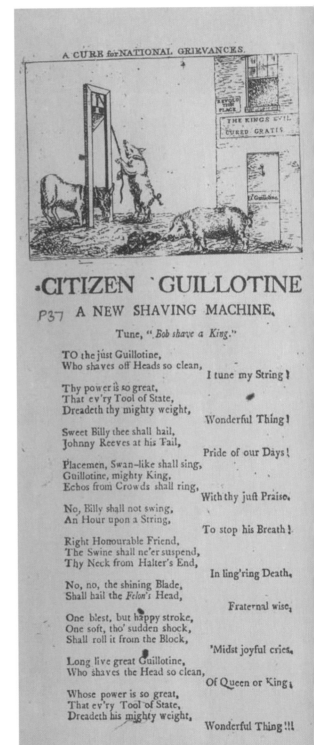

Fig. 21. Richard Lee [?], *A Cure for National Grievances* [London, Richard Lee, 1795]. Trustees of the British Museum.

Afterworld

The Gothic Travels of John Gamble (1770–1831)

Breandán Mac Suibhne

> Human reason is not, as some
> fondly suppose, a stream that
> bears us straight forward, but a
> ceaseless tide, which has ebbed
> and flowed from the beginning,
> and shall, in all probability,
> until time shall be no more.
> John Gamble[1]

September 1810 was a fine month and one Sunday morning Dr. John Gamble shook off the dust of Newtownstewart, County Tyrone, and hit the road for Strabane.[2] Born in 1770, Gamble had been reared in Strabane. He had been educated locally and then at the University of Edinburgh, from where, on graduating in 1793, he had moved to London to pursue a medical career. He had accepted a commission in the British army and seen action in the Netherlands in 1799; he

1 John Gamble, *Views of Society and Manners in the North of Ireland, in a Series of Letters Written in the Year 1818* (London, 1819), 376.
2 The following account is abridged from Anon. [John Gamble], *Sketches of History, Politics and Manners, Taken in Dublin, and the North of Ireland, in the Autumn of 1810* (London, 1811), 246–50; the italics and direct quotations are Gamble's.

Photo: Dorling Kindersley/ Getty Images.

had also served in the South Atlantic, spending three inactive years on 'the dreary rock of St. Helena'.[3] And now he was going home, not to settle, but to spend the summer months in hopes of recovering from a bout of illness. Gamble did not care for Newtownstewart. It was, he was prepared to admit, an attractive village, but there was 'more cunning and trick', he would write, 'more envy and jealousy, more heart-burnings and dissensions, more hatred and malice, more mean, pitiful and paltry contentions [in such little country villages] … [than] in the largest town in Christendom'.[4] In truth, the reason the doctor did not care for Newtownstewart was that its Churchmen (and some of its Presbyterians) had embraced Orangeism and John Gamble was no Orangeman.[5]

And so late that fine Sunday morning, Gamble left this town he had never liked to walk the eight miles to Strabane; he noted tellingly that, 'The people were going to meeting, as a place of Presbyterian worship is called, and to church, as I was turning my back on them.' Some distance out the road he was overtaken by a boy driving a car with a chest and some furniture on it. Walking behind the car were a good-looking young man and a woman. Their eyes were red and their faces inflamed and Gamble thought they had been drinking or quarrelling. Both

were crying. The man turned his head away from Gamble as if embarrassed to be seen crying, but the girl did not turn her face. 'In a woman's tears,' Gamble wrote, 'there is a softness that seeks sympathy — in a man's there is a sternness that rejects it'.

Gamble asked the woman if they travelled far, meaning if they had far to go.

'I do not,' she said. 'He does.'

'Do, Peggy darling,' interjected the young man, his Scotch twang intimating that they were Presbyterians, 'do, turn now; ye *ha* gone far enough — we *man* part, and isn't it best to have it *our*?'[6]

'I'll just *gang* the length of that *auld* tree, on the *tap* of the hill — many a sorrowful parting has been at it, and we'el put ours to the number.'

'The best of friends must sometimes part,' said Gamble, 'you will soon, I trust, have a happy meeting.'

'Never, never, *Surr*, in this *leefe*,' shot back the woman, 'when we *pert* now, my *hert* tells me it is for ever — ah! Man, man, *gin ye* had *na* been *prude*, *gin* ye had trusted to providence, and staid at *hame* — what though we could *na* get the *ferm* — what though we could *na* live in a *stane* house — they could *na* keep us out of a *scraw* one — I would have wrought for ye, and slaved late and early — and *gin* we could *na ha* got bread — we could have died together.'

3 A. Albert Campbell, *Notes on the Literary History of Strabane* (Omagh, 1902), 28–35, provides a succinct biographical sketch. Also see George O'Brien, 'The First Ulster Author: John Gamble (1770–1831)', *Éire-Ireland*, 21, 3 (1986), 131–41, and Jack Gamble, 'A Literary History of Strabane', in Jim Bradley, John Dooher and Michael Kennedy, eds., *The Fair River Valley: Strabane through the Ages* (Belfast, 2000), 250–66. C. J. Woods kindly showed me a draft of his entry on Gamble in the forthcoming *Dictionary of Irish Biography*. For extracts and commentaries, see W. J. McCormack, 'Language, Class and Gender (1780–1830)', in Seamus Deane, ed., *The Field Day Anthology of Irish Writing*, 3 vols. (Derry, 1991), vol. 1, 1106–15, and Stephen Regan, ed., *Irish Writing: An Anthology of Irish Writing in English, 1789–1939* (Oxford, 2004), 57–61, 474–75. Rolf Loeber and Magda Loeber, with Anne Mullin Burnham, *A Guide to Irish Fiction, 1650–1900* (Dublin, 2006), 482–83, lists his various works.

4 *Sketches*, 240–41. Gamble was not an admirer of Omagh either: 'Omagh (pronounced Omay, as being softer) is the assize town of the county of Tyrone; a dignity it owes more to its central situation than to any other advantage it possesses. There is a degree of gloom about it which it is more easy to feel than to describe. If I were confined to a country town, I should not chuse Omagh for my

Gamble's travel narratives are Anon. [John Gamble], *Sketches of History, Politics and Manners, Taken in Dublin, and the North of Ireland, in the Autumn of 1810* (London: C. Cradock and W. Joy, 1811); John Gamble, *A View of Society and Manners in the North of Ireland in the Summer and Autumn of 1812* (London: C. Cradock and W. Joy, 1813), and idem, *Views of Society and Manners in the North of Ireland, in a Series of Letters Written in the Year 1818* (London: Longman, Hurst, Rees, Orme, and Brown, 1819). In 1826 Baldwin, Cradock and Joy published a 'new edition' of *Sketches*, the anonymous 1810 volume, under Gamble's name. Although ostensibly a reprint, it silently incorporates three chapters from *A View*, his account of his 1812 visit; compare *A View*, 310–36, and *Sketches*, 2nd edn., 317–45. And see below, n. 7, for a significant excision. Gamble also published a pamphlet — 'A Protestant Dissenter', *Brief Observations on the Present State of Ireland; Designed as a Supplement to a Work Lately Published, Entitled, Sketches of History, Politics, and Manners, Taken in Dublin, and the North of Ireland, Principally Addressed to the English Nation* (Dublin: Thomas Courtney, 1811) — some passages of which had already appeared in *Sketches*; others reappeared, slightly emended, as the Conclusion of *A View*, 377–99, and in *Views*. Phrases from his travel narratives also echo in his various works of fiction; see below, n. 95.

prison.' See *Sketches*, 226–27; also see 225 where he describes the town as dirty, its streets irregular and the houses grotesque, and 231 where a fiddler in the inn plays 'not so well as Mr. Ware, but well enough for Omagh'. 'Mr. Ware' was possibly William Ware, organist of St. Anne's Church, Belfast, from 1776 to 1825; since Gamble's youth, his name had been synonymous in the north of Ireland with musical excellence.

5 Arriving in Newtownstewart, he had recalled how 'some time since' when there was a yeomanry review in the town, the corps, by then almost universally composed of Orangemen, had defied their officers' orders and marched through Strabane. Here, he was referring to a controversial march in August 1808. He had earlier, when at Omagh, given details of a fatal riot by Orange yeomen in 1809 that resulted in five fatalities. In both instances, he is highly critical of the Orangemen. See *Sketches*, 228–29, 241–43.

6 The Scotch twang was not exclusively Presbyterian. Gamble elsewhere renders the speech of Catholics in the same dialect. However, a discussion of emigration prompted by the encounter suggests that the young man was Presbyterian.

'*Dinna* Peggy,' said the man, '*dinna* break my *hert*, it has enough to bear already; *dinna* make me shame myself.' He again turned his head to conceal his tears. 'It is a *braave* country I'm *ganging* to, woman. There's *nae* hard landlords nor *prude* vicars there to *tak* the poor man's mite. I *war'nt* ye, I *winna* be slothful, and whene'er I earn the price of your passage, I'll send it *our*, and then wha will *pert* us?'

'You are going to America, I presume,' said Gamble.

'Yes, *Surr*, please God — this is *no* country for a poor man to *leeve* in — I thought for a *wee* bit of land — but it *nae* matter — God forgive them that wronged me, is the worst that I wish them.'

'You have been wronged then.'

'A, *Surr*, it is *nae* to seek that I could say — but we *winna* talk o' that now, for I wish to *gang* in peace with all men. I would na hae cared for myself — *a* know that man is born to trouble, as the sparks fly upwards; and *wee* God's help, I dinna fear either *hertship* or difficulty — but that poor lassie — she was aa to me in the world — and to *pert* with her is a sore tug — I *man* own it — but it was my fate, and I could na get *our* it.'

He began to whistle, for fear he should cry.

The woman walked by his side, apparently unconscious of what he was saying. She moved mechanically forward, for the large drops that every instant gathered in her eyes, and fell on the ground as she walked, must have prevented her from seeing.

'Now, Peggy, honey,' said the young man, 'we are at the tap o' the hill — the road is rugged, ye hae a *lang* way *hame*, and ye *hae* na me too.' By now he was crying again.

'I will never, never, leave ye', she said, starting from her trance, and grabbing him by the arms. 'I will never leave ye. I will go barefoot *our* the world — I will beg with ye, sterve with ye, *dee* with ye — one ship will carry us, one grave will *houlde* us — nothing but death now shall *pert* us.'

Moved by the conversation, and aware that the couple seemed exhausted by hunger as well as emotion, Gamble brought them into a little public house at the side of the road. He got them some oat-bread and butter, and whiskey and water. It would be absurd, he impressed on the distraught woman, for her to even think of going to America without making the proper preparations. Her lover was an active young man and he would soon earn enough money to take her over decently. The couple grew more composed and, leaving the public house, they parted with deep but less frantic sorrow. Gamble walked on a few paces, but the young man soon caught up with him.

'See what a beautiful day this is?' the doctor remarked; 'the sun shines on your setting off.'

'Let him shine on her I left behind,' he replied, 'and he may spare his *beems* to me — *mony* and *mony* a time we ha seen him set, from the hawthorn bush, in my father's garden; but that's over now, as well as every thing else.'

'It is not over, I hope,' responded Gamble. 'You will, I trust, have as happy hours, as you now have sorrowful ones; but if you should not, remember that affliction is the common lot, and that you have no right to expect to escape it.' No doubt thinking of the conversation that had passed in the public house, he continued: 'You have health and you have youth. You have the testimony of a good conscience; you have the approbation of your own mind, for manfully acting your part in life. Of these your enemies cannot deprive you. They will follow you to America, and gladden the wilderness where you may chance to reside. They will sweeten the rude morsel that labour procures you. They will lull you to sleep in the torrent's roar while greatness, that wants them, will find its costly viands insipid, and seek vain repose on its gilded couches, and beds of down. You think the rich are to be envied. I tell you they are more to be pitied than you. They have the lassitude, intemperance and vice — of ill-health, that folly engenders, of vice that gives no enjoyment, and of the greatest of all wants, that of having something to do. Leave them their diseases and riches; take you your poverty and health. Leave them their sensuality and gluttony, and drunkenness; take you temperance and content. Leave them their close apartments, their midnight revels, their burning tapers, their gilded canopies, their luxuriant carpets; take you the air which breathes so sweetly on you, these birds which sing around us — this immense apartment of the universe — this green and verdant earth, which heaven itself has fitted up for the gratification of man.'

And Gamble having said his piece, they shook hands and parted.

•

This chance encounter on the road to Strabane intrigues, not least as the conversation in the roadside tavern, which might fully explain the tear-stained young man's departure, is left open to conjecture. He is leaving because he can not get a farm. He might have got a farm, but he was a man of conscience, a proud man; his enemies are wealthy, lazy men, rectors and landlords. And he is leaving at a time when the Orange Order, the tool of rectors and landlords, was in its pomp. So there is the ghost of politics — youth, love and integrity against power, wealth and bigotry.

Gamble published his description of this encounter in his *Sketches of History, Politics and Manners, Taken in Dublin, and the North of Ireland, in the Autumn of 1810*; it appeared in London in 1811. The book was a success, in part because it was well written but more particularly because it appeared at a time when Ireland, most especially 'the North of Ireland', was making news in England on account of a spike in intercommunal violence, caused by Orange marches intended to provoke a reaction that would cause aspersions to be cast on Catholics' insistence that they were eligible for full citizenship. Gamble's

book was also controversial. Legal action by William Conyngham Plunket, a lawyer who had acted as a crown prosecutor in the trial of the republican leader Robert Emmet, forced booksellers to withdraw it from sale; Gamble had alluded to Emmet's reputed denunciation of Plunket as 'that viper my father warmed in his bosom', which had already been the subject of a successful case against the radical printer William Cobbett.[7] Gamble, however, produced two other books on his trips home to Strabane, one visit in 1812, the other in 1818, when it appears he returned to stay.[8] He also wrote a pamphlet, published in 1811, that argued for Catholic Emancipation, and several works of fiction, all either set in 'the North of Ireland' or involving characters from it: *Sarsfield; or, Wanderings of Youth. An Irish Tale*, 3 vols. (1814), *Howard. A Novel*, 2 vols. (1815), *Northern Irish Tales*, 2 vols. (1818) and *Charlton; or, Scenes in the North of Ireland. A Tale*, 3 vols. (1823; 2nd edn., 1827).[9]

For a modern reader, Gamble's 'tales' and novels (with the exception of *Charlton*) suffer from the weaknesses of much early nineteenth-century fiction — overwrought language, types rather than characters, predictable plots. But his books about his journeys home are a different matter. In all three of them, he introduces a memorable set of characters, including his fellow travellers — drunken sailors on the Liverpool coach, other drunks singing and snoring and a woman chewing garlic who shared the Derry mail with him, a lonely country boy who accompanies him through the mountain districts of west Tyrone — as well as people met on the roads, people like the tear-stained couple on the road from Newtownstewart, a gigantic prostitute who accosted him on the street in Drogheda, and the Monaghan beggar who, when proffered a penny, replied 'I *canna tak* it, gentlefolks always *gie* me *siller*.'[10] There are also his friends and close acquaintants, notably a dying Presbyterian minister with whom he passed a few days at Toome, a former patient whose dying niece he tended in a

7   For the controversial passage, see *Sketches*, 74–77; compare with *Sketches*, 2nd edn., 84–85, and the favourable presentation of Plunket in *Views*, 76–77, where his election as MP for Trinity is described. Plunket was later the target of Orange obloquy when he prosecuted those involved in the 'bottle riot' of 1822. There is a local connection here; Plunket's wife, Katharine McCausland (1761–1821), was a daughter of John McCausland (1735–1804) of Strabane, MP for County Donegal, 1768–76. On the suppression of the book, see McCormack, 'Language, Class and Gender', 1106, 1113 n. 11, and Maeve Ryan, '"The Reptile that had Stung Me": William Plunket and the Trial of Robert Emmet', in Anne Dolan et al., eds., *Reinterpreting Emmet: Essays on the Life and Legacy of Robert Emmet* (Dublin, 2007), 77–101, esp. 83. Gilbert and Hodges, the Dublin company at the centre of the dispute, were respectable but occasionally audacious printers and booksellers, publishing, in 1810, Thomas Moore's *Letter to the Catholics of Dublin*, which like Gamble's work, had first appeared in London, and William Cooper's letters to the exiled republican William Sampson.

The title-page of the second edition of Gamble's *Sketches* (1811).

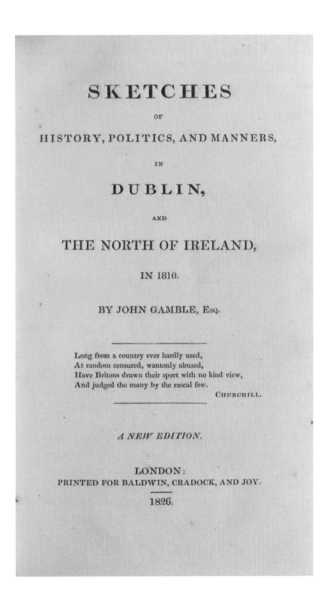

8 *Views*, 58, gives the impression he had no intention of returning to England. However, the Preface to *Charlton; or, Scenes in the North of Ireland. A Tale*, 3 vols. (1823; 2nd edn., 1827), vol. 1, v, suggests he returned on a short visit but happened to stay.

9 While Gamble's tours have occasionally been cited, his 'tales' have attracted little attention. For an exception, see the acute reading of his work in both genres in O'Brien, 'First Ulster Author'.

10 *Sketches*, 3–4 (sailors), 138–40 (prostitute), 143–46 (garlic-eater), 156 (beggar), and *A View*, 336–37 (boy).

11 *Views*, 274–78 (dying girl); *A View*, 209–57 (minister), 306–10 (spinners). Listening to the spinners leads Gamble into a discussion of the controversy over the relative merits of the settings of Irish tunes by Edward Bunting and, for Thomas Moore's *Melodies*, by Sir John Stevenson; he finds both wanting.

12 *Sketches*, 251; the italics are Gamble's, warning against the Old Light turn in Presbyterianism.

house between Castlederg and Ardstraw — he chastized his friend for discussing the girl's funeral with her — and servant girls who sang in Irish at their spinning wheels in a house near Aghyaran as he pretended to sleep by the fire.[11]

And then there is Gamble himself. He was emphatically a Dissenter partisan — 'Presbyterianism as it *now* exists in the North of Ireland, is beyond all others the religion of reason' — but a partisan who was not a bigot.[12] His fondly remembered nanny was a Catholic, he socialized and engaged intellectually with Catholics (discussing politics with them, attending Mass, visiting the pilgrimage island in Lough Derg and befriending a priest), appreciated their culture (including the Irish language, Irish music, and, remarkably, the much-derided 'Irish Wake' and 'Irish Cry') and, if at times patronizing about their political direction, he wrote with passion of their historical 'sufferings' and argued trenchantly for Catholic Emancipation.[13] There is a brutal honesty in his discussions of the Catholics' position. In 1812, when a man named Sullivan, with whom he breakfasted at an inn in Larne, informed him (before Gamble had swallowed his first cup of tea) that, despite his surname, he was a Protestant, descended from a French Huguenot, Gamble wondered: 'How must the native Irish have been treated in their ancient land, when it is thought degradation even to be descended from them[?]'[14] And later that same year, when he was in the predominantly Catholic mountains of west Tyrone, he remarked that 'in ancient times [the mountains] were the asylum of those unfortunate people, and they were not dispossessed of them, probably because no other people would live in them'. The image here is stark, its effect startling: 'Into these mountains, [they] were driven and pent up like sheep, and left upon black bog, and dun heath, and barren rock to mourn over their fallen greatness, their fertile vales, their flocks and their fields.'[15] And on another occasion, near Ballygawley, expressing irritation at travellers who attribute the 'torpor and listlessness' of the Catholic poor to 'inherent, and constitutional laziness', the effect of his imagery is more startling still: 'It is not laziness … in the common acceptation of the word; it is melancholy, it is hopelessness, it is despondency. It is a singular recollection of ancient sufferings and humiliations. It is the heart-sinking of the prisoner, to whom the act of cleaning himself becomes at length a burthen.'[16]

Gamble, it should be said, was also something of a wit. All three books are replete with wry one-liners:

An Irishman's house, like Polyphemus's den, is of easy access; the difficulty is in getting out of it.[17]

[In the North of Ireland], excessive heat is as rare as adultery.[18]

Extravagance is no more a Presbyterian's vice than distrust in Providence.[19]

And Gamble was most definitely a drinker. In 1810, the most drunken of his trips, the journey from Dublin to Strabane involved 'large potations' of wine and punch in Drogheda, where, being on the Boyne, he drank the 'Glorious and Immortal Memory' of King William, a toast he describes as 'an excuse for drunkenness upwards of a century'. At Drogheda, he got the Derry mail, which stopped to change horses in Carrickmacross. Although it was only 'about seven in the morning', Gamble was offered 'a drop of something warm, just to keep the damp out of my stomach this cold morning'; he declined. The mail stopped again to allow the passengers to breakfast at a 'well-kept' inn in Castleblayney. Here, Gamble remarks on how he preferred travelling by coach in Ireland than in England, as 'an Irish coach stops longer for meals, and is more tedious in changing horses than an English one':

You are not obliged to devour your food like a cannibal, and at length to run away like a debtor pursued by bailiffs. You are allowed a decent time for dinner; and should the goodness of the wine induce you to wish to extend it for a few minutes, the guard is seldom inexorable. His majesty's mail can wait, you may finish your *meal* at leisure.

Later, he drank whiskey (although wine was on the table) in Monaghan with some Clones Methodists and then half a pint of excellent wine — 'I would never wish to drink better wine, nor did I ever, in a coffee house in London, drink any so good' — in a disordered establishment in Rockcorry, a 'poor little

13 *Views*, 208–09 (nanny); *A View*, 326–36, and *Views*, 396–98 (cry and wake). In the latter passage, he describes the 'cry' as consisting 'but of a few words, and the music only of a few bars', which, he argues, demonstrates the magic effects that can be wrought by the simplest and least complicated means. He insists that 'the Irish Cry will be cherished, and its *affecting cadences admired, as long as plaintive melody is relished or understood*' (italics added) and sniffily dismisses the 'hymns in the Latin language, set to the Gregorian music', which many priests were then promoting, as having an allegro movement with more of the step of dancing than of death. Here, he is quoting without acknowledgement from Alexander Ross, 'Parish of Dungiven', in William Shaw Mason, comp., *A Statistical Account, or Parochial Survey of Ireland*, 3 vols. (Dublin, 1814–19), vol. 1 [1814], 283–348 (319). On the Irish language, see *A View*, 307–10, and, also, 358–59, where he mentions an old priest having told him it was 'the best language in the world for a man to make love in'. On Catholics' political direction, see *Brief Observations*, 11–12, where he deplores their leaders for keeping alive a flame 'which in the end may consume themselves'.

14 *A View*, 82–83.

15 *A View*, 303, 318–19.

16 *Sketches*, 222–23.

17 *Sketches*, 143.

18 *Sketches*, 75. Adultery was known in Louth: see *Sketches*, 132.

19 *A View*, 277.

20 Such accidents were
not uncommon. A few
months earlier, the driver
of a hack chaise and
one of the gentlemen
inside were killed when
it overturned at Douglass
Bridge, not far from
where the guard on
Gamble's coach perished.
See *London-Derry
Journal* [hereafter, *LJ*], 6
March 1810.

21 The quotations on
drinking are from
Sketches, 115–16
(Drogheda), 146
(Carrickmacross), 147
(Castleblayney), 159–61
(Monaghan), 163–64
(recalling Castleblayney),
167–68 (Rockcorry), 172
(Cootehill), 192, 194,
198 (farmer's house),
204 (Crossroads), 211
(near Aughnacloy),
212–14 (Aughnacloy),
214 (Ballygawley),
225 (Omagh), 240
(Newtownstewart), 278
(Strabane).

22 *A View*, v. Parts of this
description of his style
are repeated in *Sketches*,
2nd edn., v.

place, containing about a dozen indifferent houses'; 'drinking', he had remarked drily on entering the town, 'must be highly prized here; for out of the dozen, five or six were public ones'. At this stage, Gamble, who had got off the coach at Monaghan, was making a major diversion to visit the mother of a deceased friend, another doctor, in Cootehill, a town of which he had little to say but that the shambles was remarkably neat and that 'drunkenness' was becoming increasingly common among the young. On leaving Cootehill, he spent a night at the house of a relatively casual acquaintance; they had a 'drop of the cratur' on arrival and, after dinner washed down with a bottle of 'excellent wine' (his drunken host cut his hand trying to carve the goose), they 'continued drinking and conversing to a late hour'. The following day, he walked five miles to Crossroads, where he had breakfast in a public house but (to his relief) no alcohol, before walking to Emyvale; there, he was offered a seat by a gentleman's servant driving a jaunting car, who, letting him off a mile outside Aughnacloy, agreed with his suggestion that they 'must not part with dry lips' and joined him for some whiskey in a house at the side of the road. Gamble walked into Aughnacloy, opting to wait for the Derry mail in the lesser of the town's two inns, where he ate fish, roast lamb and sweetmeats and downed a pint of port. The mail, when it arrived, was full of noisy drunks, so he had to walk to Ballygawley. There he got accommodation in the village's only inn; it was 'shabby looking' from without but like 'a little Eden within' and the whiskey was like 'nectar'. The next morning, he walked a few miles before flagging down the Derry mail. En route, the guard, who was playing the clarinet on the roof, fell from the coach and died on the spot; the driver and passengers took the corpse into a cabin at the side of the road before proceeding.[20] At Omagh, Gamble visited the Abercorn Arms, where he dined with the landlord, a Mr. Jenkins, and enjoyed at least a tumbler of whiskey, before taking a night coach to Newtownstewart, where his supper was 'bacon and eggs … the

best relish for whiskey punch I am acquainted with'; he describes how 'I quaffed the latter off in full streams, as if they had issued from Mount Helicon'. He spent the night in Newtownstewart and the next day he drank with the departing emigrant and his girlfriend in the roadside tavern. In Strabane itself, where he was to spend the next few weeks, he was frequently invited to 'dinner and evening parties', where 'every person was at liberty to drink as he pleased', but Gamble saw no 'disposition to excess'. The wine on the table, Tenerife, Sherry, and Port, was scarcely ever touched, he wrote; 'Wine is taken without pleasure, but the approach of the punch is hailed with rapture, as it makes its appearance immediately after the cloth is removed.' 'Punch', he adds, as if by this stage the reader needs to be told, 'is the national liquor.'[21]

•

Gamble's ostensible purpose in these books is 'to make better known to the inhabitants of England, a people deserving to be known', the approach being to relate — 'by hasty sketch, by short tale, and brief dialogue' — his journeys home and the recollections and speculations provoked by things he sees and hears.[22] They are forms of travel writing but they are not the jottings of an outsider. Rather, they are the work of someone reared in the country he describes and familiar with the people and places he visits. And yet several years have passed since he was last there. More especially, then, Gamble's books are the reflections of a returned exile, a man who goes home after a long absence and finds, as the returned emigrant always finds, that familiar as the home-place may be, he has changed and it has changed and he no longer fits in; he may get back to a place, but not to a place in time:

I should never advise him who quits in early life the place of his birth, to come back in mature age in expectation of enjoyment; if he does, and has but ordinary sensibility, he will be disappointed. If such a hope has been his solace in a strange land, I pity him, for it will fail him the moment his heel touches his native earth. The scenes of his youth he may return to, but his youthful joys, like his youthful years, will return no more; like luminous vapours which mislead the benighted traveller, they shine on him from afar, only to plunge him as he approaches in darker gloom.[23]

For this reason, and because, in addition, Gamble has not been in Ireland since 1798, the year of the United Irishmen's great rising, the journey books are preoccupied with the political imaginary. The 'ghost of former days', as he puts it in the third book, haunted him on each of his trips home; things reminded him of the past but also the future as it had been imagined in the past. Strabane, as he saw it, in the 1810s — commercially (depressed, especially in 1818), culturally (moribund; life there is 'like a grass-grown lake, which stagnates by its own stillness') and politically (sectarian, if not as sectarian as Newtownstewart) — bore little resemblance to what it had been in his youth in the 1780s or, more importantly, to what he and others had then imagined it would become in the new century.[24] And as

the ghost of former days — the remembered past and the outline of the might-have-been — cast a lengthening shadow over the never imagined but actual present, so 1798, the year in which the future imagined by a generation finally disappeared, became for Gamble the point on which time had turned and still turns; it became, for him, the reason that home is not what home was supposed to have become.

Gamble's presentation of 1798 as history's pivot — as distinct from the Union of 1801 — can be read as provincialism: the loss of the Irish parliament ('Three hundred Bacchannals whose sun daily set in claret') was more grievously felt in the capital than in the country.[25] However, it is better seen as an expression of his concern for 'society and manners', that is people — 'human passions, human actions, and human beings, with all their imperfections on their heads' — and culture, more especially sociability. 'Men and women', he writes, 'are of more importance than pillars or columns'.[26] In all three books, he grieves for the decline of 'society' since the Rising — 'There is no community of feeling in Ireland …'[27] — drawing attention to the most subtle signs of diminished interaction between Catholics and

23 *Views*, 168. And compare *A View*, 276–77: 'I know nothing more calculated to draw forth more sad and mournful reflection, than a return, after a long absence, to the place where we passed our youthful days. … different habits, different manners, and different degrees of communication with the world, will hardly allow [the returned emigrant] to feel much friendship or to experience much gratification.'

24 *Views*, 168, 193.

25 *Sketches*, 58. Also see *Brief Observations*, 14–15.

26 *A View*, v.

27 *Sketches*, 279. Likewise, discussing the effects of Orangeism (253), he refers to 'the diseased state of public feeling'.

28 Marianne Elliott, *The Catholics of Ulster: A History* (Harmondsworth, 2000), 198, thinks differently, arguing that 'John Gamble's invaluable tour of 1810 … shows that the old traditions of hospitality and deference had not been eroded by the bitter experiences of the 1790s …' Elsewhere (335–36), she writes that 'The impression [in Gamble's various tours] is of roads full of human traffic, of walkers invariably seeking companionship, of hospitality to excess.' However, George O'Brien has read Gamble in similar terms to myself. See 'First Ulster Author', 140, where he observes that 'Both [Gamble's] travel books and novels are suffused with a sense of aftermath and marginality, of psychological trauma and cultural withering'.

One of the more curious aspects of Gamble's drinking is that he frequently presents himself as being more abstemious than those around him, remarking of an acquaintance in Armagh in 1818 (*Views*, 352), that 'he is no more a drinker than myself'. But the evidence of his intake suggests otherwise. Moreover, he has a telltale tendency to philosophize on alcohol, musing on its relationship to health (*A View*, 314–15), connecting heavy drinking to climate (*Views*, 291–92) and seeing a cycle of oppression, drinking and violence in Irish society (*Brief Observations*, 18). And Gamble also has a drinker's preoccupation with the quality of what he consumes. However, this foible serves one of the key purposes of his books: his repeated insistence on the 'excellence' of the drink in Ireland (particularly in such unstoried places as Rockcorry and Aughnacloy) — like his insistence on the quality of Irish inns (*Sketches*, 147–48, 163–64), coaches and so forth — becomes a put-down of English travellers who compared all things in the country unfavourably with those available in England. In that context, Gamble's commenting (*Views*, 366) that in Belfast, 'You might fancy yourself in Liverpool or Glasgow, only that the accent is a little too English for the one, and a great deal too Scotch for the other …' is a more nuanced remark than some commentators have allowed. This sentence is quoted in Paul Bew, *The Politics of Enmity: Ireland, 1789–2006* (Oxford, 2007), 565, but not the preceding one: 'As to the town itself, it is a great commercial one, and commercial towns are nearly the same all the world over.'

29 Gamble's comments on the changing attitude to inns were prompted by his observing that Pat Lynn's inn, which had once been considered the 'best kept house' in Belfast, had recently lost something of its reputation; see *A View*, 62–63. He explains, 'I should suppose, from the name (for a zealous Protestant would as soon call his son Judas as Pat) that Mr. Lynn is a Catholic'.

30 *A View*, 299–301 (absence of players). Also see *Views*, 350 (absence of musicians).

31 On Methodism, see *Sketches*, 2–3 (addiction); 160–61 ('fanaticism'); and 237–38 (preachers like quack-doctors). Also see *A View*, 343–44, and *Views*, 51, 137–47.

32 *Sketches*, 255. The psalm-singer, a Mr. McVity, conducted classes in both the cathedral and meeting house in Derry, as well as in Strabane: see *LJ*, 12 September 1809. For Gamble's appreciation of the 'noisy bawling' that typically passed for singing at Presbyterian meetings, see *A View*, 364.

33 *Sketches*, 128; *A View*, 36.

Protestants.[28] He notes, for instance, that Protestant travellers used to prefer Catholic innkeepers 'on account of their greater subserviency and civility' but were now increasingly favouring their co-religionists with their custom. Likewise, he remarks on Protestants' wonder that the 'lower-classes of Catholics' now 'give offence by what is called their rudeness and sulkiness' (he himself sees little cause for wonder — 'The man employed in bending the tough elm into a bow, need not be astonished when it flies back in his face').[29] The erosion of a common cultural life that, he avers, had existed in his youth is a recurrent theme. In 1812 he comments, 'with regret' and some surprise, that he had travelled 150 miles since arriving in Ireland and 'I have not even heard of a party of strolling players, or even a single mountebank, horse-rider, juggler, or puppet-showman, in any town, great or small, I have passed through'.[30] And he is suspicious of the new enthusiasm for religion — be it focused on church, chapel or meeting — seeing in it a divisive, disabling force. Methodism, enjoying a surge in popularity in the wake of the Rising, he views with a mixture of fascination and repulsion, representing it as an addiction, but he also frowns upon the Old Light turn in Presbyterianism and the emergence of a more Roman (less Irish) Catholicism in the same years. It is the wider social and cultural consequences of religious enthusiasm, then, that concern him.[31] On his first trip home, he reported that a travelling psalm-singer appointed by the bishop of Derry had caused the traditional popular songs 'Grammachree', 'Granua Uile', and 'The Blue Bells of Scotland' to be neglected around Strabane, as young and old, men and women, 'people who had voices and others who had none', flocked to learn hymns.[32] He is relieved to find that 'rage' is dying down, remarking that it is being replaced now by card-playing, another 'frenzy'. Ultimately, the most obvious expression of diminished sociability — the degradation of society and manners — was overt and particularly casual sectarianism. He repeatedly appears shocked by bigotry. He has no time for Orangeism: an Orange song with the refrain 'And to H[ell] with the breed for ever' appals him, for instance, and he is insulted to be offered a bunch of Orange lilies by a street-trader, replying, 'I am no party man, nor do I ever wear party colours'.[33] Likewise, a Catholic herdsman damning Presbyterians as a 'black-hearted breed' disconcerts him (although he can understand the man's bitterness at how

Although Gamble (contra Marianne Elliott's comments) was insistent on the decline of sociability since the Rising, he had no illusions about its limits before it. On his tour of 1810, for instance, he describes how, in the north of Ireland, Scotchmen had only taken possession of the valleys and fertile spots, leaving the natives the bogs and mountains, adding 'By degrees, as fear abated and rancour subsided, [the Catholic] crept slowly down, and the lowly [P]resbyterian, who was now become of consequence enough to have another to do for him, what he was once happy to do himself, allowed him to labour the land which he once possessed, and when his spirit was fairly broke to his fortunes, treated his humble hewer of wood, and drawer of water, with something that resembled kindness. He still, however, regarded him with distrust; he rarely admitted him into the house where he slept, and when he did, a large door, double locked, separated their apartments: "Never trust an Eerishman, gude troth he's a foul chap — gin ye tak him in at your boosom, he'el be oot at your sleeve." The [P]resbyterian farmer often spoke thus, many generations after he had become an Irishman himself.' See *Sketches*, 153–54; this passage is repeated in *Views*, iii–iv, as far as '… resembled kindness'. Although the concern in this essay is Gamble's attitude to the recent past, spectres from Protestant folk history — stories about 1641, references to travellers crossing Glenshane in caravans for fear of rapparees and the like — appear in all three narratives.

'they' had been quick to '*sell the pass* upon us' at Ballynahinch).[34]

Conversely, occasions when Gamble meets the old sociability are described in detail and at length and, it seems, experienced on an emotional level. The honest and open, rational and heartfelt discussion with the distraught couple on the road from Newtownstewart in 1810 is an exemplary incident, as is the time he spent that summer with his late friend's mother in Cootehill, 'talking of times that are long past, and of persons I had once known well'; so too are a few days spent near Ballymena in 1812 with a former United Irishman, reading books and talking politics, telling stories and drinking whiskey; an argument about religion and titles with an old Covenanter he meets on the road from Ballymena to Toome — the man explained his refusal to refer to his landlord by anything other than his first name by asking '*wha* ever said Mr. Mat[t]hew, or Mr. Luke, or Mr. John?' — and a couple of weeks he passed in the predominantly Catholic mountain districts around Aghyaran, where 'Life, like the mountains which sustain it, like the wind which howls over them, like the mists which ever rest upon them, and now come down in thick and drizzling rain, is solemn and lugubrious'; there, he ate with the herdsmen and servant girls, smoked their tobacco and drank their whiskey, attended a wake and funeral, worked as a doctor, listened to stories of banshees, and ghosts and *wraths* ('a shadowy representation of a living person'), and talked about politics.[35]

The weeks in the backhills moved Gamble. 'Simple and warm-hearted people!' he wrote. 'Because I had in a light work written a few lines in your favour — because I had done you a faint kind of justice, how expressive were your feelings, how warm was your gratitude, and how sincere were your thanks.'[36] On another occasion, taking leave of a Frenchman whom he had befriended in Ballymoney and with whom he had visited the Giant's Causeway on the north Antrim coast, he remarked that 'parting with those whose society has pleased, and whom in all likelihood we shall never again behold, is the tearing of a part of life's scaffolding away'.[37] And it is perhaps here, in the savouring of the shade of the old sociability and in the mourning of its passing — rather than in the discussion of 'public affairs' or the arguments for Catholic Emancipation or the memory of the dead — that Gamble's books are most decisively political.[38]

•

James Clarence Mangan was a poet and a drinker and a drug-abuser and he was an admirer of John Gamble: the Tyrone-man's

34 *A View*, 116–17; italics in original.
35 *Sketches*, 166–93 ('fleshpots of Cootehill'); *A View*, 120–208 (republican), 210–13 (Covenanter), 301–43, esp. 303 (Aghyaran).
36 *A View*, 319–20, referring to *Brief Observations*.
37 *Views*, 398.
38 While Gamble's early efforts at fiction were clumsy, the style of his journey books (thick description of 'ordinary' people, the use of dialect and what might be seen as the romancing of a destroyed world) anticipated that of Walter Scott's Waverley novels (1814–27), and that of his final and most accomplished novel, *Charlton*, might be considered to mimic it. Although an admirer of Scott (*A View*, 357; *Views*, 397–98), Gamble thought that his own 'most perfect impartiality towards my different characters, to whatever sect or party they belong' distinguished *Charlton* from Scott's work: see *Charlton*, vol. 1, v–vi. For Gamble on Moore, see *A View*, 306–10; also see *Views*, 79, and 92, where at Tara he quotes Moore's 'The Harp that Once Through Tara's Halls' as he recalls the battle there in 1798. The phrase 'gone and for ever', used by Moore in a melody composed in October 1814 to evoke the fading hope of freedom, was a borrowing from Walter Scott's *The Lady of the Lake* (1810); in his account of his 1812 journey, Gamble quotes Scott's verse and compares it to an Irish-language lament: see *A View*, 335–36.

There are many hints on Gamble's family history in his books. For instance, he mentions (*Views*, 223–24) that his grandfather had lived close to Castlegore and he relates (*Views*, 277–78) a conversation with a former patient between Derg and Ardstraw who alludes to the author having been related to Lairds, including 'Mr. Laird, the clergyman of Donaghmore'. Francis Laird (d. 1742) was Presbyterian minister of Donoughmore in 1709–42. In 1747, the Synod of Ulster removed his son, William Laird (1721–91), then minister of Ray (Manorcunningham), to the Rosemary Street congregation in Belfast. The Ray congregation took umbrage at the 'high-handed procedure' and refused to admit another minister from the Synod, allying themselves with the Secession Synod. The former patient also mentions that Gamble's 'old grandmother' was a Henderson and that both his father and his 'old uncle Sproulle' won the Lottery. This uncle, a later reference (*Views*, 409) indicates, was a doctor who attended John Macnaghton, a gentleman murderer, prior to his execution in 1761; hence, he was John Sproull (his preferred spelling), a well-regarded Strabane surgeon and a member of the committee that oversaw Crawford's Strabane Academy; see *Regulations*, 3. Some of these connections are discussed in Campbell, *Notes*, 29–30.

The title page of Gamble's *A View* (1813).

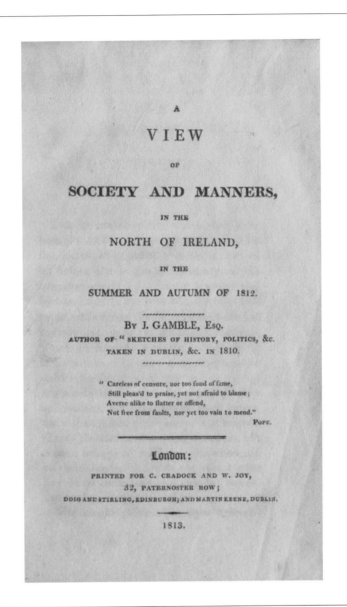

A

VIEW

OF

SOCIETY AND MANNERS,

IN THE

NORTH OF IRELAND,

IN THE

SUMMER AND AUTUMN OF 1812.

By J. GAMBLE, Esq.

AUTHOR OF " SKETCHES OF HISTORY, POLITICS, &c.
TAKEN IN DUBLIN, &c. IN 1810.

" Careless of censure, nor too fond of fame,
Still pleas'd to praise, yet not afraid to blame;
Averse alike to flatter or offend,
Not free from faults, nor yet too vain to mend."

POPE.

London:

PRINTED FOR C. CRADOCK AND W. JOY,
32, PATERNOSTER ROW;
DOIG AND STIRLING, EDINBURGH; AND MARTIN KEENE, DUBLIN.

1813.

39 The quotation is from a letter to Charles Gavan Duffy, suggesting republication of Gamble's *Northern Irish Tales* and Charles Robert Maturin's *Milesian Chief* (London, 1812). Mangan continued: 'His narratives are all domestic and exceedingly melancholy. Which county of Ulster gave him birth I wist not, but in one of his tales he apostrophises the Mourne as his own river — and in truth he seems to have drunk royally of its waves, for he is very, very mourne-ful.' Quoted in D. J. O'Donoghue, *The Life and Writings of James Clarence Mangan* (Edinburgh, 1897), 145. The defining discussion of Mangan is David Lloyd, *Nationalism and Minor Literature: James Clarence Mangan and the Emergence of Irish Cultural Nationalism* (Berkeley, 1987); the essential addendum is Seamus Deane, *Strange Country: Modernity and Nationhood in Irish Writing since 1790* (Oxford, 1997), 122–39.

'domestic and exceedingly melancholy' narratives, he told a friend, had made a 'powerful impression on me when I luxuriated (*à la* Wert[h]er) in my teens'.39 The style and subjects that so impressed Mangan — 'the mingled gloom and levity', as Gamble himself describes it, the sense of being alone or lonely at home, the flitting from what he sees to what he remembers and from what he remembers to what he fears — stemmed from a source other than

the emigrant's return to an alien home-place: John Gamble was going blind. Always 'remarkably short-sighted', he suffered 'frequent attacks' of 'almost total blindness' and he was resigned to permanently losing his sight. A Preface to his account of 1812 offers a pointed defence of his everyday subjects, his sudden shifts from sombre to light-hearted concerns and his ostensibly casual intermixing of incident, anecdote and apprehension. His flickering eyesight is the

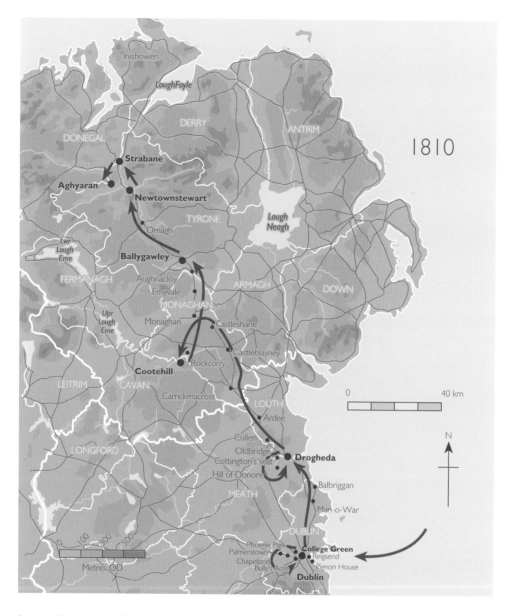

Gamble's route in 1810. Larger dots indicate places where he spent a night or more.

bottom line, 'an apology … which I dare say will be thought a sufficient one':

Even at the best … I can take little share in the business or the amusements of life, and while feeble is the light that shines on the present, I have the past to remember, and the future to apprehend. Inevitable blindness, like all other inevitable misfortunes, may be borne … But neither to be wholly blind nor entirely to see, to vibrate as it were between light and

darkness, may well throw the mind off its balance, and cause joy and sadness, mirth and melancholy, to struggle together, and contend for mastery, like the elemental particles of chaos.[40]

But here the doctor protests too much. The apparently meaningless physical and mental meanderings as he tries to get home are deceptive. All three narratives are based on extensive background reading as well as chance encounters and casual meetings

40 *A View*, v–viii. Also see Preface to *Charlton*, vol. 1, v–xi.

Gamble's route in 1812; originally bound for Newry, his ship had been wrecked on the Dublin coast.

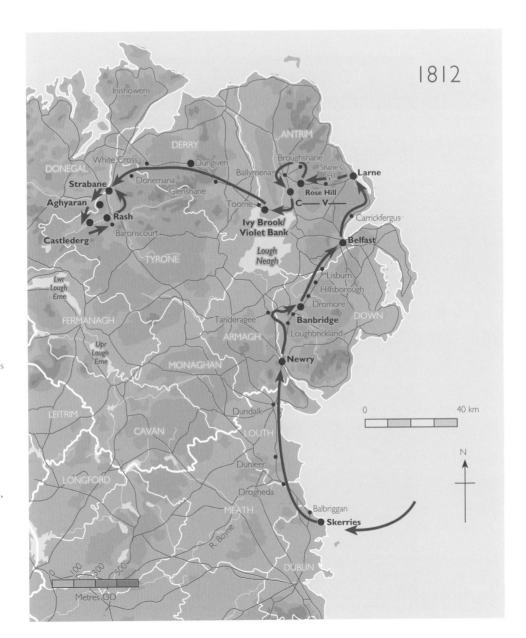

41 Gamble's journey books are replete with passages taken silently from works by other authors, on which see above, n. 13. Also see his listing of the art collection of the earl bishop of Derry, in *A View*, 295–96, culled from George Vaughan Sampson, *Statistical Survey of the County of Londonderry ...* (Dublin, 1802), 420–23. The influence of Sampson's *A Memoir, Explanatory of the Chart and Survey of the County of London-Derry, Ireland* (London, 1814), esp. 184–94, 332–59, is also very much in evidence in the 1818 volume, *Views*: the discussion of the 'character' of the three ethno-religious groups (particularly Catholic character, which both describe as 'monarchical'), concern that Catholics were replacing Protestants on the land, and conviction that power falling to Catholics would have disastrous consequences, are all strikingly similar.

42 *A View*, v, 318.

and all three make pointed interventions in contemporary political and cultural debates.[41] They are deliberate works, carefully structured to make a case (the case is often in the structure) — most obviously about the need for Catholic Emancipation — but also, it appears, to illuminate, by cumulative impressions 'rather than by formal dissertation', the connection between 'society and manners' and politics and to show that people 'do not live in the present

alone, but in the future, and in the past, and while they have hope to brighten, [they] have recollection to darken their path'.[42]

Hope guttering in dark recollection might well describe John Gamble's own 'manner', but a Gothic aspect in his journey books — not least the representation of living people in ghostly terms — owes less to that melancholy sensibility than to the particular condition of post-1798 Ireland, most especially the condition of

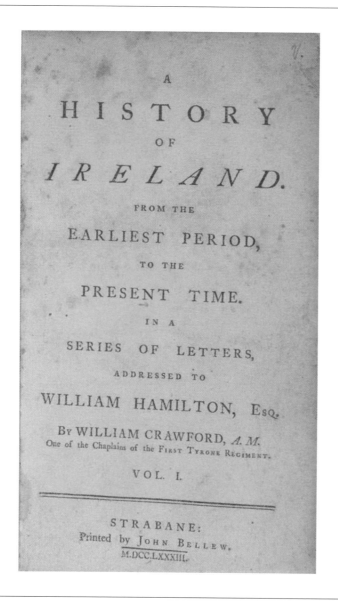

Dr. William Crawford's two volume *A History of Ireland* (1783). Crawford, the local Presbyterian minister, had been Gamble's teacher in the 1780s. He quotes without acknowledgment from Crawford's book on his tour of 1812 and includes a poignant account of Crawford's departure form Strabane in his account of his 1818 visit; see below, 102 and 109–10.

his home-place.[43] Republican rebellion and the state's repression of it (a process intensified by infringements on the right to bear arms, freedom of assembly and the freedom of the press in the five years prior to 1798) had combined with wider (though not all unconnected) social and cultural developments — such as the rise of evangelicalism — to corrode many of the institutions which, in earlier decades, had sustained reasoned discourse.[44] For instance, public houses, as Gamble himself intimates, had changed in the opening years of the new century. The Catholic publicans whom Protestants had once preferred for their meekness had, by their very presence, exercised considerable influence on society and manners — why gratuitously offend the inoffensive; why be unreasonable to reasonable men? — promoting 'conversation in mixed company', a space where people of diverse backgrounds could 'unite' — as 'the

43 Here, Gamble's home-place should be understood to mean, in the first instance, north-west Ulster but also, in a secondary sense, Presbyterian Ulster.

44 The state's assault on the press had begun in earnest in the mid-1780s; see Brian Inglis, *Freedom of the Press in Ireland, 1784–1841* (London, 1954).

The Derry edition of Thomas Paine's *Rights of Man*, Pt. 1, which was published anonymously by George Douglas. A 'cheap edition', it was subsidized by raffling a portrait of George Washington. The portrait had been brought to Derry by the artist, Charles Peale Polk, who had hoped to sell it to Frederick Augustus Hervey, Bishop of Derry. Hervey was away from home, but a group of city radicals acquired the painting; Robert Moore, a prominent member of this group, won the raffle.

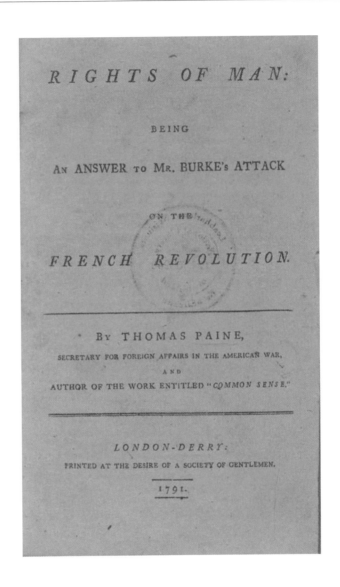

RIGHTS OF MAN:

BEING

AN ANSWER TO MR. BURKE's ATTACK

ON THE

FRENCH REVOLUTION.

BY THOMAS PAINE,

SECRETARY FOR FOREIGN AFFAIRS IN THE AMERICAN WAR,

AND

AUTHOR OF THE WORK ENTITLED "*COMMON SENSE.*"

LONDON-DERRY:

PRINTED AT THE DESIRE OF A SOCIETY OF GENTLEMEN.

1791.

45 The number of occasions on which Gamble was taken aback by a stranger opening a conversation with a sectarian comment is itself evidence of this tendency.

46 Besides public houses and public prints, institutions important to the public sphere that changed in character included barbershops, town and parish meetings, clubs and societies, not least Masonic lodges, and the Presbyterian Synod. The transformation of Northern Masonry is the subject of a fine study, Petri Mirala's *Freemasonry in Ulster, 1733–1813* (Dublin, 2007).

47 In Derry, where the late eighteenth century had seen the publication (by Douglas) of volumes of several hundred pages, the longest book published in the first two decades of the 1800s was a 168 page builder's manual; only one other book printed in the city in 1800–20 had more than 100 pages, the rest less than fifty. The book trade was stronger in Strabane, but the output was heavily evangelical.

people', 'the Irish people', and ultimately republicans. Now, with Catholics and Protestants inclining to drink with their own 'breed', there was greater latitude for sectarian expression in public houses and a greater propensity for overt animosity to the 'other' to be the hook for conversation and the basis for identification.[45]

The public prints too had changed.[46] If not fewer books, certainly shorter books and more books of inferior quality were published in Derry and Strabane in the two decades after the Rising than had been published in the twenty years prior to it.[47] Moreover, where once printers had published on diverse topics — history, politics, science — now evangelical tracts dominated their lists. Gone was the day when a regional printer would insist, as George Douglas of Derry had done in 1782, that there were 'no texts in scripture so *neglected* not to have received "explications" … over and

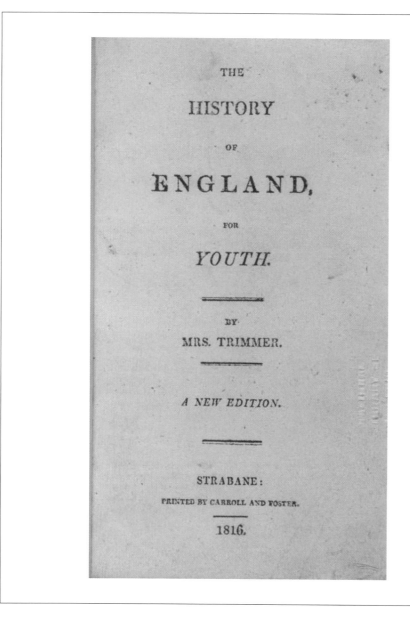

THE

HISTORY

OF

ENGLAND,

FOR

YOUTH.

BY

MRS. TRIMMER.

A NEW EDITION.

STRABANE:
PRINTED BY CARROLL AND FOSTER.

1816.

Left: The only history book published in Strabane in the first two decades of the nineteenth-century: an edition of a schoolbook by the English evangelical Sarah Trimmer.

Right: A collection of sermons by William Dickey, seceding clergyman of Carnone. Protestant sermons and devotional literature dominated the lists of Strabane printers in the years that Gamble returned to the town.

48 *LJ*, 19 March 1782; italics in original. Douglas was responding to a reader's suggestion that a corner of his 'political paper' be given over to explaining neglected religious texts.

49 On Douglas's career in Ireland America, see Breandán Mac Suibhne, 'Politicization and Paramilitarism: Northwest and Southwest Ulster, 1796–98', in Thomas Bartlett, et al., eds., *1798: A Bicentennial Perspective* (Dublin, 2003), 243–78. Citing government oppression, Douglas had relinquished editorial duties in 1786 but resumed them two years later. At this time, John Alexander, printer of the *Strabane Journal* [hereafter, *SJ*], had offered his newspaper for sale, but he failed to find a buyer and continued as editor until at least 1790: see *SJ*, 30 April 1787, and *LJ*, 21 September 1790, where he is mentioned in an advertisement. James Elliot was editor of it by the mid-1790s and was still editing it in 1801: see *SJ*, 17 August 1795; 2 March 1801. The changes in the ownership and editorial lines of the regional press had parallels elsewhere

over again.'[48] But if such 'explications' were now printers' stock-in-trade, different men were now the printers. After over a decade protesting at government's harassment of the free press, Douglas himself had sold up in 1796 and emigrated to the United States, where he settled in Baltimore, Maryland; other prominent regional printers — notably the Bellews of Strabane — also went out of business in these same years.[49] The *London-Derry Journal*, which Douglas had established in 1772 and built into the main regional paper, had passed into the hands of men who proved themselves strong supporters of the constitution in Church and state in the crisis years of 1797–99. Later, when the prospect of revolution was 'gone and for ever', William McCorkell, the new editor of the *Journal*, would countenance Catholic Emancipation, but a suspicion of Catholics' intentions and an acceptance of the state's professed neutrality still restrained his in Ulster, with both the *Belfast Newsletter* and *Newry Chronicle* being sold in the mid-1790s.

50 For McCorkell's 'editorial principles' see *LJ*, 5 December 1809, and 12 June 1810. For his hostility to the populist Catholic leaders ('hair-brained orators', 'briefless counsellors', 'the Theatrical Orators of Fish-shamble Street') who came to prominence in the 1810s, see *LJ*, 23 June 1813, where he argues that they were doing more harm than good to the Catholic cause, and *LJ*, 10 May 1814, for his insistence on the liberality of Derry Protestants. On Orange marches, compare *LJ*, 7 August 1810, and 25 September 1810, where he blames 'both sides' for the rioting that they provoked, and *LJ*, 16 July 1822, where he argues that they should be abandoned as they gave offence to Catholics.

51 On Douglas's notion of the function of the journalist, see *LJ*, 8 March 1785, where a tax increase provoked the outburst: 'So — the tax on advertisements is augmented still further — a penny stamp on every sheet of paper, and 1s. 4d. on every ten lines of advertisements! — But these News Printers are a troublesome set, and must be silenced some way or other — They publish County meetings, and Volunteer meetings and Parliamentary Intelligence — they are ever talking of Parliamentary Reform, and of Liberty and all that — they tell tales about certain great men, nay, they sometimes discover the evil deeds of certain great men! — Therefore, down with the Press!'

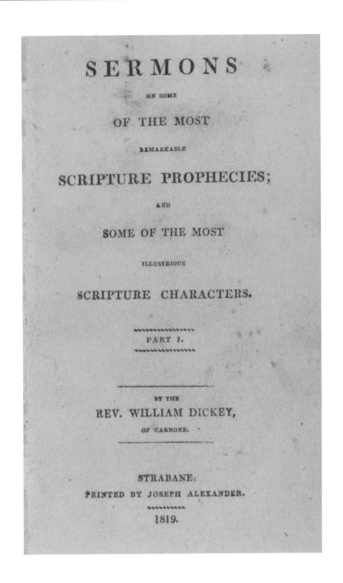

liberalism, his editorial line collapsing into an anaemic centrism. For example, McCorkell would readily concede that Orange marches were intended to give offence, but he would almost always add the weak-kneed rider that Catholics should not be so quick to take offence. And through the 1810s, he would time and again point out to his Catholic readers that they lived in a tolerant place, which was a way of saying that they should know their place — hope but not expect, desire not demand.[50] Hence, while Douglas had conceived the business of a newspaper to be monitoring 'great men' and providing 'the people' with a platform to make the case for reform, it was now the excluded, those anticipating power, not those in power, who were to be watched most carefully.[51]

And so it was that, in the 1810s, men *and* women who had devoted the 1780s and 1790s to the pursuit of a political project that had failed found, in this degraded public sphere, that their activities in those decades were no longer worthy of an honest reckoning, certainly not a fit subject for the public prints.[52] And when that which had defined the youth and, in many cases, the middle age of such people — that which had defined their *lives* — was ignored, it was almost as if they themselves had never really lived.[53] Only seldom in the first decades of the century did an obituary in the regional press even hint at a respectable person having been a rebel or a republican in former days. Those few that did were for men who died abroad, suggesting that their politics was not only not of this time, but also not of this place: the past was *in* a different country.[54] But such hints were rare; when a rebel died, even when he died abroad, the tendency was to hide the truth in a meaningless half-telling. Robert Moore (1752–1807), a wealthy ironmonger of Bishop Street, Derry, was ubiquitous in public affairs in the north-west from the 1770s through until the late 1790s. He was a Volunteer officer, who was delegated to the Dungannon convention in 1782. He was the chairman and treasurer of Derry's poor-house and infirmary, a founding member of the city's Chamber of Commerce, and a representative of his congregation at the Presbyterian Synod (1787, 1789). And by the mid-1790s, he was a key figure in the provincial leadership of the United Irishmen. Forced to go into exile in September 1798, Moore died in Baltimore, Maryland, in 1807; there at the end were Douglas, the Derry printer, and John Glendy (1755–1832), formerly Presbyterian minister of Maghera, south Derry, who, like Moore, had been a Volunteer and a United Irishman.[55] The Baltimore papers — and those of Philadelphia, New York, Boston and other cities — noticed his death and the reason he had left home:

Died — On Thursday the 18th inst. in the 55th year of his age, Mr. *Robert Moore*, a native of Ireland, and one of her exiled sons, who suffered in the

cause of freedom and humanity — this cause he maintained with all the order of a patriot till his last breath. If the most inflexible integrity, in scenes peculiarly calamitous and distressing, and the most extended philanthropy, embracing man as a brother, where he met him, united to those interesting and pleasant manners which flow from the warmest sensibilities and charities of the heart, constitute the principles of an honest man and the graces of a gentleman — this character justly belongs to the deceased. 'He was an Israelite, indeed, in whom there is no guile.'[56]

But at home, the single sentence that appeared in the *Journal* rang hollow: 'Died. … In Baltimore, Mr. Robert Moore, for many years a Respectable Merchant, of this City.'[57] Here, the book closed on the actual past, and a great lie — that 'the whole Protestant community' had been loyal — began to become history.[58] Refused ink, the republican account of what had happened in the late eighteenth century became a matter for the fireside and the hours of darkness. Accordingly, the things that were best remembered when Gamble returned to Strabane in 1810, in 1812 and in 1818 were songs, and the stories that were told often concerned rebels who had departed for America, passing out of this world and into another, or they were ghost stories — endeavours to explain what was, in the light of day, inexplicable; to say what could not be said, that those who were denied their past had in fact lived. Hence, while Gamble's drinking, descriptions of everyday life and depictions of Catholics and Presbyterians — well written, eminently quotable, easily cherry-picked — draw a certain type of researcher, a *reader* follows a half-blind man into the spectral afterworld of failed revolution, where memory (a 'true story') rebukes history (a barefaced fiction) and the living meet the dead.

52 In time, children would deny the reality of their parents' lives. For a late example, see Thomas Ainge Devyr, *The Odd Book of the Nineteenth Century …* (New York, 1882), 86. Devyr (*c.* 1805–87), the son of a Donegal Town republican, was involved in radical politics in Ireland and England before settling in the United States in the early 1840s. In Ireland on holiday in 1860, he met 'three clever educated gentlemen at Derry — whose father was known to my father when both were servant boys. When I spoke of this they shrank from the record as if their father were their disgrace — that clever, energetic man — who founded for them, the respectability which they were thus striving to guard from the supposed contamination of his name.' Devyr comments on his own family's politics but also see *LJ*, 28 May 1793, reporting Derry republican Robert Moore had presided at a meeting in Devyr's Hotel, Donegal Town.

53 See the discussion of grievable and ungrievable, real and unreal lives in Judith Butler, 'Violence, Mourning, Politics', in her *Precarious Life: The Powers of Mourning and Violence* (London, 2004), 19–49.

54 For instance, the *Strabane Morning Post*, 4 May 1824, carried the following obituary, presumably lifted from an American paper: 'Died … At Mountpleasant, Kentucky, of typhus fever, on the 7th of August last, Mr. Samuel Molyneaux, aged 63,

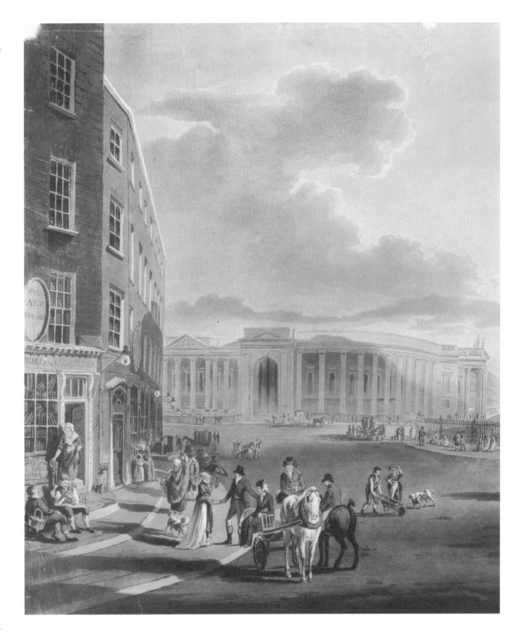

The National Bank, formerly Parliament House, from Grafton Street, c. 1807. Attrib. to J. Bluck, (fl. 1791–1819), after a drawing by James Roberts (1725–99). National Library of Ireland.

formerly a respectable farmer of British, Killead, near Antrim. He was one of the Volunteers of 82, the principles of those patriots he never abandoned. He ever was an enthusiastic friend of freedom, and this was the chief cause of his emigrating to a land of liberty. His wife died two days before him.'

55 Moore's civic and political involvements are sketched in my 'Politicization and Paramilitarism', 243–78. On his business career in the United States, see Richard Moore-Colyer, 'The Moores of Londonderry and Baltimore: A Study in Scotch-Irish Eighteenth-Century Emigration', *Familia*, 19 (2003), 11–40, esp. 15–25.

56 *Democratic Press*, 22 June 1807, quoting the *Baltimore American*; this obituary was also carried in New York's *Public Advertiser*, 22 June 1807. Other notices of his death appeared in Boston's *Columbian Centinel*, 27 June 1807, which noted he was from Derry, and the *Salem Register*, 29 June 1807, where he was described as a 'worthy Emigrant from Ireland.'

57 *LJ*, 18 August 1807.

58 The process was largely complete by the mid-1840s: see Robert Simpson, *The Annals of*

Ghosts of Former Days

The 1798 Rising is first mentioned early in Gamble's account of 1810, shortly after he has landed in Dublin. Determined not to drink whiskey on his first day in Ireland, he visited a few acquaintances in the afternoon but dined alone that evening in a box in the Ormond Tavern on Capel Street. The tavern was raucous — enlivened further by somebody calling a waiter a 'damned wriggled-eyed bastard' — with diners shouting across the room at acquaintances in other boxes ('all eating, all speaking, and, except myself, nobody listening') and Gamble, enjoying the general and what he saw as very Irish conviviality, downed a bottle of 'excellent' wine ('more than I intended on going in').[59] He spent much of the next few days in the company of an unnamed friend, drinking a 'great deal' at dinners and on excursions around the city and its suburbs; one of their first trips was an abortive search for Strongbow's house.[60] The friend, a former regimental surgeon, had been a fellow student in Edinburgh in the early 1790s.[61] Although a mere sixteen or seventeen years had passed since they had graduated, Gamble remarks that only two others from a group of twenty-five close friends from college days were still living; twenty-one, in other words, were dead. Some had drowned, others had died of yellow fever and others had fallen in duels. One had committed suicide — a man who had insulted him at a dance refusing his challenge (as his father, a church organist, was not a 'gentleman'), he had rushed into the ballroom in a frenzy and blown his own brains out. And another of the group had been executed aged twenty-six for his part in the Rising in Wexford. Gamble writes at some length about this man, John Henry Colclough (he only gives his surname), describing him in some detail and in terms that flit between affection, admiration and admonishment. He remembers him as 'a young man of considerable talents and great gentleness of manners', but vain and ambitious; 'vanity and ambition, more than conviction', Gamble avers, 'have made many young men republicans. He who thinks himself qualified to govern does not like to obey …'

'Mr. Colclough' had been a Catholic and Gamble remembers that though he thought it 'degrading as a philosopher and a republican, to wear the shackles of so contracted a religion', he used to be seen stealing privately to the only Catholic chapel in Edinburgh. He also recalls a meeting of a students' debating society which had considered the motion 'Was it a justifiable act on the part of Brutus and the other conspirators [to assassinate Caesar]?'. Colclough had taken the side of 'the great martyr of freedom', meaning the republican Brutus, in a 'long and brilliant speech, which was greatly admired and rapturously applauded by all who heard it'. For Gamble, that applause set him on the course that would lead him to his

death. He threw up medicine for the bar, but before he could complete his legal studies a small fortune was left him, and he returned to Ireland. Here, Gamble uses a theatrical metaphor that insinuates an element of unreality or artifice that will suffuse many of his discussions of the Rising; 'the stage was now erected on which so many thousand were doomed to perish; he flattered himself, no doubt, with being able to play a distinguished part, and was among the foremost who appeared on its reeking boards'. He describes his capture and how, at his trial and execution, he conducted himself with a 'calm intrepidity and dignity, tempered with mildness, which commanded the admiration and esteem of the spectators'; he refuses to credit a report that Colclough had disgraced himself on the scaffold by asking for a glass of wine to toast the king. To the extent that there is a moral in the tale it is about vanity.[62]

By the time Gamble leaves Dublin for Strabane a few days later, he has seen John Philpot Curran, the republican lawyer whose daughter Sarah had been involved with Robert Emmet, and he has been 'lucky enough' to see Henry Grattan, the politician associated with the achievement of legislative independence in 1782, on Dame Street. He has also experienced the absurdity of what then passed for politics in Ireland. Gamble prefaces his account of this absurdity with a description of horror in a graveyard; he follows it with a description of the horrors on the streets of Dublin in 1798; the same word, Golgotha, in both descriptions, frames the discussion. He and his friend, the doctor, had walked through the barracks squares of the north inner city ('The Barracks are esteemed the largest and most commodious in Europe'), the Phoenix Park and Chapelizod out to Palmerstown to attend the village fair. The approach roads to the village were thick with people, 'mostly of the lower class', and seated on the roadside were beggars who 'exhibited the most disgusting sores to excite compassion'. The fair itself was boisterous; the two doctors

Derry … (Londonderry, 1847), 224, where the author goes through considerable contortions to assert that Derry had been loyal in '1797–8–9'. Simpson argues that while 'the rebellion of 1798' was said to have been 'hatched' by 'the descendants of the first Colonists of Ulster', meaning Presbyterians, 'it can be positively asserted that the Citizens of Londonderry were not either directly or indirectly, materially implicated in the concoction, or in furthering the progress of that rebellion'.

59 *Sketches*, 18–19.
60 *Sketches*, 26, 36–37.
61 *List of the Graduates in Medicine in the University of Edinburgh from MDCCV to MDCCCLXVI* (Edinburgh, 1867) returns medical students by year of graduation, nationality and specialism; for example, in 1793: *Joannes Gamble, Hibernus. De Rheumatismo*. However, positively identifying Gamble's friend is difficult, as several doctors practising in Dublin in the 1810s had been at college in Edinburgh in the late 1780s and early 1790s. Gamble refers to him as 'Dr. P——', says that he has been a regimental surgeon in Ireland for several years, and indicates that he was at a controversial duel in Wexford in 1807, all of which may help to identify him. John Crampton, a physician attached to Dr. Stevens's Hospital, had graduated with Gamble and was still living in 1810, but he was not Dr. P——. Crampton

later became King's Professor of Materia Medica in Trinity. See R. B. McDowell and D. A. Webb, *Trinity College Dublin, 1592–1952: An Academic History*, 2nd edn. (Dublin, 2004 [1982]), 531.

62 *Sketches*, 28–30. Ironically, the duel Gamble's college friend attended in 1807 resulted in the death of a member of Colclough's extended family, John Colclough. See *Sketches*, 39–43. Although he did not complete his medical studies, John Henry Colclough had, with Gamble, been a member of the Edinburgh-based Hibernian Medical Society; see *Laws and Regulations of the Hibernian Medical Society. Instituted December 14, 1786* (Edinburgh, 1791), 21.

63 *Sketches*, 33–36 (Curran; Grattan); *Sketches*, 38–39, 43–47 (Palmerstown).

64 *Sketches*, 47–48. Brian Boru was reputed to have been buried in the Hospital Fields, popularly Bully's Acre: see *Dublin Penny Journal*, 25 August 1832. It is more likely that he was buried in Armagh. Robert Emmet was also supposed to have been interred in Bully's Acre. Thomas Gamble, rector of St. Michan's Church, ministered to Emmet on the eve of his execution and was said to have arranged for the body to be removed from that burial ground to his own church. A native of Galway, he had no known connection with John.

65 *Sketches*, 48.

drank 'excellent' wine in one of the many tents but opted to return to the city just as the fighting was breaking out.[63] On their way back to Dublin, they cut through the Hospital Fields; this was 'the burial place of the lower-class: of the poor, the artizan, and the stranger; of the unfortunate who ends his days in an hospital, the wretch who perishes on the highway, and the criminal who dies by the executioner; the outcast who had no friend, the wanderer who had no habitation …' Their ostensible object, besides making a short cut, was to the see the reputed grave of Brian Boru, the high king who had, in Patriots' imagining of the Irish past, expelled invaders at the Battle of Clontarf (1014). What they find is a shambles:

> We walked over their mouldering remains, which a little earth loosely scattered hardly concealed from our view: in some places it did not conceal them. Whether from the carelessness of interment, or the ravages of animals, the graves of several were open, and the coffins exposed; through the broken boards of which we saw their decaying bodies in every progressive state of putrefaction; in some the knees were falling from their sockets, and the eyes melting in their eye-balls, the worms crept along their fingers, and the body and face was one great mass of corruption: in others an unshapen heap of bones and ashes only remained. We turned in horror from a spectacle so hideous and revolting; from a sight so dreadful and disgusting, so mortifying and shocking to mortality; nor can I conceive how such a violation of decency could be permitted. I did not even stop to look at the tomb of Brian Barome, monarch of all Ireland, who was killed by the Danes at the battle of Clontarf, and is said to be buried there. I fled with precipitation from this Golgotha, where the air is contaminated with the exhalations of death, nor did I seem to myself to breathe freely till I was some distance from it. A little further we met the lord and lady

lieutenant, with their attendants and some other company.[64]

The constituent parts of this episode — the absence of civility (at the fair), the barbarity of neglecting the dead, the reference to the Irish king's grave and the sudden appearance of the British king's representative with his train of attendants — appear to be prefatory to a political commentary. Gamble does not explicitly offer one, concluding the chapter by imagining the dead paupers, prisoners and outcasts rising from their graves to rebuke the great and the good with mortality:

> Imagination could scarcely have formed a greater contrast than this gay and gallant party, to the quiet and silent group we just had quitted; yet they were once active and animated, though not so splendid as these are; who, in a few years, perhaps a few months, will be mute likewise in their turn. Oh! could the wand of enchantment touch the slumbering bones, and raise before them these inhabitants of the grave; could they gaze on their fleshless arms, their putrid lips, their hollow cheeks, their eyeless sockets, where the worm has now taken its abode; could they behold as in a magic glass, the reflection of what all that lives must be, how would they start affrighted and dismayed; how would their mirth and gaiety vanish, their pomp and consequence subside; how would the frivolous pursuits, the transient pleasures, the restless wishes, and busy cares, of this fleeting scene sink into the insignificance they deserve.[65]

Still, while Gamble here refrained from making a direct political comment, politics past and present come to the fore as he proceeds towards his lodgings and finds ghosts of that other Golgotha — 1798 — stalking his imagination. Having just closed one chapter with the sight of the lord lieutenant, he opens the following one by reflecting on the office — 'He is always now an English nobleman of high rank: there are no instances of a Scotchman being appointed, and I believe but one or two of an Irishman' — and recalls some men who have held it. He praises Lord Ormond (1610–88), who resisted ultra-Protestants' demands for punitive measures against Catholics in the late 1670s and early 1680s, and Lord Chesterfield (1694–1773), a scholar and wit who relaxed the Penal Laws against Catholics in the mid-1700s. The rest, with few exceptions, he dismisses as 'grave and formal courtiers, who wore bag-wigs and swords, turned on their toes, danced minuets, and laughed as seldom as they thought.' The current incumbent, he observes, seems determined to drink himself into favour ('he is what is called a five bottle man'), but in general people are rightly indifferent to lords lieutenant: 'a lord lieutenant of Ireland has no more to do with the measures of government, than the postman with the incendiary letter he is the bearer of.'[66]

Walking through the city streets, he sees caricatures of John Foster, the chancellor of the exchequer, on old walls and gateways, 'sometimes hanging, and sometimes roasting'. Foster was held responsible for an increase in taxes and the Common Council of Dublin (the Corporation) had just passed a motion ordering that his portrait be removed from their meeting room; when one alderman proposed that it should be kicked by every member, 'another genius' said it should be kicked by every man in the nation.[67] Gamble sniffs at this 'playing at football with pictures' — he has earlier noted that Grattan's portrait suffered a similar fate — and he writes scathingly of what had become, by the proroguing of the Irish parliament with the Act of Union, the most important representative body in Ireland. Being almost exclusively loyalist, it contained no difference of opinion and there being no difference of opinion, there was neither reason nor eloquence in its debates: 'There are few good speakers in the Common Council of Dublin — it is the collision of

opinions only which emits eloquence, and there can be little of argument where almost all are of one mind'. Its most conspicuous member, the rabble-rousing Henry Gifford, he reports to be a prejudiced man who expressed himself with more 'vehemence and force than is usual among English orators'. He then mocks Dublin loyalists generally as 'poor hen-hearted creatures who go about croaking about plots, and pikes, and the church, and papists'; they include 'gossipping [sic] people' who recount frightful tales of nocturnal meetings 'that have no existence but in their own imaginations' and timorous ones who frighten themselves and endeavour to frighten others with outlandish rumours of an imminent rebellion. There is no prospect whatsoever of another rebellion, Gamble argues: 'Government knows it, and every rational man who thinks must know it likewise …' The 'horrors' and 'terrors' of 1798 — most especially the experience of martial law — would deter 'every humane and thinking man' from insurrection: people were sickened and frightened, prepared to accept an imperfect constitution rather than face worse oppression:

A suppressed rebellion (as it is proverbially expressed) strengthens government — it cuts off the active and the ambitious, it frighten[s] the timorous, it sickens the humane, and for a time lays the people prostrate at the feet of government. Reconciled to lesser evils by the recollection of greater [evils], legal subjection, or even oppression, is scarcely felt by those who have just escaped from the insolence of military dominion; the fury of lawless and unbridled will.[68]

For his own part, Gamble insists that he would live content under the most despotic government 'rather than run the risk of making it better by a rebellion of even half [1798's] terrors'. Here, he recalls having been 'a very young man' in Dublin at the time of the Rising, when the city was a scene of unrelieved terror:

66 *Sketches*, 49–56; the quotations are from pages 49, 52, 54. Charles Lennox (1764–1819), duke of Richmond, the lord lieutenant seen by Gamble, held office from 1807 through 1813.
67 *Sketches*, 57. Also see *Sketches*, 126–30.
68 *Sketches*, 59–61.

69 *Sketches*, 61–62.
70 *Sketches*, 62–65. And
    compare *A View*, 343–44.

… was I to live to a patriarchal age, I shall not forget the impression it made on me; nor the gloomy sepulchral appearance Dublin presented — when all business and pleasure were suspended, when every man was a tyrant or a slave; a rebel that was suspected, a spy that suspected, or an executioner that punished; when malice and hatred, terror and doubt, fear and distrust, were on every face, and all the tender charities of nature withered and perished before the poisoned breath of party; which made no allowance for error, had no recollection of friendship, felt no gratitude for kindness, no sympathy for age, sex, sickness, or sorrow — when almost every house was a barrack, every public building a prison, and every street a golgotha, or a shambles, on the lamp posts of which some wretched fellow creature was daily suspended; who, while his limbs quivered in the agonies of death, was the subject of brutal joke and unfeeling exultation.[69]

And yet, while deploring rebellion, Gamble is ambivalent about the Rising itself. He remarks that 'though there is so much to lament and reprobate' in the memory of 1798, 'there is something likewise to admire'. The recollection of 'magnanimity, unshaken fortitude, and contempt of death' on both sides, he hopes, can obliterate the memory of 'savage excesses and midnight murders' by the republicans, *and* the 'vindictive and unrelenting vengeance, the floggings and torturings' of government. He proceeds to praise the Irish parliament for continuing its sittings 'undaunted' during the Rising and for rejecting the proposition of its more violent members 'to order the prisoners to military tribunals, and instant execution'. But he also praises the valour of the republican leaders who 'almost universally' faced death 'with a courage which was never excelled'. He mentions the execution of prominent rebels — the Sheares brothers and Billy O'Byrne — and the death in gaol of Oliver Bond, the republican leader in Dublin

whose family in St. Johnston, a few miles from Strabane, would have been known to him. He also remarks on the slow death of Edward Fitzgerald, describing him as a man esteemed for his 'courage and military conduct, his honour, humanity and candour'; he cites William Cobbett's high regard for him and quotes Mark Antony's speech over the body of Brutus, the republican who, on principle, kills his dearest friend, in Shakespeare's *Julius Caesar*:

> His life was gentle; and the elements
> So mixt in him, that nature might stand up,
> And say to all the world, 'This was a man!'[70]

The year 1798 and its aftershock, 1803, continue to unsettle Gamble's narrative as he travels north. A few miles outside Drogheda he notes that the residence of the Cottington family was 'attacked and nearly carried by the rebels in 1798', and he inspects the battery on 'Castle-mount' (that is, Millmount) to which he attributes the town remaining 'tolerably quiet' during the Rising, though 'the number of disaffected was supposed to be very great'. He also discusses the billeting of a large number of predominantly Protestant yeomanry corps on the town during the Rising; 'they all drank and caroused, swallowed wine, and whisky in pail fulls, and, in their zeal for the good old cause, I fear committed a number of bad actions'. And he describes with pity how, when some rebels who broke out of Wexford and fled north arrived in the vicinity of the town, the yeomen marched out and attacked the 'unfortunate wretches'; the courage of the yeomen, he adds, 'would have entitled them to the highest praise, had it been oftener than it was connected to humanity'. Later, passing through Castleblayney, he gives a scathing account of Andrew Thomas Blayney (1770–1834), the local landlord, who had commanded several particularly vicious yeomanry corps in the late 1790s. In spring 1797, when government had ordered a military crack-down on republicans, Lord Blayney had deployed 'his little

Thomas Russell (1767–1803).
National Library of Ireland.

71 *Sketches*, 113–14
(Cottington's), 134–37
(Drogheda), 147–51, esp.
150 (Blayney). Ironically,
Blayney, a prisoner of
war when Gamble's first
two tours appeared,
subsequently published
a travelogue of sorts,
*Narrative of a Forced
Journey through Spain
and France as a Prisoner
of War in the Years 1810
to 1814*, 3 vols. (London,
1814–16), the third
volume of which presents
his 'Observations on the
Present State of Ireland'.

72 *Sketches*, 182–89. The
republican woman
proceeds to reflect on
how 'because I am
woman, I am not to think
of this.' For another
republican woman, see *A
View*, 131–86, discussed
below.

73 The barber dismisses
Gamble's suggestion
that heavy drinking
was a great fault in a
clergyman: '*Guid* man,
guid man, it was *nathing*
to the congregation if it
was na for the slight of
others — they would na
mind *gin* he was to be
drunk, till he was near
bursting; but then it was
what other *Sacts* said
— *Ogh aye* man, the
papists, and the high kirk,
held out their fingers at
us, and gibe us sore, sore,
on his account.'

army', burning houses, crops and other provisions to bring rebel communities to heel; his tactics, Gamble surmises, were at once 'inhuman' and 'impolitic', simply augmenting the 'violence of hatred'.[71]

At Cootehill (where the people were 'outrageously loyal — disagreeably so I was about to say, but checked myself'), he remembered the dead friend who had been a doctor there in 1797. Back then, the inhabitants 'were supposed to have rather a democratic tendency' and his friend got himself mixed up with a 'United

Irishwoman' who, at a 'house-warming' where rebel songs were sung and seditious toasts drunk, called for the assassination of loyalists and scorned him for not feeling like a republican:

'You may wear your hair close, you may sing what songs, and dance what tunes you please, but I tell you, you are no true croppy — you *reason*, but a republican,' said she with animation, 'feels — for his bleeding country — for the exile in the foreign land — for the prisoner in a

74 *Sketches*, 219–20. The judge was Baron George. James Quinn, *Soul on Fire: A Life of Thomas Russell* (Dublin, 2002), 297, 301 n. 64, notes that Russell's 'literary work' passed into the hands of John Dubourdieu (1753–1839), rector of Annahilt, County Down. Dubourdieu was the author of the *Statistical Survey of the County Down* (Dublin, 1802) and that of Antrim (Dublin, 1812). His father, Saumarez (1716–1812), had kept a classical school at Lisburn, where his students had included George Vaughan Sampson and William Sampson of Derry, the former an author whose works were sources for Gamble's journey books, and the latter a republican lawyer. John Dubourdieu married the Sampsons' sister, Margaret. And his brother, Saumarez (1766–1801), graduated from Edinburgh with Gamble in 1793, became surgeon to the Longford Militia and died unmarried in 1801. On the family, see H. B. Swanzy, comp., *Succession Lists of the Diocese of Dromore*, ed. J. B. Leslie (Belfast, 1933), 142–44, and *Clergy of Connor, from Patrician Times to the Present Day, Based on the Succession Lists Compiled by Canon J. B. Leslie* (Dundalk, 1993), 312–13.

75 *Sketches*, 229–30. 'There were many others [among the Irish peers] who could have been much better spared.'

76 *Charlton*, vol. 3, 244.

dungeon — for the victim on the scaffold; for the wretched wanderer without habitation or name, whose house has been burned, whose wife has been outraged, and property destroyed, by the vile agents of lawless and brutal power …'

Gamble admits to having himself known this woman a few years later, when she was married. 'I never was in company with a more amiable woman', he reflected. 'The enthusiasm of the hour had passed away, and given place to the sober business of human life. Occupied with domestic employment, and domestic happiness, she thought little of those evils she once thought great.'[72]

Three days after leaving Cootehill, when an elderly barber with a bad eye who was trimming his beard in the shabby inn at Ballygawley chanced to mention that his congregation's former minister had a weakness for whiskey ('he's *our* fond of the *wee drap*'[73]) but knew the Bible from Genesis to Revelations, Gamble recalled 'a story I had heard of an unfortunate enthusiast of the name of Russell, who was being executed at Downpatrick, in the year of 1803, for being concerned in the insurrection of that period': before the judge had passed sentence, Russell — Thomas Russell, a friend of Wolfe Tone and a founder of the United Irishmen — had told the judge that he expected to hang, but that he was in the process of writing a commentary on the Book of Revelations and he would be grateful if he would be allowed a few weeks to finish it. Gamble, who bought the barber a glass of whiskey before heading off to Omagh, remarks that: 'Had his lordship allowed him to live until he had succeeded in making this portion of the Scripture intelligible, he would probably have lived as long as any person in court.'[74] And finally, at Rash, two miles from Omagh, passing a demesne that once belonged to Luke Gardiner, Lord Mountjoy, Gamble observes that the late lord was killed leading the Dublin Militia against the rebels in the Battle of New Ross in 1798. He notes too that Lord O'Neill, 'another northern lord', fell at Antrim a few days later. Both, he says, were the most amiable of men. It would not have been as great a loss, he intimates, had some other members of the House of Lords been dispatched.[75]

•

The 'Rebellion' is also a presence in Gamble's other journey books, his visits of 1812 and 1818, and it is the subject of his most accomplished work of fiction, *Charlton* (1823; 2nd edn., 1827). In this three-volume novel, a Presbyterian doctor, apparently from Donegal or west Tyrone, becomes involved in the United Irishmen, survives the Rising and, when things settle down, comes to regard the effort at revolution, 'in which he had so strangely got entangled, its idle hopes and wishes, as a phantom that had vanished, or tale that is told'.[76] But while Gamble insists on the historicity of this 'fiction', flagging his extensive use of contemporary song as a mark of its authenticity, it is in his account of his 1812 journey that the real and the imagined *appear* most blurred as he relates, in ghostly prose, stories told him about the Rising by close and casual acquaintances; these stories, together with his own recollections of late eighteenth-century politics, account for perhaps a third of the book. On this visit Gamble had sailed from Liverpool for Newry, but his ship had been wrecked near Skerries and he had then taken a circuitous route home, travelling north through Newry and Banbridge to Belfast and Ballymena; then to Toome and Dungiven and finally on to Strabane. The Rising was first brought to mind at Banbridge. Sitting at the market-house on 13 July, drinking tea with a 'genteel looking man' whom he had engaged in conversation, Gamble was startled when a yeomanry corps, on catching sight of his companion, suddenly started playing 'Croppies Lie Down'. The man, smiling, explained that he had been suspected of being a United Irishman in 1798. Gamble continued chatting with this 'intelligent man', whom he found 'perfectly awakened from the reveries of republicanism, if he ever indulged in them'; his new friend took him to the public library of which he was a committee member and later they drank punch 'until a late hour'.[77]

The following day, Gamble walked to the house of an acquaintance, a Presbyterian minister, two miles from Banbridge on the Dromore Road. On arrival, he found that this 'virtuous' friend had died the previous week. Invited to stay by the bereaved family, he spent some time rooting through the deceased man's library. The books were 'mostly Treatises on Divinity and Reviews', but on one of the shelves he found 'a parcel of Dublin newspapers, mouldy, and in some places moth-eaten[,] published in the years 1796 and 1797. They were a series of a well-known print called *The Press*; and seemed to the full as revolutionary, as some publications of the present day.' Gamble comments: 'I looked over a few of them, and was much gratified with the talent they displayed, as I lamented its misapplication'. He then proceeds to quote a long piece of 'ingenious levity', a republican polemic in the form of a letter from Patrick O'Blunder to John Bull, the length (six pages) of the extract and that it had been published on the eve of the Rising, a testimony to his own ambivalence.[78]

The dead friend, although not named by Gamble, can be readily identified. He was Nathaniel Shaw (1759–1812), minister of the main congregation in Banbridge since 1790, who had died at Henry Hill on 3 or 4 July, just over a week before Gamble's arrival.[79] That Shaw had been a republican is a reminder of the social, cultural and political milieu in which Gamble himself had been formed in the 1780s and 1790s. However, that he was dead and, politically, had been dead since 1798, intimates Gamble's sense of a wider change.[80] Indeed, Shaw is the second friend that Gamble had failed to meet on this trip. En route to Banbridge, he had turned off the main Belfast road to call on the Presbyterian minister of Tandragee (properly Clare), also unnamed but clearly Robert Adams (*c*. 1785–1840), a native of Ardstraw, west Tyrone. It was 12 July, the town was a perfect 'orange grove', doors and windows decorated with Orange lilies, and the streets crowded with people commemorating the Battle of the Boyne (1690). Adams was away from home and his meeting house was closed, the congregation having ostracized him for supporting a petition in favour of

77 Richard Linn, *A History of Banbridge*, ed. W. S. Kerr (Banbridge, 1935), 6–7, intimates that the Banbridge Reading Society, formed by the 'leading men of the town and parish' in 1795, was associated with the United Irishmen.

78 *A View*, 42–53; italics added. *The Press* was a republican newspaper, published in Dublin from September 1797 to its suppression in March 1798. 'Patrick O'Blunder, to John Bull, Esq.', which Gamble reproduces verbatim (47–53), appeared on the front page of *The Press*, 18 November 1797. It was subsequently reproduced in Anon., *The Beauties of* The Press (London, 1800), 202–06.

79 *A History of Congregations in the Presbyterian Church in Ireland, 1610–1982* (Belfast, 1982), 109, gives Shaw's date of death as 4 July, but James McConnell, comp., *Fasti of the Irish Presbyterian Church, 1613–1840* (Belfast, 1951), 230, as 3 July. Gamble called on 14 July (he was in Tandragee two days earlier on 12 July) and refers to Shaw having died 'about a week ago'. David W. Miller kindly helped me to identify Shaw.

80 Here, *A View*, 43–44, a neighbouring Presbyterian minister who was visiting the 'house of mourning', tells Gamble of having recently attended a wake that was disrupted by a 'travelling Jew', a partner in a 'respectable mercantile house in the city', meaning London, who had come to Ireland a few days earlier. The incident may have happened, but

Bizarrely, given the tension between real and imagined in the 1812 volume, this tour *became* fiction when it was attributed to Daniel O'Connell (and quoted and paraphrased at length, as if written by him) in the English hack Robert Huish's *The Memoirs, Private and Political, of Daniel O'Connell, Esq., from the Year 1776 to the Close of the Proceedings in Parliament for the Repeal of the Union. Compiled from Official Documents* (London, 1836), 316–71 (55 of 732 pages). This section ('Diary of a Tour in the North of Ireland'), which was illustrated with a map, was discussed inconclusively in *Notes and Queries*, 7th ser., 5 (1888), 267 (by Matthew Russell, SJ) and 391 (by W. J. Fitzpatrick); 7th ser., 6 (1889), 173 (Juverna) and 411–12 (Fitzpatrick), without any connection being made to Gamble. However, years earlier, Thomas D'Arcy McGee had identified a similar problem in Huish's 'memoirs', the presentation of several pages of a speech by Charles Phillips to the Electors of Sligo (1818) as a speech by O'Connell in Kerry. See his *Historical Sketches of O'Connell and His Friends … with a Glance at the Future Destiny of Ireland*, 4th edn. (Boston, 1854), 35n. Also see Gamble, *Sketches*, 2nd edn. [1826], v, where he alludes to his first journey book having been 'freely borrowed from by all descriptions of my contemporaries, speechmakers as well as writers … with as little notice taken of me as Vesputius [*sic*] took of Columbus'. And so it continues: Bew, *Politics of Enmity*, 86 n. 182, attributes *Sketches* to a 'J. Gault'.

the 'wandering Jew' was a well-established figure in Christian oral tradition and literature, enjoying a new ubiquity in early nineteenth-century Gothic. This figure is sometimes conceived as a cipher for a penitent, he having been cursed to wander the earth forever for mocking Christ at his crucifixion. Hence, whether the encounter happened or not, Gamble's introduction of such a literary figure prior to his representation of Shaw's life as having ended in 1798 distresses his narrative's claim to reportage.

81 Here, *A View*, 36–37, Gamble remarked: 'The county of Armagh Presbyterians are the very Spadassins of Protestantism.' *Spadassin* is French for bully or bravo, especially a hired assassin. Adams had been licensed in Strabane in 1806. The dispute in which Adams was embroiled dragged on for over four years, ending when he resigned in 1816: see *History of Congregations*, 296–97, and McConnell, *Fasti*, 187. Neil Jarman, 'The Orange Arch: Creating Tradition in Ulster', *Folklore*, 112 (2001), 1–21, 5, is mistaken when he reads Gamble as expressing 'delight' at the Orange displays in Tandragee.

82 *A View*, 58 (Castlereagh), 71 (Simms), 83 (Larne), 120 (Ballymena). To these references can be added Gamble mentioning the musician Edward Bunting and two 'literary men', William Hamilton Drummond and William Drennan, all three of whom had some involvement with

the extension of civil rights to Catholics.[81] One friend dead — indeed, dead before he died — and another passing out of the public sphere, still minister but not ministering, a spectral figure: Gamble is now beginning his most sustained reflection on the remains of republicanism.

Over the next few days, as Gamble continues his journey home, he repeatedly alludes to events and individuals connected to the Rising. In north Down, he mentions the popular hostility towards Lord Castlereagh (the conservative statesman was a member of a local gentry family) for having 'turned renegado' and renounced the liberal patriotism of his youth. Two miles outside Belfast, he breakfasts at a house that belonged to a Mr. Simms, whom he surmises was a prominent republican, exiled with other 'misguided leaders of the United Irish' to Fort George in 1799, and as he passes through Larne and Ballymena he notes that there were battles at each of these towns during the Rising.[82] But 1798 becomes a decidedly disturbing presence when he leaves Ballymena, and calls at the house of Mr. C——, a bleacher belonging to the 'second class of Irish gentry' living at C—— Vale, a two-and-a-half-hour walk off the 'great road', south and west of the town. Gamble did not know this man. He had been given a letter of introduction to him by another man with whom he had stopped at Rosehill, outside Ballymena. Mr. C——'s house was in a glen, watered by a brook, with a mountain in front and a lake behind.[83] He spends several days here, reading his host's books during the day and, at night, 'drinking his whiskey and listening to his stories'. Mr. C——, he writes, 'is a Presbyterian and was a Volunteer. He was, of course, strongly suspected of being a United Irishman and fame even conferred on him the dignified title of Adjutant-General of the County.' In the late 1790s, he was called before a magistrate when a man swore that he had seen him drilling rebels in white shirts at the lake behind his house. He was released, however, when he explained to the

magistrate that the witness was a notorious drunkard who rarely made it home from a fair or market, but lay in a bog or ditch where 'he might fancy a thousand imaginary things'. Gamble neither confirms nor denies that his host had been a rebel, enigmatically alluding to people having often seen ghosts by the lake:

The rushes shaken by the wind of the borders of the lake … and the flocks of wild fowl which sometimes passed over it, had from time in memorial, been mistaken by the midnight wanderer for troops of ghosts, who spread their white robes to the wind, and hearkened to the music of that hollow blast. The transition from ghosts to rebels was easy …

Mr. C—— was re-arrested in 1798 when a disgruntled former employee swore that he had been a delegate at a provincial meeting of the United Irishmen. The local magistrate sent him to B[elfast] but, after six weeks in prison, he was again released when the presiding officer, an Englishman, ruled that he had no case to answer. On this occasion, he stayed in the courtroom to observe the next trial, that of a forty-year-old countryman, who had been taken in arms. The case against the man was conclusive and he was found guilty. Asked if he had anything to say on his own behalf, the man delivered a bitter speech from the dock, asking why he should hang and his landlord, Lord L[ondonderry], father of Castlereagh, who was present in the courtroom, should not, as it was he who had made him 'an enthusiast in politics':

I that stand here a spectacle to this court, and soon will be to God and holy angels, had once as little thought as any one in it that I should ever do so. … I minded the plough as my father and grandfather did before me … And I married a wife, who was the comfort of my life, though I am now the sorrow of hers; and I had three brave children to welcome me when I came home among them at night. And if my meal was homely, the blessing of the Lord was on it, and I eat [*sic*] it in content, and I didn't trouble my head about politics or matters of state, except to wish success to my brethren in America; and that I did do, and won't go for to deny it now. And my Lord, there he sits, came to me his own self, and said to me 'Andrew, why don't you do like your neighbours, and become a volunteer?' And I said, 'my Lord, I have no time for such vagaries, I have a wife and three children to support, and can afford neither the money nor the time.' And you said, it was a shame that I should do nothing for the good of my country; that you were a volunteer, and that all your tenants must become volunteers. And I became a volunteer, and learned my exercise, and went to field days, and reviews; and his Lordship made fine speeches to us, and said we were the admiration of the world, and that now we had got a free trade, we must strive to get a free constitution. And when I used to go to N[ewtownards] to pay rent, there were piles of pamphlets in the office; and the agent would make me take handfuls of them for myself and neighbours to read; and I did read them, and became convinced that nothing but reform could save the country. And I did take the United Irishman's oath, and I did fight at S[aintfield], and for that I am to die. But if I deserve death, what does he deserve who sits yonder — he was learned and I am ignorant — he was a great gentleman and I am a poor farmer — he found me at the plough, and he brought me to the gallows — he led me into this, and my blood be upon his head and on his children's for ever.[84]

Mr. C——'s most extended story is related by Gamble in ghostly terms.[85] It begins in 1797 with an old man, Mr. H——, lying on his deathbed. His twenty-year-old son, William, is by the bedside; so too is Mr.

C——. The dying man was a Presbyterian who had been an Irish Volunteer, carried arms and written and spoken on the cause of reform; he had given his son high ideas of civil liberty and taught him that to resist bad government was a duty, but now he tells him these things are of no importance and he makes his son promise to renounce politics. William, unknown to his father, had taken the United Irishmen's oath of secrecy, a preliminary step to full membership, but he now abandons politics. After a relationship with a rector's daughter is destroyed by an argument with her father about Bonaparte, he again socialized with his republican friends. A nineteen-year-old United Irishwoman, Miss Harriet W——, seduced him at a party and he joined the society. The couple were to marry in June 1798, after the planned insurrection. By now, Harriet had second thoughts about rebellion: 'she no longer saw in revolution, a bloodless pageant, but a mournful sepulchre, in the dark vaults of which repose the conquered, while echo only prolongs the heavy steps of the conquerors, who stalk in mournful silence over their heads'. She pleads with William not to turn out in arms, but he insists he must. He put on his 'fatal garment of green', which he had once put on before to impress her. Now, she thinks it a 'winding sheet'; 'his green uniform was no longer a flowing robe of triumph, but clung to him like a shroud'.

William made his way to the rebel camp at Ballynahinch with the small party of men he commanded. The night before the battle, as many in the camp got drunk, he lay awake thinking of his father's dying words. In the rout of the following day, he was severely wounded in the head and shoulder; he fled from the battlefield and, after riding for some hours, hid in a ditch in the mountains while soldiers with blood-stained bayonets searched for rebels. After midnight, he stole to the cabin of a man who had been a labourer for his father; the labourer and his wife dressed his wounds and put him to sleep in their bed. He stayed for two days,

the United Irishmen. However, he only alludes to Drennan being best known as a 'writer of politics'; see *A View*, 66–68. And see *A View*, 115–20, where a Catholic driving pigs refers to the Battle of Ballynahinch.

83 I have not securely identified Mr. C—— or C—— Vale. *A View*, 123, indicates that he was a widower in 1810, with two sons and no daughter. It is likely that he was one of the Cussicks of Crevilly Valley or, possibly, one of the Careys of Careyvale. I am grateful to Eul Dunlop for the latter suggestion.

84 *A View*, 128–30.

85 What follows is abridged from *A View*, 131–86.

86 The verses are from 'William and Margaret' (1723), an adaptation, attributed to the Scottish poet David Mallet (1705–65), of a traditional ballad.

and then wearing some of the man's old clothes, he went to see Harriet; she arranged for him to hide in the cowhouse of one of her uncle's tenants but, in late June, when she was making arrangements to get him out of the country, a cavalry party intercepted her near the hiding place. They threatened to rape her, but she was now 'more a corpse than a living being' and oblivious to their threats. They searched the house and cowhouse, threatened, abused and struck the tenant, but he would not betray the man hiding in his cowhouse. Then the sergeant threatened to rape the tenant's own daughter. The old man pointed to the cowhouse and threw himself in agony on the ground.

William was taken to B[elfast] on horseback; too weak to support himself, he was tied to the rider. In B[elfast], he was lodged in the same prison as Mr. C——, who got him a cell of his own and some basic necessities. After a few days, he was taken to court on a chair and tried by court martial; 'His head was tied up. His countenance was ghastly and pale.' Harriet was present in the court; the trial was over in a few moments and he was condemned to death. About ten, the night before the execution, Mr. C—— got permission to visit the condemned man and his lover with a bottle of wine and some other light refreshment. William was sleeping; Harriet, described as a 'mourner', was sitting on the bed. Mr. C—— gave her some wine. Some time later, William woke and asked, 'What hour is it?' He was told it was midnight: 'Ah! midnight,' he repeated, 'the hour at which ghosts quit their graves to visit those they loved'. He shuddered and paused, perhaps reflecting that at that hour the following night 'he would be that object from which the imagination of his mistress, even, would start in horror and affright'. Harriet must have thought something similar for she started to sing 'with a voice and manner almost superhuman' as she walked to and fro, backwards and forwards, in the cell:

That face, alas! no more is fair,
That lip is no longer red;

Dark are my eyes, now clos'd in death,
And every charm is fled.

William cried, 'Sing it, Harriet, sing it!', tossing himself on the bed. And Harriet sang:

The hungry worm my sister is,
This winding sheet I wear,
And cold and weary lasts our night,
'Till that last morn appear.[86]

After he had calmed the young woman, Mr. C—— was taken back to his own cell. Between eleven and twelve the following morning he was permitted to see the couple again. There was a clergyman now with them, but they paid little heed to him. Harriet was dressed in white. They talked at intervals, falling into long 'fits of abstraction'; William's mouth would tremble on occasion and he would frequently get up and walk rapidly back and forward. The gaoler came at one o'clock. Harriet was allowed to sit beside William as the car moved through the streets of B[elfast]; Mr. C—— walked behind reading the Thirty-eighth Psalm. At the gallows, she stood beside him, herself mute and motionless and her eyes closed, as he was hanged; her whole frame then stiffened like marble. She was carried away and for several years was insensible to everything passing around her. Gamble remarks that 'From this state she is (I think unhappily) reviving', adding:

The heart which received so rude a shock will never taste happiness, and can only, if it shakes off sorrow, settle into torpor or indifference — the earth will be without form — the autumn without fruit, and the spring without fragrance. Sorrow tears but it enlarges the heart — indifference shrivels it up. Melancholy is the repose of the soul, indifference is its death.

•

Leaving Mr. C—— of C—— Vale, Gamble walked as far as a place he calls Violet

Bank to visit an old friend whom he had not seen for 'nearly fourteen years', that being, in 1812, since the year of the Rising. This friend, whom he calls Mr. S——, was an elderly Presbyterian minister who, according to Gamble, had been sixty years attached to one congregation. As such, he is easily identifiable as Robert Scott (1732–1813), then living at Ivy Brook, for which Violet Bank seems a plausible error or deliberate disguise. Scott belonged to the generation that had come of age in the middle years of the eighteenth century when, as Jacobitism went from being a force to a farce and Ireland experienced a protracted period without open war, Presbyterians had come to a sense of themselves as Irish: in adulthood, this same generation would decry Britain's invasions of Ireland's commercial and constitutional freedom, and provide 'moral' leadership to the Volunteer movement. Scott had been ordained to this congregation, properly Duneane and Grange (popularly Toome), in 1762. Like Mr. C——, and the dead Nathaniel Shaw, Scott was a republican or, to be consistent with the idea that republicans had 'died' as political actors

in 1798, he *had been* a republican. Indeed, Scott had been arrested in 1798 on a charge of high treason but acquitted when brought to trial (though Gamble says none of that). He had continued as minister of Toome for a decade after the Rising, only resigning from active ministry in November 1808.[87] His successor was Henry Cooke, a young man later to become a key figure in steering the Irish Presbyterian Church to a more conservative theological and political position. In 1808, however, the bitter young man's narrow Old Light opinions did not find favour with the congregation. Cooke left Toome in March 1810 and Scott, it appears, returned to ministry.[88]

Scott's daughter did not at first recognize Gamble when he arrived at the house, but when he identified himself, she took him to the garden where her father was sitting in the sun by his beehives.[89] He was asleep, his long hair, 'white as the stricken flax', shading his forehead, and Gamble, as he watched him sleep, remarked on how little he had changed since he had seen him last. On waking, Scott brought Gamble into his house and then into his room or study. Again, as in the dead minister's house at

87 *History of Congregations*, 454; McConnell, *Fasti*, 172. For his death at Ivybrook, on 17 April 1813, see *Belfast Newsletter*, 17 May 1813. Scott was a native of Balteagh, an area where Gamble had relatives. Ian McBride includes Scott (but not Shaw) in his useful list of ministers suspected of republicanism in the 1790s: *Scripture Politics: Ulster Presbyterianism and Irish Radicalism in the Late Eighteenth Century* (Oxford, 1998), 232–36.

88 For an account of Cooke's time in Duneane, by his son-in-law, see J. L. Porter, *The Life and Times of Henry Cooke, DD, LLD* (London, 1871), 26–28, where Scott is represented as an old man, who had 'never been distinguished for energy, either mental or physical; and his views, if he had any clear or decided views on points of doctrine, were believed to be Arian. Religious indifference pervaded the whole community. There was still the form of Christianity, but there was nothing of the spirit. A withering heresy paralysed the whole community.' Porter represents Cooke as being 'almost starved' out of the parish by Scott and his supporters.

The subtlety with which Gamble alludes to the private and the public impact of 1798 — such as when he arrives at Scott's — is a feature of his three journey books. For instance, in Armagh, in 1818, looking over an acquaintance's books, he writes (italics added): 'I opened the dimmed leaves of *twenty* wearisome years, and think [*sic*] of my youth's hopes, dimmed now as they. How our tastes differ with different periods of our existence, and how dull and unprofitable seemed to me just now the *Anna St. Ives* of Holcroft, which I read then with so much pleasure, and possibly reckoned among the happiest efforts of human genius. It is a feeble transcript of the philosophy of Godwin, whose opinions are brought forward in a ballet of action, and Miss Anna St. Ives is a kind of metaphysical columbine, who twists and twirls herself about in the display of them.' See *Views*, 352–53. *Anna St. Ives*, 7 vols. (1792) is a once popular novel by Thomas Holcroft (1745–1809), a novelist and playwright who enjoyed critical and commercial success in London in the 1780s. Prominent in pro-Jacobin circles in the city, Holcroft had been arrested for treason in 1794 but was released without being brought to trial. Hence, he was one of the celebrated radicals of London in the years when Gamble, a young doctor, arrived from Edinburgh. Holcroft had fallen into poverty when his audience deserted him in the late 1790s. Two years prior to the visit on which Gamble mentioned him, William Hazlitt had completed *Memoirs of the Late Thomas Holcroft*, 3 vols. (London, 1816), which went some way to recover Holcroft's reputation. Interestingly, at least one contemporary critic had earlier detected the influence of both Godwin and Holcroft in Gamble's fiction: see the review of *Howard* and *Sarsfield* in the *Augustan Review*, 1, 7 (1815), 670–78.

89 Scott's daughter gave Gamble 'a cordial though, perhaps, a melancholy welcome', causing him to remark that 'it is sorrowful to meet as we are beginning to grow old, the friends we have known in our youthful days'. His recurrent preoccupation — the failure of life to turn out as had been expected, the failure of the future to be born — here resurfaced. 'Fourteen years,' he wrote, 'are a great death stride in the life of man — how few can look back upon them with pleasure, how few can contemplate them without despondence, when they reflect how little they performed of what, elate in youth and hope, they expected when they looked forward to them.'

90 Possibly meaning the *Monthly Review* (1749–1845), an influential London literary journal.

91 *A View*, 217–18.

92 Tristram Stuart, *Bloodless Revolution: A Cultural History of Vegetarianism from 1600 to Modern Times* (London and New York, 2007 [2006]), esp. 239–43, provides a useful account of vegetarianism in Edinburgh University.

93 *A View*, 236–57.

Banbridge, it was as if time had stopped fourteen years earlier. Scott's room 'appeared as if it were as little changed as himself — the spectacles lay on the table as I had formerly seen them — and I believe the identical book was there likewise, it was a volume of monthly reviews[90] — a volume once highly prized in the North of Ireland, for the same reason that it was disapproved of by Doctor Johnson — the liberality of its opinions on religious and political subjects'. The man himself the same, the same book on the table, his glasses in the same place as fourteen years earlier: life had ended in 1798; or put another way, the public world may have changed, but the inner, private world had frozen. It was now teatime, and they sat down to a meatless dinner: 'flesh meat in my revered friend's house was an article rarely to be met with — for sixty years he had not tasted it, nor did he like to see others take it — his food was vegetables, bread, milk, butter, and honey'.[91] It too was a quiet but audible reference: vegetarianism was both moral and medical (and Edinburgh University, where Gamble had trained, was the 'headquarters of medical vegetarianism') but it was also political, having been an element in many radical counter-cultures from the middle of the eighteenth century.[92]

Gamble spent six days in this house where time had stood still. Judging from his narrative, much of his conversation with the old man concerned the early stages of his clerical career, when his New Light theology — 'more rational, more liberal and infinitely more humane' than dreary Old Light doctrines — had made it difficult for him to get a congregation, but how, once placed, he had earned the respect and affection of his people.[93] And yet the Rising still cast a shadow. Scott told Gamble how in 'the harvest of 1798', possibly a euphemism for the Rising, a stranger had applied to him for work as a labourer. After a few weeks, he learned from a reward notice in a newspaper that this man was a rebel who had been implicated in a robbery. Scott, 'feeling as an Irishman', could not bear to

give him up. He told him he wished him no harm, offered him his wages, tended his wounds which were crawling with maggots and told him to go his way. Moved by this humane gesture, the man confessed that he had been conspiring with one of the other servants, a man named Dennis, to rob him. Scott dismissed Dennis, but did not report him to the authorities. The following year, 1799, seven men ambushed Scott as he was travelling to a town some thirty miles from Toome. Dennis was among the would-be robbers; they 'were mostly desperadoes, who had been concerned in the rebellion, and a life of violence and plunder was become natural to them'. When Scott recognized Dennis, one of his colleagues knocked him unconscious. He woke in a cave on a mountainside. Dennis was standing guard over him. He had remembered Scott's kindness the previous year and he had prevented the others from killing him, telling them what a charitable man he was 'to all sects'. And he now assured Scott that he was as safe as if he were on his own potato ridge. Scott passed the night in the torch-lit cave, eating and drinking with his captors, who included Catholics and Protestants, before sleeping on a bed of heath. The following morning he was blindfolded and placed on his horse. Two of the group escorted him across rough country, leaving him five hundred yards from the town to which he had been going.

A few weeks later, Scott received a message from Dennis, telling him that he had been arrested and was to hang for robbery. He asked Scott to assist in burying him. Scott went to the gaol. It was a scene of noise and confusion. A crowd of country people was gathered at the grated door of Dennis's cell. Dennis himself was standing on his coffin, begging for money to bury his corpse and pray his soul out of purgatory: 'He rated those who were tardy in drawing out their purses, scolded others who had already given for not standing back to make room for newcomers; wept, preached and prayed, all in the course of a few minutes.'

A man in the cell with Dennis was to hang with him; he was a Protestant. The following day, Dennis and this friend were taken under military escort to the place where they had committed the robbery. There, they were allowed to rest themselves in a cabin, where they put on 'the dead dress'; that is, the shroud and cap with a black ribbon worn by men to their execution. The dead dress gave the condemned men 'the look of a spectre, as the imagination forms it, or of a corpse newly raised from the tomb'. Dennis came out of the cabin with a great show of fortitude but collapsed on seeing the other man attired like a corpse; both men were then hanged.

Scott rode home after the executions. He woke the next day at 'grey morning' — his term for dawn. He thought he heard a noise in the room and drew back the bed curtains. A figure like one of the hanged men, in its shroud and dead cap, stood pale and sad in the window. Scott rubbed his eyes and strove to wake himself. He turned himself in the bed, stretched himself forward and tried to penetrate the gloom. The figure did not, as he imagined it would, melt into thin air. It moved its eyes. It opened and shut its mouth. It seemed to be preparing to speak. Scott lay speechless. The phantom approached the bed and fell on its knees. 'Master,' it said, 'remember I have saved your life, now save mine.'

The phantom was Dennis. Having fainted on sight of his comrade in the dead dress, he had to be supported on the car as he was being executed and, as a result, he had swung gently off it; also, he was a tall man, and his feet at times had touched the ground as he hung. After hanging the minimum specified time, he had been cut down and given to his friends to bury. They had taken him to a nearby cabin and used various 'vulgar methods' to revive him: his feet were put in warm water, he was blooded with a rusty lancet, whiskey was rubbed into his skin, applied to his lips and nostrils, and poured down his throat and then, when he opened his eyes, milk was given to him from a woman's breast.

That night Dennis, 'having so unexpectedly returned among the living', decided to go to Scott's house at Toome, a distance of four miles across the fields. He met nobody, but if he had, the dead dress would have been his protection, 'for every one would have run from him as from a ghost'. But he did not need its protection:

....

Gamble cites scripture (Isaiah 7:15, 'Butter and honey shall ye eat, that you may fly evil and choose the good.') in explaining Scott's vegetarianism, and then contrasts his health and serenity with the condition of 'the sensual and beastly gormandizer [sic] of a metropolis, who with greasy hands, and blood-stained mouth, dozes snorting over the table, covered with the hecatomb of animals which are murdered to his rapacious maw, and pays the penalty of his barbarity, in his habitude, his stupidity and lethargy, his face distorted out of all human resemblance, and his body tortured with the gravel and gout'. Although not himself a vegetarian, Gamble had qualms about meat-eating and hunting for sport; note, for example, his comments on hunting in *Views*, 402–04, and *Sketches*, 192, where he says the sight of butchers and raw meat reminds him of cannibalism, and 198, where he finds a 'bloody goose' which he had been obliged to eat has 'taken possession of my imagination'. Towards the end of his 1812 tour, he praises the 'vegetable diet' (vegetables and milk, potatoes, butter, onions and oaten bread) in the mountain districts of west Tyrone, attributing the longevity and 'mild, humane and affectionate' character of the people to their diet (*A View*, 312–16). Elsewhere, he deplores the Irish and English preference for rare meat, contrasting it with the French tendency to 'conceal the nature of the food, and to weaken, as much as possible, in the imagination, the idea of a living animal' (*A View*, 120–21). And he expresses a preference for the 'Irish breakfast' — rich cream, butter, sweet cakes, preserved strawberries — over the 'brutal custom' increasingly prevalent in England of bringing flesh meat ('dead animal') to the table (*A View*, 71–72).

94 *A View*, 219–36.

95 *A View*, 33, 118–20. The displayed quotation is recycled in *Charlton*, vol. 2, 185–86.

96 For instance, *A View*, 118–20, represents 'the Presbyterian' contemplating revolution as estranged from his true self: 'Government did not know him — the Catholic did not know him — perhaps he did not know himself.' For an example of Gamble's use of types, see *Sketches*, 287: 'It is astonishing how little idea Presbyterians have of pastoral beauty — the Catholic has a thousand times more fancy — but a Presbyterian minds only the main chance.'

97 *Views*, 295–96. Gamble's general depiction of Volunteering was based on his recollection of the movement in the north-west in the 1780s. His main points — that companies were relatively autonomous of landlords and associated with the rise of a sense of nationhood — are at once consistent with contemporary sources and at variance with the interpretation in the 'revisionist' scholarship of the 1970s and 1980s. On Volunteering in the region (and a critique of revisionist work), see Breandán Mac Suibhne, 'Whiskey, Potatoes and Paddies: Volunteering and the Construction of Irish Identity, 1778–84', in Peter Jupp and Eoin Magennis, eds., *The Crowd in Irish History* (New York, 2000), 45–82.

'few people in any country would be willing to lead to the gallows a man just escaped from it — few people in Ireland would refuse to run some risk to save him from it'. He knew the room where his master slept; he had opened the window and stepped into the room from the garden.

Scott hid Dennis for some time in his house and then got him on board a vessel bound for the United States. He later became a porter in Baltimore, Maryland, the city that harboured many of the republicans who left Derry quay in the wake of the Rising — most notably Robert Moore and John Glendy — and which George Douglas, the Derry printer, had also made his home. Gamble commented: 'When time has thrown its dark mantle over the origin of their family, the descendants of poor hanged Dennis may rank with the greatest in America.'[94]

•

In these various forms — fact (the journey books) and fiction (*Charlton*) and fact repeated in the style of fiction, especially that of a ghost story (a fiction that *must* be a 'true story') — Gamble makes attempts, sometimes as asides but occasionally in extended analyses, at explaining the transformation which his home-place had undergone in his lifetime. Few of these efforts are in themselves compelling nor are they entirely consistent — in some places he emphatically emphasizes one factor as *the* cause of a development and elsewhere another. Most particularly, he vacillates on the extent of Presbyterian involvement in the Rising itself: at one point in 1812 he says that the 'Presbyterians of the north were not much less deeply and universally engaged in the rebellion than the Catholics of the south', but later in the same visit he represents them as balking at the last moment, refusing to countenance violence:

As long as it was uniting, and writing, and speaking, he took the lead; but when the rubicon was to be passed, when the

final decision was to be taken, when the fatal sword was to be unsheathed — then his moral sense resumed its influence, then the voice of conscience was harkened to, then his feelings and his prejudices, which were slumbering only, awoke.[95]

Moreover, as evident in that last quotation, Gamble had a tendency to write in terms of types — 'the Catholic' is emotional and artistic; 'the Presbyterian' rational and scientific — resulting at times in a dull cultural determinism but also a certain ambiguity: however many Presbyterians rose, 'the Presbyterian' did not.[96] Still, taken together, his efforts at explaining change — variously stressing economics, culture, and national and international politics — form the outline of a total history of the politics of identity in Ireland, more especially in the North, in the late eighteenth and early nineteenth centuries, while also being themselves part of the phenomenon he is explaining.

Gamble's account of the rise of radical Patriotism is straightforward. People, concerned with grievances more apparent than real, had achieved a no less illusory independence in the 'Revolution of 1782'. In 1818, for instance, he writes:

About forty years ago, the Presbyterians of Ulster, who, humanly speaking, had so few real evils to complain of, heated their fancies, with I could almost say, imaginary ones. They associated in large armed bodies, under the denomination of Volunteers, and by their formidable array having dispelled all dread of invasion with which they were threatened, they still continued together, to free themselves from the supposed political grievances of their situation. ... By the display of her force, Ulster at that time obtained privileges, which, in all probability would never have been yielded to her solicitations.[97]

Likewise, he offers a coherent account of the transition from radical Patriotism to republican separatism, locating it in the anti-climactic years of the mid-1780s. In his telling, the Volunteers had 'freed Ireland from what they conceived the tyranny and oppression of England' and achieved an 'independent parliament'. However, when that parliament failed to meet their expectations, or rather to be sufficiently dependent on themselves, they had engaged in 'wild speculations on governments and constitutions'. Government had initially repressed this 'spirit of innovation' by 'influencing Parliament, seducing some of the volunteer leaders, frightening others by displaying to them the evils of anarchy every where, and the particular evils of anarchy in Ireland'. But the spirit 'was smothered … not extinguished; it was covered, not entirely concealed; and by its concentration in the middle classes gained fresh strength'. And within a few years the French Revolution would blow it into flame.[98] In the meantime — that is, in the mid-1780s — the foisting of a large military establishment on the country and an increase of taxes, most especially on alcohol, to pay for it, had further alienated 'the people' from government, providing more kindling for revolution.[99] His main point is clear: Irish republicanism was not an import from America or France, nor the creation of a few middle-class politicos: it was deeply rooted in society and manners and the experience of bad government.

Crucially, Gamble has little of consequence to say on the failure of the Rising itself; perhaps as a former soldier, he saw conventional military history for the poor sports journalism that it is: the winning side either has more or better resources or makes better use of lesser resources. Still, in addressing the retreat from radicalism he is insightful, emphasizing, inter alia, the efficacy of government's suppression of the Rising, including the legacy of division and bitterness that government stoked; the ramifications of Napoleon's subversion of the French Republic; and changes in the leadership of the different religious groups that served to mitigate the difference between Dissenters and Churchmen

(members of the established church) and to distance Catholics from Protestants. For instance, he is sensitive to a new sense of ambition and advance in the Roman Catholic clergy. His explanation of their efforts to suppress the 'Irish Cry' — the traditional wailing at funerals of which he was himself a great admirer — is that 'circumstances having rendered them more objects of consideration', they were now 'more sensitive to ridicule'.[100] He gives an impression of a less rational, more emotional religious culture emerging among Protestants generally, most especially Churchmen, in the 1810s. Again, Methodism for Gamble was the epitome of excessive enthusiasm; he clearly finds it distasteful (though he says he does not) and it is a subject of curiosity to him. He connects its rise — and *ipso facto* the general evangelical turn in Protestantism — with the defeat of the Rising. 'Methodism of late years had greatly increased in this part of Ireland', he writes of west Tyrone on his return in 1810, continuing:

> It is a curious fact that after the last rebellion, several who were concerned in it, turned drinkers, and others died mad. Numbers became Methodists. The enthusiasm for politics gave way to the enthusiasm of religion. The high-wrought fever, which agitated the mind in the exultation of revolution, could not at all subside at once into the settled business, the sober current of life.[101]

But it is changes within Irish Presbyterianism to which Gamble is most attentive, picking up on the shifting balance of forces within the denomination that were causing it to turn in on itself — to become more evangelical in spirit and more conservative in politics. In 1818, after travelling by jaunting car from Belfast to Ballymena with several young Presbyterian clergymen returning home from the General Synod, he remarked on how the increase of the regium donum had greatly diminished their 'influence' ('perhaps at no time great')

98 *A View*, 117–18.
99 *Views*, 296–98.
100 *Views*, 396–98.
101 *A View*, 343–44. Like many contemporary Presbyterians, he had little time for Methodist preachers, presenting them as trading on credulity. In 1810, when travelling between Omagh and Newtownstewart, an area where Methodism was strong, he remarks, 'We are too fond of simplifying in judging the actions of men. We think of one cause only, when there are many. The mixture of simplicity and cunning, folly and knavery, is more frequent than people are aware of. How else should we have so many miracles, saints, quack-doctors, and methodist preachers[?]', *Sketches*, 237–38.

102 *Views*, 374–80.
Still, writing of the
Presbyterian Synod ('in
its construction the most
republican assembly
now in Europe'), he does
argue (372–73) that the
'dread of public opinion'
checks 'that disposition
to slavery, or at least
to servility', to which
'since the rebellion
which frightened, and
the augmentation of
the royal bounty, which
soothed', the Synod was
supposed to be prone.

103 *Views*, 421.

104 *Sketches*, 250–52.

105 The current
environmental crisis
has caused a number
of writers to revisit 'the
Year Without Summer',
but John D. Post, *The
Last Great Subsistence
Crisis in the Western
World* (Baltimore and
London, 1977) remains
required reading.

over their communities: people regarded the government allowance as sufficient for their support and, hence, no longer looked upon them 'as independent pastors of free men, but the servile stipendiaries of a court'. He intimates that Castlereagh's intention in paying them — 'to lull the clergy into inactivity' and to make the state secure by making them dependent on it — had succeeded. Tellingly, he notes that his 'young fellow travellers' were all 'rigidly Calvinistic in their sentiments'; 'these opinions, which a few years ago seemed to be dying away among Presbyterians, are fast reviving again'. Here, reflecting on the young men's old opinions, he makes explicit the basic point he repeatedly tries to impress on a target readership (the British middle class) with a teleological notion of progress: 'Human reason is not, as some fondly suppose, a stream that bears us straight forward, but a ceaseless tide, which has ebbed and flowed from the beginning, and shall, in all probability, until time shall be no more.' When the jaunting car reached Ballymena, and the clergymen rode off on little palfreys — horses of middling quality, generally ridden by women — which were waiting for them where the coach stopped, Gamble headed to the local inn, where he befriended a Frenchman as he waited for the Ballymoney coach.[102]

Of all Gamble's efforts to explain what was happening in Ireland in the 1810s, perhaps his most striking contribution is his flagging of the socio-economic and demographic bases for a sense among Presbyterians, which he himself shares, that they now faced cultural death, that is, that the norms and values which had defined their community would cease to be. Presbyterians, as he puts it, were 'the sturdy though decaying oak of this forlorn wilderness of man'.[103] The political project which they had nurtured for over a generation — overtly, at least from the late 1770s — had foundered in 1798 and the cultural space that had made it possible had been severely constricted; now, with their

numbers declining, the community was itself changing, and that, Gamble insisted, would have a negative impact on the wider society. This idea is first introduced in 1810 when he parts with the young man he had met outside Newtownstewart. Emigration to America, he observed as the fellow headed off for Derry, had declined in recent years, but people, particularly Presbyterians, were still leaving in large numbers, driven by landlords' exactions and drawn by the prospect of a better life. Those Presbyterians that remained at home, being rational, tended to marry comparatively late in life and rarely had large families. But 'the Catholic,' he argues, is 'more thoughtless, more improvident, more amorous, perhaps takes a wife when he is yet a lad; piles up a heap of sods into a cabin, eats potatoes, and gets children like a patriarch of old'. The result was that 'the population of Ireland is rapidly becoming more Catholic'.[104] By the end of his final trip, that of 1818, when Ireland 'was so much changed from what it was ten years ago that I can scarcely think it is the same land', his vision is grimmer. And there were reasons for the vision being grimmer. The long agricultural boom — sustained by a generation of war with America and France — had ended in 1815, when a combination of environmental and political factors — severe weather and demobilization following the final defeat of Napoleon — had precipitated an economic crisis that was soon compounded by famine and disease. A land system that, in the boom time, had encouraged owners to place tenants on bogs and mountains, where they could only ever hope to eke out a precarious existence, came close to collapse, and the region was only beginning to stabilize when Gamble came home in 1818.[105] Crucially, in the north of Ireland, this crisis raised old ghosts — both, the shade of deep historical injustice and the spectre of sectarian cataclysm — as Catholics, seeking work and food, came down from the mountains, where, in Gamble's phrase, they had been 'pent up' since the seventeenth century.

In the north-west in particular, the droves of 'mountainy' people crowding into plantation towns — Catholics now suddenly visible, at the very time Presbyterians were disappearing (by emigrating) — resonated with the biblical connotations of famine and disease.[106] And so the crisis at once unsettled Presbyterians, strengthening an apocalyptic world-view in some quarters, while also causing millenarian enthusiasms to pulse through Catholic communities. It seemed to many that a great transformation was imminent: for some Presbyterians, 'the end' was nigh, while some Catholics anticipated an end only to their own oppression.[107]

Such is the scale of the change that Gamble encounters in 1818, reality to him appears imaginary: 'so altered indeed is the condition of the country, that there are times when I scarce believe it is real, and could almost fancy myself in a dream'.[108] In the final passage of the book, he tries to isolate the factors that had produced this phantasmal actuality.[109] He now describes the prosperity which the French wars had brought to Ireland as having been, like the independence achieved in 1782, 'more apparent than real'. Its effects had been dissipated by the 'refinement in manner of living, improvement in dressing, and a taste for luxuries' that had accompanied it; 'something was gained … little was saved'.[110] More especially, increased income had been absorbed by landlords' raising of their rents to 'an enormous pitch'. The 'undue cultivation of the potato' had compounded matters, enabling people to live where nobody should have lived; 'the bleak and misty hills, fit habitation alone for shepherds and their flocks, are now thickly swarming with men'. And man, he writes, is like any other object, to be valued he must be rare: and so the men in the mountain were trodden on and oppressed. The country was now bereft of its gentry, who had decamped to London after the Union, 'leaving their poor tenantry to the mercy of servile and rapacious agents'.[111] Hence, when the economic downturn had come, and with it

famine and disease, 'society' had collapsed, appearing almost to go back in time. The law had lost its majesty. After a spate of legal actions — 'lawsuits, ejectments, distresses, imprisonments' — in the initial stages of the downturn, the courts were soon quiet as few people could afford the expense of a lawyer or expect payment if their case succeeded. Even cash dealings were being abandoned:

In many places society is transported back to the practice of the ruder ages, and payments in kind are becoming the commonest of any. A few weeks ago a relation of mine disposed of a field of corn which was ready for cutting, for which, according to the valuation of two men who viewed it, she is in December to get an equivalent quantity of oatmeal. A poor man who has a few acres of land from her, and is now nearly three years in arrears, expects, as the harvest of so favourable a one, shortly to pay a part of it, but not in money, but by giving her potatoes and turf. I know not that this has ever occurred to lawyers on circuit, as has been reported, but I am sure that surgeons and apothecaries, physicians here are pretty much out of the question, have been paid in a similar manner.[112]

And the upsurge in emigration had made the situation worse. Most of the emigrants were Presbyterians. 'The Presbyterian' had been reared with high ideas of himself. He had been taught in his youth that his ancestors, 'bearing the favoured name of Protestants, like Roman citizens in a remote province, lived on a footing of equality almost with the highest'. He could not now accommodate himself to 'the degradation wrought in his once lofty condition' and preferred to take refuge in America than accept 'unaccustomed misery' in Ireland. 'The Catholic', in contrast, rarely emigrated: 'to him the evil of the times is slight for he nor his ancestors ever knew a much better manner of living …' And the Catholic — made servile by experience — curried favour

106 For a sophisticated account of the crisis in the Strabane area, see Francis Rogan, *Observations on the Condition of the Middle and Lower Classes in the North of Ireland …* (London, 1819).

107 On Catholic mentalité in the late 1810s and early 1820s, see James S. Donnelly, Jr., 'Pastorini and Captain Rock: Millenarianism and Sectarianism in the Rockite Movement of 1821–4', in Samuel Clark and James S. Donnelly, Jr., eds., *Irish Peasants: Violence and Political Unrest, 1780–1914* (Dublin, 1983), 102–39, and Claire Connolly, 'Prince Hohenlohe's Miracles: Supernaturalism and the Irish Public Sphere', in David Duff and Catherine Jones, eds., *Scotland, Ireland and the Romantic Aesthetic* (Lewisburg, 2007), 236–57.

108 *Views*, 405.

109 *Views*, 412–23.

110 *Views*, 413–14. And compare *A View*, 200–01.

111 *Views*, 420–21.

112 *Views*, 416.

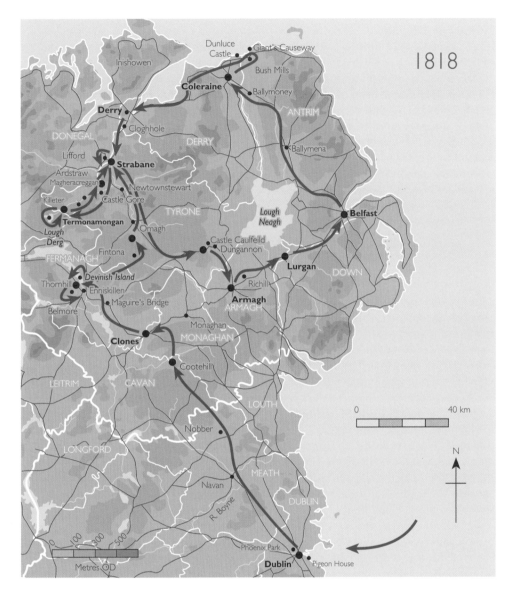

Gamble's route in 1818.

113 *Views*, 412–22. Here
Gamble echoes Sampson's
concern that poor
Catholics were being
preferred for land over
Protestants: see Sampson,
Statistical Survey, 503–
04, and *Memoir*, 336–41.

with 'delegated greatness', that is the agents
and bailiffs of absentee landlords who were
at once easily flattered and at the same time
quick to extract exorbitant rents from the
highest bidder, who were invariably the more
emotional, pliant Catholics, not the rational,
unbending Presbyterians:

> Long trampled on too and oppressed,
> [the Catholic] is subservient when he is
> not turbulent, and, thoughtless of remote
> consequences, and fondly attached to his
> own country, to the soil, to the sod as he

affectionately terms it, he eagerly takes
land at any rent, and bows down before
greatness, or its representation, in all that
lowliness of prostration, which delegated
greatness in a particular manner so loves.
In a contest for land therefore he is sure
to outbid, as by avaricious and short-
sighted policy, he is to be preferred to his
more unbending Presbyterian antagonist;
and scarcely is he settled when he takes
a wife, and begets children to inherit his
miseries, and possibly to avenge them.[113]

Hence, the 'degradation' of the 'ill-fated' Catholics was intimately connected with the emigration of the Presbyterians. A Malthusian apocalypse was imminent. But it would be war — not fever or famine or emigration, all of which 'operate too slowly' — that would check the growth in population: 'I may be wrong, and sincerely wish that I may, but I fear there is concentrated in Ireland causes sufficient to erase half the actual generation from the earth. It is a sleeping volcano, in which the fire of ages is pent up.'[114]

•

John Gamble has been described as 'a northern supporter of the United Irishmen, or at least, a supporter of their general policies'. It is an inadequate description.[115] Gamble may acknowledge and admire the heroism of executed United Irishmen and enjoy the 'society' of surviving rebels, but he repeatedly deplores rebellion — not only 'the late unfortunate rebellion' but rebellion itself, which he presents as unnatural; he may explain why people became rebels in the 1790s, but he still regrets it, regarding their republicanism, like their rebellion, as an unnecessary and unwarranted step. Politically, Gamble might be better represented as a sentimental Patriot: he writes reverentially of Henry Grattan and expresses a high regard for the old Irish parliament (if not for the Dubliners who bemoan its loss). But sentimental Patriot is no less inadequate a

description. Gamble writes from a point after the future has ended, after a politics that sought a revolutionary break with the past — the radical Patriotism that produced the phantasmal Revolution of 1782 or the republican paramilitarism that pursued the mirage of a revolution in 1798 — has decidedly passed away, but before a viable new civil politics has emerged, its emergence inhibited by the dissipation of society and manners, a dissipation that was itself, at least in part, a product of the rebellion he deplores and its suppression. And it is for this reason that Gamble's various efforts at explaining what happened in his home-place in his lifetime only ever amount to the shadow of a history. If memory rebuked the fiction that was becoming history in the early 1800s, it also called up shades that, for Gamble, are beyond an emotionally satisfying explanation, not least the most decent of men and women becoming rebels prepared to take and sacrifice life and, once the Rising is suppressed, those same decent people — or those of them who survived — passing out of the public sphere, dying in political terms. And hence the ghosts with whom Gamble sups and dines when he recalls the late 1790s.

Haunted Houses

I saw, I felt, but I cannot describe, the last moments of this horrible scene. Dragged from the mud and stones, they dashed a mangled lump of flesh right across the

114 *Views*, 422–23. Although developed at greatest length in *Views*, the idea that a political cataclysm (with a demographic dynamic) was imminent had been introduced in his accounts of his visits of 1810 and 1812; see, for example, *A View*, 380: 'In the country where I write this, and probably at no very distant period of time, there may be a most awful struggle.' Also see *Brief Observations*, 10–11.

115 McCormack, 'Language, Class and Genre', 1106. It is also an insular assessment, indicative of a tendency in 1970/1980s' Ireland to represent anybody concerned to establish the causes of discontent as a 'fellow traveller' of 'men of violence'. And it is wrong: the United Irishmen proposed the establishment of an Irish republic, yet John Gamble argues in *Brief Observations*, 13–14, that 'Any dispassionate person who considers the situation of [Ireland and England] must be convinced, that whenever society became advanced, they were intended to form one empire of which England must necessarily be the head; she was interposed between Ireland and all the rest of Europe, and through her only, could arts, knowledge, and civilization pass to the lesser state.'

116 Charles Robert Maturin, *Melmoth the Wanderer* (Oxford, 1998 [4 vols.; 1820]), 256–57. Maturin inserted a footnote to the cavalry officer's question ('Where was the victim?') and the response ('Beneath

Gamble was not to see the eruption he predicted. However, the crisis of 1815–18, which was followed by another in 1821–22, proved a tipping point in both the demographic decline and the cultural transformation of the Presbyterian community. A comment in the Preface to *Charlton*, published in 1823, might be used to extend the argument here about feeling people becoming ghosts. Gamble writes: 'I came [in 1818] to the remote part where I write this, on a visit of a few weeks, or at the most months, and I have stayed, *I think* years' (italics added). The 'I think' is curious, suggesting that, as the cultural world that had shaped him changed beyond recognition, he himself passed out of time and became ghostly. This extension of the argument is suggested by Jonathan Lear, *Radical Hope: Ethics in the Face of Cultural Devastation* (Cambridge, Mass., 2007), which was brought to my attention by Luke Gibbons.

your horse's feet'):
'this circumstance occurred in Ireland 1797, after the murder of the unfortunate Dr. Hamilton. The officer was answered, on inquiring what was that heap of mud at his horse's feet, — "The man you came for".'

117 The details of the assassination have often been confused. For instance, James Glassford, *Notes of Three Tours in Ireland in 1824 and 1826* (Bristol, 1832), 56, depicts him being killed at the Church of Ireland bishop's palace in Raphoe (not Waller's rectory in Sharon); A. T. Q. Stewart, *The Narrow Ground: Aspects of Ulster, 1609–1969* (Belfast, 1997 [1977]), 118–19, has him killed in 1798 (not 1797), and W. J. McCormack, 'Irish Gothic and After', in Deane, ed., *Field Day Anthology*, vol. 2, 831–949, 833, represents his killers as 'agrarian assassins' (not republicans).

118 William Hamilton, *Letters Concerning the Northern Coast of the County of Antrim …* (Dublin, 1786). The volume went through a number of editions in Hamilton's lifetime, including German (Leipzig, 1787) and French (Paris, 1790) translations. Several editions were published in the nineteenth century, the book serving as a guide to the Giant's Causeway.

119 William Hamilton, *Letters on the Principles of the French Democracy and Their Application and Influence on the Constitution and*

door of the house where I was. With his tongue hanging from his lacerated mouth, like that of a baited bull; with one eye torn from the socket, and dangling on his bloody cheek; with a fracture in every limb, and a wound for every pore, he still howled for 'life — life — life — mercy!' till a stone, aimed by some pitying hand, struck him down. He fell, trodden in one moment into sanguine and discoloured mud by a thousand feet. The cavalry came on, charging with fury. The crowd, saturated with cruelty and blood, gave way in grim silence. But they had not left a joint of his little finger — a hair of his head — a slip of his skin. Had Spain mor[t]gaged all her reliques from Madrid to Mon[t]serrat, from the Pyrenees to Gibraltar, she could not have recovered the paring of a nail to canonize. The officer who headed the troop dashed his horse's hoofs into a bloody formless mass, and demanded, 'Where was the victim?' He was answered, 'Beneath your horse's feet'; and they departed.
Charles Robert Maturin, *Melmoth the Wanderer* (1820)[116]

In March 1797 republicans assassinated Dr. William Hamilton (b. 1757), rector of Fánaid, in the house of Dr. John Waller at Sharon, near Newtowncunningham, some fifteen miles from Strabane.[117] Hamilton, as a magistrate and a Church of Ireland minister, was the embodiment of the constitution in Church and state. He was also very well connected. A former fellow of Trinity College Dublin and a founding member of the Royal Irish Academy, he was acquainted with leading figures in academic and ecclesiastical circles and he was respected abroad for a vulcanist treatise on the Antrim coast (1786).[118] He was well known in political circles too. He had penned a vigorous attack on republicanism, *Letters on the Principles of the French Democracy*, in 1792 and, in 1796, Dublin Castle had solicited (and greatly appreciated) his analysis of the political situation in the

north-west.[119] Indeed, Hamilton had been targeted for assassination on account of his unusually vigorous efforts to disarm United Irishmen in his own parish: at a time when wealthy loyalists were quitting their residences across north Donegal and moving into Derry, he had established a yeomanry corps, detained several prominent republicans and withstood a siege at his glebe house. Such was his profile, that in the wake of his killing, the Irish parliament voted a sizeable pension for his widow, Sarah née Walker, and nine children, and special orders were issued to General Lake to disarm Ulster.[120] In time, the writer Charles Maturin would use the details of the killing to describe a particularly gruesome murder in his sprawling Gothic novel *Melmoth the Wanderer*, and a memoir appended to a tourist's edition (1839) of 'Hamilton's *Antrim Coast*' would perpetuate the image of a loyalist martyr.[121]

Gamble met a man who had been at Sharon on the night that Hamilton was done to death. He met this man in the summer of 1812, the summer in which he wrote about the events of the late 1790s in the most ghostly terms. The day before he met him he had walked from Scott's house in Toome to Dungiven. He had stopped that night at 'a little inn or public house' where he ate a dinner of veal chops, roast mutton and boiled beef — he had only ordered the chops — washed down with a glass of whiskey, meaning parliament whiskey. 'The malt liquor,' he observed, 'was bad, as is too frequently the case in Ireland, there being little inducement to make it good, for few people seem disposed to drink it. Spirits [meaning *poitín*] and water constitute the favourite beverage at dinner, and punch after it.'

After dinner, and the bad malt liquor, Gamble went to 'the bar', where he found the landlady busy serving whiskey to a large company and the landlord reading a newspaper. He invited the landlord to take a glass of punch with him but he refused saying that he was 'under a promise' and could only take one glass in the day. Gamble knew such voluntary penance to be common; people unable to refrain from drinking, preferred to restrain it, devising oaths that were hard to break yet easy to evade. A man might swear never to drink 'except out of the hand of some lady or gentleman in his neighbourhood'; hence, 'When any merry-making is going forward in which he wishes to take his share, he waits patiently on the keeper of his conscience with a bottle of whiskey, which he puts into her or his hands, and immediately takes back again into his own.' Or else a man might swear never to drink whiskey as long as he lives; 'he soaks bread in it, and gets drunk — he does not, he conceives, drink, he only eats it'. Or perhaps a man swore neither to drink in nor out of his own house, but drinks instead with one foot either side of the threshold, and 'flatters himself that he is not forsworn.'

Before retiring, Gamble asked the landlord if he had any books. The landlord had little but sermons, and Gamble, having read the like of them in his youth, did not wish to see, never mind think of reading. He opted for a copy of 'Sir William [sic] Temple's account of the rebellion of 1641', an ultra-Protestant pornography of Catholic violence first published in 1646 of which at least ten editions had appeared since then.[122] Perusing it made him mad. 'Of all accounts of that unhappy period,' he wrote, 'his are the most partial, the most exaggerated and the most absurd. On reflection, he was not himself pleased with the performance, for he would not suffer it to pass through a second edition.' Here, a shadow has fallen across Gamble's page: the words (from 'the most partial …' to '… second edition') are an unattributed direct quotation from William Crawford's 1783 A History of Ireland.[123] Crawford (1739–1800), who had been the Presbyterian minister of Strabane in Gamble's youth, was the epitome of the activist New Light clergymen of the late eighteenth century.[124] He had been a Volunteer, serving as chaplain to the Strabane Rangers, and preaching to them on 'the connection betwixt moral courage

and virtue' when a violent confrontation between parliament and 'the people' had appeared imminent in autumn 1779.[125] He had later, in February 1782, been a delegate of the Strabane Battalion to the first Dungannon Convention, which energized the final push for 'independence'; there, he had distinguished himself by speaking strongly in support of the relaxation of the Penal Laws against Catholics.[126] Besides having been Gamble's minister in the 1780s, Crawford had also been his teacher: he had founded an academy in Strabane in 1785, which accepted students of all religions, and prepared the best of them for Scottish universities.[127] The work that Gamble now silently recalled surveyed the history of Ireland from 'our Milesian ancestors' to the achievement of legislative independence, which in 1783 had been imagined to be real, concluding with a vigorous argument for radical parliamentary reform, including the extension of the franchise to Catholics.[128] And reading Temple and remembering Crawford, as that rowdy company drank in the bar below, Gamble's mind turned to the condition of Irish Catholics:

It is impossible, without a sinking of the heart, to think of the fate of these generous and warm-hearted, though often misguided and misled people, of their sufferings, their proscriptions, their expulsions, and when actual violence had ceased, of the contempt which unceasingly pursued them — the brutal scorn, the idiot laugh, the pointed finger, which have marked with indelible letters, the Catholic character, which has made past recollection almost predominate over future hope, which with great swelling heart and thrilling anguish … But I check myself, lest my words should convey a meaning different from what I intend. Far be it from me to insinuate, or even suppose, that the Catholics are not to be gained by kindness, or that were they relieved from what they deem the degradation of their present condition,

Happiness of Britain and Ireland (Dublin, 1792).

120 On Sharon, see my 'Politicization and Paramilitarism', 263–69.

121 Maturin would have been familiar with the details of the assassination — his cousin, Henry Maturin, succeeded Hamilton as rector of Fánaid in 1797: see James B. Leslie, comp., Raphoe Clergy and Parishes (Enniskillen, 1940), 51. The memoir of Hamilton is in an edition of Letters Concerning the Antrim Coast published by Samuel Hart of Coleraine in 1839. The anonymous author of the memoir appears to have had access to Hamilton's correspondence with Castle officials in 1796–97, suggesting he may have been Robert Marshall, a friend of Hamilton who was private secretary to Thomas Pelham, the chief secretary of Ireland in 1795–98. The author also had access to Hamilton's children's papers.

122 Gamble is here (264–65) referring to John (not William) Temple's The Irish Rebellion (London, 1646). Two editions of Temple, the first since 1800, were issued that very year (1812) by London printers, one by Wilks and the other by White and Cochran; the Wilks edition had been prepared by Richard Musgrave, a leading anti-Catholic polemicist.

123 William Crawford, A History of Ireland, from the Earliest Period, to the Present Time …, 2 vols. (Strabane, 1783), vol. 2, 44. Crawford apparently began his

History in winter 1781
— that December Lord
Charlemont had offered
'assistance' to him
provided he publish
his 'intended history'
by subscription: see
Strabane, 9 December
1781, William Crawford
to Charlemont, quoted
in J. T. Gilbert, ed.,
*The Manuscripts and
Correspondence of
James, First Earl of
Charlemont*, 2 vols.
(London, 1891–94), vol.
1, 389–90. A committee
of seven 'friends',
including Charlemont
and Luke Teeling of
Lisburn, a prominent
Catholic politico, raised
600 (of a total 700)
subscriptions to support
the publication; see *A
History*, vol. 1, viii.
Also see *LJ*, 18 June
1782, where, responding
to a suggestion by
'Hibernicus', Crawford
announced that he
would extend his history
to 'the present period
— a period the boast
of Irishmen, and which
will shine with a brilliant
lustre in the annals of
the nation'.

124 For biographical details,
see McConnell, *Fasti*,
136.

125 William Crawford, *The
Connection betwixt
Courage and the Moral
Virtues Considered, in a
Sermon, Preached before
the Volunteer Company
of Strabane Rangers,
on Sunday the Twelfth
of September, 1779,
and Published at their
Desire* (Strabane, 1779).
Crawford delivered
another major sermon
during the Volunteer
epoch: *The Nature and
Happy Effects of Civil
Liberty, Considered in
a Sermon, Preached
before Colonel Stewart,
Lieut. Col. Charlton,*

From an original Profile Shade, in the Possession of the Family.

the past would many years longer occupy
that strong hold on their imagination,
which it now assuredly does. Were
present grievances removed, ancient
ones in a few years would probably only
be a subject for tales or ballads. What
event was ever more disastrous or less
honourable to a nation than that of
Flodden Field; yet a celebrated Scotch
poet has made it the subject of the only
poem resembling an epic one which his
country can boast of. Were a generous,
and, therefore, a wise system of policy
adopted towards Ireland, some future
Catholic genius might find his hero in
King William, and might deck with all

the charms of poetry, the battle of the Boyne.[129]

Having spent the night brooding over the brutal scorn, the idiot laugh, and the pointed finger that had made Irish Catholics what they were and imagining a transformation, if only Britain adopted a proper *policy* toward Ireland, Gamble woke early the next morning to set out on foot for Strabane. As he was leaving the inn, the landlord was taking his 'morning glass' and, having declined Gamble's invitation the previous evening, he now asked him to partake. Gamble, who had taken a wry view of the landlord's promise (guessing he had a large glass and gave himself a good measure), declined (he several times claims never to drink in the morning), asking instead for a draught of buttermilk.

'That's poor weakening liquor,' said the landlord, 'its enough to give a man the dropsy.'

'I was going to make the same observation of yours,' shot back the doctor, 'it is slow poison.'

'Slow indeed,' sniffed the landlord, 'I have taken it many a long year, and never found it did me any harm, but a great deal of good.'

As he walked out the door, Gamble could hear the man with the good measure muttering behind him: 'Slow poison, indeed! May be I will be stout and hearty when you are laid under the sod.'

The doctor walked ten miles before stopping for breakfast at a large house denoted by the sign of a white cross; two hundred years later, the tavern is still there, still denoted by a white cross.[130] Travellers, it occurred to Gamble, often meet crosses and 'the cross' in this instance was the breakfast, a mediocre one marred by bad tea and coarse sugar. He was soon on the road again. It was a beautiful day: 'the sun shone in mild brightness against a serene sky, in whose blue bosom I contemplated the image of aetherial repose we hope for after death'. He was overtaken by a gentleman's servant

on horseback. The horseman immediately dismounted and, 'with the civility almost universal on an Irish road', insisted that the doctor take the horse while he walked alongside him for several miles. The two men talked and it transpired, apparently quite quickly, that the servant had been present in Waller's house at Sharon when the republicans had arrived looking for William Hamilton. Gamble recollected the event; he describes it as 'almost the only murder committed in this part of the country during the late rebellion', an economical surmise given that several rebels may have been killed on that very stretch of road in a single incident in 1797.[131] And his own recollection and the report of this 'eye witness', as Gamble described him, melded into a narrative of what passed at Sharon:

Doctor Waller was an old and almost bed-ridden clergyman. Mrs. Waller was a middle-aged woman; their house was in a lonely spot, nearly a mile from any other habitation. Doctor Hamilton, fatigued, exhausted both in body and mind, arrived there on horseback an hour before it was dark. 'I am come,' said he, 'to beg the shelter of your roof for this night — to claim it rather — I am unable to go farther, nor will I leave this unless I am turned out.'

He was a rector of a parish near the sea side; he had rendered himself very obnoxious to the United Irishmen, by the opposition he gave their system, and even his friends allow that he committed a number of harsh, if not cruel actions. As rebellion became more powerful, his situation became more perilous, and it required all his address to get clear of his own house, and to pass through the different parties that were lying in wait to murder him. Mr. Waller reluctantly consented to his stopping that night in the house. After tea, Mrs. Waller, two young ladies, visitors, and Doctor Hamilton, sat down in the parlour to a rubber of whist. They had not finished the first

the Strabane Volunteers, Strabane Rangers, and Urney Forresters. On Sunday, the 19th of March, 1780. And Published at their Desire (Strabane, 1780). The companies present published resolutions demanding the repeal of the Declaratory Act, and declaring that 'We were born FREE. Liberty is our glorious birthright in support of which we are determined to risque our property and everything dear to us upon earth.' See *LJ*, 24 March 1780. For commentary on the meeting, see Strabane, 21 March 1780, James Hamilton to Abercorn, PRONI, Abercorn Papers T/2451/ IA1/13/19.

126 Patrick Rogers, *The Irish Volunteers and Catholic Emancipation (1778–1793): A Neglected Phase of Ireland's History* (London, 1934), 70.

127 On the academy, see *LJ*, 12 July; 16 August; 6 December; 13 December 1785; 11 April; 31 October 1786; 23 October; 13 November 1787, and *SJ*, 18 October; 29 November 1785; 9 May 1786. Also see Anon., *Regulations of the Strabane Academy. And an Address to the Students in General, on Opening that Seminary, Delivered on Monday, November the 7th, 1785 … by W. Crawford D.D. with an Address to the Students in the Class of Languages by W. Taggart A.M., and an Address to the Students of the Mathematical Class by J. T. Murray* (Strabane, 1785).

128 Crawford, *A History*, vol. 1, 28.

129 *A View*, 267–68.

The poem is Scott's *Marmion: A Tale of Flodden Field* (Edinburgh, 1808).

130 The premises is The Inn at the Cross, a well-known small hotel, on the Glenshane Road.

131 On this incident, near Newbuildings, see my 'Politicization and Paramilitarism', 262. Gamble also refers to Hamilton at the Giant's Causeway in 1818: *Views*, 390–91.

132 *A View*, 269–71.

133 Derry, 4 March 1797, R. G. Hill to John Beresford, National Archives of Ireland, Rebellion Papers [hereafter, NAI, RP] 620/29/29; Letterkenny, 27 March 1797, John Rea to Sackville Morgan, NAI, RP 620/29/116.

134 Derry, 7 December 1796, John Bagwell to [Edward Cooke], NAI, RP 620/26/104; Derry, Wed. night, George Hill to Edward Cooke; Examination of Patrick Baldwin, Private in the Tipperary Militia, 7 December 1796; Examination of George Hennessey, Private in the Tipperary Militia, 7 December 1796, NAI, RP 620/26/107; Information of David Dobbyn, Serjeant Tipperary Militia, 21 March 1797, NAI, RP 620/29/99; Information of Patrick Hickey, Private in the Tipperary Regiment, 23 March 1797, NAI, RP 620/29/111.

game, when the window shutters were violently thrown open, and a number of voices called loudly for the unfortunate Hamilton. He started wildly up, and rushed to the door. The men without fired. Mrs. Waller crossed the room at an instant, and received a shot in her side, of which she died a few minutes afterwards. Doctor Hamilton ran down to the cellar, where he concealed himself. The assassins with shouts of vengeance, desired him to be sent out, threatening, otherwise, to set fire to the house, and to murder everyone in it. Overcome by weakness and fear, overwhelmed with grief for the loss of his wife, and, probably, irritated against the innocent cause of her death, Doctor Waller gave the fatal mandate. The servants dragged the wretched man from the cellar — trembling, quivering, convulsed, grasping at every thing he could lay hold of. With the mortal heart-sinking which sudden and violent death inspires, he was dragged along and thrown out to his murderers, who dispatched him with as many wounds as Caesar was in the capitol. Then they mounted their horses, and rode quietly away.[132]

It is a matter-of-fact account, if inaccurate on minor details (Hamilton had sent his servant to Waller's to announce that he would be coming), moderately ambiguous (the assassination of Caesar involves both republican idealism and personal betrayal), and a little melodramatic (the horsemen riding quietly away adds a Gothic touch). Gamble appends his own speculations about the identity of the killers. Here, he makes a tendentious argument that they were Catholics who had come down from the mountains of Fánaid; they had, he writes — adding to the eerie mood — travelled over twenty miles by land and water, a common phrase in stories of the supernatural. That argument is at odds with the authorities' conviction in 1797 that only two men from Fánaid, James Friel and Robert Floyd,

were present at the killing; Friel was a Catholic, but Floyd was a Presbyterian like James Kinkaid of Newtowncunningham, the most deeply implicated suspect.[133] Gamble's rather convoluted reasoning was that nobody having been convicted of the assassination, the killers *must* have been Catholics, as Catholics were less likely to inform. Again, the official record suggests that the prime informers in the north-west were those men who could be most easily intimidated. For instance, militia-men suborned by the United Irishmen and facing summary execution once exposed, devastated the organization in the north-west; these men were predominantly Catholics.[134] But Gamble and the man who had been at Sharon should have their say:

There were probably about twenty of them. They had traversed partly by land, and partly by water, a distance of nearly thirty miles, yet, what is most singular, not one of them has ever since been discovered. It is a question, often and warmly discussed in Ireland, whether they were Catholics or Protestants. Some have supposed they were a mixture of both. I am not of that opinion; the union which took place between the two sects, was a most unnatural one. I mean unnatural, with a reference to Irish nature, modified by habit and circumstance. It was kept up only by success; misfortune, or the dread of punishment, always resolved it into its elemental particles, and mutual altercation and mistrust prevailed. On these occasions, the Protestant almost always was the informer. The fidelity of the Catholic could rarely be shaken. I do not here attribute to him greater virtue, but greater zeal. His opposition to government was, in some degree, his settled habit; it was in some degree his ordinary and habitual movement; it was the vertigo of the Protestant, and required the perpetual agitation of movement to keep it up — whenever he stood still, it subsided. He played only, if I may be permitted to use the expression, for the counter of speculative freedom, which circumstances led him to prize more than formerly. But the Catholic played for life, for what is dearer than life — he had set his all on the hazard of a die, and he played with a constancy, a fidelity, a devotedness, equal to the greatness of the stake.

Government, therefore, was probably benefitted [*sic*] rather than injured by the share the Protestant had in the rebellion, hanging, as he often did, a dead weight about the neck of his associate, restraining his efforts, and discovering his plans. The events of that day, (at least as far as the present generation are concerned)[,] have placed an everlasting bar between the two — the one has no wish to be trusted; but, if he had, no inducement, I dare say, would prevail on the other to trust him. Rebellion, therefore, should it ever again, for the misfortune of these kingdoms, take place in Ireland, would likely be confined to one great homogenous body, animated by one soul, directed to one object, and, therefore, I should conceive, infinitely more dangerous.[135]

Having raked over the events at Sharon, Gamble and the gentleman's servant stopped in Dunny Manra (Donemana), a little village whose inhabitants had been strongly republican in the 1790s (though Gamble does not say so), 'to take some refreshment'. And refreshed, they parted there. The gentleman's servant rode off to the left, up into the mountains. Gamble went forward alone, and on foot as formerly.[136]

•

The unnamed horseman was one of two men: he was Barney McCafferty or William Shiels, respectively Waller's and Hamilton's servants. When the republicans (who had already killed Waller's wife) had threatened

to burn Sharon glebe, the Wallers' cook, Mrs. Squires, had single-handedly pulled Hamilton from the cellar and ordered McCafferty to turn him out. McCafferty, without saying a word, had then dragged Hamilton by the hair to the hall door and thrust him through it.[137] Yeomanry officers who interrogated him in the hours after the attack had judged McCafferty 'a horrid savage' and lodged him in Lifford Gaol.[138] However, when McCafferty stood trial for murder at the Donegal assizes in September 1797, the presiding judge, Baron George, said there was no evidence McCafferty had any 'previous intent' to harm Hamilton. 'The case,' he said, 'was not unlike that of two men falling into the sea and having a plank, sufficient to save the life of one, but not of both; in which case ... it would be no crime for one to push the other off the plank as self-preservation was the first principle of our nature.' The jury acquitted McCafferty without leaving the box.[139] Shiels, although never charged with any offence, became the subject of innuendo in Fánaid. John Maturin, a son of Rev. Henry Maturin, Hamilton's successor, heard that Shiels, a Catholic or a convert or the descendant of a convert, dampened the powder in the pans of Hamilton's pistols. Perhaps he did, but the plot (betrayal from within by the trusted 'other') is a 'dreary steeple' in Irish Protestant polemic and there is no evidence that the authorities attached any blame to him at the time.[140] One suspects that the horseman was McCafferty, if only because a man from the Laggan was more likely than one from Fánaid to be on the road from Dungiven to Strabane.

Barney McCafferty, if he was the horseman, was a haunted man, his life defined by the horror of a single night that he would revisit time and again, even with a stranger met on a country road at the height of summer. Yet it was not McCafferty but a haunted house that would give Gamble the greatest pause. Gamble saw this house during his third documented visit to Strabane (1818). On this trip, he was more morose

135 *Sketches*, 271–73.
136 *A View*, 257–75, gives Gamble's account of the night spent in Dungiven and the encounter with the gentleman's servant.
137 *Dublin Evening Post*, 30 September 1797; *Belfast Newsletter*, 22 September 1797. McCafferty (sometimes McClafferty) and Sheils were the only male servants in the house on the night of the attack.
138 Ballymacool, 9 March 1797, John Boyd to Bob [Mansfield], NAI, RP 620/29/46, refers to McCafferty as a savage. Also see n.p., n.d. [Sharon, 3 March 1797], R. G. Hill to Earl of Cavan, NAI, RP 620/29/13, reporting the killing and that McCafferty had been arrested 'as from his manner of dragging Mr. Hamilton from the cellar, he appears to have been actuated by something more than terror.'
139 *Dublin Evening Post*, 30 September 1797.
140 James Reid Dill, *The Dill Worthies* (Belfast, 2nd. ed., 1892), 98–99.

141 *Views*, 341.
142 *Views*, 67, 95–96, 98, 104.
143 Thornhill is in the parish of Trory. The clergyman was probably William Weir, perpetual curate of Trory. He had entered Trinity College, Dublin, as a sizar, or poor student, in June 1762 and was still living in early 1818. James B. Leslie, comp., *Clogher Clergy and Parishes* (Enniskillen, 1929), 252, only lists a single child, a son, for him.
144 *Views*, 153–54.

about 'the ravages of time', 'the wreck of time', than he had been in 1810 and 1812; he was also more disillusioned with the dull realties of Irish politics and more despairing about what he saw as a dismal demographic dynamic.[141] The world-weary mood was set even before he reached Strabane. In Dublin, he met a friend from college whom he scarcely recognized, as he was so 'kneaded and moulded by the slow-moving hand of time', and in Cootehill the elderly woman with whom he stopped eight years earlier was herself now dead: 'To the little inn, I retired disconsolate and it lessened not the feeling of melancholy, that, long as I had known Cootehill, it was the first time I had ever sought, or had occasion to seek the shelter of one.' He spent two nights there, visiting places he had once known well — walking through the apparently unoccupied house in which he had stayed in 1810 (and years earlier) — thinking of 'the loss of long gone friends'. 'My sleep even was not repose,' he wrote of that last night in Cootehill, 'for all the deceased friends of my waking thoughts, clad in their burial garments, came to visit me, and to invite me to be one of them.'[142] Later, at Thornhill, outside Enniskillen, he and a distant relative, an elderly Protestant clergyman whom he had not seen for years, spent the night 'carousing'. But cold rum punch only brought on bitter melancholy:

> For a while we drained the bowl in all due jollity; but the jollity of an old man is fleeting as his few remaining years, and as the liquor exerted its influence, age's natural disposition more and more appeared. … In wine there is truth, and liquor opened wide the sluices of my kind host's eyes as well as his heart; merriment gave way to thoughtfulness and thoughtfulness to tears. In bitter anguish, he recalled to mind the friends whom are for ever gone, of whom my father was the dearest, and wept over the six fine sons by whom he was surrounded when I last saw him, and of whom only

one now remains. I know not, nor did I venture to ask, whether he mourns or rejoices over him.[143]

Arriving in Strabane, he lays eyes on his 74-year-old mother. Seeing her now, he wonders which of them has had the lonelier life — he who went alone into the wide world, or she who has spent her life in the one place, now in old age confronted at every turn by reminders of all that time has taken from her:

> We arrived in Strabane … and I again beheld the place of my birth. I beheld too the aged parent to whom I owe that birth. I beheld her with pleasure; but it was a pleasure in which there was pain; the bowed down head was stooped still lower; the dim eye was dimmed further; and the weakened limbs trembled more. It has been my lot, whether good or bad, to be a wanderer; amidst the scenes of her youth, she has grown old; never has she changed, nor perhaps wished to change her place. But the mountains which bounded her narrow horizon could not shut her out from care. It has followed her over them, and made her die a hundred times in the loss of those she has loved. Could we enter the heart, and read its secret thoughts, she dies perhaps further, as every green tree, and field, and bush, reminds her of the years that are flown. The daisied bank opposite her garden is the same on which, in happy infancy, she gathered wild flowers; and the setting sun which sheds lustre on her windows, lighted up in this very room her opening years and blooming hopes. To cheerless age, the earth no longer pours forth flowers; and neither rising nor setting sun can warm with joy the languid heart, on which is the chill of more than threescore and fourteen years.[144]

His first few days in Strabane were unsettled. He visited a 'few' old acquaintances and made his favourite walks, but he found 'every thing changed, and changed for the worse'. 'Since I was last here,' he writes, 'this town and neighbourhood have been visited by two almost of the heaviest calamities which can befal[l] human beings. Fever and famine have been let loose, and it is hard to say which has destroyed the most.' Gamble was here referring to the hunger and disease that ravaged Ireland in 1815–18, when pummelled by a combination of environmental, economic and epidemiological blows, regional society had come close to collapse. By the end of that summer, he would argue that Ireland now faced a demographic crisis that, given the country's cultural and political divisions, was liable to result in sectarian war. In the first days at home, however, it is the social dislocation that captured his attention. He himself describes how

hord[e]s of wandering beggars, impelled by the cravings of hunger, carried the distemper from door to door; and, from their wretched habiliments, wafted contagion far and wide. Almost the entire mountain population, literally speaking, took up their beds and walked; and, with their diseased blankets wrapped around them, sought in the low lands, the succour which charity could not give, but at the hazard of life.

Irish people, he remarked, have always been indulgent of beggars; and the poor in turn claimed charity 'as a matter less of favo[u]r than of right'; now, in 'frightful numbers' they had 'besieged every house, and forced their way into kitchens, parlours, and even rooms the most remote'.[145]

Against this background, he never shakes off the morose mood. He returns time and again to think about how the town has changed from a bustling happy place, a prosperous place, to a depressed, lonesome, moribund place, and to think about his friends that are gone:

[These] high hills which recall to my remembrance my receding years in morning's brightness, throw evening's lengthening shadows on my coming ones, and not these high hills only, but every green field and low bush, and wide street and narrow lane, and lone house, revives some recollection, and haunts me with the ghost of former days. If I walk upwards, I pass the ancient meeting house where I was early taught to look to heaven as a habitation, and to regard as nothing this vain and transitory world; if I go downwards I see the green lane, where still stands the deserted school-room, to which, with shining morning face, I trudged not unwillingly to school; and if I stand still, I have full in view the market-house, where I played a thousand times with companions not one of whom remains.

A few are gone to America, but by far the greater number are dead. Many by shipwreck and battle, many more by sickness, and some no doubt by sorrow; a disease which though inserted in no bill of mortality, kills more than we are aware. I walk therefore nearly as much alone as I should in the wilds of America, and somewhat I have of their solitariness too. Commerce, as well as riches, seems to have taken its flight; and in these very streets where not many years back was all the bustle of business, I wander up and down almost as undisturbed as in the fields.[146]

Standing in the town square, he recalled that it was once inhabited by 'a numerous gentry, social, hospitable and gay; but these have almost all passed away, and the houses, where so oft was heard the sounds of merriment and laughter, are fallen in ruins or mouldering in decay'. One of the now ruined houses was where, in his youth, the 'venerable old rector' lived; he could see him still in his mind's eye, 'with large grizzle wig, and gold-headed cane to prop his tottering steps', as he walked to his little rural church.[147] Near that house was the building where General Carleton, earl of

145 *Views*, 155–56.
146 *Views*, 168–69.

147 Adam Harvey (*c.* 1710–
93), rector of Strabane
in 1769–93, was the old
man here remembered.
See James B. Leslie,
comp., *Derry Clergy and
Parishes* (Enniskillen,
1937), 133, 297, 299,
and Leslie, comp.,
Raphoe, 44, 61, 126.
148 *Views*, 169–74. On
Richard Montgomery,
see Hal T. Shelton,
*General Richard
Montgomery and the
American Revolution:
From Redcoat to Rebel*
(New York, 1994);
on Alexander, see
Edith Mary Johnston-
Liik, *History of the
Irish Parliament,
1692–1800: Commons,
Constituencies and
Statutes*, 6 vols.
(Belfast, 2002), vol.
5, 276–80, and, on
his victory in the
1797 election, my
'Paramilitarism and
Politicization', 276.
The election cast a long
shadow; see Strabane,
24 October 1809, James
Hamilton to Abercorn,
PRONI, Abercorn
Papers T2541/
IA2/18/17, discussing
how tenants had voted
twelve years earlier in
'that cursed election'.
149 *Views*, 183–84.
150 *Views*, 175–84. On
the Crawfords, see
A. Atkinson, *Ireland
Exhibited to England
in a Political and Moral
Survey of Her Population
...*, 2 vols. (London,
1823), vol. 2, 187–88,
and Edward Cupples,
'Parishes of Glenavy,
Camlin and Tullyrusk', in
Mason, comp., *Statistical
Account*, vol. 2, 215–80,
esp. 270–71, 280. On
John Crawford, who
settled in Baltimore
in 1796, see David L.
Cohern, 'Crawford,
John', in *American*

Dorchester, who commanded the British at the Battle of Quebec (1775), was reputed to have been born. Gamble had little time for Carleton; he concedes that he was 'the only remarkable person which this town has produced', but says no one living in Strabane remembers anything of him but that he was born in the barracks and that his father was a collector of excise. And remembering Carleton, he remarks that Richard Montgomery, the 'gallant general' who led the Americans against him, was a brother of Alexander Montgomery, Donegal's Independent MP, who, when a boy, he had seen being chaired through the streets; he does not recall that 'Old Sandy' won his last election in 1797 by releasing republican freeholders from Lifford Gaol to vote for him, fought a duel with one of the more obnoxious local loyalists later that year and, that when he won, United Irishmen had carried him home to Convoy.[148] Gamble's eyes then falling on another neglected house, he remembered its occupant, William Crawford, Presbyterian minister, Volunteer chaplain, delegate to Dungannon, and Patriot historian. He here gives a striking description of this house, connecting its fate with Ireland and remarking that when in London the residence of the king of England had reminded him of it:

His house is now a barrack, his study a guard-room, and the windows which so often I have seen fragrant with the rose and geranium, I yesterday saw shattered and broken, hung with belts and pouches, and soldiers' coarse shirts. It is only part of a large mansion, which often in times past put me in mind of Buckingham House, or rather Buckingham House put me in mind of it. The other part has lately been fitted up as a private dwelling, and the mobbled house only looks the more hideous for this. It may be compared, as the ill-fated land, to which it belongs not unaptly has been, to a beautiful woman well-dressed to the middle, but her limbs shrunk in poverty, and covered with rags.[149]

Gamble had in his youth been a frequent caller at this house that reminded him of Ireland and on intimate terms with the extended Crawford family. He writes that when he first arrived in England, Crawford's brother, Adair Crawford (1748–95), a celebrated surgeon and chemist, had assisted him in his medical career in London; he does not volunteer the information that another brother, Alexander (1755–1823), himself a physician in Lisburn, was to become a key figure in the provincial leadership of the republican movement, or that a third brother, John (1746–1813), was one of the leading doctors in Baltimore, Maryland, and a prominent member (with Robert Moore and George Douglas) of the city's Hibernian Society.[150] William Crawford, however, Gamble now remembered as 'an excellent man', a 'pious good man', respected in Strabane by people of all religions and descriptions. A brilliant classical scholar, he 'scarcely ever' tasted ale, wine or spirits — 'his only relaxation was the tea-table, and hearing his daughter play on the piano-forte'. There was a 'sensitive delicacy' about him and if no one dared smile in his presence, people often smiled behind his back. Gamble, as a boy, had seen in his daughter's music-books how the minister had struck out every expression and word which, even by inference, could be thought to sully her innocence. It must be a puzzle to many, Gamble mused, that 'so Christian a man as he truly and unaffectedly was' should have taken so deep an interest in 'the passing transactions of this fleeting and unsatisfactory world', meaning politics, as to write *A History of Ireland*. It was an important book, the first by a Protestant to say that Irish Catholics were 'more sinned against than sinning'. But the freedom and prosperity that Crawford so confidently celebrated in 1783 had been an illusion; hindsight could only mock his vision of a bright future for Ireland. He had died aged only sixty and his family had fallen on hard times: his daughter was now a 'cheerless wanderer', having emigrated with her husband and children to America where they slipped into destitution; a son had sailed for the West Indies on a ship that sank, and his wife had died 'of the most excruciating tortures of a cancer, which corroded even to the heart's blood'.[151]

•

Such then was John Gamble's home-place: it was a place gone quiet, the push and energy spent, a place corroded even to the heart's blood — it was dead. Some of his contemporaries considered there to be a tension between fact and fiction, the real and the imagined in his representation of that home-place. For instance, writing about *A View*, his 1812 journey, one reviewer — clearly taken with Mr. C——'s story of William and Harriet — commented:

> But we really cannot tell whether he means it to be all believed or not. He assumes most fully indeed the manner of a person relating what he knows or believes to be facts, only concealing names under initials; but he begins and ends without saying any thing precisely on the subject of the authentication of the story, while he might have been sensible that a more established name than he can suppose his to be, would have been requisite for such a narrative, if it was to be given without any of the formalities of evidence. Indeed he will expect every reader to challenge the authenticity of a history so full of romantic incidents, of surprising changes of feeling, of tragical and overwhelming misery, and of retired circumstances and communications which it is impossible to conceive how the relator could know.[152]

Likewise, and in similar terms, a modern critic, concerned to relate Gamble's travel writing to the making of the Irish historical novel (not, surprisingly, the Gothic novel), has observed that towards the end of *Sketches*, that is, when Gamble reaches

Strabane in 1810, 'a curious anonymity is imposed on certain figures, as if they were to be treated not so much as particular people whose careers might be verified but as if they were references in a manifest fiction masquerading as real human beings'.[153] An argument here has been that the figures met on Gamble's tours were 'real human beings' and that, in some instances, their lives can be 'verified', but that in the case of republicans — indeed, in the case of feeling people — their lives had been rendered unreal, not by the author, but by the 'manifest fiction' which became history in the degraded society and manners that congealed post-1798.

The End

> Think of me, therefore, as of one whom
> you shall never again behold; think of
> me, if possible, with kindness; and when
> in your walks you trace fancied figures
> amidst the evening's grey mist, think of
> me as one of those — as a phantom that
> has vanished, or a tale that is told.
> John Gamble, *Charlton* (1823)[154]

Towards the end of summer 1812, John Gamble tried to sum up what he thought of his people, the people of north-west Ulster — Catholic, Protestant and Dissenter. 'The people seem highly superstitious here,' he wrote. And that was unusual; superstition, with the decline of darkness, was fading away.[155] And so Gamble set himself to explaining why his people remained unusually superstitious and, here, he rejected the idea that physical environment alone shapes culture, and looked instead to lived and imagined experience:

> The country itself may give such a
> character — awful and majestic in
> its quiescent [moments], but forlorn
> and dreary, howling with tempests,
> roaring with cataracts, and darkened
> with clouds, in its troubled moments,
> it may naturally be supposed to

National Biography, 24 vols. (New York and Oxford, 1999), vol. 5, 701–03, and Harold A. Williams, *History of the Hibernian Society of Baltimore* (Baltimore, 1957), 2–3. Also see *History of Congregations*, 761, and Campbell, *Notes*, 64–67.

151 *Views*, 182–84, includes a touching description of Crawford's farewell sermon in October 1798. It is unclear if Gamble was present, though elsewhere he indicates that he was in Ireland that year.

152 'Gamble's *View of Ireland*', *Eclectic Review*, 10 (September 1813), 229–43. Also see William Shaw Mason, *Bibliotheca Hibernicana: or, A Descriptive Catalogue of a Select Irish Library, Collected for the Right Hon. Robert Peel* (Dublin, 1823), 47, where Gamble's accounts of his tours of 1810 and 1812 are described as 'abounding in entertaining anecdote, to be perused with some caution, as the author is thought to have allowed his imagination at times to take excursions at the expense of truth.'

153 McCormack, 'Language, Class and Genre', 1106–07. Ironically, McCormack was here discussing the second edition of *Sketches*, oblivious to the fact that it silently reproduces some of the final chapters of Gamble's 1812 tour — when presented as part of his 1810 journey, these passages are a fiction. McCormack has provided a rich and suggestive reading of Gothic writing by people

(Maturin, Maxwell, Carleton, Le Fanu, Lever, Stoker, Wilde, Yeats, Synge and Bowen) 'attached to some degree to the (once) Established Church of Ireland.' See his 'Irish Gothic and After', 831–949. Gamble might be considered to have contributed to another corpus of Gothic writing — one largely produced by people from the Presbyterian community concerned with the lost opportunity (and lost history) of 1798; here, one thinks of the writings (in various genres) of Classon Emmet Porter, George Sigerson, W. G. Lyttle, R. M. Young, Florence M. Wilson and Stewart Parker.

154 *Charlton*, vol. 3, 236. The sentence is uttered, at the end of the second-last chapter, by a man going into exile after the 1798 Rising. It is echoed in the final line of the penultimate chapter (vol. 3, 244), when, years after the event, the hero has come to regard the Rising, 'its idle hopes and wishes, as a phantom that has vanished, or a tale that was told'.

155 On darkness, see A. Roger Ekirch, *At Day's Close: Night in Times Past* (New York and London, 2005), a study with a number of Irish examples. On the decline of superstition, see W. E. H. Lecky's *History of the Rise and Influence of the Spirit of Rationalism in Europe*, 2 vols. (New York, 1865), which is here of particular interest given Lecky's writings on eighteenth-century Ireland.

156 *A View*, 365.

excite corresponding emotions in the natives. A fondness for the marvellous, a shuddering at the indistinct, a superstitious dread of futurity, have been remarked in almost all of the northern nations. But beside the physical influence of climate, there has been in Ireland the moral influence of events. It was natural that the wild ideas of superstition should take possession of a people so accustomed to gloomy transactions, and that nursed to slaughter, and suckled as it were to blood, all their notions should be tinged with it. It was natural that they should turn to the phantoms of their imagination, rather than to the objects of their reason, and that these ideas (gradually softening by time) should be handed down from generation to generation, even to the present.[156]

The half-sighted doctor's point was simple: in Ireland, as in any colonial society, nursed to slaughter and suckled to blood, all ghosts are political.[157]

On a Sunday in that same summer of 1812, Gamble went to church in Strabane. He did not go inside, but wandered instead through the churchyard, looking at the tombstones. 'A church-yard is the best temple,' he explained, 'and a tombstone the best sermon — I could have heard none so good within.'

He spent over an hour there, trying 'to penetrate the darkness of the tomb':

In fancy I contemplated those sheeted tenants of the grave, each in his narrow house — I saw the changed face, the hideous yellow of the body newly buried — I saw the blackening hue of putrefaction, the decaying garments, the crawling worms of what had lain longer in the ground — I saw the green and melted mass of the next stage of this shocking process, and the consummation of all, in the little heap of dust, about to be mingled with the great mass of matter, from which it sprung.

And is this then, the history of man — is this the end of his joys, and his sorrows, his hopes and his fears — is it for this he traverses countries, and wanders over oceans — is it for this the extremes of the earth are ransacked, to procure him raiment and food — is it for this he is a villain — is it for this he inflicts misery, and sacrifices thousands to his ambition?

Is it for this beauty disdains deformity? — they are both disdained here.

Is it for this riches disdains poverty? — they are both poor here.

Is it for this fashion shrinks from vulgarity? — they are both of one fashion here.

Oh, man! In wisdom an infant, but in folly full-grown, raise your head above the stars but, your feet rest here — deck yourself with jewels, but your garment is a shroud — feed yourself with dainties, but a worm will feed upon you — build palaces, but this is your abode.[158]

For Gamble, it was an unusually frank comment on the human condition. Although a man of a decidedly humanist cast of mind, he was prone to occasional affirmations of his belief in a 'creator' and an afterlife.[159] But now, he said it as he saw it: this is it; this is the end.

Almost twenty years later, on 4 May 1831, when he had been back home in Strabane for thirteen years, Gamble walked over the bridge to Lifford to attend the funeral of Mrs. Despard Humphreys. Humphreys's daughter, Ann Jane, was married to William Gamble of Strabane, most probably a relation of John's, making his attendance something of an obligation.[160]

As he crossed the bridge, Gamble would have seen Croaghan Hill, where the Volunteers had staged field days and reviews in the early 1780s. In Lifford, as he crossed The Diamond, he would have seen the public houses where Alexander Montgomery had entertained his supporters from his first election in 1768 down to his

Dice and shaker given by James Napper Tandy to James and Andrew Stilley of Ballindrait: the Stilleys had regularly visited Tandy, when he was a prisoner in Lifford. Donegal Historical Society Museum. Photo: Vincent O'Donnell.

Ballindrait, where the dead woman was born, was home to some implacable republicans, notably brothers James (b. 1765) and Andrew Stilley, the local mill-owners. Andrew had been a county delegate to the Ulster provincial committee of the United Irishmen in the late 1790s, and both men remained active radicals after the Rising. They visited the republican celebrity, James Napper Tandy, when he was held in Lifford Gaol in 1799–1802; Andrew's frequent trips to Dublin attracted Government attention in 1808 and James attended Daniel O'Connell's duel with John D'Esterre on the Curragh in 1815. The Stilleys were cousins of Rev. James Porter (1753–98), a native of Tamnawood, Ballindrait, who became a republican propagandist and was executed at Greyabbey, County Down, in 1798, and they had sheltered his son, Alexander, in the immediate aftermath of the Rising. As late as the 1820s, the village's predominantly Presbyterian inhabitants were being fingered as troublesome. In January 1822, for instance, the Bishop of Raphoe wrote to Dublin Castle, complaining of nightly meetings in Ballindrait, 'which has always collected together the worst spirits [and] has been a constant source of annoyance & danger to the inhabitants of this part of the country …'. That same month, Sir George F. Hill, the leader of north-western loyalism, warned Dublin Castle that 'Many efforts, hitherto thank God ineffectual, have been made to produce a reorganization between Roman Catholick [and] Presbyterian upon the former United Irish principle.' Some ghosts, then, were restless.

See Raphoe, 7 January 1822, Bishop of Raphoe to William Gregory, NAI, State of the Country Papers Series 1 2359/1; Derry, 27 January 1822, Sir George Hill to William Gregory, State of the Country Papers Series 1 2360/7. On Andrew Stilley in Dublin, see 'Alphabetical List of Suspects, 1798–1803' [despite the title, it includes suspects active at specific dates *after* 1803], NAI, RP 620/12/217. There are extracts from James Stilley's conversations (in 1845) with Classon Emmet Porter (1814–85) in Robert M. Young, *Ulster in '98: Episodes and Anecdotes* (Belfast, 1893), 18–19, 58–60; also see Classon Emmet Porter, *Irish Presbyterian Biographical Sketches* (Belfast, 1883), 16–19.

157 I owe this observation (in Ireland all ghosts are political) to Seamus Deane.
158 *A View*, 375–76.
159 One contemporary reader dismissed Gamble's repeated claims to accept 'the immortality of the soul' and castigated him for 'disbelief'; see the long review of *Sarsfield* in the *British Critic*, 3 (February 1815), 208–16, where aspersion is also cast on the role of superstition in the novel.
160 On this marriage, see *Strabane Morning Post*, 24 June 1823.

161 Kinkaid jumped bail in summer 1797. Floyd was arrested in Fánaid that June, brought into Derry and then sent out of the country. Friel was taken up the following month, but released in September on giving bail; in summer 1798 he left for America, where he became clerk to the inspector of state prisons in New York. Letterkenny, 17 July 1797, John Rea to ——, NAI, RP 620/31/241; Derry, 12 June 1797, R. G. Hill to John Beresford, NAI, RP 620/31/78; Copy of Information of John Dougherty, Manor Cunningham, 9 July 1797, NAI, RP 620/31/214; New York, 20 November 1799, James Friel to Rev. James Friel, Rossnakill, NAI, RP 620/57/104; *Dublin Evening* Post, 30 September 1797.

162 On Gamble's death, see *Strabane Morning Post*, 10 May 1831. He is buried in the parish churchyard of Leckpatrick. Campbell, *Notes*, 33, also remarks on his death at a funeral.

final victory in 1797. And he would have certainly seen the hulking prison where men strongly implicated in the killing of William Hamilton had been held — James Friel and Robert Floyd of Fánaid and John Kinkaid of Newtowncunningham, none of whom was convicted yet none of whom remained at home.[161] He would have seen too the courthouse from which Barney McCafferty, the haunted man he may have met on the road to Donemana in 1812, had walked a free man having been acquitted of murdering the man he had helped to kill.

The dead woman being well known and well to do, there was probably a large attendance at the funeral — people from Strabane and Lifford, but also from the Presbyterian towns and villages of the Laggan — people from Castlefin, who, in 1798, had been among the last to relinquish their arms and people from St. Johnston, who would have known the family of Oliver Bond and shared his republicanism, but particularly people from the dead woman's own town, Ballindrait, who had ventured all and lost in 1798. All ghosts — what had actually happened in their youth denied an honest account in print, only spoken about, and then only quietly, and more often than not at night, when *true stories* were told as ghost stories.

On this occasion, the half-sighted doctor went into the church rather than wandering through the churchyard. And there on a spring day, in the church in Lifford, during the reading of the funeral service, surrounded by ghosts, John Gamble died.[162]

Mr Burke

James Gillray, *Cincinnatus in Retirement*, 1782, etching on paper,
25.8 × 35cm. Trustees of the British Museum.

CINCINNATUS in Retirement
falsely supposed to represent Jesuit-Pad driven back to h

1 From Sinéad Morrissey, 'Advice', *The State of the Prisons* (Manchester, 2005), 34.
2 Sinéad Morrissey, 'Reading the Greats', in *The State of the Prisons*, 35.

Pub.ᵈ Aug.ᵗ 23.ᵈ 1782. by E.ᵈ D'Achery S.ᵗ James's Street.

tines. see Romish Common-Wealth.

Ugly Criticism

Union and Division in Irish Literature

Claire Connolly

> You think it ugly: drawing lines
>   with a knife
> Down the backs of those
>   writers we exist to dislike.
> But it's life.[1]

Sinéad Morrissey's poem 'Advice' scrutinizes the 'ugly' object of literary criticism: the everyday business of dissecting, dividing and analysing a body of literary work. The voice of this poem (composed while Morrissey was writer-in-residence at Queen's University Belfast) might be that of the creative-writing tutor, urging the recalcitrant poet to find his or her own voice by picking a fight with the literary tradition, those 'big fish' described in the next poem in Morrissey's collection as 'the Greats'.[2] 'Advice' offers an ironical celebration of splits and divisions. It pours scorn on the notion of an 'undivided' body, understood biologically, or as literary corpus, or as cultural group or coterie:

> You think it ugly: drawing lines with a
> knife
> Down the backs of those writers we exist
> to dislike. But it's life.
>
> One is disadvantaged by illustrious
> company
> Left somehow undivided. Divide it with
> animosity.
>
> Don't be proud —
> Viciousness in poetry isn't frowned on,
> it's *allowed*.
>
> Big fish in a big sea shrink
> proportionately.
> Stake out your territory
>
> With stone walls, steamrollers, venomous
> spit
> From the throat of a luminous
> nightflower. Gerrymander it.

Divisions are to be inflicted by 'stone walls', 'steamrollers', 'spit' and — in a final sentence that itself marks a division from the preceding sound patterns — by external political agency. The term 'gerrymandered' suggests manipulated or manufactured political divisions, and carries with it more than a whisper of reference to the border between the six counties of Northern Ireland and the 26-county Republic, and to officially sanctioned sectarian political practices within the Northern state. In this final phrase, 'Advice' brings the political realities of severed states to bear upon the business of literary value.

Ugliness, lines, the body in pain: the image patterns of Morrissey's poem stand in striking relation to the terms assembled by Edmund Burke in his 1757 treatise on aesthetics, *A Philosophical Enquiry into the Origin of Our Ideas of the Sublime and Beautiful*.[3] Opening with an invocation

of 'those things which a daily and vulgar use have brought into a stale unaffecting familiarity', Burke forges a philosophical space within which the sensations can be defined and analysed. Assuming that there is a shared stratum of sensations that are nonetheless subject to cultural differences, the *Enquiry* depicts a world of highly particularized feelings within which 'the three states, of indifference, of pleasure, and of pain' may be seen to operate.[4] Many of the striking opening examples Burke produces are designed to shock readers into a grasp of his argument by forcing an imaginative participation in extreme sensations: 'Suppose ... a man ... to receive a violent blow, or to drink of some bitter potion, or to have his ears wounded with some harsh and grating sound', opens his discussion of how pain involves more than the absence of pleasure. '[S]tretch Caius upon the rack,' he invites, extending the argument to show how pleasure and pain have an existence beyond their relation to one another.[5]

The *Enquiry*'s desire to divide and thus analyse the sensations is always shadowed by subjection. Even its famous distinction between the sublime and the beautiful fails to distance either term from a 'disabling passivity': 'both the sublime and the beautiful are defined in Burke's *Enquiry* as states of subjection and domination,' argues John Whale.[6] Luke Gibbons has conclusively linked Burke's aesthetics to 'the turbulent colonial landscape of eighteenth-century Ireland', and in particular to agrarian unrest in eighteenth-century Munster.[7] Gibbons's account of the *Enquiry* stresses the formative influence of Irish places on its young author, in particular the famine-struck Cork of his boyhood and the colonial Dublin of his adolescence. Burke's aesthetic treatise was however begun in London in the 1750s, during the time he spent studying at the Middle Temple and holidaying in England and Wales. It is amidst these linked relationships and journeys — between Britain and Ireland, one the one hand, and aesthetics and politics, on the other — that

3   The collection in which 'Advice' appears enacts a wider dialogue with the eighteenth century, and in particular with the Enlightenment faith in perfectibility manifested in John Howard's plans for prison reform. Morrissey borrows the title of her collection from Howard's 1777 essay 'The State of the Prisons'.

4   Edmund Burke, *A Philosophical Enquiry into the Origin of Our Ideas of the Sublime and Beautiful* (Oxford and New York, 1990), 31.

5   'Caius is afflicted with a fit of the cholic; this man is actually in pain, stretch Caius upon the rack, he will feel a much greater pain; but does this pain arise from the removal of any pleasure?' Burke, *A Philosophical Enquiry*, 31.

6   John Whale, *Imagination under Pressure, 1789–1832: Aesthetics, Politics and Utility* (Cambridge, 2000), 22, 23.

7 Luke Gibbons, *Edmund Burke and Ireland* (Cambridge, 2003), 23.

8 Thomas Moore, *Memoirs of the Life of the Right Honourable Richard Brinsley Sheridan*, 2 vols. (London, 1825), vol. 2, 148.

9 Adam Phillips, Introduction, in Burke, *A Philosophical Enquiry*, xiv.

10 Lock cites Susannah Centlivre's play *A Bold Stroke for a Wife* (1718) and Frances Burney's novel *Cecilia* (1782) as examples, with the latter text being greatly enjoyed by Burke. See F. P. Lock, *Edmund Burke*, 2 vols. *Volume I: 1730–1784* (Oxford, 1998), 27.

11 Anne Fogarty, 'Literature in English, 1550–1690: From the Elizabethan Settlement to the Battle of the Boyne', in Margaret Kelleher and Philip O'Leary, eds., *The Cambridge History of Irish Literature*, 2 vols. (Cambridge, 2006), vol. 1, 140–90 (151); Ian Campbell Ross, 'Prose in English, 1690–1800: From the Williamite Wars to the Act of Union', in Kelleher and O'Leary, eds., *Cambridge History of Irish Literature*, vol. 1, 232–81 (249).

12 James Chandler, 'A Discipline in Shifting Perspective: Why We Need Irish Studies', *Field Day Review*, 2 (2006), 19–39 (27).

this essay locates the continuing relevance of Burke's *Enquiry* in our critical constructions of Irish literature.

'Drawing lines with a knife': Union and Division

Burke presents an especially complicated case study in what is an observably pre-Union cultural phenomenon: a writer whose career has been seen to divide in paired oppositions, chiefly between Britain/Ireland, on the one hand, and aesthetics/politics, on the other. His reputation is split between his writing on aesthetics and on politics, on cultural geography (in England, France America, India and Ireland), and on political philosophy (Burke the conservative and counter-revolutionary versus Burke the defender of local attachments turned proto-postcolonialist). Writing in the 1820s in the context of his biography of Richard Brinsley Sheridan (another figure dominated by comparable fissures), Thomas Moore describes the divided Burke in the following terms: 'His mind, indeed, lies parted asunder in his works, like some vast continent severed by a convulsion of nature, — each portion peopled by its own giant race of opinions, differing altogether in features and language, and committed in eternal hostility with each other.'[8] Moore offers an aerial survey of the fragmented territory of the Burkean imagination in language that echoes across the literary culture of eighteenth-century Ireland, evoking the well-known instabilities of narrative position in travel writing, the geographical discourse of Union and Jonathan Swift's *Gulliver's Travels*.

The figure or trope that is most commonly used to unite the divided Burke is the family romance of the mixed marriage: child of a Protestant father and a Catholic mother, Burke, we are told, carried Ireland's confessional divisions within himself and reproduced them in the intricate accounts of sympathy in his philosophical and political

writings. The text that seeks to anatomize such figures of feeling, his *Enquiry*, is, according to the psychoanalyst Adam Phillips, 'among other things, a prospective autobiography'.[9] Or, to the critic of Irish literature, a proto-national tale. Its sensuous — Phillips says 'erotic' — empiricism unites at the level of philosophical method a lived division between passion and reason that critics have traced back to Burke's early formation in east Munster. F. P. Lock has found in Burke's early upbringing 'the stuff of fiction': he compares Burke's education among Catholics, Anglicans and Quakers to the position of an eighteenth-century heroine with a philosophically or morally mixed group of guardians.[10] Yet the way in which familial, local and national dynamics are mapped onto one another within Burke's biography is closer to the narrative strategies deployed by the generation of Irish writers that came after him, in particular the national romances pioneered by Maria Edgeworth and Sydney Owenson.

In many ways, Burke's career reinforces and perpetuates a set of divisions that can be said to structure Irish literary history. To the 'divided' Burke, we can at the very least add, as exemplars of a comparable division, Edmund Spenser, Jonathan Swift and Maria Edgeworth. Since the 1980s, major advances in scholarship have helped to restore the Irish side of these writers' reputations: these would include Anne Fogarty's reading of Ireland within the 'ideological anxieties, symbolic patterns and narrative dynamics' of Spenser's *Faerie Queene*; Ian Campbell Ross's biographical and textual analyses of Swift's 'complex and troubled relationship to Ireland'; and Gibbons's book, *Edmund Burke and Ireland*.[11]

For authors to be 'Irished' or 'ReIrished' has acquired, as James Chandler points out, 'the status of quasi-disciplinary procedure' within Irish Studies.[12] Of the revisions I have mentioned, Gibbons's is perhaps most tightly bound up with the advent of Irish Studies as a critical practice. The critical energy invested in these 'shifting perspectives' is

what leads Chandler to place Irish Studies in the forefront of the overthrow of the *ancien régime* of the disciplines currently taking place across the humanities. Perhaps because of this wider revolution, in none of the cases mentioned here has a writer's reputation settled into anything like orthodoxy. In general, there remains a demand for greater equilibrium in our critical apprehension of divided *œuvres*, a sense that more work

13 Quoted in Chandler, 'A Discipline in Shifting Perspective', 27.

14 F. P. Lock, 'Burke, Ireland and India: Reason, Rhetoric and Empire', in Seán Patrick Donlan, ed., *Edmund Burke's Irish Identities* (Dublin, 2007), 154–70 (155).

15 William Parnell, *Inquiry into the Causes of Popular Discontents in Ireland*, 2nd edn. (London and Dublin, 1805), 72.

16 Chandler, 'A Discipline in Shifting Perspective', 27.

17 See Tom Furniss, *Edmund Burke's Aesthetic Ideology: Language, Gender and Political Economy in Revolution* (Cambridge, 1993), 4; Seamus Deane, 'Phantasmal France, Unreal Ireland: Sobering Reflections', in *Strange Country: Modernity and Nationhood in Irish Writing since 1790* (Oxford, 1997), 1–48 (1–2).

18 See Matthew Arnold, 'The Function of Criticism at the Present Time', in *Lectures and Essays in Criticism*, vol. 3, *The Complete Prose Works of Matthew Arnold*, ed. R. H. Super (Ann Arbor, 1962), 267.

19 Yoon Sun Lee, *Nationalism and Irony: Burke, Scott, Carlyle* (Oxford, 2004), 40. A contemporary caricature of Burke shows him using a box labelled 'Tropes' as his political armoury. See Anon., 'House-breaking, before Sun-Set', published 6 January 1789; Nicholas Robinson, *Edmund Burke: A Life in Caricature* (New Haven, 1996), 127.

must be done and a better balance must be achieved. Joseph Valente, for instance, has upbraided Irish Studies scholars for their over-Irishing of *Dracula*.[13] But however one appraises the interaction of British and Irish elements, or of aesthetics and politics in the case of these major writers, it is important to note how ideals of balance and organic unity continue to inform our understanding of the ways in which they ought to be read. Consider, for example, Lock's accusation that the 'Irish' or 'post-colonial' Burke lists too far towards one side of Burke's thought; a side of Burke that is, problematically for him, much too closely connected with our current preoccupations and prejudices. Critics from Conor Cruise O'Brien to Luke Gibbons are accused of having 'delved so deep as to obscure some of the most prominent contours of the Burkean mindscape'. Lock invokes on his own behalf the ideal scholarly perspective that could see Burke's British and conservative, as well as his Irish and humanitarian, affiliations.[14]

Readers will be able to supply other versions of this kind of complaint or criticism as it relates to texts or writers that they know well. What concerns me particularly here, however, is the problem of the divided *œuvre* more generally. Does it apply especially to our critical constructions of pre-1800 writers? Where the issue persists past the nineteenth-century heyday of the Union, we find it adheres most closely to the reputations of writers to whom the term 'Anglo-Irish' would be conventionally applied (Bram Stoker, Elizabeth Bowen). So has the Union a role or after-effect that is detectable in the literature that succeeded it? It might be argued that Act of Union itself seems, through much of the nineteenth century, to soften, if not solve, this dilemma of radical division paradoxically by enhancing the divisions and differences that the Act, in attempting legislatively to draw the two countries together, had produced. As William Parnell put it: 'the Union is a name, a sound, a fiction; there is no Union; the nominal Union is only an additional

source of discord'.[15] The public discourse of unity served to underline rather than erase Ireland's inferior role in the Union. As such, it proved a rich reserve of 'discord'.

As with the Burkean mindscape visualized by Moore and Lock, the territory of Irish Studies is often conceptualized in terms of issues of union and division, and remains closely bound up with questions of perspective. In many of the most hotly contested cases of re-Irishing, Chandler points out — citing Burke as 'an especially good case in point' — 'the question of an author being "Irishable" is intensified by the sense that, internal to his or her *œuvre*, we can find not only another side to the story but beyond this, an anticipation of what it means to be able to see or not see the story from that other side'.[16] Burke's exemplary status in Chandler's argument depends on his reputation for political prescience, itself closely related to what is often described as the supplementary or excessive character of his language.[17] The flexibility and fluidity of Burke's prose style maps onto a kind of special knowledge regarding the outcome of the political events on which he comments: Burke's style is linked to an almost improper, and, according to Matthew Arnold, 'un-English' knowledge of the future. [18] This is perhaps what Yoon Sun Lee means when she describes Burke's tropes as having a 'deterritorializing effect': Burke's prose possesses an affective force that serve to 'open up passages and connections between positions that are, in theory, diametrically opposed'.[19] Whether analysed in terms of Burke's prophetic powers or in terms of the special power of his language, what interests me here is the declension of the difference between aesthetics and politics into a linked relationship between poetry and prose, with poetry taken to exemplify the special role of literary language.

Pascale Casanova's recent work contends that it is only with James Joyce that Irish writing attains what she calls 'autonomy' within 'Irish literary space'; out of the highly politicized context of the revival, argues

William Dent, *Grand Irish Air Balloon*, 1784, etching on paper, 33.7 × 24.7 cm. Trustees of the British Museum.

20 Pascale Casanova, *The World Republic of Letters*, trans. M. B. DeBevoise (Cambridge, Mass., 2004), 315.

21 See Joe Cleary on decolonization and its effect on the world literary system sketched by Casanova: 'The World Literary System: Atlas and Epitaph', *Field Day Review*, 2 (2006), 197–219.

22 Adam Potkay, *The Passion for Happiness* (Ithaca and London, 2000), 2–3.

23 Giles Deleuze, 'He Stuttered', *Essays Clinical and Critical*, trans. Daniel W. Smith and Michael A. Greco (London and New York, 1998), 112, quoted by Susan Manning, *Fragments of Union: Making Connections in Scottish and American Writing* (Basingstoke, 2002), 257. Manning (17) relates Deleuze's interest in the 'federative and paratactic' qualities of American writing to Scottish Enlightenment theories of fragmentation and union.

Casanova, Joyce enacted a double rejection — he broke with both the language and literature of empire and with the aesthetic imperatives of cultural nationalism.[20] As Joe Cleary has shown, however, there remains a need to analyse this constitution of literary space in terms of the asymmetries instituted by the Union and perpetuated by the economic and political cleavages of the nineteenth century.[21] The emergence of

24 What is extraordinary about Swift and Burke, according to Deane, is the rhetorical energy that is expended in the service of a dying cultural formation. The conservative politics that are officially endorsed by Swift and Burke have already passed out of time or can no longer achieve realization in the (for them, fallen) present. There is a nostalgia here that is historically inflected but politically aware. For Deane, this takes the shape of a temporal pressure that is brought to bear on language, finding expression in forms of brokenness and fragmentation but also post-modern stylistic devices such as self-referentiality. Seamus Deane, 'Phantasmal France, Unreal Ireland', 2–3. See also his account of Joyce's *Dubliners*, which argues that 'immense psychic as well as rhetorical energy has to be expended on the production of stasis'. 'Dead Ends: Joyce's Finest Moments', in Derek Attridge and Marjorie Howes, eds., *Semicolonial Joyce* (Cambridge, 2000), 21–36 (21).
25 W. J. T. Mitchell, *Iconology: Image, Text, Ideology* (Chicago and London, 1986), 121–29.
26 Burke, *A Philosophical Enquiry*, 154–55.
27 Burke, *A Philosophical Enquiry*, 154–55.
28 Mitchell, *Iconology*, 123.
29 Mitchell, *Iconology*, 1.

an idea of national literature as a category belongs centrally to these dynamics of union and division. Among other things, it involved a series of divisions inflicted upon 'the wholeness of the eighteenth-century world of letters' and a resulting reorientation of the relationship between aesthetics and politics.[22]

There are of course a great many writers who, for commercial and other reasons, split their output between, say, Irish, English and Indian novels and tales. The issue, though, may be more narrowly identified as one of style: 'the foreign language within language' in Gilles Deleuze's terms.[23] The divisions that structure our understanding of writers like Spenser and Swift often boil down to the difference between the *Faerie Queene* and *A View of the Present State of Ireland*, on the one hand, or *Gulliver's Travels* and *A Modest Proposal*, on the other. Seamus Deane's account of what is most 'interesting' in Burke and Swift — the relationship between politics and style in their writings — is richly suggestive in this respect.[24] Burke's *Enquiry* itself played an important part in the creation of a category of literature that is at once aesthetic (different from other kinds of writing) and political (different from the kind of imaginative writing that has emerged in other places).

'Viciousness in poetry': National Literature between Aesthetics and Politics

W. J. T. Mitchell's reading of the *Enquiry* situates Burke's treatment of the difference between image and word in the context of the *Enquiry*'s development of the ancillary differences between prose and poetry and the beautiful and the sublime.[25] Among the examples of his contention that 'WORDS may affect without raising IMAGES', Burke offers a self-reflective commentary on the process by which words acquire meaning. Discussing a blind professor of mathematics who could give 'excellent lectures upon light and colours', Burke argues that: 'it was as easy for him to reason upon the words

as if he had been fully master of the ideas. Indeed it must be owned he could make no new discoveries by way of experiment.'[26] In attempting to capture the experience of the blind professor, Burke draws attention to his own language:

> He did nothing but what we do every day and in common discourse. When I wrote this last sentence, and used the words *every day* and *common discourse*, I had no images in my mind of any succession of time; nor of men in conference with each other; nor do I imagine the reader will have any such ideas on reading it.[27]

In showing how everyday words — which include words like 'every day' — operate independently of images raised in the mind, Burke aims for as cool as possible a criticism of figurative theories of language. In doing so, he 'wants to reassert the boundaries between texts and images' and 'to defy the prevailing Lockean notion of mental images/ideas as the referents of words'.[28] Burke inflects the post-Lockean distinction between words and images with the developing categories of the beautiful and the sublime: words as clear and modern aspire to the status of the beautiful, while images are primitive and obscure and potentially sublime. The force of Mitchell's argument, however, is to show us that Burke's anti-pictorialism results in a paradoxical state of 'sublime words and beautiful images'. Mitchell ingeniously argues that, by the end of the *Enquiry*, Burke will have reversed these values so that 'the tendency of language to arouse obscure, confused images, or no images at all, will begin to seem normative'.[29] Poetry is the ultimate expression of language free from the tyranny of images:

> Indeed so little does poetry depend for its effect on the power of raising sensible images, that I am convinced it would lose a very considerable part of its energy, if this were the necessary result of all description. Because that union of affecting words which is the most

powerful of all poetical instruments, would frequently lose its force along with its propriety and consistency, if the sensible images were always excited.[30]

The example given — the description of thunder forming in Vulcan's cavern in Virgil's *Aeneid* — involves the reader (once more) in 'affecting words' that tend toward violence and distress. Following through Burke's stress on the 'deep and lively impressions' of words, Mitchell thus captures an aspect of the *Enquiry* that tracks the threat to sympathy posed by the darkness and isolation of the sublime.

Gibbons, however, recuperates this same dynamic for a happier version of intersubjectivity. For him, the *Enquiry*'s anti-pictorialism is concerned to show how mimetic theories of language fall woefully short of comprehending 'the evocative capacity [of words] generated through social usage'. Rather than each word generating a related image or graphic representation, 'meanings are carried over from their original contexts through habit and custom, the usages which we share as members of an interpretive community'. The force of Gibbons's argument is to push forward this insight into an understanding of the power of words to generate imaginative sympathy. This bolsters his depiction of a Burke who believes in a 'flow of sympathy that emanates from the moral imagination'.[31] Gibbons embeds this discussion of the *Enquiry* within a broader understanding of Burke the theorist of community and proto-postcolonialist.

These tensions around language and community are condensed in one of the *Enquiry*'s memorable scenes of sympathy. The *Enquiry* is explicitly committed to a version of imaginative sympathy that leads towards the formation of community, as Gibbons argues. In this, Burke follows David Hume in depicting sympathy not so much as a series of acts of transfer from one individual to another, but rather as an outward radiation 'in concentric circles of diminishing intensity'.[32] Burke differs in his

account of how such circles are configured, and in particular with regard to the limits he wishes to place on 'imitation'. The *Enquiry* installs a difference between imagined and real sympathy that depends on a distinction between fiction and reality:

> We delight in seeing things, which so far from doing, our heartiest wishes would be to see redressed. This noble capital, the pride of England and of Europe, I believe no man is so strangely wicked as to desire to see destroyed by a conflagration or an earthquake, though he should be removed himself to the greatest distance from the danger. But suppose such a fatal accident to have happened, what numbers from all parts would croud to behold the ruins, and amongst them many who would have been content never to have seen London in its glory?[33]

There is a problem, however, in the figuration of sympathetic absorption as a scene of pain and ruin. Moreover, this is a scene of specifically imperial ruin, with the decline of London here, as always in the eighteenth century, echoing the decline of Rome. Imagining subjective responses to the compelling spectacle of the ruined metropolis as part of a set of feelings that are only activated in the case of distress allows Burke to dismiss 'immunity' as an inadequate explanation of the attraction of such scenes. A negative sense of one's own safety from danger is not enough, in other words, to explain either the compelling aesthetic spectacle of ruin or the auratic deficit he associates with completion, order, prosperity and commerce — all those things conventionally associated with London in its glory. The concept of 'immunity' enters Burke's argument here as a way of underlining the fiction/reality distinction but also for its potential to return thought to the body, the site where 'affecting words' make their primary impression.

The compelling spectacle of London in ruins draws the spectator to the very

30 Burke, *A Philosophical Enquiry*, 155.
31 Gibbons, *Edmund Burke and Ireland*, 27.
32 Potkay, *The Passion for Happiness*, 109.
33 Burke, *A Philosophical Enquiry*, 44.

34 Gibbons, *Edmund Burke and Ireland*, 88.

35 Burke, *A Philosophical Enquiry*, 44.

36 *Philosophy in a Time of Terror: Dialogues with Jürgen Habermas and Jacques Derrida*, interviewed by Giovanna Borradori (Chicago, 2003).

37 J. Hillis Miller, 'Derrida Enisled', *Critical Inquiry*, 33, 2 (2007), 248–76.

38 Janet Sorensen, *The Grammar of Empire in Eighteenth-Century British Writing* (Cambridge, 2000), 141.

39 Sorensen, *The Grammar of Empire*, 148.

40 Adam Potkay, *The Fate of Eloquence in the Age of Hume* (Ithaca, 1994), ch. 1.

brink of destruction even as it generates the possibility of sympathetic identification: without this tension between the roles of spectator and fellow sufferer, the full force of what Gibbons characterizes as the *Enquiry*'s 'fraught engagement with the anxieties of empire' cannot be appreciated.[34] The section concludes: 'we can feel for others whilst we suffer ourselves; and often then most when we are softened by affliction; we see with pity even distresses which we would accept in the place of our own'.[35] Accepting the distresses of others as part of one's own experience produces a version of sympathy that moves the argument towards a necessary but essentially destructive engagement with the pain of others: something very like the notion of auto-immunity.

A reference to recent mobilizations of the concept of immunity in debates about community serves to remind us of what is at stake here. Burke produces immunity as a concept in order to indicate the inadequacy of his culture's idea of tragedy. No more than aesthetic distance provided by fiction, immunity does not account for what Burke characterizes as a delighted or eager flocking to the scene of pain or distress. In terms of current theory, much of it under the sway of Jacques Derrida's late writings on the topic, immunity helps us to theorize the relationship between self and community and particularly those parts of the self that can be held back from incorporation within wider communal or national structures.[36] In J. Hillis Miller's account of these debates, Derrida is nearly unique in opposing the idea 'that the individual is and should be his social placement, with no residue or leftover that is not determined by the surrounding culture'.[37] What space Burke's *Enquiry* does make for meanings generated outside 'social placement' is found in the discussion of language, which, as suggested above, powerfully imagines, if it does not endorse, an isolationist vision of communication as part of its anxiety over the limits of imitation in the fostering of sympathy.

Burke is often studied as one of a group

of eighteenth-century theorists of language who sought to show how language is best analysed in terms of its aesthetic effects. A set of distinctions emerges in the eighteenth century between polite or 'beautiful' language, associated with proper and modest forms of communication, and impolite language, which is rude, aggressive and excessive. The supposedly central experience of polite language emerges as the object of philosophical concern, with impolite language allotted a residual or peripheral space. In depicting a version of polite language that had recourse to 'the authority of subjectively experienced aesthetic effects', Adam Smith's Glasgow University *Lectures on Rhetoric and Belles Lettres* (1748) set in motion a set of linguistic ambiguities that bear the markings of the thematics of union and division.[38] Janet Sorensen notes that the main advances in theory and practice of 'polite English' were authored by a group of what she calls 'non-English British nationals'. Scottish and Irish thinkers such as Thomas Sheridan, Hugh Blair, Adam Smith, Francis Hutcheson and Edmund Burke found in the 'amphibious discourse of aesthetics' an appealing admixture of private responses (located in the culturally particular world of the senses) and universal standards (represented in the abstractions of taste). As Sorensen puts it: 'Neither pure abstraction nor total embodiment, tasteful language appeals to subtle physical responses, forever universalizing while also relativizing them.'[39]

These linkages were underwritten, as Adam Potkay has shown, by a temporal schema, with impolite language — eloquence — consigned to the past.[40] There, however, it lays important claims to a sense of civic betterment and community. Eloquence and its political analogue, enthusiasm, thus trouble the formulation of theories of polite language. Even Hume admits to a bias in favour of enthusiasm, at least if the alternative is superstition, because the former historically has links to liberty and the dissenting tradition. In general though, Scottish culture can manage this problem

through the elaboration of cultural synthetic forms: most famously evidenced in James Macpherson's *Poems of Ossian* and Walter Scott's Waverley novels. As Potkay says of *Ossian*: 'Macpherson capitalized on this archaizing of eloquence by paradoxically

41 Potkay, *The Fate of Eloquence*, 8.
42 Katie Trumpener, *Bardic Nationalism: The Romantic Novel and the British Empire* (Princeton, 1997), 132.

43 Katherine O'Donnell, 'Gaelic Poetry, Rhetoric, Rhetoricians and Burke's Philosophical Enquiry', paper presented at the Royal Irish Academy Conference, 'Edmund Burke and Irish Literary Criticism, 1757–2007', April 2007. See also Jean Dietz Moss, '"Discordant Consensus": Old and New Rhetoric at Trinity College, Dublin', *Rhetorica*, 14, 4 (1996), 383–441.

44 I am grateful to Terence Brown for discussion of this point.

45 Stephen K. Land, *From Signs to Propositions: The Concept of Form in Eighteenth-Century Semantic Theory* (London, 1974), 48.

46 Reading Burke shortly before Home Rule, Gladstone was told that 'your *perfervidum ingenium Scoti* does not need being touched with a live coal from that Irish altar'. Quoted by Conor Cruise O'Brien, 'Introduction to the Cresset Library Edition', *Irish Affairs: Edmund Burke*, ed. Matthew Arnold (London, 1988 [1881]), xi.

47 See Moore's *Sheridan*, vol. 2, ch. 11, for his discussion of the public speaking styles of Sheridan and Edmund Burke; M. W. Savage, ed., *Sketches, Legal and Political, by the Late Right Honourable Richard Lalor Sheil*, 2 vols. (London, 1855), vol. 1, 16; letter of Mary Russell Mitford to Mrs Hofland, 17 April 1819, in *Letters of Mary Russell Mitford. Second Series*, ed. Henry Chorley, 2 vols. (London, 1872), vol. 1, 59–60: cited in http://www.british-fiction.cf.ac.uk/anecdotal/wome18-41.html.

modernizing the ancient clan: that is, the Ossianic forgeries *reconcile* the age's nostalgia for sublime eloquence and political community with its taste for subdued manners and private life.'[41] In eighteenth-century Wales, the notion of *hwyl* developed under the influence of Nonconformist religion: namely, an emotionally charged and enthusiastic form of speech that gained authority from its association with pulpit preaching but later became linked with more debased forms of oratory.

The transnational context enables a fuller appreciation of the treatment of language in Romantic Ireland, as part of what Katie Trumpener has characterized as the 'transperipheral Irish-Scottish public sphere'.[42] Burke's time at Trinity College Dublin would have exposed him to the classical model of eloquence, best known from the publications of his friend Thomas Leland, whose translation of Demosthenes appeared between 1754 and 1761 and whose *Dissertation on the Principles of Human Eloquence* was published in 1764.[43] There is a sense in which pursuing a political career in Britain created the conditions in which Burke's language came to be understood and analysed: had he remained within this Dublin context, what critics often describe as the excesses of his style might never have come to be diagnosed in these terms.[44] Such a counterfactual proposition denies, of course, the realities of British–Irish relations in the eighteenth century, but does serve to highlight how the importation of the Trinity College Dublin speaking model to the British parliament plays a part in the invention of an idea of Irish culture.

If, in Burke's *Enquiry*, there is always a sense that language will exceed its brief (Stephen Land refers to Burke's claims for 'a rhetorical surplus in language'[45]), then, in Irish literary production from the eighteenth century onwards, there is an ongoing set of worries over the issue of eloquence and its relationship to political enthusiasm.[46] Moore's biographies of both Sheridan and Lord Edward Fitzgerald continually try to divide eloquence from politicized enthusiasm. Irish Romantic drama, whether in plays by Alica LeFanu, Richard Lalor Sheil, Charles Robert Maturin or John Banim, treats the issue of eloquence at a kind of meta-level, aware of the drama's dependence on rhetorical skills yet making the power and limits of eloquence part of the thematics of the plays. Sheil believed Irish rhetorical skills were much hampered by the closure of the Trinity College Historical Society, which was suppressed by Lord Castlereagh as a consequence of the 1798 rebellion. And clear evidence of the backlash against Irish eloquence can be found in Mary Russell Mitford's description of Maturin's *Women; or, Pour et Contre* as 'a detestable book — a mere hotch potch of *Glenarvon* and *Corinne* mixed up with that indescribable nonsense which most Irishmen and Irishwomen call eloquence, and which is as like it as rouge is to the bloom of fifteen'.[47]

These linguistic tensions form the matrix from which first Romantic then modern definitions of literature itself emerge. The theories of linguistic difference elaborated by Scottish and Irish thinkers during the eighteenth century mesh with debates around taste to create a new and significant role for culture. Even opposed thinkers like Burke and Hume share a desire to widen the constituency of taste beyond the kind of élite group imagined by thinkers like Shaftesbury earlier in the century, and alike participate in the establishment of national boundaries on culture. In Irish Studies, we are familiar with a definition of Irish literature that traces its beginnings in the late eighteenth century and Maria Edgeworth's *Castle Rackrent*. But the Scottish perspective allows us to see that it is the idea of national literature itself that is being produced at this moment. Alongside *Castle Rackrent*, Edgeworth published (with her father) *An Essay on Irish Bulls*, a text that is extensively engaged with the cultural and political horizon of language in the context of the newly created United Kingdom.

The role of literature within the Union described thus far depends on debates around the representational power of language itself, and in particular the relationship between word and image. The Scottish case is important for comparison because both the Union of 1707 and the difference embodied by the role of literature within that Union are more complete. Ireland has problem areas of incompletion, one of which is crucially the idea of eloquence and enthusiasm, often diagnosed as a kind of unregulated spill-over of affecting words. This is in contrast to Jon Mee's account of the ways in which British Romantic culture worked to differentiate forms of enthusiasm from the authentically 'literary', so that 'the idea of literariness itself' came to be defined in its difference from rancour in religion and politics.[48] Mee has revalued T. E. Hulme's sceptical definition of romanticism as 'spilt religion' to show the myriad ways in which political and religious enthusiasm were subsumed into the poetics of British romanticism.[49] A residual problem within the formulation of theories of polite language — eloquence/enthusiasm — thus becomes a kind of figure for both poetry and the difference of literature, even as it accumulates connections with the experience of foreign, 'Oriental' and peripheral places.

For the Irish and Scottish writers who advanced their theories of language in terms of subjectively experienced aesthetic affects, these connections with place were often secondary to an embodiment that could lay claim to a certain universality. Later accounts of this difference, however, came to be understood increasingly in terms of national character. When Matthew Arnold reworked Burke for the post-Famine decades, he 'went further than Burke would ever have dared' in 'introducing the "Celtic" idea as a differentiating fact between Ireland and England'.[50] Arnold positions 'Celtic literature' on the cusp of definitions drawn from both linguistics and the discourse of national character. His notorious attribution of sentimentalism to the Celt — 'Sentimental, *always ready to revolt against the despotism of fact*' — is another way of absorbing all those qualities that troubled the formulation of polite language in the eighteenth century.[51]

'venomous spit / From the throat of a luminous nightflower': Theory and Tradition

Writing about Burke in the Preface to his 1881 edition of Burke's *Letters, Speeches and Tracts on Irish Affairs*, Arnold deploys the figures of difference that I have been tracing so far — Britain/Ireland, aesthetics/politics, poetry/prose — to invoke the need for a more complete English culture. In Arnold's efforts to remind his audience of the importance of Burke as the great master of English prose, the Britain/Ireland difference becomes at least partly submerged, only to resurface as irony: among the many paradoxes attendant upon the celebration of Burke the English prose stylist is its reliance upon a construction of Burke the commentator on Irish affairs. Arnold introduces Burke's political speeches to an audience that he characterizes as forgetful of his greatness. Arnold characterizes the dangers attendant upon forgetting Burke (and with him, Swift) in terms of loss and division. To lose Swift and Burke 'from our mind's circle of acquaintance' is to ignore prose at the expense of poetry (no one now forgets to read Shakespeare and Milton, Arnold argues) and to inflict a harmful division upon the national body: 'the unacquaintance shuts us out from great sources of English life, thought and language, and leaves us in consequence very imperfect and fragmentary Englishmen'.[52]

In Arnold's view, Burke's prose assumes a position within the tradition of English letters that is not unlike the role Arnold accords to Celtic literature within his broader scheme of cultural union. Arnold's famous essay 'On the Study of Celtic Literature' contends that a blending of racial types (Celtic and Saxon) within the United Kingdom is necessary for cultural

48 Jon Mee, *Romanticism, Enthusiasm and Regulation: Poetics and the Policing of Culture in the Romantic Period* (Oxford, 2003), 24–25.

49 Mee, *Romanticism, Enthusiasm and Regulation*, 4–5.

50 Seamus Deane, 'Arnold, Burke and the Celts', in *Celtic Revivals: Essays in Modern Irish Literature, 1880–1980* (London, 1985), 22.

51 Matthew Arnold, 'On the Study of Celtic Literature', *Lectures and Essays in Criticism*, vol. 3, *The Complete Prose Works of Matthew Arnold*, ed. R. H. Super (Ann Arbor, 1962), 344. Original emphasis.

52 Arnold, Preface, *Irish Affairs Edmund Burke*, xxxvii–xxxviii.

53 Arnold, 'On the Study of
Celtic Literature', 292.
54 Laura O'Connor,
*Haunted English:
the Celtic Fringe, the
British Empire and De-
Anglicization* (Baltimore,
2006), 26–27.
55 Edmund Burke,
*Reflections on the
Revolution in France*
(Harmondsworth, 1969).
56 Arnold, 'On the Study of
Celtic Literature', 293.

with its author in Wales, holidaying in
Llandudno while he watches preparations
for an *Eisteddfod*, a form of Druidic revival
conceived during the late eighteenth century
as part of an effort to revivify bardic
language and culture. Arnold muses on the
predicament of Welsh, focalized through the
imagined perspective of a 'French nursery
maid', and seen here as emblematic of the
fate of Celtic languages within the Empire:

> As I walked up and down, … looking
> at the waves as they washed this Sigeian
> land which has never had its Homer, and
> listening with curiosity to the strange,
> unfamiliar speech of its old possessors'
> obscure descendants, — bathing people,
> vegetable sellers, and donkey-boys, —
> who were all about me, suddenly I heard,
> through the stream of unknown Welsh,
> words, not English, indeed, but still
> familiar. They came from a French nursery
> maid, with some children. Profoundly
> ignorant of her relationship, this Gaulish
> Celt moved among her British cousins,
> speaking her polite neo-Latin tongue, and
> full of compassionate contempt probably,
> for the Welsh barbarians and their jargon.
> What a revolution was here! How had
> the star of this daughter of Gomer waxed,
> while the star of these Cymry, his sons,
> had waned![53]

In *Haunted English*, Laura O'Connor
expresses her outrage at Arnold's silencing
of the Welsh language in this passage.[54]
However, Arnold's treatment of Welsh
depends on his ability to imagine the
affective response of the nursery maid,
whose Frenchness alone is perhaps enough
to turn Arnold's mind to Burke: 'What
a revolution was here!' It is not only the
Burke of the *Reflections*[55] who is present
here, but also the Burke of the *Enquiry*.
Arnold refreshes Burke's distinction between
words and images for a community that has
experienced a tragic loss of the link between
proud place name and debased national
status:

> … the poor Welshman still says, in the
> genuine tongue of his ancestors, *gwyn,
> goch, craig, maes, llan, arglwydd*; but
> his land is a province, and his history
> petty, and his Saxon subduers scout his
> speech as an obstacle to civilisation;
> and the echo of all its kindred in other
> lands is growing every day fainter and
> more feeble; gone in Cornwall, going
> in Brittany and the Scotch Highlands,
> going, too, in Ireland; — and there,
> above all, the badge of the beaten race,
> the property of the vanquished. [56]

Here, Arnold imagines the feelings of a 'poor
Welshman' whose rich topological language
(*white, red, rock, field, chapel, lordship*)
raises images that exceed the political status
of his country as 'a province' whose history
has been rendered 'petty' by incorporation
within the Empire. And yet something does
happen in this mismatch between word and
image: a space opens in which the 'genuine'
'faint' and 'feeble' sounds of the Welsh
language can be heard.

The nature of this space is determined
by a sentimental relationship between past
and present. Sentiment is undoubtedly
the dominant note sounded in Arnold's
characterizations of Celtic literature,
something for which the essay has been
severely censured. Shaun Richards
specifically locates the emergence of
theoretical approaches to Irish literature
in a rejection of Arnoldian sentimentalism
allied with the emergence of a politicized
strain of criticism. Recalling splits that
took shape at the International Association
for the Study of Anglo-Irish Literature
conference of 1984, held in the University
of Graz, Richards remembers the 'mystical-
magical' version of Irish literature put
forward in the contribution of the late
Professor Robert O'Driscoll: a paper
entitled 'The Irish Literary Renaissance
in the Context of a Celtic Continuum'
(published in the conference proceedings
as 'A Greater Renaissance: The Revolt of
the Soul Against the Intellect)'. Richards's

recollections can barely contain the felt impatience at Driscoll's dated Arnoldian position: 'O'Driscoll glossed his position in the question period: "The Celts could not have invented the refrigerator", and for that we were to be grateful, irrespective of the curdled consequences.'[57]

Most recently, O'Connor insists that Arnold's admiration for the richness of the Welsh language is only the second part of a 'double move of screening out Celtic languages and apotheosizing Celtic culture onto a pedestal'. The Welsh language acquires an affective dimension in Arnold's account that positions it within the realm of the beautiful rather than the sublime. Together, the deafness to the language and its exoticization in elegy serve to 'tune out the thick texture ... of Welsh culture and sublimate it into something else, an abstract notion of the Celt, which transforms ... Wales into a spectacle of ruin'.[58] The network of Burkean meanings is suggestive. Arnold here partakes of the eighteenth-century and Romantic convention of the flight of philosophical speculation brought on by the experience of revolutionary change. What comes into view in the moment of revolutionary or colonial destruction is the previously vague — because lived as everyday and filling out our vision without need of framing — field of traditional culture.

There have been a number of scholarly efforts to rescue Arnold as an early, if flawed, theorist of multiculturalism. Robert Young, for instance, opposes what he calls 'Arnold-bashing' with the suggestion that his ethnographic politics foregrounded the role of race in the formulation of ideas of culture.[59] Comparing English, Irish, Welsh-American and African-American theorists of culture, Daniel Williams has also been concerned to show how ethnicity is integral to the late nineteenth-century construction of cultural authority, rather than something that assails culture from the outside.[60] And in an Irish context, Mary Jean Corbett proposes that 'Arnold's willingness to

FRENCH FLIGHT
Or, the Grand Monarque and the Rights of Kings
Supported in a Sublime and Beautiful
Manner.

William Dent, *French Flight; or, the Grand Monarque and the Rights of Kings Supported in a Sublime and Beautiful Manner,* 1791, etching on paper, 39 × 11.4 cm. Trustees of the British Museum.

imagine that Union could no longer be conceived as a matter of Ireland becoming more like England, but must instead proceed on principles that would newly articulate the meanings and uses of cultural difference,

57 Shaun Richards, 'Our Revels Now are Ended': Irish Studies in Britain — Origins and Aftermath', in Liam Harte and Yvonne Whelan, eds., *Ireland beyond Boundaries: Mapping Irish Studies in the Twenty-First Century* (London, 2007), 48–57 (50). See also his 'Irish Studies and the Adequacy of Theory: The Case of Brian Friel', *Yearbook of English Studies,* 35, 1 (2005), 264–78.

58 O'Connor, *Haunted English,* 28.

59 Robert J. C. Young, *Colonial Desire: Hybridity in Theory, Race and Culture* (London and New York, 1995), 87–88.

60 Daniel Williams, *Ethnicity and Cultural Authority* (Edinburgh, 2007).

61 Mary Jean Corbett,
   *Allegories of Union
   in Irish and English
   Writing, 1790–1870:
   Politics, History, and the
   Family from Edgeworth
   to Arnold* (Cambridge,
   2000), 159.

62 Quoted in Margaret
   Kelleher, 'Prose Writing
   and Drama in English,
   1830–1900: From
   Catholic Emancipation
   to the Fall of Parnell', in
   Kelleher and O'Leary,
   eds., *Cambridge History
   of Irish Literature*, vol. 1,
   449–99 (477).

63 D. P. Moran, *The
   Philosophy of Irish
   Ireland* (Dublin, 1905),
   104.

64 Seamus Deane, 'Factions
   and Fictions', in *Foreign
   Affections: Essays on
   Edmund Burke* (Cork,
   2005), 6.

65 Raymond Williams, *The
   Country and the City*
   (New York, 1973), 10.

66 Joe Cleary, 'Irish
   Modernity', in Joe Cleary
   and Claire Connolly, eds.,
   *Cambridge Companion
   to Modern Irish Culture*
   (Cambridge, 2004), 1–24
   (18).

also constitutes a powerful critique of Englishness'.[61] Perhaps this proto-Irish Studies aspect to Arnold is what the Fenian John O'Leary registered when he listed Arnold's essay among his 'best hundred Irish books' in 1886, noting that 'he is always more or less suggestive and mostly very sympathetic, even if, occasionally ... a little patronizing'.[62] D. P. Moran's comments on Arnold in his *Philosophy of Irish Ireland* are also suggestive. Moran condemns 'On the Study of Celtic Literature' as dangerous but at the same time registers its critical pliability when he bemoans how it takes the place of an indigenous Irish (specifically Irish-language) conceptualization of our traditions:

> We were all on the lookout for somebody to think for us, for we had given up that habit with our language. Matthew Arnold happily came along just in the nick of time, and in a much-quoted essay suggested, among other things, that one of the characteristics of Celtic poetry was 'natural magic' ... We seized on the phrase like hawks ... Then yet another Irish make-believe was born, and it was christened 'The Celtic Note', Mr. W. B. Yeats standing sponsor for it.[63]

What interests Moran about Arnold is his having established a principle of difference that, because muddled and mystical, created the conditions in which much sharper and more hard-edged forms of cultural and social inquiry could take shape.

For Arnold as for Burke, the taken-for-granted aspects of culture — the things that fill out the edges of vision and might be thought of as sublime — come into perspective as part of a widespread framing of national traditions, itself part of the longer history of European romanticism. In linguistic terms, words obscure, but that obscurity is in the process of acquiring a value that is bound up with ideas of affect. Tradition thus goes from a state of sublimity to one that is associated above all with

beauty: the soothing effects of custom, ritual and repetition. Seamus Deane, drawing on Burke, describes the ensuing cultural politics in the following terms:

> Tradition ... refers to ... modes of feeling that are the more precious for being out-of-time and therefore enduring, rather than in time and therefore merely fashionable or transient. Above all, such feelings, while they would seem at times to run merely from the moist to the lachrymose, were most traditional when they included within them a sense of the tragic dimension of human experience.[64]

The invocation of the 'merely' here and the discomfort with the 'moist' and the 'lachrymose' suggests that only feelings that incline towards tragedy carry complex meanings and values. Yet there is a case to be made for analysing these 'modes of feeling' in all their soggy variety. As Raymond Williams suggests, sentiment may be less a matter of 'historical error' and more one of 'historical perspective'.[65]

Deane's critical writing draws from Burke a deep and almost painful awareness of the antinomies of tradition and modernity and a conceptualization of their interrelation in the present moment (however that present is conceived). Deane's Burke spoke first to the Ireland of the 1980s and helped him to indict the paltry promises of pluralism and its shallow relationship to the history of our divided island. As Joe Cleary puts it: 'on these conundrums of Ireland and the modern, [Deane] has demonstrated, an entire national literature has battened, revisiting the vicissitudes of that problematic monotonously, occasionally with extraordinary brilliance'.[66] At the same time, though, there is a tendency to dismiss sentiment as the opposite of analysis, rather than forming a part of the condition under investigation. To put it in its most basic form, these conundrums of Ireland and the modern have an affective dimension. We might also notice here how embodied emotions constitute a realm of experience, which, in the period after the *Enquiry* was published, came to be increasingly associated with women and — via a shared discourse of ornamentalism, weakness and dependence — with oppressed national cultures. This shared conjunction is almost certainly why Ireland saw the development of the genre of the national tale, with its marshalling of affective responses, in the hands of women writers and in the shadow of the Act of Union.

For Wales to be both the territory of abstraction and of ruin brings it close to the France of the *Reflections*, devastated by the abstraction wrought by both revolutionary and colonial systems and yet, out of the devastation, producing both new and newly systematized concepts. Wales then, or the Celtic countries, can be seen via this Burkean prism as, to borrow Deane's description of France, 'the territory of theory'.[67] It may seem strange to think of the Celtic world as the site of abstraction rather than rich particularity, but Burke's role in Romantic-era culture allows us to reconcile these contradictory possibilities. Most obviously, Burke was a powerful spokesperson for the case against abstract theory made in the name of cultural particularism. As Mike Goode has recently argued, however, the turn away from abstraction (associated above all with *Reflections on the Revolution in France*) suffered a loss of cultural authority during the Peninsular and Napoleonic wars. Goode highlights accounts of Burke's defence of French culture that sought to weaken its cultural authority by underlining its gendered, national and confessional dimensions.[68] Because the rejection of theory in *Reflections* operated in what came to be a negatively characterized sentimental and chivalric mode (witness the many contemporary caricatures of its author as a sad and hopeless knight-priest figure), Romantic-era cultural politics sought a space for a less sentimental version of 'forward-looking knowledge' — a more 'manly' history.[69] The scientific models of history developed in the early years of the

new century (especially by Walter Scott) can be seen to work to exorcise a residue of sentiment that is for Goode condensed in the figure of Burke. Central to this process was a reorientation of the relationship between forms of philosophical knowledge and the national past that would allow the former to negotiate the latter without becoming subsumed by its demands: the feminized figure of the antiquary came to serve as a model for the dangers inherent in the process.

Theory, then, is neither simply the possession of centre or periphery but rather a tool to be deployed in a reclamation of the resources of national culture. From the Romantic period, this exorcism of sentiment has been coded as a necessary remasculinization of culture. In terms of the longer history of Irish literature, the problem may be identified as one of the subjective effects produced by language and the question of how to handle them in a literary tradition accustomed to tracking political rather than aesthetic issues. In manoeuvring between the related figures of difference traced throughout this essay, there is a danger that Irishness continues to be located on the side of politics, with aesthetics found elsewhere.

'Gerrymander it': Past Feeling

Burke's *Enquiry* concerns itself with the excess of affect over representation in ways that helpfully focus our attention on the role of the aesthetic in Irish literary and cultural criticism. 'Affects', according to Gilles Deleuze and Félix Guattari, 'are no longer feelings or affections; they go beyond the strength of those that undergo them'.[70] Their speculations on art as '*a bloc of sensations*' are part of a wider reconsideration of affect within literary and philosophical thought. A major aim of the argument presented here is to open up Irish literary criticism to the resources of the new scholarship on affect. Sianne Ngai's 2005 book, *Ugly Feelings*, situates her work among that of a growing

67 Deane, 'Phantasmal France, Unreal Ireland', 7.

68 Mike Goode, 'Dryasdust Antiquarianism and Soppy Masculinity: The Waverley Novels and the Gender of History', *Representations*, 82 (2003), 52–86 (61).

69 Goode, 'Dryasdust Antiquarianism and Soppy Masculinity', 61–62.

70 Gilles Deleuze and Félix Guattari, *What is Philosophy?*, trans. by Graham Burchell and Hugh Tomlinson (London and New York, 1994), 164.

71 Sianne Ngai, *Ugly Feelings* (Cambridge, Mass., 2005), 8, 3.

72 Lynn Festa, *Sentimental Figures of Empire in Eighteenth-Century Britain and France* (Baltimore, 2006), 15.

73 Ngai, *Ugly Feelings*, 22–23.

74 Festa, *Sentimental Figures of Empire*, 2.

75 Festa, *Sentimental Figures of Empire*, 54–55.

76 Siobhán Kilfeather, 'Alice Maher's Materials', *Field Day Review*, 2 (2006), 3–17 (17).

77 For this formulation, see Kevis Goodman, *Georgic Modernity and British Romanticism: Poetry and the Mediation of History* (Cambridge, 2006), 10. Goodman locates her work as part of 'a revised historicist method that reserves a place at the table for sensation and affect'.

78 Dipesh Chakrabarty, 'Modernity and the Past: A Critical Tribute to Ashis Nandy', *Habitations of Modernity: Essays in the Wake of Subaltern Studies* (Chicago, 2002), 38–47 (46).

body of critics who believe that 'emotion may be recuperated for critical praxis'. Crucially, this is a critical praxis devoted to 'the effort of thinking the aesthetic and the political together'.[71] That sentimental discourse is above all defined by having formal properties is important here — it consists of a set of literary conventions which, if they are to be recognized, will be as 'a formal aspect of a text rather than an ideological position'.[72] Ngai's book is concerned to locate and analyse not so much a collection of affective responses as a series of what she calls 'representational predicaments' that revolve around 'the exact role and status of emotion in the aesthetic encounter'.[73] In terms of the figures of difference worked through in the course of this argument, to end on sentiment is to end on the related issues of aesthetics/politics and Britain/Ireland — and to suggest a way of thinking about these topics in terms of their interrelatedness.

Contemporary post-colonialism provides compelling accounts of the linkages between emotion, aesthetics and politics. In historical terms, Lynn Festa has helped us to think about how the turning inward of sentimental discourse is inextricably linked to the turning outward of expansionist empires (France and England).[74] Sentiment is not so much cover for empire as a 'structure of feeling' that allows for 'repetition without absorption'.[75] Sentiment is thus theatrical — which in Burkean terms means it offers both a perspective on and a necessary distance from power. In more contemporary terms, appeals to aesthetics afford a degree of immunity that can function as a kind of defence against the imperatives of community. Siobhán Kilfeather has located in Alice Maher's art a powerful example of such an appeal: 'Maher's ability to reinvigorate a sense of wonder around certain objects is a historicist act. It is harder to explain why her own art goes so far beyond

simply suggesting what is already known about women, history and tradition.'[76]

The imperatives of history and tradition as the 'already known' are undoubtedly pressing. They are — as Burke knew — at once embodied and external: as such they possess the power to overwhelm individual understanding. To grasp this process, we need to realize a fuller sense — or perhaps sensation — of the power of history and tradition to inflict 'affective discomfort'.[77] Dipesh Chakrabarty, in *Habitations of Modernity*, writes of historiographical attempts to engage with — to reach out and touch — the threatened territory of tradition in terms that might have come straight from Burke's *Enquiry*. His prose carries Burke's sense of the attraction and dangers of community, enlivened with fresh anxieties about the limitations of such supposedly assured theoretical approaches as 'critical traditionalism'. The past, writes Chakrabarty, 'comes to me as taste, as embodied memory, as cultural training of the senses, as reflexes, often as things that I do not even know that I carry. It has the capacity, in other words, to take me by surprise and to overwhelm and shock me'. He goes on:

> That is why, it seems to me, that, in addition to the feeling of respect for traditions, fear and anxiety would have to be the other affects with which the modern intellectual — modernity here implying a capacity to create the future as an object of deliberate action — relates to the past.[78]

Creating the future of Irish literature in relation to its past demands reading practices alert to the full affective range embodied in texts that continue to cross borders shaped by uneven distributions of power.

C.W. Locke's cinematograph house and triple dioramic apparatus, c. 1910. Photo: Rischgitz/Getty Images.

Politics and the Cinematograph
The Boer War and the Funeral of Thomas Ashe

Denis Condon

> A. Would you use the cinematograph to foster a national spirit in Eirinn?
>
> B. Would you use it to forward the Irish-Ireland movement?
>
> C. Would you use it for political propaganda?

These questions were posed by 'Oisín' in a competition for the young readers of the column *Buidhean na hÉireann* (the Irish Brigade) in two issues of the newspaper *Sinn Féin* in late 1910 and early 1911. An anonymous 'friend of the Brigade' had offered five shillings for the best essay answering these questions. Although the winning essay, if there was one, does not seem to have been printed in the newspaper, the competition is evidence that some radical nationalists were thinking about how moving-picture technology might be used for their political purposes. The questions, however, posed as they are in a children's column, perhaps suggest an uneasiness with the seriousness of the issue, that while the cinematograph might be utilized to promote an Irish national spirit, advance the Irish-Ireland movement, and disseminate political propaganda, the new technology should not after all be put to such use. Such reluctance would not have been overly surprising, given the amount of Irish nationalist energy expended in reviving or inventing Gaelic cultural pursuits untainted by association with British domination and what may have been regarded as an undesirable foreign technology.[1]

Nevertheless, between 1896, the date of the first exhibition to an Irish audience of projected moving pictures, and the establishment of the Free State in 1921, nationalists and other political groups in Ireland did use film for political purposes. In 1914, for example, the Union Defence League equipped lecturers with three large vans with cinematographs and fold-out screens to tour Britain, with the aim of promoting the unionist cause by showing films of Edward Carson and the Ulster Volunteer Force.[2] Others with no obvious political affiliation used politics as the pretext for making films to ensure large audiences.

The concern here is the political uses of film and the filmic uses of politics in Ireland in relation to the Boer War and the funeral of Thomas Ashe. These two historical moments exemplify the interaction of politics and what would, by the end of this period, come to be called *cinema*. Specifically, in showing something of the circumstances in which the people of Dublin were at times the audience for and/or the subject of films of political events, I hope to illuminate the dialectical relationship between the production, exhibition, and reception of 'topical' films at the turn of the century and what had become commodified as 'newsreel'

films by the time of the 1916 Rising.

In order to concentrate on the closeness of factual films to politics in early twentieth-century Ireland, those fiction films that were first made in significant numbers in 1910–20 have been omitted from this discussion: their political dimensions have been discussed in other commentaries.[3] Paradoxically, early 'factual' films have received little critical attention, yet those that survive have had a busy afterlife and are familiar to a wide audience through their use by makers of historical films and television programmes. While early Irish fiction films can only be seen at the film archives that house them or in rare archival screenings elsewhere, a large body of political non-fiction film is readily available on DVD, notably in the film documentaries *Mise Éire* (1959) and *Saoirse?* (1961), directed by George Morrison for the Irish-language cultural organization Gael-Linn, and in the first episode of the landmark television history *Seven Ages* (2000), directed by Seán Ó Mórdha for the Irish national broadcaster RTÉ. Through frequent use in television programmes that illustrate Ireland in the last years of the nineteenth century and the first decade of the twentieth, the relatively few factual film images from the late colonial period have become detached from the history of their own production, distribution, exhibition and reception.

This is problematic on a number of levels. Harvey O'Brien has argued that *Mise Éire* and *Saoirse?* offer 'a depoliticized political history, built solely upon the construction of an image of the nation amenable to received nationalist mythology'.[4] For O'Brien, Morrison created a powerful myth of the 'birth of a nation' that would long exert a retarding influence on the representation of Ireland in moving pictures. Despite this, his films were important because at the very least they preserved early film material long before the establishment of the Irish Film Archive in 1992; indeed, for decades, Morrison's documentaries were ruefully described as Ireland's only film archive.[5] It is important to note, however, as indeed IFA curator Sunniva

1 *Sinn Féin*, 24 December 1910 and 7 January 1911.

2 'Pictures in Ireland. By "Paddy"', *Bioscope*, 18 June 1914.

3 In particular, see Kevin Rockett, Luke Gibbons and John Hill, *Cinema and Ireland* (London and Sydney, 1987), 7–32; and Ruth Barton, *Irish National Cinema* (London, 2004), 18–33.

4 Harvey O'Brien, *The Real Ireland: The Evolution of Ireland in Documentary Film* (Manchester, 2004), 120.

5 Martin McLoone, *Irish Film: The Emergence of a Contemporary Cinema* (London, 2000), 17.

6   Sunniva O'Flynn, 'Irish Newsreels: An Expression of National Identity?', in Roger Smither and Wolfgang Klaue, eds., *Newsreels in Film Archives: A Study Based on the FIAF Newsreels Symposium* (Trowbridge, 1996), 57 and 59.

7   *Dublin Evening Mail* [hereafter, *DEM*], 29 September 1917.

8   Rick Altman, *Silent Film Sound* (New York and Chichester, 2004), 18–23.

O'Flynn has observed, the selective nature of Morrison's act of preservation, by which he extracted the political items contained in Ireland's first newsreel series, *Irish Events*, to create his documentaries, while neglecting other items of a non-political nature seen by their first audiences.[6]

O'Flynn's insight — that political items filmed by an Irish newsreel company were first presented to their audiences as part of a series of short scenes of local interest — begins the process of re-imagining the context for these films. Whereas much about moving-picture entertainments changed in the sixteen years between the exhibitions of Boer War films and the *Irish Events* special *The Funeral of Thos. Ashe* in 1917, their essential 'variety' nature remained constant. Variety covered a wide range of entertainments — from live acts that accompanied the film, itself regarded as an 'act', in the music halls and variety theatres in the early 1900s, to the filmic variety provided by cinema programmes in the late 1910s. For O'Flynn, the typical combination of a one-minute political film along with four other one-minute films of sporting or cultural interest is likely to have lessened the impact of the political material on the audience. Besides, the audience of a late 1910s cinema programme would usually have seen this newsreel material as an accompaniment to a featured dramatic film, one or more short comedies, and perhaps a travelogue or other non-fiction 'interest' film of five to ten minutes in length. This can be seen in the programme at the Bohemian Picture House in Dublin's north-city suburb of Phibsboro for the first part of the week in which *The Funeral of Thos. Ashe* formed the *Irish Events* contribution:

> On Monday next a splendid picture by the Fox Company is announced, 'The Island of Desire', featuring George Walsh, a thrilling tale of the South Seas; a two-part Keystone comedy, 'Teddy at the Thottle', will afford plenty of fun. The Gaumont Graphic and Irish Events, with

a cartoon, will complete a really first-class picture programme.[7]

Although this helps to enhance our awareness of the historical importance of topicals, these films did provide the occasion for some remarkable political displays.

Not only did the Irish political scene undergo enormous changes between 1900 and 1917 but so too did moving pictures. Even use of the term 'cinema' to designate a venue dedicated to the exhibition of moving pictures did not become common until after 1912, and was not universal even then, many establishments preferring to call themselves picture houses. Part of what Rick Altman has called the 'identity crisis' of projected moving pictures, they emerged as a form of entertainment independent of the established media from which they had liberally borrowed, then underwent internal 'jurisdictional conflicts', and finally reached 'overdetermined solutions' to tease out these problems.[8] It would be anachronistic to call these moving pictures 'cinema' or even 'early cinema'; contemporary sources demonstrate how film shows were understood at specific moments.

Emphasis here is on the encounter between historical audiences and films, rather than on extended textual analysis of the films themselves. The aim is to challenge entrenched myths about early film entertainments. For example, it is widely believed that James Joyce established Ireland's first cinema, the Cinematograph Volta, in Dublin's Mary Street in December 1909. However, there was fixed-venue, dedicated picture entertainment in Ireland before the Volta. Between March 1908 and January 1909, for example, the Colonial Picture Combine's People's Popular Picture Palace was located at the Queen's Royal Theatre in Dublin's Brunswick (now Pearse) Street, when the venue's theatrical patent and lease had temporarily lapsed. Differing significantly from the Volta and attracting a substantially proletarian audience, this picture palace opened with a programme headed by *The Story of the Kelly Gang*, a sensational melodrama about the notorious Australian outlaw.[9] Of Irish extraction, Ned Kelly proved a popular subject and the film created a stir in an audience used to the Queen's staple stage melodramas about the deeds of Irish nationalist heroes. But an even earlier encounter between Dublin audiences and films had occurred eight years before.

The Boer War

It was the visit of Queen Victoria to Dublin in April 1900 that produced the first substantial encounter between politics and the cinematograph in Ireland. Continuity exists between street protests organized against Victoria's jubilee in June 1897, pro-Boer demonstrations that began in August 1899, and opposition to the visit of Edward VII in July 1903.[10] Of particular interest here, however, are the public demonstrations by the Irish Transvaal Committee, an organization led by James Connolly, Maud Gonne, Arthur Griffith, and John O'Leary, and supported by such figures as W. B. Yeats, Michael Davitt, and William Rooney. The last of the great pro-Boer demonstrations was held on 17 December 1899, on the eve of the arrival in Dublin of Colonial Secretary Joseph Chamberlain.[11] When the Transvaal Committee's efforts against army recruitment in early 1900 seemed to be having an effect, a two-week royal visit, to begin on 3 April 1900, was announced in an attempt to champion the British cause.[12] Dublin Corporation's decision on 14 March to deliver a loyal address to the queen led to angry scenes in the council chamber, with separatist nationalists singing 'God Save Ireland' from the gallery,[13] and on St. Patrick's Day the inauguration procession of Lord Mayor T. D. Pile was attacked in the streets.[14] A planned peaceful protest against the Victoria's visit, organized by Yeats for 4 April, was suppressed by the police.[15]

These demonstrations occurred in immediate response to, or even in advance of, events. However, it was to be some time before such resistance manifested itself in response to moving images of the queen's visit, or of the Boer War for that matter, because the speed with which a film production company could screen images of the war in British and Irish venues depended upon how quickly a camera operator could be shipped to and from 'the seat of war'. By contrast, the telegraph, while unable to transmit pictures, could deliver information rapidly between the parts of the Empire suitably connected. War films may have been screened at Dublin's Lyric in the week following the outbreak of hostilities between the Boers and the British, but the images were of the Spanish-American War, which had been under way for nearly a year and a half. When the advertisement for this act claimed that 'All Important News from the Seat of War arriving during the Performance will be Announced Nightly on the Cineograph', however, the war referred to was the conflict in South Africa, which was dominating the news. As Simon Popple has observed:

> The war itself straddled the end of the old and the beginning of the new century, and marked the end of a tradition dominated by the manual transcription of information and impressions. New media based on the technologies of the camera and the telegraph altered not only the speed with which the war could be covered but also the nature of the representation.[16]

When moving-picture representations of the conflict eventually arrived in Irish theatres and other venues, they encountered patterns of reception that had largely been established by other entertainments. From early in the war, Dublin theatre audiences voiced their displeasure at jingoistic displays by British stage performers. In January 1900, the *Irish Playgoer*'s 'Odds and Ends' column advised that 'all reference to the war and soldiers should be omitted from our entertainments for the present, seeing the divided state of our people on the matter'.[17] In February,

9 *The Story of the Kelly Gang*, Australia: Gibson and Tait, 1906; dir. Charles Tait.

10 P. J. Mathews, *Revival: The Abbey Theatre, Sinn Féin, the Gaelic League and the Co-Operative Movement* (Cork, 2003), 17–18, 66–91, 122–24.

11 Mathews, *Revival*, 72.

12 Editorial 'The Royal Visit', *Evening Telegraph* [hereafter, *ET*], 8 March 1900.

13 'Corporation and the Queen: The Lord Mayor Proposes an Address: Scenes in the Council Chamber: "God save Ireland" Sung from the Gallery', *ET*, 14 March 1900.

14 'The Lord Mayor's Procession: A Hostile Reception', *ET*, 17 March 1905.

15 Mathews, *Revival*, 89.

16 Simon Popple, '"But the Khaki-Covered Camera is the *Latest* Thing": The Boer War Cinema and Visual Culture in Britain', in Andrew Higson, ed., *Young and Innocent? The Cinema in Britain 1896–1930* (Exeter, 2002), 13–14.

17 *Irish Playgoer*, 1, 9 (1900), 4.

18 *Irish Playgoer*, 1, 14 (1900), 12.

19 'San Toy: Lively Scenes at the Gaiety — Singers Turn the Theatre into a Bear-Garden by Singing "Jingo" Songs', *Irish Playgoer*, 2, 10 (1900), 11.

20 *Irish Daily Independent*, 14 May 1900.

21 'Odds and Ends', *Irish Playgoer*, 2, 13 (1900), 2.

22 *ET*, 10 March 1900.

23 *ET*, 10 March 1900.

a writer in the same journal described the Gaiety audience as 'over sensitive': 'Our Wilkie Bard was singing a capital medley song, and the very mention of one line of "The Soldiers of the Queen" created an uproar.'[18] At the same theatre, more substantial disruption greeted the opening of the new musical comedy *San Toy*, which included such jingoistic songs as 'Private Tommy Atkins' from the 1893 musical comedy *The Gaiety Girl*:

the indefensible introduction of war glorification and jingoistic bunkum of that sort completely marred the ordinary playgoer's enjoyment on the opening night, as each reference to such caused a disturbance, which, at times, developed into quite a pandemonium of discordant sounds that completely obliterated what was taking place on the stage. This introduction of contentious matter into musical plays ought to be discontinued, especially in Dublin, where so much diversity of opinion on such-like affairs is, at present, or in fact, always to be found.[19]

It was not just the Gaiety's predominantly middle-class audience that reacted in this way. When comic singer Harriet Vernon appeared at the low-priced Lyric variety theatre on 15 May 1900 dressed as an English officer, 'though she looked exceptionally well in the uniform, a very large number of the people who were present objected, and showed that they did so in the usual way'. Despite establishing that the uniform was the problem, 'Vernon came out in the same dress and sang what a majority of the audience considered a Jingo song, with the result that during the time she was on the stage hissing was very noticeable'.[20] The *Irish Playgoer* columnist Conn comments:

I, for one, sincerely wish the war was over, in order that amusement-seekers in Dublin may again be allowed to enjoy themselves in peace ... I fear our local managers are greatly to blame for the

state of affairs that exists at present, in not compelling all companies to 'blue pencil' every Jingo allusion while here ... if this were done, I, for one, would go with a merrier heart to the theatre, knowing that I could then sit out a play without uproar and hideous noises.[21]

The same sensitivities were not apparent in Belfast, where for several weeks in late January and early February the Alhambra featured war sketches such as *Briton or Boer* and *The Union Jack*.

What appear to be the first Boer War films in Ireland were exhibited at the Lyric in March 1900 by Scott's metascope, 'the most up-to-date appliance for showing living pictures'.[22] As well as views of the battles of Spion Kop, Modder River, and Nicholson Nek, mentioned in the advertisement, the show featured general films of South Africa — 'among many others, Cape street, Port Elizabeth' — and further war-related footage, including: 'the Roslin Castle, conveying consignments of troops for the war; the "Fighting Fifth" digging trenches at Estcourt; a Skirmish with the artillery outside Ladysmith; the Lancers at the Modder River; Bridging the Tugela, and Watering the Artillery and Transport Mules; the Ambulance at Work, etc'.[23] These films do not seem to have caused anti-British demonstrations or displays of loyalty in the Lyric.

A delay in the arrival of pictures, however, could as likely have increased as reduced the resistance to them, but their mode of presentation was crucial to the audience's reception of them. When the films were presented in a neutral way — without any pro-British display by the lecturer, or the choice of jingoistic music, or the patriotic wording of titles — they could be accepted as information rather than resisted as propaganda. Reviewing the first week of 'WAR PICTURES. The Very Latest, including "Relief of Kimberly", Troops in Action, Most Thrilling Scenes' and the first showing of 'HER MAJESTY THE QUEEN's Gorgeous Entry into Dublin' at the Empire Theatre of Varieties, the unionist *Dublin Evening Mail* briefly comments that

Republican prisoners returning from British jails to an enthusiastic reception on 18 June 1917 pass Dublin's Queen's Theatre in Great Brunswick (now Pearse) Street. From *Release of the Sinn Féin Prisoners*.

they 'were greatly appreciated' and 'received with unstinted applause'.[24] A newspaper with this ideological outlook might be expected to emphasize demonstrations of loyalty and downplay shows of protest. In its review of the shows at the Empire during the second week of the run of these films, however, the same paper demonstrates that the music-hall audience could divide on political lines. On the evening of 16 April, protest broke out before the potentially explosive film material had been shown:

> Mays and Hunter, banjoists, played several charming selections, and for a moment or two the gallery threatened to become disorderly, in consequence of representations of different schools of politics, calling — some for 'Killarney' and other for 'Rule Britannia'. Eventually the banjoists played 'Killarney', and were cheered again and again.[25]

In this context, and given that the loyal element in the audience had previously been prompted to sustained applause in response to footage of the queen's visit, it seems remarkable that the pictures were not more contentious.

The nationalist *Evening Telegraph*'s strong pro-Boer stance reflected the broad nationalist position, which drew a clear analogy between the British threat to the self-determination of the Boers and that of the Irish, understood either as Home Rule or as independence. The paper gave prominence to illustrated articles on the Transvaal Irish Brigade, which fought with the Boers.[26] However, it could not ignore the fact that much larger numbers of Irish recruits fought in the British army against the Boers, and it is on such an issue that the accusations against the British establishment's manipulation of the news take an interesting turn. The *Telegraph*'s report 'A Sensational Story: Dublin Fusilier's Letter from the Front: The Boers and the Border Regiment' displays the Dublin Fusiliers as patriotic Irish men in their

24 *DEM*, 10 and 14 April 1900.
25 'The Empire Palace', *DEM*, 17 April 1900.
26 See, for example, 'The Transvaal Irish Brigade' and 'Transvaal Irish Brigade: Four of Its Sturdy Members', *ET*, 28 October 1899 and 9 December 1899.

Members of the Dublin Brigade of the Irish Republican Army fire a volley of shots above the grave of Thomas Ashe. From *The Funeral of Thos. Ashe.*

27 *ET*, 27 January 1900.
28 'Sham War Cinematograph Films', *Optical Magic Lantern Journal and Photographic Enlarger*, 11, 30 (1900), 30.
29 Robin Whalley and Peter Worden, 'Forgotten Firm: A Short Chronological Account of Mitchell and Kenyon, Cinematographers', *Film History*, 10, 1 (1998), 37–38.
30 Popple, 'The Boer War Cinema', 20.
31 Popple, 'The Boer War Cinema', 20–21.
32 *ET*, 13 April 1901. All quotations in this paragraph are from this review and an earlier, longer review titled 'The Modern Marvel Syndicate, Limited: An Interesting Show', *ET*, 9 April 1901.

readiness to tell the true story of British losses covered up by the military hierarchy.[27]

The delay in the delivery of genuine films of the war in South Africa, and the subsequent difficulty of filming a guerrilla campaign, encouraged certain film producers to shoot staged war scenes. In March 1900 the *Optical Magic Lantern Journal* lamented that 'A correspondent asks us how he is to know real from sham war films, seeing that several subjects are made at home from life models.'[28] These staged war films, the longest running series of which were produced by the Mitchell and Kenyon Company between 1900 and 1902,[29] 'draw on the standard Boer narratives, in which the patriotic behaviour of the Tommy is contrasted with the devious and unchivalrous conduct of the Boer'.[30] Staged films were joined in late 1900 by patriotic trick films, such as R. W. Paul's *Kruger's Dream of Empire*, directed by Walter R. Booth, which includes an animated dream and the disappearance of live-action figures.[31]

The first film exhibition at which protests are recorded was the Modern Marvel Syndicate's film and variety show at the Rotunda between 8 and 20 April 1901. The company was run by T. J. West, 'a gentleman long and favourably known in theatrical and amusement matters in Dublin, his association with our city extending over twenty-five years, during which time he has been very successful in his endeavours to meet the public taste'.[32] When protests were made against parts of the show, the reviews were careful to exonerate him. As well as managing the show, he delivered 'a descriptive and interesting lecture at each display'. Far from offering a damning verdict, the two substantial reviews in the *Telegraph* might be said to be generous in their attentiveness but equivocal in their praise. Their overall assessment, nevertheless, was that the 'whole show certainly makes an amusing, interesting, and wonderful entertainment'. The variety acts, consisting of singers and

Michael Collins delivers his brief oration at Ashe's graveside. From *The Funeral of Thos. Ashe.*

jugglers, were 'a pleasing adjunct to the photographic portion'. The main attraction featured the drama *Joan of Arc*,[33] which was judged to be 'both entertaining to the old and instructive to the young, and last night the display was received with loud and long well-merited applause'. But some of the accompanying topical films elicited conflicting responses from the audience:

> Some did not meet with the approval of a large section of the audience. They objected to representations of her late Majesty Queen Victoria, and scenes representing 'Our gallant soldiers, who have been fighting for the last eighteen months'. Some of those present cheered and clapped, and the remainder booed and hissed, but probably both parties were satisfied, notwithstanding the Khaki flavour of that portion of the entertainment, for, as a show, it was good, and this, the manager said, was all he wanted the audience to admit.

By the end of the week, the *Telegraph* was describing the show with no mention of audience disapproval. It seems likely that West altered the programme to make it more acceptable to the divided loyalties of Irish audiences.

Two South African-themed entertainments played seasons in Dublin to coincide with the lucrative Horse Show week in late August 1901. *Savage South Africa*, playing at the grounds on Jones's Road, was advertised as 'not a circus but real life. not pictures but reality'.[34] Its demonstrations of trick-riding and pageantry based on the Zulu wars attracted more than usual attention because of the outbreak of the Boer War, and new acts were added accordingly,[35] including a

> realistic scene descriptive of Major Allan Wilson's last stand on the banks of the Shanghani River, and the piece de resistance was afforded in the concluding spectacle dealing with the battle of Elandslaagte, in which the rattle of Maxim guns and the roll of heavier ordnance played a leading part.[36]

As the different newspaper reviews described it, audiences could read this variation on the

33 *Joan of Arc*, France: Star, 1899; dir. Georges Méliès.
34 Advertisements appear in the daily papers in the week of 29 July 1901.
35 Popple, 'The Boer War Cinema', 23.
36 '"Savage South Africa": Unique Entertainment at Jones' Road', *DEM*, 6 August 1901.

Crowds thronged the streets not only for the Sunday funeral but also for the removal of the body from the Mater Hospital to the Pro-Cathedral and the procession from the Pro-Cathedral to City Hall, when this high-angle shot of the hearse nearing College Green was taken. From *The Funeral of Thos. Ashe.*

37 'The Stage and Gallery: Poole's Myriorama', *DEM*, 24 August 1901.
38 'Poole's Myriorama', *ET*, 6 August 1901.
39 *ET*, 10 August 1901.

Wild West show as either pro-Boer or pro-British, or as apolitical spectacle.

The other South African-themed entertainment running in August 1901 was not so ambiguous in its address to its audience. One of Poole's myriorama companies, which had long-established links to Dublin, encountered difficulty because of the jingoism of its Boer war-based show of still and moving pictures. 'There are no less than seven of Messrs Poole's organisations all being exhibited to-night in various parts of the kingdom,' reports the *Evening Mail*, 'and so well is the business arranged, that no show is ever seen twice in the same town.'[37] The company that met with protests in Dublin was owned by Joseph Poole and managed by Fred Mayer. The *Evening Telegraph* offers a blunt assessment:

> The entertainment is styled 'Our Empire', and the title is entirely expressive and descriptive. The principal portion consists of scenes in the Boer war, and while the pictures as pictures are good enough, the history pourtrayed ... by them will not be of much assistance to the young student.

Of course the Myriorama was painted for a British audience who imagine that their aggression in the South African Republics has been an uninterrupted series of successes, and that the Yeomanry are the equal of Napoleon's Old Guard. Yesterday these pictures were not received with unmixed approval. But better than these unfortunate views was the photographic display in reference to the Pekin [*sic*] disturbances and scenes of general interest all over the world.[38]

The *Telegraph* reiterated its claim of controversy in its Saturday 'Music and the Drama' column at the end of the first week of the season: 'Poole's Myriorama continues to draw large houses at the Round Room, Rotunda, and the pro-British representation of South African war scenes give rise to a little excitement nightly between the patrons of the show who hold opposite views on the subject of the war.'[39]

Poole's case is illuminating because the war films were included with paintings and still photographs. In assessing the entertainment as a whole, the *Telegraph* reviewer admires them as aesthetic objects, while criticizing their use to advance the British cause. Dublin newspapers and journals pointed out the limitations of the new media technologies based on the telegraph and the photograph. '"[F]aked" snapshots of the war,' observes the *Irish Playgoer*, 'made with pictures of theatrical supers, who are made up as Boers or Englishmen as occasion demands are much more dramatic than the real ones, and find ready sale in Paris'.[40] While remarkable achievements in themselves, these media could be made to lie, whether inadvertently on occasion, to increase their entertainment value, or to suit the ideological position of the companies that produced them and screened them.

The Funeral of Thomas Ashe

In the sixteen years between the Boer War film protests and the funeral of Thomas Ashe, some significant uses of film for political purposes occurred. There were exhibitions of films covering republican commemorations at the grave of Wolfe Tone in Bodenstown, Co. Kildare, in 1913 and 1914. And some cinema-owners around the country, including the Horgan brothers of Youghal, County Cork, shot and screened films of local political groups. But the founding by Norman Whitten of his General Film Supply company after his arrival in Ireland in 1910 was of national importance. Whitten had worked in film since its earliest days, beginning his career with the British pioneer film-maker Cecil Hepworth. As the name of his company suggests, Whitten distributed films and supplied cinema and film-making equipment, but he also made many kinds of film, including: news films of events such as the funeral of Jeremiah O'Donovan Rossa in 1915; local interest films; British army recruitment films; promotional films for such companies as Court Laundry and Patterson matches. He also made a film of the 1913 Irish National

Pilgrimage to Lourdes, as well as the early Irish animated film *Ten Days' Leave*, with newspaper cartoonist Frank Leah in 1917, and the 1920 drama *Aimsir Phádraig/In the Days of St. Patrick*.

It was a film from the GFS's newsreel *Irish Events*, which ran from 1917 to 1920, that marked the spectacular public culmination of a protest in September 1917 against British government treatment of Sinn Féin prisoners in Mountjoy prison. The occasion of the protest was the death of Thomas Ashe, president of the Irish Republican Brotherhood, as a result of force-feeding while on hunger strike. In a series of demonstrations carefully stage-managed by republican leaders, Ashe's body became the emblem of a new public solidarity between the various insurgent nationalist groups that were already moving towards coalition under the Sinn Féin banner. The protest's highlight was Ashe's funeral at Glasnevin cemetery on Sunday, 30 September, the largest public demonstration since the Rising was put down in 1916, at which the Irish Volunteers marched openly under arms and fired three volleys of shots over the coffin, 'the only speech which it is proper to make above the grave of a dead Fenian'.[41]

The *Evening Herald* commended the exhibition on the evening of Ashe's funeral 'of films showing various ranges of the procession and scenes associated with it. The rifling part at the grave was included'.[42] The widespread publicity of organized events after Ashe's death allowed GFS to plan a newsreel special for their *Irish Events* serial. In what might be called a 'prequel', some of the material relating to Ashe's lying-in-state at City Hall was shown at the Rotunda on the Saturday night preceding the funeral, with the complete film, including the procession through the city to the cemetery, due for general release on the following Monday. The final film was first exhibited, however, on the night of the funeral at the Bohemian.[43] Run by Frederick Sparling, the Bohemian was a 1,000-seat cinema located on the route of the funeral procession out

40 'Odds and Ends', *Irish Playgoer*, 2, 3 (1900), 2.

41 This accounts for most of Collins's laconic oration at the graveside, reported in the daily papers; see, for example, *Irish Times*, 1 October 1917.

42 *Evening Herald* [hereafter, *EH*], 1 October 1917.

43 See advertisements in *DEM*, 29 September 1917.

44 For details of the location, management, and seating capacities of most Irish cinemas of the period, see *Cinema Yearbook 1915* (London, 1915), 94ff.

45 *Irish Limelight*, 1, 10 (1917), 8.

46 *Irish Limelight*, 1, 10 (1917), 8.

47 *DEM*, 29 September 1917. *A Modern Taming of the Shrew*, United States: New York Motion Pictures, 1915; dir. Reginald Baker.

48 'Sinn Féin Prisoners' Homecoming: Story of the Filming of Recent Remarkable Street Scenes in Dublin', *Irish Limelight*, 1, 7 (1917), 16–17. This incident is treated in more detail in Rockett, Gibbons and Hill, *Cinema and Ireland*, 34.

of the city, between Mountjoy prison and Glasnevin cemetery.[44]

Reporting on the filming of the funeral, the cinema journal *Irish Limelight* observed that people 'took part in the procession, went home to have tea, and an hour later saw themselves on the screen. Some hustle on the part of the camera men!'[45] While by no means unprecedented for important events, the speed with which Whitten prepared the film for exhibition distinguished the GFS from its competitors; in this case, from Charles McEvoy, proprietor of the Masterpiece Picture House, who also filmed the funeral but was unable to show his film until the Monday evening.[46] The theatrical exhibition of *The Funeral of Thos. Ashe* is as important as the speed of its appearance. The *Limelight* report suggests that, having taken some refreshment, mourners reassembled at the Bohemian to reconstitute the political demonstration that the funeral represented. Here, they viewed the funeral distilled to its ten-minute highlights — twice the usual length of a newsreel — all taken from advantageous viewpoints. In a sense, the exhibition at the Bohemian represented the culmination of the political protest, of the concentration of the energies and emotions that had been built up over several days. That night the spectators were freed from the limited perspective available to people in a crowd; they saw all the key events from a privileged vantage, an audience now seeing itself.

The screening of this film might seem to be a moment when the cinema assumed a key role in Irish political protest. However, little information is available on what happened in the Bohemian that night. What does survive suggests that the film would have fostered a participative form of spectatorship among the people who chose to attend its screening. 'Participative' here implies a more advanced form of interaction than took place with the Boer War films, this kind of spectatorship occurring between the subject, the producer, the exhibitor and the spectator(s) because both the subject

and the spectator(s) and, at least in early cases, the producer and the exhibitor are often remarkably allied with one another. Such an alliance between producer/exhibitor and spectator/subject does not transcend the material conditions in which the films were produced and consumed. In fact, the earliest manifestations of this participative spectatorship, when it is particularly associated with the local-view film, seems to be associated with a form of primitive accumulation in which the moving image of previously unfilmed groups is expropriated for profit.

Other factors in the first exhibition of *The Funeral of Thos. Ashe* must have worked to dissipate this participative dynamic or to make it fleeting. Advertisements for the Sunday evening show at the Bohemian, for example, describe it as 'a special long and interesting programme', featuring 'a five-part exclusive comedy-drama entitled, "A Modern Taming of the Shrew"'.[47] With the evening performance beginning at eight thirty and the funeral film screening at ten o'clock, the spectators would have experienced an hour and a half of other entertainments. There is no report that the cinema's well-publicized orchestra played dirges or patriotic tunes, although this seems very likely and happened in on similar occasions. Earlier that year, when Whitten managed to get the *Irish Events* film *Release of the Sinn Féin Prisoners* screened just hours after their arrival in Dublin on 18 June,

Some of the ex-prisoners and their friends could not resist the temptation to see themselves 'in the pictures', and a contingent marched up to the Rotunda early in the afternoon. They cheerfully acceded to the genial manager's request that they should leave their flags in the porch, and, when inside, gave every indication of enjoying not only 'their own film' but the rest of the programme.[48]

The power of the cinema to enthral its audiences is evident in this account, with

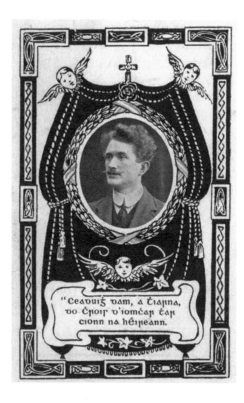

A memorial card for the hunger-striker Thomas Ashe. Courtesy of Dublin City Public Libraries.

optical perspective. Newspaper reports and photographs demonstrate that even such apparently god-like perspectives as the high-angle shots above the crowd reproduced the points of view of numerous mourners. 'Over 200,000 spectators and sympathisers thronged the route,' declares one evening newspaper, 'roofs, windows, verandas — even lamp-posts, railings, walls, hoardings, trees, statues, and monuments — every possible point of vantage was utilised by eager sightseers.'[49] The *Freeman's Journal* reported that 'residents of many houses were charging for seats at their windows, and that the sites were appreciated by those taking advantage of them was testified by the numbers who witnessed the procession from these points'.[50] The caption to a photograph in the *Freeman* reads:

> Sunday at the O'Connell Statue: The above picture gives a very good idea of the dimensions of the crowd which surged round and up the base of the O'Connell Statue on Sunday afternoon. For fully two hours before the cortege was due to pass men and boys by the score fought to obtain a good view by climbing amongst the figures which adorn the plinth, until all but the statue itself was obscured.[51]

This film and others like it address not only those who could claim this very direct form of spectatorial identification with the image, but also those who desired to witness the event. In the weeks following the funeral, apart from cinema-goers who were indifferent or hostile, it is likely that screenings of the film in Dublin and in the fifty cinemas around Ireland that subscribed to *Irish Events* would have brought together spectators who had taken part in the demonstrations as well as those who had been unable to attend.[52] From this perspective, these films are essentially local newsreels targeted at spectators who could decode them. Therefore, it was not only the actual participants who would be able to place themselves in the crowd, but also those

heightened political feeling having been, at least momentarily, forgotten in the sense of enjoyment of the other entertainments on offer. Nevertheless, it also indicates a tension that undermines the apparently smooth identification being advanced between the cinema audience and the mourners on screen. This tension is present in the *Limelight*'s suggestion that it was not the continuation of the demonstration that brought mourners to the Bohemian but the narcissistic pleasure of seeing oneself on screen, of picking oneself out of the crowd. This kind of pleasure was a particular feature of the earliest films, but early films also purposely employed the figuration of the crowd as an instance of identification.

In any event, it is unlikely that many individual mourners could have identified themselves among the throngs depicted in long shot by the funeral film. With the camera viewing events from among the spectators, it could, however, help re-create for its audience their participation in the funeral as a group by reproducing their

49 '30,000 Mourners: Incidents in Yesterday's Mighty Funeral: Facts and Figures: 3 Miles of Marchers in Massed Formation', *EH*, 1 October 1917.
50 'Thomas Ashe: Funeral in Dublin Yesterday: Impressive Scenes: Enormous Crowds Throng the Streets', *Freeman's Journal*, 1 October 1917.
51 *Freeman's Journal*, 2 October 1917.
52 *Irish Limelight*, 1, 12 (1917), cover.

53 *Irish Limelight*, 2, 4 (1918), 15.

who could fill in this 'back-story', those who would have wanted to be in the crowd and who, as a result, became virtual participants. These films worked on the desire to see oneself as a participant, whether or not one actually had been present at the event, and provided a semi-public context in which to experience this mediated participation.

When exhibited as political propaganda in jingoistic shows, the Boer War films engendered protest among nationalist audience members and displays of loyalty among unionist members. On the other hand, such *Irish Events* specials as *The Funeral of Thos. Ashe* seem more directly to offer the possibility of fostering 'a national spirit in Eirinn'. These latter films could be used to imply identification between the spectator and popular protest. In the period between the 1916 Rising and the War of Independence, GFS seems to have ensured its audience by being more obviously favourable to the nationalist cause. A 1918 listing of *Irish Events* specials features: *Irish Sinn Féin Convention*; *Funeral of Thos. Ashe*; *Release of the Sinn Féin Prisoners*; *South Armagh Election*; *Consecration of the Bishop of Limerick*; *Funeral of the Late John Redmond, M.P.*; and *Waterford Election*. 'It has been proved', boasts the advertisement, 'that topicals such as any of the above will attract a larger audience than a six-reel exclusive'.[53] In the context of wider political events and especially when they took the place of the featured attractions at the top of the cinema programme, as *The Funeral of Thos. Ashe* did at the Bohemian Picture House on 30 September 1917, the political significance of these films becomes more fully visible.

Research for this essay was made possible by funding from the Irish Research Council for the Humanities and Social Sciences.

'I will acquire an attitude not yours'
Was Frederick MacNeice a Home Ruler and Why does this Matter?

David Fitzpatrick

'Just another bourgeois liberal,
I would have said. Although
he was a great Home Ruler,
in his day.' Nick laughed.
'Not a popular position for a
Protestant clergyman, surely?'
'Carson hated him. Tried to
stop him being made bishop.'
'There you are: a fighter.'[1]

This exchange appears in John
Banville's melodrama *The
Untouchable* (1997), where
Victor Maskell (Anthony Blunt's
world-weary double-agent,
incongruously grafted onto Louis
MacNeice's Irish roots) discusses
his father with Nick, another
hybrid figure who turns out to be
the Fifth or Sixth Man. Banville's

1   John Banville, *The Untouchable*,
    rev. edn. (London, 1998), 72.
    Jon Stallworthy, *Louis MacNeice*
    (London, 1995) [hereafter,
    Stallworthy, *LM*] is among the eight
    authorities acknowledged by Banville
    (406).

John Frederick MacNeice
(1866–1942), Bishop of Down
and Connor and Dromore
(1934–42), probably late 1930s.
Photo: MacNeice Collection,
Carrickfergus Museum.

The young clergyman with his extended family, probably taken in Clonsilla, County Dublin, c. 1895. Photo: MacNeice Collection, Carrickfergus Museum.

account, though a travesty of what scholars have written about Frederick MacNeice,[2] demonstrates the pervasiveness of his posthumous reputation as an heroic outsider within the 'Black North'. Critics and biographers concur that Louis MacNeice's attitudes towards religion, morality, politics, and above all Ireland, were profoundly influenced by those of his clergyman father. Louis was both attracted and repelled by the unity and humanity of his father's world-view, sustained by his serene faith in Christ as peacemaker and reconciler. The rector (later bishop) is almost universally portrayed as a tolerant if puritanical southerner, courageously opposing all forms of sectarianism and violence, abhorring both revolutionary republicanism and Ulster unionism, and supporting Home Rule.[3] Admittedly, Frederick MacNeice's early association with the Society for Irish Church Missions to the Roman Catholics, notorious for its 'aggressive' campaign of proselytism in both Connemara and Dublin, casts some doubt upon his liberal and non-sectarian

credentials. However, it has been surmised that his parents' bruising experience of sectarian conflict while missionary teachers on Omey Island, culminating in the family's fabled flight in 1879,[4] left Frederick (then thirteen years old) with a lifelong detestation of sectarian confrontation and intolerance.[5] His mental world as an adult was that of a liberal Protestant nationalist, fundamentally at odds with the political outlook of his congregations and neighbours in Belfast and Carrickfergus.

Louis MacNeice's supposed childhood experience of alienation within Protestant Ulster is often cited in explaining his youthful repudiation of its values and symbols, his romantic identification with the West of Ireland, and his sympathy with non-violent nationalist and anti-imperialist movements. By this account, while rejecting his father's religion and morality, Louis paradoxically embraced much of his outlook on Ireland and Irish politics. The rector's presumed support for Home Rule is crucial to this widely held analysis of the poet's Irishness and

2   I have chosen the forename Frederick rather than John since the latter name seems almost never to have been used in his signature until his elevation to the bench of bishops in 1931 (though John alone appears on the birth certificate). His lifelong alternation between the initials 'F. J.' and 'J. F.' is notorious, exhibiting a family disposition to live uncomfortably with any particular name: see Stallworthy, *LM*, 5. In the notes that follow, father and son are referred to respectively as 'FM' and 'LM'. The form McNeice was invariably used until 1913, when he broke with family practice by adopting the less Scottish variant MacNeice, while sporadically using the more contracted form in signatures.

3   See, for example, Terence Brown, 'MacNeice: Father and Son', in Terence Brown and Alec Reid, eds., *Time was Away: The World of Louis MacNeice* (Dublin, 1974), 21–34 (23); Terence Brown, *Louis MacNeice: Sceptical Vision* (Dublin, 1975), 8–10; Albert Haberer, *Louis MacNeice, 1907–1963: L'Homme et la Poésie* (Talence, 1986), 15; Edna Longley, *Louis MacNeice: A Study* (London, 1988), 19, 22, and '"Defending Ireland's Soul": Protestant Writers and Irish Nationalism after Independence', in Vincent Newey and Ann Thompson, eds., *Literature and*

Nationalism (Liverpool, 1991), 198–214 (199); William T. McKinnon, *Apollo's Blended Dream: A Study of the Poetry of Louis MacNeice* (London, 1971), 9–10; Seán McMahon, 'A Heart that Leaps to a Fife Band: The Irish Poems of Louis MacNeice', *Éire–Ireland*, 11, 4 (1967), 126–39 (129–31); Robin Marsack, *The Cave of Making: The Poetry of Louis MacNeice* (Oxford, 1982), 1; Stallworthy, *LM*, 34. Among the few critics who have examined Frederick MacNeice's influence on Louis *without* the explicit attribution of nationalist sentiments are Peter McDonald, *Louis MacNeice: The Poet in His Contexts* (Oxford, 1991) and also William T. McKinnon, in his enigmatic but suggestive reappraisal of 'The Rector's Son', *Honest Ulsterman*, 73 (1983), 34–54.

4   By a family account summarized in Stallworthy, *LM*, 5, a fracas in Claddaghduff on 23 March 1879 led immediately to the 'flight from Omey': 'The following night, friends of the McNeices brought a coach to the mainland side of Omey strand, and William, Alice, and their eight children were driven the sixty miles to Galway and put onto the Dublin train.' In reality, William Lindsay McNeice appears to have departed alone, leaving his family in a state of siege on the island for several months: see Alice Jane to William McNeice, 22 May 1879, in *Galway Express*, 7 June 1879. I am grateful to Dr. Miriam Moffitt for drawing the existence of this letter to my attention.

political vision. Yet the supporting evidence is remarkably threadbare, being restricted to assertions by Louis himself, ambiguous utterances by his father in later life, and academic inferences based on possibly misleading extracts from published sermons and addresses. This article will assess the credibility of such interpretations, present fresh evidence indicating a very different political viewpoint, suggest reasons for the subsequent disregard of such evidence, and assess the consequences for our understanding of the poet's Irishness and for our reading of some of his most celebrated works.[6]

The most authoritative testimony to Frederick's nationalism is that of his son, whose imaginative and finely embroidered autobiographical writings have been so widely accepted at face value as a reliable factual source: 'My father was one of the very few Church of Ireland clergymen to be a Home Ruler. This was another reason for despising Co. Antrim and regarding myself as a displaced person. Sometimes this feeling caused an inner conflict in me.'[7] Another passage implies that Frederick's reputation as a Home Ruler was established before 1917, when his second wife was thought 'very daring' for having gone 'so far afield as my father — especially as he was a Home Ruler'.[8] These recollections were written in 1940, two decades after Home Rule had ceased to be a practical option (except for six counties of Ulster), and they reflect the 33-year-old poet's renewed respect for his father and for many aspects of both southern Ireland and Ulster. Slightly earlier testimony may be found in *Zoo* (1938), where Frederick (as a 'pacifist' and a 'Home Ruler') is set apart from Ulster's 'patronising and snobbish' gentry, that 'inferior species';[9] and also in 'Auden and MacNeice: Their Last Will and Testament' (1936):

I leave my father half my pride of blood
And also my admiration who has fixed
His pulpit out of the reach of party
    slogans
And all the sordid challenges and the

mixed
Motives of those who bring their drums
    and dragons
To silence moderation and free speech
Bawling from armoured cars and carnival
    wagons.[10]

It is notable that Louis's numerous evocations of his boyhood give no particular illustrations of his father's nationalism, and that (in Stallworthy's words) 'neither his letters home [from preparatory school] nor his parents' letters to him mention the worsening situation in Ireland'.[11] When at home, he appears to have paid little attention to political conversations, for his sister Elizabeth recalled that 'there was so much talk in the house about Carson and the [Ulster] covenant that he must have heard it though he never in later years seemed to have any memory of doing so. Of course, he heard the history of it later on'.[12] It is difficult to avoid the conclusion that Louis MacNeice's account of his father's supposed nationalism was based on adult rather than childhood observations.

It is a curious fact that Frederick MacNeice himself never advocated or endorsed Home Rule in his many published booklets and sermons. As Christopher Fauske has guardedly averred, 'MacNeice had gone to Carrickfergus with a reputation as a Home Ruler, a reputation bolstered by his stance against the Covenant, but of his politics he actually said nothing in public throughout his life'.[13] Though not strictly accurate, as I shall show, this assessment highlights the difficulty of defining the political stance of one whose politics were avowedly non-partisan. The only text that has been cited as a direct affirmation of nationalism, as distinct from a disavowal of (Unionist) party politics, is Frederick's engaging historical sketch of Carrickfergus (1928):

The extension of the franchise in 1884 made inevitable some form of Home Rule for Ireland ... Election after election gave similar results. That surely was

Frederick and his brother Ferguson John. Photo: MacNeice Collection, Carrickfergus Museum.

5 This interpretation is implicit in Stallworthy's superbly crafted biography, and explicit in Fauske's statement that 'his experience of the flight from Omey led the man later to understand the dangers of division': Christopher Fauske, *'Side by Side in a Small Country': Bishop John Frederick MacNeice and Ireland* (Newtownabbey, 2004), 4.

6 This article originated in a paper delivered to the superb conference held at the Queen's University of Belfast, in September 2007, to celebrate Louis MacNeice's centenary. There I benefited greatly from discussions with (among others) Jonathan Allison, Terence Brown, Edna and Michael Longley, Rev. J. R. B. McDonald, Peter McDonald, and Jon Stallworthy. I am especially grateful to Jane Leonard for her perceptive comments on drafts of this article. I am also indebted to the custodians of several private collections as well as many public libraries and archives; to Jon Stallworthy for permission to quote unpublished correspondence in the Bodleian Library, Oxford, where Judith Priestman was an invaluable guide; and to Helen Rankin for her generous treatment of a demanding visitor and for permission to cite material and reproduce photographs in the Carrickfergus Museum,

a writing on the wall. It was thought, however, that such warnings and verdicts could be disregarded. Arguments were reiterated for more than a generation which were a denial of the assumed meaning of democratic government. The true entity, it was urged, is Great Britain and Ireland. It is the majority in that unit that should count ... Ireland in so far as it was educated and rich was against Home Rule! Such arguments, and they had a very Prussian ring about them, did duty for a time.

MacNeice went on to dismiss Edward Carson's initial confidence that resistance in Ulster 'could defeat, and not simply delay, the whole Home Rule policy', and to deplore the growing acceptance of partition as the Ulster leaders themselves 'began to think

The rector and his second wife, Beatrice, in Carrickfergus. Photo: MacNeice Collection, Carrickfergus Museum.

MacNeice Collection (the source of all illustrations accompanying this article).

7 LM, *The Strings are False: An Unfinished Autobiography*, ed. E. R. Dodds (London, 1965), 223.

8 LM, *Strings*, 62.

9 LM, *Zoo* (London, 1938), 80.

10 LM, *Collected Poems*, ed. Peter McDonald (London, 2007), 732 [hereafter, *CP*].

11 Stallworthy, *LM*, 65. This report is currently unverifiable, as most of LM's early family correspondence was withdrawn from the Bodleian Library in December 1995. Many early letters will however appear in the *Selected Letters of Louis MacNeice*, ed. Jonathan Allison (London, forthcoming 2008).

12 Elizabeth Nicholson, 'Trees were Green', in Brown and Reid, eds., *Time was Away*, 11–20 (15). In *Strings*, however, LM claimed that 'remembering my father and Home Rule, I said I thought Carson was a pity', when challenged for his views by a 'tipsy American soldier' on a train in spring 1919 (71); he also recalled having 'heard political arguments' before the Great War, which 'were all about Orangemen and Home Rulers' (53). Elizabeth's sensitive and detailed recollections of her parents and brother stopped short of attributing nationalism

along Nationalist lines'.[14] On the face of it, this analysis demonstrates that Frederick was not merely an opponent of partition, but a pragmatist who accepted, however reluctantly, the necessity for Home Rule. We shall return to the question of whether as a younger man he had indeed, like the prophet Daniel, accurately divined the ominous writing on the wall of Belshazzar's palace, '*mene, mene, tekel, upharsin*': 'God hath numbered thy kingdom, and finished it. Thou art weighed in the balances, and found wanting. Thy kingdom is divided, and given to the Medes and the Persians.'[15]

The practical proof of Frederick's nationalism, liberalism, and non-sectarianism, as expounded by a distinguished procession of MacNeicians, relates mainly to four episodes: his public refusal to sign the Ulster Covenant in

September 1912; his espousal of an ecumenical 'League of Prayer for Ireland' between 1920 and 1924; his initiation of a similar campaign in 1935–36 in response to renewed sectarian conflict in Belfast; and his successful resistance in the same period to the government's proposal that the Union flag should officiate perpetually over Carson's grave in St. Anne's Cathedral.[16] In each case, scholars have drawn inferences from Frederick's words and actions which are by no means self-evident. Opposition to the Ulster Covenant implied rejection of the threat of violence as a political tool, but not approval of any particular political programme. Collaboration with other Protestant clergymen, in two ecumenical and non-partisan campaigns for reconciliation, was likewise consistent with unionism as well as nationalism. Finally, Frederick's refusal to sanctify Carson's legacy in the form of a flag raises the issue of which aspect of Carson's political career gave offence to his fellow southerner. In order to test the implications of these episodes for our understanding of Frederick MacNeice's politics, we must first re-examine the historical record.

As rector, Frederick joined several other local ministers on a committee to make 'arrangements for the celebration of Ulster Day in Carrickfergus' in 1912, though, 'in the absence of the text of the Covenant', he insisted that attendance at the various church services should not entail automatic endorsement of that document.[17] When addressing his congregation in St. Nicholas's church, he undoubtedly caused a sensation by declaring that he personally (like others who approached the issue 'primarily from the Church's standpoint') would not sign the Covenant, feeling that 'Ireland's greatest interest is peace, and they shrink from a policy which, as is avowed, in the last resort, means war — and worse still, civil war'. Such a course would tend to 'intensify the bitterness that many of them hoped was fast dying away'.[18] This final passage from the sermon was extracted by Frederick himself

in *Carrickfergus*, with a comment which conceals as much as it reveals: 'The ministers of religion in Carrickfergus, in permanent charges, did not sign the Covenant. They represented a minority, negligible indeed in numbers, whose conscientious scruples exposed them at the time to some adverse criticism.'[19] In a celebrated response, a butcher on the Select Vestry remarked: 'That was a grand sermon the Rector gave us. But he spoiled it all at the end by telling us he wasn't going to sign the covenant.'[20]

Oddly, no scholar appears to have scrutinized the omitted elements of that 'grand sermon', which reveal its author to have been an orthodox and unrepentant unionist. The rector declared that the opposition to Home Rule was 'democratic', working men being united by 'a common conviction that Home Rule would be a death blow to the industrial life of Ireland. In this opposition they are joined by the farmers of Ulster, and I may add of Ireland'. Even Nonconformists in Ireland (unlike Britain) opposed Home Rule, because 'they know this country, its history, its circumstances'. MacNeice eloquently endorsed the widespread fear that a predominantly Roman Catholic parliament 'could not be trusted to do justice to a Protestant minority', citing the examples of Quebec, Italy, France, and Spain:

> Is it any wonder that the Irish Roman Catholic has been described as a rebel whose feet are in British fetters and whose head is in a Roman halter? ... Are not the Bishops the patrons of the Party? Are not the Priests, almost as a rule, the chairmen of the local branches of the United Irish League?

Citing the absence of lay protests against enforcement of the infamous *Ne Temere* decree regulating 'mixed' marriages, he asked, 'Isn't the fear of the Irish Protestants a reasonable fear?', rejected all previous Irish parliaments as 'ghastly failures', and asserted that 'Ireland has self-government just as

to Frederick, while stating that 'his political opinions differed widely' from those of 'the Northern people whom he served' (14).

13 Fauske, 'Side by Side', 15.

14 FM, *Carrickfergus and Its Contacts: Some Chapters in the History of Ulster* (Belfast, 1928), 70, 75. Publication was preceded by full weekly serialization (in a prominent position and an unusually large font) in the *Carrickfergus Advertiser* [hereafter, CA], 27 January to 29 June 1928.

15 Daniel 5:25–28.

16 See, for example, George Rutherford, 'John Frederick MacNeice', *Carrickfergus and District Historical Journal*, 7 (1993), 38–46; Stallworthy, *LM*, esp. 34–37, 172–74; Fauske, 'Side by Side'.

17 CA, 6 and 20 September 1912.

18 CA, 4 October 1912; quoted in Stallworthy, *LM*, 35, and in many other studies.

19 FM, *Carrickfergus*, 72. The Covenant was, however, signed by Frederick's curate, Robert Newett Morrison, and by the two Presbyterian ministers at nearby Woodburn: Ulster Covenant, signature sheets (on line), Public Record Office of Northern Ireland [hereafter, PRONI].

20 Nicholson, 'Trees', 15.

21 *CA*, 4 October 1912.
22 Letter from Lady Elizabeth Nicholson, quoted in McKinnon, 'Rector's Son', 53.
23 *Ulster Guardian: Organ of the Liberal Party in Ireland* (Belfast), 5 October 1912 (second leader). In November 1921, the rector assisted at the dedication of a Presbyterian memorial to the *Ulster Guardian*'s ex-editor, Major William H. Davey from Carrickfergus: *CA*, 3 September 1920 (obit.), 25 November 1921.
24 *CA*, 3 October 1913.
25 *CA*, 29 May 1914.
26 See lists of officers in *CA*, 14 June 1912, 10 July 1914, 18 June 1915, 14 July 1916, 3 August 1917, and 28 June 1918. He assumed the same office in the Carrickfergus Unionist Club in 1914, but not in the following year: *CA*, 20 February 1914, 6 March 1915.

England and Scotland have'. MacNeice predicted that 'as the masses advance in prosperity and in education the desire for Home Rule and the interest in agitation will die away'. Meanwhile, 'let no word be spoken, let nothing be done to wound the feelings of our Roman Catholic neighbours ... One of the chief reasons we oppose Home Rule is because we believe it would lessen individual liberty ... And because such are our ideals, therefore, we recognise the rights of others, whether majorities or minorities, to think their own thoughts and be true to their own convictions'.[21]

MacNeice's exposition of the case for the Union is utterly conventional in its terminology and assumptions, blaming nationalist disaffection on lack of education and on clerical domination, detecting signs of opposition to Home Rule among respectable Catholics, deploring all policies tending to undermine the gradual process of Anglo-Irish reconciliation, and echoing the ideals of liberty and toleration embedded in the 'Qualifications of an Orangeman'. Far from detecting 'a writing on the wall', MacNeice in 1912 still adhered to those very arguments with their 'very Prussian ring' which he was to formulate and dismiss so scathingly in 1928. By using the passive voice to express the failed Unionist position that he had once espoused, Frederick managed to mislead credulous posterity without actually lying. Like his children, he was an accomplished rhetorician who knew when and how to be economical of truth. As Elizabeth observed so acutely: 'Both Louis and his father were very complex people, I think, and it was often hard to understand what was in their minds (though their minds were in many ways so different).'[22] Contemporaries, of course, were not so easily misled. When praising his 'brave act' in declining to sign the Covenant, a liberal weekly pointed out that 'Mr. McNeice's Unionism is of too staunch a character and has been too often manifested in his parish for him to risk being dubbed a Home Ruler because he is commended in a Home Rule organ'.[23]

Frederick's sleight of hand was not an

exercise in casuistry, but an understandable attempt to antedate the process by which he had gradually moved from optimism about the future of the Union to the conviction that it was doomed. On the first anniversary of Ulster Day, he reaffirmed his unionist ideals:

Why may not we claim, and rejoice to claim, that we are Irish, no matter what our remote ancestors called themselves, and that while remaining Irish we also can be members of a wider unity, sharers in the strength and glory of the Empire for which our fellow-countrymen have made such splendid sacrifices?

By then, however, he felt that 'a great wrong has been done on our side' through appeals 'to race hatred, and to religious, or rather irreligious bigotry'.[24] Seven months later, he warned a parade of Ulster Volunteers that they must submit, *in extremis*, to the mandate of the electorate:

And speaking as a Unionist to Unionists I say — 'We must make it plain, abundantly plain, that while we are opposed to the change of Government now proposed, and with which we are now threatened, we are no less opposed to the thought of a war which would range us against the soldiers of the King, or against our fellow-countrymen '.

In the absence of an agreement, 'then there's no alternative but to demand that the question be submitted to the people of the United Kingdom. In making such appeal we know there are risks'.[25] The rector's public commitment to the Union was expressed in his annual election as a vice-president of the East Antrim Unionist Association between 1912 and 1918.[26] But the threads of his unionism were beginning to unravel as Carson's Ulster campaign shifted inexorably from all-Ireland rejection of Home Rule towards provincialism and acceptance of partition.

By December 1918, when 'the people' of Ireland returned a republican majority

In the rectory garden.
Photo: MacNeice Collection,
Carrickfergus Museum.

while Lloyd George's coalition parties swept the polls in Britain with a bipartisan commitment to Home Rule, the existing Union had clearly lost its popular mandate. Four years later, with partition a *fait accompli* and the Union 'gone', the rector reminded the Orangemen of Carrickfergus that 'the old order whether for good or evil has passed away'. Ireland remained 'a unity geographically' and to some degree commercially, but 'political unity' could never be secured through military force. It could come only through the consent of the people themselves, North and South ... If it became clear, as it might, that what was desired was a political unity, within the British Commonwealth ... then it should be possible, with goodwill on both sides ... to find a way to a final settlement of what has been known as the Irish question.[27]

27 FM, *For Peace with Honour between North and South: An Address to Orangemen ... on Sunday, 9th July, 1922* (Carrickfergus, 1922).

Farewell to soldiers leaving Carrickfergus railway station during the Great War. Photo: MacNeice Collection, Carrickfergus Museum.

28 Consider the excited responses of numerous journalists and politicians to Bloomfield's recent revelation that he does 'not find the idea of some form of Irish unity or closer association — almost certainly after my time — in any way unthinkable in principle. But what is conceivably acceptable in principle would have to be mutually acceptable in practice'; *Irish Times*, 24 August 2007. In January 1922, Craig expressed a similar view to Michael Collins: 'For the present an all-Ireland Parliament was out of the question, possibly in years to come — 10, 20, or 50 years — Ulster might be tempted to join with the South ... If he were convinced it were in the interests of the people of Ulster, he would frankly tell them of his views, but should such an eventuality arise, he would not feel justified himself in taking part in an all-Ireland Parliament'; Cabinet Conclusions, 26 January 1922, in PRONI, CAB 4/30/9, quoted in Patrick Buckland, *James Craig, Lord Craigavon* (Dublin, 1980), 57.

Far from being a repudiation of his earlier beliefs, this cautious contemplation of unity by consent, within the Commonwealth, in the indefinite future, echoed the sentiments of a procession of liberal unionists in Northern Ireland stretching from Sir James Craig to Sir Kenneth Bloomfield. It is astonishing that, even today, such innocuous utterances arouse a frenzy of excitement as signs of either progressive or subversive thinking, according to viewpoint.[28]

In July 1920, when Frederick MacNeice inaugurated his first ecumenical crusade for peace and reconciliation among all religious groups throughout Ireland, no practical possibility remained of keeping 'southern Ireland' within the Union. Rather than campaigning against partition, also a lost cause, the rector attempted to mobilize Christians of all denominations,

'Roman Catholic and Protestant alike', in a succession of enterprises designed to create 'a new outlook in Ireland' and to curtail the accelerating cycle of reprisals and counter-reprisals. The campaigns of 1920–24 and 1935–36 were exceptional only for their non-sectarian rhetoric, which carefully avoided both selective ascription of blame and expressions of selective empathy. Otherwise, the Christian message broadcast by MacNeice and his fellow ministers was indistinguishable from that of countless sermons addressed to all denominations. The appeals for priestly collaboration in these crusades brought no response, though in late 1920 the parish priest of Carrickfergus commended his Protestant fellow clergymen for helping to keep the town 'free from the evils that have arisen out of the recent labour troubles', by 'assiduously preaching peace and a Christian

Louis and his stepmother in wartime Carrickfergus. Photo: MacNeice Collection, Carrickfergus Museum.

tolerance of the rights of their neighbours'.[29] MacNeice's Catholic counterpart as bishop of Down and Connor (Dr. Daniel Mageean) continued to portray his flock as guiltless victims of Protestant persecution while uttering his own separate appeal for peace in July 1935.[30] Though MacNeice's campaigns drew rapturous responses from the Catholic press and indignation from some diehard Ulster loyalists, his private assessment of Catholic leaders such as Bishop Mageean was far from laudatory. As 'Daddie' wrote to Louis and his then wife, Mary, in September 1936: 'Yes, I fear the R.C. bishop & I were a bit mixed up in the English papers. He was given credit for some of my appeals for fairmindedness &c, & I suffered occasionally because of some of his criticisms & attacks!'[31] Though an eloquent advocate of ecumenical co-operation and eventual reunion among the Protestant

29 Revd. George McKay to Very Revd. Patrick Convery, published in *CA*, 10 December 1920 (from *Irish News*).
30 *Belfast News Letter* [hereafter, *BNL*], 22 July 1935.
31 FM to LM and Mary, 16 September 1935: LM Papers, Box 7, Bodleian Library (uncatalogued).
32 FM, *Reunion: The Open Door: A Call from Ireland* (Belfast, 1929), esp. sermon delivered in Trinity College, Dublin, 10 March 1929.
33 Carrickfergus RFC Minute Book, 13 September 1909: in private hands. I am grateful to Jane Leonard for alerting me to this fact. Sixteen years later, both the rector and the then parish priest attended the funeral of a former Congregationalist minister: *CA*, 20 February 1925.

Louis and his first wife, Mary, standing with Frederick and Beatrice at Bishopscourt, Waterford, 25 August 1932. Photo: MacNeice Collection, Carrickfergus Museum.

34 Grand Chaplains and Deputy Grand Chaplains [hereafter, GC and DGC] of the Loyal Orange Institution included the Methodist cosignatory of the appeals of 1920, James Ritchie, DGC for Fermanagh (1938–41) and a leading Antrim Orangeman in 1920; and three of the fifteen clergy who distributed 'A Message of Peace' to Belfast shipyard workers in July 1935 (William Shaw Kerr, dean of Belfast, GC for Ireland; Canon Robert Cyril Hamilton Glover Elliott, DGC for Ireland from 1940; and John McCaffrey, a Methodist minister and DGC for Londonderry City in 1922): *CA*, 16 July 1920; *BNL*, 23 July 1935; Grand Orange Lodge of Ireland [hereafter, GOLI], *Report of the Half-Yearly Meeting* (December 1935, et al.).

35 *Northern Whig*, 22 February 1936. These rolls of honour, though ascribed to the 36th (Ulster) Division in the board's statement, were presumably the eight volumes of *Ireland's Memorial Records, 1914–1918* (Dublin, 1923). For letters to MacNeice from the deans of eleven English cathedrals, in response to his enquiry about precedents (not in file), see FM Papers, Bodleian Library, dep. c. 759.

36 FM to LM, 24 February 1936: LM Papers, Box 7, Bodleian Library (uncatalogued).

Churches, Frederick was less sanguine about the prospects for rapprochement with the Church of Rome.[32] His only known public collaboration with a priest involved the game that was later to obsess his son: in September 1909, both the rector and the parish priest of Carrickfergus were enrolled as 'Vice-Presidents or Patrons' of the town's Rugby Football Club.[33] Otherwise, Frederick's non-sectarian partnerships were restricted to other Protestant denominations, several of his clerical collaborators being prominent Orangemen.[34]

MacNeice's reputation as a liberal dissentient from Ulster orthodoxy was enhanced by the decision of the Belfast Cathedral Board, which he chaired, to withhold permission for the permanent display of a Union flag above Carson's tomb. The ostensible justification for resisting Craigavon's proposal was the lack of precedent in other cathedrals for setting such emblems over civilian tombs or monuments, and the board eventually mollified its detractors by agreeing to place a flag over the memorial rolls of honour at the west end of the cathedral.[35] Remarking on this compromise in a letter to Louis, 'Daddie' found 'much to rejoice over: the Clergy, in the main, and the respectable people, include the working men, are with us'.[36] It is far from clear that the bishop had been primarily responsible for the board's unexpected declaration of independence, and the *Irish News* mused that 'of all those who were engaged in the matter on the side of the Board he [the bishop] was probably the least consulted or responsible'.[37] MacNeice was nevertheless criticized by a Catholic correspondent for approving Carson's burial in the cathedral in the first place, so allowing St. Anne's to 'become a fashionable graveyard for "sham statesmen"'.[38] 'Sincere Churchmen' of his own persuasion also deplored the conversion of a place of worship into a 'Mausoleum' for 'political pilgrims', while pointing out that 'Ulster pilgrims from Monaghan, Cavan and Donegal' would inevitably be reminded of 'a broken covenant'.[39]

MacNeice was careful to avoid any public slight upon Carson's memory, expressing 'deep regret' at the death of 'one of the outstanding figures of his day, and one whose great gifts of head and heart gave him a place of his own in the hearts of multitudes'.[40] The bishop played an admittedly minor part in the funeral service, uttering the final words of prayer after the lowering of the coffin, over which a Methodist minister had emptied the contents of a 'silver bowl presented by the Northern Ireland Cabinet and containing soil from each of the Six Counties'.[41] This narrative was characteristically improved by Louis in a letter to Anthony Blunt, alleging that his father 'had to sprinkle earth from the 6 Northern Counties on the coffin of ... his lifelong bête noir [*sic*] out of a large gold chalice.'[42] Despite the bishop's measured responses to these rituals of veneration in his cathedral, there is no reason to doubt the sincerity of his remark (in a letter to his daughter) that Carson would 'be remembered as the man who broke the unity of Ireland'.[43] This statement is generally assumed to refer to the unity promised for Ireland under Home Rule. In reality, it surely arose from the sense of betrayal felt by former 'Southern Unionists' with respect to those who opted for Home Rule in Northern Ireland, while ditching their southern brethren and antagonizing nationalists throughout

Ireland. This betrayal was aptly symbolized by the selection of soil from six counties (rather than nine or thirty-two) in tribute to the arch-partitionist. Carson's offence was to shatter Frederick MacNeice's dream of winning over Catholic minds and hearts to the ideals of the Union.

If Frederick MacNeice was never a Home Ruler, neither was he unreservedly liberal in matters of faith. Not only was he reared among the 'soupers' (proselytizers) and 'jumpers' (converts) of Connemara, but he followed the example of his parents and three elder siblings by taking paid employment with the Irish Church Missions. After two years' training and teaching with the Missions in Dublin, he went on to teach at a Protestant boys' orphanage in Ballyconree, near Clifden in County Galway, close to the Mission school where his future wife, Lily, worked for over a decade before their marriage in 1902.[44] Frederick's father remained as a scripture reader with the Missions in Dublin until his retirement in 1905; and his widowed father-in-law, a zealous convert from Connemara, lived with Frederick and Lily in Belfast until his death in the following year. Far from severing his connection with the Missions and their aggressive sectarianism after the mythic flight from Omey, Frederick maintained an active connection with the society throughout his career. His congregations in Belfast and Carrickfergus raised subscriptions for its work on at least seven occasions between 1903 and 1928; he served as an executive member of the Belfast Auxiliary for several years after 1907; and, like most Irish bishops, he became a vice-president of the society, upon his elevation in 1931.[45]

On several occasions, he invited T. C. Hammond, an incorrigible proselytizer and Orangeman who became superintendent of the Dublin Missions, to address his congregation in Carrickfergus.[46] Hammond was among the preachers at a festival in aid of the Missions staged in thirty-one churches in the Belfast region on 10 February 1935, the Sunday after Frederick's enthronement

37 *Irish News*, 14 December 1935; cf. *BNL*, 14 December 1935.

38 Francis J. McKenna to FM, 28 October 1935: FM Papers, Bodleian Library, dep. c. 759.

39 Extract from 'Parish Notes' by Canon Marable Williams (incumbent of St. Luke's and precentor of Connor), in *Lower Falls Magazine*, December 1935: *Irish News*, 5 December 1935, 6 January 1936.

40 *BNL*, 23 October 1935, echoing his tribute to the living statesman in *Carrickfergus*, 71: 'He had great qualities of head and heart; he had courage, enthusiasm, quickness, eloquence.'

41 *In Memoriam: Last Honours to Ulster's Leader, Lord Carson of Duncairn* (Belfast, 1935), 5, 24–25, 29, from *Belfast Telegraph*, 26 October 1935; *BNL*, 28 October 1935.

42 LM to Blunt, 9 December 1935, as quoted in Stallworthy, *LM*, 173.

43 Nicholson, 'Trees', 16.

44 See Society for Irish Church Missions to the Roman Catholics [hereafter, ICM], annual MSS Agency Books, 1856–1905: ICM, Dublin.

45 ICM, annual *Report of the Committee ... with a List of Subscribers to the Irish Branch* (Dublin, 1896–1939): virtually full set at ICM, Dublin.

46 FM, Diary, 12, 13 July 1913: FM Papers, Bodleian Library, dep. c. 758; *CA*, 25 October 1918. Thomas Chatterton Hammond (1877–1961), curate, then incumbent of St. Kevin's, Dublin (1903–19); superintendent, Dublin Missions (1919–36); principal, Moore

Theological College, Sydney (1939–49); archdeacon of Sydney (1949–61). During his years at St. Kevin's, 'more converts had been received out of the Church of Rome than in any other parish church in Ireland': A. E. Hughes, *Lift up a Standard: The Centenary Story of the Irish Church Missions* (London, 1948), 38; see also Warren Nelson, *T. C. Hammond: Irish Christian; His Life and Legacy in Ireland and Australia* (Edinburgh, 1994) and *Clergy of Dublin and Glendalough: Biographical Succession Lists*, comp. J. B. Leslie, ed. W. J. R. Wallace (Belfast, 2001), 700.

47 *BNL*, 9, 12 February 1935.

48 MacNeice was elected as a DGC for Belfast for the years 1903–09 (except 1905) and as a district chaplain for Belfast Districts nos. 6, 10, 3, and 1 for various years (successively as a member of Lodges 410, 631, and 938). Though giving various initials, it may be shown that all of these returns refer to FM. See officer lists in GOLI, *Reports*, and in annual reports of Belfast County Grand Lodge.

49 *CA*, 6 August 1909.

50 *CA*, 21 April 1911; LOL 1537, Minute Books and Roll Books: in private hands.

51 *CA*, 12 July 1912. Five men were eventually imprisoned following attacks on thirty-three houses, only four of which belonged to Protestants: *CA*, 27 December 1912.

52 *CA*, 2 February, 1 March 1912.

53 *CA*, 15 January 1915.

54 *CA*, 26 March 1920. He

in St. Anne's Cathedral. Though unable to attend the annual meeting of the Belfast Auxiliary on the following day, the bishop wrote: 'that the work of the Missions was primarily a work of witness for the faith in its primative [*sic*], uncorrupted form ... He knew well that all who supported the Missions in Belfast and elsewhere had as their aim the uplifting of Christ, the King of Love.'[47] In his campaigns for peace and reconciliation, Frederick applied the techniques perfected by Alexander Dallas, founder of the organization, whose marketing strategies included massive mailshots and distribution of a multitude of handbills to supplement incessant exhortations from the pulpit and through the press. Though MacNeice's parishes in Belfast and Carrickfergus presented limited opportunities for the conversion of Roman Catholics, the rapid growth of secularism among nominal Protestants presented a more urgent challenge to ministers struggling to save souls through more efficient dissemination of the gospel of Jesus Christ as expounded in the 'open Bible'. He came to see secularism rather than popery as the principal threat to salvation, just as partition supplanted Home Rule as the principal threat to liberty in Ireland. Though modifying his strategies as external conditions changed, Frederick MacNeice remained profoundly true to his youthful ideals in both faith and politics.

The quintessential embodiment of both all-Ireland unionism and evangelical Protestantism was, of course, the Loyal Orange Institution. It is, therefore, scarcely surprising that MacNeice belonged to three Orange lodges in Belfast between 1903 and 1909, acting as a chaplain for no less than four of the city's ten District Lodges.[48] Within a year of his controversial appointment as rector, 'Bro. Rev. F. J. McNeice' was welcomed by the brethren of Carrickfergus Total Abstinence LOL 1537, whereupon 'he assured the lodge of his sympathy and assistance whenever called on'.[49] Though an infrequent attender who

appears never to have paid dues, he presided over the unfurling of a new banner on Easter Monday, 1911, served as lodge chaplain for the years 1912 and 1913, and last appeared on the roll in 1915.[50] After a rare outburst of violence against Catholic windows in July 1912, he exhorted a meeting of local Orangemen and unionists to 'assist the local [Constabulary] force in the event of assistance being required'. The meeting obediently resolved to enrol the brethren and club members as special constables, who were to help preserve the peace 'by placing themselves each evening in different parts of the town'.[51] Lily MacNeice had recently presided over an Orange bazaar, after which both husband and wife were effusively thanked for their services. In response, Frederick reminded the brethren that

the society was not a political, but a religious society. They opposed Home Rule because they believed it meant Rome Rule ... Convince them that Home Rule was not Rome Rule and that it would benefit the country and they would be Home Rulers. And to prove that Home Rule really was Rome Rule, he spoke about the Ne Temere decree as an example.[52]

In January 1915, LOL 1537 was one of the few local organizations to publish a resolution of condolence after Lily's death, in remembrance of 'the valuable services rendered to the lodge by her, and of the esteem and respect in which she was held by the brethren'.[53] As late as March 1920, though evidently no longer an active Orangeman, MacNeice revisited the Orange Hall to witness his sister-in-law unveiling a roll of honour for local brethren who had served in the Great War.[54]

Frederick took little interest in the ostentatious celebrations each Twelfth of July, and was only once reported among the chaplains seen 'on or near the platform', at the Castlereagh field in 1902. He therefore witnessed the epic confrontation between Colonel Edward Saunderson and Thomas

Sloan which eventually led to the creation of the Independent Orange Order and a serious rift in Belfast unionism.[55] MacNeice seems never to have had a public part in the East Antrim demonstrations, apart from apologizing for his absence in 1920.[56] Though addressing at least three July 'anniversary services' for Orangemen in Carrickfergus in 1909, 1917, and 1922,[57] he used these occasions to preach the virtues of temperance, tolerance, internationalism, reconciliation, and respect for law and order, paying scant attention to the customary commemorative themes. Already, in 1909, he wished 'to God we had the strength and wisdom not only to remember but to forget. Surely there is no true wisdom in recalling year after year the story of wrongs inflicted on Protestants in 1641, or any other rebellion'.[58] For MacNeice, Orangeism was a potentially useful tool in promoting godliness, sobriety, and respectability among workers of all Protestant denominations, offering access to a far broader range of souls than that reachable from the pulpit of St. Nicholas's. Like so many Orange chaplains, he regarded the order as a 'religious' rather than a 'political' institution, concentrating on the cultivation of morality within the lodge rather than the assertion of supremacy outside it.

So long as Orangeism did not stand in the way of Irish unity within the Union, MacNeice remained involved. As the institution followed Carson's lead towards acceptance of partition, he dissociated himself from its inner counsels and transferred his fraternal enthusiasm to freemasonry. By 1935, he was regarded as an antagonist by many leading Orangemen, especially when he applauded clerical 'aloofness from party politics' and warned that 'the influence that is gained by a clergyman in the political sphere lessens his influence in the spiritual sphere'.[59] In response to widespread protests, some by his own clergy, he declared:

> I was not thinking of the Orange Order, and I was not insinuating anything

whatsoever ... The Orange society is not a political society ... I know well that many most excellent men have used the opportunity, which membership of the society has given them, in advocating the basic principles of Christian revelation.[60]

MacNeice himself was, of course, among those 'most excellent men'. When pursuing his campaign for peace in the shipyards a few weeks later, he made a 'very special appeal' to Orangemen, offering a remarkably positive account of the order:

> I witnessed the great procession on the Twelfth of July. It was magnificent. I was deeply impressed by its orderliness, one might say, the solemnity of it. I feel sure that the thousands of splendid men whom I saw at close quarters were and are lovers of order and justice and peace. I believe that those men, worthily led, could more than any other men now find a way, an honourable way, out of a vicious circle. I implore the leaders of the Orange Society not to let such an opportunity go by.[61]

At the very apogee of his liberal reputation, it is clear that the moral ideals of Orangeism had not lost their allure for the lord bishop of Down and Connor and Dromore.

The father that Louis MacNeice put behind him as a rebellious adolescent, and re-embraced as a tormented adult, was not in my view the liberal, non-sectarian nationalist with whom MacNeicians have become so familiar. During Louis's early childhood, Frederick remained a conventional all-Ireland unionist and Orangeman. As Louis matured, his father's political and religious priorities were changing in response to the catastrophic effects of war and revolution, all other objectives being subordinated to the necessity for peaceful reconciliation of both international and local antagonists. Frederick's post-war sermons and addresses were remarkable in the Irish context not for their content but for their irenic tone,

was one of five clergymen present, 'in addition to the brethren', at the unveiling by Dorinda Florence, wife of the second Mrs. MacNeice's brother, Thomas MacGregor Greer. She was a leading figure in the Ulster Women's Unionist Council and (by 1927) in the Carrickfergus Women's Loyal Orange Lodge No. 7: *CA*, 7 January 1927. Mrs. Greer was perhaps the 'Belfast aunt, lately engaged in gun-running', with whom Louis and John Hilton dined in September 1928: LM, *Strings*, 269; Stallworthy, *LM*, 124–25; Dorinda MacGregor Greer, Diary, 24–25 April 1914, in PRONI, D/2339/4/8/23.

55 *BNL*, 14 July 1902.

56 *CA*, 16 July 1920.

57 *CA*, 16 July 1909, 13 July 1917, 14 July 1922. In 1927, he conducted another anniversary service but engaged a special preacher for the occasion: *CA*, 15 July 1927.

58 *CA*, 16 July 1909.

59 *BNL*, 1 July 1935; Rutherford, 'John Frederick MacNeice', 41–42.

60 Letter from FM, 8 July 1935, in *BNL*, 9 July 1935.

61 *BNL*, 22 July 1935, reprinted in FM, *Our First Loyalty* (Belfast, 1937), 61–68. In 1938, however, he watched 'a very large procession', from the front of St. Thomas's rectory and then from the junction of the Lisburn and Malone roads, exclaiming 'But what does it all mean, and why are Clergymen in it?' See FM, Diary, 12 July 1938: FM Papers, Bodleian Library, dep. c. 758.

62 LM, *Strings*, 78–79; Stallworthy, *LM*, 71.

63 'Belfast' (September 1931) and 'Autumn Journal, XVI' (1938), in *CP*, 25, 138.

64 LM, 'Northern Ireland and Her People', 148–49, in LM, *Selected Prose of Louis MacNeice*, ed. Alan Heuser (Oxford, 1990), 143–53.

65 'The Gardener' (summer 1939), in *CP*, 188–90; LM, *Strings*, 47–48; LM, 'Childhood Memories' (recorded for BBC, Belfast, 2 July 1963), in LM, *Selected Prose*, 267–73 (269). Archie White's mark appears among the Carrickfergus signatures to the Ulster Covenant: PRONI.

66 'Belfast' (September 1931), 'Valediction' (January 1934), 'Autumn Journal, XVI' (1938), and 'Prologue' (1959) to 'The Character of Ireland' (uncompleted book of essays), in *CP*, 25, 10, 138, 779; cf. LM's jeer that 'the potboy priests and the birds of prey were still the dominant caste' in Dublin, September 1939: *Strings*, 213.

67 'The Truisms' (1961), in *CP*, 565.

from which all elements of rancour and partisanship were excised. Indeed, a neglected aspect of Louis's early rejection of his father is his adoption of a bitterly censorious style, whereas in later life he emulated his father's preference for measured words and balanced judgements. Yet, tolerant and broad-minded though he was, Frederick remained to the end a son of the Irish Church Missions, a loyal subject of the monarch, a celebrant of the moral and political mission embodied in the British Empire, and an upholder of many of the tenets of Orangeism. In rejecting his father, Louis was also rejecting the Loyal Orange Institution. This provides a vital subtext for that curious passage in *The Strings are False* where Louis (aged thirteen) panders to his headmaster at Sherborne by agreeing that the Twelfth was 'all mumbo-jumbo', thus offending a teacher from darkest Portadown: 'Oh this division of allegiance! That the Twelfth of July was mumbo-jumbo was true, and my father thought so too, but the moment Mr. Cameron [*recte* Lindsay] appeared I felt rather guilty and cheap.'[62] In truth, he was surely betraying not only his teacher but also his father, the former Orange chaplain. This could not be made explicit, since by 1940, when the account was composed, Louis was in effect collaborating with his father in the attempt to redraft Frederick's biography and to obscure the less palatable elements of his earlier career.

The poet's own view of Orangeism was becoming more benign, and closer to his father's attitude in later life. The Twelfth was no longer a nightmarish 'banging of Orange drums' or 'voodoo of the Orange bands / Drawing an iron net through darkest Ulster',[63] but 'an emotional safety-valve' or 'catharsis' for men who were privately 'quiet and unemotional'. The Orangeman's ideal, so Louis declared in 1944, was to be 'a decent wee man' — 'unostentatious, sober, industrious, scrupulously honest, and genuinely charitable'.[64] Echoes of Orangeism and the Irish Church Missions suffused Louis's poetry and prose throughout his career, as in the affectionate tributes to Archie White, rectory gardener and Orangeman,[65] and those Dallas-like references to 'the garish Virgin', 'your dolled-up Virgins', 'the garish altar', and 'cormorants / Waiting to pounce like priests'.[66] These elements belonged to the MacNeice heritage just as much as the virtues of sobriety, tolerance, breadth of vision, and hatred of violence with which they coexisted in Frederick's mental world. There was more in the celebrated 'box of truisms' than one might have supposed:

His father gave him a box of truisms
Shaped like a coffin, then his father died;
The truisms remained on the mantelpiece
As wooden as the playbox they had been
    packed in
Or that other his father skulked inside.

When the prodigal son returned to bless his parental home, it was the Orange verities of civil and religious liberty, symbolized by the open Bible, which 'flew and perched on his shoulders' and nourished the tree that 'sprouted from his father's grave'.[67]

Intrude

Snapped

Thomas Allen's Pulp Fictions

Seamus Deane

An exhibition of photographs cannot escape being an exhibition of photography. That is, the technology of reproduction, especially when it is highly sophisticated, as here, is always on show *as a technology*. The elaborateness of the set-up and the design is so painstaking that we feel we are looking at prints that bear the unmistakable mark of something individually handcrafted while also having the equal and opposite mark of the mass-produced, a mark that belongs to photography itself. These photographs present us with images from American pulp fiction (westerns, detective stories, war romances, science fiction) that initially illustrated the stories themselves and that have now been cut out and mounted, seeming to rise in three-dimensional space as in children's pop-up books, to be

photographed. But the crude figures don't entirely leave the wood-pulp pages in which they were first realized; their passage from print-illustration via cut-out arrangement to the two-dimensional photograph that dramatizes the relations between material and imaginative production provides a commentary on the capacity and the limits of representation.

In one sense these are images that are playful, familiar and even stale, refreshed by being drenched in a new technological wave. Yet they still transmit a sense of trouble, lightly indicated in the punning, ambiguous titles, repeated in the transgressions from image to book to the 'real', accelerating the allure they once had as popular stereotypes of men and women, precisely *because* they are so dated through being so knowingly updated — isn't this what 'retro' is? — into this glossy new medium. The criss-cross between book and photograph is at the heart of the comic element, with square-

jawed males and curvy females rising or striding from the dog-eared paper and limp covers into the afterlife/former life of the stereotype (*Intrude*), images that have been deeply imprinted into our consciousness by repetition in different popular media. The glaring typography of the book covers, spines, blurbs and titles and the well-thumbed pages indicate cheapness, mass-production values, sensationalism. But Thomas Allen's photographs are not at all derisive. They do, though, have a strange effect; these images, which once were so slick and modern, now appear as poses from the ancient ritual of being 'modern', of the limited repertoire of gesture developed in early mass-consumer production. Their self-conscious modernity now looks as sculpted and histrionic as the acting styles of the movies of the 1920s and 1930s. The clarity of the poses belongs to the world of sexual fantasy, to popular fiction and to the cinema. Allen reminds us of this by his

Stranger

miniaturization of the human figures or by the enlargement of the book sizes; the ratio between them, and the transition from the represented — especially when it makes claims to being 'realistic', tough-guy-no-nonsense-nothin'-fancy presentation — to the 'real' is always a fake but necessary element; you can't let anyone, man or woman, on to a screen or a page unless they are already made up as manly men or as sexy women. So the images are always front loaded; their startling obviousness is what alerts us to the gender weight they carry, although their popular appeal in part depends upon their ease, their refusal to appear to be carrying anything culturally 'heavy' or 'symbolic'.

Cowboys and detectives of the hard-boiled kind in dime novels, like cowboys and gangsters in movies, are specifically American heroes with specifically American locations for their colportage morality. The open country of the Wild West or the wide

main street of the frontier town and its rowdy bar, with the frail swing-to doors that scarcely divide street from bar or the sober, solitary step of the law from the drunken uproar of the lawless, is a plainly charted territory, full of clear divisions between the natural and the civilized, rooted in a stalwart system of moral decisiveness that comes out of the barrel of a six-gun held by a man wearing a star (*Posse*). Coming through that door, which is more like a hinge or a membrane, the cowboy or gunman walks out of and into, into and out of, the real and imagined (*Stranger*, *Loaded*). The shoot-out for the sovereignty of the main street between the good and the bad man at high noon is the iconic image, although we must remember too the hidden audience of the fearful townsfolk that casts the unrinsable stain of the watcher, tense and ashamed, on the brightness of the image. And in these photos the implied (or explicit) onlooker, the viewer, belongs to that grouping; the very

Left: *Dark Hunger*

Right: *Jackpot*

act of looking sends a ripple of voyeurism across the photograph, itself the product of a watching eye, a lens, a chosen focus (*Dark Hunger*). The sidelong glance of the eyes indicates sexual desire but also a warp in that desire — sex for money, furtive secrecy, betrayal, the 'sexpot' pose of the femme fatale who is always unmarriageable (*Jackpot*, *Explorer*, *Breathtaking*). The strong male, in his army uniform or in his rumpled tough-guy pose, with his cigarette in the corner of his mouth and his desire in the corner of his eyes, is presented in such standard images as a dupe, trapped; yet his sexual success is indisputably one of the rewards for his toughness.

The sheer violence of the gangster or of war makes a Wild West morality appear more archaic and, as a consequence, more sentimentally prized. Killing is regularly eroticized in all media, but the taste for violence cannot always be presented as pathological. For it is a characteristic, as one example, of the city machine (both in the political sense, and as 'organized' crime), for which the tommy gun is the emblem; it is aimed at a specific target but can hit anyone and it leaves its acne everywhere, particularly on its companion machine, the motor car, shrouded in punctured chrome and glass, its slumped victims wreathed in sirens and lights. The morality of the sheriff or marshal has difficulty in surviving such conditions; those who embody it, like Raymond Chandler's Marlowe, are given to us as men who find themselves in a world where virtue itself has become archaic — and they with it. In the reversals of these stereotypes and locations, between high morality and low technology, high technology and low morality, the hero equipped with six-gun or tommy gun, the soldier or sailor at leisure out of the war zone where his moral solidarity can be challenged (see *Mate*, *Explorer*), we can see the American movie and publishing industries forging an ideology for American foreign policy. The

critical and frail linkages between sexual glamour, moral conduct and violence need to be soldered over and over again.

Violence is not disapproved of in these photos; it has an attraction that is obviously sexual and in which women — dames, broads, *femmes fatales*, 'nice' girls — play the assigned roles of the desired and of the desiring and provide the stimulus for that whole economy of action in which physical strength, usually allied with moral straightforwardness (and thus not a characteristic of the male detective), is celebrated. Boxing (echoed in the fist-fight that always leaves knuckles undamaged, see *Red*) is the sport in which violence can best be legitimized, open-air brawls turned into fenced rituals, with moral and

physical strength now menaced by intrigue, sexual temptation and urban corruption (*Knockout*, inside back-cover); the predators that surround a boxer wear big suits over thin frames, big overcoats draped over the suits, drink and smoke a lot, and still survive the boxer who usually finishes wheezing, shuffling, brain-dead, consumptive, his morality as ruined as his health. Of course,

if the boxer is white (like Gene Tunney), he can avoid all this, he can be not only moral but gentlemanly, possessed of a textbook expertise (*Spar*). He is really a sheriff or marshal; he needs to maintain his distance from his opponent and from the world; so he fights from the upright, open stance and favours the punishing, stern straight left.

In the conventional narratives where

Red

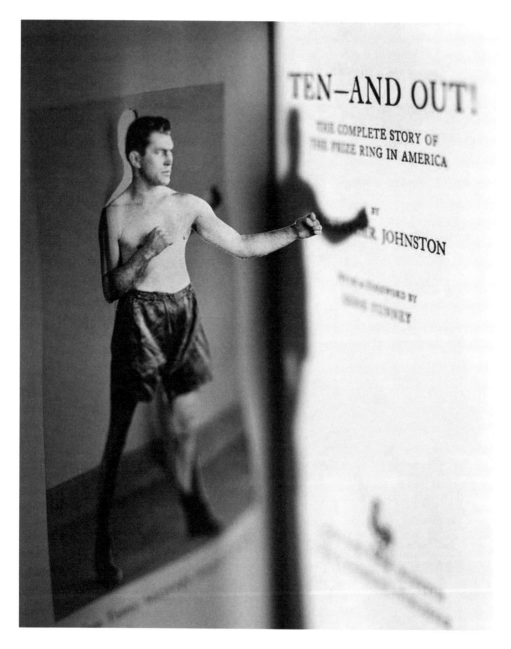

these images preside, the degradation
and complicity of women in a world of
unlawful violence is an inescapable, even
a stimulating, energy; whereas in a lawful
world, where violence is much more discreet,
then the function of women is to enforce
discretion in that and in personal and social
behaviour generally. It is the love of a good
woman that provides the male with the
sentimental education that makes him a
fit defender of that orderly world. In the
degraded world, the relationships of men
and women are sheerly sexual, commercial,
understood as forms of violence in which
the male always predominates because of
his greater physical strength; whereas the
converse is (almost always) the case in the
world of law and order. Gender is a value
system that works both ways, for and
against the licit/illicit. We clearly recognize

Fathom

cowboys, detectives and their dames or broads in today's war propaganda, give or take a few small changes in dress codes and a huge transformation in technology. Or, it may be that a deeper change has occurred. The belief that the reproduction of nature is more and more within our grasp revives the old belief in progress, now born again in the light of new economies and new technologies. This may have affected our notion of desire, turning it heliotropically towards the ambition to 'become all we can be', making us admirers of what drives people to be driven. The Big Sleep; the dream out of which the diver, horizontally trapped in the vertical riffling of the book pages and the theatre curtain, which merge into one another, forever seeks to surface, clasping the treasure box he has found, aiming for the moment of breaking the surface, of waking, which is to break into where we are, through the gloss (*Fathom*). But then that would be 'history', not representation, and would take away our treasured role as voyeurs, the watchers for whom the sharpest pleasure is not to be an agent. Let somebody else step out into high noon and become a counter-image of ourselves, one that we can watch from our dark inner room as it emulsifies, clarifies, comes up into focus.

Ivan Armstrong, *Ewa Skalska*, etching, 29.3 × 20.6 cm; Belfast Print Workshop © the artist.

Minding Ourselves
A New Face for
Irish Studies

Michael Cronin

The writer and critic Arland Ussher in the *The Face and Mind of Ireland* (1950) set about the not wholly original task of explaining Ireland to his English readers. Explanation and conflict are invariably the terrible twins of history, one arguing why the other is unavoidable. Thus, in Ireland and England, from Cambrensis to Céitinn, and from Fynes Morrison to Bernadette Devlin, the reasons for conquest or resistance are carefully rehearsed on the page, an indispensable counterpoint to the slaughter in the fields or the violence on the streets. Ussher is, however, writing in more peaceable times, his mid-twentieth-century Ireland a kind of Arnoldian haven of predictable unpredictability. The mood is more serene but much still needs to explained. In drawing up a psycho-social portrait of the Irishman, Ussher makes much of the former's 'artistic temperament'. This is, in Ussher's view, more a question of attitude than achievement and the returns are more imagined than real:

> The Irishman is a bohemian and a *je m'en foûtiste* [*sic*] in his way of living, somewhat of a play-actor (or 'playboy') alike in action and passion, seeing existence as a *show* — while remaining as far as possible uninvolved. No man is more realistic or cynical conversationally than the artist type of man, but with all his sense of reality he is usually a failure in actual life, because he is not oriented to a world of facts and duties; and the same is true of the Irishman — he is like the king who never said a foolish thing and never did a wise one.[1]

Ussher is all too obviously drawing on the time-worn binary of dreamy Celts and practical Saxons but what is important in the context of any discussion of the future of Irish Studies is that he believes the Irish are different. His book is turned towards a repeated affirmation of what we might term 'Irish exceptionalism', the ways in which the Irish are believed to be utterly distinct from the English and other Europeans. One reason for affirming the difference, though not one Ussher had in mind, was to persuade tourists to come and see what it was that made the Irish so different. Indeed two years after the publication of Ussher's book the Irish Tourist Board/Bord Fáilte was set up to see how the world of 'facts and duties' might profit from the reputation of the artistic type of men.[2] But what of Irish exceptionalism now?

In a four-year survey of more than 28,000 holidaymakers, entitled *Marketing Insights — Image of the Island of Ireland* produced in February 2006 by Tourism Ireland, the successor to Bord Fáilte, the authors of the report found that what mainly disappointed tourists was that Ireland was not 'unique enough'. Compared to many Eastern European destinations, Ireland fared poorly in conspicuous exoticism.

Mark Henry, Tourism Ireland's director of central marketing, noted in his comments on the results of the survey that for British tourists, 'Five or 10 years ago, Ireland was greatly different from their domestic holidays. Now a lot of retail outlets in Ireland are British, so tourists are less likely to see the sort of uniquely Irish-run stores that they might have seen eight or 10 years ago.'[3] If Irish cities looked remarkably like many other British and European cities, what was so exceptional about Ireland any more? Had the arrival of the world of 'facts and duties' in globalized Ireland meant that the only exceptionable thing about Ireland in the developed world was that it was unexceptional? This crisis of Irish exceptionalism is not, however, only a cause of concern for tourism marketing executives anxiously seeking bed-nights but has equally fundamental implications for the present state and future growth of Irish Studies.

Research thrives on enigmas and good research questions are ones we are generally at a loss to answer. If there were easy answers, there would be little point in expending time and energy trying to answer them. For this reason, Ireland for the last three decades of the twentieth century was deeply attractive as a site of scholarly inquiry. The country in the context of the developed world was an anomaly. First, there was the economic anomaly of a country which despite proximity to British markets and membership of the European Economic Community consistently failed to achieve satisfactory levels of economic growth, had the highest net outward migration rate of EEC member states and experienced record levels of public debt. Joe Lee's *Ireland: Politics and Society 1912–1985* was a forceful indictment of the scale of independent Ireland's economic failure, and the title of a collection of essays edited by Therese Caherty and published in 1992 was eloquent, *Is Ireland a Third World Country?*.[4]

Second, there was the social anomaly of a state in Western Europe that banned all forms of artificial contraception, prohibited civil divorce, made sexual activity between

1   Arland Ussher, *The Face and Mind of Ireland* (New York, 1950), 169; his emphasis.
2   Barbara O'Connor and Michael Cronin, *Tourism in Ireland: A Critical Analysis* (Cork, 1993).
3   Alison Healy, 'Tourists say Ireland not Unique Enough', *Irish Times*, 2 February 2006.
4   Joseph J. Lee, *Ireland 1912–1985: Politics and Society* (Cambridge, 1989); Therese Caherty, ed., *Is Ireland a Third World Country?* (Belfast, 1992).

David Connolly, *St Petersburg View*, lithograph, 41 × 31cm; Cork Printmakers © the artist.

consenting adult homosexuals a criminal offence and tolerated high levels of clerical interventionism in the educational and health services. The signal failure to separate Church and state and the aggressive policing of private morality made Ireland conspicuously different from the more general drift towards liberal legislation in post-war Europe.

Third, there was the seeming political anomaly of a country mired in ethnic conflict, linked to questions of religion and territory, where thousands of people lost their lives or were seriously injured and where militarization was an inescapable fact of everyday life in Northern Ireland. The presence of these 'wars of religion' in the pre-Bosnia, pre-9/11 secular vision of an Enlightenment world appeared both scandalous and perplexing. Therefore, as an economic, social and political anomaly, Ireland was puzzling to the growing numbers of students and scholars attracted to Irish Studies in the last three decades of

the twentieth century. The discourse of Irish exceptionalism that sustained Ussher in his musings on Irish history and character was equally applicable to the seeming aberrations of late modern Ireland. In this respect, then, Irish Studies did not have to look far to see why it was different from other country studies.

The difficulty for Irish Studies in the early twenty-first century is that what is different is that Ireland is no longer so different. *The Economist* declared in 2005 that Ireland was the best place in the world to live, while spectacular economic growth made Ireland by the dawn of the new century one of the wealthiest countries on the planet:

Between 1991 and 2003 the Irish economy grew by an average of 6.8 per cent per annum, peaking at 11.1 per cent in 1999. Unemployment fell from 18 per cent in the late 1980s to 4.2 per cent in 2005, and the Irish Debt/GDP ratio fell from 92 per cent in 1993 to 38 per cent

Raymond Henshaw, *Anushiya*, screenprint, 40.2 × 29.3 cm; Belfast Print Workshop © the artist.

in 1999. Throughout the 1990s Irish living standards rose dramatically to the point where the country is now, at least by some measures, one of the richest in the world, and has the fourth highest GDP per capita in the world.[5]

If Ireland was no longer so anomalous in economic terms, changes to social legislation in the 1990s, permitting, for example, the sale of contraceptives, removing the prohibition on divorce, and decriminalizing homosexuality, meant that Irish legislation in areas of private morality was closer to the European norm. The ceasefires of 1994 and 1997, the Good Friday and St. Andrews agreements, the decommissioning of weapons and most recently the establishment of a power-sharing assembly in Northern Ireland mean that military conflict is no longer a salient feature of political life on the island. But is what is good for Ireland, necessarily good for Irish Studies? If Ireland becomes more and more like any country of comparable size in the developed world, fully integrated into the global economy with the standard freedoms of a liberal democracy, is there any particular reason why Ireland should still remain worthy of investigation or analysis? Does the end to Irish exceptionalism spell the end of Irish Studies?

Disciplinary Expansion

Irish Studies needs to be reconfigured to take account of the new context in which Ireland finds itself, and that new circumstances offer new opportunities. It is no surprise that in trying to establish why Ireland was so different for so long, the disciplines that occupied pride of place in Irish Studies were history and literature. The historians could try and explain what had happened to make the Irish the anomalous crew that they were and the writers and literary critics could try and describe what it felt like to inhabit and make sense of this world of difference. Violent, political conflict involving a stand-off between British and Irish nationalism

5   Kieran Keohane and Carmen Kühling, *Cosmopolitan Ireland: Globalization and Quality of Life* (London, 2007), 1.

John Kelly, *Alien (Belfast)*, lithograph, 41 × 31 cm; Cork Printmakers © the artist.

6 Paul Gillespie, 'World more Integrated than ever in 2002 Despite Economic Turmoil', *Irish Times*, 13 March 2004.

invested historians and literary critics with even more authority as the polemicists on both sides sought to marshal the arguments of history and theory to lend credibility and authority to their positions. However, as the economic, political and social anomalies begin to recede from view what becomes more pressing are questions of typicality, generality and comparability. In other words, what becomes of increasing relevance is not the way in which the Irish were radically different from everybody else but rather now that they are like many other advanced developed societies, what can be learned from the similarities to these societies.

The A. T. Kearney/Foreign Policy Globalization Index ranks 62 countries (representing 96 per cent of the world's GDP and 84 per cent of the world's population) for 14 variables in 4 groupings: economic integration; personal contact; technological connectivity; and political engagement. Ireland emerged at the top of this index as the most globalized country in the world for three years in a row, 2000, 2001 and 2002.[6] In

this context, the narrow disciplinary focus of Irish Studies to date is no longer sustainable. This is not to say, for a moment, that history or literature have nothing to say about these altered circumstances, quite the contrary. However, it is now time for the full range of the human and social sciences (examples might be economics, sociology, psychology, business studies, modern languages, anthropology, philosophy) to be brought to bear on the subject matter of Ireland. In a sense, the fundamental shift in thinking is moving from the figure of typicality emerging against the ground of atypicality (hunting for elements of the 'modern' in Irish life and writing) to considering the figure of what is specific or atypical against the ground of typicality. Examples of the latter might be the specific role of the Irish military in post-Cold War international politics or the particular constraints around the soap-opera genre in minority-language broadcasting practices. In a report on the future of Irish Studies the group examining Irish Studies in the non-anglophone world identified the following core notions as needing the broader cross-disciplinary investigation envisaged here:

- **Transformation** (eg moving from one kind of economy to another, moving from a situation of violent conflict to one of relative peace etc.)
- **Hybridity** (Ireland's long experience of identity politics now more relevant than ever due to changing migration patterns)
- **Diversity** (the elements of Irish literature, culture and society that make a distinctive contribution to European and world culture)
- **Peripherality** (the experience of a small nation in the area of peacekeeping, development aid, UN power politics, EU negotiations etc.).[7]

These are all notions where an abundant body of research in the human and social sciences could both illuminate and invigorate Irish Studies and most importantly, ensure the area's continuing relevance to the major debates of our time.

The Diasporic and the Diffusive

If the object of Irish Studies has changed beyond all recognition, an embodiment of the change was Mary Robinson, whose election as president of Ireland signalled the advent of a markedly different set of values on the Irish political scene. One consistent theme of her presidency was the Irish diaspora. If Éamon de Valera was doomed to be forever associated with twirling maidens dancing at crossroads hops, Robinson would be linked to the candle in the window of Áras an Uachtaráin symbolically lighting the way at Christmas for millions of Irish emigrants to their island point of origin.[8] The gesture was not merely symbolic, however, and related to a desire to retrieve a lost or largely ignored dimension to Irish culture: the existence of a substantial Irish diaspora living outside of Ireland. In 1995, when President Robinson addressed the joint

Houses of the Oireachtas, the title of her speech was 'Cherishing the Diaspora'. This diaspora, remembered once a year in the photogenic bonhomie of St. Patrick's Day, was largely marginalized in Irish life and did not impinge in any major way on the consciousness of those living and practising politics on the island. Robinson argued that their role was more central than previously thought and that: 'Our relation with the diaspora beyond our shores is one which can instruct our society in the values of diversity, tolerance and fair-mindedness.'[9]

By 1996, 'Ireland and Its Diaspora' was the theme selected by the Irish Stand at the Frankfurt Book Fair, the most important book fair in the world, where Ireland was the main guest. The diasporic theme dominated the 1990s, as researchers, columnists, politicians of various hues drew public and scholarly attention to the lives and contributions of the millions of people of Irish descent who had settled in various parts of the world. In 2000 Alan Gilsenan and David Roberts directed a five-part television series entitled somewhat misleadingly *The Irish Empire*, where they offered viewers a summary account of the lives and fates of the Irish who had left the shores of Erin for a better life elsewhere.[10] Though the series did look briefly at the Irish presence in Africa, India, the Caribbean and South America, the focus was overwhelmingly on the anglophone countries of destination, namely Britain, the United States, Canada and Australia. This in one sense is hardly surprising, since that is where most of the Irish went. The anglophone hegemony has also traditionally been a feature of Irish Studies, where outside of Ireland itself scholars from Britain and North America have by and large tended to dominate the area.

The second major challenge for Irish Studies, therefore, in addition to disciplinary expansionism is to engage in a shift from diasporic to what I would term *diffusive* perspectives on Irish culture. What is intended by the term *diffusive* is a way of capturing the influence of Irish cultural

7   Christine Hunt Mahony, et al., eds., *The Future of Irish Studies: Report of the Irish Forum* (Prague, 2006), 26.

8   Olivia O'Leary and Helen Burke , *Mary Robinson: The Authorised Biography* (London, 1998), 196–98.

9   O'Leary and Burke, *Mary Robinson*, 196.

10 Alan Gilsenan and David Roberts, *The Irish Empire* (London, 2000), broadcast on BBC (1999).

Amelia Norman, *Mé Féin/Myself*, photo intaglio, 34.5 × 25 cm; Cork Printmakers © the artist.

activity on the different literatures, languages and polities of the world outside of the increasingly well-documented networks of an Irish anglophone diaspora. The focus of a diffusive perspective would in fact be exclusively on the Irish presence in the non-anglophone world. It is of course the non-anglophone world where most of humanity live, thus offering obvious growth opportunities for Irish Studies as an area of scholarship and inquiry. What then might research from a diffusive perspective look like and what kinds of things might it investigate? We might begin to answer this question by asking another. What do one of Spain's greatest living writers, a former president of Hungary and a German bankrupt all have in common? Javier Marías, Árpád Göncz and Felix Paul Greve have all translated works by Irish writers and contributed to the strong international reputation that Irish literature enjoys in the world today. One of the often forgotten paradoxes of writing is that it is translation rather than the originals themselves that make writers famous. Without the work of translators in many different languages most readers on the planet would not be aware of the writings of a Joyce, a Beckett, a Yeats, a Ní Dhomhnaill or a Doyle. The Irish themselves are generally unaware of the extraordinary amount of translation activity of Irish writing in English and Irish into other languages which is and has been going on over many centuries. In addition, the labours of those who do so much to promote Irish writing abroad through translation are generally unsung.

In 2002 a group of researchers in the Centre for Translation and Textual Studies at Dublin City University decided to build a public, freely available, online resource that would give the first true picture of the extent of the translation of Irish literature abroad and also give a public profile to the translators of the literature. The purpose was not only to provide information to scholars but to help organizers of Irish literary festivals in other countries with compiling reading lists and bibliographies, to assist literary translators in identifying whether a work had already been translated and what works needed to be translated, to help strengthen the growth of Irish Studies in non

Terence Gravett, *The Wearing of the Green*, screenprint, 28.7 × 21 cm; Belfast Print Workshop © the artist.

English-speaking countries and to highlight domestically an often invisible dimension to Irish writing. The project was named TRASNA from the Irish word for 'across', as the aim was to emphasize the way in which literature goes across the boundaries of nation, language and geographical region. There were two parts to the project, the online bibliography, which lists all the details relating to Irish works in translation, and the online biographical database known as TRASNABIO, which gives biographical information on translators of Irish literature.

The scale of what the research team has unearthed shows just how extensive the impact of Irish literature has been in translation. The online bibliography as it currently stands includes over 16,000 entries on 350 writers who have been translated into more than 60 languages. It is now the largest national database of its kind in the world. Jonathan Swift, for example, with 1,161 entries, has been translated into a total of 47 different languages. Among the languages into which Irish writing has been translated are French, Spanish, German, Italian,

Russian, Chinese, Japanese, Greek, Polish, Dutch, Turkish, Portuguese, Urdu, Serbian, Croatian, Catalan, Icelandic, Assamese, Sinhala, Gujarati, Bengali, Georgian, Persian, Romanian, Norwegian, Hungarian, Bulgarian, Ukrainian, Swedish, Lithuanian, Danish, Galician, Finnish, Macedonian, Kirghiz, Azeri, Telugu, Malayalam, Tadjik, Kannada, Basque, Albanian, Tamil, Indonesian, Moldovan, Slovak, Slovenian, Czech, Flemish, Scots Gaelic, Glosa, Hebrew, Korean, Latin, Latvian, Marathi, Occitan, Welsh and Uzbek.

The 200 plus online biographies that have been compiled of the translators show that the translators have come from all sectors of society, from national presidents to full-time revolutionaries, and are often acutely aware of the importance of bringing Irish writing to their own country in their own language. As TRASNABIO was the first translator biographical database of its kind anywhere, it was important to provide as much information as possible on the translators who do so much for the literature of a country that only rarely acknowledges

Veronica Wallis, *Gold is the New Green*, drypoint and aquatint, 31.3 × 22 cm; Belfast Print Workshop © the artist.

11 Rose-Marie Vassallo, private e-mail communication to Rita McCann, 17 January 2005.

their achievement or their contribution to the spread of Irish literature. As Rose-Marie Vassallo, a French translator of Peadar O'Donnell and Siobhán Parkinson, put it in an e-mail to one researcher:

> ... what I think is crucial is to make translation visible at long last! Dammit, people read translated texts everyday and never realize that those were born in another language! Our little persons are not that important, although, of course, translation being a living thing, we translators certainly are part of the context.[11]

Part of the context of how we think about Ireland must be how Ireland appears in different contexts. Over the last decade there has been much talk about the Irish diaspora and subsequently about Ireland as one of the most globalized countries on the planet. However, a great deal of the attention on Ireland's relations with elsewhere is bound up with the anglophone world, as can be seen in the kinds of news stories and celebrities that appear on Irish television screens and the kinds of literature that get into Irish bookshops. As a result, Irish people's interest in how others respond to them tends to focus almost exclusively on British and American reactions or opinions. All this may be understandable because of language economy (no need for translation) but it does the country and its literature a great disservice, in that other forms of reaction, other kinds of feedback, other ways of interpreting Ireland and its writing remain largely invisible in the public sphere in Ireland.

Part of this problem is to do with a lack of awareness, simply not knowing what is out there in other languages about Ireland and its culture. An aim of the TRASNA project was to bridge the information gap, so that absence of knowledge about what others are doing was no longer a barrier to cultural self-understanding. But what the project also showed is that the literary history of any country is at a very deep level not so much national as transnational. In other words, there was a need to move away from an obsessive concern with what happened to Irish writing on the island of Ireland and look more closely at what happened when it travelled elsewhere. Looking at how translated Irish literature influenced Czech responses to totalitarianism, for example, or the development of the Brazilian novel, would reveal as much about Home as about Away. As changed economic and political circumstances have made Ireland think again about its position in the world, it is important to show that in the very substantial body of Irish literature in translation there was an unique opportunity to move away from a predominantly Anglocentric diasporic purview to a more inclusive diffusive perspective.

Extrinsic and Intrinsic Alterity

Disciplinary expansion, the broadening out from a diasporic to a diffusive perspective, suggests the third major transformation for Irish Studies, which is to do with the shift from *extrinsic alterity* to *intrinsic alterity*. What I understand by this move is a greater attention in the study of Irish culture to those elements within the culture that speak of contact with the wider world rather than seeing foreignness, difference or alterity as elements without, or external to, the culture. In a sense, this paradigm shift mirrors the demographic shift in Ireland itself where a country with the highest net emigration rate in the European Union in the 1980s found itself with the highest net immigration rate by the start of the new century.[12] The foreign is no longer over there or beyond the waves (extrinsic alterity) but next door, across the street, in the local corner shop (intrinsic alterity). One immediate consequence of the arrival of new migrants in Ireland has been a dramatic increase in the number and size of foreign-language communities in Ireland and there are now estimated to be approximately 160 different languages spoken in the country.[13] The

altered nature of Ireland's linguistic present has brought in its wake a revisiting of Ireland's multilingual past. Evidence for this can be seen in two volumes of essays: *The Languages of Ireland*, co-edited by myself and Cormac Ó Cuilleanáin; and *Language and Tradition in Ireland*, co-edited by Maria Tymoczko and Colin Ireland.[14] Tymoczko and Ireland stress the flexible, adaptable and inventive nature of *tradition*, which they contrast with the tendentious reduction of the term by Eric Hobsbawm and others to essentialist, timeless immobility and go on to trace the outlines of a history of linguistic mixing for Ireland, which is explored in detail for a number of languages in *The Languages of Ireland*:

> From the pre-Celtic languages and the various dialects of the Celtic invaders to the integration of Latin after the conversion of the Irish to Christianity by British clerics, from the linguistic diversity encountered by Irish missionaries abroad to the assimilation of Scandinavian dialects introduced by the Vikings, the early history of Ireland is rich in multilingualism. The Anglo-Norman conquest brought still other languages to Ireland at the end of the twelfth century, with armies and settlers speaking more than one dialect of French, Occitan, Welsh, Flemish, and English.[15]

Thus, an effect of the marked increase in multilingualism in Ireland over the last decade has been to make visible elements of the Irish multilingual past, so that language change is presented less as a threat to the founding languages of the nation (to borrow a Canadian term) and a more as part of an Irish multilingual tradition that has been largely, though not exclusively, overshadowed by the rivalry between English and Irish. Developments in the present, then, are likely in the future to further bring to the fore the particular variety and richness of Ireland's multilingual past. Significantly, as part of the events to mark Ireland's presidency of the EU

12 Martin Ruhs, *Emerging Trends and Patterns in the Immigration and Employment of Non-EU Nationals: What the Data Reveal* (2004); http://www.policyinstitute.tcd.ie, accessed 23 May 2007.

13 Michael Cronin, 'Babel Átha Cliath: The Languages of Dublin', *New Hibernia Review*, 8, 4 (2004), 9–22.

14 Michael Cronin and Cormac Ó Cuilleanáin, eds., *The Languages of Ireland* (Dublin, 2003); Maria Tymoczko and Colin Ireland, eds., *Language and Tradition in Ireland: Continuities and Displacements* (Amherst and Boston, 2003).

15 Tymoczko and Ireland, *Language and Tradition in Ireland*, 1.

16 Paul Fussell, *Abroad: British Literary Travelling between the Wars* (New York, 1980), 11.
17 Bernard Share, *Far Green Fields: Fifteen Hundred Years of Irish Travel Writing* (Belfast, 1992).

The images that accompany this essay were exhibited in *10 x 10: Identity in Contemporary Ireland*, in the Lavit Gallery, Cork, in March 2008. The exhibition featured works by artists attached to the Belfast Print Workshop and Cork Printmakers.

in 2004, the European Commission building in Brussels hosted an exhibition curated by the poet Peter Sirr, which had as its theme the multilingual heritage of the island of Ireland. In this way, the growing emphasis on internal alterity, on already existing instances of internal interlingual and intercultural contact, opens up new areas of research and offers further cross-disciplinary for researchers in Irish Studies.

A further dimension to internal alterity is the post-Independence tradition of Irish travel writing. Paul Fussell, in *Abroad: British Literary Travelling between the Wars*, speaks of the diasporic conditions of inter-war literary modernism, the many English-speaking writers who decided I Hate It Here:

> This diaspora seems one of the signals of literary modernism, as we can infer from virtually no modern writers remaining where he's 'supposed' to be except perhaps Proust — we think of Pound in London, Paris and Italy; Eliot in London; Joyce in Trieste and Paris; Mann ultimately in the United States.[16]

For the American critic, literary modernism and twentieth-century travel writing owe their common origin to this unhousedness, this compulsive desire to be elsewhere. It is of course the permanency of being elsewhere that underscores the drama of exile, the condition of a Joyce or Beckett on the European Continent. Travel, however, defines itself in the moment of return, in the sighting of Ithaca after the trials of difference. This dimension to Irish nomadic experience in the twentieth century has, however, been curiously disregarded. Travel writing about Ireland has been the focus of critical attention, whether this writing has been work of Irish or foreign travel writers but, in contrast, commentary on travel writing by Irish writers travelling elsewhere in the modern period has been relatively sparse. The oversight is significant and points to a danger in Irish diasporic studies where only certain forms of movement are privileged in analysis. The permanent move to Canada but not the sojourn in Sicily, the emigrants' letters home from Australia but not the visit to Berlin, become objects of critical inquiry. Irrevocability risks becoming a talisman of authenticity (real travel [exile] v. superficial travel [tourism]) and concentration on the Irish in New Communities may narrow the world to encounters with varieties of anglophone Irishness and neglect individual Irish experiences of a multilingual and multicultural planet. And yet one of the striking features of Irish writing in the modern period has been the continual presence of the travel genre, from Jane Francesca Wilde's *Driftwood from Scandinavia* (1884) to Kate O'Brien's *Farewell Spain* (1937), Monk Gibbon's *Swiss Enchantment* (1950) to Seán O'Faoláin's *A Route to Sicily* (1953) and Colm Tóibín's *The Sign of the Cross: Travels in Catholic Europe* (1994). With the notable exception of Bernard Share's anthology of Irish travel writing, *Far Green Fields: Fifteen Hundred Years of Irish Travel Writing*, this is writing in the English and Irish language in Ireland that has been almost singularly absent as a distinct category from books, dictionaries, guides and anthologies of twentieth-century Irish literature.[17] Thus, rather than focusing continually on how others have seen the Irish, much remains to be done on how the Irish have seen others, a task that is all the more urgent as the others have now come to live amongst the Irish.

A changed Ireland of necessity means a changed Irish Studies. It means that Irish Studies must not only deal with a transformed present but must look afresh at the Irish past, both near and remote. Broadening the disciplinary range, embracing the diffusive dimension to Irish cultural impact and bringing experiences of internal alterity to the fore would mean, if nothing else, a new Portrait for the Irish Artist.

The Lane Bequest

Giving Art to Dublin

Fintan Cullen

1 *Irish Times*, 17 June
   1998. See also Robert
   O'Byrne, *Hugh Lane
   1875–1915* (Dublin,
   2000), 242–43, and
   Senan Molony, *Lusitania:
   An Irish Tragedy* (Cork,
   2004), 45.
2 Robert O'Byrne, *Hugh
   Lane's Legacy at the
   National Gallery of
   Ireland* (Dublin, 2000);
   see also Peter Somerville-
   Large, *1854–2004: The
   Story of the National
   Gallery of Ireland*
   (Dublin, 2004), ch. 20.

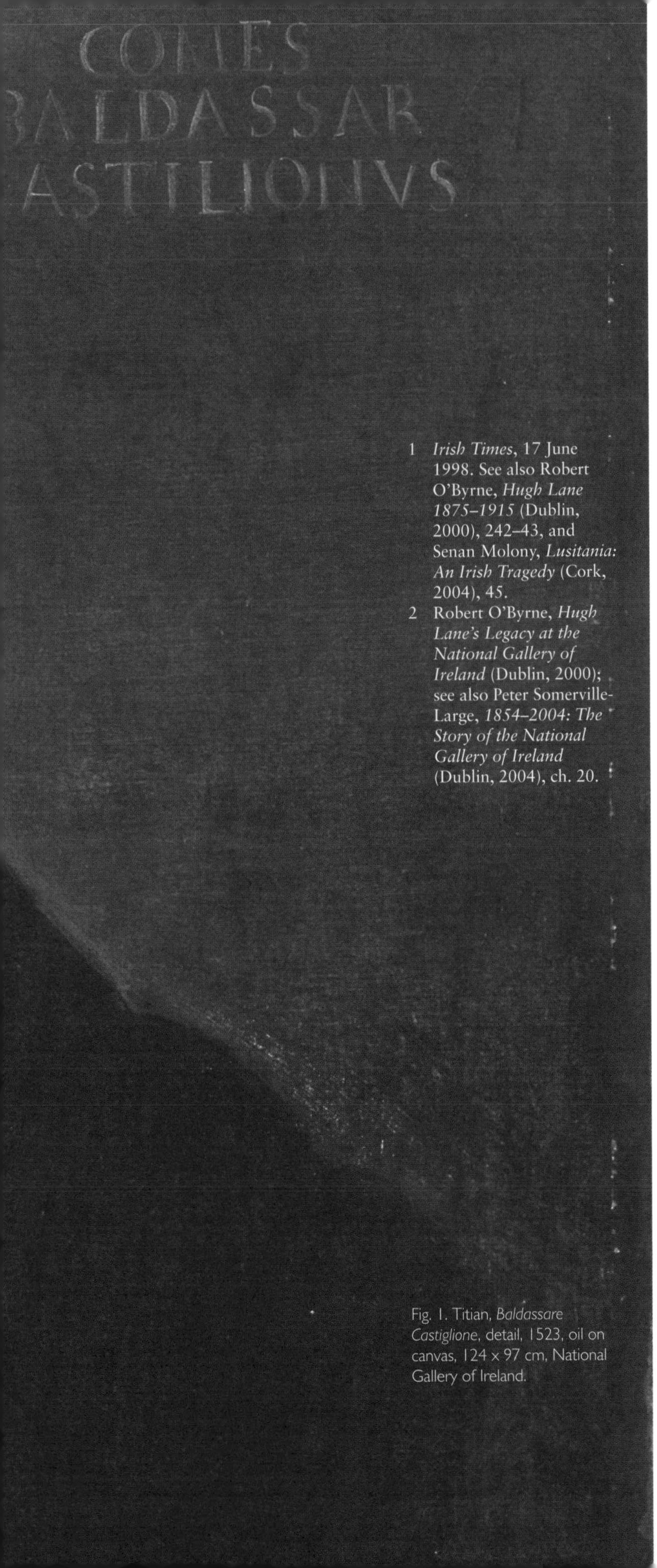

Rumour has it that in May 1915, when Sir Hugh Lane went down with the *Lusitania* off the Old Head of Kinsale, he had with him a selection of Old Master paintings, perhaps 'stored in protective lead cylinders'.[1] According to one story, Lane, at the time director of the National Gallery of Ireland, was returning from New York with a Rubens and a Titian; another account claims that he was transporting a crate of paintings by French Impressionist artists such as Claude Monet and Pierre-Auguste Renoir. We will probably never know. In 1914 Lane had placed on loan Titian's *Portrait of Baldassare Castiglione* at the National Gallery (fig. 1), which in 1917, two years after his death, became part of a generous bequest of over forty Old Master paintings.[2] In 1908, in the expectation that the city of Dublin would erect a purpose-

Fig. 1. Titian, *Baldassare Castiglione*, detail, 1523, oil on canvas, 124 × 97 cm, National Gallery of Ireland.

Fig. 2. Sir Hugh Lane in court uniform as Director of the National Gallery of Ireland, c. 1914, Dublin City Gallery/The Hugh Lane.

Fig. 3. John Butler Yeats, *George Moore giving his memorial lecture at the RHA*, 1904, pencil on paper, Berg Collection, New York Public Library.

built art gallery, Lane (fig. 2) had deposited thirty-nine paintings, including works by Monet and Edouard Manet, in a temporary Municipal Gallery of Modern Art. A couple of years later, annoyed by Dublin Corporation's failure to provide 'a suitable building' for his paintings in the city,[3] he bequeathed all thirty-nine works to London's National Gallery.[4] Controversially, however, after Lane's death an unwitnessed codicil to his will reversing this decision was found in his desk in the National Gallery of Ireland. Despite this 'codicil of forgiveness', as his aunt Lady Augusta Gregory represented it, the paintings are still legally owned by London.[5] However, a number of sharing agreements have been struck between the two cities, the most recent, dating from 1993 (updated in 2007), preventing the intolerable situation suggested by the *Burlington Magazine* that the paintings should be 'shuttled from one [gallery] to the other like the children of divorced parents'.[6]

The Lane saga — his collecting of art, the great philanthropic gesture of giving it away, and the ensuing cultural/political problems arising from his disputed bequest — have the makings of a stirring national tale. Lane's attempts to create a gallery of modern art for Dublin and bequeath it with some key French paintings from recent decades has been seen as a determinedly modernist act, which fits perfectly with the Celtic revival of the late nineteenth and early twentieth centuries.[7] Roy Foster in his biography of W. B. Yeats neatly explains the city's loss of the pictures in terms of the 'pusillanimity' of the Dublin Corporation, the 'enmity' of William Martin Murphy, a wealthy newspaper proprietor and the 'arrogance' of Lane himself.[8] In time, for Yeats and others, the saga became a stick with which to attack the British establishment and also Catholic middle-class Dublin, with the poet declaring that the Lane pictures were 'something that all Ireland wanted'.[9] But Yeats's remark was not made until five months after Lane's death.

3   The term 'a suitable building' appears in the famous codicil, written in 1915, in which Lane bequeathed the pictures to Dublin, see Thomas Bodkin, *Hugh Lane and His Pictures* (Dublin, 1956), 43. In his Prefatory Notice to the first *Illustrated Catalogue of the Municipal Gallery of Modern Art* (Dublin, 1908), ix, Lane had called for 'a suitable site' for 'the promised permanent building'. This catalogue was reprinted by the Friends of the National Collections of Ireland and the Hugh Lane Municipal Gallery of Modern Art, Dublin, in 1984.

4   Lane's problems in persuading Dublin Corporation to take an interest in supporting a gallery of modern art were not unique. In the first decade and a half

Fig. 4. Édouard Manet, *Eva Gonzalès*, 1870, oil on canvas, 191 × 133 cm, National Gallery, London.

Fig. 5, overleaf: detail.

of the century, many prominent curators in Germany, from Hugo von Tschudi in Berlin and Munich to Gustav Pauli in Bremen, ran into difficulties with civic authorities. The situation was no better in England, where, in Leeds and Brighton, supporters of modernism, such as Frank Rutter and Henry Roberts, were 'driven to fury' by conservative aldermanic taste. See James J. Sheehan, *Museums in the German Art World from the End of the Old Regime to the Rise of Modernism* (Oxford and New York, 2000), 167; Michael F. Zimmerman, 'A Tormented Friendship: French Impressionism in Germany', in Charles W. Haxthausen, ed., *The Two Art Histories: The Museum and the University* (New Haven and London, 2002), 162–82; Giles Waterfield, 'For an Excellent Purpose: Museums and Their Publics in Britain 1850–1914', Paul Mellon Lectures, 2007, No. 6, delivered at the National Gallery, London, 14 February 2007 (unpublished). See also John House, *Impressionism for England: Samuel Courtauld as Patron and Collector* (London, 1994).

I

Comments by two individuals who supported Lane's pictures being given to Dublin provide useful starting points for an appraisal of Lane's reasons for making his gift. One statement on what became known as Lane's 'Conditional Gift of Continental Pictures' is by the writer George Moore (fig. 3), which he made in a public lecture in December 1904

in support of Lane's gallery plans. The other comments are by Éamon de Valera, first in a letter to Lady Gregory on 15 June 1928, when he was leader of the opposition party Fianna Fáil, and then as Taoiseach a decade later, as recorded in a memorandum by Sir Edward Harding, permanent undersecretary at the Dominions Office in London.

In his lecture, Moore proclaimed that Manet's portrait of Eva Gonzalès (fig. 4) 'is what Dublin needs'.[10] The 1870 painting, had been borrowed in 1904 by Lane from the Parisian dealer Paul Durand-Ruel for exhibition in Dublin at the Royal Hibernian Academy (RHA) in Lower Abbey Street and to form the nucleus of a gallery of modern art. Two years later, Lane bought the painting from Durand-Ruel and it became one of the most famous of the thirty-nine contested pictures.[11] Kenneth McConkey has referred to Moore's statement as an 'extraordinary utterance',[12] and of course we must understand Moore's claim as part of a campaign for the creation of a gallery of modern art. But why did Moore think that the Manet was a picture that Dublin needed? For his lecture, delivered in the Large Exhibition Room of the RHA, and published two years later in 1906, Moore had been asked to choose between two Manets then on loan to Dublin and suggest which one should be purchased for the city. The two paintings were *Eva Gonzalès* and *The Old Musicians*, the latter now in the National Gallery of Art, Washington, DC. Turning to *Eva Gonzalès,* Moore said:

> To anyone who knows Manet's work it possesses all the qualities which we associate with Manet; the eye that sees clearly and quickly is as apparent in one picture as in the other ... Mademoiselle Gonzales' rounded white arm is ... courageously stated, for it is entirely without sexual appeal, and I am afraid the picture will to many people seem vulgar for that very reason ... That portrait is an article of faith. It says: 'Be not ashamed of anything, but to be ashamed.' Never did Manet paint more unashamedly. There are Manets that I like more, but the portrait of Mademoiselle Gonzales is what Dublin needs. In Dublin everyone is afraid to confess himself. Is it not clear that whosoever paints like that confesses himself unashamed; he who admires that picture is already half free — the shackles are broken, and will fall presently. Therefore I hope it

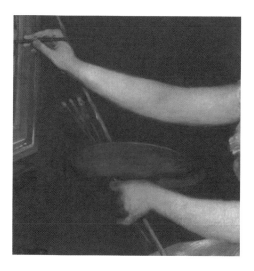

will be Mademoiselle Gonzales that will be purchased, for it will perhaps bring about the crisis we are longing for — that spiritual crisis when men shall begin once more to think out life for themselves, when men shall return to nature naked and unashamed.[13]

When first shown at the Paris Salon in 1870, Manet's portrait was severely criticized for representing the contemporary and not the ideal body, and the artist was accused on that account of ridiculing the respectable. A lot of attention focused on what one critic referred to as the 'impossible' arms of the sitter (fig. 5), which indicate 'inappropriate nakedness and the unseemly sexualisation of an identifiable contemporary woman',[14] which, interestingly, is at odds with Moore's observation that the 'rounded white arm ... is entirely without sexual appeal'.

To Moore, Manet was fundamentally revolutionary, and he greatly upset many in his 1904 Dublin audience by his candid admiration of the portrait and its painter. Adrian Frazier, in his recent biography, has argued that Moore regarded *Eva Gonzalès* as a suitable painting for Dublin city to purchase for its new gallery precisely because it showed 'courage, candor, and shamelessness, with an almost childish innocence'. In suggesting that the portrait exhorted the viewer to 'Be not ashamed of anything, but to be

5 Lady Gregory, *Sir Hugh Lane: His Life and Legacy* (Gerrards Cross, 1973 [1921]), ch. 17.

6 Editorial, *Burlington Magazine*, 126 (1984), 131. For a brief account of the various agreements, see Barbara Dawson, 'Hugh Lane and the Origins of the Collection', in *Images and Insights* (Dublin, 1993), 30. My thanks to Barbara Dawson for clarifying the latest agreement.

7 This is certainly the thrust of Jeanne Sheehy, *The Rediscovery of Ireland's Past: The Celtic Revival 1830–1930* (London, 1980), ch. 7.

8 R. F. Foster, *W. B. Yeats: A Life. I. The Apprentice Mage* (Oxford and New York, 1997), 497.

9 Quoted in R. F. Foster, *W. B. Yeats: A Life. II. The Arch Poet* (Oxford and New York, 2003), 26.

10 George Moore, *Reminiscences of the Impressionist Painters* (Dublin, 1906), 20; see also Adrian Frazier, *George Moore, 1852–1933* (New Haven and London, 2000), 339.

11 Martin Davies (and Cecil Gould), *National Gallery Catalogues: French School, Early 19th-Century, Impressionist, Post-Impressionists etc.* (London, 1970), 90. See also Caroline Durand-Ruel Godfroy, 'Durand-Ruel's Influence on the Impressionist Collections of European Museums', in Ann Dumas and Michael E. Shapiro, eds., *Impressionism: Paintings Collected by European Museums* (New York, 1999), 34–35.

12 Kenneth McConkey, 'Some Men and a Picture', in *Memory and Desire: Painting in*

Britain and Ireland at the Turn of the Twentieth Century (Aldershot, 2002), 224.

13 Moore, *Reminiscences of the Impressionist Painters*, 19–20.

14 Tamar Garb, *The Painted Face: Portraits of Women in France 1814–1914* (New Haven and London, 2007), 86 and ch. 2.

15 Frazier, *George Moore*, 338–44. R. F. Foster discusses Moore's 1904 lecture and what Moore has to say about Manet in '"Old Ireland and Himself": William Orpen and the Conflicts of Irish Identity', *Estudios Irlandeses* (2005), 43–44 (www.estudiosirlandeses. org, accessed 30 October 2007).

16 Quoted in Foster, *W. B. Yeats: A Life. II*, 302.

17 See, for example, the treatment of Mainie Jellett when she exhibited some abstract paintings in Dublin, Fintan Cullen, *Visual Politics: The Representation of Ireland 1750–1930* (Cork, 1997), 166–67. See also John Turpin, 'Visual Culture and Catholicism in the Irish Free State, 1922–1949', *Journal of Ecclesiastical History*, 57, 1 (2006), 55–77.

18 Quoted in Anne Kelly, 'The Lane Bequest: A British–Irish Cultural Conflict Revisited', *Journal of the History of Collections*, 16, 1 (2004), 102; quoting from National Archives, Kew, DO35/899/3, Dominions Office Memorandum, Sir Edward Harding, 19 May 1938.

19 George Moore, *Hail and Farewell: Vale* (London, 1933), 93. For the background to Moore's 1904 lecture, see F. S. L. Lyons, 'George Moore

ashamed', Moore appeared to his audience to be avowing a form of freethinking, hostile to Roman Catholicism and, indeed, to all forms of Christian bourgeois respectability. The presence of Manet's great portrait in Dublin would, for Moore, aid the spread of a welcome 'atheism and instinctual liberation'.[15]

In 1928 de Valera was being encouraged by Lady Gregory to take an interest in the Lane case. He wrote to her, claiming to be fully committed to founding a gallery to house the foreign paintings, a facility, he said, 'which in its architecture and in its content [would express] that love for the arts which has ever been a characteristic of the Gael'.[16] In a decade when deep social conservatism stifled innovation in the visual arts,[17] what did de Valera mean by this comment? Its insincerity becomes clear a decade later, when de Valera, then in power, acknowledged to Harding, an English civil servant, that, while he advocated the return of the Lane pictures to Ireland, he himself 'knew nothing about pictures, and did not know whether these were good or bad ones'.[18]

Despite Moore's and de Valera's support of the return of Lane's paintings to Dublin, neither man had much understanding of what Lane had been trying to do. In 1904, when Lane spoke to Moore about his wish to create a modern collection for Dublin, it was, he said, because, 'I am Lady Gregory's nephew, and must be doing something for Ireland.'[19] Lane's motives were romantic and admirable. In the summer of 1904 he organized a major exhibition of Irish art, both historical and contemporary, in London's Guildhall Art Gallery. A few years later, in 1908, he organized a more modest display of recent Irish art at the model Irish village of Ballymaclinton in London's White City. Lane believed that he was doing something for Irish art by organizing exhibitions, alerting people to what was being produced, and that, in purchasing recent French art, he was also making available a wider range of visual stimuli to both Irish artists and the Irish

public. Moore took this further; he regarded Lane's conditional gift to Dublin of Manet's portrait, in its singular shamelessness, as a subversive act. In his 1904 lecture, Moore would also exclaim:

I believe that a gallery of Impressionist pictures would be more likely than any other pictures to send a man to France, and that is the great point. Everyone must go to France. France is the source of all the arts ... We learn in France to appreciate not only art – we learn to appreciate life, to look upon life as an incomparable gift. In some café, in some Nouvelle Athènes, named though it be not in Baedeker nor marked on any traveller's chart, the young man's soul will be exalted to praise life. Art is but praise of life, and it is only through the arts that we can praise life.[20]

De Valera, on the other hand, had no sympathy for the Lane campaign *per se*. His interest was in politics, not in art. As his comments to Lady Gregory and to Harding imply, when it came to the repatriation of the thirty-nine Lane pictures, their importance was entirely political. In the 1938 memorandum, de Valera is recorded as admitting his ignorance of art. In paraphrasing Harding's comments, Anne Kelly has written that de Valera had suggested to London that:

'artistic circles' in Dublin were very anxious for the return of the pictures and their return would have an excellent effect on opinion in Ireland. He [de Valera] was assured that privately there was 'considerable sympathy' that the pictures should go to Dublin. It was hoped to take the matter up but that legislation would be required.[21]

Lane's gift (and Dublin wanting or not wanting the pictures) has been much discussed by art and cultural historians.[22] However, his reasons for wanting to give

certain pictures to Dublin remain obscure. Here, an effort is made to relate his wish to gift works of art to Dublin to similar acts of philanthropy in the city, prior to the great controversy over the building of a designated gallery in Dublin. But such philanthropic activity needs to be seen in the context of a wider history — that of the display of and access to art, most especially contemporary art, in Ireland in the period dating from the great Irish Industrial Exhibition held in Dublin in 1853.

II

Hugh Lane's efforts to bring contemporary art to Dublin were by no means unprecedented. In the aftermath of London's Great Exhibition of 1851 there had been comparable if smaller-scale exhibitions in several Irish cities.[23] Notably, in 1852 Cork's Exchange Building was enlarged to host a National Exhibition of the Arts, Manufactures and Products of Ireland, in which 567 works were displayed.[24] A year

and Edward Martyn', *Hermathena*, 98 (1964), 9–32.

20 Moore, *Reminiscences of the Impressionist Painters*, 42–43.

21 Harding's Memorandum, paraphrased by Kelly, 'The Lane Bequest', 102.

22 Bodkin, *Hugh Lane and His Pictures*; Sheehy, *The Rediscovery of Ireland's Past*, ch. 7; S. B. Kennedy, *Irish Art and Modernism, 1880–1950* (Belfast, 1991), ch. 1; Marta Herrero, *Irish Intellectuals and Aesthetics: The Making of a Modern Art Collection* (Dublin, 2007), ch. 2.

23 Leon Litvack, 'Exhibiting Ireland, 1851–3: Colonial Mimicry in London, Cork and Dublin', in Glenn Hooper and Leon Litvack, eds., *Ireland in the Nineteenth Century: Regional Identity* (Dublin, 2000), 57. In the same volume, see also, A. Jamie Saris, 'Imagining Ireland in the Great Exhibition of 1853', 66–86.

24 Ann M. Stewart, ed., *Irish Art Loan Exhibitions 1765–1927*, 3 vols. (Dublin, 1990), vol. 1, xv.

Fig. 6. John Hogan, *Hibernia with a bust of Lord Cloncurry*, 1844, marble, 148 cm ht., University College Dublin.

Fig. 7. James Mahony, *Queen Victoria and Prince Albert in the Fine Arts Hall of the Dublin Industrial Exhibition 1853*, 1853, watercolour on paper, 62.8 × 81 cm, National Gallery of Ireland.

25 Aluin C. Davies, 'Ireland's Crystal Palace, 1853', in J. M. Goldstrom and L. A. Clarkson, eds., *Irish Population, Economy, and Society: Essays in Honour of the Late K. H. Connell* (Oxford, 1981), 251.

26 The bringing together of the names of Dargan and Lane in terms of their art philanthropy was mentioned in 1924 in the *First Annual Report, The Friends of the National Collections of Ireland*, quoted in Harold Clarke and Aidan O'Flanagan, eds., *75 Years of Giving: The Friends of the National Collections of Ireland. Works Donated by the Friends to the Public Collections of Ireland* (Dublin, 1999), 11.

27 *Art Journal*, 5 (1853), 117, 162, 262, 302.

28 Dargan is reported to have offered £20,000 to the Royal Dublin Society to stage the Dublin Industrial Exhibition (about €6 million in today's money), see Somerville-Large, *Story of the National Gallery of Ireland*, 39.

29 Davies, 'Ireland's Crystal Palace', 269. See also, Catherine de Courcy, *The Foundation of the National Gallery of Ireland* (Dublin, 1985).

later, on 12 May, Dublin launched a huge Irish Industrial Exhibition on Leinster Lawn, where 1,356 works were shown. Commonly known as the Dargan Exhibition after William Dargan, 'Ireland's leading railway magnate' and the event's chief patron,[25] it was dominated by paintings and sculpture.

The Dargan Exhibition is a key event in the historical development of art institutions in Ireland, not least as it led directly to the creation of the National Gallery of Ireland and its emergence as the major depository of Old Master (as distinct from contemporary) paintings in the country. Importantly, however, the Dargan Exhibition had included a large collection of Irish and foreign contemporary works.[26] In 1853 the London-based *Art Journal* frequently lauded Dargan's 'patriotism' and noted that 'several schools of modern Europe will be worthily represented; and we repeat our conviction that the collection will be THE BEST THAT HAS EVER BEEN BROUGHT TOGETHER UNDER ONE ROOF'. The journal claimed the 'indefatigable zeal' of Dargan's secretaries 'in bringing together so large and excellent an assemblage of works of modern art to be absolutely astonishing'.[27] In turn, Dargan's generous backing of the exhibition acted as a stimulus to others to support public access to the visual arts.[28] Most obviously, a public testimonial to thank him for his patronage raised £5,000 towards the erection of a Public Gallery of Art, which in 1864 became the National Gallery.[29]

Like the Great Exhibition in London, Dublin's 1853 spectacle included an array of contemporary statues by Irish sculptors; indeed, contemporary sculpture had a particularly dominant presence in the exhibition. This interest in exhibiting recent art was especially emphasized in the accompanying exhibition catalogue, which invited 'the Irish public to make themselves

Fig. 8. Philip Henry Delamotte, *The Dublin Exhibition, 1853*, 1853, collodion negative, Swansea Museum, Wales.

acquainted with the Modern Schools, almost all of which were represented by examples of considerable excellence'.[30] In its discussion of the display of modern sculpture, the catalogue could claim that among

> these examples it is with no slight satisfaction that the Irish critic finds himself not merely attracted, but compelled to give the first place to one or two works of Irish artists, — men, too, who are not mere accidental offshoots of our people, but really and thoroughly Irish in whatever part of the world they reside.[31]

Works by John Hogan (fig. 6) and many other Irish artists were on display and can be seen on the left- and right-hand side of James Mahony's large watercolour, which celebrates Queen Victoria's visit to the Fine Arts Hall (fig. 7). Hogan's *Hibernia with a Bust of Lord Cloncurry,* visible on the immediate left of Mahony's painting, offered a suitably national theme: a coronet- and laurel-crowned female allegorical representation of Ireland affectionately places her left arm around the bust of Cloncurry, while her right hand quietly plucks the strings of an Irish harp as she rests a foot on an Irish wolfhound.[32] A former United Irishman and occasional supporter of Daniel O'Connell's movement to repeal the Act of Union, Cloncurry, who died in October 1853, 'did his best to cultivate and reward Irish talent'.[33] He lived to see the great exhibition in Dublin and was delighted to lend Hogan's marble group, which, he informed the sculptor, 'will cause the artist's fame to stand unrivalled in your own country'.[34] The exhibition catalogue went so far as to suggest that Hogan's sculpture 'might well adorn the Hall of an Irish National Gallery, if we had one'.[35] Smaller pieces by Hogan of an equally 'national' type were displayed in a room adjoining the Fine Arts Hall, where an idealized bust of the recently deceased Daniel O'Connell was shown amongst marbles on display after the antique and contemporary paintings,

as can be seen in Philip Henry Delamotte's contemporaneous photograph (fig. 8).[36]

Amidst the bog-oak furniture, reproduction Celtic jewellery, and examples of Irish industry, the Dublin exhibition made recent Irish and continental art easily accessible to the viewing public.[37] Indeed, in the two categories of sculpture and painting, modern works dominated by a ratio of at least 2 to 1. Large works, such as the imperialist *Last Stand of the 44th at Cabul, in 1842,* by Michael Angelo Hayes, or Francis Danby's biblical extravaganza *The Deluge* were on display, but one could also view much smaller and more intensely national images, such as Joseph Patrick Haverty's *Irish Piper* dating from the mid-1840s (fig. 9) and Nicholas Crowley's portrait *Daniel O'Connell, Painted during His Imprisonment in Richmond Prison, in 1844.*[38] Of the foreign art on display, loans were organized from Prussia, Belgium, France and the Netherlands. Amongst these exhibits was work by one of the leading German sculptors of the time, Christian Daniel Rauch, who was especially celebrated in the exhibition catalogue for his plaster-cast representation of *Victory (About to Throw a Garland),* the original of which had been completed in 1844.[39] German painting was represented by Andreas Achenbach, a leading landscape artist, two of whose works were loaned by the crown prince of Prussia.[40]

If the Dargan Exhibition brought contemporary Irish and foreign art to wider attention in Dublin in the mid-nineteenth century, the RHA also made its contribution. *The Village Scribe* (fig. 10), a painting by James Brenan exhibited at the academy in 1882, can stand as an exemplary statement on the acceptability of contemporary indigenous Irish scenes in public exhibitions for much of the late nineteenth and early twentieth centuries.[41] The RHA was a bastion of conservative values with a strict adherence to academic norms and it had no distinctly 'Irish' agenda. Yet the academy's exhibition lists for the nineteenth century

30 J. Sproule, ed., *The Irish Industrial Exhibition of 1853: A Detailed Catalogue of Its Contents* (Dublin, 1854), 422.

31 Sproule, ed., *Irish Industrial Exhibition,* 422.

32 John Turpin, *John Hogan: Irish Neoclassical Sculptor in Rome 1800–1858* (Dublin, 1982), 77–78, 179–80.

33 Valentine Browne Lawless, second Baron Cloncurry (1773–1853), *Oxford Dictionary of National Biography,* www.oxforddnb.com, accessed 6 October 2007.

34 Letter from Cloncurry to Hogan, 27 May 1853, in W. J. Fitzpatrick, *The Life, Times and Contemporaries of Lord Cloncurry* (Dublin, 1855), 582.

35 Sproule, ed., *Irish Industrial Exhibition,* 428. See also Paula Murphy, 'British Sculpture at the Early Universal Exhibitions: Ireland Sustaining Britain', *Sculpture Journal,* 3 (1999), 64–73, esp. n57.

36 For the Hogan bust of O'Connell, see Turpin, *John Hogan,* 156 and 161. The statuary after the antique include *Spinario,* or *Boy Extracting a Thorn from His Foot,* and the *Crouching Venus,* both by Giacomo Vanelli, see Sproule, ed., *Irish Industrial Exhibition,* nos. 101 and 102, both now in the National Gallery of Ireland (nos. 8085 and 8186), presented in 1863. The contemporary paintings have not, as yet, been identified.

Fig. 9. Joseph Haverty, *The Blind Piper*, c. 1845, oil on canvas, 76 × 59 cm, National Gallery of Ireland.

37 Nancy Netzer, 'Picturing an Exhibition: James Mahony's Watercolors of the Irish Industrial Exhibition of 1853', in Adele M. Dalsimer, ed., *Visualizing Ireland: National Identity and the Pictorial Tradition* (Boston and London, 1993), 88–98. For wood engravings of the exhibited bog-oak furniture and Celtic jewellery, see 'Appendix with an Illustrated Catalogue to the Exhibition of Art and Industry in Dublin', *Art Journal*, 5 (1853), 39 and 47.

38 Stewart, ed., *Irish Art Loan Exhibitions*, vol. 1, 166, 174, 310, 315.

39 Sproule, ed., *Irish Industrial Exhibition*, 425–26, illustrated, 427; marble, with wings, now in the National Gallery, Berlin, see, *Nationalgalerie Berlin. Das XIX. Jahrhundert. Katalog der Ausgestellten Werke* (Berlin, 2001), 329.

40 Sproule, ed., *Irish Industrial Exhibition*, 442–43.

41 On Brenan's paintings, see Claudia Kinmonth, *Irish Rural Interiors in Art* (New Haven and London, 2006), 256–58.

Fig. 10. James Brenan, *The Village Scribe*, 1881, oil on canvas, 24 × 29 cm, Brian P. Burns Collection.

reveal many Irish subjects, although they are by no means in the majority.[42] The exhibition of Brenan's painting in 1882, when Irish nationalists were enjoying unprecedented electoral success, reflected a marked shift in the cultural mood. A rural interior, it shows a people culturally confident and at ease in their own environment. Indeed, Brenan's inclusion of a quotation in Irish in the catalogue entry underscores that self-assurance; the village scribe is being addressed by the seated woman:

> *Dubhairt an bhean —*
> *Tá lá fada geal agad*
> *Tá páipear breagh glan agad*
> *Ta do phagha ar do bhos agad*
> *Agus bidheadh do gnó a gceart agad.*

The woman said —
You have a long bright day
You have fine clean paper
You have your pay in your fist
And may you get on with your job.[43]

Based in Cork in the 1880s, Brenan was well versed in international developments in the art world. Earlier, he had worked in England, and indeed had worked as a decorator on the Pompeian Room at the Great Exhibition in London.[44] His subsequent paintings of rural interiors owe a debt to a fellow Irish artist, William Mulready, who had died in 1863 but whose work Brenan would have seen in London. Mulready was a mainstay of the annual exhibitions at the Royal Academy of Arts and his fame rested on his scenes of rural incidents — a schoolroom, boys fighting, lovers exchanging verses. His work is tinged by romance, an idyllic rural world untroubled by modern realities. Brenan's

42 For more on this, see Fintan Cullen, 'Union and Display in Nineteenth-Century Ireland', in Dana Arnold, ed., *Cultural Identities and the Aesthetics of Britishness* (Manchester and New York, 2004), 120. For the RHA and its nineteenth-century problems, see Walter Strickland, *A Dictionary of Irish Artists*, 2 vols. (Dublin, 1913), vol. 2, 613–18; Peter Murray, 'Trouble at Mill: George Petrie and the Royal Hibernian Academy', *Martello Arts Review*, *Special Issue on the Royal Hibernian Academy of Arts, 1991* (Dublin, 1990), 14–22; also, Cyril Barrett and Jeanne Sheehy, 'Visual Arts and Society, 1851–1900', in W. E. Vaughan, ed., *A New History of Ireland, VI, Ireland under the Union, II, 1870–1921* (Oxford, 1996), 443–44. See also Ann M. Stewart, *Royal Hibernian Academy of Arts, Index of Exhibitors and Their Works, 1826-1979*, 3 vols. (Dublin, 1986).

43 Translation from Adele M. Dalsimer and Vera Kreilkamp, eds., *America's Eye: Irish Paintings from the Collection of Brian P. Burns* (Boston, 1996), 88.

44 Strickland, *Dictionary of Irish Artists*, vol. 1, 77, and Anne Crookshank and the Knight of Glin, *Ireland's Painters 1600–1940* (New Haven and London, 2002), 231. See also Peter Murray, 'Artist and Artisan: James Brenan as Art Educator', in Dalsimer and Kreilkamp, eds., *America's Eye*, 40–46.

45 *Illustrated Catalogue*, vii. For a useful discussion on the relationship between 'Patriotism and the Art Exhibition', see Francis Haskell, *The Ephemeral Museum: Old Master Paintings and the Rise of the Art Exhibition* (New Haven and London, 2000), ch. 6.

46 *Illustrated Catalogue*, ix.

47 On Lane's portrait commissions, see Fintan Cullen, *The Irish Face: Redefining the Irish Portrait* (London, 2004), 65–69.

48 'The Municipal Gallery Revisited', 1937; Peter Allt and Russell K. Alspach, eds. *The Variorum Edition of the Poems of W.B. Yeats* (New York, 1957), 602.

49 For Mancini and Lane, see O'Byrne, *Hugh Lane*, 94–97. For Lady Gregory's account of sitting for Mancini, see Gregory, *Lane: His Life and Legacy*, 79–80. For Mancini's technique, see Ulrich W. Hiesinger, *Antonio Mancini: Nineteenth-Century Italian Master* (New Haven and London, 2007), 66–67.

rural interiors of forty or more years later have definite formal comparisons with his Irish predecessor — the box-like room with similar lighting, the arrangement of the characters — but his vision is more specific, more localized. In *The Village Scribe*, the Irish-speaking and most probably illiterate standing man and his seated wife are dictating a letter in Irish to a scribe who is presumably writing in English. This cultural transformation is occurring because of the harsh reality of emigration: the child of the Irish-speaking parents has left Ireland and may never return. The letter written by the village scribe is thus a vital means of maintaining family and cultural ties.

III

Like his nineteenth-century predecessors, a key ingredient in the development of Lane's plans for a gallery of modern art was a patriotic desire to build a collection for Ireland. In the opening paragraph of his Prefatory Notice to the 1908 *Illustrated Catalogue* of the Dublin Municipal Gallery of Modern Art, he stated that the

> project of founding a Gallery of Modern Art in Dublin is no longer an idea, it is now an accomplished fact. Till to-day Ireland was the only country in Europe that had no Gallery of Modern Art. There is not even a single accessible private collection of Modern Pictures in this country. That reproach is now removed.[45]

Lane went on to say that he planned to hand over his 'collection of pictures and drawings of the British Schools … and Rodin's Masterpiece, 'L'Age d'Airain' … a group of portraits of contemporary Irishmen and women … [and] my collection of pictures by Continental artists'. And it was here that he also warned of the conditional nature of his gift:

> [I] intend to present the most of them,

provided that the promised permanent building is erected on a suitable site within the next few years. This collection includes a selection of the Forbes and Durand Ruel pictures, bought by me after the Royal Hibernian Academy Winter exhibition, and some important examples of Manet, Renoir, Mancini, etc., which I have purchased to make this Gallery widely representative of the greatest painters of the nineteenth century.[46]

Exhibited in a Georgian terraced house, formerly known as Clonmell House, on Dublin's Harcourt Street, the paintings were arranged in distinct sections — Irish Painters, British Schools, French Barbizon School and French Impressionists. They included Manet's *Eva Gonzalès* and Renoir's *Umbrellas* (*Les Parapluies*), which were only on loan to the new gallery. Other exhibits were unconditional Lane gifts, with examples of work by Irish, British and American artists such as Frank O'Meara, Walter Osborne, Albert Moore, George Frederic Watts, Wilson Steer and James McNeill Whistler as well as gifts of some Constables and Corots from the prince and princess of Wales. On the staircase, Lane hung a selection of portraits, mainly by John Butler Yeats and William Orpen. The former was represented by portraits of his son, W.B. Yeats, and John Millington Synge, while Orpen's subjects ranged from the Fenian Michael Davitt to the Unionist J. P. Mahaffy.[47] One of Lane's favourite contemporary artists, the now forgotten and distinctly odd Italian painter Antonio Mancini, was represented in this collection of portraits by an oil of Lady Gregory, which years later W. B. Yeats would refer to, rather generously, as a 'great ebullient portrait'.[48] Viewing his sitter through his distinctive perspective grid (he called it a *graticola* or *grille*), Mancini represented Lane's aunt on a canvas heavily encrusted with impasto.[49] The new Municipal collection also contained a small number of prints and drawings and sculpture. The

Fig. 11. Auguste Rodin, *The Age of Bronze*, 1876–77, original plaster work; bronze, 1904, 170 cm, ht, Dublin City Gallery/The Hugh Lane.

50 See Neil Sharp, 'The *Wrong* Twigs for an Eagle's Nest? Architecture, Nationalism and Sir Hugh Lane's Scheme for a Gallery of Modern Art, Dublin, 1904–13', in Michaela Giebelhausen, ed., *The Architecture of the Museum: Symbolic Structures, Urban Contexts* (Manchester and New York, 2003), 38–39.

51 For Mancini's portrait of Lane, see Hiesinger, *Mancini*, 85, 87, for the *Portrait of the Artist's Father* or *The Maker of Figures*, plate 25.

52 Giles Waterfield, *Palaces of Art: Art Galleries in Britain 1790–1990* (London, 1991), 61–62. For Ricketts and Shannon remembering Lane's penchant for interior design, see Gregory, *Lane: His Life and Legacy*, 168–69. Lane had included Shannon in his 1904 exhibition of Irish artists at London's Guildhall (Gregory, *Lane: His Life and Legacy*, 54) and both Shannon and Ricketts presented paintings to the Municipal Gallery, see *Illustrated Catalogue*, 8 and 15.

53 For Tschudi, see Françoise Forster-Hahn, 'Shrine of Art or Signature of a New Nation? The National Gallery(ies) in Berlin, 1848–1968', in Gwendolyn Wright, ed., *The Formation of National Collections of Art and Archaeology* (Washington, DC, 1996),

works on paper included drawings by Giovanni Segantini, Jean-François Millet, Augustus John, Max Beerbohm, Edward Burne-Jones and prints by Alphonse Legros, Whistler and George Clausen. The sculpture collection was dominated by Rodin's *Age of Bronze* (fig. 11), a silhouette of which also graced the vivid green cover of the catalogue. It was an eclectic collection and to all intents and purposes it was an exercise in cultural reconciliation. Its aim was to bring contemporary Ireland and Europe closer together, just as Dargan had done in 1853, by attracting loans from the newly formed Prussian museums in Berlin and other European centres.

The day after the opening of the gallery, the *Irish Independent* carried a series of

93–95. For photographs of Tschudi's installations and a list of the paintings and sculpture on display in Berlin in 1908, see Barbara Paul, *Hugo von Tschudi und die Moderne Französische Kunst im Deutschen Kaiserreich* (Mainz, 1993), 221–23. From 1902, in the Museum Folkwang in Hagen, North-Rhine Westphalia, Karl Ernst Osthaus also placed Rodin's *Age of Bronze* and a Renoir full length (now in Essen) within a contemporary hang; see Dumas and Shapiro, *Impressionism*, 60–61. Today there are more than fifty bronze casts of Rodin's *Age of Bronze*, see Antoinette le Normand-Romain, *Rodin* (London, 2006), 206. In 1906 Lane had arranged for the casting through Rodin himself, see O'Byrne, *Hugh Lane, 1875–1915*, 83–84. Tschudi had done much the same in 1903, see Paul, *Tschudi*, 361.

54 Arsène Alexandre, 'L'art de donner un musée,' *Le Figaro*, 20 March 1908: '*Seulement, si M. de Tschudi a créé à la Galerie nationale de Berlin une section d'art moderne très remarquable, et cela avec le concours d'amis très riches … Hugh Lane, lui, a créé un musée entire à Dublin, sans le secours de personne.*' [While Mr de Tschudi has created a very remarkable section of modern art at the National Gallery in Berlin, and with the help of very rich friends… Hugh Lane, himself, has created an entire museum in Dublin, without anyone's help.] In Gregory, *Lane: His Life and Legacy*, 23.

hand-drawn sketches of the interior of the building.[50] *The Age of Bronze* is visible at the turn of the stairs leading to the first floor and looking out towards the portraits of Irish celebrities. On the first floor, and in what the *Independent* refers to as 'A Corner of the French Room', the paper's sketch shows Manet's *Eva Gonzalès* balanced with Mancini's full length portrait of Lane himself, with another, smaller, Mancini portrait of the artist's father hanging in between.[51] In his preference for showing different Schools in distinct sections, displayed in relatively uncluttered suites of rooms, with each work of art given its own space, Lane's Dublin hang was in keeping with avant-garde fashions for the exhibition of pictures. In the early years of the twentieth century, Lane's London friends Charles Ricketts and Charles Hazelwood Shannon were experimenting in their apartment in Holland Park, which Lane is known to have visited, with neutral colours and a well-spaced aestheticism.[52] Equally, in the new Municipal Gallery, with its gently classical interior, the single row of hanging paintings, and most especially the privileging of Manet and Renoir, one is reminded of the virtually contemporaneous hang created by Hugo von Tschudi in Berlin's National Gallery. Despite official opposition, Tschudi hung paintings by Manet and Renoir in single lines above the dado and placed Rodin's *Age of Bronze* in the centre of the room.[53] Only two months after the opening of the Dublin gallery, this similarity between Lane and Tschudi in the hanging of modern paintings was remarked upon by the art critic of *Le Figaro*.[54] Both curators were using modern art, and in both cases that meant Manet, Renoir and Rodin, to offer new aesthetic solutions to the display of the visual. Given that he was operating out of an eighteenth-century town house, Lane's innovations in display were quite modest. Rugs, vases of flowers and period furniture featured throughout the Harcourt Street gallery, while Tschudi's rooms in Berlin were less obviously domestic.

In the Dublin gallery and in keeping with the cultural influences of the time — a portrait of Douglas Hyde, the founder of the Gaelic League, by John Butler Yeats was displayed on the staircase — the cover and section headings in the *Illustrated Catalogue* appeared in both Irish and English. Such bilingualism was later explained by Lane's friend Tom Bodkin as 'typical of Lane … for he sought quite sincerely to conciliate every kind of opinion that might be used to further his work'.[55] The juxtaposition of portraits of old Land Leaguers such as Davitt and Trinity Unionists such as Mahaffy was yet another demonstration of a movement towards conciliation. On a grander scale, Lane was attempting to satisfy the newly empowered Catholic middle class who dominated Dublin Corporation and were owners and managers of the gallery, while also placating his own particular caste, the Anglo-Irish community. Although he organized the display of the 1908 gallery, he was but its honorary director. The chairman of the Committee of Management was an alderman, Thomas Kelly, a member of Sinn Féin who, along with fellow city representatives, sat around the table with grandees such as the earl of Drogheda, at the time a representative Irish peer who took the Tory whip. As an example of what F. S. L. Lyons has termed the 'cultural fusion' that was current in Irish life in the first decade of the twentieth century, the list of subscribers to the new gallery included the prince and princess of Wales, the earl of Mayo and many other Irish peers, but also United States President Theodore Roosevelt, and independent thinkers such as Countess Markievicz, George Bernard Shaw, George Russell and Jack B. Yeats.[56]

Just as the *Irish Independent* had carried a story on the opening of the gallery, the *Irish Times* also offered an analysis of Lane's achievement:

Assembled in one of the great old houses which recall the former glories of Dublin, this gathering of peers, professors, Sinn Feiners, and Gaelic Leaguers felt the true inspiration of citizenship, and forgot their daily differences. It would be hard to find three men who look at life from more different points of view than Dr Mahaffy, Alderman Kelly, and Mr Stephen Gwynn. Yesterday, however, they were joined by the spirit of citizenship. Their theme was the future greatness of Dublin, and the duty of civic pride, and we sincerely hope that their words will find an echo in the hearts of all our people.[57]

Such themes of reconciliation also appear years later in Lady Gregory's hagiography, *Hugh Lane's Life and Achievement* (1921). She wrote of how her nephew had hoped that

someone might from time to time give a picture in memory of one who had been dear in friendship or near in blood. And this in Ireland would be a happy thing to do, rather than to place a monument before the eyes of a congregation of one or other creed, as though — and this, thank God, is not customary — Protestant could not hold Catholic, or Catholic Protestant, in honour and affectionate regard. The Gallery knows no such divisions, but is wide and liberal for all. A tranquil landscape by Stott of Oldham was thus given by me and my son to the memory of an old friend who had been kind to us ... And lately, to Hugh's own memory, and as a symbol of ultimate reconcilement, a friend who had stood by him through all his work for the Gallery has given and put up their portraits of John Redmond and Edward Carson, those stout fighters for South and North.[58]

Unfortunately, such reconciliation was illusory. It just did not happen. The reactions of George Moore and Éamon de Valera to Lane's intended gift to Dublin of recent French paintings indicate the great divisions between the two cultural groups. Although born a Catholic, Moore's 1904 comments on the welcome subversiveness of Manet's *Eva Gonzalès* represented an Ascendancy

disregard for the local and the indigenous. Equally, given de Valera's preoccupation with nationalism, his attitude to the fate of the Lane pictures was dominated by what Lyons has referred to as 'a single criterion — whether it helped or hindered the breaking of the English connection'.[59]

Although the gallery was open until 10 p.m. every weekday and to 6 p.m. on a Sunday, and although W. B. Yeats could later claim that it was 'well attended, and among the rest by working people', wider support was not easy to obtain.[60] In his memoirs, the English critic and curator Frank Rutter recalled being invited to Dublin for the gallery opening and being asked to lecture:

My chief recollection of this visit was the utter incredulity on the part of the citizens of Dublin that the pictures given to them could be of any real value. The view generally entertained was expressed by some Irish cousins of mine who came to see me after my lecture. 'Of course,' said they, 'we understand you've got to crack them up in public. You are Lane's friend. But you can tell us. They aren't any good really, are they? They can't be. If they were any good they wouldn't be in Dublin.' Nothing I could say would remove these suspicions, and they went away telling me I was 'very loyal' to my friend, and wondering to themselves exactly what his 'little game' was.[61]

Despite Dublin Corporation having made him an honorary freeman of the city in 1908 and that in the following year he received a knighthood in the king's Birthday Honours list, Lane never succeeded in uniting the various Irish camps.[62] As such, Lane's 'little game', as Rutter's Irish cousins called it, failed. The municipal authorities never built the gallery he wanted and the French pictures are still officially owned by London's National Gallery. Moore might have thought that Manet's *Eva Gonzalès* was the picture that Dublin needed but Dublin did not listen. And when de Valera claimed

55 Bodkin, *Hugh Lane and His Pictures*, 19. See also Lucy McDiarmid, *The Irish Art of Controversy* (Dublin, 2005), ch. 1.

56 The *Illustrated Catalogue* lists the Committee of Management and the subscribers, v, 60–61. See F. S. L. Lyons, *Culture and Anarchy in Ireland 1890–1939* (Oxford, 1979), 57; see also Sharp, 'The *Wrong* Twigs for an Eagle's Nest?', 37.

57 *Irish Times*, 21 January 1908. For further newspaper accounts of the January 1908 opening of the gallery, see Herrero, *Irish Intellectuals and Aesthetics*, 51–55.

58 Gregory, *Lane: His Life and Legacy*, 70. The Stott in question was *An October Morning*, see *Illustrated Catalogue*, 13, illustrated, no. 72. The portraits were by John Lavery, see his *The Life of a Painter* (London, 1940), 208.

59 Lyons, *Culture and Anarchy*, 82.

60 *Illustrated Catalogue*, ix; W. B. Yeats, letter to *Observer*, 21 January 1917, quoted in Gregory, *Lane Life and Legacy*, 235.

61 Frank Rutter, *Since I was Twenty-Five* (London, 1927), 175.

62 Bodkin, *Hugh Lane and His Pictures*, 24, and O'Byrne, *Hugh Lane*, 109, 117.

63 For criticism of the porch, see Maurice Craig, *Dublin 1660–1860* (Dublin, 1980), 224. An added indication of municipal change in 1933 was that the former Rutland Square became Parnell Square, see Yvonne Whelan, *Reinventing Modern Dublin: Streetscape, Iconography and the Politics of Identity* (Dublin, 2003), 221.

64 Barbara Dawson, 'The Hugh Lane revisited', in Margarita Cappock, ed., *Dublin City Gallery: The Hugh Lane* (London and New York, 2006), 11.

65 McDiarmid, *Irish Art of Controversy*, 12.

66 Bruce Arnold, 'A Controversial Bequest', *Irish Book Review*, 1, 1 (2005), 25.

67 McDiarmid, *Irish Art of Controversy*, 39.

68 Senia Pašeta, *Before the Revolution: Nationalism, Social Change and Ireland's Catholic Élite, 1879–1922* (Cork, 1999), 132–33.

that he was fully committed to founding a gallery that would reflect a characteristic Irish love for the arts, the 'promised' building never materialized. Instead, in 1933, a year after Fianna Fáil came to power, Charlemont House, an eighteenth-century town house designed by William Chambers, was refitted as the Municipal Gallery of Modern Art, an inappropriate porch was added to its Parnell Square façade, and a room was made available for the Lane pictures.[63] To add insult to injury, as one of the most recent books on the gallery informs us, the gallery 'did not have a purchasing budget until 1974', seventy years after Lane had first exhibited *Eva Gonzalès* in Dublin.[64]

In a recent essay on the Lane controversy, Lucy McDiarmid has suggested that 'Giving was the great central fact of Lane's life: it took him away from luxury goods and gained him entrance into a public realm of philanthropy'.[65] Bruce Arnold has rejected that statement, claiming that the 'central fact of [Lane's] life was getting, not giving. He was a superbly gifted dealer ... dedicated to the art and craft of trading in works of art. He made money, acquired paintings, and then gave them away.'[66] To a degree, both views have credit. In reviewing the details of Lane's gifting paintings to the

city of Dublin and to the Irish nation, it is certain that one has to move beyond the uncritical partisanship of Lady Gregory, who, as McDiarmid entertainingly puts it, 'devoted hours to taking tea with the wives of powerful men, begging them to convince their husbands of Ireland's right to the paintings'.[67] Lane did give and Lane did make money but his efforts to establish a gallery in Dublin were comparable to the stance taken by his contemporary, the ever pragmatic intellectual nationalist Tom Kettle. In wanting to give a Manet to Dublin, Lane, like Kettle, was of the opinion that in order for Ireland to become 'deeply Irish she must become European'. Expanding on that, in the first issue of his newspaper, the *Nationist*, Kettle in 1905 urged his readers 'to accept Ireland as a great complex fact; an organism with all the complications of modern society'. [68]

A shorter version of this essay was delivered at the conference 'Art, City, Spectacle: The 1857 Manchester Art-Treasures Exhibition Revisited', held at the University of Manchester, 9–10 November 2007. For comment and information, I am grateful to Helen Rees Leahy, Giles Waterfield and Anthony Hamber. I am also grateful to Roy Foster, Anne Kelly and Ruth Kenny.

O'FARRELL Ltd

FRANCIS O'FARRELL
CIGAR IMPORTERS
ANALYSTS

Éamon de Valera leads his cabinet in saluting the colours at a 1916 commemoration, General Post Office, Dublin, Easter 1940. Photo: Hans Wild/Time Life Pictures/Getty Images.

'A statue's there to mark the place'
Cú Chulainn in the GPO

Robert Tracy

From the central window of Dublin's General Post Office, a bronze statue faces passers-by on O'Connell Street. A little less than life size, it depicts an athletic young man, nearly naked. His head and body have slumped forward, but he is still almost upright, held up by a strip of cloth across his chest, which binds him to a pillar-stone. His right arm holds a sword, his left a round shield, but he can no longer raise them. He is exhausted, clearly dead or dying, pierced by many wounds, lapsing into unconsciousness for the last time. A carrion crow, bird of ill omen, is settling on his right shoulder, sensing that death has come. The figure suggests conventional images of Christ on the Cross.

Those who pause to read the tablets in English and Irish that flank the statue learn that the subject is *The Death of Cuchulain*, by the sculptor Oliver Sheppard. They learn also that the statue is 'a memorial to the participants in the 1916 Rising'. It commemorates the rebels who seized the GPO on Easter Monday, 1916, and proclaimed Ireland a sovereign republic, independent of British rule. Here Patrick Pearse, provisional president of the republic, and soldiers of the Irish Volunteers and the Irish Citizen Army, held off units of the British army for five days, until the building was in flames around them. Survivors who escaped to a house in nearby Moore Street continued the battle until Saturday, when Pearse surrendered to avoid further bloodshed. He was tried by a British military tribunal and executed a few days later, as were most of the other leaders of the Rising, an act that the British government hoped would put an end to Irish rebellion for the foreseeable future. Members of the rank and file from the Post Office and the other rebel positions in Dublin were sent to prison in England. It was one more failed Irish rebellion, a seventh added to the six previous rebellions, which Pearse had cited in the Proclamation and in an earlier political pamphlet, *The Separatist Idea*, had called 'the chain of the Separatist tradition ... never once snapped during the centuries',[1] a sacred tradition that each Irish generation must re-enact.

Pearse had argued the necessity of rebellion, whether or not there was much chance of success. Each failed rebellion kept alive 'the Fenian flame' of resistance to British rule[2] and so would inspire its successor, thus keeping alive 'the Spirit of the Nation'. His poems, plays, and political pamphlets frequently refer to blood sacrifice. 'The old heart of the earth needed to be warmed with the red wine of the battlefields,' he wrote, late in 1915,[3] celebrating the bloodshed of the First World War. Joseph Connolly, leader of the Irish Volunteers in Belfast and later a

prominent member of Fianna Fáil, recalled meeting Pearse in 1914 and hearing him 'propounding clearly his doctrine of the need for the blood sacrifice and the necessity for the re-baptism of the country for the salvation of the national soul'.[4]

There had been practical arguments for a rebellion at Easter, but in Catholic Ireland the chosen date also suggested a symbolism of heroic sacrifice, of defeat that might eventually turn into a victory. When he led his force into the GPO on that Easter Monday, Pearse knew that the Rising was almost certain to fail and would lead to his own death. The planned muster of Volunteers all over Ireland, which was to result in the capture of police barracks and other public buildings, had been countermanded. The national Rising he had planned had already been thwarted.

The passer-by who does not already know the heroic legends of ancient Ireland, and the reworking of those legends by W. B. Yeats and his associates during the Irish literary revival in the early years of the twentieth century, reads that the dying warrior of Sheppard's statue is Cú Chulainn, the great doomed hero of the *Táin Bó Cuailnge*, and the sinister crow on his shoulder is the Morrigu, or Great Queen, goddess of battles and feaster on the bodies of the dead. Surrounded and outnumbered in his last battle, Cú Chulainn, the tablets explain, fastened himself upright to a pillar-stone with a strip of cloth, that he might die facing his enemies; 'only when a raven perched on his shoulder did they dare approach'.

Oliver Sheppard (1865–1941) was Yeats's fellow student and friend at the Dublin Metropolitan School of Art in 1884–85.[5] His *Bard Oisin and Niamh* (1895) depicts the protagonists of Yeats's *The Wanderings of Oisin* (1889). Yeats would later champion Sheppard's work in a letter to the Dublin *Daily Express*.[6] In 1901, he wrote urging Sheppard to leave England and return to Dublin to teach modelling at the Metropolitan School of Art and take part in the new cultural movement:

1 Padraic H. Pearse, *Collected Works: Political Writings and Speeches* (Dublin, 1922), 238.

2 Pearse, *Collected Works*, 205.

3 Pearse, *Collected Works*, 216.

4 Joseph Connolly, *Memoirs of Senator Joseph Connolly 1885–1961: A Founder of Modern Ireland*, ed. J. Anthony Gaughan (Dublin, 1996), 94.

5 R. F. Foster, *W. B. Yeats: A Life. I: The Apprentice Mage 1865–1914* (Oxford and New York, 1997), 36.

6 W. B. Yeats (14 September 1898), *Collected Letters of W. B. Yeats 2 (1896-1900)*, eds. Warwick Gould, John Kelly, and Deirdre Toomey (Oxford 1997), 269–70.

7 Quoted in John Turpin, *Oliver Sheppard 1865–1941: Symbolist Sculptor of the Irish Cultural Revival* (Dublin, 2000), 19.

8 Turpin, *Oliver Sheppard*, 23.

9 *Irish Times* [hereafter, *IT*], 27 April 1935.

10 Lady Gregory, *Cuchulain of Muirthemne* (Gerrards Cross, 1973 [1902]), 272; Douglas Hyde, *A Literary History of Ireland* (London, 1980 [1899]), 341–53; 'Brislech Mór Maige Muirtheimne [The Great Defeat on the Plain of Muirthemne]', *Gaelic Journal*, 11, 128, 132–35 (May, September–November 1901), 81–83, 145–47, 161–64, 177–80. 'Dergruathar Chonaill Chearnaig, The Bloody Raid of Conall Cearnach', *Gaelic Journal*, 11, 123–27 (December 1900–April 1901), 1–3, 17–19, 33–36, 49–52, 65–67; Whitley Stokes, ed. and trans., 'Aided Conculaind, The Death of Cuchulain', *Révue Celtique*, 3 (1877), 175–85.

11 Gregory, *Cuchulain*, 256.

12 Francis Shaw, 'The Canon of Irish History — A Challenge', *Studies*, 61 (1972), 124.

13 William Irwin Thompson, *The Imagination of an Insurrection: Dublin, Easter 1916* (New York, 1972), 75.

I feel it is our duty to get as much talent into Ireland as we can in the present crisis ... Our country's course feels certain ... The artistic and literary movement, in which I include the Gaelic movement, has changed the face of the town. There is quite a strong little group of writers and artists now ... Thus in Ireland you would be known, the living forces of Ireland shaped and shaping.[7]

Sheppard settled in Ireland for the rest of his life, teaching sculpture, carrying out private commissions, and producing public art: memorials in Wexford and Enniscorthy to the republican rebels of 1798; portrait busts of, among others, John O'Leary, James Clarence Mangan, George Russell (Æ), Patrick Pearse and Cathal Brugha; and subjects from Irish mythology.

Sheppard had been drawn to Cú Chulainn as early as 1897, when he exhibited *The Training of Cuchulain* at the Royal Hibernian Academy. Once resettled in Dublin, he became a regular at the Abbey Theatre,[8] and so presumably came to know Yeats's early plays about Cú Chulainn, *On Baile's Strand* (1904) and *The Green Helmet* (1910). He certainly knew Lady Gregory's *Cuchulain of Muirthemne* (1902) a version of the *Táin*. The statue in the GPO was, in fact, modelled in 1911–12, and embodied Sheppard's enthusiastic response when he first read Lady Gregory's book and 'was struck by [Cú Chulainn's] suitability as a sculptor's theme'.[9]

The particular episode that Sheppard chose to depict is not, in fact, from the *Táin*. 'Death of Cuchulain', the last chapter of *Cuchulain of Muirthemne*, draws on legends about Cú Chulainn after the great battles of the *Táin* were over. Lady Gregory cites as her sources 'Brislech Mor Magh Muirthemne and *Deargruatar Conaill Cearnaig* — published in *Gaelic Journal*, 1901; S[tandish] Hayes O'Grady in Miss [Eleanor] Hull's *Cuchullin Saga* [1898]; Whitley Stokes, *Révue Celtique*; an unpublished MS in Dr. [Douglas] Hyde's possession.' She also drew on Douglas Hyde's *A Literary History of Ireland* (1899).[10]

After Cú Chulainn defeated Queen Maeve's attack on Ulster, as recorded in the *Táin*, Maeve plotted revenge. She led another army against Ulster when she knew that Cú Chulainn alone would be capable of fighting, and sent witches to entice him with visions of an invading army. He resisted their spells for a time, but finally refused to wait for reinforcements and went against his united enemies with only his charioteer. Mortally wounded at last, unable to stand, he tied himself to a

pillar-stone ... with his breast-belt, that way he would not meet his death lying down, but would meet it standing up. Then his enemies came round about him, but they were in dread of going close to him for they were not sure but he might be still alive.

Only when 'a bird came and settled on his shoulder'[11] do they realize he is dead, and cut off his head and right hand.

Sheppard's statue, then, depicts the end of a heroic fight against overwhelming odds, but also an imprudent fight, which the hero failed to postpone until allies could join him. He went into battle to obey a complex code of honour and to become a heroic exemplar, knowing that to do so would bring about his own death. It is thus an appropriate memorial to Pearse and the other leaders of the Easter Rising, but especially to Pearse, who had refused to postpone the Rising despite the near certainty of failure. He had often spoken of death in battle as redemptive of Ireland's honour and described the death of Cú Chulainn as symbolizing 'the redemption of man by a sinless God ... it is like a retelling (or is it a foretelling?) of the story of Calvary'.[12]

Pearse was fascinated by the legend of Cú Chulainn. He had taken an oath at the age of ten to emulate Cú Chulainn in the fight for Irish freedom.[13] At St. Enda's, the bilingual school for boys he founded in 1908, Pearse's students performed in dramatic pageants which he wrote for them: *Mac-Ghníomharta Chuchulain* (The Boy Deeds of Cuchulain, 1909), and a pageant from the Cú Chulainn saga in 1913.[14] Just inside the school entrance a painting by Edwin Morrow depicted an episode from the *Táin*: the young Cú Chulainn taking arms for the first time, after he had learned that the man who took arms on that day would earn great fame, but would also die young. Around the hero ran the words of Cú Chulainn's response: 'I care not though I were to live but one day and one night provided my fame and my deeds live after me.'[15] That response became the school's motto.

Pearse's 'ideal Irishman,' his friend Stephen MacKenna remembered, 'whom he thought might become a living reality in our day, was a Cuchulain baptized.'[16] Pearse wrote that in the early days of St. Enda's, 'I spoke oftenest to our boys of Cuchulainn and his compeers of the Gaelic prime'. After 1910, when the school moved to Rathfarnham, he began to speak more often of Robert Emmet and his brave, futile effort to provoke a rising in 1803.[17] But Desmond Ryan noted that 'Cuchulain moved' with the school and 'settled down' as 'an invisible member of the school staff'.[18]

The Easter Rising and its suppression left the GPO a gutted wreck, and so it remained for some years, during Ireland's War of Independence (1919–21) and Civil War (1922–23), and throughout the 1920s. The Civil War was fought between those who accepted the 1922 Treaty with Great Britain, which established the Irish Free State as an independent dominion under the British crown, and those who would accept only the independent Irish republic that Pearse had proclaimed in 1916. It was fought with that intense bitterness engendered when men who have been united in a successful struggle then disagree about the way to use their victory. The division over the Treaty and the subsequent Civil War defined Irish politics for many years, and shaped modern Ireland's two main political parties.

For the first ten years of the Free State, the Dáil, or parliament, was dominated by the pro-Treaty party, Cumann na nGaedheal, led by William T. Cosgrave. Éamon de Valera and his fellow republicans, who had rejected the Treaty, continued to seek and win election to the Dáil, but were unable to take their seats because they refused to take the oath of loyalty to the British king, which the Treaty imposed. De Valera and most of his followers finally took the oath in 1927, however, and entered the Dáil. In February 1932, his party, Fianna Fáil, won the general election, and he became president of the Executive Council, or prime minister, a position he would soon rename with an old Irish word for leader, *taoiseach*. He would be Taoiseach until 1948, and again from 1951 until 1959. In September 1933, his Cumann na nGaedheal opponents merged with the short-lived Centre Party and Eoin O'Duffy's fascist Blueshirts to form the United Ireland Party, better known as Fine Gael. Once in power, de Valera quickly moved to make the role of the British king and government meaningless in Ireland. Without repudiating the Treaty, or explicitly violating it, he worked to make Ireland in all but name the republic he had fought for in 1916 and had campaigned for since. In a series of carefully planned steps towards a republic completely independent from Britain, the loyalty oath was the first to go, soon followed by the crown representative, the right of appeal to the British Privy Council, and other relics of imperial rule.

The reopening of the restored GPO in 1929 gave de Valera an opportunity to remind his countrymen of the events of 1916, to stress the republican ideal for which Pearse and his followers had fought, and especially to lay claim to 1916 for himself and his own party. In March 1933, the first modest references to a 1916 memorial appeared in the letter column of de Valera's own newspaper, the *Irish Press*. One John Brennan declared: 'it is about time that the G.P.O. in Dublin bore some memorial to the men who fought for us there in 1916'. Brennan suggested that the text of Pearse's

14 Ruth Dudley Edwards, *Patrick Pearse: The Triumph of Failure* (Dublin, 1990 [1977]), 123, 172.

15 Edwards, *Patrick Pearse*, 117.

16 Martin Daly [Stephen McKenna], *Memories of the Dead* (Dublin, n.d. [1919 or 1920]), 17.

17 Edwards, *Patrick Pearse*, 135

18 Desmond Ryan, *A Man Called Pearse* (Dublin, 1919), 83.

19 *Irish Press* [hereafter, *IP*], 6 March 1933.

20 *IP*, 8 March 1933.

21 Tim Pat Coogan, *Éamon de Valera: The Man Who Was Ireland* (New York, 1993), 649.

22 Coogan, *de Valera*, 698.

23 Coogan, *de Valera*, 501.

24 Coogan, *de Valera*, 394, 501–05.

Proclamation of the Irish Republic 'should certainly be engraved on a tablet outside the G.P.O., and a memorial tablet bearing the names of all who fell in action in the G.P.O., and those of the garrison who were executed, should be placed inside the building'.[19] 'John Brennan' was the pen name, or *nom de guerre*, of Madame Sidney Gifford Czira, who wrote frequently for the *Irish Press* at the time. Her sister Muriel was the widow of Thomas MacDonagh, and her sister Grace the widow of Joseph Plunkett; both men were among the signers of the Proclamation of the Irish Republic and had been court-martialled and executed by British firing squads after the defeat of the Rising. Long a fervent nationalist, Czira clearly also had strong personal reasons for wishing to honour the men of 1916, but it is probable that she wrote her letter at de Valera's instigation.

Brennan's letter was immediately seconded by a letter from Liam Mac Fhionnlaoigh (William McGinley), writing as secretary of the Associated Easter Week Men from the organization's Eustace Street headquarters, and by an editorial headed 'Memorials', commending Brennan's letter and supporting 'the proposal that this historic building should carry on its walls for our people and for foreign visitors a memorial to mighty days'.[20] The editorial, which also suggested that an original copy of the Proclamation be displayed, was probably written by de Valera, and certainly reflected his views.

We can only speculate as to what went on in de Valera's mind as he considered a suitable memorial. He knew little of the visual arts, and he already had developed the vision problems that would make an eye operation necessary in 1936.[21] Nor did he know much about literature, even Irish literature — a close associate, Maurice Moynihan, doubted whether 'he ever read a serious novel in his life'.[22] Though eager to revive Irish as the nation's language, he had no interest in either the ancient heroic literature of Ireland or the Irish literary revival. His aesthetic theory is summed up

in his evaluation of the poems of Thomas Davis: 'His poetry accomplished the stirring of the people and thus it was good poetry.'[23] De Valera's only recorded comments on the writers of the revival are attacks on Sean O'Casey for 'defam[ing] our values' in *The Plough and the Stars* (1926), and misrepresenting 'the struggle for national independence'. In the *Irish Independent* (7 April 1934), he was quoted as declaring that 'he had never set foot in the Abbey Theatre' and 'had no knowledge whatever of the plays produced there'.[24] Apart from politics, his only interest was abstruse mathematical speculations.

The suggestion that Sheppard's statue of the dying Cú Chulainn be cast in bronze and placed in the GPO came from John Leo Burke, de Valera's close friend, personal legal adviser, and perhaps his only link with literary and artistic Dublin. Burke, a prominent Dublin solicitor, advised the government in 1932–33 in its complex negotiations with Great Britain over the collection and payment of land annuities owed to the British government by Irish farmers. For a time he was solicitor to the attorney general. Among the leaders of the new Ireland, there were few with any knowledge of literature or art. Burke made himself a kind of ambassador between the new men and Ireland's artists. He persuaded de Valera and his wife, Sinéad Ní Fhlannagáin, to sit for portraits by Seán O'Sullivan, and to commission drawings of their children. Burke himself commissioned O'Sullivan to sketch a number of distinguished contemporaries; these drawings are now in the National Gallery of Ireland, where Burke was for many years a member of the board of governors. His artist friends included Sheppard, Evie Hone, Albert Power, Patrick Hennessy, and Jack B. Yeats.

Burke was also a regular at the Abbey and Gate theatres. Among his literary friends were Lennox Robinson, Padraic Colum, and especially T. C. Murray, who usually included Burke among those he invited to hear him read a new play. In the diary that preserves so much information about Dublin's theatre world, Joseph Holloway describes Burke as 'the centre of the literary and artistic gossip of the town'.[25] Burke's other friendships included the famous tenor Count John McCormack, and members of both sides in the great political division: Maud Gonne MacBride, Seán MacEntee, Seán T. O'Kelly, and Arthur Clery among the republicans; William T. Cosgrave and John A. Costello on the other side.

Burke often visited Sheppard's studio, and he had long admired *The Death of Cuchulain*, which had remained there, cast in plaster but unsold, for many years. When proposals were first floated in the *Irish Press* for placing a tablet to 1916 in the GPO, there were discussions about a 1916 memorial in the Executive Council.[26] These discussions presumably prompted Burke's suggestion to de Valera that *The Death of Cuchulain* would suitably commemorate Pearse and his comrades. He was able to cite Pearse's own admiration for Sheppard's work, expressed in comments on the sculptor's *Inis Fáil*, shown at the Royal Hibernian Academy in 1901 and again at the Gaelic League's 1906 Oireachtas:

> Oliver Sheppard is the greatest poet and one of the most creative minds in Ireland to-day; he dreams beautiful dreams of Eire, he has tender reveries of her past, ambitions mighty things for her future: and all these dreams, and reveries, and ambitions he has the power of fixing in bronze or marble, giving enduring expression as well to the most evanescent fancies of a singularly emotional and changeful temperament as to the deeper and stronger yearnings of an earnest man ...[27]

Burke was aware of this passage from Pearse's review of the 1906 Oireachtas art exhibition, and would quote it in a leaflet he issued in 1937, as part of his successful campaign to purchase *Inis Fáil* for the nation

and have it cast in bronze. He was also able to remind de Valera that Willie Pearse, executed with his brother after the Rising, had studied sculpture with Sheppard at the Metropolitan School of Art. De Valera may have been aware that he himself had recently been described by Seán O'Faoláin as 'A Cuchulain of Easter Week'.[28]

How much Burke may have said about Cú Chulainn's rash heroism, and how much de Valera knew about the ancient hero, is unknown, but it is curious that de Valera never mentioned Cú Chulainn's name — or Oliver Sheppard's — in his dedication speech at the statue's unveiling. He spoke only of a 'beautiful piece of sculpture, the creation of Irish genius, symbolizing the dauntless courage and abiding constancy of our people ... [that] ... will commemorate "1916" modestly, indeed, but fittingly'.[29]

Burke brought de Valera to Sheppard's studio to view the statue, where, according to the *Irish Times*, he 'immediately decided to secure it for the nation'.[30] No doubt the decision was a little more considered, but on 29 May 1934, the Executive Council agreed 'to have Oliver Sheppard's *The Death of Cuchulain* cast in bronze for erection in the G.P.O. as a 1916 memorial'.[31] The letter was accompanied by seven letters of support, which Burke had obtained from prominent Irish artists; unfortunately these letters have disappeared. On 10 August 1934, late in the afternoon of the last day of the 1933–34 session, de Valera's minister of finance, Seán MacEntee, announced the Executive Council's decision to the Dáil, described the arrangements for casting the statue in Belgium, and moved that the Dáil vote £1,000 for the project.

The opposition was quick to object to what it saw as an attempt by de Valera and his party to hijack the potent memory of the Rising and its symbolism. Cosgrave, who had himself fought in the GPO in Easter Week, complained that Sheppard's statue had been chosen in secret and that the timing of the request for funds on the last day of session made any serious discussion impossible:

25 Holloway's diary entry, 9 January 1943, National Library of Ireland (NLI) MSS 2009, 62.

26 *IP*, 8 March 1933.

27 *An Claidheamh Soluis*, 8, 22 (1906), 7 (unsigned; original in English).

28 Seán O'Faoláin, *The Life Story of Éamon de Valera* (Dublin, 1933), 28–30.

29 *IT*, 22 April 1935.

30 *IT*, 26 April 1935.

31 Letter dated 30 May 1934, to Rúnaí [private secretary] to Minister, Posts and Telegraphs, National Archives of Ireland [hereafter, NAI], S6405.

32 Dáil Éireann Debates [hereafter, DÉD], vol. 53, 10 August 1934, 2505–10.

33 DÉD, vol. 53, 10 August 1934, 2505–10.

34 DÉD, vol. 53, 10 August 1934, 2505–10.

35 NAI, S6405; Cabinet 7/177 12.10.34, item 1.

Oliver Sheppard's *The Death of Cuchulain*. Photo: An Post.

When there are divisions — and bitter divisions — amongst the people is not the time to initiate a proposal of this sort. ... It is certainly treating the House with scant courtesy, and the people with no consideration at all, to produce at the end of a session and practically without a moment's notice a *fait accompli* in connection with this matter.

He also objected to the site, and questioned whether 'the time is actually ripe for the erection of a single monument or memorial to the exclusion of others'.[32] MacEntee, conscious that his party enjoyed a comfortable majority, blandly described the statue 'as by no means a national monument to the men of 1916' but intended 'merely to commemorate the fact that in 1916 the headquarters of the Provisional Government of the Second Irish Republic was situated in the Post Office'. He gave his assurance that 'people who are competent to judge' had declared Sheppard's work to be 'of outstanding artistic merit' and insisted that it

> ... is intended to be merely a feature of the building and not, as I have already said, in any sense a national monument to commemorate 1916 in general. I think it is fitting that something should be erected in the Post Office to mark its special relationship to the events of 1916.[33]

Cosgrave was not mollified. 'There is a Party and there is a Party view,' he declared: 'those fellows are out of office now. Let us show some form to the public in connection with this. This is ours, and so on.'[34] The Dáil then voted the requested sum.

With the casting under way, the Executive Council appointed a committee in October[35] to choose a suitable inscription for a tablet beneath the statue. Committee members included de Valera and his vice-president, Seán T. O'Kelly, and the ministers of finance (Seán MacEntee), agriculture (James Ryan), post and telegraphs (Gerald Boland), and lands (Joseph Connolly). All save Connolly had been 'out' in 1916, O'Kelly and Ryan as members of the GPO garrison. In January 1935, they recommended that the tablet contain the third paragraph of Pearse's Proclamation,[36] followed by the names of its seven signatories, all executed after the Rising: Thomas J. Clarke, Seán MacDiarmada, Thomas MacDonagh, P. H. Pearse, Éamonn Ceannt, James Connolly, and Joseph Plunkett. The chosen text could be read as an implicit rebuke to those who had accepted the 1922 Treaty:

> We declare the right of the people of Ireland to the ownership of Ireland, and to the unfettered control of Irish destinies, to be sovereign and indefeasible. The long usurpation of that right by a foreign people and government has not extinguished the right, nor can it ever be extinguished except by the destruction of the Irish people. In every generation the Irish people have asserted their right to national freedom and sovereignty: six times during the past three hundred years they have asserted it in arms. Standing on that fundamental right and again asserting it in arms in the face of the world, we hereby proclaim the Irish Republic as a Sovereign Independent State, and we pledge our lives and the lives of our comrades-in-arms to the cause of its freedom, of its welfare, and of its exaltation among the nations.[37]

At the end of March 1935, the Department of Public Works reported that *The Death of Cuchulain* had been set up in the GPO and approved by de Valera and by Sheppard. The pedestal was about to be installed, as was the tablet, 'in accordance with the views of the President.'[38] Statue, tablet, and marble pedestal had cost £820. With the completion of the project, de Valera prepared for an indoor ceremony to unveil the statue and present it to the Irish people.

The planned ceremony, its purpose, and its guest list immediately became an issue for the opposition party in the Dáil. On 4 April, Fine Gael's Richard Mulcahy, who had led the armed forces that defeated de Valera's republicans in 1922–23, formally asked de Valera for information about 'a body calling itself the Easter Week Memorial Committee', which was inviting, with advertisements in the *Irish Press*, 'all national organizations to participate in the unveiling ceremony of the Easter Memorial to the men and women of 1916', to be 'unveiled by President de Valera on Easter Sunday, the 21st April next'.[39]

His question was probably provoked by that morning's *Irish Times*, which described at some length the arrangements for unveiling *The Death of Cuchulain* in the GPO. De Valera and his ministers would attend an open-air Mass at Portobello Barracks with the troops. There would be a parade from Parnell Square to the GPO, headed by 'officers and men of the 1916 garrison' marching in units according to their stations during the Rising. De Valera and the other members of government would arrive at eleven thirty with a mounted escort, and the statue would be unveiled on the stroke of noon, the moment when Pearse began to read the Proclamation in 1916. 'All classes of organized associations' were again invited to participate in the parade. Invitations to the actualunveiling inside the GPO, where space was limited, would go to government ministers and their parliamentary secretaries, ministers from all previous governments back to 1919 and the first Dáil, all present Dáil deputies and senators, former Dáil deputies who had fought in 1916, relatives of those killed in action or executed, and 'Volunteers who actually participated' in the Rising. A bugle call and drum roll from inside would announce the moment of unveiling, to be followed by a fanfare of trumpets from the roof, the firing of a *feu de joie*, the playing of the national anthem, 'The Soldier's Song', and three rifle volleys from 1916 men stationed on the roof. The ceremony would be followed by a parade of the Free State Defence Forces, 2,000 Regulars and 4,500 Volunteers, the largest military display in Dublin since the departure of the British.[40]

36 NAI, S6405, Cabinet 7/101 22.1.35, item 4.
37 *Proclamation of the Irish Republic, Irish Historical Documents since 1800*, eds. Alan O'Day and John Stevenson (Dublin: Gill and Macmillan, 1992), 160.
38 NAI, S6405.
39 DÉD, vol. 55, 4 April 1935, 1889–92.

40 *IT*, 4 April 1935.
41 DÉD, vol. 55, 4 April 1935, 1889–92, and 11 April 1935, 2313–16, 2435–62.
42 42 *IT*, 18 April 1935.
43 43 *IT*, 15 April 1935.
44 *IT*, 17 April 1935; last sentence omitted in *IT* but in original, NAI: S6405/C.
45 NAI, S6405/C.
46 *IT*, 15 April 1935.

Aware of all this planning, Mulcahy demanded to know whether the Easter Week Memorial Committee was an official government committee, who its members were, who had formed it, and to whom invitations were to be issued. De Valera was evasive about the committee's nature and membership and rejected Mulcahy's charge that a public monument paid for with public money had been taken over by the Fianna Fáil party. De Valera, Mulcahy complained, 'tells us what he does not know but he does not tell us what he knows'. Mulcahy and other opposition members raised the issue again, and at length, on 11 April, without much success. [41]

De Valera eventually sent invitations 'on behalf of the Government of the Irish Free State' to attend 'the unveiling of Oliver Sheppard's statue "the Death of Cuchulain"' at the General Post Office on Easter Sunday (21 April) 1935. In the event, Cosgrave, Costello and other members of the opposition declined invitations to attend what they considered to be both a co-option of the 1916 legacy and a Fianna Fáil party rally. 'The time is not yet ripe for an adequate commemoration of 1916', Cosgrave declared, citing 'division' and contemporary political ill will in the statement he released to the *Irish Times*: 'It is not possible to hide these national humiliations today, or to cover them with a veil lifted from the bronze statue of Cuchulain.'[42] Mulcahy simply announced, 'I am not going'.[43] The chief justice pleaded illness, and the president of the High Court found that he would be away from Dublin. De Valera also received spirited refusals, for vastly different reasons, from Oliver Gogarty and Maud Gonne MacBride. 'Sir, I have received your invitation to a commemoration of a proclamation of a Republic in the G.P.O.', wrote Gogarty on 15 April, with studied distaste: 'I must refuse to assist you in playing Hamlet when your Republicans are howling for Macbeth. In view of my experience of them, I consider your invitation to me personally an impertinence.'[44]

Maud Gonne was more formal, but equally dismissive: 'Madame Gonne MacBride regrets that for reasons the President and the Government of the Free State are aware of, she cannot accept their invitation to be present at the ceremony at the General Post Office on Easter Sunday, 21st April, 1935.'[45] Unlike the resentful supporters of the opposition party, who distrusted de Valera's republican leanings, she scorned him for betraying the ideals of the Rising by not being republican enough, by taking the oath and working within the framework of the Treaty. She told the *Irish Times* that she 'hoped all true Irish Republicans would not go near the General Post Office on Sunday next', where their presence would 'desecrate the memory' of 1916.[46]

United Ireland, the paper of Fine Gael, fired a final salvo on 20 April. A lengthy front-page editorial celebrated the extraordinary heroism of 1916 as a 'blood sacrifice' that had saved 'the flickering flame of that intense national self-consciousness and enthusiasm which had survived the defeats and disappointments of centuries' from dying out. 'The men of 1916 ... not only freed Ireland but preserved Ireland.' A partisan effort to 'exploit' their memory was 'AN UNSEEMLY SCRAMBLE' when 'the Communistic I.R.A.' did so, but this year 'the men who for the time being constitute the Government of the State ... have decided to outdo all that has heretofore been done by partisan bodies to desecrate the memory of Easter Week'. The paper complained that *The Death of Cuchulain* 'was not even specially designed, [but] ... was made many years ago. It lay ready to hand, however, and could be unveiled when it suited the political purposes of the Government, whereas, a specially sculptured piece might not have been completed for some years'. As for Cú Chulainn, he was hardly 'a suitable symbol' of 1916:

He did not even fight, as Finn MacCumhaill is reputed to have fought at times, against foreigners ... HE FOUGHT ONLY IRISHMEN ... WHY THE 19TH ANNIVERSARY? ... If political tactics were not the deciding factor … one would expect any special celebration to be timed for the twentieth or the twenty-fifth anniversary.

The editorial also complained that the committee in charge of the event did not include anyone from the 'great Opposition Party', despite its many 'leading members' who had 'actually fought in 1916' and that '[w]orst of all', Fianna Fáil would also treat the occasion as a chance to raise money; there would be 'the jingle of collecting boxes' as well as the military parade and the firing of salutes. The *United Ireland* declined to urge a boycott of the whole affair, but suggested that 'all who have any sense of fitness will take part, if they do take part, with a certain repugnance and a deep feeling of sorrow that what might have been a great national manifestation of love and reverence should have been cheapened and degraded'.[47]

De Valera's Executive Council was of course present on Easter Sunday, as were Fianna Fáil deputies and relatives of the 1916 leaders, Pearse's mother prominent among them. John Leo Burke was there, described on the official guest list as 'Originator of the Memorial'. Sheppard was unfortunately ill with pneumonia and could not attend.[48] None of the writers and artists then working in Dublin was invited, not even W. B. Yeats, despite his Nobel Prize and the several plays he had written about Cú Chulainn. Given his increasingly conservative politics after 1922, he might well have declined.

The Free State army duly marched on Easter Sunday morning, bands played, drums rolled, bugles and trumpets sounded, volleys and salutes were fired, and no doubt collecting boxes jingled. De Valera's dedication speech was fully reported next day in the Dublin papers. The text from which he read survives in the de Valera archive at Dublin's Franciscan House of Studies. He wrote the speech himself, had it typed, and then made revisions on the

typescript, a sign that he took considerable pains with it.[49] Those members of the opposition who declined to attend the dedication and unveiling would find in the speech much to disturb them when they read it over breakfast on Easter Monday. It was a subtle but emphatic assertion that de Valera and his party were the legitimate heirs of 1916, and were determined to preserve and extend their legacy. Though speaking as the Irish Free State's head of government, de Valera suggested that the government itself was a work in progress, a stage that would lead eventually to the achievement of Pearse's republic. Given the steps he was taking and would take to evade the Treaty and gradually distance Ireland from Great Britain and the crown, it is, in hindsight, a clear statement of intentions:

> From this place nineteen years ago the Republic of Ireland was proclaimed … the beginning of one of Ireland's most glorious and sustained efforts for independence. It has been a reproach to us that the spot has remained so long unmarked. To-day we remove the reproach. All who enter this hall henceforth will be reminded of the deed enacted here. A beautiful piece of sculpture, the creation of Irish genius, symbolizing the dauntless courage and abiding constancy of our people, will commemorate it modestly, indeed, but fittingly. The time to raise a proud national monument to the work that was here begun and to those who inspired and participated in it has not yet come. Such a monument can be raised only when the work is triumphantly completed. [50]

In this speech, de Valera clearly responded to Cosgrave's recent claim that the time for a memorial to 1916 had not yet arrived, because of the enduring bitter political divisions that now separated those who had earlier fought side by side in the War of Independence. De Valera agreed that the time for 'a proud national monument'

47 *United Ireland*, 20 April 1935.
48 *IT*, 22 April 1935.
49 Information from the late Breandán Mac Giolla Choille, Franciscan House of Studies, Dublin.
50 *IT*, 22 April 1935.

1941: Éamon de Valera inspecting troops outside the General Post Office on the 25th anniversary of the 1916 Rising. Photo: Keystone/Getty Images.

51 51 T. D., A. M. and D. B. Sullivan, eds., *Speeches from the Dock* (Dublin, 1968), 42–43.

had not arrived, but he implied a different reason: the Free State was only a provisional arrangement, the result of a flawed Treaty. His listeners, well versed in Irish patriotic oratory, would have recognized in his words an echo of a speech then memorized by most Irish schoolchildren, Robert Emmet's defiant words to the court that condemned him to death in 1803:

Let no man write my epitaph; for as no man who knows my motives dare now vindicate them, let not prejudice or ignorance asperse them. Let them and me rest in obscurity and peace, and my tomb remain uninscribed, and my memory in oblivion, until other times and other men can do justice to my character. When my country takes her place among the nations of the earth, *then, and not till then*, let my epitaph be written.[51]

De Valera went on to read the third paragraph of the Proclamation, as quoted on the yet unveiled tablet. He recalled the 1918 parliamentary elections, when the Irish people voted overwhelmingly for Sinn Féin candidates, who pledged that they would not enter the British parliament, but would meet in Dublin as Dáil Éireann, the independent parliament of Ireland. He left unsaid the charge that the members of that assembly who voted to accept the Treaty had betrayed their trust, and again he implied that the Free State government was only a provisional arrangement, a framework within which the vision of 1916 could be realized: 'here again to-day, proud of our association with ... [the signers of the Proclamation] ... and with their work, once more as the elected representatives of the majority of the Irish people, we proclaim our unchangeable devotion to their ideals, and dedicate ourselves anew to their uncompleted task'. He quoted again from the Proclamation, noting its guarantees of civil and religious freedom and equality, and its promise to ignore 'the differences carefully fostered by an alien government, which have divided a minority from the majority in the past'— differences that the provisions of the Treaty perpetuated. Ireland could be united again behind the 'lofty aims' of 1916, he claimed:

The work of Easter Week can never be undone. Even those who do not feel any yearning for independence themselves must realize that there can never be a turning back. Before 1916 Ireland might have been content for a time with something less than independence. After 1916 that is impossible.

In his peroration, de Valera shifted into 'the language to which the leaders of the 1916 rising were so faithful, and from which there came to them the real spirit of nationhood'. Speaking in Irish, he declared that

Ireland will not be satisfied until the country is absolutely free of foreign domination, North, South, East and West. ... It is for us to prepare ourselves, not alone to win freedom, but to ensure that we shall be worthy of it ... I now unveil this memorial to the men who gave their lives for Ireland in the rising of 1916, and to commemorate also the proclamation of the Irish Republic at that time. I hope that it will serve to keep in the minds of the youth of this country the great deeds of those who went before us, and that it will also serve to spur us on to emulate their valour and their sacrifice.[52]

The *Irish Times* also records that there was a parade 'after a fairly long wait', of about a thousand 'persons who refused to participate in the official celebrations', IRA members and 'extreme Republicans' who shared Maud Gonne MacBride's scorn for de Valera's compromises, and marched past the GPO on their way to the republican plot in Glasnevin cemetery.

And so Sheppard's *Death of Cuchulain* was set up, dedicated, and unveiled. Thanks to John Leo Burke, the men and women of 1916 are not unworthily commemorated, by a monument infinitely preferable to the kind of Republican *pietà* then in vogue, with Erin or Cathleen Ní Houlihan cradling a fallen Volunteer on her knees. *The Death of Cuchulain* is certainly preferable to Sheppard's *Inis Fáil*, which is overburdened with symbolic content.

The choice and placement of *The Death of Cuchulain* as the 1916 memorial had another consequence. Yeats would have seen the plaster cast of the statue in Sheppard's studio. We do not know if he ever saw it cast in bronze and in place at the GPO. But at the end of his life he was brooding on 1916, and his own possible responsibility for the Rising. 'Did that play of mine send out / Certain men the English shot?' he asks in 'The Man and the Echo', published in January 1939, the month and year of his death. He was thinking of his *Cathleen ni Houlihan* (1902), in which Cathleen, played in the first production by Maud Gonne, calls on young men to die for Ireland even when there is no chance of victory. Pearse certainly had 'that play' in mind as he planned the Rising, and he responded to Cathleen's appeal in an almost literal way. 'When I was a child I believed that there was actually a woman called Erin,' he tells us in *The Spiritual Nation*, written in January 1916:

and had Mr. Yeats' 'Kathleen Ni Houlihan' been then written and had I seen it, I should have taken it not as an allegory, but as a representation of a thing that might happen any day in any house. This I no longer believe as a physical possibility. ... But I believe that there is really a spiritual tradition which is the soul of Ireland.[53]

52 *IT*, 22 April 1935. The newspaper notes that de Valera finished his speech at 11.57.
53 Edwards, *Patrick Pearse*, 254; Pearse, *Collected Works*, 300–01.

54 W. B. Yeats, *Autobiographies*, ed. William H. O'Donnell and Douglas N. Archibald (New York, 1999), 90–91.

55 W. B. Yeats to E.S. Heald, 28 June 1938, in *The Letters of W. B. Yeats*, ed. Allan Wade (London, 1954), 911.

56 W. B. Yeats, 'The Statues', in *The Variorum Edition of the Poems of W. B. Yeats*, eds. Peter Allt and Russell K. Alspach (New York, 1957), 610–11.

57 W. B. Yeats, *The Death of Cuchulain*, in *The Variorum Edition of the Plays of W. B. Yeats*, ed. Russell K. Alspach (New York, 1966), 1063.

For Yeats, who had celebrated Cú Chulainn in plays and poems, the presence of Sheppard's *The Death of Cuchulain* in the Post Office as a memorial to Pearse and his comrades acted to associate the ancient hero's determination to fight against overwhelming odds with Cathleen Ni Houlihan's call to fight even though victory is unlikely. Pearse shared these commitments. The statue also recalled Yeats's own days in the Metropolitan School of Art modelling class, where he had learned about proportional measurement and the sculptor's use of the plummet, with Sheppard as fellow student.[54] Late in June 1938, he sent a new poem, 'The Statues', to his last lover, Edith Shackleton Heald, explaining in the accompanying letter that 'Cuchulain is in the last stanza because Pearse and some of his followers had a cult of him. The Government has put a statue of Cuchulain in the rebuilt post office to commemorate this.'[55]

'The Statues' celebrates the physical specificity and precise calculations of Graeco-Roman sculpture and the European tradition it establishes, in contrast to 'Asiatic vague immensities':

> When Pearse summoned Cuchulain to his
>   side
> What stalked through the Post Office?
>   What intellect,
> What calculation, number, measurement
>   replied?[56]

Yeats implies that Cú Chulainn, given physical form, the 'lineaments of a plummet-measured face', by the 'calculation, number, measurement' of the unnamed Oliver Sheppard, makes manifest that spirit, source of energy, emanation, that Pearse was able to summon from literature, from art, to sustain him and his followers in their time of crisis. Pearse, Cú Chulainn, and Sheppard's careful craftsmanship, combine as the matrix of the poem.

Yeats returned again to this complex merger of artistic form, heroic energy, and the actual fighting at the GPO, in his last play,

to which he gave the name of Sheppard's sculpture: *The Death of Cuchulain*. In the play, written October–December 1938, he follows the version of the hero's death that had inspired Sheppard when he read Lady Gregory's *Cuchulain of Muirthemne*. Here too Cú Chulainn ties himself upright to a pillar-stone to face his enemies alone. Yeats's play ends after Cú Chulainn dies, with three shabby street singers mourning the physical disappearance of the great 'ancient race' of such heroes, their survival only as emanations; however, it suggests that there are dimensions beyond ordinary reality, that the thought of Cú Chulainn infused the fighters of 1916 with his reckless heroism. Sheppard in bronze, Yeats in verse have given form to that thought:

> Are those things that men adore and loathe
> Their sole reality?
> What stood in the Post Office
> With Pearse and Connolly?
> What comes out of the mountain
> Where men first shed their blood?
> Who thought Cuchulain till it seemed
> He stood where they had stood?
> No body like his body
> Has modern woman borne,
> But an old man looking on life
> Imagines it in scorn.
> A statue's there to mark the place,
> By Oliver Sheppard done.
> So ends the tale that the harlot
> Sang to the beggar-man.[57]

Idir Dhá Chomhairle/ Between Two Minds

Interculturality in Literary Criticism in Irish

Máirín Nic Eoin

Two interlinked debates — one about linguistic standards and another about literary form — have animated Irish-language literary criticism since the commencement of the revival movement in the late nineteenth century. They have both played a role in shaping a modern literature in Irish and they have also defined two key features of criticism in the language: its commitment to, and vested interest in, the fate of the language itself; and its anxiety about the bilingual and intercultural context in which writers of the language have been working.

There would not be a modern

Máirtín Ó Cadhain.
Photo: courtesy Cló Iar-Chonnachta.

Seosamh Mac Grianna. Photo: courtesy Cló Iar-Chonnachta.

literature in Irish without the language revival movement. Indeed, that very literature is one of the most tangible cultural achievements of that movement and, depending on one's commitment to multilinguality, arguably one of the most positive. One gets the sense from Irish-language criticism, however, that modern literature in Irish remains in a constant state of emergence. Its continued existence can never be taken for granted — and writers' awareness of the endangered nature of their literary medium is reflected in a sense of critical responsibility or engagement resulting in a perceived need to exhort and encourage writers, to predict future trends and thereby to play an active role in the shaping of what was, or what has, yet to come.

At the same time, Irish-language criticism, while it tends to revolve around a number of clearly recognizable cultural themes and preoccupations, has never been monological. It was marked from the outset by the most intense and passionate of debates, sometimes about issues (such as font, orthography and the authority of

1 See Philip O'Leary, *The Prose Literature of the Gaelic Revival, 1881–1921: Ideology and Innovation* (University Park, Penn., 1994) and *Gaelic Prose in the Free State 1922–1939* (Dublin, 2004); Gearóid Denvir, 'Ó Shíolteagasc go Critic: Litríocht Dhioscúrsúil na Gaeilge san Aois Seo', *Léachtaí Cholm Cille*, 26 (1996), 178–218; Brian Ó Conchubhair, 'The Gaelic Font Controversy: The Gaelic League's (Post-Colonial) Crux', *Irish University Review*, 33, 1 (2003), 46–63.

2 Richard Henebry, 'A Plea for Prose', *Gaelic Journal/Irisleabhar na Gaedhilge*, 4, 40 (1892), 143.

3 Henebry, 'Plea for Prose', 143.

4 Richard Henebry, 'Revival Irish', *Leader*, 17 (1908–09), 302–05, 326–27, 351–54, 378–80, 398–402, 423–34, 446–47, 470, 492–93, 522–24, 543–44, 564–65, 587–88, 613–14; 'Revival Irish' *Leader*, 18 (1909), 14–15, 39–40, 58–59, 84–86, 110–11.

5 Gearóid Ó Crualaoich, 'An Nuafhilíocht Ghaeilge: Dearcadh Dána', *Innti*, 10 (1986), 64.

6 Ó Crualaoich, 'An Nuafhilíocht Ghaeilge', 66.

dialect forms) which would seem trivial to a contemporary reader but which were of huge cultural importance to those directly involved in them and are typical of the kinds of issue facing the literature of language communities that have become minoritized.[1] Some cultural positions, such as association of the language with rural communities and traditions, were articulated so often that they became synonymous with the Irish-language literary movement, yet there was always room for dissenting voices and a suspicion about critical consensus. Over the 'long' twentieth century, it is the work of those who challenged the dominant ideology of their own period that has best survived. Moreover, criticism has never been in danger of becoming institutionalized or cut off from the realities of practising writers. Literary criticism was for long seen to be on the periphery of academic scholarship in the language, and it was the creative writers, both within and outside the academy, who were to the fore in creating and sustaining a vibrant critical discourse.

Language Quests and Language Questions

Over more than a century, one can trace a strand of anxiety about the nature and standard of language acceptable in a modern literature in Irish. This is visible from the 1890s, in, say, the writings of Waterford-born linguist, critic and controversialist Dr. Richard Henebry through to the work of contemporary critics such as Gearóid Ó Crualaoich. In the *Gaelic Journal* in 1892, Henebry attacked the poetry of the Gaelic revival as nothing but 'Correct, commonplace English sentiment, thought, expression ... with a miserably tortured poor shred of Irish for veneering.'[2] Henebry commanded prospective writers of Irish to reject such an amalgam: 'But there must be no foreign admixture. English idiom, mannerism, style, system of thought, must be rigidly eschewed.'[3] He published a more sustained treatise on 'Revival Irish' seventeen years later in the *Leader*; in it he

reiterated both the condemnation of English influence and the message of de-anglicization.[4] Almost eighty years later, Ó Crualaoich, in a controversial article in the poetry magazine *Innti*, made a similar judgement about contemporary poetry in Irish:

> *'Béarla a fhoghlaim ar dtúis' an chomhairle is críonna a chuirfeá ar an Seapáineach aonteangach a dteastódh uaidh élí féin a chur in oiriúint chun brí a bhaint as an gcuid is mó ar fad de nualitríocht na hÉireann idir Ghaeilge is Bhéarla, idir bhéarsaíocht agus phrós.*[5]

'Learn English first' would be the best advice you could give to a monolingual Japanese person who wished to prepare himself/herself for an understanding of most modern Irish literature, both in Irish and in English, both verse and prose.

Most Irish-language poets are functioning outside of what Ó Crualaoich terms *dioscúrsa na Gaeilge* (Irish-language discourse), and the exceptions he cites, Nuala Ní Dhomhnaill and Michael Hartnett, illustrate his understanding of 'truly Gaelic' contemporary poetry as poetry in communion with a historical Irish-language poetic tradition. While both Henebry and Ó Crualaoich in essence reach the same critical conclusion, Ó Crualaoich's greater understanding of the sociolinguistic context of modern writing in Irish allows him to conclude with a recognition that the biculturality of the contemporary poet in Irish is a biculturality of the marginalized:

> *Is é cás an fhile Ghaelaigh, sa mhéid gur ann dó/di in aon chor ar na saoltaibh seo, bheith 'bicultural', stractha idir dhá shaol, dhá theanga, dhá mheon, bheith 'as riocht' go mór, bheith eolgaiseach ar imeall na beatha, ar bhuile, ar thost síoraí, ar an neamhní.*[6]

It is the fate of the Gaelic poet, in so much as he or she exists at all at present, to be 'bicultural', torn between two worlds, two tongues, two minds, to be greatly 'out of kilt', to know the margins of life, to know madness, endless silence, nothingness.

Henebry's 'decolonizing' stance was a dominant one in critical practice in Irish for much of the twentieth century. Indeed, it faced no significant challenge until the 1960s when it was acknowledged that the cultural values on which it was based hindered a proper critical evaluation of the work of many of the most accomplished Irish-language writers. Henebry himself is best remembered for the arguments that he lost. His most controversial proposal — that contemporary writers should return to the literary standard of classical Irish — was firmly rejected from the outset in favour of the more pragmatic position taken by an tAthair Peadar Ua Laoghaire, a highly influential Cork-born native speaker and revivalist who believed that a modern literature should be based on *caint na ndaoine*, or the language as it was spoken in the Irish-speaking districts.[7] This emphasis on *caint na ndaoine* made a quite different version of linguistic authenticity and linguistic purity the central and overriding concern of literary criticism in Irish for decades. Among the consequences was a fetishization of the native speaker, a privileging of filiation over affiliation, and an unresolved tension between centre and periphery, between the urban and the rural, between standard and dialect. Gaeltacht writers such as Ua Laoghaire and Séamus Ó Grianna were hailed as exemplars and non-native speakers were assessed on their ability to disguise their learner status by successfully mimicking a particular regional idiom.

Very few second-language writers escaped criticism on linguistic grounds, but the preoccupation with linguistic purity was also limiting for Gaeltacht writers, perhaps demonstrating that demotic standards are rarely acceptable to literary élites. Most of Henebry's criticism was directed at the

writings of non-native speakers, but his linguistic purism extended so far as to lead him to claim as early as 1908 that it is only 'one possessing P. Canon O'Leary's marked gift of the language sense that can prevail against the overpowering dominance of foreign idiom'.[8] Gaeltacht writers, acutely aware of the changing speech styles in their own native districts, used their work as a bulwark against, and as a critique of, such tendencies. Ó Grianna was an extreme example. In the words of critic Ailbhe Ó Corráin:

He modelled his language on the diction of the most idiomatic speakers from his own area and refused to countenance anything in his work which was not native to his own dialect. Indeed, it is perhaps true to say that he wrote the language not of his own generation but rather that of his parents' and grandparents' generation and he was highly critical of the Irish of younger people from the *Gaeltacht*, which he regarded as already to some extent corrupt and debased.[9]

This concern about the spoken language of native speakers was expressed regularly throughout the twentieth century and has come to the fore in recent work by linguists, creative writers and critics.[10] But the context of the debate has changed utterly, however, as more Gaeltacht writers ignore the strictures of former generations of revivalists and attempt more realistic depictions of language as spoken in Gaeltacht regions. These depictions include code-mixing, code-switching and other manifestations of the language contact situation in which Irish has for centuries been written and spoken. Critical response to these developments has been wary, mainly because of the critics' vested interest (as teachers, college lecturers, publishers) in the survival of the purer forms and in the survival of a sustainable and distinguishable Irish-speaking language group. Certain fundamental questions,

7   For a discussion of that particular debate, see Cathal Ó Háinle, 'Ó Chaint na nDaoine go dtí an Caighdeán Oifigiúil', in Kim McCone, Damian McManus, Cathal Ó Háinle, Nicholas Williams and Liam Breatnach, eds., *Stair na Gaeilge* (Maigh Nuad, 1994), 745–93, esp. 754–64.

8   Henebry, 'Revival Irish', *Leader*, 17 (1908-09), 302–03.

9   Ailbhe Ó Corráin, 'Language as a Reflection of Changing Ireland: Developments in Modern Irish Prose Writing', in Birgit Bramsbäck, ed., *Homage to Ireland: Aspects of Culture, Literature and Language* (Uppsala, 1990), 100–01. See also Ó Corráin 'Teanga Mháire', in Nollaig Mac Congáil, ed., *Jonneen Khordaroy Answers Critics* (Baile Átha Cliath, 1992), 94–107.

10 See Máirín Nic Eoin, 'Íonghlaineacht Teanga: Fadhb an Bhéarla i gCritic Liteartha na Gaeilge' and '"Idir Dhá Theanga": An Chruthaitheacht Liteartha agus an Contanam Dátheangach', in *'Trén bhFearann Breac': An Díláithriú Cultúir agus Nualitríocht na Gaeilge* (Baile Átha Cliath, 2005), chs. 2 and 8 respectively.

11 See O'Leary, *Gaelic Prose in the Irish Free State*, 37–69.

12 Daniel Corkery,'On Anglo-Irish Literature', in *Synge and Anglo-Irish Literature* (Cork, 1931), 1–27.

13 Domhnall Ó Corcora, 'Filidheacht na Gaedhilge — A Cineál', in Risteárd Ó Foghludha, ed., *Éigse na Máighe* (Baile Átha Cliath, 1952), 7–29; 'Smaointe Fánacha ar an bhFilíocht', *Feasta* (Eanáir 1954), 9; (Feabhra 1954), 10; (Márta 1954), 5, 19, (Aibreán 1954), 10, 20; (Bealtaine 1954), 9–10; (Meitheamh 1954), 13; (Iúil 1954), 13–14; (Meán Fómhair 1954), 2–3.

14 For a discussion of *An Béal Bocht* as post-colonial critique, see Louis de Paor, 'Myles na gCopaleen agus Drochshampla na nDealeabhar', *Irish Review*, 23 (1998), 24–32; Sarah E. McKibben, '*An Béal Bocht*: Mouthing off at National Identity', *Éire-Ireland*, 38, 1–2 (2003), 37–53.

15 See, in particular, his 1930 essays 'Teanga na Tíre' and 'Gaeil agus Gaelainn', in Breandán Ó Conaire, ed., *Bloghanna ón mBlascaod* (Baile Átha Cliath, 1997), 170–71, 183.

Máirtín Ó Direáin. Photo: courtesy Cló Iar-Chonnachta.

arising from the position of Irish as a minoritized language, cannot be avoided. For example, can one have an Irish-language literature that goes against the grain of revivalist ideology? Can one afford to jettison the authority of literature as standard-bearer in the face of what some commentators now see as a process of creolization? For an endangered language, victim of an unequal linguistic encounter, is there a viable alternative to literary purism?

There has also been a considerable shift in relation to another aspect of this concern about linguistic standards. For long, a concern with linguistic authenticity came hand in hand with a preoccupation with the appropriateness of certain subjects and themes for Irish-language literature. Concern for purity of expression often masked a predilection for romanticized, heroic or moralistic narratives of humble Irish-speaking life on the economically impoverished western seaboard. A large and repetitive body of literary commentary developed (particularly in the 1920s and 1930s) around the concept of 'Gaelachas' and what constituted a truly Gaelic world-view,[11] so that Daniel Corkery's formulations on what constituted 'the Irish national being' in *Synge and Anglo-Irish Literature*[12] and on what constituted truly Gaelic literature in his various essays in Irish[13] were merely a reiteration of what were widely believed to be defining characteristics of Gaelic life and culture. What Philip O'Leary's ground-breaking volumes have revealed is the sheer volume of nativist propaganda faced by the modernizers, among whom can be counted Patrick Pearse and Pádraic Ó Conaire in the early years of the century, through to Seosamh Mac Grianna, Donn Piatt, Liam Ó Rinn, Brian Ó Nualláin/Myles na gCopaleen, Máirtín Ó Cadhain and many significant others in the later post-Independence period. For decades, writing in Irish strove to live up to the expectations and prescriptions of a cultural nationalist agenda that was both limiting and pervasive.

However, most of the nativist commentators whom O'Leary discusses are known today only in scholarly and academic circles, while the work of the most significant of the modernizers is still being read, discussed, taught and enjoyed by a contemporary audience. It is significant also that those literary works that were to become canonical examples of Gaelic Ireland in all its purity and nobility of spirit — the Blasket Island autobiographies — carried within them the material for the most radical of post-colonial parodies, that of Myles na gCopaleen's *An Béal Bocht* (1941), where the huge gap between the ideals and obsessions of the language movement and the economic realities of Gaeltacht life are brilliantly captured.[14] After that, nativist assumptions were never again so secure. Furthermore, even Tomás Ó Criomhthain, whose *An tOileánach* (1929) was the key text parodied in *An Béal Bocht*, was himself very aware of the gap between the efforts of the language movement and the economic reality of Gaeltacht life in independent Ireland.[15] Such an awareness informs the work of all the significant twentieth-century Gaeltacht writers, including Ó Criomhthain's son Seán and his grandson Pádraig Ua Maoileoin.

Máire Mac an tSaoi. Photo: courtesy Cló Iar-Chonnachta.

There was another irony here, in that the ideology that laid the basis for a national attempt to revive Irish did not include a strategy for dealing with the creative endeavours of those who were the success stories of that attempt — those who, through the efforts of the school system in the post-Independence period, became active bilinguals, competent and confident enough to consider writing in Irish a real possibility. Yet it was the work of these accomplished non-native, or semi-native, speakers that fundamentally challenged the decolonizing thrust of much early twentieth-century critical commentary. A classic example can be found in the early critical response to the work of Cork-born poet Seán Ó Ríordáin. Ó Ríordáin was deprived, by the span of a generation, of a 'true' Gaeltacht upbringing. Born in 1916 to an English-speaking mother, he spent his earliest years in the bilingual breac-Ghaeltacht community of Baile Bhuirne in West Cork before the household moved to Cork city when he was in his mid-teens. His embrace of Irish, as articulated in his poetry and prose writings, can be seen, on the one hand, in essentialist and nativist terms as an attempted decolonization of the mind, a linguistic homecoming and a retrieval of a sense of lost personal and national identity. It can, on the other hand, also be interpreted as part of a lifelong

16 Máire Mhac an tSaoi, 'Filíocht Sheáin Uí Ríordáin', *Feasta* (Márta 1953), 17–19.
17 Seán Ó Tuama, 'An Forum: Filíocht Sheáin Uí Ríordáin', *Feasta* (Aibreán 1953), 16.
18 Máirtín Ó Direáin, 'Ríordánachas agus eile', *Feasta* (Bealtaine 1953), 14–15.
19 Tomás Ó Floinn, 'Filíocht Sheáin Uí Ríordáin', in Liam Prút, ed., *Cion Fir: Aistí Thomáis Uí Fhloinn in Comhar* (Baile Átha Cliath, 1997), 144; first published in *Comhar* (Bealtaine 1953).

20 Declan Kiberd, 'Seán Ó
Ríordáin: File Angla-
Éireannach?', in Eoghan
Ó hAnluain, ed., *An
Duine is Dual: Aistí ar
Sheán Ó Ríordáin* (Baile
Átha Cliath, 1980),
90–111.
21 Eibhlín Nic Ghearailt,
*Seán Ó Ríordáin agus
'An Striapach Allúrach'*
(Baile Átha Cliath, 1988).
22 Frank Sewell, 'Seán
Ó Ríordáin: Joycery-
Corkery-Sorcery', *Irish
Review*, 23 (1998),
42–61.
23 Stiofán Ó Cadhla, *Cá
bhfuil Éire? Guth an
Ghaisce i bPrós Sheáin
Uí Ríordáin* (Baile Átha
Cliath, 1998).

spiritual journey, a conscious act of identity construction and cultural positioning. It is indicative of the critical climate still prevailing in Ireland in the early 1950s that when the young poet Máire Mhac an tSaoi attacked what she held to be Ó Ríordáin's misuse of language in his first collection *Eireaball Spideoige* — exhorting him, with the conviction of the true nativist, to cease writing until he had filled his head with the kind of Gaeltacht Irish necessary for him to be accepted as a true Irish-language poet[16] — one of his strongest defenders, Seán Ó Tuama, felt it necessary to stress his Gaeltacht filiation.[17] Others defended his use of language on the grounds of artistic freedom, the poet Máirtín Ó Direáin (himself a native speaker) in particular challenging any critic who would impose limitations on the work of the imagination.[18] Only one critic at that time articulated a more nuanced understanding of Ó Ríordáin's cultural position. That was Tomás Ó Floinn who, writing in May 1953, responded to the critical reception of *Eireaball Spideoige* thus:

Tá sé míréasúnta a bheith ag éileamh ar dhuine nach cainteoir ó dhúchas é filíocht a scríobh faoi mar a scríobhfadh cainteoir dúchais í. Agus ní fios cé acu is measa lucht a cháinte nó lucht a chosanta mar is é an ní céanna atá á éileamh ag an dá dhream. Ní hé go bhfuilim ag cosaint a lochtanna, ach go bhfuilim ag glacadh leo mar chuid dá dhéantús, mar chuid de dhlúth agus d'inneach an fhile nár tógadh go hiomlán le Gaeilge ach gur mian leis, ar a shon san, a chuid filíochta a cheapadh sa teanga sin.[19]

It is unreasonable to demand of a non-native speaker that he write poetry as if he was a native speaker. And I don't know who is worse, those who fault him or those who defend him, because they are both looking for the same thing. It is not that I am defending his faults, but that I accept them as part of his work, as an integral part of the make-up of a poet who was not raised fully through Irish but who wishes, nevertheless, to compose poetry in that language.

It was not until the late twentieth century that critics would openly celebrate Ó Ríordáin's creative achievement in terms of his interculturality and his attempts to marry a personal voyage of discovery with a process of linguistic retrieval and cultural re-affirmation. Declan Kiberd, writing in 1980, termed him an 'Anglo-Irish' poet, so marked were the influences of the English poetic tradition on his work,[20] and Eibhlín Nic Ghearailt subsequently undertook a study of Ó Ríordáin's major non-Gaelic influences.[21] Frank Sewell has since written very perceptively of Ó Ríordáin's engagement with the language in terms of a spiritual journey, a search for 'the true self and true self-expression' where language could function as bedrock of identity only if the concept of *dúchas* (nativeness) could be extended so that the poet would be concerned less with successfully locating himself within a predefined cultural and linguistic tradition than with devising means whereby he could extend that tradition in new directions.[22] Ó Ríordáin was himself very aware that the extension of the concept of *dúchas* he was suggesting, though necessary, was extremely problematic as long as the language was so threatened. Ó Ríordáin's prose works are important for an understanding of his creative and political dilemma. Stiofán Ó Cadhla's penetrating analysis of his journalism explores Ó Ríordáin's attempt to reconcile a decolonizing politics of cultural affirmation with an acceptance of post-colonial interculturality.[23] For Ó Ríordáin — as for most Irish-language writers — the most urgent question was: how does one come to terms with the minoritization and marginalization of a language regarded as key to cultural identity and effective self-expression?

•

The 1960s saw a change of direction in Irish-language writing, with the emergence

Louis de Paor. Photo: courtesy Cló Iar-Chonnachta.

of a new kind of non-Gaeltacht writer. Notably, the young poets who established the poetry magazine *Innti* while students in University College Cork, although inspired by Ó Ríordáin, shared none of his anxieties about their own linguistic and cultural backgrounds. Poets such as Cork-city born Michael Davitt embraced the language with a greater sense of self-confidence, associating it with 1960s freedoms rather than with post-Independence pieties and recognizing in it the potential for new kinds of cultural and linguistic fusion. Their journey west to the Gaeltacht was experienced as a voyage of discovery, never as a homecoming, and their political commitment to the language was motivated more by the civil rights movements of the period than by the cultural nationalism of a former generation.[24] Also in the same decade other writers, such as east Galway-born Eoghan Ó Tuairisc and West Cork-born Diarmaid Ó Súilleabháin, challenged the critical orthodoxy by openly proclaiming that their standards could not be those of the Gaeltacht and by demanding a creative freedom that would acknowledge hybridity and reject the strictures of the linguistic purists. Ó Tuairisc outlined his view

of the cultural position of Irish writers in both languages in a 1975 article on Patrick Kavanagh's poem 'Stony Grey Soil', where he articulated a theory of post-colonial hybridity almost a decade before Homi Bhabha was to publish his oft-cited essays on the subject:

> *Tá an fhadhb chéanna le fuascailt i nduibheagán ár n-anama againn go léir: conas is féidir an tSacsainis atá d'inneach ionainn* (mandril, plough, coulter, bank, burgled ...) *a chomhghaolú leis an Ghaeilge a shaolaítear i gcuisle na cuimhne linn* (Mullahinsha, Drummeril ...)?
>
> *Níl gar againn cultúr amháin acu a shéanadh agus luí go hiomlán leis an chultúr eile. Níl gar againn an Phlandáil a chur ar ceal: ní acmhainn dúinn ach oiread an oidhreacht Cheilteach a ligean le gaoth. Tá an dá oidhreacht fite i bhfíodóireacht ár n-aigne, agus níl dul astu.*
>
> *Maidir le réiteach, ní mian liom a bheith dogmach. Tógfaidh sé cúpla céad bliain eile, mo thuairim, chun an scitsifréin (an chríochdheighilt phearsantachta atá de smior ionainn) a leigheas agus an tÉireannach a fhuineadh as an nua.*[25]

24 For an excellent insight into the change of direction in Irish-language poetry marked by the *Innti* generation, see Eoghan Ó hAnluain, 'Nuafhilíocht na Gaeilge 1966–1986: Úire agus Buaine', *Léachtaí Cholm Cille*, 17 (1986), 7–24. For a discussion of the work of two key figures to emerge in that period, Michael Davitt and Liam Ó Muirthile, see Tadhg Ó Dúshláine, 'Michael Davitt: *Pontifex Maximus Poesis Corcagiensis*', in Micheál Ó Cearúil, ed., *An Aimsir Óg* (Baile Átha Cliath, 1999), 134–50; '*Mearú Uilix Chorcaí*', in Micheál Ó Cearúil, ed., *Aimsir Óg: Cuid a Dó* (Baile Átha Cliath, 2000), 360–70.

25 'Stony Grey Soil: Dándearcadh ar Éigean an Dá Chultúr', in Eoghan Ó Tuairisc, *Religio Poetae agus Aistí Eile*, ed. Máirín Nic Eoin (Baile Átha Cliath, 1987), 163; first published in *Feasta* (Samhain 1975).

26 Diarmaid Ó Súilleabháin, 'Bí Tú Féin, a Úrscéalaí', *Comhar* (Iúil 1965), 19–22.

27 See Diarmaid Ó Súilleabháin, 'An Uain Bheo', *Irisleabhar Mhá Nuad* (1972), 65–69; Éamon Ó Ciosáin, 'Diarmaid Ó Súilleabháin — Geit as an nGaeilge?', *Nua-Aois* (1979), 25–36.

28 Tomás Ó Floinn, 'Filíocht idir dhá Theanga', in Prút, ed., *Cion Fir*, 306; first published in *Comhar* (Meán Fómhair 1964).

29 Pádraigín Riggs, 'Caint na nDaoine: An Chaint agus na Daoine', in Ó Cearúil, ed., *Aimsir Óg: Cuid a Dó* (Baile Átha Cliath, 2000), 78–90.

We are all confronted with the same problem: how to reconcile the Saxon strain within us (mandril, plough, coulter, bank, burgled ...) with the Irish language which lives on in the pulse of memory (Mullahinsha, Drummeril ...)?

We cannot deny one of those cultures and adhere solely to the other culture. We cannot undo the Plantation: we cannot afford either to throw our Celtic heritage to the winds. The two heritages are entwined in the weave of our minds and we cannot avoid them.

As for a solution, I don't mean to be dogmatic. It will take several hundred years, in my view, to heal the schizophrenia (the psychic partition which goes to our core) and to reshape the Irish person.

Ó Súilleabháin had already gone a step further when, in an 1965 essay, he encouraged non-Gaeltacht writers to forget about aping Gaeltacht language or Gaeltacht themes and to be, above all, 'true to themselves'.[26] Ó Súilleabháin put this decidedly non-nativist concept of cultural authenticity into practice in his own work. His highly individual narrative style attracted attention from the outset and came to be seen as part of a very conscious attempt to 'startle the Irish language' by extending the scope of expression in new directions. A major motivation for such innovation was Ó Súilleabháin's determination to depict through Irish those social situations and relationships that would not normally be associated with the language.[27] Dozens of writers have followed his lead and the critical climate of condemnation with which he was faced in the sixties has been replaced by a greater acceptance of all kinds of linguistic experimentation.

Tomás Ó Floinn too was a key figure in this critical shift. He was one of the first critics to openly acknowledge and discuss the difficulty of responding to literary works that were, in his own words, *idir dhá theanga* (between two tongues). In a 1961 review of a collection by Armagh-born poet Réamonn Ó Muireadhaigh, he gives voice to the dilemma of the critic who finds he is dealing with an Irish-language poetry whose idiom and metaphorical structure is often based on English. He doesn't have the critical apparatus to evaluate such poetry. And yet, when he poses the general question at the end of the review whether poetry produced by a non-native speaker can be effective or not, his response is definitively positive:

> ... *cén éifeacht is féidir a bheith le filíocht a scríobhtar i dteanga a d'fhoghlaim an file? Ardéifeacht, in ainneoin ceataí agus laigeachtaí, bac agus bacadraíl, mí-labhairt, claonlabhairt agus dearbhéigeart labhartha na teanga idir dhá theanga: in ainneoin an Bhéarla ina Ghaeilge agus na Gaeilge ó Bhéarla.*[28]

> ... how effective can poetry be when it is written in a language the poet learned? Very effective, despite the awkwardness and weaknesses, the barriers and hindrances, the bad speech, perverse speech and out-and-out incorrectness of a language between two languages: despite the English being Irished and the Irish from English.

The Irish-language critic can no longer ignore the presence of both languages in the Irish-language text. In the words of critic Pádraigín Riggs: '*Ní féidir* aontíos an dá theanga a shéanadh' (*One cannot* deny the coexistence of the two languages).[29] Critics are now beginning to analyse the literary styles of both Gaeltacht and non-Gaeltacht writers in the context of the particular social situations depicted and the ideological stances adopted in their writing, and both writers and critics have acknowledged, with varying degrees of enthusiasm or reluctance, the creative potential of the mixed or in-between forms.

Still, the early concern with linguistic standards remains and is frequently expressed by publishers and editors anxious to develop Irish-language readerships. A number of important critical issues have been raised in recent years. In his capacity as poetry editor of *Innti*, Michael Davitt, himself one of those poets who has been acclaimed for his ability to creatively incorporate a range of linguistic styles and registers in his depictions of the Irish bilingual continuum, expressed his anxiety about a perceived gap between the highly cultivated literary style of much contemporary poetry and the anarchic mixed forms now common in the Gaeltacht. Should the writer be a conservative, a defender of standards, an exemplar, or should the literary text reflect the changes occurring in the spoken tongue?[30] Likewise, critic and publisher Caoilfhionn Nic Pháidín has raised the question of the role of the printed word at a time when electronic media have given public recognition to the less pure forms?[31]

Issues of minoritization and of language endangerment are recurring preoccupations in contemporary writing in Irish. Post-colonial critical theory, especially on topics such as hybridity and cross-culturality, helps us to understand the complex cultural context of such preoccupations. However, the uneven power relations between imperial and indigenous languages, which make hybridity and cross-culturality problematic for minoritized linguistic groups, are seldom given due recognition in post-colonial criticism. Writing from a position of minority, Irish-language writers are aware of the precariousness of their cultural position. While they may celebrate and exploit the both/and position of having *idir Ghaeilge agus Bhéarla* (*both* Irish and English), there is still a strong tendency amongst writers, especially non-native speakers, to feel that they are floundering somewhere *idir Gaeilge agus Béarla* (*between* Irish and English). In the context of forced hybridity, most Irish-language writers feel their cultural mission is to challenge the hegemony of the world-dominant language by developing (and thereby revalorizing and protecting) the minority language. There is, moreover, a palpable awareness that the development

of a minority language as a modern medium of expression involves a constant process of translation, and that awareness in turn accounts for a growing critical interest in the practice and theory of translation.

In Search of Form

In Irish-language criticism concern with literary form revolves around the relationship of the Irish language historically to the development of particular genres. Richard Henebry, being a traditionalist and nativist, saw no room for innovation in the Irish literature of his time. His best-known critical judgement was his condemnation of the unconventional (in terms of the Irish storytelling tradition) opening of Patrick Pearse's short story 'Íosagán'.[32] For Henebry, a modern Irish literature should be based on native models, and where prose was concerned, such models as were provided by the folk tradition. This was a view supported enthusiastically by folklorists such as Séamas Ó Duilearga and by many of those involved in the creation and publication of literature in Irish.[33] Critic Aisling Ní Dhonnchadha has documented the influence of the folktale on the development of the short story in Irish — and the gradual movement (inspired particularly by the critical writings of Pearse, Ó Conaire and Thomas MacDonagh) away from the folk models.[34] Much early revivalist publication was motivated by a desire to provide suitable models for prospective writers. Énrí Ó Muirgheasa, in his introduction to the song collection *Céad de Cheoltaibh Uladh* in 1915, for example, outlined his view of the exemplary nature of the material therein:

> This is the first volume of modern Irish Ulster poetry ever published. Collections of songs and poems by living Irish writers have, no doubt, appeared in recent years, but their contents can not be regarded as Irish poetry. In their ideas, their metres, their petty end-rhyme, and

30 Michael Davitt, 'Eagarfhocal', *Innti*, 15 (1996), 3–4.

31 Caoilfhionn Nic Pháidín, '"Cén Fáth Nach?" — Ó Chanúint go Críol', in Róisín Ní Mhianáin, ed., *Idir Lúibíní: Aistí ar an Léitheoireacht agus ar an Litearthacht* (Baile Átha Cliath, 2003), 115–29.

32 Henebry, 'Revival Irish', *Leader*, 17 (1908-09), 564.

33 Séamas Ó Duilearga, 'Ó'n bhFear Eagair', *Béaloideas*, 1 (1927–28), 3–6. For critical commentary, see Máirín Nic Eoin, 'Béaloideasóirí, Cainteoirí Dúchais agus Scoláirí', in *An Litríocht Réigiúnach* (Baile Átha Cliath, 1982), 33–41; O'Leary, 'The Real and Better Ireland: Rural Life in Gaelic Prose', in *Gaelic Prose in the Irish Free State*, 90–164, esp. 119–22.

34 Aisling Ní Dhonnchadha, *An Gearrscéal sa Ghaeilge 1898–1940* (Baile Átha Cliath, 1981), esp. 30–127.

35 Énrí Ó Muirgheasa, *Céad de Cheoltaibh Uladh* (Baile Átha Cliath, 1915), ix.

36 Pádraig de Brún, 'Ars Scribendi', *Humanitas* (Márta 1930), 2–5; Domhnall Ó Corcora, 'Na hEorpaigh Seo Againne', *Humanitas* (Meitheamh 1930), 2–6; Pádraig de Brún, 'An Sean-Rud Séidte', *Humanitas* (Meán Fomhair 1930), 3–7; Domhnall Ó Corcora, 'Buailim Sciath — An Sean-Rud Séidte', *Humanitas* (Márta 1931), 3–8.

37 de Brún, 'Ars Scribendi', 4.

38 Liam Ó Rinn, *Mo Chara Stiofán* (Baile Átha Cliath, 1939), 34–35.

39 Seán Ó Tuama, *An Grá in Amhráin na nDaoine* (Baile Átha Cliath, 1960); Mícheál Mac Craith, *Lorg na hIasachta ar na Dánta Grá* (Baile Átha Cliath, 1989). See also Mícheál Mac Craith, 'Gaelic Ireland and the Renaissance', in Glanmor Williams and Robert Owen Jones, eds., *The Celts and the Renaissance: Tradition and Innovation* (Cardiff, 1990), 57–89.

above all, in the complete absence of internal assonance — that most essential characteristic of modern Irish verse — they are as English as Moore's *Melodies*, and are merely Irish in the accident of the words being Irish. Their writers — good Irishmen and ardent lovers of the Irish Language — are not, withal, men steeped in the wealth of Irish poetic literature of the last three hundred years, and their productions are not a new and natural leafing and branching of that once luxurious tree, but are rather shoots of English origin grafted on to it, and never destined to bear either flowers or fruit.[35]

Daniel Corkery took up this theme with his nativist interpretation of what a modern literature in Irish should be. Corkery's confrontation with Pádraig de Brún in the short-lived journal *Humanitas* (1930–31) is typical of critical debate in the early 1930s.[36] Where Corkery rejoiced in what he saw as the independence of the Gaelic tradition from European influence — the fact that the Renaissance never impinged on literature in Irish was a fact to be celebrated — de Brún lamented the consequent insularity of Irish literature and proposed a project of translation so that Irish writers and readers could gain access to the classics of the European tradition without having to rely on English versions. De Brún was as much concerned with defending modern Gaelic literature from *contemporary* European influence as he was with exposing the Irish language to the humanistic values of Greek or Renaissance literature. Referring to the type of literary text that should be translated into Irish, for example, de Brún rejected modern fiction and poetry:

Ach tá dearmhad mór orainn má mheasaimid gurab iad nua-scéalta agus nua-fhilidheacht Shasana agus na hEorpa is ceart dúinn d'aistriú. Ní bhíonn ionta soin, do ghnáth, ach críonacht agus tuirse na haigne síbhialta. Ní haon tsamplaí geinearálta iad; níl adhbhar oideachais

ionta. Agus dá fheabhas iad, níl ionta ach caitheamh aimsire.[37]

But we are mistaken if we think that we should translate modern English or European stories or poetry. All they contain, usually, is the decadence and weariness of the civilised mind. They are not general exemplars; they have no educational content. And however good they may be, they are merely of recreational value.

Translator and classicist Stephen McKenna, as portrayed by his intellectual soul-friend Liam Ó Rinn in *Mo Chara Stiofán* (1939), similarly considered European languages and the European literary tradition as bulwarks against (what he saw as) the pervasive influence of English and of English literature on contemporary Irish-speaking Ireland.[38] No translation project could seriously diminish the force of such influence, however, and it is ironic that, while *Humanitas* was progressive enough to encourage an interest in European literature and a comparative approach to literary studies, subsequent comparative literary studies have led to a radical reinterpretation of de Brún's initial premise. (Seán Ó Tuama's findings in his seminal study *An Grá in Amhráin na nDaoine* [1960], for example, where he traced the origins of the love-song tradition in Irish to medieval French, has subsequently been substantially revised by Mícheál Mac Craith, who has demonstrated, through detailed textual analysis, the influence of English Elizabethan poetry and Renaissance ideas on late medieval Irish love poetry.[39]) The attraction of Corkery's position at the time may have been that it was clear and unequivocal. The rejection of *all* outside influence was hardly a much more extreme position than the rejection of that which was, for the twentieth-century writer in Irish, clearly the most powerful and unavoidable of literary and cultural influences. De-anglicization was still the dominant critical stance at mid-century and it affected all aspects of critical commentary, especially questions of literary form and style, as is clear from the values expressed by poet and editor Séamas Ó Céileachair in his 1956 anthology *Nuafhilí (1942–1952)*:

> *Toisc a leithne is atá an Béarla labhartha agus scríofa níl aon ní is contúirtí dúinn ná é. Ní ceart do na filí a gcuid tinfidh (inspioráide) a thógáil ó fhilíocht an Bhéarla. Caithfidh siad bheith aireach, leis, ar rithimí a thiocfadh ina gceann ar eagla go mba mhacallaí ón mBéarla iad. Ba cheart dóibh bheith seachantach, freisin, ar léirmheas ó dhaoine ag a bhfuil an Béarla mar shlat tomhais.*[40]

Because of the all-pervasiveness of spoken and written English, nothing is more dangerous to us than it. Poets should not take their inspiration from English poetry. They must be careful too lest the rhythms that enter their heads are echoes from the English. They must avoid also the critical opinions of people whose yardstick is English.

Perhaps such hard-held cultural positions masked an underlying acceptance that what was being proposed was a kind of mission impossible. Certainly, most modern poets were to depart dramatically from the native forms, metres and rhythms to develop their own individual versions of free verse, and most would have been in general accord with Máirtín Ó Direáin when, in defence of Ó Ríordáin, he rejected as impractical the suggestion that the modern poet can follow in the footsteps of the Irish-language poets of former times because: 'Tá an bhearna ró-mhór' (The gap is too wide).[41] As late as 1986, however, Ó Crualaoich's discussion of *dioscúrsa na Gaeilge* still displays a nativist concern with contemporary poets' engagement with the native tradition. While he acknowledges the biculturality of the Irish-language poet, and the fact that many contemporary practitioners are not native speakers of the language, his concern is with

the persistence of a poetic voice that is truly Gaelic, in tune with a *mentalité* he sees as embedded historically in the Gaelic poetic tradition.

●

Corkery's concept of *dúchas* and his views that Gaelic literature was and should be *dúchasach* (especially in the sense of being non-derivative) ran counter to certain important strands in revivalist thinking about the function of a modern literature in Irish. Whatever chance existed that a modern poetry in the language could evolve uninfluenced by developments in English, the situation where prose was concerned was different, in that there was no unbroken chain of native literary models. With the oral storytelling tradition as the only readily available exemplar, the critical question was not whether one should borrow or not, but how to facilitate a process that would rapidly produce those literary genres, especially the novel and the play, which were absent from the Gaelic literary tradition.

There is an inherent irony running through the debates about the form and content of these new genres as they were to enter the Irish-language tradition for the first time at the beginning of the twentieth century. As long as *Gaelachas* was to be associated solely with the lives and lifestyles of peripheral rural communities, the language was doomed. Unless the language could produce plays, novels, short stories, which would satisfy the standards laid down by majority languages such as English, its literature was fated to remain in the realm of the folkloristic, the rustic, the pre-modern. The revivalist potential of what were widely recognized as popular genres was also acknowledged. If writers could satisfy the tastes of urban readers by providing them with the kinds of urban realist novel they desired, then literature would be functioning as a genuine revivalist tool, producing a readership, reclaiming the urban landscape for Irish, developing lexical fields suited

40 Séamas Ó Céileachair, 'Brollach', *Nuafhilí (1942-1952)* (Baile Átha Cliath, 1956), vi.

41 Ó Direáin, 'Ríordánachas', 14.

42 Patrick Pearse, 'About Literature', *An Claidheamh Soluis* (26 Bealtaine 1906), 7.

43 Thomas MacDonagh, *Literature in Ireland: Studies Irish and Anglo-Irish* (Nenagh, 1966 [1916]), 113–14.

to the depiction of traditionally non-Irish-speaking environments. To be truly modern, literature in Irish would have to open itself to outside influence, a position held almost from the outset by the most significant critical voices. The first of these was Pearse, who by 1906 had rejected the narrow nativist position in favour of a cultural openness to European and contemporary influences:

> Irish literature, if it is to live and grow, must get into contact on the one hand with its own past and on the other with the mind of contemporary Europe. It must draw the sap of its life from the soil of Ireland: but it must be open on every side to the free air of heaven.
> We would have our literature modern not only in the sense of freely borrowing every modern form which it does not possess and which it is capable of assimilating, but also in texture, tone and outlook. This is the twentieth century; and no literature can take root in the twentieth century which is not of the twentieth century.[42]

It was recognized very early on that such a process of borrowing was not going to be an easy one, and the views expressed by MacDonagh in his *Literature in Ireland* (1916) demonstrated a concern with how the language movement could encourage writers to depart from the native forms in the direction of bourgeois literary values. His discussion of Gaelic drama is indicative of the cultural contradictions in the critical climate of the period:

> One cannot, with all the good will and all the good money in the world, produce literature to order, but one can lay down canons of criticism, one can strive to keep the way clear for the coming of a good thing by correcting false impressions, and — what is more to the point in this matter — one can set up good models and display them, when the models are at hand and the pedestals empty.

> … Writers of plays in Irish want to produce dramas of a certain kind — very distinctively Irish, very characteristic in the right sense, but still of the same kind as certain plays in other languages — to take the example nearest home, as certain plays about Ireland written in English. They want to produce such dramas, but they have not studied the models which have been followed by the writers of the plays in English. They have done little or nothing towards mastering their craft, and they have failed in their endeavour. … Judging from all but one of the plays sent in for the Oireachtas some years ago, when I was adjudicator, the authors have no conception of what a play is. It is unfortunate that the one exception, which was the work of a man who does understand the craft, and was in every way admirable, was of a cosmopolitan description, not at all so Gaelic in character as several plays written in English. The others were for the most part stories or essays written in the form of dialogues or catechisms. They had no dramatic sequence or balance. The situations did not flow from the characters, as they do inevitably in all good drama. There is such a thing as stage-craft. The dramatist must learn his craft as a dramatist over and above his craft as a writer, and before he begins he must have in him the makings of a dramatist and a conception of dramatic art.[43]

The irony here is that what is being rejected is the influence of the same native oral tradition hailed by other commentators. The difficulties faced by those concerned with the creation of a modern literature are reflected in the titles of certain Oireachtas competitions, where writers are challenged to break away from established forms and to write *Gearrscéal de shaghas ar bith ach béaloideas* (Any sort of short story except folklore, 1899), *Scéal bunaithe ar an saol in Éirinn faoi láthair* (A story based on contemporary Irish life, 1900), *Gearrscéal faoi shaol na linne in Éirinn* (A short story on life in Ireland at present, 1913).[44] In such a context, it is hardly surprising that critical writings became prescriptive, exhorting would-be writers to produce short stories, novels, plays in Irish in a manner in keeping with the contemporary expectations of English-speaking readers. Books such as Seoirse Mac Clúin's *An Litríocht* (1926) and Liam Ó Rinn's *Peann agus Pár* (1940) were produced as textbooks or manuals for the reader or would-be writer.[45] Mac Clúin's examples are almost all taken from the English literary canon, while Ó Rinn's book — the work of one of the most perceptive critics of his period — is modelled on popular handbooks in English. A minority of critical voices actually grappled with the contemporary sociolinguistic reality and suggested creative means to surmount it. For example, Micheál Mac Liammóir, writing in 1940 about the future of Irish-language drama, proposed a rejection of realism in favour of an expressionism that might facilitate the development of an altogether new Irish-language theatre of the imagination.[46]

Concern about the limitations of realism — and the difficulties associated with the development of an urban realist strand in modern Irish literature — were reiterated throughout the twentieth century. The fate of the realist novel became the central focus of an ongoing debate. Critics Seán Ó Tuama and Breandán Ó Doibhlin applied sociological and psychological insights to their discussions of the modern literature, accounting for the prevalence or otherwise of certain literary genres in terms of Irish social life in general and in terms of the increasingly marginal position of the language and the language community.[47] Ó Tuama's suggestion in 1976 — 'It may also be that, with the success of *Cré na Cille*, the fantasy or non-realistic novel will continue to be seen for a long time as the most viable novel-genre for the writer of Irish in modern Ireland'[48] — seems to have proven accurate,

and yet, when such a view was reiterated in a negative review of a novel by well-known journalist Breandán Ó hEithir in 1989, it generated a public debate in which the tensions associated with the representation of English-speaking Ireland through Irish were rehearsed once again.[49]

One outcome of critical anxiety about the vitality or otherwise of particular genres was a preoccupation with literary convention. Again there are ironies associated with this approach, especially in relation to the novel, where few of the most significant works to emerge have escaped the kind of genre criticism — based largely on English critical texts such as Ian Watt's *The Rise of the Novel* (1957) and E. M. Forster's *Aspects of the Novel* (1927) — which would place doubt on their categorization as novels in the first place. It took the critic Alan Titley, himself an accomplished novelist, to point out that the most characteristic feature of the novel is its novelty and that it should not be expected that any genre would develop in a minoritized language like Irish as it did in the literatures of the major world languages.[50] A greater critical understanding has been developing of the various forces which affected (and which still affect) the development of particular genres in Irish: the forces determining the prevalence of autobiography, for example, or the circumstances that have led to a preponderance of introspective, philosophical or psychological novels.[51] Recent criticism seeks to engage with the literary and linguistic reality and to develop critical paradigms that will account for the evolution of particular forms in the context of the language's marginalized and minoritized status. Examples can be found in the work of Caoimhín Mac Giolla Léith and Máire Ní Annracháin and particularly in their mutually illuminating explorations of the self-reflexive and anti-realist strands in modern and contemporary Irish-language fiction.[52] Their approaches are different — Mac Giolla Léith looks to alternative traditions within the history of the European

44 See Donncha Ó Súilleabháin, 'Cruthú Litríochta agus Freastal ar Éilimh' and 'Buaiteoirí Duaiseanna Liteartha an Oireachtais 1897–1924: Gearrscéalta agus Úrscéalta' in *Scéal an Oireachtais 1897–1924* (Baile Átha Cliath, 1984), 58–67; 172–76.

45 Seoirse Mac Clúin, *An Litríocht: Infhiucha ar Phrionnsabail, Fuirmeacha agus Léirmheastóireacht na Litríochta* (Baile Átha Cliath, 1926); Liam Ó Rinn, *Peann agus Pár* (Baile Átha Cliath, 1940).

46 'Drámaíocht Ghaeilge san Am atá le Teacht' [1940], in Micheál Mac Liammóir, *Ceo Meala Lá Seaca* (Baile Átha Cliath, 1952), 227–40.

47 Seán Ó Tuama, 'The Other Tradition: Some Highlights of Modern Fiction in Irish', in Patrick Rafroidi and Maurice Harmon, eds., *The Irish Novel in Our Time* (Lille, 1976), 31–47, and 'Úrscéalta agus Faisnéisí Beatha na Gaeilge: Na Buaicphointí', *Scríobh*, 5 (1981), 148–60; Breandán Ó Doibhlin, 'Smaointe ar Chúrsaí na Próslitríochta', *Comhar* (Lúnasa 1984), 22–24, and 'Glasnost nó Perestroika? Inspioráid agus Ceird an Úrscéalaí Ghaeilge', *Léachtaí Cholm Cille*, 21 (1991), 139–53.

48 Ó Tuama, 'The Other Tradition', 47.

49 For an account of this debate, see Máirín Nic Eoin, '"Ar Thóir na Foirme": Idir an Réalachas Sóisialta agus an Réaltacht Fhíorúil', in '*Trén bhFearann Breac*', 421–25.

Nuala Ní Dhomhnaill. Photo: courtesy Cló Iar-Chonnachta.

50 Alan Titley, 'Mála an Éithigh', *Léachtaí Cholm Cille*, 21 (1991), 184–206.

51 See Máirín Nic Eoin, *An Litríocht Réigiúnach* (Baile Átha Cliath, 1982) and 'From *Lieux de Mémoire* to Narratives of Self-Invention: Twentieth-Century Gaelic Autobiography', in Liam Harte, ed., *Modern Irish Autobiography: Self, Nation and Society* (London, 2007), 132–55; and Ó Doibhlin, 'Smaointe ar Chúrsaí na Próslitríochta' and 'Glasnost nó Perestroika?'.

52 Caoimhín Mac Giolla Léith, '"Is Cuma Faoin Scéal": Gné d'Úrscéalaíocht na Gaeilge', *Léachtaí Cholm Cille*, 21 (1991), 6–26; Máire Ní Annracháin, 'An tSuibiacht Abú, an tSuibiacht Amú', *Oghma*, 6 (1994), 11–22; 'Litríocht na Gaeilge i dTreo na Mílaoise', in Ó Cearúil, ed., *An Aimsir Óg*, 14–24.

novel, while Ní Annracháin applies modern linguistic, psychoanalytical and Marxist perspectives to a study of the de-centred subject in contemporary Irish-language fiction — but both concur in exposing the limitations of nineteenth-century realism as an appropriate critical paradigm for twentieth-century prose writing in Irish. It is clear that the focus of the critique has altered dramatically and it may be the case that from now on less attention will be paid to the perceived absences or gaps in the literary record and more to the qualities and characteristics of the literature that *has* emerged in the language.

Conclusion

Many other perspectives should be brought to bear on this discussion. The influence of other modern and contemporary literatures on Irish-language writers should be taken into account, for example, as should the destabilization of literary genre associated with post-modernist aesthetics. The kinds of comparative studies that would place modern literature in Irish in the context of developments in other minoritized languages, both within the Celtic language group and elsewhere, have yet to appear. Comparisons with Irish literature in English would also further illuminate the full range of literary responses to the bilingual cultural heritage outlined by Ó Tuairisc in 1975. It is clear, however, that contemporary Irish-language criticism has certainly, whether by choice or by circumstance, moved beyond the cultural nationalist discourse of decolonization and its attendant binary oppositions. It is not that it has reached, or perhaps ever can reach, a stage where the medium of expression itself can be taken for granted. Certain revivalist concerns will always be present, especially concern about the relationships between literature and literacy, between authorship and readership, between publication and reception. Just as the Irish-speaking community has had to come to terms with its status as a minority, so does Irish-language criticism have to accept its status as a minority discourse, struggling to maintain a visible, palpable and audible presence in the face of a growing movement towards cultural homogenization. In the process of developing as a minority discourse with real explanatory power, cultural issues that tended to be avoided in the past — such as the centrality of translation, the inevitability of hybridity and the challenges of intercultural and interlingual communication — have now become central critical issues. While the creative writer may choose to reflect or to transcend current linguistic realities, the critic must account for such choices and illuminate the field of influences in which they are made.

REVIEWS

1 Laurence Mordekhai
Thomas, *Vessels of Evil:
American Slavery and the
Holocaust* (Philadelphia,
1993), 125.

Crow tipi frame, c. 1910. Photo: Richard
Albert Throssel (1882–1933), courtesy of
the American Heritage Center, University of
Wyoming.

'Mourn — and then Onward!'

Luke Gibbons

*Radical Hope:
Ethics in the Face of Cultural Devastation*
Jonathan Lear
Cambridge, Mass.: Harvard
University Press, 2006
197 pages. ISBN 978-0-674-02329-1

In *Vessels of Evil: American
Slavery and the Holocaust*
(1993), the African-American
Jewish scholar Laurence
Mordekhai Thomas suggested
that on the scales of oppression
and injustice, death is not always
the worst fate: 'It is simply
false that surviving is always
rationally preferable to death.'[1]
Living on one's knees, stripped of
all dignity and self-respect, is a
more lethal form of annihilation
than the destruction of millions
of members of one's community.
For this reason, the calculus
often drawn up to compare the
loss of life in the Holocaust
with the Atlantic passage — six
million or ten million? — is
beside the point, for what counts
in the end is the long-term
impact of catastrophe on both
cultures. It is at this juncture

Plenty Coups. Photo: Richard Albert Throssel (1882–1933), courtesy of the American Heritage Center, University of Wyoming.

that Thomas's argument takes a controversial turn, for in terms of its consequences, the Shoah, he contends, did not take as great a toll on Jewish culture as did slavery on the subsequent history of African Americans:

> Recovering the traditions of Judaism was not a concern that plagued Jews who settled in what became the nation of Israel or in the United States or anywhere else. No one wondered what counted as a Bar Mitzvah or Bat Mitzvah or how to perform them. No one wondered what rituals to perform for Pesach, or what the Four Questions of Pesach were. After the Holocaust, the Jewish tradition, in all its richness, was left very much intact.[2]

The same could hardly be said of African-American culture in the aftermath of slavery. Invoking Orlando Patterson's influential (and equally contested) concept of 'natal alienation', Thomas argues that black culture experienced the slow strangulation of 'social death', depriving successive generations of the rich array of social and cultural achievements that remained the preserve of the dominant white class in the United States.[3]

Though Jonathan Lear does not use the phrase 'social death' — or its cognate 'ethnocide' — such concepts are at the heart of *Radical Hope: Ethics in the Face of Cultural Devastation*. His book exemplifies the best features of recent breakthrough works in philosophy: it is analytically

2 Thomas, *Vessels of Evil*, 153.
3 See Orlando Patterson, *Slavery and Social Death: A Comparative Study* (Cambridge, 1982).

4 Jonathan Lear, *Radical Hope: Ethics in the Face of Cultural Devastation* (Cambridge, Mass., 2006), 2; my italics. The quotation is taken from Frank B. Linderman, *Plenty Coups: Chief of the Crows* (Lincoln, 1962), 311.

5 Lear, *Radical Hope*, 24.

6 Lear, *Radical Hope*, 32, 34; Lear's italics.

7 Thomas Kuhn, *The Structure of Scientific Revolutions*, 3rd edn. (Chicago, 1996).

rigorous, yet grounded in both history and anthropology, and open to world-views other than those safely ensconced in the Western academy. It deals with the cultural catastrophe that befell the Crow Indians in Montana and Wyoming in the nineteenth century, a series of disasters that not only destroyed the things they valued — tradition, territory, the buffalo and beaver, warrior prowess and courage, a nomadic way of life — but also their sense of value itself. Sequestered initially by the Fort Laramie Treaty of 1851 in an area the size of England (33 million acres), Crow territory was reduced to 2 million acres by 1882. Depleted by disease, starvation and the pressures of an alien land allotment system in the 1880s, the Crows were eventually moved to a reservation. Lear's analysis is prompted by a cryptic remark of the great Crow chief, Plenty Coups, who lived, and led his people, through the calamity: 'When the buffalo went away the hearts of my people fell to the ground, and they could not lift them up again. *After this nothing happened.* There was little singing anywhere.'[4] What does it mean to say that history ended and 'nothing happened', when in fact the Crows did survive into the twentieth century, albeit as shadows of their former selves?

It is tempting at the outset to suggest that they survived as human beings — just about — but not *as Crows*, as a people whose culture was the very eco-system of their lives. The fate of the Crows can perhaps be seen as a trailer for George Romero's film *Night of the Living Dead* (1968), with the reservation, and the parcelled allotment system seen as open-air precursors of the zombie-like shopping mall. Lear's account of cultural devastation serves as an important rejoinder to those constructions of society based on the beliefs of liberal individualism, according to which the suppression of actual forms of life — screening the texture of cultural differences behind a 'veil of ignorance' (John Rawls) — is a precondition for taking one's place in civil society. Such putative forms of freedom, or abstract

equality, are appropriately figured in the deracinated image of the Alberto Giacometti stick man who is the bearer of fundamental human rights, designated by Giorgio Agamben as *homo sacer*. Drawing on a version of Thomas's analysis, Lear imagines, as against what actually happened, what a Crow holocaust might have been like. The vast majority of the Crows would have of course have been liquidated, but if some pockets of people, or even one individual, had managed to survive 'they would still have the conceptual resources to understand what had happened'.[5] In the case of cultural catastrophe, this would not be possible, as the categories for even making sense of loss would have disintegrated along with physical bodies:

> [T]he problem goes deeper than competing narratives. The issue is that the Crows ... lost the concepts with which they could have constructed a narrative. This is a *real loss*, not just one that is described from a certain point of view. It is the *real loss of a point of view* ... What we have in this case is not an unfortunate occurrence, not even a devastating occurrence like the holocaust; it is a breakdown in the field in which occurrences occur.[6]

The Crows underwent what might be described as a fundamental paradigm shift in consciousness but unlike its counterpart in the philosophy of science,[7] they did not experience just a shift in consciousness about the world. They lost the consciousness of *their* world. The rupture was within experience itself. Drawing on concepts of practical reason elaborated by Candace Volger, Lear recounts how the Crow went about the ordinary business of everyday life, labouring, cooking, mending, eating, drinking, and so on, but in a manner that would suggest they were only partly living:

> The social group may endure, and one may identify with being a member of that

group — thus a member of the tribe can still think of him- or herself as a Crow — but the possibility of constituting oneself as a certain kind of subject suddenly becomes problematic.[8]

It was the Crow's distinctive social rituals and customs that succumbed most of all to the onslaught, not least the practice of gaining 'coups' in mastering an opponent in battle through the symbolic act of hitting him with a 'coup-stick' before armed combat (the source of Plenty Coups's prowess in the tribe). The Sun Dance, an integral component of the culture, also fell into disuse, and one of the options facing the Crow at this stage was to continue the performance, 'though the point of the dance has been lost. The ritual continues, though no one can say what it is *for.*'[9]

It is in this context that some of the problems in Lear's analysis begin to emerge. It is far from clear that the power of rituals, still less the performative impact of dance, depends on an awareness of their meaning or 'point' — if indeed they can always be said to have a meaning that can be defined or described by instrumental reason. No doubt, rituals can outlive their usefulness if the whole world of which they are a part disintegrates, but this does not follow as a matter of course. As Joseph Roach shows in his *Cities of the Dead: Circum-Atlantic Performance* (1996), not least of the sources of revitalization in African-American culture were the performative energies of dance and music, the rhythms and tonalities of the body that remained when everything else had been destroyed.[10] Many of these practices were remnants of earlier African rituals that did not survive the brutalities of the Atlantic passage but which nonetheless persisted in vestigial, somatic form — and were no less resonant for that. Undertows from submerged pasts operated as both 'retentions' and 'surrogations', counter-currents that unsettled the still waters of 'social death', when, because of the social paralysis of the plantations, so much seemed lost.

Lear shows how the true horror of cultural devastation goes 'all the way down', beyond surface manifestations of identity. He contrasts ascriptions of ethnicity in much of contemporary identity politics, where cultural markers are chosen like so many designer labels, with the kind of true Crow subjectivity that once went to the heart of their existence. This subjectivity did not depend merely on occupying a social role; it required deep immersion in the ideals of a culture, precisely the kind of identification that goes 'all the way down'. When a culture collapses, 'this is a problem that penetrates deeply into one's inner life'[11] — such life designated at times by Lear as subjectivity in its conventional individualist mode. Yet there is a difficulty in depicting Native Americans as having the kind of introspective mental life characteristic of Western modernity — not to mention its deeply subjective, Protestant variants. To establish the extent of the existential crisis the Crows lived through, Lear draws, with telling effect, on Kierkegaard's 'suspension of the teleological'. The soul-searching of Kierkegaard — or Hamlet — is not only for Danes, of course, but one has to ask whether modes of thought with universal claims always transfer unproblematically to other cultures or, indeed, to the universe as it actually stands. Does Kierkegaardian interiority correspond to Crow inner life at all?

The issue was a matter of life and death as the Crows underwent assimilation into the American way of life. The systematic campaign to refashion Native-American culture along Western individualist lines between the 1880s and 1930s — to convert communal land into private property (or 'allotments'), and to reconstitute communal identity in terms of self-regarding possessive individualism — gave effect to a slow cultural ethnocide that took up where extermination left off. The Carlisle Industrial School for Indians (1879–1918) in Pennsylvania became the showcase for the implantation of inner life into refractory Native Americans, leading its

8   Lear, *Radical Hope*, 44.
9   Lear, *Radical Hope*, 36; italics in original.
10 Joseph Roach, *Cities of the Dead: Circum-Atlantic Performance* (New York, 1996).
11 Lear, *Radical Hope*, 48.

Crow prisoners confined to a reservation, January 1887. Photo: Getty Images/Hulton Archive.

12 Cited in Joel Pfister, *Individuality Incorporated: Indians in the Multicultural Modern* (Durham, 2004), 20.
13 Pfister, *Individuality Incorporated*, 44.
14 Lear, *Radical Hope*, 61.
15 Lear, *Radical Hope*, 63.
16 Lear, *Radical Hope*, 65.

superintendent, Colonel Richard Henry Pratt, to famously pronounce that 'all the Indian there is in the race should be dead. Kill the Indian in him, and save the man.'[12] The regime at Carlisle took the colonel at his word, as Luther Standing Bear, a survivor of the first class, recollected in sorrow: 'The change in clothing, housing, food, and confinement combined with lonesomeness was too much, and in three years nearly one half of the children from the Plains were dead and through with all earthly schools.'[13]

This is the sort of cultural asphyxiation Lear analyses with acuity from a philosophical point of view. Yet, from the perspective of cultural history, it is clear that it was not the want of subjectivity but its *imposition* that was killing the Indian softly with its inner song. Though not addressing the issue directly, Lear's 'philosophical anthropology' (as he terms it) negotiates the complexities of Indian culture as it manifested itself in such activities as hoping and dreaming, or moral states such as courage and shame, but tends to construe them in mental, rather than cultural, terms (if one can make such a distinction). In

one passage, Lear recounts how the Crow woman Pretty Shield expressed shame at inflicting corporal punishment on her children (corporal punishment was *de rigueur* at Carlisle), leading her to lament: 'I am trying to live life I do not understand.'[14] There is clearly a lack of 'fit' here between the Crow's hollowed existence on the reservation and what remained of their forms of life, but it does not follow that what was missing was a connection with their deep subjectivity.

The complex interweaving of inner and outer lives is explored by Lear in his analysis of the roles of shame and courage in Crow culture. Linking conceptions of courage with the avoidance of shame, he notes that a tribal upbringing cultivated 'an internalized shame-mechanism that reflects the Crow understanding of courage',[15] and it is this inner recess that survives in the event of cultural collapse: 'there are ways in which a person brought up in a culture's traditional understanding of courage might draw upon his own inner resources to broaden his understanding of what courage might be'.[16] Would this formulation lack

'Cold Grave'. December 1890: mass burial of Sioux Indians killed at Wounded Knee, South Dakota. Photo: Getty Images/ Hulton Archive.

any of its validity if it suggested that one might fall back on one's *cultural* as well as personal resources to meet the exigencies of a new order in which both self and society faced disintegration? Cultures have interior histories or 'hidden transcripts' (in James C. Scott's phrase) [17] just as much as individuals, and these may be as important in providing resources of hope as inner psychological reserves. What is at stake here is not the existence of mental states, or subjectivity, but the relation of such private worlds to 'outer', collective practices, the forms of life of a society. Though shame, unlike guilt, is an overtly social mechanism, in that one loses face before others, a measure of internalization may still take place since the actual presence of others is not required. As Bernard Williams notes in *Shame and Necessity* (cited with approval by Lear): 'Even if shame and its motivations always involve in some way or other an idea of the gaze of another, it is important that for many of its operations the imagined gaze of an imagined other will do.'[18]

There is still, however, a difference between two kinds of internalization: one, compatible with Crow culture, internalizes the presence of others, maintaining a relationship to *specific* others; the alternative, associated with advanced Western individualism, cultivates a detached or *generalized* other, thus laying the basis for self-regulation abstracted from the company of others, real or imagined. The former is the source of solidarity and corresponds — broadly speaking — to what might be seen a communal moral code; the latter, to the type of self-interested ego institutionalized at Carlisle, and repugnant to Native-American forms of life. The contrast between the two modes is brought out by an incident in Sophocles *Ajax*, cited again by both Williams and Lear, in which the hero, having prided himself on his courage at killing Greek warriors, discovers to his dismay that under a spell of Athena's, he has been killing sheep all along:

> He could not go on living ... in virtue of the relations between what he expected of the world and what the world expects of a man who expects that of it. 'The World' there is represented in him by an internalized other, and *it is not merely any other* ... the other in him does represent *a real world*, in which he would have to live if he went on living.[19]

17 James C. Scott, *Domination and the Arts of Resistance: Hidden Transcripts* (New Haven, 1990).

18 Bernard Williams, *Shame and Necessity* (Berkeley, 1994), 82, cited in Lear, *Radical Hope*, 85.

19 Williams, *Shame and Necessity*, 84-5, cited in Lear, *Radical Hope*, 87; my italics.

20 Lear, *Radical Hope*, 96.
21 Lear, *Radical Hope*, 43.
22 In several extended
passages in his book, Lear
acknowledges the social
structuring of the self,
as in the following: 'If
one were simply to leap
from the thick concepts
of one's culture into
the ethical concepts of
another culture, it would
seem that one would
experience not only a
radical discontinuity
with the past; one would
experience a rip in the
fabric of one's self. If
we think of the self as
partially constituted by its
most basic commitments,
then in jettisoning those
commitments one would
be disrupting one's most
basic sense of being'
(65). The difficulty here
lies in the sense in which
'partially constituted'
accounts for 'one's most
basic sense of being'.
23 Lear, *Radical Hope*, 77.
24 Lear, *Radical Hope*, 125.

Of course, Lear is correct to emphasize that this real world was facing imminent collapse but to the extent that the Crows survived *as Crows* — to the extent that their 'subjectivity' endured the catastrophe — traces of this culture lived on in individuals, in however truncated or attenuated a form.

For survival to take place, Lear writes, 'we would have to understand the Crow as somehow transcending their own subjectivity',[20] but it was perhaps more imperative to transcend subjectivity itself to retain connections with the energies of an endangered culture. As Lear writes: 'This was more than a mere psychological matter of "identifying" oneself in a particular way. It required a steadfast commitment stretching over much of one's life to organize one's life in relation to those ideals'.[21] Subjectivity, in this sense, is commingled with, and negotiated through, profound social attachments, as is the case in most non-Western (or 'pre-modern') cultures.[22] It is in this sense that the dream-vision which lies at the heart of Crow experience — and Lear's analysis — also 'transcends' the boundaries of the individual by virtue of its shadowy, external provenance. Recounting a series of oracular dream-visions that seemed to provide intimations of a dark future, which Chief Plenty Coups had as a young boy, Lear describes in some detail how such dreams were not simply private experiences but intersubjective and communal. One dream, presaging the disappearance of the buffalo, was brought back to the elders of the tribe by the nine-year-old Plenty Coups:

It is not unreasonable to suppose that a sensitive nine-year-old was attuned to the anxiety in his community and that he was able to dream what he was not in a position to think. And he dreamt it on the tribe's behalf. Plenty Coup's dream seems to have been an integral part of a process by which the tribe metabolized its shared anxiety. It helps, I think, to conceptualize the anxiety not as specifically located in this or that person but as diffused

throughout the tribe. It is the tribe that is anxious.[23]

In a related manner, Lear analyses with considerable sensitivity another dream that Plenty Coups had as a young boy following the death of his beloved older brother at the hands of the Sioux. In this vision, the young Plenty Coups was taken in hand by the Dwarf-chief, the head of the Little People whom the Crow believed lived in the hills of Montana — where stone arrowheads have been found (the Crows made their own arrowheads of bone). The Dwarf-chief reassured the young warrior that if he sharpened his senses in relation to his surroundings, he would prevail in the future as a chief to lead his people. Drawing both on D. W. Winnicott's concept of the 'transitional object', which occupies an indeterminate zone between the child's inner and outer worlds, and Sigmund Freud's late notion of 'ego-ideals', Lear comments:

Psychologically speaking, the Little People function as transitional figures for young Plenty Coups: because they are taken to exist as some aspect of the spirit world, the question whether their voices come from inside or outside is left vague. We can think of these voices as the voices of an emerging ego-ideal.[24]

The possibility that the dreams come from outside the self may have to do not just with their otherworldly provenance but with their *collective* form: their giving voice to a structure of feeling 'diffused throughout the tribe', as in the earlier dream of the buffalo. It is through these shards of solidarity that fractured cultures often find the remnants of hope, even when their world is falling to pieces.

Lear's absorbing study is at its best when he identifies such submerged forms — in excess of subjectivity, as it were — in the outlines of the 'radical hope' that lies at the centre of his book. Because of the incommensurability of life-worlds — the

November 1940: a sign at Wounded Knee, South Dakota, where US troops massacred 250 Native Americans in 1890. Photo: John Vachon/Library of Congress/Getty Images.

shifting tectonic plates before and after a calamity — hope itself 'may outstrip the concepts with which we seek to understand it'.[25] In marked contrast to optimism, which is driven by wishful projections of the future, hope is open-ended, allowing us to go on by virtue of its own striving for definition. To the extent that it is more expansive than wish fulfilment, it also transcends the ego, emanating less from the interiority of the self than from an orientation towards the other — if not, indeed, *from* the other. In that line of thought stretching from Plato to Freud that claims or suggests that it is our sense of our imperfection as human beings that instills a longing for what we lack, Lear points to a material basis in the outward reach of desire in early childhood:

> We instinctively reach out to parental figures for emotional and nutritional sustenance that, in the moment, we lack the resources to understand. This is the archaic prototype of radical hope: in infancy we are reaching out for a source of goodness, though we as yet lack the

concepts with which to understand what we are reaching out for.[26]

Hope, in this sense, does not always require a clear — 'conscious' — grasp of the future, but is impelled by a version of the 'kinaesthetic imagination' (Roach's term) — the will to go on, or even to shuffle on, as in the slow motions of the Ghost Dance (see below). While the future may be inscrutable in the midst of cultural collapse, it is important to emphasize that there is no absolute discontinuity — any more than there is complete incommensurability in Thomas Kuhn's notion of 'paradigm shifts' in the philosophy of science. Cultural devastation that seems complete in terms of 'content' — a substantive core of truths and values — may still meet resistance not so much in subjectivity but in the recalcitrance of 'form': the aesthetic or cultural materiality of practices containing, so to speak, a mind of their own. It is this 'form' or material substratum that prevents hope from being simply blind faith, irrespective of whether or not it has a religious basis. Participants in

25 Lear, *Radical Hope*, 120.
26 Lear, *Radical Hope*, 122.

27 Roach, *Cities of the Dead*, 55–71.
28 Lear, *Radical Hope*, 142.
29 Lear, *Radical Hope*, 145.
30 Lear, *Radical Hope*, 149.
31 Lear himself seems to agree with this version later, criticizing the Ghost Dance for its lack of agency: 'It is the hallmark of the wishful that the world will be magically transformed — into conformity with how would like it to be — without having to take any realistic steps to bring it about' (150–51). For recent scholarship on the phenomenon, reiterating the contemporary judgement by the ethnographer James Mooney that it was not a pretext for armed insurrection, see Jeffrey Ostler, *The Plains Sioux and U.S. Colonialism from Lewis and Clark to Wounded Knee* (Cambridge, 2004), chs. 11–15, and James Mooney's classic ethnographic account, *The Ghost-Dance Religion and the Sioux Outbreak of 1890*, Fourteenth Annual Report of the Bureau of Ethnology, 1892–93, pt. 2 (Washington, DC, 1896)
32 Lear, *Radical Hope*, 151.

patterns of culture — 'performers' — may not have a conscious grasp of what these forms are 'for', and there may indeed be nothing conscious about them at all. As Roach suggests, the inscriptions of residual African practices onto Christian funeral ceremonies among slaves in New Orleans, such as a granddaughter throwing herself into the grave at a funeral, was not a calibrated strategy of resistance, but was nonetheless perceived, like other wayward customs, as preserving havens of black autonomy in the face of total domination. Even when the gesture and rhythms of the intractable body were appropriated in subsequent generations by white culture — such as, Roach suggests, in Elvis's notorious gyrations, and rock 'n' roll generally — they were still regarded as constituting an affront to white respectability and to puritan conceptions of self (or racial) control.[27]

Though admirable throughout in its nuanced response to the values and life forms of the Crow, and in particular to their redoubtable courage, Lear's empathy is less apparent in the case of Plains Indians such as the Sioux and the Cheyenne, who chose heroism of a different kind — to go down fighting, even in the face of insuperable odds. This is surprising at one level, for much of the book is based on the argument that death is not the ultimate indignity: 'better to die on your feet than live on your knees', as La Pasionara (Dolores Ibarurri) is reported to have proclaimed during the Spanish Civil War. Towards the end of his book, Lear contrasts the Crow mode of survival, laying down arms and making peace with their conquerors, with the tragic denouement of the Ghost Dance among the Lakota Sioux, the traditional enemies of the Crow, which ended on the killing fields of Wounded Knee in 1890: 'The Crow were wiser [than the Sioux and Cheyenne]', Plenty Coups is reported as saying:

> We knew the white men were strong, without number in their own country, and there was no good in fighting them

... Our decision was reached, not because we loved the white man who was already crowding other tribes in our country, or because we hated the Sioux, Cheyenne and Arapahoe, but because we plainly saw that this course was the only one which might save our beautiful country for us.[28]

Lear glosses this as implying 'not just that it was psychologically advantageous not to give into despair but also that it would have been a mistake to do so. It would also have been a mistake to "go down fighting".'[29] But is it a mistake to go down fighting? Lear is perhaps too harsh in his judgement on the millenarianism of the Ghost Dance, representing it as little more than wish-projection, false optimism, on the part of militant Native-American tribes in the South and the West who resisted incarceration in reservations in the 1890s. His account of the dance is misleading, in that it appears to confirm the authorities' view at the time that it was an alibi for armed insurrection, and hence should be suppressed accordingly.

Writing of Wovoca, the Paiute prophet in the South-West whose visions originally inspired the Ghost Dance, Lear states that he claimed to be the son of God, 'who has returned to punish the whites and restore the Indians to their previous life': 'According to this messiah, in the following spring (1891), he would wipe out all the whites in a catastrophe ... The dance was ecstatic: participants would dance into a frenzy ... and abandoned all other activities in order to bring about this cataclysm.'[30] This was not, in fact, the case: deliverance was not placed in the hands of the Indians themselves but was to be brought about by external forces, whether natural or supernatural.[31] To be sure, the Sioux envisaged a world without the white man but this need not be taken literally, 'mistaken for reality',[32] any more than the dream-content of Plenty Coups's visions recounted earlier should be taken at face value. The Ghost Dance might be viewed more productively as an attempt not so much (literally) to restore an irretrievable

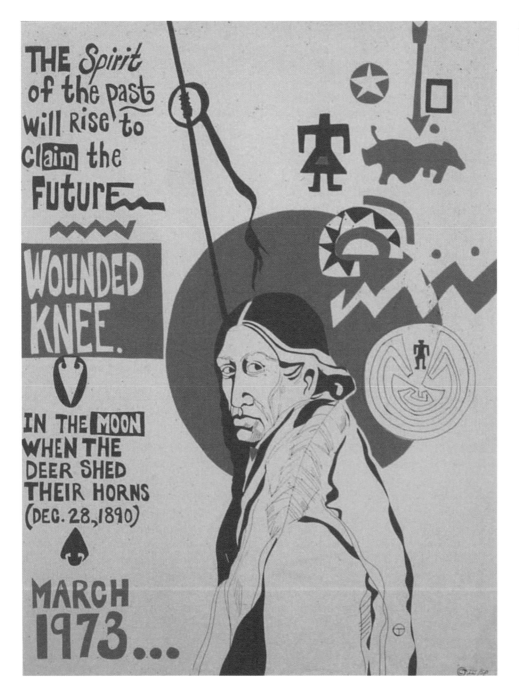

A poster commemorating the massacre of Wounded Knee. Photo: MPI/Getty Images.

past but to prevent the past from being entirely eliminated — the fate facing the Crows. As Roach argues:

> This amends somewhat the idea that ... the Plains Indians danced for the repossession of territory, though that is true; they also danced to possess themselves again of the spirit of their ancestors, to possess again their memories, to possess again their communities. They danced to resist the reduction to the status of commodities. In other words, they danced — and they still dance — to

33 Roach, *Cities of the Dead*, 209–11.

34 Pfister, *Individuality Incorporated*, 125.

35 Frederick Hoxie, *Parading through History: The Making of the Crow Nation in America, 1805–1935* (Cambridge, 1995), 331. The citation in the local newspaper is from the *Hardin Tribune*, 4 May 1934.

36 Lear, *Radical Hope*, 64–65.

37 As Hoxie points out, Yellowtail's support for Collier led to divisions within the Crows, and in recent decades Collier's advocacy of top-down Western-style democracy and the welfare state was still a matter of contention (see Vine Deloria, Jr., *Custer Died for Your Sins: An Indian Manifesto* [New York, 1969], 145).

possess again a heritage that some people would rather see buried alive.[33]

Ironically, one of the threats presented by the Ghost Dance lay in its vernacular engagement with Christianity. This represented an appropriation of the new world that Indians were due to enter *on their own terms*. As Joel Pfister explains, while the individualizing regime at Carlisle sought to instill 'what it meant to be "sinful" as an effective way of structuring consciences, guilt, and self-monitoring along Christian lines', what it feared most was that Indians might take Christianity — or modernity — into their own hands, giving them a specific Native-American stamp:

> What riled Pratt most of all were 'Indians' who had evolved beyond being 'Indians' (as he thought he understood them) into 'individuals', but who then continued to Indianize themselves. This sort of impenitent Indianism disrupted commonly held evolutionary assumptions that being individual was more progressive then being 'Indian'.[34]

It may be that such resilience as the Crows showed in the face of enormous adversity came from the tenacity with which they held on to remnants of their own past, not least their determination to hold on to communal land values.

Towards the end of the book, Lear pits younger Crow leaders such as Robert Yellowtail against the wisdom of Plenty Coups, arguing that the former, a white-educated lawyer, saw allotment as a way to avoid further white encroachment. This does less than justice to the remarkable young

lawyer who was perhaps the first Indian activist to fully utilize the language of 'rights' for Native-American causes. On Yellowtail's appointment as superintendent of the Crow Agency in 1934 — the first Native American to assume such a position — the local newspaper nervously reported that while he 'foreswore the ways of his forefathers' on entering law school, he continued to defend the Indian's rights to 'dress, live and worship as he chooses', regardless of his (or her) degree of 'civilization'. 'This statement,' writes Frederick Hoxie, 'captured Yellowtail's appeal to both Indians and whites: he had long been an advocate of democratic decision making, constitutional rights and Indian enterprise, but he was also a product of the social, economic and religious atmosphere the Crows had created on the reservation during his lifetime'.[35] As Lear himself describes this appropriation of the new order as a means of cultural survival: 'The issue [here] would then be one not simply of going over to the thick concepts of another culture, but of drawing on their traditions in novel ways in the face of novel challenges.'[36]

While not constituting the stuff of legend like Plenty Coups, Robert Yellowtail was instrumental in a coup of his own, playing a key role in the appointment of the radical activist John Collier as commissioner of Indian Affairs under Franklin D. Roosevelt's New Deal administration. It was under Collier's fundamental restructuring of Indian affairs that the iniquitous policy of private allotments, coercive individualism in Indian lands, and the assault on Indian culture, was finally abandoned.[37] Some of the wishful thinking of the Ghost Dance had come true after all.

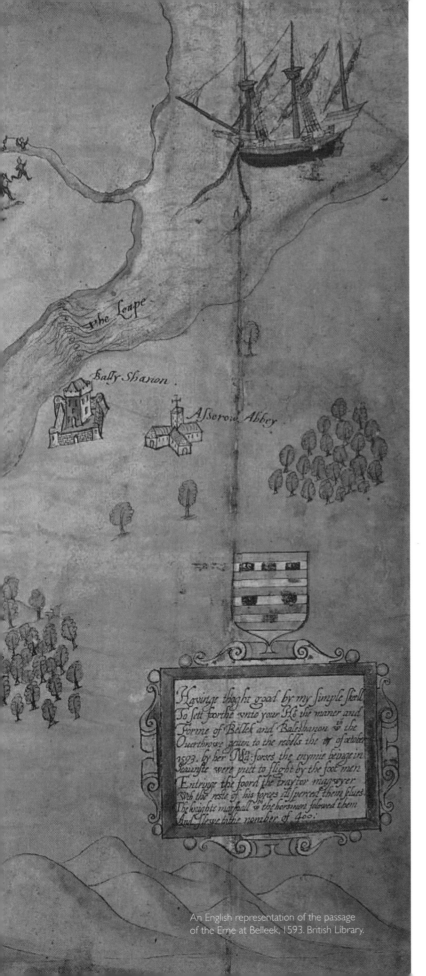

An English representation of the passage of the Erne at Belleek, 1593. British Library.

Reckoning with the English

Patrick Griffin

Contested Island:
Ireland 1460–1630
S. J. Connolly
Oxford: Oxford University Press, 2007
426 pages. ISBN 978-0-198208-16-7

Map-Making, Landscapes, and Memory:
A Geography of Colonial and Early Modern
Ireland, c. 1530–1750
Field Day Critical Conditions
W. J. Smyth
Cork: Cork University Press, 2006
760 pages. ISBN 978-1-859183-97-7

The history of Ireland appears more and more like the history of America. At first blush, such a statement seems absurd. Historically, and this is not news, America became more and more like Ireland. For instance, it has become a commonplace in the literature of the early modern Atlantic that Ireland and America were linked in profound ways, but Ireland almost always acted as precursor. Irishmen and women ventured to America throughout its colonial period, greening the Atlantic and presumably America in the process. Both struggled in the

The Arrival of the English in Virginia, from 'Admiranda Narratio ...', 1585–88 (coloured engraving). Service Historique de la Marine, Vincennes, France; Bridgeman Art Library.

eighteenth century with their status within the British state; but the Irish did so first, presumably offering models of resistance to British rule. And, of course, the Elizabethan conquest of Ireland served as a laboratory for the first settlement of America. So axiomatic has this last point become — much more so than the other two Atlantic bonds — that it lies beyond debate. Sean Connolly's new book, *Contested Island: Ireland 1460–1630*, is not centrally concerned with America. Nor is William Smyth's *Map-Making, Landscapes, and Memory: A Geography of Colonial and Early Modern Ireland, c. 1530–1750*. Yet both suggest that the tables are turning on the nature of the bonds between Ireland and America in the early modern period of conquest and settlement. But as these books demonstrate, it's not so much that America took the lead in the historical relationship; rather, America's historians did.

Indeed, to evaluate the work of Connolly and Smyth in light of how we now think of the 'encounter' between natives and newcomers, of the nature of English imperial ambition, and of the implications of English

settlement in a foreign land, we should first cross the ocean to Virginia. Stimulated by the 400th anniversary of the settlement of Jamestown, scholars have drawn on path-breaking work done over the last generation to rethink what each of these dynamics mean. What used to be a simple story of triumph, then a simplistic one of perdition, has by now evolved into a sophisticated and ambivalent one.

Consider the latest take on Jamestown.[1] The focus used to be on the English who arrived in 1607, encouraging us to see the event as a mythic moment or a fiasco. No longer. Instead of demonizing or celebrating, we understand. In May of that year, less than four months before the Flight of the Earls, a little over 100 men and boys from England landed at a place which they would call Jamestown but the local Indians knew as Tsenacommacah. The surrounding region, watered by rivers emptying into Chesapeake Bay, supported more than 15,000 people. By all accounts, the natives possessed a sophisticated culture and had encountered Europeans before. They were led by a man of considerable abilities. Powhatan, as he

1 This account of Jamestown is based on two of the best studies that appeared to commemorate the 400th anniversary, James Horn, *A Land as God Made It: Jamestown and Birth of America* (New York, 2005); and Karen Kupperman, *The Jamestown Project* (New York, 2007). The best older account, still excellent, is Edmund Morgan's *American Slavery, American Freedom: The Ordeal of Colonial Virginia* (New York, 1975). On the change from old to new, see Charlotte Hays, 'American Originals: Descendants of Jamestown Settlers Meet and Greet', *Wall Street Journal*, 18 May 2007. Similarly, see Jill Lepore, 'Our Town', *New Yorker*, 2 April 2007.

The Siege of Enniskillen, 1594, as represented by John Thomas, a soldier serving under the English commander, Captain George Bingham. British Library.

2   On Indian conceptions of space, see April Hatfield, *Atlantic Virginia: Intercolonial Relations in the Seventeenth Century* (Philadelphia, 2004).

3   Andrew Fitzmaurice, *Humanism and America: An Intellectual History of English Colonization, 1500–1625* (Cambridge, 2003), 12–13, 37; Anthony Pagden, *Lords of All the World: Ideologies of Empire in Spain, Britain, and France, c. 1500–c. 1800* (New Haven, 1998); J. H. Elliott, *Empires of the Atlantic World: Britain and Spain in America, 1492–1830* (New Haven, 2006); and Peter Mancall, *Hakluyt's Promise: An Elizabethan's Obsession for an English America* (New Haven, 2007).

was called, ruled at least thirty tribes in the region through intimidation and violence. These Indians had no affinity for bonding; Indianness as a concept was unthinkable. Powhatan also relied on patronage to hold his confederation together. Subchiefs placed in each village under his control doled out the goods that Powhatan had bestowed on them. In this 'gifting' culture, passing out things, rather than accumulating them, represented the surest path to securing power. In this regard, Powhatan had few equals. He was master of a violent world of warlords and vassals. He also imposed his rule over peoples and groups, less than over land and territory. He did not see his world as if it were a map on a page.[2]

The Englishmen had not reckoned on settling amid such an organized people. Nor could they recognize the sophistication of Powhatan's people. We know that they regarded Indians as their inferiors, a savage people — literally 'wood's dwellers' — better suited to an imagined state of nature than to their notion of civil society. They saw Powhatan's people as idolatrous drudges and his land as a place to be exploited and settled by a better people, who would and could do all in their power to improve what God had put there. There was nothing new about this jaundiced way of seeing the 'other'. Spaniards viewed natives this way, as did the French. The idea that the world was divided between civility and barbarity was as old as the classical world, and was only intensified by the European encounter with indigenous peoples during the 'Age of Discovery'. Armed with this enduring sensibility, the English understood the 'New World' as a place to be 'improved'. And so from the earliest days of settlement, Captain John Smith set off to explore the region, to see what riches it could offer and to map it so as to exploit it. By mapping it, he made it English. This ideology underwrote settlement.[3]

But Powhatan did not see things this way. In fact, he viewed these strange-looking interlopers not as exotic or superior but as useful and subservient. Powhatan planned to employ the goods they brought with them, especially copper, to extend his power to other regions. He hoped to get his hands on their guns to overawe those who would stand in his way. And he believed that the

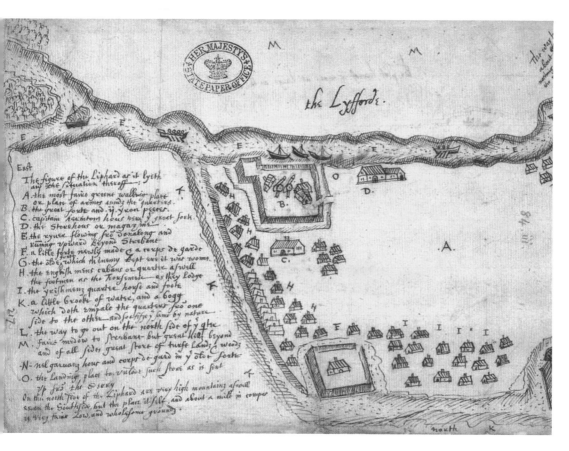

A plan of the English settlement at Lifford, County Donegal, 1600. Public Record Office, London.

English were another tribe to be brought into tributary status to him. He would have been a fool to think otherwise. The newcomers were dying at an appalling rate from dysentery, saltwater poisoning, and 'mere famine', as one put it. Powhatan then played a game of 'good cop, bad cop' with them, dispatching emissaries with gifts of corn one day and raiding parties the next. The message was clear. The English, their silly rituals of possession as well as their map-making to the contrary, stayed in Tsenacommacah at Powhatan's pleasure. Conquest, after all, did not define the early years, and neither group, despite English ideological pretensions, lay beyond any sort of cultural or racial pale. Both groups struggled to make sense of one another, groping for a metaphorical middle ground between cultures. And at this stage, Indians held the upper hand.[4]

The poisonous ideology espoused by the English proved almost incidental to what was really happening on the ground. Ideologies of conquest were simple and straightforward, but complexity and ambiguity defined the period. In other words, we've come a long way over the past generation when it comes to characterizing the initial encounter between natives and newcomers in America. Of course, we used to view the 'discovery' of what would become the United States in almost providential terms. The Indians resisted for a while, but they did so against inevitability. This interpretation reached its high-water mark at the end of the nineteenth century, with the work of George Bancroft and especially Frederick Jackson Turner, the father of the frontier thesis.[5] More recently, we have turned this exceptionalist narrative on its head, arguing that racism and greed decimated Indian cultures, thereby paving the way for conquest, formally celebrated in 1992 with the 500th anniversary of

4 Peter Wood, Introduction, in G. A. Waselkov, ed., *Powhatan's Mantle: Indians in the Colonial Southeast* (Omaha, 2006). On these themes, also see Karen Kupperman, *Indians and English: Facing off in Early America* (Ithaca, 2000).

5 On this, see my *American Leviathan: Empire, Nation, and Revolutionary Frontier* (New York, 2007).

6 For the best analysis of 1492 and 1992, see the essays by James Axtell in *Beyond 1492: Encounters in Colonial North America* (New York, 1992).

7 Richard White, *The Middle Ground: Indians, Empires, and Republics in the Great Lakes Region, 1650–1815* (Cambridge, 1991). Also see James Merrell, *The Indians' New World: Catawbas and Their Neighbors from First Contact through the Era of Removal* (New York, 1991).

8 Qualifiers include James Merrell, *Into the American Woods: Negotiators on the Pennsylvania Frontier* (New York, 2000); and Gregory Dowd, *War under Heaven: Pontiac, the Indian Nations, and the British Empire* (Baltimore, 2004).

9 For the sequence, see D. B. Quinn, *The Elizabethans and the Irish* (Ithaca, 1966), and *Voyages and Colonizing Enterprises of Sir Humphrey Gilbert* (London, 1940); Nicholas Canny, *The Elizabethan Conquest of Ireland: A Pattern Established, 1565–76* (London, 1976), as well as his path-breaking article 'The Ideology of English Colonization: From Ireland to America', *William and Mary Quarterly*, 3rd ser., 30 (1973), 575–98. The sequence is explained in Patrick Griffin, 'Richard Hakluyt, Chicken Little, and the Ends of Atlantic History', *Reviews in American History*, 35 (2007), 325–34.

10 Nicholas Canny, 'The Politics of History: Writing Early Modern History in Parnellite Ireland', *The Parnell Lecture, 2004–05: Magdalene College Occasional Paper*, 34 (Cambridge, 2005). Some have argued that the conquest paradigm is at the heart of an 'Irish exceptionalism' and has fostered a sense of 'Irish essentialism'. On this, see Donald Akenson, *If the Irish Ran the World: Montserrat, 1630–1730* (Montreal, 1997), 173–75.

11 Introduction, in Ciaran Brady and Jane Ohlmeyer, eds., *British Interventions in Early Modern Ireland* (Cambridge, 2005), 10. On problems with this theme of conquest, see also the work of Steven Ellis, who concludes that the Tudor plantations and takeover of Ireland's political apparatus and state Church amounted to a 'failure'. See *Tudor Ireland: Crown, Community, and the*

Columbus's 'conquest' of America.[6] Now we see things differently again. Indians did not represent some essentialized group of people beyond time, the proverbial noble savages, unable to cope with newcomers espousing foreign ways of understanding things, people, and the land. Like all people, natives adapted. They learned to assimilate and to take advantage of the market. When it came to European goods, Indians proved discriminating shoppers, melding new imperatives with older traditions quite easily. As the historian Richard White argues, natives and newcomers from the moment of first contact through the early nineteenth century continually created 'middle grounds' between two cultures. According to our conventional wisdom these days, people learned to find merit in each other's cultures. Indians embraced white ways, dressing as Europeans, using their goods, adopting their notions of land, and worshipping like them. Euro-Americans also 'went native' from time to time, adopting Indian notions of warfare, eating Indian foods, dressing like Indians, and marrying them.[7] No doubt, lately some have suggested that we need to qualify our use of 'the middle ground', that it can obscure the essential features of what happened to native communities. But the blunt instrument of conquest can no longer be employed.[8]

Let's return to Ireland. What does it have to do with the story? A great deal. Ireland after all served as laboratory for American settlement. And we know that the transatlantic process resembled a sequence. The English would conquer Ireland, and after learning a thing or two there, would settle America. The great historian D. B. Quinn did pioneering work in uncovering the sequence, arguing that English adventurers who were intent on seizing opportunities anywhere on the globe turned their attention decisively to America only after their experience conquering Ireland. And Nicholas Canny demonstrated the cultural pathologies — the ideologies — that underwrote the sequence.[9] But what happens to the sequence if we do

not view American settlement as inexorable? Do we have to reconsider the Irish case if the American case is not so straightforward? American scholars are no longer so sure of the American side of the equation.

Neither are historians so sure of the Irish side. Indeed, the tale of native and newcomer for the early modern period in Ireland is beginning to undergo a similar transformation. The old narrative of conquest dominated the whole enterprise of early modern Irish history. For generations, Irish historians assumed that the kingdom was, would be, or was in the process of being conquered. In the nineteenth century, historians with unionist and nationalist sympathies could agree upon little else but the notion that early modern conquest created the salient features and fissures of the kingdom. They held radically different ideas of its meaning, but found common ground in seeing its centrality to a 'disputed national grand narrative'. The earliest revisionists who focused on the seventeenth century, such as R. Dudley Edwards and T. W. Moody, both of whom sought to bring archival rigour and dispassion to the study of the Irish past, also could not escape these assumptions. Nor did they try.[10] This should not surprise us. As Jane Ohlmeyer and Ciaran Brady argue, even revisionists have trouble moving beyond what they call 'the paradigm of conquest and appropriation'. This motif, they argue, tends to drive the study of sixteenth- and seventeenth-century Irish history, and largely goes unquestioned because it underscores what all regard as a critical truth of the Irish past.[11] It represents the great fact of early modern Irish history, the place where debate — and Irish sense of self — begins and ends.

Sean Connolly jumps into this debate with two feet. In doing so, he plays to his strengths. A bit of a contrarian, Connolly has had some pretty pointed things to say about Irish historiography. More than a decade ago, he played the part of Ireland's J. C. D. Clark, suggesting that we should view Ireland less as a British problem and more within a European *ancien régime* framework.[12] The issue for Connolly was proper context. In his estimation, a European context better explained Ireland's eighteenth century than a 'new' British one, then all the rage. In *Contested Island*, Connolly is playing the role of contrarian once more, in this instance contesting the conquest paradigm. In many ways the book amounts to an unrelenting if crafty attack on the old standby. The title of the book says it all. Ireland in the fifteenth century was a contested island of warlords and competition, a world of the descendants of English medieval settlers degenerating and currying favour with the Irish in their midst, of Highland Scots mercenaries coming and going, and of Gaelic Irish looking for any ally in this jostling world of power and position. Some 'Old English' families had gone native several generations earlier. Some of the old Gaelic families were wholly anglicized. In fact, the old tried and true distinctions between groups do not do this kaleidoscopic world justice. The book ends the same way. After what should have been the period of conquest, we find so-called 'New' English settlers intermarrying with the Irish and adopting their language. New groups of Scots only added to the competitive mix. Both created alliances and forged accommodations with the Irish. If anything, by 1640 Protestants were literally and figuratively disarmed, one group of many on a complex island.

Therefore, even after the so-called — and this term crops up quite a bit — Elizabethan conquest and Jacobean plantation, Ireland was as much as it had been: a 'contested island'. In between beginning and end, the story hinges on disorder. We have been led to believe that the English were able to assert their power in Ireland by the time Elizabeth died. For Connolly, however, the state's failure to do so — even if it wanted to, which is another matter — ensured that Ireland teetered between disorder and chaos. Thomas Hobbes would have been at home here. Once Henry VIII declared himself king

of Ireland, all hell broke loose, or better, new players joined an already raucous chorus. Following Steven Ellis's and Ciaran Brady's lead, Connolly argues that the king's English and allied Irish subjects began dismantling an old system of accommodation without fully implementing a new one.[13] The destruction of the house of Kildare — the bedrock of the idea of lordship over Ireland — did not amount to some great watershed. It simply initiated a heightened period of competition in an already competitive world. Endemic and complex feuding merely incorporated new players from across the sea, ensuring that no single actor — not even a state — could impose effective authority. Far from dictating the course of events, the English, it seemed, had gone native.

Ambiguity is the defining characteristic of the period and of this book. Connolly believes that the earliest plantation strategy represented no strategy at all. Each was prosecuted for pragmatic and defensive purposes. Each proved limited in scope, scale, and intent. None of the early schemes represented ends in and of themselves. Even the plantations in Munster of the 1580s, long seen as templates for later larger plans, were not ideologically driven, justified by a racist ideology, or particularly effective. As Connolly points out, only those Irish deemed traitors lost their lands, and loyal Irish subjects could settle on lands surrendered. No doubt, brutality defined these years. The English were, however, doing nothing new or exceptional. Ireland, after all, was a violent place before they came; and if we compare Ireland to the Continent, the level of bloodshed does not seem all that pronounced. Intervention in Ireland by the English only elevated the ruthlessness of Irish warfare to policy. Connolly presents us with a place where English authority was ever uncertain and intent was ambiguous, where rival shifting factions — Irish of different stripes and English of different stripes — vied for power. 'Loyalties and identity were highly fluid,' he argues, and '[i]nstincts

Conflict of Cultures, 1470–1603 (London, 1985), 315–16. It proves difficult to move beyond the conquest paradigm, even if we define it as 'intervention' or even as we acknowledge its unevenness as a process and its contingent quality, and even as we try to resurrect the agency and cultural survivals of indigenous peoples. Breandán Ó Buachalla, notably in *Aisling Ghéar: Na Stíobhartaigh agus an tAos Léinn, 1603–1788* (Baile Átha Cliath, 1996), and Éamonn Ó Ciardha, in *Ireland and the Jacobite Cause: A Fatal Attachment* (Dublin, 2003), have made these claims for early modern Ireland. Eerily enough, this tension between oppression and agency replicates debates in American historiography about slaves and slavery and even about Native Americans and the nature of the encounter. On this parallel, though one has to read between the lines, see Breandán Ó Buachalla, 'James Our True King: The Ideology of Irish Royalism in the Seventeenth Century', in D. G Boyce, R. Eccleshall, and V. Geoghegan, eds., *Political Thought in Ireland in the Seventeenth Century* (London, 1993).

12 Sean Connolly, *Religion, Law, and Power: The Making of Protestant Ireland* (Oxford, 1992).

13 Sean Connolly, *Contested Island: Ireland 1460–1630* (Oxford, 2007), 74.

14 Connolly, *Contested Island*, 90.

15 Éamonn Duffy, *The Stripping of the Altars: Traditional Religion in England, 1400–1580* (New Haven, 1992). For the futile and pathetic efforts of the Puritans, see James Axtell, *The Invasion Within: The Contest of Cultures in Colonial North America* (New York, 1986).

16 Connolly, *Contested Island*, 126–70.

17 Connolly, *Contested Island*, 278.

had not yet hardened into clearly defined ideologies.'[14]

The act of crossing boundaries defined this place-in-time. Almost perversely, turning old verities on their head, Connolly shows how the prelate entrusted with anglicizing the Irish Church under Henry VIII married a local Catholic woman and fathered three children with her. In an even more striking inversion to conventional understandings, the grandsons of Edmund Spenser — the man long considered the architect of English conquest — became Catholic. For Connolly, Spenser's views prove exceptional — going native does not. And why shouldn't this be the case? According to Connolly, Protestantization under Elizabeth was never really tried. His Ireland appears a great deal like Éamonn Duffy's England, but one that could or would not be regimented. Reformers, in this regard, achieved the same level of success as the Puritans among the Indians in New England — very little, in other words. Few proved willing or able to strip the altars.[15]

Connolly's characterization of the Nine Years War sums up his treatment of the period. Connolly concedes that by the end of the sixteenth century, relations had taken a turn for the worse. Fears of Spain did not lead to new policies; rather, new Irish settlers profiteering in the vacuum of power that Ireland had become did. The kingdom's problems stemmed from too much private interest run amok and intensified feuding. In a chapter entitled the 'Wars of Ireland', we in fact witness little of the expected warfare, only more of the same sorts of vendettas, alliances, and naked power grabs that defined Irish society for a long period of time, in this instance heightened by the failure of the state to assert control. Impotence not imperial hubris, therefore, underscored conflict. The war that did occur did not involve two simply delineated sides: Irish v. English. Its violence was not exceptional, nor was it rooted in ideology. It was not marked by 'the development of a radically new anthropological perspective on the Gaelic

Irish, but rather the results of a long-term process of corrosive dillusionment'.[16] In this context, the plans for the reform of Irish society epitomized in surrender and regrant were failing. Self-interested Gaelic warlords had all too successfully ensnared the English in their rivalries. The subsequent 'flight' of the earls — not really a flight at all but part of a pattern of Irish military migration to the Continent — did usher in a new phase for Ulster but not for some Spenserian reasons. Once declared traitors, their lands were forfeit. The flight did not represent the end result or logical implications of conquest, but, if anything, gestured toward a new beginning. The flight certainly did not signal some sort of ideological shift.

Connolly concedes that the accession of James VI and I to the throne initiated a transition, and plantation became a state-sponsored enterprise. But Connolly does not see a strategy of conquest even at this juncture. Now more cognizant of threats on the marches, James's government sought to pacify and bring order to both Ireland and Scotland by cutting off the points of connection in Ulster between Gaelic warlords and their Highland allies. The plantation of Ulster did not bring an end to a 'contested island'. As Connolly puts it, 'a whole new layer was thus added to the already complex pattern of ethnic, religious, and political division that existed within Irish society'.[17] Change, no doubt, lay on the horizon. But events, not ideology, would drive the process. Willy-nilly, Ireland would become an anomalous kingdom or third appendage in the archipelago, a place of, dare we say it, ambiguous status.

No wonder then that the old standby of Ireland as precursor for American settlement is stood on its head by Connolly. Since Ireland did not represent 'a theatre for colonial expansion' but a 'problem of government', it is difficult to argue that it represented a precedent for the settlement of Virginia. Closer links — and here Connolly goes back to his Eurocentric roots — existed between military actions in the Netherlands and aggression in Ireland and Virginia. Most Englishmen looked toward the Continent and the Mediterranean for their useful models. The Atlantic, for Connolly, lies on the periphery. Even the older view that ideas about the Irish informed views about Indians — as savages — should be taken with a grain of salt because this interpretation assumes 'a coherent colonizing mentality' that did not exist.[18] We cannot draw parallels between the Irish and Indians, he suggests, or between events in Ireland and process in America. Ever the contrarian, he suggests no tangible link existed between Ireland and America.

Connolly's book is sure to provoke. It is smart and insightful. It also frustrates, though in some measure this had to be one of his aims. He raises all sorts of fascinating questions that he leaves unanswered. How and when will the end come? Or will it come at all? Do we need ideology to have conquest? Does ideology shape and form social reality or does it reflect and react to the sequence of events? He plans to write a sequel to this volume. But if we take this book on its own merits, as a stand alone project, it's clear that Connolly quite skilfully dodges these sorts of questions. That said, they also transfix him. Throughout the book, he plays with these ideas, teasing us at those junctures when the old narrative seems to be rearing its head only to lop it off again and again. The effect can be as frustrating as it is enlivening. Indeed, instead of thinking of Connolly as a contrarian or as an arch-revisionist, we do better to characterize him as an iconoclast. Ambiguity defines all. For Connolly, nothing is inevitable or foreordained. He eschews any sort of teleology, instead sticking with contingency. Events, not process, he argues, drive his narrative. 'It avoids the passive voice,' he writes, 'that great transformer of event into process.' He adds that 'if this book remains an exercise in a traditional genre, the general narrative survey, it is at least a self-conscious one'.[19] But the question remains: do we lose the clear-cut sense, the essential features of the landscape if we are mired in ambivalence?

And he knows that this is the question, even if he refuses to engage it. Make no mistake about it: this book has a powerful purpose. The passive voice, one imagines, could lead to all sorts of ideological explanations for what happened to Ireland in the early modern period. But to opt to ignore or de-emphasize ideology, however justifiable, is to choose another ideology, especially given the centrality of the conquest narrative to Irish historical memory.

•

William Smyth relies on an older, tried and true model. And if Connolly wields a scalpel too craftily, Smyth uses a sledge hammer unabashedly. In *Map-Making, Landscapes, and Memory: A Geography of Colonial and Early Modern Ireland c. 1530–1750*, Smyth seeks nothing less than to uncover the mapping of conquest and the ideologies, notions of land, and culture that underscored it. Smyth approaches the early modern period from the point of view of a cultural geographer informed by post-modern ethnographic theory. But this is a work of history, and the subtitle does not lie. Smyth comfortably conflates the terms 'colonial' and 'early modern', seeing them as analogous. In contrast to Connolly, little ambiguity marks these pages. Ireland would be conquered, and 'early modern' scientific and geographic notions would underscore colonization. In many ways, Smyth has produced a — literal — tour de force, a powerful, unsentimental, and unapologetic study of the geography of conquest.

Although Smyth focuses on the use of the map in conquering Ireland, he also renders interesting readings of other sorts of texts, such as the 1641 depositions and the census of 1659. Case studies of the mapping of Dublin, Kilkenny, and Tipperary follow, demonstrating how a world was turned upside down in a few generations. For all the complexity of its constituent parts, however, this is a simple story. Crossing boundaries — real or metaphorical — was

18 Connolly, *Contested Island*, 264–65.
19 Connolly, *Contested Island*, 3.

20 William Smyth, *Map-Making, Landscapes, and Memory: A Geography of Colonial and Early Modern Ireland, c. 1530–1750* (Cork, 2006), 55.

21 Smyth, *Map-Making, Landscapes, and Memory*, 115.

22 Smyth, *Map-Making, Landscapes, and Memory*, 123.

a dynamic feared and condemned by all. The case studies and documentary evidence he enlists support this finding. Given Smyth's reliance on maps, which by their nature create or codify boundaries, and his assumption rather than dissection of conquest, such a conclusion is foreordained. Maps, after all, entailed and inscribed power, especially in a world characterized by zero-sum relationships. Maps served as tools and symbols of military conquest and of plantation. In this way, they mirrored, clarified, and justified intent.

Maps, then, reflected ideology as they shaped it. As maps were becoming more exact and modern, as geography was overtaking cosmography as a way of understanding space, England's agenda was becoming imperial. To chart was to dominate. Complex maps underscored the need for accurate intelligence for marauding armies and invasion fleets. Empty spaces on maps revealed ignorance of space but also suggested the savagery of a land peopled by wood's dwellers or the opportunities available to the would-be planter. As Smyth puts it, the emerging science of map-making in Ireland 'turns the landscape into a permanent documentary record to be indexed and filed away in cards and maps for the use of future rulers and administrators'. A map is 'a strategic instrument for administering territories and ... a key weapon in creating and sustaining state power'. [20]

Interestingly, the very questions that Connolly dodges are the ones that Smyth assumes as fact. Smyth, in fact, goes further, arguing that geographic determinism was especially pronounced in Ireland. Here two irreconcilable cultures clashed. An individualistic, expansive, scientific, modern, market-oriented, and 'graphic and perspective based' world-view confronted a more communal, conservative, traditional, oral, literate, and myth-making culture. One needed to make maps to conceive of the space, which one sought to dominate; the other relied on histories, place names, and genealogies to define shifting contours of spatial boundaries. In early modern Ireland, map confronted memory. The older Irish way of doing things may have looked messy to 'civilized' Englishmen, but it had its own logic, purpose, and sense of order and stability. With conquest, no longer. Imposing graphic and simplistic representations of space on a complex and sophisticated notion of landscape allowed land to be emptied and the conqueror to claim victory. Irish language and culture, which had been attuned to the woods, as Smyth suggests, now found itself at sea in its own land, overwhelmed by the normatively defined civility of the conqueror.

Military conquest prepared the way for all sorts of imperialism. The English divided the country into useful and rational administrative units. They imposed their law. They planted their people. They transformed economy. They destroyed culture. And they cleared the woods with abandon. Maps made it all possible. By 1603, the 'new conquistadores', as Smyth calls them, were 'in secure possession of Ireland'. This was an Elizabethan conquest, which James VI and I only 'intensified'. All that happened afterwards stemmed from the twinned processes of mapping and invasion. Take 1641 as an example. Although he describes the events of 1641 as a spliced 'rising/rebellion', Smyth believes they heralded the end of Irish Ireland. The conquerors enjoyed the advantage of 'state terror' on their side, and the famous depositions ensured that the rising/rebellion would be publicized around the broader Protestant world as a massacre of innocent Protestants at the hands of the 'wild Irish'. The depositions, like maps, also became 'documents of conquest'.[21] Indeed, the depositions represented, as Smyth argues, 'a major part of the war' itself.[22] As the American historian Jill Lepore argues in her study of King Philip's War in New England, which saw massacres and the publication of narratives eerily similar to those published after 1641, 'writing about war can be almost as difficult as waging it and, often enough, is essential to winning it'. Recording atrocities reinscribes conquest. In New England after 1675, Indians were rendered as irredeemable savages, regardless of tribe.[23] In Ireland, through the act of writing, the vanquished would be remembered and reinscribed as 'Irish Papists', whether or not they were 'Old English' or 'Gaelic Irish'. Writing about war canonized what had been happening for generations. As one deposition, this one from Cavan, related, rebels were wont to say 'Virginia will become Aughanure again'.[24] This was a world 'with little middle ground'.[25]

Oliver Cromwell only continued this inexorable process in a more efficient fashion. Smyth discusses these dynamics through the census of 1659, by analysis of the ways in which Ireland was mapped in the mid-seventeenth century, and by close examinations of three regions. 'A fully colonial Ireland,' he writes, 'in the grips of military occupation and dictatorship and now to be subject to an all-embracing plantation, required comprehensive island-wide mapping.'[26] William Petty, who would lay Ireland out on a dissecting table, region by region, would see to the 'cartographic conquest' of the whole island on the heels of the Cromwellian conquest. It would be he who would write the *Political Anatomy of Ireland* and would serve as a founding member of that arm of the modernizing project, London's Royal Society. These sections, as well as the rest of the book which looks ahead to the eighteenth century, read almost like epilogues to a story finished soon after it has begun. If we understand the role of maps and ideology, we understand the early modern Irish past.

Almost fittingly, the book ends in America. Here the lesson is clear. Ireland acted as both model for future colonization and safety valve for Ireland. Hundreds of thousands would travel to Britain's New World possessions before the American Revolution in the wake of the conquest of Ireland. And forms of rule that would govern Ireland would be imported to America, eventually leading to the

American Revolution in one and the Patriot movement and 1798 in the other. Through conquest, Ireland 'becomes an integral part of the European-controlled Atlantic world, yet — uniquely amongst western European countries — becomes a colonized rather than a colonizing country'.[27] Ireland was more than 'this famous island set in a Virginian sea';[28] its past suggested a connection between Ireland and America in the minds of colonizers. The Irish example of a totalizing colonial plan ensured that the 'stage was set' and 'seeds were planted' for Virginia.[29] What followed was a discernible 'sequence' of conquest and settlement. Munster fell, followed by Virginia and then Ulster. Colonization of Newfoundland preceded plantations in Wexford and Longford, culminating in Barbados, Plymouth, and Massachusetts Bay. The same inexorable process gripped these regions with the same grim results. All these regions became frontiers to an expanding and expansive England.

Smyth's post-revisionism would seem the antidote to Connolly's arch-revisionism. But such is not necessarily the case. If Connolly presents us with a sometimes frustratingly ambiguous book, Smyth's unambiguous clarity and purpose prove a bit too overdetermined. For the historian, one problem with Smyth's analysis is that it assumes what it seeks to explain. Invoking Foucault quite often, Smyth argues that power is everywhere, that discourses are determinative, and that the imperially normative conquers all. But if power lies everywhere and explains everything, it becomes axiomatic. With conquest and ideology assumed, maps can explain all that Smyth would have us believe. If blank and poorly delineated, they demonstrate a conqueror's intent. If filled with place names and detail, they illustrate conquest as a *fait accompli*. This does not mean that Smyth is wrong. Rather, he is captive to teleology. The first sentence of the book says it all: 'The New English colonization of Ireland from the 1530s onwards may be seen as the equivalent of a major continental

23 Jill Lepore, *The Name of War: King Philip's War and the Origins of American Identity* (New York, 1999), ix.

24 Smyth, *Map-Making, Landscapes, and Memory*, 137.

25 Smyth, *Map-Making, Landscapes, and Memory*, 139.

26 Smyth, *Map-Making, Landscapes, and Memory*, 165.

27 Smyth, *Map-Making, Landscapes, and Memory*, 345.

28 Smyth, *Map-Making, Landscapes, and Memory*, 421.

29 Smyth, *Map-Making, Landscapes, and Memory*, 425.

30 Smyth, *Map-Making, Landscapes, and Memory*, xix.
31 Smyth, *Map-Making, Landscapes, and Memory*, 19.
32 Alan Taylor, *American Colonies* (New York, 2001), xv.
33 Nicholas Canny, *Making Ireland British, 1580– 1650* (Oxford, 2003).

invasion that transformed the island from Malin Head to Rosslare and from Fair Head to Cape Clear.'[30] And he aims to make 'the documents of conquest speak'.[31] Teleology, of course, stands as the enemy of contingency. But in all fairness to Smyth, maps do not lead to contingent history. More to the point, a purely contingent history of Ireland may obscure the more significant processes at work.

In truth, we need both contingency and teleology. As the American historian Alan Taylor argues, as he struggled to see American colonial history as more than the history of 'a proto-United States', 'rejecting teleology ... to wallow in pure contingency is an equal folly. Hindsight affords a pattern to change over time that readers reasonably seek from the historian.' Only after disaggregating event from broad narrative can reconstruction and historicization begin; but events without framework prove equally problematic.[32] Both Connolly and Smyth stand guilty on this score. Smyth won't entertain the possibilities of a middle ground or of meaningful continuities. From the start, his story revolves around conflict. Connolly ends his account in 1630, on the very eve of all hell breaking loose. All we have then is middle ground and no change over time. Perhaps what is needed is the clarity of Smyth combined with the craft of Connolly.

Can there be a meaningful middle ground between the two positions? Ireland's answer to Alan Taylor may be Nicholas Canny. To be sure, like Canny's earliest work surveying the nature of the Elizabethan 'conquest' of Ireland, his major book, *Making Ireland British, 1580–1650* (2003), dwells a great deal on violence and especially on ideology.[33] That said, he has complicated our understandings of conquest. Canny has demonstrated how an ideology of conquest developed by fits and starts and did not emerge full-blown with the first furtive attempts at plantation; also how that ideology would by the mid-seventeenth century garner support and become the defining characteristic of English engagement

with Ireland during the early modern period. In making this point, he has illustrated how the process of British state formation, or really the story of English expansion into the marches, did not occur as a consensual dynamic, as some suggest. Conflict, in fact, defined it. But conquest did not. Plans for plantation were never fully carried out. Ireland was never effectively 'reformed', even after Spenser's dark vision was finally adopted by Cromwell and his army. Making Ireland British failed. What he presents us with is a story of ambiguity told against the backdrop of an unambiguous ideology. Ideas ultimately fail to account for the complexity on the ground.

Canny complicates the story even further, agreeing with Connolly that perhaps a European context offers the best solution for making sense of Ireland, but he does so in the service of the 'new' British paradigm only to undermine the broad sense of consensus that underscores it. In many ways the ideologies that led to 1641 and Cromwell's conquest did not grow from Irish, English, or British sources, contexts, or events, but from European ideas. Britishness represented the regional variation of a European humanist discourse, violent by its very nature, applied in Ireland. It was not modern, nor necessarily scientific. It was most certainly not a Protestant discourse. It did not stem from the disorder of Irish society. Canny's Ireland is not an exceptional outpost, but part of the fabric of Europe; but its distinctive history will be defined by engagement with the English state, however contingent the nature of that engagement might have been. Fittingly enough, Canny's work echoes that of the American historian James Merrell who in his classic *The Indians' New World* described a process of conquest that was defined by contingency, boundary crossing, and the whir of events, and that ultimately failed. Only by framing the question as one of conquest from the beginning, both Canny and Merrell suggest, can we evaluate it as process and understand the meanings of contingency.

John Smith's 1612 map of Virginia, with Powhatan, the Indian leader, depicted in the top right, from *A Map of Virginia: With a Description of the Countrey, the Commodities, People, Government and Religion* (Oxford, 1612).

Where does this situate Canny on the old colonization sequence that he and D. B. Quinn established? Does Ireland still act as precursor? Well, probably not. If conquest, even as an ideology, had little purchase by the 1640s, it stands to reason that it did not animate English efforts in America. Perhaps the best we can do is to suggest that Canny gestures towards an Ireland as parallel to America. Similar dynamics would grip both societies, particularly as the state became more involved in warfare and plantation in both regions. Even if 'conquest' was not fully realized, it was clear by the latter half of the seventeenth century — the 1660s in Ireland and 1676 for America — that Englishmen ruled both the eastern littoral of North America and the kingdom of Ireland.

The same, of course, holds true for the changing ways that historians view these parallel processes. In point of fact, American historians did not inform or influence Connolly, Smyth, or even the American-trained Canny, for that matter. American and Irish historians shifted in tandem, coming to similar conclusions, albeit for

different reasons, about parallel dynamics. This change in sensibilities tells us a great deal more about Ireland and America today than it does about what happened in the sixteenth- and seventeenth-century English Atlantic. Connolly's arch-revisionism, Smyth's strident post-revisionism, and Canny's complicated story are only possible in a post-modern Ireland, one divided between those who would rather forget a narrative based on victimhood and conquest and those who would embrace it all the more. The same holds true for America. Middle grounds only make sense in a post-civil-rights United States.

But the similarities between Ireland and America can only take us so far. For all of our Atlantic pretensions, Ireland is not really like America. For in Ireland, as the old saying goes, the natives did not die. American stories of accommodation are always told against the backdrop of the reality that the Indians would lose. The Indians of the Chesapeake would not have a 'hidden' eighteenth century or a nineteenth century that would bring a 'hidden'

Tsenacommacah to a close, a subsequent history, in other words, that was refracted through the events of the sixteenth and seventeenth centuries. These people would not live to resist in any meaningful way the mapping of their lands. The early story of the creation of middle grounds always seems to fall apart. For the Powhatans, it all happened pretty quickly. Within a generation of settlement, the Powhatans would be overrun and massacred, the remnants of their people pushed beyond a line to the west. Most simply died of disease. Many tragically became dependent on English goods. Settlers and the state, albeit an at-times reluctant state, saw to the rest. By 1623, settlers had retaliated for the 'Good Friday massacre' of 1622, which saw a third of the settler population killed. Settlers would strike again in 1644, leading the governor to declare that Indians should not live to the east of the fall line in the colony. By 1676, with Bacon's Rebellion — really a complex struggle between élites, poor men on the margins, and Indians — the Powhatans and all Indians in the region were effectively finished as a people.

Charting such a grim reality by exploring the flow of events in the light of the ideology of race arguably offers a model for how we should conceive of the pasts of Ireland and of America. In America throughout the colonial period, middle grounds succumbed to rigid frontiers, as lines of settlers encouraged by the state moved a people compromised by disease and dependency off the land. Such a process was replayed again and again over the course of seventeenth and eighteenth centuries. Space, then, stood as the great dividing line in society. Ireland, on the other hand, where natives held their own, had become something of a perpetual borderland between and among cultures with its mix of conflict and accommodation sustained by a more proximate state. Status, which determined the viability of middle grounds in this context, played the role that space did in America largely because effective spatial lines could not be sustained. Some events — the stuff of

contingency — determined the ability to cross boundaries in both societies. Others created the conditions for the erection of rigid spatial or status frontiers. Such an arrangement in America was underscored increasingly by race, the other in Ireland by confession. But the defining markers of process are beside the point. For the Irish in these circumstances, going native, while always happening, often proved troubling, especially after traumatic events like 1641. For America, mixing tended to end with the erection of fixed boundaries between native and newcomer. The markers used to explain and justify each arrangement — one based on essential characteristics, one usually based on culture and religion — reflected these realities.

It is no surprise that these differing notions of frontier/borderland also form the core of identity in each nation, as well as the parameters of meaningful debate about each nation's past. Both are deemed to be distinctive but in different, though telling, ways. America's distinctiveness is based on planting civility; Ireland's on being a victim of it. Think only of the different meanings associated with 1607: the 'Flight of the Earls' and what is called by some 'America's 400th anniversary'. No matter where we stand, we must take notice of both events. If we downplay the significance of the Flight or lament it, we are trapped in a debate between two sides of the same exceptionalist coin: whether or not, or to what degree, Ireland was a colonized European country. The same applies for celebrating or denigrating the landing at Jamestown, tied up as it is with an American narrative of settlement. We may argue about the meanings of settlement and colonization, but we'll always be debating within these frameworks, hovering around them like vultures. For better or worse, they define who we are. And this fact ensures that, generations from now, Irishmen and women and Americans will still be arguing about the merits of conquest and middle grounds. Maybe, after all, the two nations are more alike than we had thought.

Civil War 'contrabands', fugitive slaves who were emancipated upon reaching the North, possibly in Freedman's Village, Arlington, Virginia, mid-1860s. Photo: Hulton Archive/Getty Images.

'My countrymen are all mankind'

Bruce Nelson

Ireland, Slavery and Anti-Slavery, 1612–1865
Nini Rodgers
Basingstoke and New York: Palgrave Macmillan, 2007
403 pages. ISBN 978-0-333-77099-3

In the early 1840s Daniel O'Connell waged two parallel campaigns — first, to win Repeal of the Union for the Irish people, and second, to persuade Irish immigrants in the United States to join him in condemning, and working for the abolition of, chattel slavery in the American South. In addressing the second of these two grand themes, O'Connell spoke the familiar moral language of transatlantic abolitionism, but he also sought to redefine the meaning of 'Irishness', by claiming that his beloved country had a long and distinctive, even unique, history of opposition to slavery. It was, he maintained, 'the first of all the nations of the earth that abolished the dealing in slaves'. It 'never was stained with negro slave-trading,' 'never committed an offence against the men of color', 'never fitted out a single vessel for the traffic in blood on the African coast'. O'Connell rejoiced that while Liverpool was crowded with slave ships and thus 'tainted with slavery', 'not a single slaver ever sailed from Dublin, or Drogheda, or Belfast, or Waterford, or Cork, or any other port in Ireland'. He argued that this proud history had, in important respects, shaped the Irish people and defined their national character.[1]

It turns out that O'Connell was wrong in making at least some of these claims. He was right in his assertion that slave ships did not sail from Irish ports during the heyday of the African slave trade, although that apparently owed more to restrictions imposed by the British parliament than to moral qualms among Irish merchants. But he was wrong in his assumption that Irish society remained untouched by slavery during the seventeenth, eighteenth, and nineteenth centuries. Slavery was integral to the economy of the Atlantic World, and Ireland was an integral part of that world. According to historian Nini Rodgers, slavery had a 'formative influence on Irish life', in the eighteenth century in particular. Moreover, the lives and fortunes of thousands of Irishwomen and men — mainly merchants, sailors, and settlers — were directly, and intimately, linked to the 'peculiar institution'.[2]

All of this becomes abundantly clear in Rodgers's *Ireland, Slavery and Anti-Slavery, 1612–1865* (2007). Rodgers, who taught for many years at Queen's University Belfast and is now an honorary senior research fellow in history there, had previously written a number of important articles and essays about Ireland's relationship to slavery and anti-slavery in the late eighteenth and early nineteenth centuries.[3] But her book reveals a depth of learning and a level of engagement with her subject that sets a new standard. Henceforth, those who venture onto the terrain of Ireland's relationship to slavery will, necessarily, take her arguments and conclusions as their starting point.[4]

The fact that Irishmen and women became part of the emigrant stream to the Americas in the seventeenth century made it inevitable that Ireland would be touched by the development of chattel slavery. Rodgers asserts that 'the Irish speaking, labouring poor of Munster' were among the earliest emigrants to cross the Atlantic; and this trend became more pronounced in mid-century, when Cromwell's draconian military campaign in Ireland 'swept Irish prisoners and vagrants into servitude.'[5] The need for willing, or even unwilling, hands on tobacco and sugar plantations made the Irish a desirable source of indentured labour. But relative to their English, Scottish, and Welsh counterparts, they quickly developed a reputation as lazy and disobedient.[6] In 1661, authorities on the island of Barbados complained of their 'bold extravagancy and wandering' and, even more so, of their 'profligate tendency' in 'joining themselves to runaway slaves'. As early as 1655, there had been reports that '"several Irish servants and Negroes were in rebellion", hiding in thickets and plundering estates'.[7] Conflict between England and its continental, and Catholic, rivals accentuated this tendency toward rebelliousness. When England and France went to war in 1666, and the West Indies became part of the theatre of conflict, Irish servants on St. Christopher and Montserrat rose up and destroyed English-owned plantations. In 1689, in the context of the geopolitical conflict that pitted Jacobites against Williamites in Britain and Ireland, '130 armed Irishmen' transferred their allegiance to the French forces on St. Christopher and joined them in burning and sacking the English district of the island in 'a true jacquerie'.[8]

Rodgers is keenly aware of the Irish reputation for turbulence and subversion in the islands of the West Indies, but she rejects any suggestion that as an oppressed 'race', the Catholic Irish felt a special sense of affinity with enslaved Africans. 'In the last resort,' she maintains, 'the Irish did not make common cause with the slaves. Only the wildest of them in their wildest moments were driven to it. They were white and wished to exercise

1 *Daniel O'Connell upon American Slavery, with Other Irish Testimonies* (New York, 1860), 7, 17; Daniel O'Connell, *Loyal National Repeal Association* ('To … [the] Executive Committee of the Cincinnati Repeal Association', 11 October 1843) (Boston, [1843?]), 8; *Liberator*, 9 June 1843; Bruce Nelson, '"Come Out of Such a Land, You Irishmen": Daniel O'Connell, American Slavery, and the Making of the "Irish Race"', *Éire-Ireland*, 42 (2007), 74.

2 Nini Rodgers, *Ireland, Slavery and Anti-Slavery, 1612–1865* (Basingstoke and New York, 2007), 196.

3 Nini Rodgers, 'Equiano in Belfast: A Study of the Anti-Slavery Ethos in a Northern Town', *Slavery and Abolition*, 18 (1997), 73–89; 'Ireland and the Black Atlantic in the Eighteenth Century', *Irish Historical Studies*, 23 (2000), 174–92; 'Two Quakers and a Utilitarian: The Reaction of Three Irish Women Writers to the Problem of Slavery, 1789–1807', *Proceedings of the Royal Irish Academy*, 100c (2000), 137–57; 'Richard Robert Madden: An Irish Anti-Slavery Activist in the Americas', in Oonagh Walsh, ed., *Ireland Abroad: Politics and Professions in the Nineteenth Century* (Dublin, 2003), 119–31.

4 Rodgers and the rapidly growing cadre of scholars who are writing on Ireland, slavery, and abolition have a distinguished predecessor in Douglas C. Riach, whose unpublished PhD dissertation has been an invaluable guide to the subject. See Douglas

Peter, a former slave, revealing scars on his back from whippings. 'Overseer Artayou Carrier whipped me. I was 2 months in bed sore from the whipping. My master come after I was whipped; he discharged the overseer'; spoken by Peter as he sat for the photograph, having enlisted in the Union Army. Photo: War Department/ US National Archives/Time Life Pictures/Getty Images.

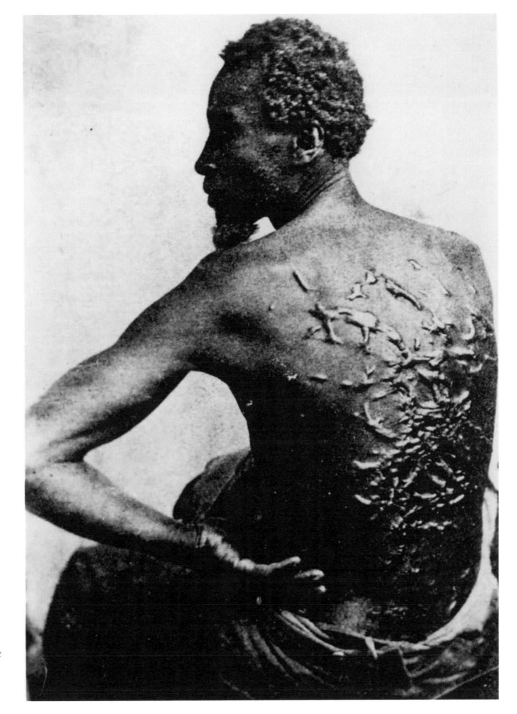

Cameron Riach, 'Ireland and the Campaign against American Slavery, 1830–1860', University of Edinburgh, 1975, and his most important articles and essays: 'Daniel O'Connell and American Anti-Slavery', *Irish Historical Studies*, 20 (1976), 3–25; 'O'Connell and Slavery', in Donal McCartney, ed., *The World of Daniel O'Connell* (Dublin and Cork, 1980), 175–85; 'Richard Davis Webb and Antislavery in Ireland', in Lewis Perry and Michael Fellman, eds., *Antislavery Reconsidered: New Perspectives on the Abolitionists* (Baton Rouge, 1979), 149–67.

5 Rodgers, *Ireland, Slavery and Anti-Slavery*, 35, 36.

6 Hilary McD. Beckles, '"A Riotous and Unruly Lot": Irish Indentured Servants and Freemen in the English West Indies, 1644–1713', *William and Mary Quarterly*, 3rd ser., 47 (1990), 503–22, and *White Servitude and Black Slavery in Barbados, 1627–1715* (Knoxville, 1989), 8, 38–39, 98–114.

7 Rodgers, *Ireland, Slavery and Anti-Slavery*, 43.

8 Donald Harman Akenson, *If the Irish Ran the World: Montserrat, 1630–1730* (Liverpool, 1997), 134.

9 Rodgers, *Ireland, Slavery and Anti-Slavery*, 44.

the advantage it conferred upon them.'[9] Moreover, she follows Donald Harman Akenson in pointing to the Irish triumph — as planters — on Montserrat. According to Akenson, Montserrat 'registered the highest concentration of persons of Irish ethnicity of any colony in the history of both the first and second English empires'. Irish settlers not only became the majority of the island's sugar planters; they prospered, he argues, mainly because 'they well knew how to be hard and efficient slave masters'.[10]

At the end of the seventeenth century and the beginning of the eighteenth, Montserrat was subjected to a succession of penal laws that denied its Irish Catholic residents access to public office but did not interfere with their right to accumulate property. Ironically, it appears that the prohibition against holding public office served to accentuate the entrepreneurial acumen of Catholic planters; for in Rodgers's words, 'the most remarkable fortunes on the island were ... made by members of the Catholic community'.[11] An outstanding example is Nicholas Tuite, the son of an Irish immigrant from County Westmeath, who accumulated 100 acres of land and 41 slaves on Montserrat but found even greater opportunity as a merchant and shipowner, carrying slaves and provisions from island to island. Ultimately, Tuite concentrated his energy and resources on the Danish island of St. Croix, where by 1766 he owned or shared in the ownership of fourteen plantations. So great was his achievement that, in 1760, he journeyed to Copenhagen, where King Frederick V paid tribute to his role in the development of Denmark's Caribbean empire.

More typical were the hundreds, or perhaps thousands, of Irishmen who came to the islands of the Caribbean as indentured servants and free wage labourers and soon became plantation overseers or small planters. In 1760, an Irish Catholic priest on St. Croix reported that 'about one hundred lads of our country' were serving as overseers on the island; surely there were many more on a larger island such as Jamaica.[12] Nonetheless, Tuite had many Irish counterparts: men who became wealthy through the ownership of plantations, or the trade in provisions and slaves, or a combination of the two. Many of these men developed a cosmopolitan outlook that defies easy generalizations about national identity. For example, Antoine Walsh died on St. Domingue in 1763, but lived most of his life in the ports of Saint-Malo and

Nantes, where he was a leading member of the prosperous Irish community in France. The son of a Dublin-born merchant who emigrated to France and became involved in the slave trade, Antoine Walsh was an *armateur*, or outfitter of ships that sailed to Africa to buy slaves for transport to the plantation societies of the Americas. Rodgers estimates that he was the 'fifth most successful slaver in France', and that during his career he 'purchased over 12,000 Africans for export across the Atlantic'.[13] Walsh was ennobled by the French monarchy, but he also remained proudly Irish, a patron of the Irish College in Nantes and an active Jacobite who participated directly in the rebellion of 1745.

To what extent was Irish society affected by the activities of men such as Nicholas Tuite, Antoine Walsh, and other Irish emigrants who were directly involved in plantation slavery or in the multifaceted trade that nourished and sustained it? Rodgers readily acknowledges that 'not much in the way of slave trade profits trickled back to Ireland', but she also emphasizes that the provision trade with the West Indies — the sale of butter, salted beef and pork, and other agricultural products — had 'an enormous impact on Munster and to a lesser extent on Connaught'.[14] As the Irish at home gradually developed a taste first for tobacco and then for sugar, they became connected, at some level, to the plantation economy and its slave-labour system. By the middle of the eighteenth century, sugar had become Ireland's most valuable import, and two-thirds of its sugar supply was refined in Dublin. Sugar was instrumental in the rise of the Catholic middle class, Rodgers argues, and the Catholic middle class became the foundation stone of O'Connell's campaign for Catholic Emancipation and Repeal of the Union. Indirectly, then, Negro slavery impacted Irish society in the eighteenth century and became intertwined with its patterns of production and consumption. But slavery also touched Ireland more directly. Historian William A. Hart estimates that there were

10 Akenson, *If the Irish Ran the World*, 107, 119.

11 Rodgers, *Ireland, Slavery and Anti-Slavery*, 55.

12 Orla Power, 'The "Quadripartite Concern" of St. Croix, 1751–1757: An Irish Catholic Plantation in the Danish West Indies', paper presented at conference on 'The Irish in the Atlantic World', College of Charleston, Charleston, 27 February– 2 March 2007, 15.

13 Rodgers, *Ireland, Slavery and Anti-Slavery*, 106, 111.

14 Rodgers, *Ireland, Slavery and Anti-Slavery*, 113, 121.

Frederick Douglass (1817–95),
c. 1879: journalist, author,
former slave and abolitionist.
Photo: Library of Congress/
Getty Images.

more than 2,000 Africans and people of African descent in Ireland during the second half of the century, more than in most European countries, including France. Most blacks were concentrated in Dublin and other port cities. A few were musicians and actors; some were drummers in British regiments; most were domestic servants, and for much of the eighteenth century at least some of these servants were slaves.

Hart argues that in retrospect 'there is no disguising the existence of slavery in Ireland at this time, nor that it was restricted, in practice, to black people from Africa and the East Indies'. Insofar as there was slavery, however, its boundaries were porous; the path from slave to indentured servant to free wage labourer was, in relative terms, easily travelled; and there was no Irish legislation relating to slavery. Newspaper references to blacks as slaves virtually disappeared in the early 1770s, at about the time of Britain's famed Somerset case (1772), which was widely interpreted to mean that Negro slaves were entitled to freedom when they set foot on British soil.[15]

By the 1780s, moreover, anti-slavery had emerged as a new and powerful motif among Ireland's educated classes. The Abbé Raynal's *History of the East and West Indies*, which welcomed the 'impending storm' of slave revolt, became one of the bestselling books in the country. In 1788, at the behest of a group of Quaker merchants, the Dublin Chamber of Commerce passed a resolution calling the slave trade 'odious' and suggesting that 'the traffic in human species does not appear ever to have been carried on from this kingdom'.[16] This compelling but erroneous view was popularized further by Mary Birkett, a Quaker whose family had moved from England to Ireland in 1784, when she was nine years old. At age seventeen, Birkett published a long poem, *The African Slave Trade Addressed to Her Own Sex*, in which she claimed that, in sharp contrast to her native England, Ireland had always remained free of the trade in slaves. It was through Birkett, Rodgers claims, that 'the idea of Ireland as a lover of the oppressed everywhere ... permanently entered the nationalist psyche'.[17]

Although Rodgers believes that slavery had a 'formative influence on Irish life', she argues that anti-slavery was a minor force in Irish society. In England the abolitionist movement helped to generate the widespread conviction that slavery was an evil institution that must be eradicated immediately

— hence the historic legislation of 1833 abolishing slavery everywhere in the British Empire. But in Ireland anti-slavery was — according to Rodgers — a mere 'diversion, a foreign import for intellectuals who thrilled to feel themselves ... part of the world's most moral cause'.[18] Irish anti-slavery groups were 'tiny'; Irish churches, Catholic and Protestant, did not really embrace the cause; even the Quakers found it divisive. She invokes David Hempton, the pre-eminent historian of Methodism in Ireland and Britain, to support her contention that anti-slavery in Ireland was 'a cause for faddists and oddities along with cruelty to animals and pacifism'.[19]

Clearly, Rodgers is relentlessly unsentimental about the character, and fate, of anti-slavery in Ireland. A part of her purpose seems to be to prove O'Connell, and Mary Birkett, and various and sundry post-modernists and practitioners of cultural studies, wrong in their belief that the Irish people felt a special sense of affinity with victims of oppression in other parts of the world. While her treatment of Ireland and slavery offers much new evidence and opens up fresh lines of inquiry, her portrayal of Ireland and anti-slavery seems to foreclose the possibility of contingency and to treat questions that require further analysis merely as foregone conclusions. It is important, I believe, to examine anti-slavery in Ireland from a perspective that challenges Rodgers' bleak portrait, while also exploring the convergence of historical circumstances and forces that contributed to its decline and marginalization.

Anti-slavery had three main pillars in Ireland. It developed first among members of the Religious Society of Friends (the Quakers) in the 1780s. The Quakers were a small sect. In the early nineteenth century, they had about 4,500 adherents in Ireland, with perhaps 650 of them living in Dublin. Many Quakers were descended from veterans of Cromwell's army, who, in the aftermath of their ruthless suppression of the Irish Catholic uprising of the 1640s,

15 W. A. Hart, 'Africans in Eighteenth-Century Ireland', *Irish Historical Studies*, 33 (2002), 19–32 (24); personal communication from William A. Hart, 31 October 2006.

16 Rodgers, *Ireland, Slavery and Anti-Slavery*, 181. Rodgers devotes her first chapter (7–26) to the existence of slavery and the slave trade in early Ireland; and there are numerous references to slavery, and the trade in slaves, in Dáibhí Ó Cróinín, ed., *A New History of Ireland*, vol. 1: *Prehistoric and Early Ireland* (Oxford, 2005).

17 Rodgers, *Ireland, Slavery and Anti-Slavery*, 181, 242.

18 Rodgers, *Ireland, Slavery and Anti-Slavery*, 275.

19 Rodgers, *Ireland, Slavery and Anti-Slavery*, 276; David Hempton, *Religion and Political Culture in Britain and Ireland: from the Glorious Revolution to the Decline of Empire* (Cambridge, 1996), 96. Hempton does not use the words 'faddists and oddities'. Rather, in describing a strand of Presbyterian radicalism in the late eighteenth century, he refers to 'a kind of high-minded Dissenting cantankerousness in its hostility to war, slavery and blood sports'.

E. W. Clay, *O'Connell's Call and Pat's Reply*, 1843, lithograph on wove paper; 31.1 x 46.5 cm. Library of Congress.

O'CONNELL'S CALL AND PATS REPLY.

20 David Brion Davis, 'The Quaker Ethic and the Antislavery International', in *The Problem of Slavery in the Age of Revolution, 1770–1823* (Ithaca, 1975), 213–54; Christopher Leslie Brown, *Moral Capital: Foundations of British Abolitionism* (Chapel Hill, 2006). On Ireland, in particular, see Richard S. Harrison, 'Irish Quaker Perspectives on the Anti-Slavery Movement', *Journal of the Friends' Historical Society*, 56 (1993), 106–25.

21 Anthony J. Barker, *Captain Charles Stuart: Anglo-American Abolitionist* (Baton Rouge, 1986), 46–48; Harrison, 'Irish Quaker Perspectives', 112.

settled on confiscated lands, renounced war, and built a religious community that was set apart from the world and yet deeply engaged with it. Over time they became legendary for their economic success; and their commitment to philanthropic endeavour earned them widespread respect. They were also part of an international network that linked them closely to their co-religionists in England and North America. Through these affiliations they emerged as leaders of the transatlantic anti-slavery movement, especially in its early stages.[20]

By the late 1820s zealous evangelicals from a number of Protestant denominations were turning their attention to slavery and beginning to address it in their own distinctive way. In 1829, evangelical Protestants took the lead in founding the Dublin Negro's Friend Society, and several of the society's organizers began a tour of Irish cities and towns that engendered an

unprecedented commitment to immediate abolition. Many of the society's mass meetings were held in Protestant churches — most often, in Methodist meeting houses. In fact, the leadership and membership of the Dublin (soon to be Hibernian) Negro's Friend Society overlapped to a significant degree with that of the Hibernian Bible Society, which was notoriously anti-Catholic in ethos and intent.[21]

The third major pillar of the evolving anti-slavery movement in Ireland was Daniel O'Connell himself. O'Connell had become committed to the cause of abolition by the mid-1820s, and he played a leading role in the parliamentary campaign to outlaw slavery in the British Empire. Without asking permission of anyone in the hierarchy of the Catholic Church, he identified Catholicism with abolition and adopted the evangelical trait of 'looking at Slavery as a Sin, wherever it exists, and ... declaring war against it, over the whole globe'.[22] It is a testimony to the depth of O'Connell's commitment that he increased his own involvement in the movement at the very moment when evangelical anti-slavery was taking off, even though he was keenly aware of the 'Orange' coloration of Irish Protestantism's 'Second Reformation' and he believed that the Wesleyan Methodists, in particular, were the determined enemies of Catholicism and of the religious liberty he cherished. 'In the long struggle the Catholics of Ireland made for the abolition of the laws that infringed freedom of conscience', he reminded them, '*you* never gave us any assistance. On the contrary, you were found in the adverse ranks, active, persevering, virulent!'[23]

It is undeniable that, apart from O'Connell and a few other Catholics such as the civil servant, widely travelled author, and historian Richard Robert Madden, anti-slavery in Ireland was overwhelmingly Protestant in character. In a country that was 80 per cent Catholic, and divided by sectarian antagonisms, this was a major problem for the movement. It may even be true that at least some of Ireland's leading abolitionists were 'oddities', as Rodgers charges. Along with a few close relatives and friends, the Dublin Quaker Richard Davis Webb was at the centre of a reform circle that took up causes such as 'slavery, temperance, British India, anti-opium, anti-capital punishment, anti-corn law, mesmerism, cold-water cure'; indeed, so many causes that its members became known as 'Anti-Everythingarians'.[24]

But if they were oddities, they clearly were not faddists. On the contrary, what characterized the Dublin trio of Webb, Richard Allen, and James Haughton was their long-standing devotion to anti-slavery. It became the cause that defined their lives. In 1840, after attending the World's Anti-Slavery Convention in London, they became disciples of the radical abolitionist William Lloyd Garrison, who was reviled by a wide swathe of public opinion in the United States. Webb hailed 'Garrison's reformation'

as more important than Luther's; his wife Hannah believed that the Boston prophet was seeking 'a world in which there would be no slavery, no king, no beggars, no lawyers, no doctors, no soldiers, no palaces, no prisons, no creeds, no sects, no weary or grinding labor, no luxurious idleness ... no restraint but moral restraint, no constraining power but love'.[25] Ultimately, Webb became deeply frustrated with the quietism and timidity that increasingly characterized the Irish Quaker community, and in 1851 he left the enveloping warmth of the sect into which he had been born forty-six years earlier.

To dismiss the Webbs and their associates as mere oddities obscures the extent to which they were able to make Ireland a hospitable place for visiting representatives of the transatlantic abolitionist movement. One of the most notable visitors was Charles Lenox Remond, a free black and faithful Garrisonian from Salem, Massachusetts, who arrived in Ireland in May 1841 and stayed for nearly six months. Far more than in England and Scotland, he encountered 'receptive and overflowing crowds', not only in Dublin, but in Wexford, Waterford, Limerick, Belfast, and other cities and towns. Webb reported that Remond addressed six meetings in Dublin; all of them were well attended. At one, in particular, 'the room was crowded almost to suffocation, but the attention and zeal of the audience could not be surpassed'. From Dublin, Remond journeyed south to Wexford, where he spoke to three crowded meetings. He then delivered five lectures in Waterford, where the number of people clamouring to hear him was so large that his hosts finally had to begin charging admission, in order to keep the attendance manageable. Then it was on to Limerick, where he gave three lectures, to a bigger audience each time. Webb, a veteran of many such events, reported that the last of these gatherings was the 'most crowded and the most attentive meeting I ever attended'.[26]

Four years later, Frederick Douglass made an even greater impression. A fugitive slave who was well on his way to becoming

22 Barker, *Captain Charles Stuart*, 46.

23 Daniel O'Connell, 'To the Ministers and Office-Bearers of the Wesleyan Methodist Societies in Manchester', London, 6 July 1839, in Daniel O'Connell, ed., *A Full Report of the Proceedings of the Great Meeting of the Catholics of London, Held at Freemason's Hall, on the Fifteenth Day of July, 1839, with an Address to the English People, and the Letters to the Wesleyan Methodists by Mr. O'Connell* (London, 1839), 40. According to David Hempton, 'the true significance of Irish Methodism in the first half of the nineteenth century lay ... in its front line position in the great evangelical crusade against Roman Catholicism'. D. N. Hempton, 'The Methodist Crusade in Ireland, 1795–1845', *Irish Historical Studies*, 22 (1980), 33–48 (35).

24 Hannah Maria Wigham, *A Christian Philanthropist of Dublin: A Memoir of Richard Allen* (London, 1886), 14. For an evocative recollection of the world of the Dublin Quaker reformers, see Alfred Webb, *The Autobiography of a Quaker Nationalist*, ed. Marie-Louise Legg (Cork, 1999), 17–32, and Riach, 'Richard Davis Webb and Antislavery in Ireland'.

25 Clare Taylor, ed., *British and American Abolitionists: An Episode in Transatlantic Understanding* (Edinburgh, 1974), 120; Riach, 'Richard Davis Webb and Antislavery in Ireland', 156.

26 C. Peter Ripley, et al., eds., *The Black Abolitionist Papers*, vol. 1: *The British Isles, 1830–1865* (Chapel Hill, 1985), 97; *Liberator*, 24 September 1841.

27 John W. Blassingame, ed., *The Frederick Douglass Papers*, series one: *Speeches, Debates, and Interviews*, vol. 1 (New Haven, 1979), 42, 44.

28 Blassingame, ed., *The Frederick* Douglass *Papers*, series one, vol. 1, 56.

29 'Letters to Antislavery Workers and Agencies [Part 1]: Frederick Douglass', *Journal of Negro History*, 10 (1925), 656–57.

30 Frederick Douglass, *My Bondage and My Freedom* (New York, 2003), 15.

31 Rodgers, *Ireland, Slavery and Anti-Slavery*, 272.

32 O'Connell, *Loyal National Repeal Association*, 7.

one of the great orators of the nineteenth century, Douglass delivered more than fifty lectures in most of Ireland's largest cities and towns to audiences that responded with 'Great sensation', 'Great applause', and 'tremendous cheers'.[27] For someone who only recently had been a slave himself, this reception was overwhelming. 'Seven years ago I was ranked among the beasts and creeping things', he told an audience in Cork; 'to-night I am ... here as a man and a brother'.[28] In his correspondence, he went much further, contrasting the omnipresence of racism in the United States with the 'total absence of all manifestations of prejudice against me, on account of my color', in Ireland. 'I can truly say, I have spent some of the happiest moments of my life since landing in this country', he wrote to Garrison on 1 January 1846:

> In the Southern part of the United States, I was a slave, thought of and spoken of as property ... In the Northern States, a fugitive slave, liable to be hunted at any moment like a felon ... doomed by an inveterate prejudice of color to insult and outrage on every hand ... But now behold the change! ... Instead of a democratic government, I am under a monarchical government. Instead of the bright blue sky of America, I am covered with the soft grey fog of the Emerald Isle. I breathe and lo! the chattel becomes a man. I gaze around in vain for one who will question my equal humanity, claim me as his slave, or offer me an insult ... I find no difficulty here in obtaining admission into any place of worship, instruction or amusement, on equal terms with people as white as any I ever saw in the United States.[29]

In fact, Douglass encountered a far more complex and fractured society in Ireland than this euphoric portrait suggests. But as someone who had crossed the Atlantic in part to avoid the long arm of the American 'slave catchers' who were eager to return escaped chattel to their masters in the South,

his reception in Ireland (and in Scotland and England) made an indelible impression. For the rest of his life, he continued to believe that his sojourn abroad had been a major turning point in his personal and intellectual development. Here he had first 'breathed an atmosphere congenial to the longings of his spirit, and felt his manhood free and unrestricted'. Here he recalled being received 'not only as an equal, but as a recognized man of genius'.[30]

The other larger than life figure in the narrative of anti-slavery in Ireland is, of course, O'Connell. As a Catholic, what was his role in a predominantly Protestant social movement? Surely his reputation as Ireland's Liberator, his strategic position as the leader of a genuine mass mobilization for Repeal of the Union, and his status as Ireland's — indeed, Europe's — leading Catholic layman gave abolition a platform that went far beyond anything the Webbs' Hibernian Anti-Slavery Society could provide. Rodgers acknowledges that O'Connell was Ireland's greatest contribution to the abolitionist movement. But she makes a sharp distinction between the 1830s, when he was among the leaders of a triumphant campaign to abolish slavery in the British Empire, and the 1840s, when, she writes, 'anti-slavery gave him endless trouble'.[31] She is referring in part to the ideological and strategic questions that divided the movement in the United States, Britain, and, to a lesser extent, Ireland; and to the quarrel between O'Connell and supporters of Repeal in the United States over his accusation that Irish immigrants who compromised in any way with slavery could not have the 'genuine feelings of Irishmen'.[32] O'Connell's Loyal National Repeal Association desperately needed the financial support that Irish Americans were eager to provide. But as his denunciations of the crimes of the White Republic became louder and ever more extreme, the entire Repeal apparatus in the United States fell apart.

And as it fell apart, famine ravaged Ireland. It not only caused unprecedented deprivation among the Irish people; it helped to generate a new discourse of human suffering that highlighted the misery of the 'white slaves' of Ireland and alleged that, in comparison, the Negro slave's lot was one of safety, security, and relative ease and comfort. Even before the Great Famine, having seen 'the Indian in his forests, and the negro in his chains', the French aristocrat Gustave de Beaumont had been shocked to encounter 'the very extreme of human wretchedness' in 'unfortunate Ireland'.[33] But de Beaumont had not sought to play one suffering and victimized people against another. His sympathy extended equally to the Indian, the Negro, and the Irish peasant. Now a new generation of polemicists sought to build a wall between black bondage and Irish 'slavery'. Douglass was dismayed by this development. But even he was compelled to ask himself whose cause he should espouse, when Ireland's poor were *more* wretched than he had been as the chattel property of his master in Maryland. 'I see much here to remind me of my former condition,' he told Garrison, 'and I confess I should be ashamed to lift up my voice against American slavery, but that I know the cause of humanity is one the world over.'[34]

O'Connell barely survived the winter of 'Black '47', and he died in May during an aborted pilgrimage to Rome. Historians tell us that for the last several years of his life, his physical condition had left him more and more incapacitated, and that a deepening spiritual anxiety had become a major deterrent to any effective engagement with his ongoing political agenda. As early as October 1843, his acquiescence in the government's prohibition of the massive Repeal meeting scheduled for Clontarf had left him bruised and rudderless. His imprisonment for three months in 1844 only added to his physical travail. His biographer Denis Gwynn tells us that by the end of that year, 'he was already a broken man'.[35]

It is all the more remarkable, then, that O'Connell continued to address the issue of slavery with extraordinary clarity and vigour during much of this period. This was nowhere more apparent than when he welcomed

Douglass to a Repeal meeting in Dublin in September 1845 and introduced him to the audience as the 'black O'Connell of the United States'. It was here that the Liberator issued one of his most famous perorations; it was here that he declared, 'wherever tyranny exists, I am the foe of the tyrant; wherever oppression shows itself, I am the foe of the oppressor; wherever slavery rears its head, I am the enemy of the system … My sympathy with distress … extends itself to every corner of the earth.' Douglass marvelled at these words, of course, but what stands out in retrospect is his sense of O'Connell's strength and radiance. He spoke for more than an hour, with no hint of weakness, anxiety, or distraction. On the contrary, 'the fire of freedom was burning in his mighty heart', Douglass told Garrison. 'I have heard many speakers within the last four years — speakers of the first order; but I confess, I have never heard one by whom I was more completely captivated than by Mr. O'Connell'.[36]

But could O'Connell have won Catholic Ireland to the cause of anti-slavery? In the countryside, the cottiers and labourers who made up the bulk of the rural population were, of necessity, preoccupied with questions of day-to-day survival in an increasingly precarious environment. But in the cities and towns where the Repeal campaign was taking root, O'Connell had some success in building a bridge between internal and external concerns. At Repeal meetings in Dublin, he made questions of slavery and abolition a frequent subject of discussion and debate. As he denounced chattel slavery as 'the greatest crime that can be committed by humanity against humanity' and described himself as 'the friend of liberty in every clime, class, and colour', his overwhelmingly Catholic audiences burst into applause and cheered aloud. Moved by his eloquence, Irishmen and women wrote to friends and family in America asking how it was that they could oppose O'Connell's criticism of the 'enemies of liberty', how it was that they had ceased to be Irish.[37]

In 1841, when Dublin Quakers drafted a

33 Gustave de Beaumont, *Ireland: Social, Political, and Religious*, with an Introduction by Tom Garvin and Andreas Hess (Cambridge, Mass., 2006), 130.

34 'Letters to Antislavery Workers and Agencies [Part 1]: Frederick Douglass', 672.

35 James E. Guilfoyle, 'The Religious Development of Daniel O'Connell, II: The Making of a Devotional Catholic', *New Hibernia Review*, 2 (1998), 114–32; Denis Gwynn, *Daniel O'Connell*, rev. centenary edn. (Cork, 1947), 241.

36 'Letters to Antislavery Workers and Agencies [Part 1]: Frederick Douglass', 662.

Benjamin Robert Haydon, *The Anti-Slavery Society Convention*, 1840, oil on canvas, 1841, 297 × 384 cm, National Portrait Gallery, London. Philanthropist Thomas Clarkson (1760–1846) is speaking; Daniel O'Connell is visible in the top left.

37 *Liberator*, 2 May 1845;
David T. Gleeson, *The Irish in the South, 1815–1877* (Chapel Hill, 2001), 125–26, 129.

38 Riach, 'Richard Davis Webb and Antislavery in Ireland', 162; John F. Quinn, '"Three Cheers for the Abolitionist Pope!": American Reaction to Gregory XVI's Condemnation of the Slave Trade, 1840–1860', *Catholic Historical Review*, 90 (2004), 81; *Liberator*, 18 March 1842.

letter calling on Irish emigrants in the United States to join with the abolitionists in seeking the overthrow of slavery, the Liberator quickly added his signature, as did R. R. Madden and Ireland's Apostle of Temperance, the Capuchin Father Theobald Mathew. O'Connell's Repeal wardens played the leading role in circulating the 'Irish Address', which suggests that although the infrastructure of abolitionism in Ireland was overwhelmingly Protestant in membership and ethos, many — perhaps most — signers of the letter were Catholic. This becomes vividly clear from the report of a Repeal warden in Kells, County Meath, who claimed that he had obtained 500 signatures. 'Everybody here is willing to abolish slavery,' he wrote, except for 'the vile faction that always kept this country ... in bondage. For instance, I called [on] two I believe [to be] Orangemen' and when they saw that O'Connell's name was first on the petition 'they walked away and would not sign'. Overall, the many Catholic signatories may have included large numbers of Catholic clergymen. Allen reported from Dublin that a single individual had secured the signatures of a Catholic bishop and seventy-two priests. 'How many, then', Garrison's *Liberator* asked triumphantly, 'are [included] among the sixty thousand names that are appended to the Address?'[38]

But the institutional Church in Ireland

remained resolutely silent as the controversy over slavery swirled around it. The Irish bishops were, in important respects, caught in a pincer between the Vatican and the rapidly expanding presence and power of the Catholic Church in the United States. The overwhelming concern of the members of the Irish hierarchy was to build up the personnel and infrastructure of devotional Catholicism in their own country, and to fend off the challenge represented by the aggressive, proselytizing thrust of Irish Protestantism's Second Reformation. Insofar as they paused to consider the question of slavery and anti-slavery, they could hardly ignore the fact that their friends and compatriots in the American hierarchy — Irish-born men such as John England in South Carolina and John Hughes in New York — were denouncing abolitionism not only as a danger to social order but as quintessentially Protestant.

In Rome, meanwhile, the Church retreated from a stance that had, for a brief moment, given great encouragement to opponents of slavery. In 1839 Pope Gregory XVI issued *In Supremo*, an Apostolic Letter that unequivocally condemned the slave trade and appeared — to many readers — to identify the institution of slavery as equally 'unworthy of the Christian name'. Abolitionists seized on the letter's vehement admonition 'that none henceforth dare to subject to slavery ... Indians, negroes, or other classes of men' as decisive proof that the Pope had sided with them. In fact, *In Supremo* issued no injunction to free any of the millions of men, women, and children who were already enslaved, and the American Catholic hierarchy quickly mounted a counteroffensive aimed at demonstrating that the Apostolic Letter had no bearing upon 'domestic slavery as it exists in the southern states and in other parts of the Christian world'.[39] Thereafter, Rome remained more or less silent on the question of slavery until the passage of the last secular abolition legislation of the nineteenth century, Brazil's 'Golden Law' of 1888. As the Catholic theologian John T. Noonan

has acknowledged, 'Only after the cultures of Europe and America changed through the abolitionists' agency and only after the laws of every civilized land eliminated the practice, did Catholic moral doctrine decisively repudiate slavery as immoral. Only in 1890 did Pope Leo XIII attack the institution itself.'[40]

We can conclude, then, that while anti-slavery in Ireland had some triumphant moments, it was undone by a complex array of forces and circumstances, including the coming of the Great Famine, the death of O'Connell, the rise of a competing narrative of *white* slavery and suffering, the persistent silence of the Irish Catholic Church, and, lest we forget, the emergence of powerful pro-slavery voices in Irish America. All of this may appear to have been foreordained, but if so, we must also acknowledge that O'Connell and Douglass were like comets in the night sky, but comets that kept on burning. The Dublin Quaker reformers could not match their extraordinary charisma and would not have aspired to. But the 'inner light' burned within them for a lifetime. Remarkably, as late as 1883, when he was in his eighty-first year, Richard Allen visited the United States and spoke to students at Fisk University, in Nashville, Tennessee, a school that was steeped in the ethos of abolitionism and whose students were likely to be the children of slaves (in some cases, former slaves themselves). 'For more than fifty years I was engaged in the anti-slavery cause', he told the assembled student body, 'first for the emancipation of [British] slaves in the West Indies, and then for those in America. ... I am thankful that in the good providence of God I am here; [and] that I see what I do'.[41]

In an era of increasingly intense and narrowly focused nationalism, these men helped lay the foundations of a different kind of national sensibility, one that sought to transcend nationalism's exclusions and to create instead an Irishness that was generous, inclusive, rooted in their native soil but global in its reach. Later in the nineteenth century, the politics and vision of

39 *Letters of the Late Bishop England to the Hon. John Forsyth on the Subject of Domestic Slavery* (New York, 1969), xi, iv, v; Quinn, '"Three Cheers for the Abolitionist Pope!"'; Robert Emmett Curran, 'Rome, the American Church, and Slavery', in Joseph C. Linck and Raymond J. Kupke, eds., *Building the Church in America* (Washington, DC, 1999), 30–49.

40 John T. Noonan, Jr., 'Development in Moral Doctrine', *Theological Studies*, 54 (December 1993), 664–67, 673–75 (675).

41 Wigham, *A Christian Philanthropist of Dublin*, 219.

42 James P. Rodechko, *Patrick Ford and His Search for America* (New York, 1976), 28-32; Bruce Nelson, 'Irish Nationalism, Irish Americans, and the "Social" Question, 1916–1923', *boundary 2*, 31 (2004), 153–56 (155).

43 Alfred Webb, 'Presidential Address at the Tenth Indian National Congress, Madras', in his *Indian Affairs: Speeches of Alfred Webb, Esq, M.P., President, Tenth Indian National Congress* (Bombay, 1895), 10–11.

Patrick Ford and Michael Davitt were rooted in this sensibility. Fittingly enough, Ford, an Irish Catholic emigrant from Galway, settled in Boston and worked as a printer's assistant for Garrison and the *Liberator* before starting his own abolitionist newspaper and then enlisting in the Union Army during the American Civil War. In the late 1870s and 1880s, Ford and Davitt would dedicate themselves to the struggle for land reform in Ireland while repeatedly reaffirming their commitment to 'Universal Justice and the Rights of Humanity'.[42]

But perhaps the last word should belong to Alfred Webb, the oldest son of Richard and Hannah Webb, who became a distinctive and important figure in the ranks of Irish nationalism, one who could share a platform with Parnell while also sharing his parents' concern with alleviating suffering far beyond Ireland's shores. In recognition of his dual role as nationalist and internationalist, Alfred Webb was elected honorary president of the Indian National Congress in 1894. In his presidential address, he defined himself for his audience by pointing to the example and legacy of O'Connell and Garrison. 'I was nurtured in the conflict against American slavery', he told the assembled delegates in Bombay:

In the words of William Lloyd Garrison, the founder of that movement, 'My country is the world; my countrymen are all mankind.' To aid in the elevation of my native land has been the endeavour of my riper years. [But] in the words of Daniel O'Connell, 'My sympathies are not confined to my own green island. I am a friend to civil and religious liberty all over the world.'[43]

Plato's Cave?

Deirdre McMahon

A Game with Sharpened Knives
Neil Belton
London: Weidenfeld and Nicolson, 2005
320 pages. ISBN 0-297643-59-2

Propaganda, Censorship and Irish Neutrality in the Second World War
Robert Cole
Edinburgh: Edinburgh University Press, 2006
196 pages. ISBN 0-748-62277-2

The Emergency:
Neutral Ireland 1939–45
Brian Girvin
Basingstoke: Macmillan, 2006
385 pages. ISBN 978-1-405000-10-9

'Mise an Fear Cheoil':
Séamus Ennis — Dialann Taistil 1942–46
Séamus Mac Aonghusa
Edited by Ríonach Uí Ógáin
Indreabhán: Cló Iar-Chonnachta, 2007
490 pages. ISBN 978-1-905560-07-3

Dublin Nazi No. 1:
The Life of Adolf Mahr
Gerry Mullins
With a Foreword by Cathal O'Shannon
Dublin: Liberties Press, 2007
253 pages. ISBN 978-1-905483-19-8

That Neutral Island:
A Cultural History of Ireland during the Second World War
Clair Wills
London: Faber and Faber, 2007
502 pages. ISBN 978-0-571221-05-9

Clair Wills's compelling new study, *That Neutral Island: A Cultural History of Ireland during the Second World War*, includes political and social as well as cultural history. She has researched an impressive array of source material — official and private records, the national and provincial press, literature, memoirs and biographies, high and popular culture, and ephemera such as advertisements and posters. Her study challenges one of the iconic images of Irish neutrality, that of F. S. L. Lyons in *Ireland since the Famine* in 1971, when he wrote:

> It was as if an entire people had been condemned to live in Plato's cave, with their backs to the fire of life and deriving their only knowledge of what went on outside from the flickering shadows thrown on the wall ... When after six years they emerged, dazzled, from the cave into the light of day, it was to a new and vastly different world.[1]

Wills presents the conflicting perceptions of neutrality in her evocative opening pages, where she compares and contrasts the wartime experiences of her Irish mother, in West Cork, and her English father, on the outskirts of London. The farm, which her Cork grandfather had bought from the Land Commission, 'was the model on which Fianna Fáil hoped to build a new, fair, if frugal, agrarian society'.[2] The family subsisted on their own crops and the small income from the sale of milk, eggs and pigs, boosted by the older children's earnings. For the boys there was rabbit-snaring and seasonal agricultural work for the county council; for the girls, domestic service in the home of the local minister. 'Except for the unaccountable fact that my grandfather had been born a Protestant (though he had long since converted), the family came close to embodying the ideal of a self-sufficient, rural, devout and independent Ireland', writes Wills.[3] Her mother's principal memories of entertainment during the Emergency were occasional visits to the cinema, music

sessions in neighbours' homes, card-playing, Sunday night patterns, turkey-drives, fair days, dances in the town hall and the round of social activities centred on the local church. Frugality was the order of the day. Transport difficulties made delivery of the *Cork Examiner* sporadic, while listening to the radio became impossible because of the difficulty of obtaining batteries.

Wills's father was evacuated to Wales early in the war but returned to London, spending nights in the Anderson shelter during air raids. His life was more disrupted than her mother's but also more varied. He made frequent visits to the local British Restaurant for dried egg and chips, made models of the British and German planes battling overhead, listened daily to music, comedy and drama on the BBC, and watched films and newsreels of the war at the local cinema.

If the contrast seems emblematic of the distinction between living inside and outside the war, it is one of the major themes of Wills's book that Irish neutrality was not synonymous with peace. The war was distant from the concerns of most Irish people but their daily lives were shaped by the political, social, economic and cultural pressures of trying to survive in the midst of a world war.

To the British, and later the Americans, neutrality was seen as an extreme expression of isolationism and Irish perverseness. It was also seen as a betrayal and Wills perceptively remarks how often the rhetoric of adultery was used in this context. In his 1951 novel, *The Cruel Sea*, Nicholas Monsarrat, in a contemptuous reference to Ireland, wrote that 'there are degrees of neutrality, just as there are degrees of unfaithfulness: one may forgive a woman an occasional cold spell, but not her continued and smiling repose in another man's arms'.[4] British and American visitors to Dublin during the war recalled a city of light, luxury and plenty, with the strong implication that beneath all this lay a moral darkness, Dublin fiddling while Europe burned. Dubliners knew this was a partial picture at best and that within a few yards

1 F. S. L. Lyons, *Ireland since the Famine* (London, 1971), 557–58.
2 Clair Wills, *That Neutral Island: A Cultural History of Ireland during the Second World War* (London, 2007), 1.
3 Ibid.
4 Monsarrat quoted in Wills, *That Neutral Island*, 118.

of the Gresham, the Shelbourne and other fashionable watering holes, there existed dire poverty, which worsened during the war.

A more profound sense of ambivalence permeated cultural and artistic opinion, about which Wills writes incisively. The generation of writers born in and around the first decade of the twentieth century — Patrick Kavanagh, Flann O'Brien, Seán O'Faoláin, Frank O'Connor, Máirtín Ó Cadhain, Séamus Ó Néill — educated at the colleges of the National University and the teacher-training colleges, reached artistic maturity during the war. They were more confident but also more cynical about the new state. Wills observes that the social role of literature developed very differently in 1930s Ireland than in Britain and America. Because political theory and sociology were underdeveloped disciplines in Ireland, literature was recording Irish life.

Not surprisingly, one of the most striking aspects of Irish writing in the period was the preference for documentary work, polemic, commentary, reportage and propaganda in both print and broadcasting. The war cut off Irish writers from British publishing outlets but this stimulated a wartime literary renaissance, which, for all the anxieties about intellectual torpor, was evidence of an energy and dynamism that was resisting stagnation. This was particularly evident in Irish-language writing.

In the early years of the war, as Wills makes clear, neutrality caused few problems for writers like Hubert Butler, Kate O'Brien, Louis MacNeice, Elizabeth Bowen and Denis Johnston. But as the war intensified and criticism of Ireland and the Irish became ever more shrill, the conflict of loyalties became acute. Kate O'Brien's novel, *The Last of the Summer,* set in the summer of 1939, refracts

A survivor from the *Athenia*, which had been torpedoed by a German submarine, comes ashore at Galway, 6 September 1939. Photo: Central Press/ Getty Images.

Irish neutrality through the more hardened prism of 1943, when it was published, thus distorting how Irish neutrality was actually perceived immediately after the outbreak of war. Wills devotes considerable attention to MacNeice and his 'convoluted self-justification' about the war in 1939–40. By 1943, however, like Kate O'Brien he saw Irish neutrality as an evasion and a shirking of responsibility. Wills writes about popular culture with equal insight: from the recruiting pageants of 'Step Together' and 'Roll of the Drum' to *Ireland's Own* (full of make-do-and-mend tips) and the huge popularity of amateur drama throughout the country (especially with women). She analyses wartime plays like Robert Collis's *Marrowbone Lane* (1939), George Shiels's *The Rugged Path* (1940), and Paul Vincent Carroll's *The Strings, My Lord, are False* (1941), which enjoyed enormous success. Wills's study of the regional press is particularly productive as she shows that

the censor's blue pencil was less in evidence in their columns than in the national papers like the *Irish Times*.

The grind of daily life — the lack of tea and petrol, the inedible black bread, the damp turf, the exhausting train journeys, compulsory tillage, smuggling and the black market, the ubiquitous 'glimmer man' — affected every class. But there were other changes in Irish society which Wills considers. There was the growth of women's organizations like the Irish Countrywomen's Association and the Irish Housewives' Association. The need for better cookery and nutrition promoted the career of Maura Laverty, whose *Home Economy* (1941) and *Never No More* (1942) were bestsellers. Although the number of people who had radios was particularly small along the western seaboard (one in thirty for Donegal, Galway and Kerry), the high emigration to Britain from the west of Ireland during the war ensured that some of the most isolated

5   Wills, *That Neutral Island*, 10–11.

6   Wills, *That Neutral Island*, 11.

7   Séamus Mac Aonghusa, '*Mise an Fear Cheoil*': *Séamus Ennis — Dialann Taistil 1942–46*, ed. Ríonach Uí Ógáin (Indreabhán, 2007), *passim*.

8   Mac Aonghusa, '*Mise an Fear Cheoil*', 145.

and remote areas of Ireland were now in closer contact with Britain than ever before.

But the western seaboard was also experiencing a grimmer contact with the war. In the most moving and haunting chapter of the book, Wills recounts what happened when the victims of the Battle of the Atlantic began to wash ashore. In October 1940 the sheer number of corpses overwhelmed the authorities in Donegal. Many bodies were spotted far out to sea by distressed observers on the land but could not be recovered; others had to be hauled from inaccessible rocks and coves and even then identification was often impossible because of advanced decomposition. Gardaí up and down the west coast received heart-rending requests from relatives overseas for information about sons or husbands whose bodies might have been washed ashore.

By 1943 for most people their Emergency existence was circumscribed by restrictive legislation, censorship, shortages, and rationing. For the worst-hit, it meant poverty, illness, unemployment, and emigration. Wills concludes that 'one version of Ireland's wartime story is that it is all about absence — the absence of conflict, of supplies, of social dynamism, of contact with "the outside world" '.[5] But she believes that this perspective has masked the material and psychic impoverishment that the war wrought in Ireland, and which continued long after it ended. The effects of poverty, massive emigration, the decline of rural areas, the suppression of debate through censorship, and of political dissent through a series of repressive measures including internment, 'persisted like a silent damage to the culture throughout the 1950s'.[6] Her book sets the benchmark for future studies of Emergency Ireland.

The wartime diaries of Seamus Ennis have resonances of many of the experiences described by Clair Wills. At the outbreak of war Ennis was working at the Three Candles printing firm in Dublin but lost his job because of the paper shortage. He was contemplating joining the British army when, in 1942, he was invited to work for the Folklore Commission, collecting traditional music and songs in Galway, Mayo and Donegal. As Ríonach uí Ógáin observes in her Introduction, Ennis made frequent references to the daily problems of rationing, endless train journeys, the lack of tea, fuel and petrol, but there was little about the war itself and what it meant to him and the people he met on his travels. On the surface it often reads like an idyllic existence: 'airneáil agus seanchas cois tine', cutting turf and cycling through some of the most beautiful landscapes in Ireland despite the frequent references to 'drochlá báistí agus stoirme chruaidh', punctures, leaking shoes and lodgings.[7] Nevertheless, there are some intriguing glimpses of the war and the wider world: on Tory Island, Ennis noticed that the song 'Óró na Buachaillí' now had an extra verse about the boys who had gone to Scotland; in Derry in January 1944 'chonaic me pictiúr, *Hitler's Children*, ab fhiú a fheiceáil. Pictiúir de phropaganda a bhí ann, ach léirigh sé an *Reich* sa nGearmáin ó thús' [I saw a film, *Hitler's Children*, worth seeing. It was a propaganda film, but it explained the *Reich* in Germany from the beginning.]; near Falcarragh he was shown the mountain where a plane crashed earlier in the war, killing everyone on board; in Gaoth Dobhair in March 1944 he met 82-year-old Síle Gallagher, who, with her husband and family, had spent many years in Scotland. Her children were now in the United States and Scotland: 'Chaith Síle cuid mhó dá saol in Albain ... Shiúil sí cuid mhór de na bailte móra agus tá tuiscint mhaith aici ar an saol amuigh.'[8] She gave him some precious tea before he left, tea from one of her children in America, which Ennis drank with relish.

The war figures more frequently in Ennis's diaries as it nears the end; he mentions the death of Hitler and the capture of Berlin and Hamburg. While staying in Carna, he wrote on 8 May, 'scéal ar an bpáipéar inniu go bhfuil an cogadh thart. Níl de shuim ag seandaoine ann ach "Caidé go bhfairsingí an tae?!!"'. [Report in the paper that the war was over. The old people were only interested in when tea supplies would be restored.][9] On 16 May he described one of the memorable codas of the war, de Valera's reply to Churchill:

> *Chuas siar tigh na gClochartach i gCarna san oíche ag éisteacht le hóráid an Taoisigh — ní go róthirim a tháinig mé abhaile, ach ó ba chearr siar é níorbh fhiú liom an óráid a ligean tharam gan é a chloisteáil. Ní ina aiféala a bhí mé mar ba bhreá liom a óráid.*[10]

[In the evening I went to the Cloherty house in Carna to listen to the Taoiseach's speech — I was none to dry when I got home; although it was a good way away, it wasn't worth missing the speech. I didn't regret it as I enjoyed the speech.]

Reading the diaries, there is something immensely ironic, and sad, about Ennis collecting the remnants of one dying culture while another was blowing itself to smithereens.

There is one area of wartime culture (in the widest sense of the word) that Wills does not discuss in any detail: the Dublin Institute of Advanced Studies, widely derided as de Valera's folly in 1939–40. It drew to Dublin a polyglot, cosmopolitan group of scientists, most notably the physicist Erwin Schrödinger, winner of the Nobel Prize in 1933, who became director of the School of Theoretical Physics. The wartime colloquia organized by Schrödinger and his colleague Walter Heitler attracted the most prestigious names in physics, including Paul Dirac, Max Born and Kathleen Lonsdale. In 1943, Schrödinger delivered his seminal lecture series, *What is Life?*, on quantum theory and its implications for genetics. The lectures at Trinity were attended by so many people (including de Valera) that they had to be repeated. His first years in Dublin are the subject of Neil Belton's 2005 novel, *A Game with Sharpened Knives*. It paints a monotonously monochrome picture of

Dublin, its 'watchfulness and foreboding', 'sadness', 'leaden air', 'grey skies', the 'forsaken air' of Clontarf, 'the village of lost causes'. De Valera and his government appear like a sinister chorus:

> As he thought about his last conversation with [de Valera], his oracular turns, his careful admissions of weakness, Schrödinger had a clear image, as in an enlarged photograph, of men behind the leader deep in shadows, vague shapes in the apparently empty air of a darkened room. Their indistinct pressure disturbed Schrödinger's image of the man. If the picture were developed differently these ghostly figures behind him might come into the foreground, changing the picture in an instant ...[11]

Later in the novel Belton attempts to link quantum theory with the 'endless despairing quibble' of wartime Dublin when Schrödinger explains the difficulty of living in Ireland:

> Reality seems to flicker. Reality *cannot* flicker, but here it does. If the quantum of energy were much larger than it is we'd see the world for what it is: a superimposed shimmer of wave paths, all there simultaneously, all the paths of light visible at once ... Of course we don't see any of that, because in our gross world quantum effects are so small. Not here, though, not in your country. We see the interference of waves about to break, a slow motion in which the possibilities are open and undecided. It's like being suspended in a fluid, sensitive to every flux. We know that there is a direction, that time will produce a clear answer as to where we were and what we were doing, but it never seems to happen. I cannot stand it any more, it is driving me out of my mind.[12]

The novel is infused with Lyons's 'Plato's cave' view of wartime Ireland and it stops

9   Mac Aonghusa, '*Mise an Fear Cheoil*', 233.
10 Mac Aonghusa, '*Mise an Fear Cheoil*', 236.
11 Neil Belton, *A Game with Sharpened Knives* (London, 2005), 192.
12 Belton, *A Game with Sharpened Knives*, 275.

13 Robert Cole,
*Propaganda, Censorship
and Irish Neutrality in
the Second World War*
(Edinburgh, 2006), ix–x.

14 Balfour, quoted in Cole,
*Propaganda, Censorship
and Irish Neutrality*, 1.

15 Cole, *Propaganda,
Censorship and Irish
Neutrality*, 2.

16 Bernstein, quoted in Cole,
*Propaganda, Censorship
and Irish Neutrality*, 115.

before the excitement of *What is Life?*
which challenged Lyons's picture of wartime
stagnation. Schrödinger spent sixteen happy
and productive years at the DIAS before
returning to Austria.

In the battle for the hearts and minds
of Irish opinion on neutrality, propaganda
and censorship were vital weapons. In
1996 censorship was analysed by Dónal
Ó Drisceoil in his *Censorship in Ireland,
1939–45: Neutrality, Politics and Society*.
Robert Cole's rationale for his new study,
*Propaganda, Censorship and Irish Neutrality
in the Second World War*, is that it fills
the gap 'where the vital propaganda-
censorship aspect of relations between
neutral Eire and belligerent nations in wartime is concerned'.[13] He quotes Michael
Balfour's definition of propaganda, 'the art
of inducing people to leap to conclusions
without examining the evidence',[14] and
thinks it an apt one for the war of words
over Irish neutrality.

Allied official propaganda took some
time to get started but the British press was
'trained on Eire virtually from day one'.[15]
Indeed so virulent was the press comment
that by mid-September 1939 the British
government was issuing D-Notices banning
certain articles and cartoons. The British
press posed a serious problem for the Irish
censors because of its dominant presence in
the Irish market. Despite this, Cole thinks
the Irish censors had considerable success
in suppressing what they considered to be
the most objectionable comments in British
newspapers. They also watched the post,
theatre, films, posters and advertising.
The job of the postal censor (who worked
closely with the British security authorities)
was especially onerous: in July 1942, for
example, the cross-border (between the
North and the South) post alone consisted
of 32,000 letters and postcards, 576 parcels
and 690 newspapers.

There was less censorship in
broadcasting. The Irish newspapers gave
BBC listings right throughout the war
and the government could have jammed

the BBC and other stations but did not.
There were plans to expand broadcasting
co-operation between BBC London, BBC
Northern Ireland and Radio Éireann but
these foundered on the opposition of BBC
Northern Ireland. Frank O'Connor was also
refused a permit to go to London to make
a BBC broadcast — perhaps because of his
left-wing past.

Cole shows that before Pearl Harbor there
was considerable anti-British propaganda
in the Irish-American press, although one
opinion poll in January 1941 showed that
40 per cent of Irish Americans opposed Irish
neutrality. Even after Pearl Harbor, there
remained a strong core of anti-British feeling
in the US, fuelled by the reverses in the Far
East in early 1942, which were blamed on
British weakness. However, a Gallup poll
on 22 February 1942 showed that 70 per
cent of Irish Americans wanted the Irish to
agree to the use of their ports by the Allies.
The *Gaelic American* dismissed anyone who
accepted the poll as a 'Gallup stoodge'. There
was a delay in distributing US Office of War
Information material in Dublin. The official
news bulletin, *Letter from America,* was
circulated to clergy, teachers, government
officials, lawyers and anyone else who asked
for it. Hollywood films were being pushed
by the OWI but Sidney Bernstein, the British
Ministry of Information Films liaison with
Hollywood, complained that many of these
films did not provide a realistic view of
America: 'Phony war romances and dramas
haven't their place in this war, for it is not
a phony war.'[16] Bernstein wanted more
films like *Mrs Miniver,* which was hardly a
contender in the realism stakes.

Cole clearly enjoys discussing John
Betjeman (or Sean O'Betjeman as he
occasionally signed his name) who entered
the scene in June 1940 when the Empire
Division of the Ministry of Information
dispatched him to Dublin to report on Irish
opinion and how British propaganda might
be improved. His suggestions included a
Catholic Truth Society pamphlet on the
persecution of Polish Catholics and getting

the racing fraternity on Britain's side, neither of which saw the light of day. Betjeman was to return as press attaché in early 1941 when he established good connections with the *Irish Independent* and provided stories about concentration camps, prisons, spies, torture, informers and conscripted labour. Betjeman realized that the Irish were suspicious of direct British propaganda, and that it was better to work for improved Anglo-Irish relations, treat Irish nationalism with respect, ease the Irish sense of being cut off from the world, circulate informational rather than promotional materials, visit Irish officials, stop anti-Irish cartoons, and work closely with the Americans.

However, one wonders how reliable Betjeman's judgement was. Here Cole's unfamiliarity with the *dramatis personae*, especially on the Irish side, leads him to cite Betjeman rather too uncritically. There are several references by Betjeman to the alleged pro-German sympathies of the diplomat T. J. Kiernan and his wife, the singer Delia Murphy. Yet near the end of the book Cole refers to Delia Murphy's decoration for helping escaping British POWs when her husband was Irish minister to the Vatican. Cole also needs to be more discriminating about the views of the American minister in Dublin, David Gray, who thought that Frederick Boland, the assistant secretary of the Department of External Affairs, was 'pro-Axis and turned over to the German and Italian legations anything that might interest them'.[17] The charges were baseless and nothing in Boland's career, then or later, indicated the slightest sympathy with the Axis. Gray, a man of considerable charm and ebullience (as his papers testify), became increasingly deranged about neutrality in general and de Valera in particular.

Cole's chapters are arranged chronologically and by 1942 the themes become repetitive. There was revived British optimism after Pearl Harbor that Irish neutrality could not survive US entry into the war, but that soon subsided. The object of Allied propaganda was to persuade

Irish opinion of the errors of neutrality but this was clearly a dead duck by 1943. It was rather more successful in persuading British and American opinion that Irish neutrality favoured the Germans rather than the Allies. There was little for Betjeman to do and he left in Dublin in October 1943; the Irish government gave him a farewell dinner. He was succeeded by the dyspeptic Ross Williamson, who moaned about 'this horrible little country' and the 'absolute second-ratedness of everybody', but concluded in 1944 that most Irish people still supported neutrality, were glad not to be in the war and held de Valera in high regard. He hated Gray and hoped that he 'will be shot before long'.[18] Alas for Williamson, Gray stayed in Ireland until 1947, returning to the US where he lived until his death in 1968 at the ripe old age of ninety-eight, producing a voluminous but unpublishable memoir, 'Behind the Emerald Curtain', still fulminating about de Valera.

Irish-German wartime and post-war relations have received scholarly attention over the last decade in David O'Donoghue's *Hitler's Irish Voices* (1998); Cathy Molohan's *Germany and Ireland 1945–55* (1999); Andreas Roth's *Mr Bewley in Berlin* (2000); J. P. Duggan's *Herr Hempel at the German Legation, 1937–45* (2003) and Mervyn O'Driscoll's *Ireland, Germany and the Nazis, 1919–39* (2004). Gerry Mullins's *Dublin Nazi No. 1: The Life of Adolf Mahr* looks at the man who became director of the National Museum in 1934, the same year that he founded the Irish branch of the Nazi party, which he had joined the previous year. Mahr's story and that of his family is a fascinating one.

He was born in Trent, then under Austrian rule, now in northern Italy (Trento), to Sudeten German parents. He was a distinguished archaeologist and was president of the British Prehistory Society in the late 1930s. In the summer of 1939 he and his family returned to Austria for a holiday and were stranded there when war broke out. Although he tried to return to Ireland, his Nazi activities had already attracted the

17 Cole, *Propaganda, Censorship and Irish Neutrality*, 111.

18 Cole, *Propaganda, Censorship and Irish Neutrality*, 173.

19 Cathal O'Shannon, Foreword, in Gerry Mullins, *Dublin Nazi No. 1: The Life of Adolf Mahr* (Dublin, 2007), 11.

20 O'Shannon, Foreword, 11.

Swastika Laundry, Ballsbridge, Dublin. Photo: Getty Images.

attention of the Irish security authorities and his return was vetoed. The latter part of Mullins's book describes what happened to Mahr's remarkable children during and after the war, an altogether more inspiring story than that of their sour and embittered father.

If Mullins had confined himself to this story, it would have been a better book. Unfortunately, his lack of experience as a historian is compounded by his sketchy knowledge of both the Irish and German contexts. The same can be said for Cathal O'Shannon's Foreword. 'This is a book I have been waiting half my lifetime for,' he announces dramatically. Why? Well, he wanted to read more about Nazis in Ireland like Mahr and Fritz Brase (first director of the Army School of Music) 'and the rag tag and bobtail of some of those who were brought here by the Irish government to build the mighty Shannon Scheme'.[19] Surely the latter were brought by Siemens and not by the Irish government? As for being 'rag tag and bobtail', most were skilled engineers and technicians who returned home when the Scheme was completed. O'Shannon

writes that he 'lived in an Ireland that was not just anti-British and anti-Allied but also significantly sympathetic to Germany. Irish governments, pre- and post-de Valera, sought out Germans to come to Ireland and the new Free State, rather than the former colonial ruling classes'.[20] These are rather sweeping generalizations for which no evidence is adduced; unfortunately this is a failing that pervades the rest of the book.

There are maddening omissions. When was Mahr born? What did he study at university, surely an important fact in any consideration of his career as an archaeologist? Where does he fit in the wider context of Austro-German-Irish cultural relations going back to the closing decades of the previous century? Annoying as these omissions are, they are dwarfed by a rather more disturbing agenda that gradually unfolds in the book: the highly tendentious attempt to link Mahr and de Valera as fellow Nazi sympathizers. In 1935, according to Mullins, the Irish Nazis seceded from the British body 'so as not to offend the new de Valera government, which was unhappy about any Irish organisation being subservient to a British one'. The only evidence cited for this claim is a lecture given by Rudolf Muhs in London in 2005. Later, Mullins writes that

> Mahr and de Valera could be forgiven for not seeing the grave dangers posed by Hitler's rise to power ... Of course the Machiavellian de Valera, who lived the maxim 'keep one's friends close, and one's enemies closer', may have felt it prudent to maintain good relations with Hitler's top man in Ireland ... Dev and Mahr worked in adjacent buildings, attended some of the same functions, and shared an interest in politics and archaeology.[21]

De Valera also kept a good working relationship with the German minister, Hempel, and 'probably adopted that other maxim "my enemy's enemy is my friend". De Valera may have reasoned that a showdown between Britain and Germany might help to bring about a united Ireland — as long as Germany won'.[22]

On the Austrian Anschluss in 1938, Mullins suggests that 'the annexation of a small nation by a larger, more powerful one should have sounded alarm bells for de Valera and his government ... It is possible that Dev felt political sympathy with Mahr'.[23] Later Mullins writes of a wartime report on Ireland compiled by Mahr that it had 'a heavy republican tone ... his plans for Ireland read like a de Valera or an IRA manifesto ... Conspiracy theorists might wonder whether Dev was his co-scriptwriter'.[24] Since de Valera was in distant Dublin in 1941, there are certain logistical problems, conspiracy theories apart, about him being Mahr's co-scriptwriter (the co-scriptwriters were actually Francis Stuart and Frank Ryan). But Mullins's glib linking of de Valera to the IRA shows a basic ignorance of the political and ideological differences that had developed between the two by 1941.

When Mahr was finally arrested by the British in January 1946, Mullins indulges in even more fantastical conspiracy theories and wonders if the arrest was 'a favour, to prevent any further embarrassment to [de Valera's] administration'.[25] Mullins expresses particular animus against Colonel Dan Bryan, the canny and efficient head of G2 (Irish Military Intelligence), who consistently advised de Valera not to let Mahr back to Ireland. Mullins argues that Bryan was pursuing a vendetta against Mahr and had no real evidence against him. But Mahr's wartime career as head of the Irland-Redaktion radio station was well known after the war and constituted damning evidence of his work for the Nazi regime. In November 1947 he sent a letter to his 'personal friend' de Valera defending himself against these charges. There was no reply.

There is a prevalence of speculative terms in all of these accounts — could be, may have, probably, possible, might. They reveal the paucity of Mullins's research. He does not cite O'Driscoll's key work on the period. If he had bothered to consult the de Valera Papers or the Dan Bryan Papers in University College Dublin Archives or the records of the Department of External Affairs in the National Archives, he might have found answers to some of these speculations and discovered just what, if any, was the extent of the friendship between Mahr and de Valera that he seems so anxious to establish, but unable to prove beyond the geographical propinquity of their offices in Merrion Street.

Brian Girvin is the author of *Between Two Worlds: Politics and Economy in Independent Ireland* (1989) and he is editor (with Geoffrey Roberts) of *Ireland and the Second World War: Politics. Society and Remembrance* (2000). He and Roberts were involved in the ground-breaking Volunteers Project, set up in University College Cork in 1995 with the aim of examining the experience of Irish citizens who contributed to the Allied war effort, either by military service or war work in Britain. Most of the essays in *Ireland and the Second World War* came out of the Volunteers Project. The title of his new book, *The Emergency: Neutral Ireland 1939–45*,

21 Mullins, *Dublin Nazi No. 1*, 66–67.

22 Mullins, *Dublin Nazi No. 1*, 66–67.

23 Mullins, *Dublin Nazi No. 1*, 74.

24 Mullins, *Dublin Nazi No. 1*, 114–15.

25 Mullins, *Dublin Nazi No. 1*, 176.

26 Brian Girvin, *The Emergency: Neutral Ireland 1939–45* (Basingstoke, 2006), 30–31.

27 Girvin, *The Emergency*, 30–31.

28 Girvin, *The Emergency*, 335.

29 Girvin, *The Emergency*, 49.

30 In 1927, several members of O'Sullivan family of Adrigole, west Cork, died from starvation, allegedly neglected by officials on account of their republican politics. The incident became the subject of a novel by Peadar O'Donnell, *Adrigoole* (1929).

31 Girvin, *The Emergency*, 73.

32 Memoirs of Admiral John Godfrey, Churchill College Archives Centre, Cambridge.

promises a more comprehensive study than is actually delivered; what we get is a rather arid diplomatic history, which goes over a lot of ground covered by other historians in recent years.

One of the most problematical aspects of the book is Girvin's treatment of de Valera, of whom he writes that 'the passions he aroused seem strange at this historical distance, yet they were a key feature of Irish politics for most of the twentieth century ... His strength was his fortitude in the face of adversity'.[26] Girvin also notes that where admirers saw de Valera's steely determination and leadership qualities, others saw 'a narrow and dogmatic mind framed by the most insular aspects of Irish nationalism'.[27] Girvin is critical of the recent tendency to debunk de Valera and appreciates that 'there are now signs of a more sensitive reappraisal of the man and his era'.[28] He comments rightly on the danger of seeing de Valera as a 'unique dictator' and attributing to him everything that went right or wrong between 1916 and 1959. However, this is largely the image conveyed in the book, not helped by the fact that two of Girvin's chapter titles refer to that hoary old cliché, 'De Valera's Ireland'. In large and small ways, Girvin writes, 'the Ireland that Fianna Fáil created in the course of the 1930s was less liberal, less tolerant and less secular than that inherited from Cumann na nGaedheal, though it was politically more democratic and inclusive'.[29] He does not explain how the 1930s were supposedly less liberal and tolerant than the 1920s (the decade of film and book censorship, the abolition of divorce, the cut in old age pensions, Adrigole,[30] etc. etc.).

Like Cole, Girvin underlines the importance of the Dublin-based diplomats, especially the British Representative, Sir John Maffey and the American Minister David Gray. Maffey, an old India and Sudan hand, was an invaluable source of sane advice and information, which often helped to take the wind out of Churchill's belligerent sails. He could be critical of de Valera, as

Girvin notes, but when crises did occur 'he had established his position as the key interlocutor between Ireland and Britain and was largely trusted by both sides'.[31]

The same could not be said for his American counterpart. Like Cole, Girvin tends to take Gray at face value and to ignore the increasing signs of unreliability, paranoia and obsession in his reports from Dublin; he does not mention, for example, the séances Gray held at his residence in the Phoenix Park, at one of which Roosevelt's dead mother put in an appearance. Girvin also makes use of the reports (which were read by Irish Intelligence) of the Czechoslovak consul in Dublin, D. K. Kostal, who reported in May 1940 that support for Hitler was evident in the general Irish population and that there was widespread approval of Lord Haw Haw's broadcasts. Interestingly, Cole states that when Betjeman arrived the following month he found that Irish people thought Haw Haw a wonderful joke and listened to him because the BBC was so dull.

The big question hovering over British and American policy was whether the ports were really so vital. Girvin never addresses this fundamental point although he writes that Maffey had doubts in July 1940. Admiral John Godfrey, director of British Naval Intelligence, wrote in his memoirs that 'by the end of 1941 the matter was dead as far as we were concerned, somewhat to the disappointment of the Irish, who talked about their ports incessantly, and disliked the idea that their acquisition did not any longer seem to be a matter of importance to us'.[32] This opinion was shared by the American chiefs of staff when they made a strategic assessment of the ports in August 1943. They concluded that bases in southern Ireland were of little use as long as the French Atlantic coast was in German hands, as ships travelling by the south of Ireland would be an easy target for German submarines based in the Bay of Biscay. If de Valera did agree to give access to the ports, then Allied forces would have to be diverted to protect the defenceless Irish hinterland. Instead of requesting the use of the ports, the chiefs of staff recommended that they should be made available *only if* the US ever needed them.[33]

Concerning the offer of unity in June 1940 in return for ending neutrality, Girvin observes somewhat mystifyingly that 'it may not have been a feasible solution but it did represent an opportunity for substantial change'.[34] It is worth noting that a similar offer was made to the Indian Congress Party in 1942, a promise of independence in exchange for co-operation in the war effort. One of de Valera's reasons for refusing the offer of unity was his conviction that once the wartime emergency was over the offer would be reneged upon. It was a view shared by Gandhi, who famously described the offer to congress as a post-dated cheque on a failing bank. Their scepticism about Churchill's sincerity was borne out by his later contemptuous comment on the 1942 offer that 'we made it when in a hole and can disavow it because it was not accepted at the time'.[35]

But would Irish public opinion have agreed to exchange neutrality for unity? Girvin claims that the de Valera government manipulated public opinion for its own ends. Well of course it did, so did every government. What Girvin particularly deprecates — 'an extraordinary aspect of de Valera and Fianna Fáil's behaviour' — was the 'sense of insecurity which they promoted ... anxiety was a permanent feature of Irish public life from May 1940 to August 1945'. Girvin sees this as an attempt both to orchestrate support for government and to undermine challenges from opposing groups. He also strongly disputes the argument that Irish neutrality was in the national interest, as this could not equate to party or government interests. Irish neutrality, he claims, 'had little to do with national interest and everything to do with ideology'.[36]

The argument as to whether Ireland should have abandoned neutrality and supported the Allies surfaces from time to time in the correspondence columns of the *Irish Times*. Girvin and Roberts firmly believe that de Valera should have abandoned

neutrality. They dispute the threat of internal conflict that might have ensued if Ireland had entered the war. But as Eunan O'Halpin has argued, to a large section of Irish public opinion in 1939 Britain was not a bastion of democracy in need of reinforcement against tyranny but the country that had unleashed the Black and Tans against them and continued to aid and abet the repression of nationalists in Northern Ireland. The Irish élite's experience of repression was at British hands, not German or Italian.[37] The War of Independence was succeeded by the Civil War, a war of great cruelty and bitterness, which had ended only sixteen years before in 1923. That war had led to a further decade of political unrest which only subsided in the mid-1930s. For the vast majority of the Irish people, any prospect of a return to those horrors was unthinkable.

Girvin also tends to see the debate in almost exclusively Anglo-American-Irish terms. At the beginning of the war every small European state wanted to stay neutral, especially the small, newly independent states that had emerged after the First World War. This was equally true of states in Asia and Latin America. One might also point to the way Ireland was treated as compared to neutral Sweden, Switzerland, Turkey and the Iberian dictatorships, towards which Churchill was considerably more circumspect. But then Ireland was the only European neutral that he did not have to be nice to; attacking the Irish now and then was probably therapeutic. Girvin argues that the Irish could have done a lot more to support the Allies short of going to war, but given the extensive material that has been released in Irish, British and American archives over the last decade and more, this argument cannot be sustained. De Valera was determined that though the country was neutral, he would never allow it to be used as a base of attack against Britain, a policy he had enunciated as far back as 1920, and he kept to that. The Irish government put no restriction on its nationals joining the Allied forces or working in British war industries and it gave

33 Quoted in T. Ryle Dwyer, *Irish Neutrality and the USA* (Dublin, 1977), 174.

34 Girvin, *The Emergency*, 135.

35 John Barnes and David Nicholson, eds., *The Empire at Bay: The Leo Amery Diaries 1929–45* (London, 1988), 1040.

36 Girvin, *The Emergency*, 324.

37 Eunan O'Halpin, *Defending Ireland: The Irish State and Its Enemies* (Oxford, 1999), 151; *Judging Dev*, RTÉ Radio 1, 18 November 2007.

38 Girvin, *The Emergency*, 329.
39 *Irish Times*, 14 May 1945.
40 Martin Gilbert, *Winston S. Churchill 1945–1965: 'Never Despair'* (London, 1988), 364–72. Churchill included these comments about Ireland in a 1952 edition of his biography of his father, *Lord Randolph Churchill*.

unstinting co-operation in areas like postal censorship, coast-watching, subversion and espionage. A majority of the British Cabinet in 1939 and thereafter, despite Churchill's jeremiads, considered it preferable to have the Irish as a co-operative neutral rather than run the risk of another wartime insurgency.

In a rather apocalyptic conclusion, 'The End of de Valera's Ireland', Girvin portrays neutrality as the fount of all the country's post-war ills. He argues that the main legacies of the Emergency were isolationism and lost opportunity which almost led to the destruction of Irish society, which, paradoxically, he also sees as 'safe, stable and conservative'. Somewhat puzzlingly, he locates the roots of isolationism in the 1930s, a decade when Ireland played a leading role at the League of Nations. In consequence of this isolationism, 'policymakers in Ireland could not or would not see the challenge the new Europe provided or the opportunities which it offered'.[38] This statement ignores how hamstrung Irish policymakers were in any consideration of the Common Market by their almost complete dependence on British markets and sterling.

In the history of neutrality, de Valera is of course the dominant personality on the Irish side, but in the books under review one wishes that Churchill received rather more attention. In certain respects he and de Valera were mirror images of one another: they came to symbolize their countries at a critical time; they were aware of their place in history; they each came to Anglo-Irish relations burdened with a weight of historical baggage. Churchill had a pernicious influence on Irish policy in 1940-41 (as he did on India throughout the war) and his hectoring only reinforced Irish suspicions of British aims. These were confirmed in his famous broadcast at the end of the war when he praised British self-restraint: 'His Majesty's Government never laid a violent hand on them, though at times it would have been quite easy and natural, and we left the de Valera Government to frolic with

the Germans and later with the Japanese representatives to their heart's content.'[39]

However, although Churchill continued to criticize neutrality in his war memoirs, privately his views do not seem to have been as hostile. In the final volume of his official biography published in 1988, Martin Gilbert printed the remarkable but rather bizarre document that Churchill wrote, and which was known within the Churchill family as 'The Dream'. One evening at Chartwell in November 1947, when Churchill was attempting to copy a painting of Lord Randolph Churchill, the ghost of his father suddenly appeared and they had a conversation about events since his death in 1895. What happened to Ireland, asked Lord Randolph, the player of the Orange card in 1886, did they get Home Rule?

'The South got it, but Ulster stayed with us'.

'Are the South a republic?'

'No one knows what they are. They are neither in nor out of the Empire. But they are much more friendly to us than they used to be. They have built up a cultured Roman Catholic system in the South. There has been no anarchy or confusion. They are getting more happy and prosperous. The bitter past is fading.'

'Ah', he said, 'how vexed the Tories were with me when I observed that there was no English statesman who had not had his hour of Home Rule'. Then after a pause, 'What about the Home Rule meaning "Rome Rule"?'

'It certainly does, but they like it. And the Catholic Church has now become a great champion of individual liberty.'

'You must be living in a very happy age. A Golden Age, it seems'.[40]

Nearly all of these books have benefited from the opening of Irish official and private archives since the 1980s and they reveal how much we still have to understand about a period which shaped every sphere of modern Irish society.

Charles Henry Cook (c. 1830–1906), St Patrick's Day, oil on canvas, 1867, 86.4 × 111.7 cm, National Library of Ireland.

Ireland's Difficulty, the Novelist's Opportunity?

Sean Ryder

Catholic Emancipations:
Irish Fiction from Thomas Moore
to James Joyce
Emer Nolan
Syracuse: Syracuse University Press, 2007
xxiv + 240 pages. ISBN 0-815-63175-8

Thomas Moore saw bright prospects for the Irish novel in the nineteenth century: 'Ireland bids fair to be the great mart of fiction,' he wrote in the *Edinburgh Review* in 1826. Unfortunately for Moore, what was good for novelists was not necessarily good for poets; as he saw it, the growth of fiction was accompanied by the desertion of 'the fair springs of Poesy' across Europe, and the impossibility of creating poetry at all in Ireland in its present condition. 'The same causes,' he complains, 'that have embittered and degraded the history of Ireland, so as to render it incapable of furnishing any safe or worthy theme for the poet, have brought the character of its

Thomas Moore, artist unknown, sometimes attributed to Martin Archer Shee, oil on canvas, *c.* 1800–05, 73.7 × 62.2 cm, National Portrait Gallery, London.

people, both moral and social, to a state which is eminently favourable to the more humble aspirations of the novelist.'[1]

This formulation of Ireland's difficulty as the novelist's opportunity is an interesting reversal of the famous renunciation of fiction by Maria Edgeworth, who complained that party and sectarian division made it impossible to produce fiction in Ireland in the 1820s. Moore too acknowledged the 'great concert of discord' produced by Ireland's colonial condition, but, unlike

1   Thomas Moore, 'Irish Novels', *Edinburgh Review*, 43 (1826), 356–72.

2 Moore, 'Irish Novels', 358–59.
3 Terry Eagleton, *Heathcliff and the Great Hunger* (London, 1995), 203.

Edgeworth, believed that the results — the 'inverted and unnatural' institutions, the gentry's 'vulgar arrogance', the people's historically induced 'low, circumventing cunning' — were all valuable grist to the mill of fiction (as opposed to poetry), and that in combination with the 'lively temperament of the whole nation' there is 'plenty of small game for the satirist and observer of character'. If the novelist's role is to be a 'sketcher of human nature', then no country could provide 'more original subjects for his pencil, more mixtures of lights and shadows, or more of that sort of picturesqueness, towards which (in morals as well as painting), utility and order are the last ingredients requisite'. And politics, far from being a distraction to a fictional narrative, Moore assumes to be essential to the understanding of those manners and morals. For him, the recent fiction of John and Michael Banim and other Irish authors did not transcend politics but made a necessary vehicle for them: 'It is pleasant after ages of bad romance in politics, to find thus, at last, good politics in romance.'[2]

Set alongside the mostly negative assessments of the early nineteenth-century Irish novel by previous generations of critics, one might think Moore's comments to be strangely utopian, misguided, or facile. At worst, the usual story goes, the nineteenth-century Irish novel is just a clumsy and practically unreadable attempt to imitate the great realist novel that flourished in England and continental Europe. At best, it is a heroic failure that simply found it impossible to represent the turbulent and recalcitrant conditions produced by a colonial history within the formal conventions of the classic realist text, what Terry Eagleton calls the 'contention ... between English convention and Irish experience'.[3] This 'failure' may even have its own virtue — in so far as it confirms the value of an insurgency that disrupts English literary forms as well as colonial political and economic structures. It is commonplace to argue that these novels' plots are incoherent or circular, constantly interrupted by digression or prolixity. The characterizations are shallow and typological rather than individualized and organic. The writing is uneven in register and voice, the moral structure marred by political concerns. The writing may even be 'duplicitous', in the sense of calling for the rejection of native barbaric violence and superstition while in fact generating reader sympathy for those very energies of the unreformed past — like Milton, being of the devil's party without knowing it.

Interestingly, Moore's own benchmark for fiction did not correspond to that of the realist novel. Instead of the features of bourgeois realism — for instance, the narrative of individual progress, social improvability, harmony between the individual and society, reader identification with character, and a reduction of politics to a career option or plot device — Moore imagines the novel to be a mixture of social satire, incidental variety, character 'observation' (rather than identification), all crafted into a form that has a utilitarian dimension. He assumes that political conflict and historical intrusion are part of the very fabric of the life to be represented, and therefore inescapably part of the fiction. In such writing there may be little distinction between foreground and background, characters may take on allegorical meaning, and human behaviour may be deeply shaped by collective activity and communal structures.

Moore's comments point to the fact that the realist novel was not the only model available to or valued by Irish novelists in the nineteenth century, and that using it as a benchmark may be severely to distort the purpose and achievement of much nineteenth-century fiction. Recent critical commentary has reflected similar thinking by paying much more attention to the extensive presence of non-realist genres of sensation fiction, gothic, melodrama, historical romance, didactic 'improvement' fiction and the picaresque in Irish writing — seeing in these forms alternative Irish traditions that may in fact have been more successful and robust, even

Outward Bound (Dublin), Erskine Nicol (1824–1904), lithograph, 34.2 × 27.6 cm, National Library of Ireland. This popular image can be seen above the piper in Cook's *St. Patrick's Day*.

if they cannot be assimilated to a Leavisite canon based on classic realist principles.[4]

Emer Nolan's stimulating new book returns us to the issue of Irish realism — but not to simply rehearse the existing arguments about its limitations in an Irish context.

Instead, Nolan performs the more difficult task of finding ways in which the attempts at realism by certain Irish Catholic authors may in fact have had some emancipatory aspects. She pays due respect to the fact that these authors themselves took the realist

4   See Jacqueline Belanger, ed., *The Irish Novel in the Nineteenth Century* (Dublin, 2005) for a good sample of recent trends; see also J. H. Murphy, *Catholic Fiction and Social Reality in Ireland, 1873–1922* (London, 1997).

novel as a benchmark, and were conscious of the problems and difficulties they faced. She reads her selected authors — especially Moore, Gerald Griffin, the Banim brothers, Charles Kickham, Canon Sheehan and Gerald O'Donovan — as engaged in more or less deliberate attempts to develop a prose form with a dual purpose; on the one hand, capable of imagining a modernizing Irish society in the process of political, religious and economic 'emancipation', while on the other hand, retaining sight of the valuable elements of pre-modern social and cultural formations that persist in Irish rural culture. Their project is a kind of literary equivalent of O'Connellism, in which the native bourgeoisie seek to establish modern forms of civil society (and thus be emancipated from the past), yet paradoxically remain culturally distinct from a 'modern' imperial culture (in order to be emancipated from political and cultural oppression). Thus the very cultural phenomena (the rituals, traditions, social structures, religion) that must be valorized as signs of post-colonial national distinction are also those that potentially undermine the building of a modern nation.

There is obviously a powerful tension between these demands, with consequences for literary form that are normally read as aesthetic failure by critics. But by adopting a wider frame as Nolan does, the picture becomes a much more interesting reflection on the intersections of representational form, political strategy, nation-building and modernization.

Thomas Moore is Nolan's starting point. But she is less interested in Moore's theories of fiction, or indeed his one real novel (a strange philosophical-theological-antiquarian-Orientalist romance set in early Christian Egypt, entitled *The Epicurean*), than she is in his hybrid work *Memoirs of Captain Rock* (1824). Much of *Captain Rock* was certainly not intended to be understood as 'fiction'. The bulk of the text is the Captain's account of several hundred years of Irish history — less a novel than an urgent attempt to set straight the historical record of Anglo-Irish relations. But in the framing devices Moore uses to chronicle this historiography, Nolan detects certain representational strategies that bear strongly on the development of Irish fiction right through the century. By 'narrating a history of collective consciousness',[5] Moore gives voice and agency to the rural, Catholic, communal, 'Whiteboy' identity without demonizing, sentimentalizing, individualizing or pathologizing it. The result is more dialogic than is usual in nineteenth-century Irish fiction, since Rock's Irish voice addresses his English interlocutor unapologetically, with confidence, and with an entirely coherent 'subaltern' narrative of Irish history.

One effect of this technique, and one where Nolan sees particular originality in Moore, is to validate the communal, the carnivalesque, the customary, and even the rebellious without relegating them to modernity's category of the primitive, as is common in other nineteenth-century writers, even those sympathetic to the national or Catholic cause. Each of the authors Nolan surveys, however, are shown to have difficulty achieving this — each novel is a struggle to negotiate between the desire for emancipatory modernization and the anxiety about its consequences for Irish culture.

The Banim brothers and Griffin are caught in a bind whereby their determination to assert the essential civility of the Irish (in order that they might be seen to qualify for the responsibilities of modernity) is disturbed by the vitality and attraction of the less civil, even criminal characters that populate the Ireland they represent. Griffin's exemplary modern Catholic hero in *The Collegians* is so shallow when set beside the more vital if chaotic and dark 'villain' of the novel that he seems to be merely 'lip-synching the music of modernity',[6] as if Griffin himself cannot write a script for him to believe in. Like Kickham (whom, Nolan reminds us, was probably the bestselling Irish author until the 1950s at least), they cannot bring themselves to abandon the energy of the

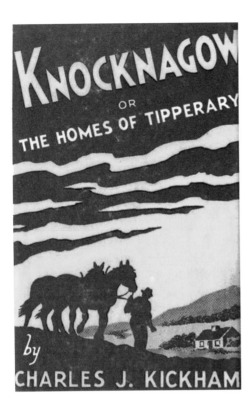

6 Nolan, *Catholic Emancipations*, 177.

7 Nolan, *Catholic Emancipations*, 177.

8 Nolan, *Catholic Emancipations*, 179.

9 Nolan, *Catholic Emancipations*, xx.

the Church's participation in a crude modernization that had no respect for collectivity and tradition. Emily Lawless in *Grania* is shown to have adopted elements of the heroic individual of classic realism in order to represent a woman's story with something like the power of a Jane Eyre, but is brought up short by the genre's inability to fully represent the context of rural Irish life, including the Irish language. At the same time, George Moore and the early Joyce (like many after them) finally abandon realism for a naturalist style that bleakly subverts realism's optimistic assumptions, casting doubt over any emancipatory possibilities at all in Ireland. Yet, for Nolan, it is eventually Joyce who has real success in bringing into harmony both modernity and pre- or non-modern forms of Irish cultural practice — by opting for the much riskier and ambitious formal experimentation that earlier writers would not or could not perform. In the creative flux of *Finnegans Wake* especially, the artificial but powerful distinction between what the nineteenth century sometimes defined as Protestant culture and Catholic anarchy is finally dissolved: 'the masses achieve consciousness'.[8]

Partly Nolan's book is an attempt to counter old assumptions about the nineteenth-century Irish novel's 'failure'; partly it is an attempt to model a new way of evaluating the purpose and effect of such fiction; and partly its aim is 'to supply a missing chapter in the prehistory of Joyce's distinctive modernism'.[9] Its multiple ambitions are its strength but also an occasional source of frustration: while the close readings of the individual texts are remarkably clear-sighted and fresh, the larger implications of the analysis of this very diverse but highly select range of texts sometimes beg for further development. The theoretical arguments that knit together the disparate writers and historical periods (from the Act of Union to the Celtic Tiger) have sometimes to be left as indicative statements rather than fully demonstrated theses. For example, Nolan notes pithily

unassimilated folk, while simultaneously believing that modernization in the form of discipline and progress held the key to national development. The dilemma is captured by Nolan's quip that 'Kickham hoped that Irish peasants could be hard-working and provident, and still dance at the crossroads'.[7] This situation, however, is not simply a paralysing contradiction. Kickham's *Knocknagow* provided a powerful vision of modern pastoral for a post-Famine survivor class of aspirants to Irish nationhood and proprietorship, in terms that supported a usable, if problematic, Irish version of modernity.

The Catholic novelists of the later part of the century had somewhat different conditions to deal with, following Catholicism's resurgence and assertion of institutional power, and the emergence of peasant proprietorship. Some, like Sheehan and O'Donovan, created their own versions of the tension between modernization and older cultural forms, expressing through realistic modes their anxieties about

10 Nolan, *Catholic Emancipations*, 178.

11 There are some interesting preliminary comments on literary Catholicism in Joe Cleary, 'The Nineteenth-Century Irish Novel: Notes and Speculations on Literary History', in Belanger, ed., *Irish Novel in the Nineteenth Century*, 213–19.

12 David Lloyd, 'Afterword: Hardress Cregan's Dream — For Another History of the Irish Novel', in Belanger, ed., *Irish Novel in the Nineteenth Century*, 229–37 (236–37).

that the perception of the Catholic Irish as a violent and indisciplined race before the Famine quickly transmuted into its opposite — a perception that they were the most repressed and sexless people in Western Europe in the wake of Catholic consolidation in the late nineteenth-century. And now, having been for a while the avatars of de Valera's anti-materialist vision, the Irish are perceived to be model consumers, 'taking with gusto to the accelerated consumption of the post-boom economy'. 'These,' she notes, 'are recognizable stages of the process of becoming fully incorporated into the system of global capitalism.'[10] This argument about the longer trajectory of modernity in Ireland flashes through the book, but is not always firmly attached to the literary historical detail being discussed — it does, however, give the book a rich suggestiveness that should make it valuable even to those working outside the field of the nineteenth century.

In a similar way, the term 'Irish Catholic fiction' itself raises significant issues that Nolan does not have space to explore in full. While she admits to using the term 'Catholic' in primarily a sociological and political sense rather than a denominational one, it is difficult not to wonder whether there are circumstances when 'Catholic' in 'Catholic fiction' might signify more than nationalist political sympathies and family background. What happens if we apply the term as a doctrinal or theological perceptive, or as a name for the intended or actual audience? Were there multiple ways of being Catholic in terms of class and gender that might have a bearing on the production and reception of fiction? The scene is complicated: William Carleton grew up within a Catholic sensibility and culture, and made Irish Catholicism a theme of his fiction, but for a Protestant audience and an anti-Catholic purpose. Catholic authors like James Clarence Mangan published prose in Protestant journals like the *Dublin University Magazine* and sometimes registered the influence of continental Catholic writing. In some ways, Moore's

Epicurean is far more of a 'Catholic' novel than his *Memoirs of Captain Rock*, and Joyce's *Portrait* (rather than *Ulysses* or *Finnegans Wake*) is the Irish novel that makes it on to international lists of 'Catholic fiction' in the company of Graham Greene, François Mauriac and Evelyn Waugh. Why did Ireland's Catholic authors not only produce something quite different to the classic realist novel, but also something quite different to the European Catholic novel? And what effect, if any, did the widely circulated pietistic literature that kept nineteenth-century nationalist publishers like James Duffy in business have on Catholic culture, writing and politics?[11]

The reason for dwelling on this particular issue is not so much to signal the limits of Nolan's approach as it is to show how her study opens up and provides occasion for further questions. In a recent essay describing the possibilities for a productive critique of the nineteenth-century novel, David Lloyd suggests that 'both the Irish novel of the period and the criticism of it seem constantly haunted by the acknowledgement of failure or of inadequacy to models it seeks to emulate' — this despite the recent critical reorientations that take a more positive view of the Irish novel's fragmented, disrupted forms. He argues that there is little point in trying to redeem these works aesthetically; instead, our reading of them should helpfully propel us towards a critical antagonism with the dominant literary forms that these novels 'fail to live up to' or partly reject, and that continue to legitimate forms of domination even now.[12] Nolan's insightful work makes a unique engagement with the Irish realist novel that illuminates the strategic possibilities as well as limitations of that literary form, and helps us see the ways in which struggles with representation have ramifications in the wider cultural and political spheres. In all these respects, this is a highly important book.

Bardic Realities

Peter McQuillan

Irish Bardic Poetry and Rhetorical Reality
Michelle O'Riordan
Cork: Cork University Press, 2007
xxvi + 458 pages. ISBN 978-1-85918-414-7

It has long been axiomatic that Irish poetry of the High Middle Ages, in particular official court or 'bardic' poetry, was less susceptible to foreign influences than either the prose of the period or other types of poetry practised during the so-called 'classical' period (thirteenth to seventeenth centuries). This book goes some way towards an overhaul of this accepted wisdom and reinforces the conclusions of various scholars over the past number of years that literature in Irish was very much a part of the European mainstream — see, for example, Mícheál Mac Craith, *Lorg na hIasachta ar na Dánta Grá*, on the poetry of courtly love, and Tadhg Ó Dúshláine, *An Eoraip agus Litríocht na Gaeilge 1600–50*, on the influence of the baroque aesthetic on devotional and political literature.[1] Like Mac Craith's study, this book

1 Mícheál Mac Craith, *Lorg na hIasachta ar na Dánta Grá* (Baile Átha Cliath, 1989); Tadhg Ó Dúshláine, *An Eoraip agus Litríocht na Gaeilge 1600–50* (Baile Átha Cliath, 1987).

Royal Irish Academy, 23F16/99. Image courtesy of Irish Script on Screen, Dublin Institute for Advanced Studies.

is concerned with a literary manifestation of a particular aristocratic courtly ethos, while it is similar to aspects of Ó Dúshláine's in its concern with the manipulation of a common store of rhetorical figures and tropes for textual effect.

Essentially, O'Riordan is engaged in the exploration of a shared European aesthetic, which, she argues, informs the praise poetry of the medieval and early modern periods in Ireland. To this end, she posits what has been in effect a 'missing link' in our understanding of what constituted the training of Irish poets. Chapter 1 sets the scene historically with the recognition that Irish as a vernacular had long been 'Latinized'; O'Riordan goes on to argue for a basic 'continuity of contact' between Ireland, Britain and Europe during the entire medieval period. In that context, the Anglo-Norman invasion, far from being disruptive, actually intensifies existing trends. In fact, in the explosion of European literary vernaculars in the High Middle Ages, Ireland had already a head start — the Old Irish grammatical tract *Auraicept na nÉces* is presented as a case study of this process. O'Riordan here builds on previous work on the aesthetics of bardic composition (P. A. Breatnach);[2] on medieval Irish literary theory (Poppe and Sims-Williams),[3] as well as teaching practice (McManus).[4]

Irish grammarians and versifiers left behind a series of linguistic and grammatical tracts.[5] They were, however, largely silent on other aspects of the poets' creative process, in particular the rhetorical structuring of composition. In chapter 2 O'Riordan traces this missing link to the European mainland of the late twelfth and early thirteenth centuries, to the treatises of Matthew of Vendôme (*Ars Versificatoria*, *c.* 1175), Geoffrey of Vinsauf (*Poetria Nova*, *c.* 1208) and John of Garland (*Parisiana Poetria*, *c.* 1234), all of which are largely concerned with the intersection between grammar and rhetoric. Coinciding with the transition of rhetoric from a public/ civic to an academic discipline and the rise of a scholastic curriculum, these treatises are

situated within the context of the European 'preceptive' movement, where specific advice is given to prospective authors regarding the style and subject matter appropriate to composition through the formal analysis of literary style. Fundamental to Matthew's tract, for example, is the process of *inventio*, the finding of an appropriate subject from among the storehouse of traditional themes of composition. In general, the emphasis is on finding the appropriate treatment and description of a subject within the set confines of a genre: 'originality' is not the aim. Once the 'conception' of a composition has been addressed, the discussion moves on to consider grammatical ('the invention of words') and rhetorical aspects of composition. The latter are divided in familiar fashion into figures (dealing mostly with manipulation of morphology and syntax) and tropes (metaphor, metonymy, synecdoche, allegory, and so on). There is also a section on metrics, including a discussion of metrical faults (something entirely familiar from Irish tradition). Despite some differences, the other two treatises cover much the same type of material.

The remainder of the book presents a series of case studies, which are designed to contextualize Irish bardic practice within this high medieval literary synthesis. Chapter 3 takes a poem by the well-known fourteenth-century poet Gofraidh Fionn Ó Dálaigh, *Beir eólas dúinn a Dhomhnaill*, composed for Domhnall Mac Carrthaigh, *rígdamna* of Desmond. The *inventio* of the poem is an exhortation to the dedicatee to lead his people out of their West Munster 'home' to Cashel, historic centre of the Munster high-kingship, in the east of the province. Here we see that the poet draws on the 'topical reserve' of his culture to find an entirely appropriate *inventio*: this is what, according to Geoffrey of Vinsauf, should be circumscribed by the 'mind's inner compass' before the poet attempts to compose. While it may bear little relation to fourteenth-century political reality, its *literary* (and cultural) reality is established by the history,

2 Pádraig A. Breatnach, 'The Aesthetics of Irish Bardic Composition: An Analysis of *Fuaras iongnadh, a fhir chumainn* by Fearghal Óg Mac an Bhaird', *Cambrian Medieval Celtic Studies*, 42 (2001), 51–72.

3 Erich Poppe and Patrick Sims-Williams, 'Medieval Irish Literary Theory and Criticism', in A. Minnis and I. Johnson, eds., *The Cambridge History of Literary Criticism* (Cambridge, 2005), ii, 291–309.

4 Damien McManus, 'The Bardic Poet as Teacher, Student and Critic: A Context for the Grammatical Tracts', in C. G. Ó hÁinle and D.E. Meeks eds., *Unity in Diversity: Studies in Irish and Scottish Gaelic Language, Literature and History* (Dublin, 1997), 97–123.

5 For a summary and discussion see, for example, various articles by Brian Ó Cuív such as: 'Linguistic Terminology in the Irish Bardic Tracts', *Transactions of the Philological Society*, 64 (1965), 141–64, and 'The Linguistic Training of the Medieval Irish Poet', *Celtica*, 10 (1973), 114–40.

6   Edited by Lambert
    McKenna in *The Book
    of Magauran* (Dublin,
    1947), 152–67.

7   See P. A. Breatnach, 'The
    Chief's Poet', *Proceedings
    of the Royal Irish
    Academy*, 83C, 3 (1983),
    37–79, for a discussion of
    Irish terms relating to this.

or *senchas*, of the McCarthys and their erstwhile association with and possession of the high-kingship of Munster. This literary appropriateness is augmented by the poet's use of a suitable apologue or *uirscéal*, that of Moses leading the Israelites out of their Egyptian captivity, as well as his evocation of a mytho-historical Eóganacht itinerary — the journey that is delineated resonates with the topography of an imagined, largely pseudo-historical past that therefore bears a certain timeless quality. Once the poem is under way, we see evidence of the poet's characteristic delight in the exploitation of linguistic forms: the first few stanzas are informed by the device of *metaplasm* (juxtaposition of words that look similar and may be conceptually similar but are formally different), in this case *eol/eolas* 'knowledge/direction', and *seol* 'send', 'embark'. This device enhances the representation of the sense of anticipation that attends an imminent journey or expedition, further intensified by the use of various types of repetition or 'dwelling' on the topic that attend it (*commoratio*).

The discussion in chapter 4 further augments this sense of the *literariness* of bardic composition. It is a close reading of 'a poem of complaint' composed by one Ádhamh Ó Fialán for an early fourteenth-century Ulster lord, Tomás Mac Shamhradháin.[6] The poem represents a characteristic instance of bardic dissatisfaction — the poet's patron has failed to fulfil, through the appropriate remuneration, his side of the reciprocal contract that exists between him and the poet. In this case, the poet seeks restitution of cattle that he had originally received in exchange for a poem. O'Riordan's approach is that in the absence of any evidence apart from the poem itself, the theft of the cattle remains 'notional', more of a literary pretext for the exposition of the poet–patron relationship: it is the poem's *inventio*, in other words. The author's analysis of the text emphasizes at every turn the felicitousness of the poet's invention and his adroitness at exploiting a

multitude of rhetorical figures and tropes: from the use of maxim and aphorism (*sententia*) at the opening of the poem, as the poet instructs his lord in the *teagasg flatha* tradition of advice to a prince, to the poet's use of the technique of *licentia*, a 'frankness of speech' that is tempered by, for example, understatement (*litotes*) and self-denying ordinances (*occultatio/paralipsis*), whereby the poet pretends not to praise his patron while actually doing so), as well as other types of ambiguity, irony, innuendo and flattery. Thus, in O'Riordan's formulation, complaint functions less as the obverse of praise than as a foil for it, a means of deliberating upon, reassessing and renewing the poet–patron nexus. Later in the poem, Ó Fialán shows his virtuosity by embarking on a litany of his patron's triumphs in war (*caithréim*), which gives him ample scope to deploy various rhetorical techniques based on repetition (*repetitio*): straight repetition of a word (*conduplicatio*); repeating the final word of a phrase at the beginning of the next (*gradatio*) and other metaplasmic variations in form.

Chapter 5 returns us to the European mainland and engages in a comparison, on a number of levels, between Irish bardic poets and the medieval troubadours. Various parallels are drawn: the preoccupation of both groups with rank and status, the contractual nature of the relationship between artist and patron, the 'indulgence' and special favour expected by the poet from his lord,[7] as well as the conventional literary conceit of the poet as the patron's lover or spouse. This last aspect is developed in an Irish context in chapter 6, entitled 'Lovers' Quarrels'. Here three poems are discussed, all by Ó hUiginn poets. The *inventio* of each of these poems is that the poet feels slighted or undermined by his lord and O'Riordan analyses them as good illustrations of *licentia* or *permissio* — the art of addressing a topic candidly but by modulating the tone through ambiguity, innuendo and flattery. The first is by the early fifteenth-century Tadhg Óg Ó hUiginn addressed to Uilleog Búrc. Central here is the attribution of blame to others, to those who surround the patron rather than to the lord himself. This enables the poet to speak frankly to his own concerns without implicating Búrc too far. In the course of the poem, the tone shifts from complaint, through blandishment, accusation and threat to a plea for reconciliation by means of the poet's own art. Again, O'Riordan emphasizes the literariness of this endeavour — we have no independent way of knowing if any such falling-out over a drunken word resulting in the poet's imprisonment by Búrc ever took place, but the poem nonetheless makes perfect sense on its own rhetorical terms. The two poems discussed for Tadhg Dall Ó hUiginn (*c.* 1545–91) are 'A theachtaire théid ar sliabh' and 'Cóir Dé eadram is Uilliam' which their original editor, Eleanor Knott (1922), has suggested were both dedicated to an 'unidentifiable' William Burke (possibly son of Seán, to whom Tadhg Dall addressed his famous poem 'Fearann cloidhimh críoch Bhanbha' in the 1570s). In any event, O'Riordan argues that the very vagueness of these compositions in referential terms enhances the poet's exploitation of the classic features of the complaint 'genre' — abandonment, puzzlement and a desire for reconciliation. In the latter poem, O'Riordan highlights Ó hUiginn's effective use of the device of *paralipsis* or *occultatio*, disavowing in order to emphasize: essentially the poet here damns his lord with faint praise.

Chapter 7 takes us in a somewhat different direction: 'Poems about Poetry'. Here we find the poets at their most self-aware and, indeed, self-aggrandizing. Four poems are discussed in this chapter, three of them from the late sixteenth or early seventeenth centuries.[8] These poems, according to O'Riordan, read like didactic exercises cast in the form of a dialogue between either master and pupil or between argumentative peers, on the technical and linguistic rights and wrongs of bardic composition. She first discusses a fourteenth-century poem by Gofraidh Fionn Ó Dálaigh ('Madh fiafraidheach budh feasach'),

which, she maintains, functions as a kind of deep background against which the later three compositions can be assessed. She points again to a multitude of rhetorical devices employed by the poet in opening the poem, from the initial proverbial-type opening (*sententia*) to the use of various types of repetition essential to the question-and-answer format of the composition: *epanaphora* (essentially *anaphora*, repetition of a word or phrase at the beginning of a line), *conduplicatio* (simple repetition of words), *gradatio* (the incremental building of climax, here through repeated questions introduced by *Cá mhéad?* 'How many?'), and *divisio* (answering the basic question by positing a series of ancillary questions). The questions referred to concern, initially, the proper inflection of Irish nouns and the first nine stanzas establish the basic *inventio* of the poem: the teacher asks the questions, the pupil cannot answer, and therefore he must proceed to the serious business of instruction. O'Riordan notes that in so doing, the poet Ó Dálaigh places himself within the medieval rhetorical tradition in that the material of the poem itself is designed to illustrate the grammatical points being taught (a practice found in the three medieval treatises alluded to above).

Of course it might be argued that this approach to texts in terms of literariness suits some poems better than others and here we could take Tadhg Dall as a case in point. In the poem discussed by O'Riordan, mentioned above, 'A theachtaire théid ar sliabh', it seems to me that a literary as opposed to a literal reading enhances our appreciation and understanding of the poet's intentions. As had been already pointed out by Knott, the meaning of the piece hinges around the interplay of the terms *fíach* 'due, debt' and *geall* 'pledge, surety, mortgage'. In brief summary: the poet sends his messenger in secret to his patron, Uilliam Búrc, to ask him to assist him in his helplessness: for the past two or three years, in his patron's absence, he has been paying everyone's debts (*fiacha*), as well as his own. For this he has

8 Edited by Lambert McKenna in *Studies*, 40 (1951), 93–96; 217–22; 352–63

9 O'Riordan, *Irish Bardic Poetry and Rhetorial Reality*, xvii.
10 See my *Native and Natural: Aspects of the Concepts of Right and Freedom in Irish*, Field Day Critical Conditions (Cork, 2004).

gone to the courthouse to seek redress (even that process costs him further). He returns from the court with a good warrant and shows his patent to some 'servants' (*lucht seirbhísi*, their precise remit or allegiance is perhaps deliberately vague here). With their reaction, however, he loses hope; moreover 'his captain' and the sheriff can do nothing for him; he is advised to face up to his creditors (or to entrust himself to them, in the Irish: *bísi i leith lucht na bhfiach*). The poet then laments that, not only can he not clear his debts, but that one pledge or mortgage (*éngheall*) does not buy him credit and he is subjected to various usurious practices: it is as if he is being charged twice and three times on everyone's debt; even when he redeems his pledge it is passed on to another creditor; finally the president of the court laments that it is beyond his power to help the poet who has to keep paying. But for the poet it is not primarily the money that concerns him, it is the indignity he is made to suffer: his herdsmen, horse boys and servants all abandon him and the poet closes his argument by returning to the lament of Búrc's (his *compánach*) absence. He finishes with a rather conventional stanza of eulogy, epithets such as 'the lion cub of Loch Con' being used to describe the absent patron.

This poem is discussed by O'Riordan within the general context of what she calls 'bardic love' — in particular, the re-establishment of the terms of personal intimacy between poet and patron when the poet feels that that intimacy has been slighted. Of primary interest here are these 'terms': Ó hUiginn is employing the language of financial indebtedness and legal obligation in order to make his point *metaphorically* and we need not be concerned about the existence or otherwise of an actual material debt in 'real-life' terms. An interesting comparison here might be Sonnet 134 by Shakespeare, Ó hUiginn's contemporary, where the poet declares himself 'mortgaged' to his lover's will — he addresses her as 'thou usurer', while the poet's friend who also loves her is

now a 'debtor' for the poet's sake. Just how common, I would like to know, is the use of metaphors of financial indebtedness for unrequited love in Renaissance Europe? In any event, O'Riordan's approach encourages a reading that, I feel, potentially enriches our understanding of sixteenth-century literature and enables us to ask further questions about that literature.

That this would be the case for other specimens of sixteenth-century and early seventeenth-century poetry in Irish will be more hotly contested. In fairness to O'Riordan, she does not set out to discuss 'political' poems as such, and there is no need to rehearse here the views of, for example, Marc Caball and Breandán Ó Buachalla, which were occasioned by the appearance of O'Riordan's first book in 1990. However, it does seem at times in the current book that the shadow of depoliticized reading still lurks in the background. The title of the book is in this respect perhaps somewhat provocative, *Irish Bardic Poetry and Rhetorical Reality*. 'Reality' here translates as a literary plausibility based on culture-specific factors, choosing a theme or topic that is 'realistic' although it might never have happened (but *could* have). The question then arises of how to interpret this literary 'reality' in the light of alleged contiguous 'facts' of the outside world (in O'Riordan's view 'political context' is a 'fact-oriented' mode of interpretation: 'the poem then represents "facts"'[9]). I would argue, however, that political context is not reducible to 'facts' and that consideration of such contexts typically demands a reading that is sensitive to the *symbolic* content of the poetry, a reading which, in other words, takes a more 'anthropological' view of a more long-term cultural meaning that transcends immediate political 'realities'.[10] Staying with the poetry of Tadhg Dall, what is the rhetorical reality of his poem of exhortation ('D'fhior cogaidh comhailtear síothchán', 'To a man of war is peace observed') to Brian na Múrtha Ó Ruairc, lord of Bréifne, composed in the late 1580s when Ó Ruairc had fallen foul of the president of Connacht,

Royal Irish Academy,
23F16/129. Image courtesy of
Irish Script on Screen, Dublin
Institute for Advanced Studies.

Sir Richard Bingham, for assistance rendered
to survivors of the shipwrecked Armada
off the north-west coast of Ireland? (One
survivor, Francisco de Cuellar, refers to 'el
gran señor Ruerge'.) Here again, the poem
shows a number of rhetorical features such as
those discussed above: the opening *sententia*,
the use of paradox, irony and *anaphora*
(the poet typically launches each incitement
with an imperative form of some kind) as
well as a lengthy apologue, derived from
Aesop, on the treachery of the lion who
having invited all the animals to his cave on
the pretext of a feast, proceeds to kill them,
all the save the fox who has the cunning
to escape with his life (he sees footprints
going into the cave but none coming out).
In other words, the bellicosity of Ó Ruairc
will force the English to sue for peace, but
this will be merely a prelude to such an act
of treachery on their part, so forewarned is
forearmed. In her discussion in chapter 3 of
the apologue used by Gofraidh Fionn in his
poem to Mac Carrthaigh (Moses leading his
people out of Egypt, just as the dedicatee
will lead the McCarthys back to Cashel),
O'Riordan emphasizes the literariness of
its use in accordance with the precepts of

the rhetoricians, especially in respect of
'plausibility' — while the McCarthy claim to
Cashel in the fourteenth century is hardly in
the realm of political realism, it is nonetheless
plausible in a historical and literary sense
and it also resonates with contemporary
Gael–Gall antagonisms (Cashel being in
Butler territory at this point). She therefore
draws the conclusion that the apologue 'does
not ... encourage the notion that the poet
had a function of political exhortation'.[11]
Possibly so in this particular instance,
although I am not certain how much we can
ever recover the cognitive and affective terms
of the reception of such poetry. However,
could O'Riordan 'plausibly' have analysed
Tadhg Dall's sixteenth-century apologue in
this same light given its immediate political
context and bearing in mind, as Cathal Ó
hÁinle has pointed out in relation to this
very poem,[12] that the 1570s had witnessed
incidents of precisely the kind that the poet
is warning Ó Ruairc against, the massacre of
the followers of Brian Ua Néill at the hands
of the earl of Essex in 1574 and the summary
mass execution at Mullaghmast (Mullach
Maistean) in 1577 (both recorded by the
Four Masters)? In addition, I have argued

11 O'Riordan, *Bardic Poetry
and Rhetorical Reality*,
94–95.
12 Cathal Ó Háinle,
Promhadh Pinn (Má
Nuad, 1978), 46–48.

13 McQuillan, *Native and Natural*.

14 See Patricia Palmer's evocative account, incorporating both poem and execution, in *Language and Conquest in Early Modern Ireland* (Cambridge, 2004), 212–16.

15 Marc Caball, *Poets and Politics: Reaction and Continuity in Irish Poetry, 1558–1625*, Field Day Critical Conditions (Cork, 1998).

16 Clare Carroll, *Circe's Cup: Cultural Transformations in Early Modern Ireland*, Field Day Critical Conditions (Cork, 2001).

17 Quoted by O'Riordan, *Irish Bardic Poetry and Rhetorical Realities*, 72, from Jane Baltzell Kopp's translation.

elsewhere[13] that the rhetorical fulcrum of this poem is provided by the poet's invocation of the symbolic ideological centre of the Gaelic polity's sense of unity: Tara, Midhe, Uisneach and other sites associated with the high-kingship. That this 'high-kingship' was never realized in the historical record does not diminish its ideological cogency, especially in the Ireland of the 1570s and 1580s. How then did the 'rhetorical reality' of Ó hUiginn's *gríosughudh ... chum cogaidh a n-aghaidh na banriaghna Eisiobel* ('incitement to war against the queen Elizabeth', as one manuscript prefaces the poem) reverberate in Ó Ruairc's head as he stood in the dock in London awaiting his execution for high treason, an event whose depiction by John Stow presents it as a ghoulish and gruesome reverse mirror image of the apocalyptic diction of Tadhg Dall's exhortation ('his members and bowels burned in the fire, his heart taken out and holden up by the hang-man, naming it to be the Arch-traytor's heart'[14])?

Somewhat in the same vein, the book concludes with a fine discussion of two poems written in the last throes of the bardic era, when, as O Riordan puts it, the medieval prescriptive arts were being abandoned and literary tastes were changing, in Ireland as in Europe. One of these poems is by Eochaidh Ó hEodhasa (d. 1616), 'Ionmholta malairt bhisigh' and O'Riordan gives an excellent analysis of the poem's structure, highlighting not least its moments of irony. She again accords this poem a more literary than literal reading, in other words

emphasizing an aesthetic shift among poets themselves rather than a wholesale collapse of their cultural world. I have no quibbles with this interpretation: there is no denying the pervasively whimsical tone of the poem. However, as Caball has pointed out,[15] by the time of the Ulster Plantation the tone of such poems has changed radically as a result of plantation, dislocation of the nobility and the spread of English common law. We should also note that, conversant as Ó hEodhasa was with the preceptive rhetorical tradition, he had also, as Clare Carroll has argued, read his Machiavelli.[16]

However, I do not wish to finish on a negative note because this is an important book which deserves a warm welcome on its own terms. I had a sense of revitalized engagement and enjoyment in reading O'Riordan's analysis of the various poems presented here. And certainly, it puts to rest the curious notion (I cannot remember the original source but one sees it recycled from time to time) that Irish poets of the bardic period were but little concerned with the compositions as integrated or cohesive wholes or units, the individual verse as a rhetorical unit, so to speak, standing in more or less random juxtaposition with its companions. To give the final word to Geoffrey of Vinsauf: 'Let the mind's inner compass circumscribe the whole area of the subject matter in advance'.[17] In the poems presented in this book, O'Riordan has most elegantly shown how Irish poets could triumphantly realize the precepts of medieval scholastic teaching.

Dony McManus's *Linesman Pulling Rope* (1999), City Quay, Dublin. Photo: Axiom Photographic Agency/Getty Images.

The Lack of the Liberal

Terry Eagleton

Luck and the Irish:
A Brief History of Change, 1970–2000
R. F. Foster
Harmondsworth: Allen Lane, 2007
240 pages. ISBN 978-0-713997-83-5

In the culture wars between nationalists and revisionists (or 'revisionists', as Roy Foster scare-quotedly has it), a spot of vulgar Marxism can concentrate the mind wonderfully. Anti-colonial revolutions in the twentieth century have been largely the work of the petty bourgeoisie, allied with forces to the left of them which, as is the way with bourgeois revolutions, usually end up being sold down the political river. Marxism was the first mass political movement to champion such anti-colonial aspirations, just as it was the first mass political movement to wave the flag for women's emancipation. But in doing so, it sought to furnish the forces of national independence with a rather less parochial, more inclusive and internationalist world-view than the nationalism to which they were typically in thrall. In this, it was to prove singularly unsuccessful.

Even so, the political Left challenged the limits of nationalist ideology while continuing to support the right of peoples to govern themselves — a right which it regarded like liberalism, feminism, democracy and republicanism as part of the precious heritage of bourgeois Enlightenment. You can support a political project while criticizing some of its ideological expressions. Liberals like Roy Foster support feminism, while no doubt rejecting what they would see as its more 'extreme' ideological manifestations. One takes it that he is no more a fan of bra-burning than he is of Brendan Bradshaw. But in the liberal camp, what goes for feminism does not necessarily go for national liberation. We hear an enormous amount from liberal revisionists about the crimes and follies of nationalism, but scarcely a word about the virtues of anti-colonial rebellion from India to Angola. True to our post-modern times, the political and economic find themselves displaced by the cultural and ideological — as they are, too, by emollient revisionist accounts of Anglo-Irish landlordism or Northern unionism which see them as cultural and ethnic groups somewhat akin to the disabled or immigrant Poles, rather than as dominant social and economic classes.

By contrast with the political Left, liberals have been more equivocal about whether, say, their proper aversion to Islamic nationalism is coupled with a desire to rid Iraq of an illegal imperial invader. They thus tend to be more selective than the political Left about the middle-class Enlightenment of which they are, even more obviously than the Left, the contemporary heirs. For the Left, it is simply inconsistent to be a good Enlightenment liberal yet to oppose the emancipation of colonized nations. Anti-colonialism is simply a form of democracy. Whether this is the case with Roy Foster, Tom Dunne, or Joep Leerssen, however,

is rather less apparent. It is certainly not unambiguously the case when it comes to Ireland. And there are, of course, those cross-grained creatures who are anti-colonial in every instance but their own, just as there are those who wish to see tower blocks sprout in everyone else's back garden.

Few thinkers have waxed more enthusiastic about the bourgeoisie than Marx. You can tell a Marxist by his or her admiration for the middle class. Marx regarded them as the most revolutionary force in human history, and never ceased to lavish praise on their magnificent achievements in the cause of human emancipation. But the middle classes have particular reason to be embarrassed by such commendation. As they grow older, they wax somewhat coy about their own insurrectionary heritage, rather like respectable young trainee accountants who squirm when their parents fondly recall the brutish antics of their childhood. If the middle classes wreak political havoc from time to time, it is ironically in the name of order and stability. If they tear the political world to pieces, it is to create the kind of peaceable, well-disciplined, conservative regimes within which their consuming passion — the accumulation of profit — can be most vigorously pursued. Revolutionary origins are bad for business. The values that founded the state now prove an obstacle to its flourishing, as former sans-culottes get their feet under ministerial desks and talk of collective liberation gives way to the language of individual liberty. Neither violence nor heroism is any longer tolerable.

In the transition from bandits to bankers, militants to managers, Shelley to Trollope, the bourgeoisie, like children in the grip of Freud's so-called family romance syndrome, are constrained to draw a veil over their own tainted origins, thrusting this squalid narrative of aggression and illegality into the political unconscious. Only in the occasional liberal society — the United States springs to mind — can this running battle between poetry and prose, the epic and the pragmatic, be successfully resolved, as entrepreneurialism in Texas or Arizona becomes a new form of heroism. Appealing to the founding fathers in the States is as much a conservative gesture as a radical one. In most of the middle-class world, however, the more amnesiac you grow about the real sources of your own power (invasion, usurpation, insurrection, extermination, and so on), the more your sovereignty is perfected. It is a doctrine promulgated all the way from Pascal and David Hume to Kant and Burke. For this theory, all political authority thrives on a certain willed oblivion or merciful forgetfulness, rather as for Nietzsche, Schopenhauer and Freud all constructive action depends on a certain salutary repression.

Or, if not outright oblivion, then at least on what Freud called 'secondary revision'. Discreditable political pedigrees may be too recent to be easily erasable, as Burke recognized of the Anglo-Irish Ascendancy in contrast to his adopted England. But as one phase of middle-class society yields to another, and the insurance brokers gradually take over from the insurrectionists, that earlier history can at least be mocked, massaged, downplayed and discredited by a post-revolutionary generation of middle-class ideologues in full-blooded Oedipal revolt against the founding fathers. Revisionism is not, to be sure, simply a reflex of historical conditions, which is why this particular Marxist narrative has a smack of vulgarity about it. Only paid-up Foucaultians hold that the truth is simply a function of interests. But historians have generally found it as hard to historicize themselves as physicians have proved inept at self-healing, which is why this story is one they might do worse than bend an ear to. If it is unlikely that they will, it is because liberal pragmatists like Foster are averse to large theoretical abstractions, except when it comes to such notions as 'the uniqueness of the individual', 'the rights of property', 'the rich diversity of humankind', 'the values of Western civilisation', and so forth. They

are equally critical of inflexible absolutes. In fact, the founding principles of liberalism are just as absolute and inflexible as those of Seventh-Day Adventism, a point which by no means automatically constitutes a criticism of the creed. It is good that most liberals believe torture to be absolutely wrong.

In other respects, however, liberals do indeed elevate to absolute status values that are clearly relative. Foster himself seems to take it for granted in post-modern style that diversity and plurality are always unequivocal goods, whereas there are those rather less generously open-ended souls among us who hold that five fascist parties or a rash of aristocracies are a good deal worse than one. If diversity, plurality, flexibility and inclusiveness can indeed be precious values, they are also the mantras of a late capitalism which needs for its own purposes to break down barriers and loosen up old allegiances; and the true pluralists are those who feel the need to say both things together, rather than remain blind to the material basis of their own beliefs. The doctrine that honest doubt is preferable to firm conviction; that firm conviction is always only a heartbeat away from authoritarianism; that the truth generally lies in the middle; that there are no important conflicts in which one side must absolutely win and the other absolutely lose; that a readiness to compromise in the spirit of realism is always to be commended, and that resistance to this counsel is inherently a vice — all of these abstract, inflexible, one-sided, grossly generalizing liberal dogmas must surely be thrown open to a genuinely free play of the mind.

It is, to be sure, important to deflate grandiose nationalist claims, just as it is important to refute cynical revisionist debunking. In one sense, however, nothing more dramatic has happened in these disputes than the replacement of middle-class nationalists with middle-class liberals. Fundamental power-relations remain largely unaltered. The task of the political Left is not so much to take sides in this somewhat parochial squabble as to comment on its historical foundation. There are many affinities between these two warring camps. Roy Foster is quite as hostile to the Left as arch-nationalist D. P. Moran. Revealingly, he refers in this book to the former Irish Communist Party apparatchik Mick O'Riordan, leader of a notably toothless, arthritic, tamely reformist bunch of leftists, as belonging to 'the wilder shores of radicalism', which is rather like mistaking Sean Connolly for James Connolly. (It should be added, however, that O'Riordan fought with great courage against Franco. Foster, however, does not like heroes, which presumably means that he is as averse to Oliver Tambo as he is to Patrick Pearse.) There is also a well-bred sneer at leftist political demonstrations, which played a key role in ending the Vietnam War, as 'quintessential act(s) of 1960s agitprop theatre'. Both parties to this contention tend to be doughty supporters of capitalism; both are sceptical of older mythologies, whether colonialist or nationalist; both view the kind of history that preceded them as ideologically distorting; both regard themselves as in the van of modernity; both tend to be believers in historical progress. In fact, Foster is not entirely without a certain Irish chauvinism himself, having regularly labelled as 'bandwaggoners' those non-Irish commentators on Irish affairs with whose views he disagrees. We, poor Sassenach souls, are bogus Irish, rather than full-blooded, authentic specimens of the race.

One vital difference between the two camps is that nationalists are upfront about their ideology, sometimes stridently so, whereas liberals on the whole are not. In fact, in their hearts liberals do not regard their beliefs as ideological at all, which is one reason why it is so exasperatingly difficult to argue with them. Ideology, like halitosis, is what other people have. Foster speaks in this book of an Irish Labour Party 'uninfected' by ideology, as though socialism is on a level with typhoid. It is not hard to see why liberals tend to be blind to their

own partisanship. For one thing, liberalism is supposed to be defined by its *anti-*partisanship or disinterestedness. A liberal like Edna Longley might serve to exemplify such an admirable lack of sectarian animus. For another thing, liberal thought is supposed to be about living, breathing, unique, flesh-and-blood individuals, not rebarbative dogmas or coercive collectivities. In fact, of course, it constitutes a belief system every bit as abstract as nuclear physics, if not quite so difficult to grasp. As for collectivities, Foster writes here sniffily of Irish republicans who 'identify with nation, tribe, church or party', heedless of the fact that free liberal spirits like himself are every bit as tribal on their protected reservations in Oxbridge and Camden Town as anything to be found in the interior of Borneo. To an outsider, the shared mindset of most middle-class liberals is every bit as striking as the cloned opinions of the Church of Latter-Day Saints.

At one point in his argument, Foster notes rather plaintively that some people use the word 'liberal' as a term of abuse. As far as Marxists go, it would be more accurate to describe it as at once a term of abuse and admiration. Classical liberalism is a tale of exhilarating emancipation from the prelates, autocrats and patriarchs, insisting as it did on the scandalous revolutionary truth that men and women were free, equal, autonomous and endowed with inalienable rights simply by virtue of belonging to the human species. Which is to say, simply by virtue of the kind of bodies they had. This is one of the most astonishingly radical insights ever to see the light of day, though it had a precedent in Judaeo-Christianity. In its heyday, liberalism was far more of a revolutionary movement than socialism has ever managed to be. It also fostered an atomistic notion of the self, an extrinsicist, austerely contractual view of human relations, an anaemically utilitarian ethics, a self-satisfied faith in progress and civility, a Panglossian purblindness to the more malign, recalcitrant aspects of human

Oisín Kelly's *Jim Larkin* (1977), O'Connell Street, Dublin. Photo: Stockbyte/Getty Images.

nature, a doctrinal suspicion of doctrine, an alienated view of the extra-individual sphere, and a witheringly negative view of power, the state, society, freedom, tradition and communality. (As far as the liberal suspicion of doctrine goes, Foster thinks that Kant's celebrated comment on the 'crooked timber of humanity' serves to illustrate this point, whereas, as Perry Anderson has pointed out in the case of Isaiah Berlin, this constitutes a misreading of the passage in question.)

Liberal belief has been largely blind to the ways in which freedom for some has involved oppression or exploitation for

THE CAUSE OF LABOUR IS THE CAUSE OF IRELAND · THE CAUSE OF IRELAND IS THE CAUSE OF LA

Éamonn O'Doherty's *James Connolly*, Beresford Place, Dublin.

many others, and has perversely championed a form of social and economic life that rides roughshod over some of the very values it holds most dear. So it is that Foster is an ardent supporter of both individual liberty and business schools. It is the economic and political doctrines of liberalism that have sent Western tanks into Baghdad, just as it is the ethical and cultural doctrines of liberalism that have been summoned in some quarters to protest against that undertaking. This view of middle-class liberalism, one might venture, is rather more subtle, complex and nuanced than the black-and-white polarities of Foster, Longley, Leerssen and Colm Tóibín when it comes to their own political adversaries, despite their ceaseless reminders to others to be subtle, complex, nuanced and even-handed.

The Left does not regard liberal values as timeless absolutes insulated from critical scrutiny. Instead, it inquires into their historical basis, along with their virtues and defects, and asks how these two things may be interrelated. The traditional term for this approach is 'dialectical', a word that one can imagine Foster using about as easily as one can imagine him singing 'Danny Boy'. It means, among other things, paying homage to one's opponent, which marks the difference between the Left's attitude to liberalism and liberalism's attitude to the Left. Socialists want to build on the great liberal heritage in order eventually to reach beyond it. They are as committed to its values as any Mill, Arnold or Russell; it is just that they see the need for radical change if those values are ever to have a hope of being universalized.

For their part, liberals are supposed to see all sides of the story; but it is remarkable how quickly those who protest against fixed oppositions resort to just this habit of mind when confronted with an ideological opponent. Irish liberal revisionists are not celebrated for bringing to bear on their own principles the kind of sceptical, flexible, open-minded investigation to which they subject the beliefs of others. Yet this is precisely what their liberalism requires of them, which is where the creed starts to hurt. A good liberal must be so liberal as to have real trouble in being a liberal. They don't like labels, for one thing. Foster, unlike his great liberal near-namesake E. M. Forster, reveals scarcely a scrap of such self-awareness, thus demonstrating that even the finest of intelligences can be occasionally rendered obtuse by ideology. Instead, he appears to believe that his views are simple, hard-headed common sense, and sets up an eminently self-serving opposition between fair-minded liberals and bigoted nationalists, as though Ruth Dudley Edwards was less prejudiced than Frederick Ryan. The truth is that, like most liberals, Foster is nervous of political conviction as such, not just of its nationalist varieties. Like most liberals, too, he does not seem to recognize just what a privileged position this is. There are those who have no need for political conviction, and those who cannot survive without it. One might expect a pluralist and pragmatist to be more sensitive to such distinctions.

One might also expect a pragmatist like Foster to be more contextual about what counts as political realism and idealism. He is naturally allergic to the idealist rhetoric of Irish nationalism; but he does not seem to notice that the United States, a nation of which one imagines he is for the most part a political ally, is rife with enough earnest, high-minded, portentous ideological wind-baggery to make even the most devoted Platonist flinch. It is a discourse that has wreaked rather more damage around the globe than Jim Larkin ever did. Those who refuse to adapt their political ideals to contemporary reality are almost always in Foster's eyes 'diehards', 'irredentists' and 'irreconcilables'. So indeed they sometimes are; but one would expect, once again, that a liberal pluralist with a distaste for grand narratives might be a little less grandly generalizing. Not long ago, in the darkest days of apartheid, one might plausibly have accused members of the South African National Congress of clinging to their absurdly abstract ideals and failing to reconcile themselves to political reality. There were times when Martin Luther King looked like the most flaky sort of utopianist. If the US occupation of Iraq is still in place in fifty years' time, would it be gritty realism to embrace it and fanatical purism to object to it? Foster is amusingly sardonic in this book about the reinvention of a befuddled Celticism; it is a pity that all he has to pit against it is a Blairite pragmatism.

Liberal revisionists are above all card-carrying modernizers. The distinction between moderates and fanatics can be easily mapped on to one between the up-to-date and the archaic. As a historian, Foster trades in the past; as an ideologue, he greets much of it with contempt. (There is a distinction here between R. F. Foster and Roy Foster, the former representing the dispassionate historian, the latter signalling the opinionated commentator.) 'Modernization', probably the most vacuous, all-purpose term in the sociological lexicon, is for liberal revisionists generally benign, as opposed to those who have noticed that it is usually a euphemism for capitalism and its latest autocratic requirements. In any case, that system, with its urge to illimitable growth, is now beginning to look distinctly archaic in the light of ecological findings. And a mode of production that time after time has so plainly demonstrated its inability to feed the world is surely ripe for surpassing. Traditional Ireland for the more vulgar sort of revisionist is largely a place of myths, priests and stubbornly unmodernizable Micks, all of them distressingly remote from middle-class Dublin. Yet modernization is itself among other things a form of mythology, as Horkheimer and Adorno point out, and there are secularized priests galore, some of them even more sinister than the clerical variety.

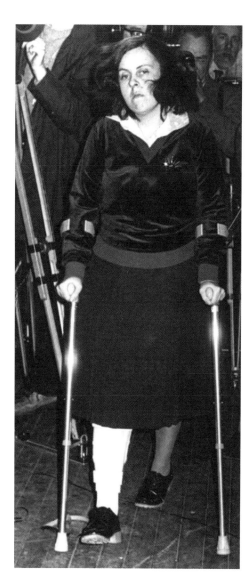

itself. Even demythologizing history-writing has its origin in fifth-century Athens, in the steely realism of Thucydides. Republicanism is among the most ancient forms of politics. Liberalism is a discourse much older than nationalism, which sees itself as nothing if not modern and is in some respects quite right to do so. Liberalism is also of course a good deal longer in the tooth than Marxism. Slavery was bang up-to-date in its own day, and the fascists were programmatic modernizers. Many of the artistic avant garde were political reactionaries.

Foster speaks in *Luck and the Irish* of 'antediluvian' labour practices, like any purple-jowled *Daily Telegraph* editorialist; but there is a distinctly modern quality about seeking to defend oneself against speed-up, neglect of safety measures and intensified exploitation. Modern multicultural identities can be every bit as coercive and constraining as some pre-modern concepts of selfhood. A chapter in this book on the loosening grip of religion in Ireland fails properly to balance the precious gains of this secularization with the loss of a certain spirituality, as the country shifts from comely maidens to hard-faced executives. For some observers, though not for Foster, true modernization in Ireland would involve completing the process of decolonization. Not all nostalgia is self-indulgent. In some respects, the past was indeed superior to the present, just as in other respects the opposite is the case. Atavists and progressivists are alike tunnel-visioned. Walter Benjamin even managed to forge nostalgia into a revolutionary concept, aware that what stirs men and women to revolt is not dreams of liberated grandchildren but memories of oppressed ancestors. The Angel of History is driven backwards into the future with its horror-struck gaze fastened on the catastrophe of the past. Foster quotes Charles Haughey on not being a prisoner of one's past; but there are also ways of using the past to interrogate the present, and in doing so, make for a finer future. Those callow triumphalists who can discern little catastrophe in the past — who

Any lecturer rash enough to declare, say, that the paper clip was invented in 1908 will most certainly be greeted by a riposte from the back of the hall that a fossilized version of one has just been unearthed from an Etruscan tomb. Historians are mostly aware that there is not all that much new under the sun; that the very word 'modern' descends to us from classical antiquity; and that the brave avant-gardist notion of breaking with past history has a very long history indeed. No epoch other than modernity characterizes itself, bizarrely, simply by its temporal coincidence with cannot see the force of Schopenhauer's brutally just observation that most men and women in history would probably have been better off never having been born — are likely to embrace a future that is no more than a mildly improved version of the present. 'The present with more options', as one post-modernist excitedly declared. The real political divisions of our time are between end-of-ideology idealists like Foster, who seem to believe that no world-shaking changes are now required of history, and those political realists who recognize that our condition is so dire that only such a deep-seated transformation could feasibly repair it. Progressives tend to believe that the truth is not as bad as it has been painted; radicals believe that the truth is almost always worse than one had imagined.

Luck and the Irish begins with a lively summary of the Great Irish Leap Forward, which concludes that this has been largely beneficial but which by no means overlooks the case against such a sanguine estimate. On the one hand, the country can boast a growth rate outperforming that of other EU nations; on the other hand, it has the highest proportion of relative poverty among EU nations, and tops the league table of inequality. There is a typically perceptive account of the current state of religion in the country, which ignores the fact that since nobody in their right mind would swallow the superstitious nonsense that mostly passes for Christianity in the country, the Irish tend to buy their atheism or agnosticism on the cheap. The Catholic Church has oppressed them not only in ways too wearily familiar to recount, but also, rather more subtly, by depriving them in its theological illiteracy of any version of the Christian gospel that might remotely challenge them.

A chapter on the fortunes of Fianna Fáil devotes rather too much attention to the rise and fall of Charles Haughey. There follows an account of the Troubles, which devotes a couple of cursory sentences to the injustices against which the Catholics saw themselves as battling, before launching rather more

gleefully into an assault on Bernadette McAliskey, Desmond Greaves and a motley collection of other political enemies. There is an enjoyable satirical polemic against the Provos, but very little on loyalist violence. The redneck views of the later Conor Cruise O'Brien are passed over in discreet silence. A 'Platonically pure' Irish nationalism is sternly upbraided, but as with 'virulent bubonic plague', it is hard to know quite what other strain is supposed to exist. Easter 1916 is accused of putting paid 'to any possibility of an autonomous Ireland that might include the North', as though the Northern unionists would have selflessly transcended their own material interests and cheerfully rallied under the banner of independence if only there had been less talk in Dublin of blood sacrifice and rosary beads. Erudite and absorbing though it is, the survey suffers from the kind of problem one would confront in, say, reading Roger Scruton on comprehensive education: one knows more or less what is going to be said. 'Moderniser was apparently calling to moderniser across the petrified forest of cross-border politics', Foster writes rather absurdly of Terence O'Neill and Seán Lemass, as though they were pigeons rather than politicians.

The book ends with a scintillating survey of contemporary Irish culture, complete with some wonderful cameos and lightning thumbnail sketches (Van Morrison as 'an edgy Belfast fusion of blues music and baroque Dylanism'). Foster is surely right to claim that Irish drama today has equalled its revivalist forebears (some might say considerably surpassed it), and sees how the novel, once thought to play second fiddle in Irish culture to the short story, has evolved into a major cultural phenomenon. There is some overhyping of Bob Geldof, a man thoroughly detested by most Green activists, along with a hilarious account of the Irish Pub (though that is part of modernization as well). *Luck and the Irish* is stylish, funny, witty, compulsively readable and marvellously well-informed. Pity about the ideological blinkers.

Jack B. Yeats, unpublished illustration of the 1798 centennial celebration, Coloony, County Sligo. Private collection.

Once Upon a Time in the West

Gearóid Ó Tuathaigh

Irish Folk History and Social Memory
Guy Beiner
Madison: University of Wisconsin Press, 2007
xix + 466 pages. ISBN 978-0-299-21820-1

The moment of conception of this work was, as the author tells us, dramatic:

> One dreary day, in the autumn of 1997, I stepped out of the Modern Irish History Department at University College Dublin, to which I had recently arrived, walked down the corridors of the Arts Faculty and opened a door into Aladdin's cave. Inside I found not only a thousand and one tales, but also many more — each waiting to take me on a magic carpet ride and show me wonders beyond belief. I had discovered the archive of the Department of Irish Folklore.[1]

Almost a decade after this first enchantment, the fruits of Guy Beiner's excavations have now appeared in a book of impressive scholarship and striking originality: his own claim, that the work 'audaciously proposes to turn modern Irish history (and by extension, history at large) on its head',[2] scarcely seems exaggerated.

The image of moving from the darkness of an academic history department to the light of folklore archives is echoed at other points in the book, as Beiner chastises Irish historians for their reluctance — indeed failure — to engage this rich resource for Irish historical studies, specifically for the study of popular historical traditions (a historiography of oral or folk history, as Beiner calls it). These strictures, with a few notable exceptions, are in large measure justified. Certainly, while scholars of various disciplines, including historians, have been more willing in recent years to engage literary material in both vernaculars bearing on the culture-conflict of the early modern period in Ireland, and on the world-view of the dispossessed as it is found in eighteenth-century verse, for example, the use of the archives of the Irish Folklore Commission (IFC) as a source for the exploration of 'history from below' in nineteenth-century Ireland has been disappointingly limited. The folklore of the Famine provides a lonely exception to this general neglect.[3]

In considering the reluctance of Irish historians to make use of the folklore archive in their researches, Beiner quotes Cathal Póirtéir's comment that there was lacking an 'acceptable methodology'.[4] Beiner does not seem altogether convinced of this explanation. Nor should he be. The main elements of his own methodology — the intellectual procedures through which he examines and interprets the source material — are not impossibly arcane or inaccessible. He has familiarized himself with key domains of critical theory, on memory, tradition, cultural transmission and history (its truth claims, its procedures and practices, its forms), drawn from a range of different academic disciplines — anthropology, sociology, cultural geography, psychology, literary and cultural theory, and history itself.

The concept of 'social memory' is the presiding idea of Beiner's examination of the construction and transmission of the story of the Year of the French/*Bliain na bhFrancach* by the communities directly affected by the events of the French expedition to the West of Ireland in support of the United Irish rising of 1798. The particular novelty of his approach lies in his use of an 'archaeology of social memory', which entails 'setting out to retrace the origins of traditions ... [starting] with the period in which the sources were collected and [moving] backwards towards the original events'.[5] Resisting any clear-cut distinction between 'positivist and interpretative investigation of oral history', Beiner's study 'deliberately integrates both approaches in its analysis of oral traditions, which are considered both as recollections of events in the past [in this case, 1798] and as representations of the ways these recollections were subsequently narrated in local communities'.[6] His purpose is to explain 'how provincial communities directly affected by the French invasion remembered historical events', and the discussion 'oscillates between the study of an actual past and interpretative representations of the past in the changing context of an ethnographic present'.[7] The challenge is to 'transcend present-minded discourses, "excavate" recollections of the past, and recontextualize them'.[8]

This excavation required the examination of a very wide range of utterances on the Year of the French recorded among the provincial communities that lived (at the time and since) in the counties in Connacht and the north midlands along or adjacent to the route taken by the French military force (and the Irish rebels who joined them) as it moved from its landing point near Killala in County Mayo on 22 August 1798, south through Castlebar, north again through Sligo and Leitrim and east to the final defeat and surrender of the Franco-Irish rebel army by crown forces at Ballinamuck, County Longford on 8 September 1798. The grim reckoning on 23 September for the rebel

1 Guy Beiner, *Remembering the Year of the French: Irish Folk History and Social Memory* (Madison, 2007), xi. The Department of Irish Folklore incorporates the archive of the Irish Folklore Commission (IFC), by which its records are identified. An important study, published since Beiner went to press, is Mícheál Briody, *The Irish Folklore Commission 1935–1970: History, Ideology and Methodology* (Helsinki. 2007).

2 Beiner, *Remembering the Year of the French*, xii.

3 The first use of the IFC material on the Famine was by the literary critic, Roger McHugh, 'The Famine in Folklore', in R. D. Edwards and T. D. Williams, eds., *The Great Famine* (Dublin, 1956), 391–406. For more recent use, see Cormac Ó Gráda, *An Drochshaol: Béaloideas agus Amhráin* (Baile Átha Cliath. 1994), and *Black '47 and Beyond: The Great Irish Famine in History, Economy and Memory* (Princeton, 1999), esp. 194–225. Also selections of folklore by Cathal Póirtéir, ed., *Famine Echoes* (Dublin, 1995) and *Glórtha ón nGorta* (Baile Átha Cliath, 1995).

4 Cathal Póirtéir, 'Folk Memory and the Famine', in Cathal Póirtéir, ed., *The Great Irish Famine* (Cork and Dublin, 1995), 231.

5 Beiner, *Remembering the Year of the French*, 317.

6 Beiner, *Remembering the Year of the French*, 23.

7 Beiner, *Remembering the Year of the French*, 8.

8 Beiner, *Remembering the Year of the French*, 316.

Sesquicentennial of the Battle of Ballinamuck, 19 September 1948. Photo: National Photographic Archive, National Library of Ireland.

9   Tom Dunne, ed., *The Writer as Witness* (Cork, 1987), 1.

forces who remained at Killala constitutes the final chapter of the remarkable story of *Bliain na bhFrancach* (in fact, scarcely a month) for the people of the West and the north midlands.

The point of departure for this excavation is the 1930s. That is to say, the bulk of the sources for the folk history of the Year of the French are, firstly, the collections of folklore made by Dr. Richard Hayes in the mid-1930s for his path-breaking book *The Last Invasion of Ireland: When Connacht Rose* (published in 1937, with a revised new edition in 1939); secondly, the material in the Main Collection of the IFC collected in the field by its own collectors, mainly from the 1930s to 1950; and thirdly, the material collected in 1937–38 in a special initiative in which the IFC succeeded in getting the co-operation of the teachers and the participation of the senior children in some 5,000 primary schools in the state in generating a rich body of folklore, known as the Schools' Manuscript Collection. In addition to this core material, Beiner has examined an exceptionally wide range of ancillary material pertaining to all aspects of the folk traditions of 1798 in Connacht–north Leinster and their

transmission down to our own time. It is an impressive achievement.

Is it the case, then, that this methodology of excavation and recontextualization, and the source material indicated, were until now entirely beyond the analytical command of most Irish historians? It is true that, in contrast to their acknowledgement of the need for familiarity with economic theory and skills of quantification in dealing with certain topics in economic and social change, Irish historians were generally slow to engage literary and cultural theory and its implications for the writing of history. The positivist approach, 'practical history' based on close, context-sensitive reading of written sources, held sway in Irish historical scholarship from the 1930s. As late as 1987, Tom Dunne could complain that historians had 'made surprisingly little contribution to the extensive modern theoretical debate about the nature of historical understanding', and that a 'general lack of theoretical appraisal has been a damaging feature of Irish, as of British historical writing ... '[9]

The intellectual climate was already changing when this was written, and the situation has altered significantly in

Paddy Óg Liath Ó Súilleabháin being recorded by Tadhg Ó Murchú of Coimisiún Bhéaloideas Éireann/Irish Folklore Commission, County Kerry, 1948. Photo: Kevin Danaher, Department of Irish Folklore, University College Dublin.

recent decades. The Field Day project and publications (the pamphlets, Anthology and monographs) were a catalyst and a challenge for new interdisciplinary approaches. The growth of interdisciplinary sites of debate and inquiry, such as Irish Studies and Post-colonial Studies programmes, facilitated, through conferences, curriculum design and team-teaching, a more regular intercourse between historians and scholars of other disciplines. Dedicated societies (with publications) were established for the study of both eighteenth- and nineteenth-century Ireland, each constituting an interdisciplinary forum. The urgent and abrasive debates on historical consciousness, memory, and the 'uses of the past' in the context of identity politics and violent conflict in Northern Ireland, drew in scholars from different disciplines. Historians were drawn into their own, largely 'domestic' dispute on 'revisionism' in Irish history (though the range of issues — conceptual, methodological and expository — raised by Beiner draws attention to the relatively narrow terms in which much of the debate on revisionism

in Irish history was conducted from the 1970s to the 1990s).[10] Key texts, by cultural critics, demanded response across academic disciplines.[11] Defensive postures were still struck, but a growing number of academic historians eventually began to show a more bracing reflexivity on the claims of their discipline and on their own practices.

The Famine sesquicentenary in the mid-1990s inspired reflection and debate on historical consciousness and memory, commemoration and representation, while addressing epistemological, conceptual and methodological aspects of the 'historical turn' in cultural studies.[12] It was, as Niall Ó Ciosáin remarks, a case of 'history writing … becoming more "cultural", [while] other disciplines concerned with culture were becoming more historical' — a development that saw 'a growing interdisciplinarity in historical writings about culture, with increased citations of anthropologists and literary and social theorists by historians on the one hand, and a major turn to historical topics by those non-historians on the other'.[13] Joep Leerssen was again

10 cf. Ciarán Brady, ed., *Interpreting Irish History: The Debate on Historical Revisionism* (Dublin, 1994).

11 Examples would include J. Th. Leerssen, *Mere Irish and Fíor-Ghael: Studies in the Idea of Irish Nationality, Its Development and Literary Expression prior to the Nineteenth Century* (Amsterdam, 1986; Cork, 1996), and W. J. McCormack, *Ascendancy and Tradition in Anglo-Irish Literary History from 1789 to 1939* (Oxford, 1985).

12 The most useful bibliography is in Ó Gráda, *Black '47 and Beyond.*

13 Editor's Introduction in Niall Ó Ciosáin, ed., *Explaining Change in Cultural History* (Dublin, 2005), 4–5.

14 Joep Leerssen, *Remembrance and Imagination: Patterns in the Historical and Literary Representation of Ireland in the Nineteenth Century* (Cork, 1996).

15 Ian McBride, ed., *History and Memory in Modern Ireland* (Cambridge, 2001) supplies a representative sample.

16 In, respectively, R. F. Foster, *The Irish Story* (London, 2001); Kevin Whelan, *The Tree of Liberty* (Cork, 1996), and Tom Dunne, *Rebellions: Memoir, Memory and 1798* (Dublin, 2004). We may note in passing the prominence of 'outsiders' to the Irish academy at key moments of originality and challenge in source-criticism and interpretative direction in historical–cultural studies of modern Ireland — George-Denis Zimmermann, J. Th. Leerssen, and now Guy Beiner.

17 This is not to say, of course, that historical consciousness was in any simple way the 'cause' of violent conflict in Northern Ireland.

prominent in addressing a grand sweep of nineteenth-century remembrance practices,[14] while a more recent surge in studies of 'sites' of memory, commemorations, collective memory and remembrance has been prompted by the seminal texts by Pierre Nora and Jay Winter, as well as by the burgeoning debate on memory and history-writing in the particular context of Irish Studies.[15] Irish historians have interrogated the narrative structure of 'the story of Ireland' and 'the politics of memory', while source-criticism, remembrance and subjectivity have been deployed together in historiographical reflections on 1798.[16] The number of recalcitrant minutemen patrolling the discipline boundaries has continued to decline. Differences remain, of course, in discipline perspectives and in the 'working languages' of various discourses; but there is nowadays more attentive reading and listening across disciplines than was the case a generation ago.

If the lack of an 'acceptable methodology' does not provide an entirely satisfactory answer, then perhaps we ought to consider other factors that might explain why Beiner was virtually undisturbed by historians during his researches in the IFC archive, and why the source material from which he has mined such a rich analysis of the complexity of social memory of a dramatic episode in Irish history lay virtually undisturbed, at least by historians, for decades. An element of plain snobbery, social no less than intellectual, cannot be discounted. Historians of the Irish academy were trained, dispassionate, strongly imbued (at least from the 1930s) with a reverence for the Rankean valuation of the written record. They recoiled from the unstable evidence gathered by amateur enthusiasts, generated in oral performance and as part of social ritual, from witnesses whose subjectivity vitiated their accounts of historical events, and whose narratives frequently employed rhetorical tropes which scientific history found uncongenial.

A more considerable obstacle was the

linguistically disabled condition of many professional historians in investigating many aspects of Irish history — in particular, the history of *mentalités* and subaltern history — during the long period of decisive language-shift between the seventeenth and nineteenth centuries. Specifically in relation to the archive of the IFC, as late as 1970, as Beiner reminds us, some 80 per cent of the Main Collection comprised items in the Irish language. And while the Schools' Collection of 1937–38, including its material on *Bliain na bhFrancach*, was overwhelmingly in English, any scholar seeking to use the full resource of the IFC (and of certain ancillary folklore material) on the French episode of 1798 would have needed competence in both Irish and English. This requirement limited the number of Irish historians of the modern period likely to undertake serious research in the folklore archive.

There is, perhaps, a further anxiety, with ethical and intellectual moorings, greatly exacerbated during the decades of violent conflict in Northern Ireland, which rendered folk history suspect to Irish professional historians. Most Irish historians were distressed by the justification, by various parties to the Northern conflict, of their recourse to armed struggle through reference to their own reading or version of Irish history.[17] Revulsion, on ethical grounds, at the use of violence, was accompanied by outrage on intellectual grounds that the version of history being invoked was mistaken, unsound, distorted, false: in short, that it was an abuse of 'history', as practised by professionals, an abuse that, in certain important respects, originated in the shortcomings and unreliability of 'popular' history. Prominent among these failings was popular history's defective understanding of 'time' in historical understanding.

In 1983 the distinguished historian Oliver MacDonagh proposed that a central issue in Anglo-Irish relations was the different and incompatible notions of time present in the Irish and the British sense of their histories. There was a cyclical, patterned

A French bayonet and five-franc coin minted in Year 6 of the French Republic which were found on French Hill, near Castlebar, County Mayo, in 1876. The coin was worn as a medallion in the centennial celebration and it is now displayed in Daly's Bar, Mulrany, County Mayo.

timelessness to the Irish view of history. In essence, the characteristic Irish attitude could 'be described as an absence of a developmental or sequential view of past events. ... this rendered and renders the past an arsenal of weapons with which to defend both inveterate prejudice and that ignorance which wishes only to remain invincible'.[18] In the public debate on the past within Ireland the professional historians were determined to confront these other ahistorical understandings, these other versions of history with a defective concept of historical time. For his part, Beiner, in discussing calendar and time in folk history, acknowledges this fundamental difference: 'While academic historiography is, by and large, grounded in the concept of linear chronological time, social memory integrates various frameworks and rhythms of time.'[19]

This unsettling understanding of time in folk narratives, together with the formidable array of motifs, images and references characteristic of such narratives, must have reinforced the instincts of professional historians that this 'unstable' folk material would not prove a hospitable site for their established practices of historical inquiry and explanation.

Whatever weight we may apportion to these various factors that may have inhibited Irish historians up to recently from using the resource of the IFC in their accounts of historical episodes and the historiography attaching to them, Beiner's work should challenge them to reconsider whether this resource might not have new insights to yield on other episodes in recent Irish history where a 'history from below' perspective would have particular value — one may instance the Irish land war.

Beiner, it must be said, makes claims for the particular suitability of his own case study, *Bliain na bhFrancach* as remembered in the West and the north midlands, for the kind of 'historical archaeology', based on the notion of social memory, that he has attempted. The relative neglect of the western episode, its relegation to the margins of an emerging Irish nationalist historiography of 1798 as a whole, confers a number of advantages on the story for the student of folk history. As he puts it, whereas the legacies of Ninety-Eight in south-east Leinster and north-east Ulster 'have been publicly contested and subjected to overt political manipulations, by contrast, it may seem that the social memory of 1798 in the West was less exposed to politicization'.[20] The advantages of relative neglect, until late

18 Oliver MacDonagh, *States of Mind: A Study in Anglo-Irish Conflict 1780–1980* (London, 1983), 6–7.
19 Beiner, *Remembering the Year of the French*, 124.
20 Beiner, *Remembering the Year of the French*, 10.

21 See, in particular, Niall Ó Ciosáin, 'Famine Memory and the Popular Representation of Scarcity', in McBride, ed., *History and Memory in Modern Ireland*, 95–117.

22 Beiner, *Remembering the Year of the French*, 42.

23 Beiner, *Remembering the Year of the French*, 226.

in the nineteenth century, of the western episode in metropolitan or hegemonic nationalist narratives of the story of 1798 and its significance, Beiner sees as applying to both of the stated purposes of his study, the positivist and the interpretative. Implicit in his argument is the suggestion that folklore on the events of 1798 in the West, collected from informants in the 1930s whose age permitted a chain of transmission to be traced directly back to the aftermath of Ninety-Eight in those very communities in the West directly affected by the French expedition, has more pristine elements in it (recovering new, alternative or corrective 'information' on the actual events of 1798 at local level) than might be the case for the rebellion in the south-east or north-east; and that it has also proved more robustly resistant to imposed nationalist historiography than other areas, and more vigorous in negotiating the transmission of local folklore as it encountered printed history, formal education (school history) or the heightened moments of nationally directed collective remembrance and official commemorations of 1798 (notably the centenary commemoration in 1898).

It may be noted, in Beiner's favour, that the collection of folklore on 1798 for the IFC Main Collection (from the 1930s to the 1950s), and in the Schools' Collection of 1937–38, did not involve a specific and detailed questionnaire on 1798, unlike the special questionnaire devised for collecting folklore on the Famine, the 'directive' nature of which has been highlighted as problematic in studies of the folk memory of the Famine.[21] In fact, the guidelines distributed by the IFC to the schools made no explicit reference at all to 1798. Yet, in assessing what folk history was available to Hayes and the IFC collectors of the 1930s, we must remember that the affected counties of the French march from Killala to Ballinamuck by no means constituted an 'uncontaminated' corridor for the transmission of folk history. Indeed, the 'reconstructions' of

the folk history of the Year of the French had involved embellishment and omission from the very aftermath of the event. The widespread reluctance of people to speak of the events of Ninety-Eight, in the decades immediately after the rebellion, was noted by contemporaries, including the collectors of local 'lore' for the topographical division of the Ordnance Survey, before the work of that division was suspended in 1842. As a nationalist movement began to mobilize mass support and promulgate an 'official' version of Irish history, the story of Ninety-Eight was absorbed (and constantly reinterpreted) in the evolving 'nationalist' history — by the Young Irelanders, the Fenians, and the Land League/Home Rule movement. With increasing literacy in English, and a continuing language-shift throughout parts of the area that witnessed the Year of the French, the reception of 'official' Irish nationalist history by the folk history of the countryside must have been a very complex process.

One category of folk remembrance that was in short supply in the folk collections of the 1930s was that reflecting a loyalist reading of Ninety-Eight. As Beiner notes:

> Corresponding to a wider postcolonial pattern, characteristic of newly liberated countries that promoted the cultural heritage of the dominant emancipated population and rejected traditions associated with previous hegemonies, oral traditions of Protestant minorities and of populations that had been loyal to the Crown — though undeniably an integral part of Irish history — were not subject to extensive documentation and study ...[22]

Whether the elision of such loyalist folk history had occurred earlier, as successive infusions of nationalist 'official' history impacted on the transmission of local folk history, is a question considered by Beiner, particularly in the context of what he terms 'recalcitrant remembrances'.[23] This term is applied to 'nonconforming references',

1798 monument, Ballinamuck,
County Longford (unveiled
1928).

24 Beiner, *Remembering the Year of the French*, 262.
25 Beiner, *Remembering the Year of the French*, 320.
26 Beiner, *Remembering the Year of the French*, 306.

or narratives that did not conform to the prevalent orthodoxies that emerged within the regional folk history, and that persisted due to 'the diversity of folk historiography'. Beiner's discussion of recalcitrance is suggestive, and is one of the few themes in the book that might have been explored at greater length.

More obvious questions arise in relation to key moments of the interaction between nationalist Ireland's 'official' commemorations of Ninety-Eight and the folk history. Not surprisingly, the ideologically freighted centenary commemoration in 1898 had an especially drastic impact on the reconstruction of nationalist Ireland's official version of the events, the meaning, and the inspirational 'logic' of Ninety-Eight (the current generation 'owing it' to the heroes and martyrs of Ninety-Eight to realize their vision, et cetera); and its impact on the folklore of the French episode in the West is clearly a vital issue in any evaluation of the status of the folk traditions of *Bliain na bhFrancach* available for recording by Hayes and by the agents of the IFC almost 40 years later. Beiner acknowledges that by the 1930s 'folklore was impregnated with centennial influences'.[24] But the scale of the negotiation and reconstruction of the local folk history of *Bliain na bhFrancach* provoked by the 'official' history of Ninety-Eight that washed over nationalist Ireland in 1898 strains Beiner's careful interpretation of folk tradition to the limit. His survey of recent scholarship on the centenary commemorations is characteristically sharp and thorough, and he does not seek to conceal or to evade the implications of this powerful mediation of Ninety-Eight for the folklore deposit collected in the 1930s. The evidence presented admits of more than one conclusion. But Beiner remains adamant that, while 'folk history was rarely, if ever, completely independent from the pervasive influences of "official" history, yet it maintained a degree of autonomy'.[25] He is in no doubt that: 'Influences of nationalist commemoration permeated folk history, but

the negotiations that reconstructed social memory did not result in its obliteration, and despite an excess of celebrations, monuments, publications and educational programs, local oral traditions persisted into the twentieth century.'[26] This is a judgement based upon a careful reading of a rich and varied body of evidence.

The 'positivist' findings of Beiner's excavation of the folk traditions of *Bliain na bhFrancach* lead him to conclude: that, in the provincial narratives of the event, local incidents predominate, local heroes/leaders (the Franco-Irish officer, Colonel Henry O'Kane, the insurgent General George Blake, the Irish pikeman Robin Gill of Edenmore, and other local rebels; the patriot priests, particularly Fr. James Conroy, Fr. Manus Sweeney and Fr. Myles Prendergast) loom much larger and generate richer legends than, for example, the French commander General Humbert; that local incidents are brought by the folk tradition into sharper relief (in some instances into the light of 'history' for the first time) than in mainstream nationalist historiography of the rebellion; that the role of women in the rebellion in the West and the north midlands was more extensive, varied and interesting than the 'official' histories of 1798 record; that local folk history accommodates a variety of perspectives and complex readings of popular attitudes to the French (not universally supportive), to defiance and discretion in local responses to the rebellion, and to the class and religious dimensions of the event, as they registered with people at local level.

The results, despite all the caveats that Beiner and the reader might register on the perils of seeking to recover historically positivist data on 1798 from folklore accounts recorded, in many instances, some 140 years later, generally justify the claim that this source may indeed 'recover' hidden histories, at local level, of events hitherto unknown or, in terms of official historiography, underdeveloped episodes during *Bliain na bhFrancach*. Indeed, this résumé of the positivist findings does scant justice to the subtlety of Beiner's examination of a wide and disparate range of utterances on the western theatre of rebellion in 1798, all the while employing insights and explanatory frameworks drawn from the critical literature on folklore and related disciplines. Few would seek to deny that our understanding of the mosaic of 1798 is all the richer for the recovery of these narratives of 'democratic' history.

It should be emphasized that in his exhaustive excavation of the various genres of folklore (forms of history-telling) that registered *Bliain na bhFrancach*, Beiner examines not only *seanchas* ('orally-preserved social-historical tradition'), tales and mini-histories, but also songs, poems and ballads of the people, in both vernaculars, rhymes, proverbs and sayings, prophecies, toasts and other genres. He also discusses loyalist songs, all the more valuable for the relative dearth of folk history from a loyalist perspective contained in the IFC or Hayes's collections from the 1930s.

Likewise, in considering the interpretative aspect of the folk history of *Bliain na bhFrancach* — that is, the transmission and constant reworking of local 'versions' of the event — Beiner's review of the evidence encompasses the history-tellers (*seanchaithe*, local historians and folk collectors), the vernacular landscape (where the author conducts an assured exercise in 'commemorative microtoponomy'), souvenirs and mementos, monuments, commemorations, the mediation of school history and education, all the while carefully and sensitively recontextualizing the negotiation of each stage of the transmission, in the light of all the surviving evidence. While his general conclusion is that 'social memory was not a passive recipient of official commemoration discourse', nevertheless, 'the pressures on local traditions to conform to an imposing national metanarrative'[27] were already powerful before the establishment of the Irish state, and must have strengthened

further after 1922, even allowing for the possibility that the indifferent quality of history teaching in the schools (and the virtual absence of local history in the syllabus) may have assisted local folk history in retaining its regenerative vitality, at least up to the 1930s.

The reworking of folk traditions in later decades (since the 1930s) presents further obvious challenges of interpretation, as print and visual media increasingly dominate the construction and dissemination of historical accounts. Indeed, Beiner acknowledges that already by the 1930s folk history was deeply impregnated with 'official' history. He perceptively notes a striking moment in the sesquicentenary commemoration of Ninety-Eight in Mayo:

> A commemorative booklet produced for the Castlebar celebrations included extensive quotations from his [Hayes's] monumental book, *The Last Invasion of Ireland*, and also reproduced the entire text of a lecture on 'Castlebar and the Rising of 1798', which Hayes had delivered in the town a decade earlier (17 March 1938). The historian, who previously had travelled through the area and listened to people recount traditions of Ninety-Eight, was now informing them authoritatively about their past.[28]

The more recent remembrances of Ninety-Eight in the later twentieth century — in particular, the bicentenary events, publications and memorials — are briefly considered in an Epilogue that is free of the asperity that marked some of the academic exchanges on the legacy and meaning of Ninety-Eight during the bicentenary year.[29]

The kind of excavation that Guy Beiner has attempted encounters difficulties at every step. There is the obvious paradox that 'the study of oral history entails the unconscious shift from performance to text'.[30] Moreover, he confesses that:

> Unlike standard archaeological evidence,

27 Beiner, *Remembering the Year of the French*, 280.

28 Beiner, *Remembering the Year of the French*, 269.

29 A compendious reflection on the bicentenary debates is Thomas Bartlett, et al., eds., *1798: A Bicentenary Perspective* (Dublin, 2003).

30 Beiner, *Remembering the Year of the French*, 23.

31 Beiner, *Remembering the Year of the French*, 320.

32 Beiner, *Remembering the Year of the French*, 317, 258.

33 Beiner, *Remembering the Year of the French*, 5.

34 *Galway Advertiser*, 6 March 2008.

oral traditions are not concrete objects. Moreover, the validity of applying literary deconstructive analysis to oral narratives, which are not stable texts, is questionable. ... At some level, the archaeological analogy falters, as it aims to inspect reconstructions based on components that have not only transformed over time but were also transmogrified when they were collected. Multiple, often contradictory narratives coexisted in folk history ...[31]

Indeed, 'bricolage' and 'kaleidoscope' are but two of the words Beiner uses as he seeks to characterize the nature of his excavation of social memory.

The constant challenge of recontextualizing the very broad spectrum of utterances and representations in the folk history of *Bliain na bhFrancach* throughout the two centuries that followed the event, carries risks at every point along the regenerative continuum of transmission. Here again Beiner concedes that 'recontextualization of oral traditions is often speculative and inconclusive', and that, 'Positively tracing the spread of information into folklore may prove elusive ...'[32] One has no sense, however, that these concessions are offered simply to disarm the critic. Beiner remains convinced, all risks and difficulties notwithstanding, that: 'By interrogating the ways by which provincial communities narrated, interpreted, reconstructed and commemorated their pasts, it is possible to uncover traces of vernacular historiographies and discover practices of popular remembrance, which are distinct though not entirely independent of national historiography and commemoration.'[33] In my view, Beiner has dealt with these difficulties and risks with a sustained intellectual subtlety and a scruple for evidence that is deeply impressive.

The book is generally well produced, with generous provision for references and an ample bibliography, though some of the plates are dull and there are typographical errors (including some misplaced accents on words in Irish) that occasionally irritate. But it would be churlish to dwell on a few relatively minor blemishes. Beiner and his publisher are deserving of the gratitude of all who value an inclusive and scrupulous approach to historical inquiry, for a work that is theoretically informed, analytically sharp and original, and firmly grounded in scholarship across an impressive range of rich and challenging primary and secondary source material.

The final word from Beiner salutes the continuing generative capacity of folk history to reconstruct the story of *Bliain na bhFrancach* (the event itself and the history of its transmission), in dialogue with the constantly changing imperatives of an ethnographic 'present'. He is unlikely to be surprised, therefore, or scandalized, by a notice in a western provincial paper of 6 March 2008, announcing a new play by a Liam Heffron, titled *The Year of the French*, in the following terms:

It is 1798 in Mayo, and Mathew Tone is depressed. It's difficult enough being the ignored younger brother of Theobald Wolfe Tone, but now he's stuck with 700 homesick Frenchmen, six months late for the rebellion, in the wrong end of the country ... and it's raining. Again. Can things get any worse?[34]

The remembrance of the Year of the French continues.

Contributors

John Barrell is Professor of English at the Centre for Eighteenth-Century Studies at the University of York. His most recent books are *Imagining the King's Death: Figurative Treason and Fantasies of Regicide 1793–1796* (2000) and *The Spirit of Despotism: Invasions of Privacy in the 1790s* (2006).

Pascale Casanova is the author of *The World Republic of Letters* (2005) and *Samuel Beckett: Anatomy of a Literary Revolution* (2007). She is associate researcher at the Centre for Research on Art and Language in Paris and a literary critic.

Denis Condon is a Government of Ireland Fellow in the Centre for Media Studies in the National University of Ireland, Maynooth. Irish Academic Press will publish his *The Cinematograph in Ireland, 1895–1921* in 2009.

Claire Connolly is editor (with Joe Cleary) of *The Cambridge Companion to Modern Irish Culture* (2005) and (with Malcolm Ballin) of *Irish Periodical Culture, 1937–1972* (2008). She teaches English at Cardiff University.

Michael Cronin writes on language and translation. His books include *Translation and Identity* (2001) and *An Ghaeilge san Aois Nua/Irish in the New Century* (2005). He is Director of the Centre for Translation and Textual Studies at Dublin City University.

Fintan Cullen is Professor of Art History at the University of Nottingham. His books include *The Irish Face: Redefining the Irish Portrait* (2004) and (with John Morrison) *A Shared Legacy: Essays on Irish and Scottish Art and Visual Culture* (2005).

Seamus Deane is the editor of *The Field Day Anthology of Irish Writing*, 3 vols. (1991) and author of numerous books in literary history, including *Strange Country: Modernity and Nationhood in Irish Writing since 1790* (1997) and *Foreign Affections: Essays on Edmund Burke* (2005). He was the inaugural Keough Chair of Irish Studies at the University of Notre Dame.

Terry Eagleton is Professor of English in the University of Manchester. Among his many books, several have achieved a canonical status, such as *Literary Theory: An Introduction* (1983), *The Ideology of the Aesthetic* (1990) and, in relation to Irish culture, *Heathcliff and the Great Hunger* (1995). His most recent book is *The Meaning of Life* (2007).

David Fitzpatrick is Professor of Modern History at Trinity College Dublin. His books include *Harry Boland's Irish Revolution* (2003). Lilliput Press will publish his biography of Frederick MacNeice in 2008.

Luke Gibbons is the Keough Family Chair of Irish Studies at the University of Notre Dame. He is the author of *Transformations in Irish Culture* (1996), *The Quiet Man* (2002), *Edmund Burke and Ireland* (2004), and *Gaelic Gothic* (2006).

Breandán Mac Suibhne is a social and cultural historian. He is editor (with David Dickson) of Hugh Dorian, *The Outer Edge of Ulster* (2000, 2001), and (with Seamus Deane) he edits *Field Day Review* (2005–).

Deirdre McMahon writes on Irish foreign policy and is editor (with Michael Kennedy) of *Obligations and Responsibilities: Ireland and the United Nations, 1955–2005* (2005). She teaches in the University of Limerick, where she is a director of the Centre for Historical Research.

Peter McQuillan is Professor of Irish at the University of Notre Dame. His *Native and Natural: Aspects of the Concepts of Right and Freedom in Irish* (2004) was published in the Field Day Critical Conditions series.

Toril Moi is the author of *Sexual/Textual Politics: Feminist Literary Theory* (1985; 2002), *Simone de Beauvoir: The Making of an Intellectual Woman* (1994); and *What Is a Woman? And Other Essays* (1999). She is the editor of *The Kristeva Reader* (1986), and of *French Feminist Thought* (1987). Her *Henrik Ibsen and the Birth of Modernism: Art, Theater, Philosophy* (2006) won the MLA's Scaglione Prize for Comparative Literary Studies in 2007.

Bruce Nelson is a labour historian. He is author of *Workers on the Waterfront: Seamen, Longshoremen, and Unionism in the 1930s* (1988) and *Divided We Stand: American Workers and the Struggle for Black Equality* (2001) and teaches at Dartmouth College.

Máirín Nic Eoin has published several major books on literature in Irish, most recently *B'Ait Leo Bean: Gnéithe den Idé-eolaíocht Inscne i dTraidisiún Liteartha na Gaeilge* (1998), a study of the ideology of gender, and *'Trén bhFearann Breac': An Díláithriú Cultúir agus Nualitríocht na Gaeilge* (2005), on cultural dislocation in modern writing.

Gearóid Ó Tuathaigh has written extensively on modern history, including a key text, *Ireland before the Famine, 1798–1848* (1972). His most recent book is (with Lillis Ó Laoire and Seán Ó Súilleabháin) *Pobal na Gaeltachta: A Scéal agus a Dhán* (2001). He is Professor of History at the National University of Ireland, Galway.

Sean Ryder writes on nineteenth-century Irish culture and literature, and on the theory and practice of textual editing. His books include *James Clarence Mangan: Selected Writings* (2004) and several collections of essays on Irish and colonial themes. He is Director of the Thomas Moore Hypermedia Archive at the National University of Ireland, Galway.

Robert Tracy is Professor Emeritus of English and of Celtic Studies at the University of California, Berkeley. His publications include *Trollope's Later Novels* (1978) and *The Unappeasable Host: Studies in Irish Identities* (1998). He has also published editions of works by Synge, Trollope, Le Fanu and Flann O'Brien.

Thomas Moore
Memoirs of Captain Rock

Thomas Moore's **MEMOIRS OF CAPTAIN ROCK** gives Irish rebellion one of its most memorable representations in fiction. Its blend of literary and historical elements secured it a place among the innovatory hybrid works of the Romantic age such as the national tale and the historical novel. This eye-opening edition — enhanced by learned editing, a perspicuous introduction and shrewd notes — will win new readers for what was, in its time, a phenomenally successful publication.
James Chandler, University of Chicago

THOMAS MOORE (1779–1852) was Ireland's 'national poet' in the century before Yeats. His *Irish Melodies* (1808-34), composed and performed for an English audience, 'to sweeten Ireland's wrong' secured him worldwide fame. But **MEMOIRS OF CAPTAIN ROCK** (1824) was a sudden and brilliant variation on 'the-smile-and-the-tear' rhetoric of the *Melodies*. Its attribution of Irish violence to the British state's support for a rapacious Protestant minority and its savage military and legal repression of a Catholic majority inverted Tory platitudes and helped to make the brutal realities of Irish life a subject of serious public debate. Six editions were printed in London in 1824 alone; other editions appeared in Paris, Berlin, New York and Philadelphia. This annotated edition, edited and introduced by **Emer Nolan** of the National University of Ireland, Maynooth, is the first to be published in Ireland. It is available in paperback and hardback from all good bookstores and from **www.fielddaybooks.com**.